Emergent Economies, Divergent Paths

The economies of South Korea and Taiwan in the second half of the twentieth century are to scholars of economic development what the economy of Britain in the late eighteenth and early nineteenth centuries is to economic historians. This book, a collaboration between a leading trade economist and a leading economic sociologist specializing in East Asia, offers a fresh, original explanation of the development paths of post–World War II Korea and Taiwan. The ambitions of the authors go beyond this, however. They use these cases to reshape the way economists, sociologists, and political scientists will think about economic organization in the future. They offer nothing less than a theory of, and extended evidence for, how capitalist economies become organized. One of the principal empirical findings is that a primary cause for the industrialization of East Asia is the retail revolution in the United States and the demand-responsiveness of Asian manufacturers.

Robert C. Feenstra is a Professor in the Department of Economics at the University of California, Davis. He also directs the International Trade and Investment Program at the National Bureau of Economic Research in Cambridge, Massachusetts. He is the former editor of the *Journal of International Economics* and an associate editor of the *American Economic Review*. Feenstra has published more than seventy articles in international trade and edited eight books.

Gary G. Hamilton is a Professor of Sociology at the Jackson School of International Studies at the University of Washington. He has published numerous books and articles, including most recently *Cosmopolitan Capitalists: Hong Kong and the Chinese Diaspora at the End of the Twentieth Century*, editor and contributor (1999), *The Economic Organization of East Asian Capitalism* with Marco Orrù and Nicole Biggart (1997), and *Asian Business Networks*, editor (1996).

Structural Analysis in the Social Sciences

The series *Structural Analysis in the Social Sciences* presents approaches that explain social behavior and institutions by reference to relations among such concrete entities as persons and organizations. This contrasts with at least four other popular strategies: (a) reductionist attempts to explain by a focus on individuals alone; (b) explanations stressing the causal primacy of such abstract concepts as ideas, values, mental harmonies, and cognitive maps (thus, "structuralism" on the Continent should be distinguished from structural analysis in the present sense); (c) technological and material determination; (d) explanation using "variables" as the main analytic concepts (as in the "structural equation" models that dominated much of the sociology of the 1970s), where structure is that connecting variables rather that actual social entities.

The social network approach is an important example of the strategy of structural analysis; the series also draws on social science theory and research that is not framed explicitly in network terms, but stresses the importance of relations rather than the atomization of reduction or the determination of ideas, technology, or material conditions. Though the structural perspective has become extremely popular and influential in all the social sciences, it does not have a coherent identity, and no series yet pulls together such work under a single rubric. By bringing the achievements of structurally oriented scholars to a wider public, the *Structural Analysis* series hopes to encourage the use of this very fruitful approach.

Mark Granovetter

Other Books in the Series:

(*continued after index*)

Structural Analysis in the Social Sciences 29

Emergent Economies, Divergent Paths

Economic Organization and International Trade in South Korea and Taiwan

ROBERT C. FEENSTRA
University of California, Davis

GARY G. HAMILTON
University of Washington

CAMBRIDGE
UNIVERSITY PRESS

CAMBRIDGE UNIVERSITY PRESS
Cambridge, New York, Melbourne, Madrid, Cape Town, Singapore, São Paulo

Cambridge University Press
40 West 20th Street, New York, NY 10011-4211, USA

www.cambridge.org
Information on this title: www.cambridge.org/9780521622097

First published 2006

Printed in the United States of America

A catalog record for this publication is available from the British Library.

Library of Congress Cataloging in Publication Data

Feenstra, Robert C.
Emergent economies, divergent paths : economic organization and international trade in
South Korea and Taiwan / Robert C. Feenstra, Gary G. Hamilton.
   p.   cm. – (Structural analysis in the social sciences)
Includes bibliographical references and index.
ISBN-13: 978-0-521-62209-7 (hardback)
ISBN-10: 0-521-62209-3 (hardback)
1. Korea (South) – Economic conditions.   2. Taiwan – Economic
conditions – 1945–   3. Korea (South) – Commerce.   4. Taiwan – Commerce.
I. Hamilton, Gary G.   II. Title.   III. Series.
HC467.F44   2006
330.95124'9 – dc22   2005030036

ISBN-13   978-0-521-62209-7 hardback
ISBN-10   0-521-62209-3 hardback

To Gail and Eleanor

Contents

ix

Acknowledgments

This book began at the coffeehouse at the University of California, Davis, where we first met each other in the early 1990s. At that time, Feenstra was pondering the links between market structure and international trade patterns: a topic that was much in vogue in the economics literature, but for which empirical applications were hard to come by. Hamilton, meanwhile, had been active investigating the differing structures of business groups in Asia, much of this work in collaboration with Nicole Woolsey Biggart. In the process, he had accumulated a rich collection of firm-level data at the Institute of Governmental Affairs. Since, by market structure, economists mean the concentration and behavior of firms, then what better application than to contrast the radically different structures of business groups in South Korea and Taiwan? Thus, a collaboration was born that has lasted more than a decade and resulted in this book.

It would not have happened without the gracious assistance of many people. First, we wish to thank Alan Olmstead, Director, and Jean Stratford, Director of Research Services, at the Institute of Governmental Affairs, University of California, Davis, along with Shelagh Matthews Mackay and other staff at IGA. They have managed a countless number of grants, conferences, visiting scholars, research assistants, datasets, and other requests that have allowed us to continue our research across time, space, and disciplines. We can only hope that others will be able to enjoy the same benefits from affiliation with IGA that we have gained.

Intellectually, we owe a great debt to Nicole Woolsey Biggart and Cheng-shu Kao, who have contributed to this project from the start. Other coauthors, too, have been instrumental in carrying this work forward, and some of these began as graduate students and research assistants at Davis: from the economics department, William Zeile, Tzu-Han (Maria) Yang, Dorsati Madani, and Shunli Yao, all of whom have made significant contributions to the project, and from the sociology department the same is true for Yinhwa Chu, Holin Lin, and also Eun Mee Lim and

Wai-keung Chung, who followed Hamilton in his move to the University of Washington in 1993. We also wish to single out Deng-Shing Huang, who helped us at a crucial point in developing the model that we use in Chapter 3 and detailed in Appendix A, and Misha Petrovic, who worked tirelessly on developing and formatting the figures in Chapters 4 and 6 and who commented extensively and insightfully on all the chapters. Many other people have taken time to comment on one or more of the chapters or have helped with our many questions about Korea and Taiwan, and while some of these are acknowledged in our references, we also wish to thank Mary Brinton, Wei-an Chang, Chieh-hsuan Chen, Loretta Fung, Eun Mee Kim, Hyuk-Rae Kim, Seok-Choon Lew, Victor Nee, Richard Swedberg, and Harrison White.

Finally, we are grateful to James Rauch and Mark Granovetter for their unfailing support. Rauch organized several conferences bringing together sociologists and economists, where we could present our preliminary results, and he and Granovetter both provided detailed comments at various stages of the project. There is no question in our minds that the analysis in this book could not have been done by one of us acting alone: it represents a genuine collaboration across the two disciplines that is relatively rare, but very fruitful for us. We are indebted to Rauch, Granovetter, and other scholars who are encouraging of this type of collaboration, and trust that our research will find an interested readership in both disciplines.

We wish to recognize the support of the Ford Foundation and the National Science Foundation for grants that supported the research leading to this book. We began to write this book in earnest during the year (1999–2000) that Hamilton was a Fellow at the Center for Advanced Studies in the Behavioral Science. He gratefully acknowledges the opportunities provided by the Center.

An early version of Chapter 1 is "The Organization of Economies," pp. 153–80 in *The New Institutionalism in Sociology*, edited by Victor Nee and Mary Brinton, 2nd ed., Stanford: Stanford University Press, 2001. Early versions of Chapters 3 and 4 are found in "The Organization of the Taiwanese and South Korean Economies: A Comparative Equilibrium Analysis," pp. 86–142 in *Networks and Markets*, edited by James Rauch and Alessandra Casella, New York: Russell Sage, 2001. In addition, the full mathematical exposition of the model, "A Market-Power Based Model of Business Groups," appears in *Journal of Economic Behavior and Organization*, 51, pp. 459–85, 2003. That appears in the book as Appendix A. Material on the Korean financial crisis contained in Chapter 3 and Appendix D appeared as "*Chaebol* and Catastrophe: A New View of Korean Business Groups and Their Role in the Financial Crisis," *Asian Economic Papers*, 1(2), 2002, pp. 1–45.

Introduction

This book began as a study of the business groups in South Korea and Taiwan, but has grown into something much more. Business groups – affiliations of firms, usually with some degree of common ownership – have been a favorite topic of study among a number of economists (who have had a principal interest in the *keiretsu* in Japan, but also the groups found elsewhere in Asia) and economic sociologists (including one of the authors), as well as political scientists and area specialists. In economics, the traditional explanation for these groups has been that they are a response to *market failure*; because the market for capital or entrepreneurial skill or some other asset does not function well within the economy at large, business groups allocate this scarce resource among affiliated firms, thereby substituting managerial initiative for market mechanisms. In political science, rather than being a function of market processes, these groups are explained as being the creation of government mandates, expressed by preferential policies toward business groups and the entrepreneurs who establish them. In sociology, the explanations also downplay purely market processes, but make these groups the outcome of background institutional environments in which political and social institutions place parameters on how economies operate.

On the surface, these various explanations have little in common. Obviously, they are all shaped by the disciplinary gaze of the analysts and the countries they observe. Economists first noticed business groups in developing countries (for example, Leff, 1978), where market failures at an early stage of development are a standard diagnosis, and business groups conveniently fit into that framework. Political scientists, and political economists more generally, working especially on South Korea (for example, Woo, 1991, Evans, 1995), like to identify "historical moments" (such as General Park's meeting with Korean entrepreneurs in 1961) that define the relationship between the government and nascent groups, which then propel them onto the national stage. Meanwhile, sociologists have been

1

satisfied with showing that the network structure of the groups mirrors the broader social structure of the societies in which they are found (for example, Hamilton and Biggart, 1988). Having found a "fit" for their theories in one country or comparison group, each discipline has been more or less content to apply the same or similar explanations to all other cases, which treats them as extensions of the initial countries studied.

As we progressed in our research, however, we discovered that business groups are shaped in quite different ways both *within,* as well as *across* countries, and that these differences are more than just a matter of degree. Any explanation for business groups must recognize and be able to explain these differences. Although some analysts noted cross-country differences and variously attempted to explain them, none of the typical explanations predicted or even recognized intra-country differences.

Cross-country differences are especially apparent for South Korea and Taiwan. In Korea, these groups are called *chaebol,* a term represented by the same Chinese characters as the infamous pre–World War II business groups in Japan, the *zaibatsu,* which literally means "money clique." In Taiwan, the large groups are usually called *guanxi chiye,* which means "related industries." Both sets of business groups consist of separate and independently constituted firms that are linked together by individual and family ownership. The *chaebol* of South Korea, however, are much larger and more vertically integrated than the business groups in Taiwan. They are also differently integrated into the rest of the national economy. Business groups in Taiwan are located primarily in the upstream markets and the service sectors, and thus are dependent on and integrated with other firms of all sizes in the Taiwan's economy. In contrast, Korean *chaebol,* particularly the largest groups, form a more self-sufficient set of firms, integrating both upstream and downstream member firms into cohesive production sets. The differences in organization between these two very advanced capitalist economies are so pronounced and lead to such contrasting economic outcomes that they provide "natural" cases that can be used to test any theory of the business groups.

Developing an explanation for these cross-country differences was the initial goal of our research. Going into the research, we both felt that any valid explanation for business groups had to be sufficient at the economic level, but also take social and political factors seriously. We, therefore, avoided the temptation to appeal to existing theories, thereby pitting one discipline against another. Instead, we decided to start on the empirical end first. We were informed by detailed firm-level data on the business groups found in South Korea and Taiwan. Rather than analyzing their ownership structure or the purely financial linkages among firms, we instead focused on the *flow of intermediate and final goods among firms* within a group. For Korea, that information was available from a published source, whereas for publicly listed firms in Taiwan, this information was included in reports filed with the stock exchange.[1] Using this as a starting point, we began to analyze the internal structure of the business groups: what goods were sold between affiliated firms and how much of each. A significant portion of internal sales often go to trading companies found within many groups, but even after correcting for this, there is still an extraordinary level of *internal sales* within the groups, which is especially so for Korea. These are not final goods being sold to consumers, but rather, are intermediate inputs being produced by one firm in a group and then sold to another for further processing.

These intra-group transactions led us to our first, and most obvious, hypothesis, namely that business groups benefit from preferential access to intermediate inputs produced by their member firms and sold internally within the group. But in order for the group alone to benefit from such trades, it must be the case that these intermediate inputs are not sold on the same terms to firms *outside* of the business group. In other words, the groups must be either withholding intermediate inputs from external sale, or alternatively, charging prices for external sale that exceed the price when the input is transferred within a group. So the converse hypothesis is that the business groups are exercising *market power* in their sale of intermediate inputs to other groups. We found that this hypothesis fits the anecdotal evidence for both Japan and Korea. For Japan, there were allegations from American firms in the 1980s that the business groups were more likely to purchase internally, from their own firms, than buy from the United States and that this was a form of trade barrier between the countries.[2] For South Korea in the 1990s, the Korean Fair Trade Commission actively investigated and fined business groups who were found to treat their member firms preferentially – buying and selling at prices different than those used for non-member firms – which was treated as an unfair business practice.[3] Without passing judgment on whether this practice is "fair" or not, it demonstrates the privileged status that group membership bestows on firms through the trade of goods between them.

[1] As explained in Chapter 4, the primary source for the 1989 Korean data is the volume *1990 Chaebol Analysis Report (Chaebol Boon Suk Bo Go Seo* in Korean) published by Korea Investors Service, Inc. The intra-group transactions for Taiwan were collected from company annual reports for 1994 filed with the Taiwan stock exchange, and when that information was incomplete, additional information was collected by contacting the groups. These data on the Korean and Taiwanese business groups are freely available from the Center for International Data at the University of California, Davis, www.internationaldata.org (choose "Asia").

[2] See the contrasting viewpoint of Bhagwati (1992), along with the empirical studies by Lawrence (1991) and Fung (1991).

[3] Some of these cases are described in Appendix B.

With this hypothesis – that group membership brings preferential access to goods produced by affiliated firms, and conversely, that sales outside the groups occur at higher prices – we had already veered far, far away from the conventional views of business groups in economics and elsewhere. While it is true that charging prices significantly above costs is sometimes considered a form of "market failure," which the business groups can avoid in their internal sales, this *market power* explanation for business groups is mentioned only rarely in the literature.[4] An example is Ghemawat and Khanna (1998), who include it as one of four reasons for business groups to occur, whereas Khanna (2000) concludes that evidence on this explanation is "lacking." It is perhaps understandable that for the "main bank" groups in Japan, the internal trade of *goods* would be treated as being of secondary importance to *financial flows* within the group. But that should not be true for the *vertical keiretsu* in Japan, such as Toyota and its suppliers, where the transfers of inputs within the group are of fundamental importance. Our theory is based on such internal trades of inputs within groups and is, therefore, particularly appropriate for vertically oriented business groups, but as will become apparent, our theory has a much broader applicability than vertical integration.

At a deeper level, the reason that our *market power* explanation for business groups has hardly been explored in economics is that current writing rejects the idea that businesses need to vertically integrate in order to obtain the gains from preferential trades between them. There is an old example (used by Stigler, 1951) of a coal mine charging monopoly prices to a downstream steel mill. Rather than paying monopoly prices, the steel mill would be more efficient if it purchased the coal at its true cost, which would automatically occur if the steel mill owned the coal mine, and then paid the mining costs. Therefore, a vertically integrated mill and mine would capture the gains from the internal sale of coal. But more recent scholarship (starting with Williamson, 1971, p. 115, for example) has questioned whether we really need *common ownership* of the mine and the mill to obtain the same result. Could not the steel company instead go to the mine owner and negotiate a contract whereby the true costs were paid per ton of coal and then some *additional* lump-sum payment is made to the mine owner reflecting the fact that the per-ton price is so low? By varying the prices and lump-sum payment in this contract, the two businesses ought to be able to obtain a result that mirrors the internal sale of coal under common ownership, but without the common

---

[4] Leff (1978, p. 667) concludes that "The institution of the group is thus an intrafirm mechanism for dealing with deficiencies in the markets for primary factors, risk, and intermediate products in the developing countries," and describes how vertical integration can be used to offset high input prices. He is therefore including a "market power" explanation for group within his general "market failure" argument.

ownership! In other words, the steel mill and coal mine do not need to merge; they can just write a contract to achieve the gains from the efficient trade of the coal between them.

If we apply this logic to business groups, it would suggest that they do not need to have common ownership in order to achieve the gains from efficient trade of inputs; some form of contract could be used instead. We have no argument with the idea that common ownership is not needed in business groups, and in fact, the degree of cross-ownership in some business groups is quite low. But, in this logic, the nature of the "contract" used between the firms is usually left unexplored, and it is unclear whether it is intended to be a written contract or just an understanding between firms. In either case, there must be a mechanism to *enforce* such a contract. This brings us to our second hypothesis: The crucial function of business groups is that they provide an *authority structure for enforcing efficient trades of intermediate inputs*. Again, this hypothesis has its converse. Efficient trades cannot be arranged between firms *outside* of the same business group; instead, these trades will occur at prices above costs, and will reflect the relative market power of the transacting firms. In a sense, we are fully agreeing with the aphorism of Adam Smith in the *Wealth of Nations* that "People of the same trade seldom meet together, even for merriment and diversion, but the conversation ends in a conspiracy against the public, or in some contrivance to raise prices,"[5] but are revising this to a context where *business groups* rather than handicraft trades provide the authority structure, as in the following: People of the same [business group] trade seldom meet together ... but the conversation ends in a conspiracy against [other groups], or in some contrivance to raise prices.

With the twin hypotheses of market power and authority, we arrived at a working definition of business groups, but this working definition was still only a start. The next, and most important, question was to determine what the *organization* of these groups would be. If business groups provide member firms with preferential access to intermediate inputs, which are utilized in final goods that are sold to the public, then how large should such groups be, and what range of upstream and downstream products should they produce? These are difficult questions to address because the answer for one group *depends on what other groups are doing*. If it is the case that most business groups are charging very high prices for the external sale of their inputs, essentially relying on themselves for intermediate inputs in "one set" production systems, then that may well be the best strategy for any other group to take. But alternatively, if most groups are selling intermediate inputs at prices only slightly above costs,

[5] Adam Smith, 1776, *The Wealth of Nations*, Book 1, Chapter X (I.10.82).

then the best strategy for any other group would be to not only purchase these available inputs, but perhaps also sell its own intermediate inputs at moderate prices as well.

It takes a formal model to sort out what the best strategies for the business groups actually are, but the suggestions we are making turn out to be correct. There is a "reflexivity" in the structure of groups, whereby each group can only determine its prices for external sale of inputs by reference to what other groups are doing, and furthermore, the outcome of this reflexive process *need not be unique.* Rather, the formal model shows that there are a small number of alternative configurations of business groups that are stable and represent fully rational responses to all economic forces. In theoretical terms, this result means that capitalist economies do not necessarily converge toward one type of optimally efficient economic organization, but rather that a small number of differently organized economies are consistent with profit-maximizing theories of capitalism. The fact that there are only a few outcomes, each of which has a coherent structure, is an example of **emergence**: a well-ordered structure arising out of an interactive physical or social process.

Making this argument precise is the goal of the business group model we shall present in Part I. The model is both economic (each group pursues its best interests) and sociological (each group exercises authority over its members), but the finding that there are several, stable organizational outcomes goes beyond what either discipline has suggested. The "market failure" approach in economics and its more modern statement in transactions costs (Williamson, 1975, 1985) suggest that organizational outcomes are determined as an efficient response to the market failure. We make no such claim for the various outcomes from our model. Although one organizational outcome may be better than another, there is no reason to expect that it will be somehow "selected" because of its inherent efficiency. Sociologists following Granovetter's (1985) "embeddedness" thesis reject the transactions-cost explanation for organization as too functionalist and see the organization of firms as being determined by a host of external conditions and relationships impacting firms. As a consequence, the set of conceivable organizational outcomes is presumed to be large, with the actual outcome being historically contingent and subsequently path dependent. The embeddedness approach, therefore, contains no conception of economic organization that would limit the range of possibilities, so much so that every society might have its own unique configuration of successful business groups. In contrast, our theory suggests that there are only a small number of organizational outcomes for configurations of business groups that are consistent with our assumptions that business groups be economically viable, in the sense that they are acting in their self-interest and that all markets clear simultaneously.

Our theory, however, does not specify the reasons that one outcome is found in one society and not in another.

We are certainly not the first to argue that organizational processes may lead to multiple outcomes. A number of prominent economists (Anderson, Arrow, and Pines, 1988, Arthur, 1994, Arthur, Durlauf, and Lane, 1997, Greif, Milgrom, and Weingast, 1994, Greif, 1994, Krugman, 1996, Luhmann, 1995, McLaren, 2000, Rauch and Casella, 2001, Rosser, 1999), as well as a few sociologists (White, 2002) have theorized emergent organizational features in economies. We are among the first, however, to demonstrate that organizational features are central to an adequate understanding of the Asian economies and that the predictions of a relatively simple model can mirror the actual organization of groups in South Korea and Taiwan.

Arguing that economic organization is not fully determined by market forces begs the question of what factors do most contribute to outcomes. Marx's phrase about history applies here: People make history, but not as they please. Why do some sets of choices have large cumulative effects for economic development and other choices seem not to matter as much? As Arthur (1994, p. xiii) notes, "the key obstacle to an increasing returns economics has been the 'selection problem' – determining how an equilibrium comes to be selected over time when there are multiple equilibria to choose from." That is the question we address in Part II of the book.

In effect, we ask in Part II: Why does the model, outlined and tested in Part I, work so well? We begin by examining the initial decades after World War II and the Korean War. It was during these years that the economic organization of these countries formed into separate capitalist trajectories. The reasons for the divergence, however, are not apparent from a simple recounting of historical events. Indeed, feeling they know the development story, a generation of scholars has told the recent histories of these countries by privileging certain political and economic factors, and ignoring almost everything else. Our task, however, is to account for the development of organizational configuration of firms, and for this it is important to disentangle proximate events and unchanging conditions from underlying causes. We show from a comparative examination that the trajectories are not the inevitable outcome of cultural and social institutions, that, in other words, the Koreans and Taiwanese do not just act that way. Alternative outcomes are not only conceivable, but also actually exist in the form of economies of Mainland China and North Korea, as well as overseas economies in which Chinese and Korean operate as minorities. We also demonstrate from a historical comparison that these organizational outcomes cannot be accounted for strictly in terms of so-called "historical moments," decisive events that change all subsequent history. Rather, we show that the small differences existing between Taiwan and Korea in the initial stages of development emerged, under *the influence of a globalizing world economy*, into progressively larger differences as development progressed.

The key point in the analysis in Part II is what caused these small differences to become large differences as time and development progressed. Continuing our empirical focus on the economic activity of business groups, rather than on existing theories of development, we closely examined what these two economies, and respective business groups, actually produced. This focus led us to a detailed analysis of exports, what we call "trade data archeology," from 1972 until 1985. We show that in the earliest period of import data, from 1972 to 1975, South Korea and Taiwan exported similar and often identical products (as defined by the 7-digit product codes) to the United States, but after 1975, the two exports from the two countries began to diverge. South Korean exports are increasingly concentrated in categories consisting of products that could be mass-produced (for example, in garments: men's shirts, as opposed to women's fashion), and often, but not always, were final products ready for consumer use, such as microwave ovens, video machines (VCRs), tires, and automobiles. In contrast, within the same product categories, Taiwanese exports tended to be component parts, goods having short product cycles (for example, in garments: women's clothes), and some fairly complex final products that can be assembled from standardized components (for example, computers, TVs, and bicycles), this in addition to a considerable range of relatively inexpensive, simply made consumer products.

This analysis of trade data reveals a sudden and accelerating expansion of U.S.-bound exports from South Korea and Taiwan that began in the late 1960s and that does not level off until the mid- to late 1980s, twenty years of extraordinary growth. The rapid emergence of these exports was highly concentrated in only a few product categories, and within these categories during this twenty-year period export products began clearly to diverge, as each economy began to specialize in particular types of production capabilities and the products compatible with those capabilities.

Our conclusion from this analysis of the export patterns is that, in contrast to the "supply side" narratives, it must be *increasing demand* that drove economic growth in South Korea and Taiwan. But what explains this rising demand? There is considerable, but very scattered material suggesting that the driving factors for Asian growth are to be located in the reorganization of the retail sectors in the United States, which resulted in an increasingly concentrated retail sector consisting of mainly new types of brand-name merchandisers (for example, Nike, The Gap) and discount retailers (Wal-Mart, Home Depot). In the literature, this trend is known as lean retailing, in which the merchandisers and retailers make direct (non-market) connections with manufacturing firms over which they can exert some control and pricing power. The important technological underpinnings of this "retail revolution" were inventory management systems based on computerization, scanning, and uniform product codes, and alongside these technological changes there was the establishment of major buyers for products from Asia, or "intermediary demand." Our third hypothesis is that the emergent, and yet divergent economic organization in these two economies was due not to "market failures" or to government policies, but rather to the differential impact of increasing global demand, expressed by intermediaries.

To demonstrate these divergent patterns of growth, we examine the "global matching" between such retailers in the United States and firms in South Korea and Taiwan. In the initial years of growth, foreign contract buyers sought out, ordered, sometimes assisted, and often supervised the Asian manufacture of differentiated goods later sold in the United States. Rapidly expanding demand encouraged Asian entrepreneurs to use available resources to construct production networks that would satisfy and even increase demand for their products and that, through the use of authority and market power, would assure some measure of predictable continuity in the future. Their early successes in responding to big buyers, in turn, created additional demand for wider ranges and greater quantities of products. This self-reinforcing cycle of selective matching in the context of increasing demand for exports led very quickly to the development of divergent economic trajectories. Once economic players (for example, entrepreneurs as well as government officials) saw themselves as participants in a common economic arena, the economic organization of both countries became increasingly rationalized both organizationally and economically.

In the context of a rapidly emerging economic organization, we further argue that state officials unwittingly became a primary force behind rationalizing the *status quo* and fixing the economy in a trajectory of growth. They fashioned economic policies that sometimes succeeded and sometimes failed. The policies that worked to reinforce and rationalize the existing trajectory of growth usually succeeded, and the policies attempting to change the existing organization in substantial ways usually failed, sometimes disastrously. Most policies made no difference one way or another. As a consequence, the sum total of the governments' efforts tended to encompass, encourage, and stabilize the existing patterns of organization and growth.

In summary, the business group model we present in Part I is substantiated by our analysis of trade flows in Part II. Linking these trade flows to the actions of retailers and other big buyers in the United States is needed to explain how the divergent economic organizations came to be established in South Korea and Taiwan. Our approach in Part II is heavily empirical, relying on the most disaggregate trade statistics collected by the U.S. Customs Service, which have proven to be useful to a recent generation of trade economists and can hopefully be utilized by other analysts as well.[6] A specific hypothesis we can test using these data is that Korea has *less product variety in exports* than Taiwan. This hypothesis is implied by our theoretical model of business groups, and finds strong support when tested using the disaggregate U.S. import data from both countries. In many markets, Korea is exporting fewer products than Taiwan, but in larger volume. This hypothesis is consistent with the observation that the very large *chaebol* found in Korea have sought to be "world leaders" in particular products and dominate in those export markets, but that resource constraints in the economy put limits on the *overall number of products* that can be produced and exported. By devoting enormous resources to products such as microwaves, cars, and semiconductors, it is impossible that Korea can also fill all the smaller "niche" markets that are served so effectively by the Taiwanese firms.

In Part II we also draw on descriptions of the regulatory changes in the United States and evidence of network linkages between big buyers and exporters in Asia, and future research may be able to further quantify and document these linkages. This material all goes beyond the strict confines of our business group model, with its narrow focus on internal transactions within the groups, and it can be expected that future scholarship will formalize the influence of global demand on economic organization, using the hypotheses that we suggest. As we say in the concluding chapter, our research findings should lead to a reevaluation of the connection between local economies and global capitalism, in particular the developmental state theories of economic development.

We started our research with a goal to better understand Asian business groups. We ended with a desire to better understand how all economies, local and global, come to be organized and how they change over time. This is an elusive, difficult goal, for which this book is merely a first step. We believe, however, that it is an important step because it changes the focus of analysis away from separate and often contradictory disciplinary views to a more integrated perspective in which economics and sociology work hand in glove to create an informed interpretation of economic organization. In the next chapter, we outline the theoretical foundations for this integrated perspective.

---

[6] The U.S. trade data we utilize can be downloaded from the Center for International Data at the University of California, Davis, www.internationaldata.org (choose "Data"). See also the documentation in Feenstra (1996) and Feenstra, Romalis, and Schott (2002).

Part I

Business Groups and Economic Organization

1

The Problem of Economic Organization

Most theories of economic organization, regardless of discipline, involve a sleight of hand. Theorists begin by assuming the existence of decision-making individuals. They then provide these actors with inner motivations: desire for gain, for power, or for social honor and reputation. Driven by these motivations, economic actors are then set in motion. They plot strategy; they use guile. They act on their interests; they interact in trusting ways. Seeking to maximize, they also respond to incentives and constraints put in place by powerful people, such as state planners or heads of state banking systems or the CEOs of the largest firms. Whatever these actors do and however they respond shape the calculations and subsequent actions of others. Assuming all similarly motivated individuals act more or less alike, economic theorists then posit an orderly, organized economy, conceived, for example, as a capitalist economy composed of independent and competitive firms. When theorized in this fashion, economic organization is pulled, like a rabbit from a hat, out of aggregated individual decisions.

Attempts to induce societal level organization from individual actions are common enough in every social science. In sociology, anthropology, and political science, theorists often, in a single bound, make the same leap from individual behavior to social and political structure. In these disciplines, however, the reverse trick is equally widespread: The inner motivations and actions of individuals are produced, as if by magic, from descriptions of the whole. Remember Karl Marx's famous line in the Preface to *Das Kapital*: "Here individuals are dealt with only in so far as they are the personifications of economic categories, embodiments of particular class relations and class interests."

Although common in other social sciences, in economics the efforts to deduce individual actions from descriptions of collective wholes are less prevalent because of the influence of classical and neoclassical paradigms, which are wedded to economic individualism. Indeed, the famous invisible

13

hand of Adam Smith shows us that the outcomes of a perfectly competitive economy with millions of firms will be the same, theoretically, as one arising from a benevolent planner seeking to maximize the public interests. In this way, the outcomes of an entire economy are reduced to that of a single agent maximizing the appropriate measure of social welfare. This commonplace mental experiment explains why economic theorists are often satisfied with modeling the structure of entire economies by the stereotyped calculations of individual agents.[1] Without questioning the usefulness of these simplifying assumptions for modeling purposes, they certainly do not do justice to the wide variation in the ways that firms, business groups, and entire economies are organized (Granovetter, 1994, Crouch and Streeck, 1997, Hollingsworth and Boyer, 1997, Whitley, 1999, Quack, et al., 2000).

In this book, we argue that the many and diverse ways economies are organized cannot be properly understood by using theories that generate economic organization either from bottom-up aggregations of individual behavior or from a characterization of collective wholes. Instead, we show that economic organization represents the interconnectedness and dynamic interplay of markets within and across economies that arises from the competitive struggles among firms. We show that such a cross-market interplay of people and firms produces emergent effects that cannot be easily captured with stylized agents representing entire economies or in simple bottom-up aggregations, both conceptions of which assume that every player is like every other player. To paraphrase Friedrich Hayek (1967, pp. 96–105), we conclude, therefore, that economic organization **emerges** as part of a "spontaneous order" that is "the results of human action but not of human design."

In this chapter, we summarize theories of economic organization that assume individual aggregation, particularly those developed by the new institutionalist economists and by their counterparts in economic sociology. Contributions in both these disciplines arose from dissatisfaction

---

[1] As Granovetter (1985) notes, there is "an irony of great theoretical importance" that both inductive approaches based on methodological individualism ("undersocialized conception" of human nature) and deductive approaches based a priori conceptions of unified wholes ("oversocialized conception" of human nature) produce similar results:

> Both have in common a conception of action and decision carried out by atomized actors. In the undersocialized account, atomization results from narrow utilitarian pursuit of self-interest; in the oversocialized one, from the fact that behavioral patterns have been internalized and ongoing social relations thus have only peripheral effects on behavior...Under- and oversocialized resolutions of the problem of order thus merge in their atomization of actors from the immediate social context.

Granovetter further adds that this allows economic theorists to "lurch directly from an undersocialized to an oversocialized state."

with the minimalist conception of economic organization found in the economic paradigm that posits perfect competition. However, the enthusiasm of these theorists for their respective explanations led them away from a central feature of capitalist economies that the competitive paradigm sought to explain, namely the interconnectedness of markets, as conceived in economics conventionally through the price system.

Our own approach, the theoretical justification of which we introduce in this chapter and then describe more fully in later chapters, incorporates many of the key insights from institutional and sociological theories into an alternative explanation for the organization of economic activity. Economically active people, ranging from businesspeople to state officials, are embedded in ongoing organized environments in which economic processes and competitive struggles are as important as social and political institutions. In such settings, economic calculability, as introduced and generalized across firms and markets through a variety of means, including complex price systems (for example, the price of capital, of ownership as represented by equity markets, of labor, as well as of goods themselves), plays an important role as a force shaping an economy's existing or emerging economic organization. To the extent that people and firms are connected within and across markets through such calculations, we can talk about an "economically organized economy" or, more simply, "economic organization," as we use that term in this book. We suggest that routine economic calculations in such organized settings involve a reflexive process in which participants are constantly objectifying their own position relative to others in that setting and taking actions based on those comparisons. Such reflexive actions are self-reinforcing in the sense that they are jointly constructed and mutually maintained. An organized economy grows from the self-fulfilling anticipations of interacting participants who are both competing and doing business with one another. If people want to succeed in such a rationalized economic environment, for whatever reasons, they are drawn into playing by the rules and standards of the activities in which they are engaged, necessarily taking those rules and standards for granted as a part of their decision-making environment. To the extent that they do so, economic organization emerges through competitive interaction and takes on a momentum that no individual or set of individuals can necessarily control or easily predict.

Bottom-up Theories of Economic Organization: The Marshallian Frame

Not that long ago, many economists would have agreed with George Stigler's aphorism (1968, p. 1), "there is no such subject as industrial organization." Stigler thought industrial organization is not a viable subject because the content of this particular area is entirely subsumed in standard microeconomic theory. Like most economists of his day, Stigler based his theoretical assumptions on a view of perfect competition most closely associated with Alfred Marshall. In contrast to Léon Walras' theory of general equilibrium, in which all markets in an economy are interrelated, Marshallian economics is founded on theories of partial equilibrium.[2] Marshallian economists examine an economy market by market, industrial sector by industrial sector, and for each market or sector, they conceptualize equilibrium models in which "the ensemble of all buyers and all sellers [in that market] determine price" (Stigler, 1968, p. 9). For the purpose of equilibrium analysis, they view each market as being independent of all other markets. Hence, Marshallian economics is a theory of economies based on partial equilibria.

Given this narrowed focus, a Marshallian competitive market economy has three characteristics: large numbers of buyers and sellers for the same product, an independence of action for all parties, and complete participant knowledge of all market activity. In the ideal market situation that meets these criteria, firms have an optimum size, which is a function of two factors: the demand for a product and the economies of scale needed to produce it (Stigler, 1968, p. 69). When markets are not fully competitive, for any reason, then firm size is also influenced by additional constraints being placed upon market interaction that go beyond the demand factors of production. Such constraints typically come from factors relating to the product, such as technological or capital barriers to entry, product differentiation, and advertising, and from non-economic factors corrupting market competition, such as market collusions in the form of cartels and political intervention (Chamberlin, 1962 [1933], Robinson, 1969 [1933], Scherer and Ross, 1990). When such constraints exist, conditions of imperfect competition, sometimes referred to as "market failures," give rise to specific industrial organizations (for example, monopoly or oligopoly), which in turn influences market performance (for example, the price and quality of goods). However, when markets are perfectly competitive, then Marshallian economics predicts that firms are essentially "price-takers"; that is, they are passive reflections of market forces.

---

[2] Marshall's view of economics was, of course, quite broad, and he clearly acknowledged that the economy as a whole was best conceived through general equilibrium theory. As Niehans (1990, pp. 240–1) reminds us, however, "The important point is that Marshall, though starting from a general equilibrium framework, did not bother to work this out in detail, as Walras did, but rather used the beam of partial analysis to shed concentrated light on different areas of the economic system."

The New Institutional Economics

In the past several decades, economists have greatly revised the foundations of Marshallian economics. The economists most responsible for this revision have styled themselves as the "new institutionalists." Although not a cohesive theoretical group, these economists, in general, no longer see firms as passive receivers of economic signals. Instead, drawing their theoretical spirit from an early article by Ronald Coase (1937), they see firms as agents actively setting prices, making markets for their products, and also creating optimal organizations for non-market transactions. In his original article (1937, p. 388), Coase triangulates Alfred Marshall's initial concern with organization as a factor of production, Joan Robinson's work on markets characterized by imperfect competition in a Marshallian sense, and Frank Knight's insights on market uncertainty and entrepreneurial risk-taking. Focusing on the costs of inter-firm transactions, Coase makes firms the primary agents in establishing the boundary between market and non-market transactions and makes factors external to "normal" market activity (for example, the non-market cost of engaging in market activity) the primary focus of the firms' decision making.

Coase's 1937 article stirred little interest until the early 1970s, when a number of economists began to question the neoclassical assumptions about competitive firms as simple price takers. In raising these questions, they did not abandon a Marshallian partial equilibrium framework, but rather reworked this framework, correcting what they considered to be faulty assumptions and expanding the theoretical scope to take in topics that economists had never before addressed. Most theorists initially concentrated on the nature of firms in relation to markets (see, for example, Williamson 1975).

Agency theory and transaction cost theory were the two principal institutional perspectives that took shape in the 1970s and 1980s. Agency theorists reconceptualized the main actors in the economy: firms and their decision-making parts, the shareholders, the boards of directors, the salaried managers, and labor (Jensen and Meckling, 1976, Alchian and Demsetz, 1972). These theorists typically examined incentives that induce actors to behave in predictable ways, and they concluded that organizations are, in reality, incentive structures that various sets of actors have knowingly created and to which the same or other sets of actors knowingly respond. Transaction cost theorists reconceptualized the dyadic interactions among firms in a market. These theorists primarily specified the conditions under which firms would prefer organizational to market solutions to their economic problems, and they concluded that economic organizations and societal institutions (for example, legal and regulatory frameworks) represent solutions to transaction cost inefficiencies (Williamson, 1975, North, 1990, North and Thomas, 1973).

Whatever their particular emphases, the new institutional economists concentrated their efforts on explaining the nature and economic roles of maximizing firms as well as of decision-making, risk-taking entrepreneurs in creating and making markets work. As interest grew in institutional arguments, these theorists flipped the Marshallian paradigm. They increasingly theorized the nature of organization and downplayed the role of price systems in equilibrating markets (Putterman, 1986, Williamson and Winter, 1993). As Harold Demsetz (1993, p. 159), one of the first of the new institutional economists, put it, "the preoccupation of economists with the price system ... undermines serious consideration of the firm as a problem solving institution."

Downplaying the assumption that markets represent price-setting equilibria, the new institutionalists began to expand their definition of markets beyond anything that Marshall would recognize as a competitive market. Reducing equilibrium to metaphor, they discovered maximizing, market-like behavior in households and family planning (Becker, 1981, 1988), in public agencies, in race relations, in foreign relations (Olson, 1982), in gift exchanges (Akerlof, 1984), and in winner-take-all contests (Frank and Cook, 1995). Without the discipline of a price structure, markets could be portrayed as any means–end rationality, so much so that game playing became the analog for market behavior. Most aspects of society were viewed as game-theoretic terrains where firms, entrepreneurs, and individuals of all types served as the principal players on that terrain, the *deus ex machina*, moving societal institutions to and fro, and thus creating the organizational structures that maximize individual goals and constrain individual cupidity. In this rather grand vision of the world, the Marshallian partial equilibrium frame served, and continues to serve metaphorically, as the institutionalist vehicle to generate interpretations of large-scale economic and social organizations of entire economies and even of global configurations.

A few examples of this line of thinking will help illustrate the leap that the new institutional economists, as well as the rational choice advocates, take in jumping from a level of analysis that, as Williamson (1994, p. 92) notes, deals predominantly with "dyadic contractual relations" all the way to the organization of entire economies.[3] As we will discuss in

---

[3] As Williamson (1994, pp. 92–3) states, "Transaction cost economies deals predominantly with dyadic contractual relations. Viewing the firms as a nexus of contracts, the object is to prescribe the best transaction/governance structure between the firm and its intermediate product market suppliers, between the firms and its workers, between the firm and finance, etc. Japanese economic organization appears to be more complicated." But, Williamson continues, "transaction cost economics can help to explicate the complementaries [between Japanese and U.S. economic organization.]"

Chapter 2, it is widely known that large business networks provide the organizational structure of many Asian economies, the Japanese economy included. Among the many explanations for these business networks, the new institutional economists offer a typical bottom-up explanation that starts by stereotyping firms and interfirm behavior, and then aggregating the results to produce an overall economic structure. First, they argue that business groups are outcomes of market imperfections (Leff, 1978, Chandler, 1984, Jorgensen, et al., 1986, Khanna and Palepu, 1999, 2000a, 2000b). This classification allows them to treat business groups as the functional equivalents of Western corporations (Chandler, 1984, p. 22) and as organizations that reflect imperfections in emerging markets. The usual explanation infers a causal link between the transactional problems that exist among firms and the organization of the entire economy. Akira Goto (1982, p. 69), one of the first to make this causal connection, argues that "the (Japanese) group is an institutional device designed to cope with market failure as well as internal organizational failure. Under certain circumstances, transactions within a group of firms are more efficient than transactions through the market or transactions through the internal organization of the firm." Accordingly, Goto maintains that the post-war Japanese economy and its principal engines, the business groups, have performed more efficiently than economies organized through "the market mode or internal organization mode of the carrying out of transactions." Imai (1992), Aoki (1984, 1988, 1990, 1992), and Williamson (1991 and 1994) have developed somewhat different versions of firm-centered explanations of Japanese business organization, each starting with assertions about the "nature" of the Japanese firm or interfirm network and then generating a rationale for the organization of the entire economy.

Similar transaction cost and agency-centered explanations of societal-level economic organization have been offered for the industrial structures of Chile and India (Khanna and Palepu, 1999, 2000a), for differences in industrial organization between countries (Caves, 1989, Levy, 1991), for global networks of multinational firms (Caves, 1995), for the organizations structuring international trade regimes (Yarbrough and Yarbrough, 1987), for the organization of trade in the Middle Ages (Greif, Milgrom, and Weingast, 1994, Greif, 1994, Greif, forthcoming), for "the rise of the Western world" (North and Thomas, 1973), and for "the economic institutions of capitalism" (Williamson, 1985). As the focus of analysis moves from actual or metaphorical (for example, ruler and subjects) dyadic interactions between agents to the organization of entire economies and societies, most theorists begin to posit the independent effects of institutions and cultures, making the organization of the whole arise from the aggregated effects of institutions on actors.

Economic Sociology

Economic sociology, particularly those works based on the theoretical premises of Mark Granovetter's (1985) embeddedness perspective, presents a sociological version of the bottom-up theories of economic organization. As economists broadened the definition of market behavior to include all behavior, they ventured into intellectual territory that other social sciences had already claimed. This encroachment inspired a spirited reaction, some in favor, but others very much against economic theorizing. Those in favor formed a rather substantial group of interdisciplinary scholars (Hechter, 1987, Kiser and Hechter, 1991, 1998, Elster, 1986, Coleman, 1990, Cook and Levi, 1990, Brinton and Nee, 2001) who promoted rational-choice theory as the intellectual extension of institutional economics outside of economics. Those against this form of theorizing, however, were less unified, except in their response to treat economists and rational choice theorists as intruders and economic models as totally inadequate (see, for example, Hirsch, Michaels, and Friedman, 1990, Somers, 1998). One group of opponents working on economic development went to great lengths to argue that the state (via its functionaries), and not the market, was the principal actor creating capitalist development (Evans, Rueschemeyer, and Skocpol, 1985, Amsden, 1989, Wade, 1990, Haggard, 1990, Evans, 1995). Another group gathered around Amitai Etzioni's Durkheimian vision of a new economics based on "the moral dimension" (1988). Yet another group sided with the Karl Polanyi's critique of economic universalism (Dalton, 1969, Block and Somers, 1984, Block, 1990, Baum, 1996, Blyth, 2002). However, the largest and, arguably, the most influential group of scholars (see Friedland and Robertson, 1988, Swedberg, 1993, Smelser and Swedberg, 1994) aligned themselves theoretically with Mark Granovetter's (1985) work on embeddedness.

In the two decades since its publication, Granovetter's seminal article, "Economic Action and Social Structure: The Problem of Embeddedness" (1985) has become the core theoretical statement of economic sociology.[4] In this article, Granovetter's target of attack is the institutional economists' notion of actor agency. Granovetter maintains that economic theories, epitomized by Oliver Williamson's transaction cost theory, rest on false assumptions that each actor is independent from all others and that each attempts to maximize his or her gains often at the expense of

---

[4] This sub-field has developed so quickly that a compendium, *The Handbook of Economic Sociology*, was published less than ten years after the publication of Granovetter's seminal article. The editors felt *The Handbook* was needed in order to summarize recent advances and to advertise the promise of economic sociology in the future, and thus giving legitimacy to economic sociology as coherent, delineated field of study. A second edition of *The Handbook* (2005) has recently appeared.

others. Such a Hobbesian view of the economy, according to Granovetter, is simply wrong. He argues that the opposite point of view, that of societal roles determining individual actions, is also incorrect.

The most accurate conception, he says, lies between these two extremes. In this "middle-of the road" conception, people's real-life activities provide a sociological foundation for economic action. To Granovetter, that is what embeddedness means. Out of people's real-life activities, consisting of "concrete personal relations and structure (or 'networks') of such relations," comes the "production of trust in economic life" (1985, pp. 400–1). These social relations, "rather than institutional arrangements or generalized morality" (1985, p. 401; see also Granovetter, 1994), generate order in the economy, and this order represents patterns of small firms, vertical integration of big firms, and the structure of business groups. In other words, the order represents macro-level economic organization.

Although Granovetter inveighs against Williamson's economistic conception of agency, it is important to note that both Williamson and Granovetter generate economic organization from the bottom-up interaction of economic participants in the economy. The crucial difference between the two points of view rests on the nature of the interactions between economic actors. On the one hand, Williamson argues that the nature of the transaction itself suggests a course of action that "rational" participants should follow. In this regard, transaction cost theory employs game theoretic or rational choice models. The exchange situation generates its own logic, which induces participants to respond to the situation and to the possible actions of others. In calculating how to respond to exchange situations, entrepreneurs continually adjust the transactional context, including changing the organization of their firms, in order to maximize their economic advantages and minimize their disadvantages. As Williamson (1981, p. 568) stated, "There are so many kinds of organization because transactions differ so greatly and efficiency is realized only if governance structures are tailored to the specific needs of each type of transaction."

Firm-level economic organization, therefore, represents the rational responses of transacting actors at any one point in time. The organization of transacting firms generated at this point in time will, in turn, have effects on actor calculation at a later point in time. According to the transaction cost perspective, therefore, industrial organization (for example, the organization of a sector or an entire economy) is rational economic decisions aggregated and re-aggregated over time. Characterized in this way, industrial organization serves as a set of constraints that influences but does not determine each subsequent transaction decision. Because each transaction represents a move or a countermove in a fluid economic context, each transactional set has the potential for altering the organization of the economic sector. For transaction cost theory, the transaction remains the key focus of analysis, and aggregation from the micro- to the macro-level of analysis remains the presumed causal path by which sectors and economies become organized.

On the other hand, in the 1985 article, Granovetter argues that the organization of an industry or an economy reflects the social organization of its participants. In making this claim for social embeddedness, Granovetter is very careful to focus on the ongoing interaction among economic participants. He wants to portray economic actors as being neither mindless game players who only respond to a narrow economic frame (which he calls an "under-socialized conception of human action") nor equally mindless social actors who represent only social roles (which he call an "over-socialized conception of human action"). Arguing for the realism of the middle way, Granovetter wants his economic actors to be rationally acting individuals whose objective thinking is socially and historically bounded.

By embedding his economic actors in previously existing social networks, thus fulfilling his requirement for trust among actors, Granovetter makes economic organization independent of the economic activity in which actors are engaged. Economic activity is simply assumed to occur, but does not have a constituting role in how the activities are organized.[5] Like Williamson's transaction cost theory, economic organization becomes an artifact of prior institutional and social conditions, an outcome of the paraphernalia of capitalism rather than of the capitalist activities themselves.

As long as Granovetter remains locked in debate with Williamson, who serves as a proxy for other economists as well, Granovetter's embeddedness theory constitutes a sociological version of a bottom-up theory: Interaction among "properly" socialized individuals creates the social organization that defines trust in an economy and that, in turn, leads to macro-level economic organization. Thus, Granovetter, like Williamson, views economic organization as an outcome produced by interactions among economic actors, with the crucial difference between the two theories being the nature of human nature. Williamson, in fact, has recognized

---

[5] One of the pillars on which Granovetter (Granovetter and Swedberg, 1992, p. 6) builds his economic sociology is the assertion that "economic action is a form of social action." Although we certainly agree with this assertion, and although he incorporates some elements of the Weberian analysis that we also employ, Granovetter in his more recent writings (for example, 2002) moves the focus of his analysis from networks per se to the social and institutional foundations of the relationships embodied in the networks. The institutions constitute the relationships that in turn become the working elements of the networks in which the economic activity becomes embedded.

the similarities between the embeddedness approach and transaction cost theory and has incorporated elements of the embeddedness approach into his own work. Granovetter's "entire argument," says Williamson (1994, p. 85) "is consistent with, and much of it has been anticipated by, transaction cost reasoning. Transaction cost economics and embeddedness reasoning are evidently complementary in many respects."

In his recent writings, Granovetter (1990, 2002) has expressed increasing discomfort with the concept of embeddedness and especially with the way the embeddedness perspective has developed, in the past fifteen years or so, into more formal network analyses. He remarked that had he known he was writing such a seminal piece as the 1985 article has turned out to be, he would have written it quite differently.[6] His discomfort arises from the ambiguous relationship between networks and institutions. In the original article, he implied that the gap between the two was substantial and significant, but in the most recent writings, he has worked to close this gap in two ways.

First, he argues that the appropriate location for network analysis is at the meso-level. Specific historical outcomes often result from particular arrangements of network ties (Burt, 1992, Granovetter and McGuire, 1998) or of the historical actors' positions in a series of networks (Padgett and Ansell, 1993). Granovetter's own work on how people locate jobs (1995a) and on the historical causes for public utilities (Granovetter and McGuire, 1998), as well as his endorsement (Granovetter, 2002) of Burt's theory of structural holes (Burt, 1992), suggest that network relationships and the particular structural arrangement of ties represent proximate causes of events that may have very long-term and path dependent consequences.[7] At this level of analysis, Granovetter (1990, 2002) has warned repeatedly that simply evoking network structure (that is, centrality or structural holes) is causally insufficient without a more developed sociological understanding of the historical context. Instead, he argues that network analysis should be less formal and methodological and more linked to standard sociological concerns with power, social structure, and institutions than is now the case.

Second, in calling for a sociological understanding of context, Granovetter wants to move an embeddedness perspective away from the structural arrangement of networks to the institutional foundations of

---

[6] Personal communication. A similar comment is found in his unpublished reply to Greta Krippner (2001), which was delivered in a workshop on "The Next Great Transformation? Karl Polanyi and the Critique of Globalization" held at The Center for History, Society, and Culture, University of California, Davis on April 12–13, 2002.

[7] Granovetter, in fact, makes this point in the 1985 article (p. 506) and then reiterates it in later works (2002).

economic action. An example of this emphasis is his analysis of business groups (1994, 1995, forthcoming), which we will discuss more fully in the next chapter. Granovetter, however, is not alone in this quest. Indeed, quite a number of other theorists have taken the lead in formulating institutional foundations for economic sociology. For example, Richard Whitley (1992, 1999) contends that a society's "dominant institutions develop interdependently with particular business-system characteristics to generate and reproduce distinctive forms of economic organization" (1999, p. 54), resulting in, for instance, the formation of three distinct business systems in Asia (Japanese, Korean, and Chinese) (1992) and a number of distinctive systems in Europe and the United States (1999). Nicole Biggart and Mauro Guillen (1999, p. 235, our emphasis; also Guillen, 2001) claim that "institutional arenas – whether the firm, the industry, or the society – are internally coherent and are based on **organizing logics** that inform action and meaning." Within developing economies, these organizing logics lead to more or less consistent patterns of firm and inter-firm organizations and to "societal competitive advantages" (or disadvantages) vis-à-vis patterns of economic organization based on other organizing logics. Arguing for a view of institutions that is based on incentive and control structures, Neil Fligstein (2001) proposes that the state and leading firms impose stability and organizational order on individual markets, as well as entire economies. He (Fligstein, 2001, p. 40) states, "Initial formation of policy domains and the rules they create affecting property rights, governance structures, and rules of exchange shape the development of new markets because they produce cultural templates that determine how to organize a given society."[8]

---

[8] Fligstein's book, *The Architecture of Markets: An Economic Sociology of Twenty-First-Century Capitalist Societies* (2001), is one of the most recent and best-developed treatises reiterating the role of institutions in competitive economies. It is also one of the clearest articulations of a sociological argument developed within a Marshallian framework that is then generalized to the economy as a whole. Fligstein (2001) develops what he says is a "new view" arising from a "basic insight" that a market in which "structured exchange" occurs should be considered as an "organizational field." A market, as an organizational field, is one that has a "self-reproducing role structure." Stated in its most concise form (Fligstein, 2002, p. 67, 2001, pp. 67–98), this role structure is "a status hierarchy of producers. In this hierarchy, large and dominant firms control the market by engaging in forms of competition that preserve their position and allow smaller firms to find niches. The hierarchy is based on a set of understandings held by all market actors about what their possible moves 'mean' and about the purpose of these moves: to reproduce the positions of firms." Fields are structured politically through actions of the state and economically and culturally through the actions of dominant firms, so that within any one field competition and price are stabilized and controlled. The partial equilibrium framework of Fligstein's theory is clear from his field-by-field analysis of markets, his notion of self-reproducing (that is, equilibriating) role structures, and his belief that markets have an inherent tendency towards stability, in this case a kind of coerced equilibrium created by the state and dominant firms in each market. Also see Chapter 2 for an additional discussion of Fligstein's conception of the impact of exterior institutions on economic organization.

These and other theorists arguing for an institutional theory of entire economies (for example, Hollingsworth and Boyer, 1997, Berger and Dore, 1996, and Quack, Morgan, and Whitley, 2000) uniformly draw a distinction between an economic or neoliberal view and their own institutional perspective. Paralleling Granovetter's critique of Williamson, these theorists criticize economists for failing to incorporate social, political, and cultural institutions into an interpretation of capitalist economies. The underlying assumptions in all these various institutional theories are that different societal institutions create different forms of capitalism, that these differences among societal institutions are essentially national differences, and that the differences in capitalist economic organization are present at outset of capitalist development and persist overtime. These assumptions lead theorists to proclaim that "comparative advantages" of businesses are "generated by a firm's societal and institutional environment at the national level" (Quack and Morgan, 2000, p. 3) and that "(t)he initial configuration of institutions and the balance of power between government officials, capitalists, and workers at (the outset of capitalist development) account for the persistence of, and differences between, national capitalisms" (Fligstein, 2001, p. 40).

In making these arguments, the macro-institutional theorists are to Douglass North (1990) what Granovetter is to Williamson: They generate a theory of entire economies from a more or less static view of institutions and institutional arrangements. What Williamson noted about Granovetter's interpretation can also be said for the macro-level interpretations as well: In many respects, they are complementary interpretations, both sets relying heavily on the assumption that the institutional "rules of the game" shape the organization of economies (North, 1990). **Insofar as they are used to interpret macro-level economic organization,** transaction cost and embeddedness theories are indeed two sides of the same coin. They both commit the same errors: First, they presuppose prior conditions (for example, incentive structures, social networks, overarching institutions, organizational logics) to get the economic process underway. For transaction cost theory, an institutional environment in which costs are calculated precedes the transactions, and for the embeddedness perspective, social networks in which trust can be calculated (or an institutional environment creating an organizing logic) precede and structure subsequent economic activity. Second, even after the action is underway, neither transaction cost nor embeddedness theories isolate the mechanisms involved whereby a given incentive or transaction cost or a particular kind of social network creates ongoing complexly organized and ever-changing economies. The sleight of hand that we mentioned at the first of this chapter comes in the announcement that the trick could be done without ever revealing how the two are actually connected. The partial equilibrium frame in which they both operate obscures the gap between relatively static theoretical formulations and ever-changing and often rapidly emergent capitalist economies in which nothing is ever static.

This problem of conceptualizing economic organization is exactly the problem of using a Marshallian frame to induce, by analogy, a characterization of the whole. The organizational whole is conceptualized as being separate from the antecedent and continuing processes of organizing, and is used, *ex post facto*, to explain how the economy became organized. From this point of view, therefore, an organized economic order is more concrete than and prior to the process by which it came to be an organized whole. Moreover, this manner of conceptualizing economic organization has the consequence of viewing ongoing economic organization, at any one point in time, as an organized whole that can be described as a static object without regard to the processes of organization that give it the appearance of an organized order.

In the same way that partial equilibrium theories can be used to explain prices in specific markets, the new institutional theories, whether economic or sociological, are best used to interpret proximate causes of interactional outcomes in a small space – the dyadic transaction, a structural hole in a single network – all in a historical setting. Specific outcomes can be causally explained in terms of perceived cost savings or trust or friendship ties or sets of laws. However, when these same sets of causes are aggregated over the entire population of actors, then organization is produced without the process of organizing.

In contrast to these institutional views, the goal in this book is to understand the organizing process. As we will show, competitive struggles among firms and interconnections across markets and across economies are central aspects of the process by which economies become organized. A part of our task is to understand how institutions, market efficiencies, and embeddedness are crucial and integral to the organizing process. Our position, then, is not to abandon institutional theories, but rather to make them part of the action, and thereby to collapse the artificial dichotomy between economy and society. As Granovetter (2002) himself recognizes, this position is implicit in the embeddedness perspective. Insofar as "rational" decisions of economic actors are socially, historically, and situationally constructed, then the interaction among actors in the economy involves not merely exchange situations and their aggregated effects or social interactions and their reproduction at the macro-level. Rather, organizationally conceived, interactions (for example, competition among firms) also involve reflexive interpretations of the exchange, of the exchange process, of the subjects involved in the exchange, and of the economic context in which the exchange takes place. In other words, economic activities always involve economically as well as socially defined participants acting in organizational environments in which their own actions, as well as those of others, can be meaningfully and self-consciously objectified and interpreted. We argue in the following chapters that the actual process of organizing, given some economic content to the interaction (in addition to whatever social or political content may also exist), has independent and emergent effects on individual and firm-level actions. Because this level of organization constitutes both intra- and inter-firm interactions, it needs to be theorized and conceptually distinguished from both bottom-up and top-down theories of economic organization.

Economic Organization as the Integration of Markets: The Walrasian Frame

In 1954, Kenneth Arrow and Gerard Debreu presented a formal theory proving the "existence of an equilibrium for a competitive economy" (1954, p. 265). Many regard this proof as the culmination of general equilibrium theories that were initially formulated by Léon Walras in the 1870s. A few years ago, in an interview with Richard Swedberg, Arrow (1990, p. 149) said he believed that "general equilibrium theory will not be the site of a cooperation between economics and sociology; rather microscopic analysis, or game theory, provides a better avenue." To date, this prediction has proven true, largely because at the microscopic level economists and sociologists can bracket the phenomena they wish to study, invoke the *ceteris paribus* clause, and then analyze and argue about the effects of firms, entrepreneurs, and networks on outcomes in restricted fields. In this kind of analysis, questions about agency, particularly questions about the nature of human nature and the rationality of the economic actor, become very important aspects of the explanations.

Although useful within narrow Marshallian frames, such bottom-up theories of economic organization offer distorted views of the ways economies actually work. One of the problems of the new institutional economics is that theorists equate economic organization with a theory of the firm. This equation makes the theory of the firm into a theory of agency without a corresponding theory of the economic environment in which agency occurs, an environment that is, in conceptual terms, analytically independent of agents but is empirically constituted by them.[9] Economic organization disappears into the firm; outside the firm

---

[9] We should note that the new institutional economists typically locate institutions outside of the economic playing field. Established as constraints or incentives, such institutions are presumed exogenously to shape the internal behavior of players within each sector of economic activity. Assuming a Marshallian frame, the institutional theorists then proceed

is the world of impersonal market transactions. As Samuel Bowles (1986, p. 352) describes, this view of economic organization, what he calls the Coasian view, depicts "the capitalist economy as a multiplicity of mini-command economies operating in a sea of market exchanges." This view, he continues, is "radically different from the Walrasian [view]."

It is our opinion that a very important site for economists and sociologists to meet and work together is precisely in the analysis of entire economies, which is what we call the "Walrasian frame." The Walrasian view conceptualizes an economy as a set of interconnected markets that has systemic dimensions. To describe our use of this perspective, we need first to outline the Walrasian view as it is represented in general equilibrium theory. We will then suggest that if the formal assumptions imposed by general equilibrium theory are loosened, making it more amenable to empirical applications in the real world, then a Walrasian view of how economies work also contains a useful characterization of societal-level economic organization. Within the Walrasian view, economic organization becomes the process-driven, price-sensitive integration of firms across markets and sectors that internally arise from the participants' engagement in ongoing competitive economic activity.

General Equilibrium Theory

General equilibrium theory assumes that the analyst must step outside the narrow frame of self-interested actors and their intentions. This necessity can be described mathematically as an "over-determined set of simultaneous equations," in the sense that "the existence of n partial equilibria does not in any way guarantee general equilibrium for the whole economy made up of n markets" (Blaug, 1985, p. 571). In other words, the assumption that equilibrium exists in each of n markets (an assumption of Marshallian economics) neither acknowledges nor works out the consequences of the interconnectedness of all markets. Thus, as Arrow (1968, p. 376) notes, underlying general equilibrium theory is the "notion that

---

narrowly to examine the interaction between incentive structure (external environment) and agency (conceptualized typically as the firm) within the scope of the sector. In this characterization, economic players or even networks of players are not oriented to other players or other networks of players in this or in other sector. Rather, their presumed focus is on the incentive structure, which is external and imposed on them.

A Walrasian frame, however, presumes that the main economic environment is established by the economic players themselves through their intra-market and cross-market connections. Were externally imposed incentives imposed in one sector of activity, the Walrasian analysis would then concern how those incentives changed the economic environment across sectors, that is, how a change in one area would affect all other areas. In the Walrasian conception, then, the economic environment is seen to be the multiple activities in which the economic players are engaged.

through the workings of an entire system effects may be very different from, and even opposed to, [human] intentions."[10]

Walrasian economics is, therefore, the attempt to specify how buyers and sellers in all markets simultaneously affect each other. Walras (1977) believed that such simultaneity, when one conceives of the economy as a closed system, would move towards, but not instantly result in, a general equilibrium. Markets in an economy are composed of overlapping sets of buyers and sellers. People are simultaneously producers of goods (for example, through their wage labor) and consumers of goods. Markets must continuously adjust price and wage structures according to what is happening in other markets. A change in the price of raw commodities will change the price of final goods. A change in the cost of labor will change the demand for goods, which will also change their price. This process of mutual adjustment across markets, believed Walras, pushes the entire economy, by gradual steps, towards an equilibrated price structure. Walras called this step-wise movement toward equilibrium "*tâtonnement*" or "groping." Walras' theory of *tâtonnement* was his way to describe the process of trial and error by which buyers and sellers across all markets groped their way towards a price structure without anyone knowing in advance what the final outcome would be. Early on, Walras realized that there was no one equilibrium solution, but rather multiple equilibria were possible. The final equilibrium solution would always be contingent on earlier conditions.

The assumptions underlying Walrasian economics led economists towards an increasingly mathematical conception of general equilibrium theory and away from Walras' original desire to explain how economies actually worked.[11] Walras' theory of *tâtonnement* was especially ridiculed

---

[10] For some recent and particularly revealing research on the topic that "aggregate market behavior (does) not mirror the characteristics of the individual transactions" (Casella, 2001, p. 196), see Rauch and Casella, 2001.

[11] Walras' goal of using general equilibrium theory to approximate real-world economics is evident in the following passage from his *Elements of Pure Economics or The Theory of Social Wealth* (1977, p. 380):

"Finally, in order to come still more closely to reality, we must ... adopt ... the hypothesis of a continuous market. Thus, we pass from the static to the dynamic state. For this purpose we shall now suppose that the annual production and consumption ... change from instant to instant along with the basic data of the problem. ... Every hour, nay, every minute, portions of these different classes of circulating capital are disappearing and reappearing. Personal capital, capital goods proper and money also disappear and reappear, in a similar manner, but much more slowly. ... Such is the continuous market, which is perpetually tending towards equilibrium without ever actually attaining it, because the market has no other way of approaching equilibrium except by groping, and, before the goal is reached, it has to renew its efforts and start over again, all the basic data of the problem, e.g., the initial quantities possessed, the utilities of goods and services, the technical coefficients, the excess of income over consumption, the working capital requirements, etc., having changed in the meantime. Viewed in this way, the market is

on the grounds that the process of mutual adjustment seemed more meta-physical than scientific; some likened Walras' idea of groping to an economy's having a fictitious auctioneer who mysteriously adjudicated prices for sellers in response to the calls from buyers.[12] As we will argue below, this intermediation between buyers and sellers is a lot less mysterious than critics suggest and is, in fact, a fundamental aspect of modern capitalist economies. The proponents of general equilibrium theory, however, were more interested in mathematical solutions than real-world processes, and so moved away from intermediation and abandoned the gradualism of *tâtonnement*, by assuming perfect knowledge in the present of one's future production and consumption possibilities (Debreu, 1959, p. xi). Such an assumption allowed a mathematical solution to the simultaneous equations (Arrow and Debreu, 1954, Debreu, 1959), but further removed the idea of the interconnectedness of all markets, as embodied in general equilibrium theory, from being useful in empirical assessments of economies, except in the most general ways. Equally important, this formalized version of general equilibrium theory has only a rudimentary theory of the firm.

The reason that Walrasian general equilibrium theory lacks a theory of the firm is that it dispenses with one of the key assumptions used in the Marshallian frame – economies of scale. As we discussed earlier, the optimum size of the firm under the partial equilibrium approach is established by balancing economies of scale with demand for a product: if economies of scale are strong relative to the potential market size, then a natural monopoly prevails; whereas if economies of scale are weak, then many firms can enter, approximating a competitive outcome. The former outcome – natural monopoly – is incompatible with Walrasian general equilibrium, however, for two reasons. First, a monopoly is obviously not a price taker, so the whole idea of having equilibrium prices established

---

like a lake agitated by the wind, where the water is incessantly seeking its level without ever reaching it."

[12] Critics of Walras' concept of groping locate the fictitious auctioneer in Walras' idealized notion of tickets (1977, p. 242).

"In order to work out [a] rigorous a description of the process of groping [toward equilibrium], ... we have only to imagine, on the one hand, that entrepreneurs use *tickets* ['*bons*'] to represent the successive quantities of products which are first determined at random and then increased or decreased according as there is an excess of selling price over cost of productions or vice versa until selling price and cost are equal; and, on the other hand, that landowners, workers and capitalists also use tickets to represent the successive quantities of services [which they offer] at prices first cried at random and then raised or lowered according as there is an excess of demand over offer or vice versa, until the two become equal."

We should note in passing that Walras' idealized ticketed price calls makes intuitively more sense as a model of the real world than Arrow and Debreu's assumption (Debreu, 1959) that all actors have perfect knowledge in the present of their future production and consumption possibilities.

by a *tâtonnement* process would need to be rethought. Second, and even more serious, a strong economy of scale introduces certain mathematical difficulties that make it impossible to prove in formal terms the existence of equilibrium. So the whole construction of equilibrium across many markets simultaneously comes crashing down like a house of cards when economies of scale are strong. How, then, are we to make progress in understanding the organization of firms, and of economies, in general equilibrium?

Reintroducing Firms: Monopolistic Competition

The answer that has developed over the past twenty-five years is to consider a weaker version of economies of scale: large enough so that each firm must achieve some minimum size to be viable, but small enough so that it is easy for additional firms to enter the market. Theorists assume that the new firms entering the market can sell products that are differentiated in some dimension from other products sold in that market. This means that the various firms have some ability to set their own prices. These twin assumptions of product differentiation and the free entry of firms are the hallmark of "monopolistic competition," due to Chamberlin, 1962 [1933] and Robinson, 1969 [1933]. As its name suggests, this framework combines features of perfect competition, through the free entry of firms, and monopoly, through economies of scale, product differentiation and price setting. Economists of the early Chicago School were not particularly impressed with this synthesis, however, and believed that the polar opposites of perfect competition and monopoly (or with several firms, oligopoly) were good enough to understand most real-world markets. This may be true in a Marshallian, partial equilibrium frame, but is most certainly *not true* in a Walrasian, general equilibrium frame. What was not realized for some years was that the monopolistically competitive framework would allow for the proof of equilibrium over many markets simultaneously (Hart, 1985) and moreover, could be adapted to introduce certain organizational issues, as we discuss below.

The usefulness of the monopolistic competition model was not fully recognized until a mathematical version of that model was developed by Spence (1976), Dixit and Stiglitz (1977) and Lancaster (1979), two of whom later won the Nobel Prize in economics. These writings were still in a partial equilibrium frame, but due to their clear mathematical formulation, allowed for an extension to general equilibrium in the years that followed. That extension has been applied to a number of fields in economics, of which we briefly discuss three: international trade, growth, and economic geography.

Before turning to these applications of the monopolistic competition model, we note that there is an alternative to its use: to derive implications of increasing returns to scale, we might instead abandon a general equilibrium framework, and replace it with some other criterion for the survival of firms. That is the approach taken by Brian Arthur (1989, 1994) and work in evolutionary economics (for example, Nelson and Winters, 1982). These models are dynamic in nature, but only rarely include price competition between firms. Instead, the entry and exit of firms are modeled by some specified process, and the goal of these analyses is to see where this dynamic process converges. We can call this convergence (if it exists) an "equilibrium," but not in the Walrasian sense. This class of models has been very effective at demonstrating the idea of *path dependence*, whereby initial conditions in the dynamic system have a lasting effect on the eventual equilibrium. This means that the equilibrium cannot be unique: even slight differences in initial conditions can have large effects on the final outcomes. But it turns out that these features of multiple equilibria and path dependence can also be derived from models that respect price competition and Walrasian equilibrium, once that framework is extended to allow for monopolistic competition.

International Trade

Up until the early 1980s, George Stigler's (1968, p. 1) observation that "there is no such subject as industrial organization," could equally well be applied to the field of international trade: there was no such thing as *traders* in the theory. Despite the deep insights of the theories, such as comparative advantage and mutual gains from trade, there was no role for firms, let alone economic organization more generally, to have any effect at all on trade patterns between countries. This limitation was recognized by at least some, but advances in the theory had to wait for the corresponding advances in industrial organization. These came with the development of analytical models of monopolistic competition, which were quickly imported into the field of international trade (Krugman, 1979, 1980, 1981, Helpman and Krugman, 1985). These models explored the general equilibrium implications of product differentiation, which for the first time allowed firms to have an impact on trade patterns.

A second-generation of models followed quickly, which abandoned the large-numbers assumption of monopolistic competition, and instead supposed that the number of firms competing in an international market might be rather small (Boeing versus Airbus is a favorite example). While it was initially thought that these models would hold insights for "strategic" trade policy, so that competitive advantage could be created by government support of firms, the lessons for trade policy proved to be complex and often contradictory (Grossman, 1992, Krugman, 1994a). Accordingly, interest has returned to the earlier, monopolistic competition models with large numbers of firms.[13]

The model that we develop in this book is a natural extension of the large-numbers monopolistic competition models. However, in contrast to these models, we allow groups of firms – what we call "business groups" – to *jointly maximize profits* over all intermediate inputs and final goods produced by the group. Helpman and Krugman (1985, pp. 220–2) recognized that these models had the potential to include economic organization in their discussion of "industrial complexes," but this idea was not pursued further in the trade context; instead, the upstream and downstream linkages between firms became a building block of the new models in economic geography. We are, therefore, returning to large-numbers monopolistic competition model, and introducing the ability of firms to align themselves with others when this is desirable. The equilibrium concept we use is closest in spirit to the work in industrial organization by Perry (1988, pp. 229–35), though also anticipated by the early work of Caves (1974). Introducing cross-firm relations into the monopolistic competition model is the natural vehicle to include economic organization, and, as we shall find, has a solid empirical basis in the economies of Korea and Taiwan.

Very recently, trade economists have gone beyond the monopolistic competition model and begun to merge modern variants of transactions cost theories into Walrasian, general equilibrium models (McLaren, 2000, Grossman and Helpman, 2002, 2004, 2005a,b, Marin and Verdier, 2002, 2003, Antràs, 2003, 2005, Puga and Trefler, 2002). To give an idea of the results in this evolving area, consider first the modern version of transactions costs known as the "property rights" model (Grossman and Hart, 1986, Hart and Moore, 1990, 1999). In this model, parties make some investment of time and effort into a project and then bargain over the returns available from it. For example, it might be a manager bargaining with the headquarters of a firm over the profits available. In this dyadic setting, if the bargaining breaks down, the manager can seek employment elsewhere, and the returns from this *outside option* most certainly affect the investment of time and effort that the manager is willing to make initially: if the returns from the outside option reward prior investments, then the manager will be more willing to make these investments, which is regarded as a more efficient outcome. In the partial equilibrium setting used in industrial organization, the returns to the outside option

---

[13] The most recent work has moved beyond the firm as the organizational unit, to consider genuine traders and the networks created by their interaction (Casella and Rauch, 1997, 2000, Rauch, 1999, Rauch and Casella, 1998, Rauch and Trindade, 2002).

are treated as determined outside of the model. But in the recent general equilibrium versions, the returns to the outside option can be determined within the model: when there are *many parties willing to hire the manager*, then his or her outside options are better, leading to a more efficient outcome. In other words, *thick markets* with many participants lead to more desirable outcomes in the general equilibrium model (McLaren, 2000, Grossman and Helpman, 2002).

The finding that market thickness has an impact on efficiency illustrates how a rudimentary aspect of economic organization enters into these recent models. Obviously, there is much more work to be done. If more participants in a market lead to better outcomes, then institutions or social groups that allow for the collection and sharing of information between their members must also make a difference; in other words, networks must matter. These have also been introduced into simple trade models (Casella and Rauch, 2002, Rauch, 1999, Rauch and Casella, 2001, 2003, Rauch and Trindade, 2002, 2003). Furthermore, since firms will want to be linked with good partners abroad, we can expect that agents will find it profitable to undertake this matching activity. A model along these lines is developed by Rauch and Watson (2004), where individuals with expertise choose to become "international trade intermediaries." This also creates a role for governments to support such intermediation activities through trade fairs and associations, for example. Evidently, these ideas are bringing the *trader* back into international trade, where he or she should have been all along! We will build on these ideas in Chapter 7.

Economic Growth

The revolution of theories used within international trade has its counterpart in those used to explain economic growth. The dominant growth model for many years, due to Solow (1956), had the same emphasis on resource allocation, with no role for individual firms, as those used in international trade. A re-examination of that framework was prompted by the extraordinary growth of the Asian economies, which appeared to rely on an alternative paradigm. The models that were developed again drew upon the monopolistic competition framework, and turned these firms into dynamic entities, constantly striving to develop new products through research and development (Romer, 1990, Grossman and Helpman, 1991). Although the mathematical details were new, the motivation for the models was as old as the ideas of Adam Smith, who argued that the specialization of products was limited by the extent of the market: remove this limitation, and further specialization could occur, which could therefore expand productivity and income, leading to even further innovation, etc. in a virtuous circle. Thus argued the new "endogenous growth" models, which enjoyed an unparalleled intensity of research activity during the late 1980s and 1990s.

Along with the models came an enormous degree of empirical work devoted to testing the hypothesis that, conditional on structural variables, poorer countries would grow faster to catch up to richer countries. With titles like "I just ran two million regressions" (Sali-i-Martin, 1997), this work left no stone unturned in the search for proximate causes of growth. Surprisingly, despite the focus of the theories on the microeconomic structure of the market, the empirical work used much the same macro variables as had the Solow growth model: GDP growth, total factor productivity, aggregate investment, and so forth. Indeed, a significant group of researchers came to the conclusion that the original Solow growth model, extended to allow for human capital, did just as well at accounting for growth patterns as anything the new growth theory had to offer (Mankiw, Romer, and Wiel, 1992). This conclusion was even echoed in the Asian context by Krugman (1994a and 1994b) and Young (1993, 1995), who argued that the rapid growth of these economies was, after all, just due to capital accumulation, and nothing to get excited about! The subsequent financial crisis, and decade-long recession in Japan, appeared to confirm the idea that these economies did not possess any special capacity for productivity growth, and certainly did not pose a competitive challenge to America.

Before the "new" growth models become "conventional," and their insights are treated as no different from orthodoxy, we think it is important to return to the microeconomic structure of these models as the engine of growth: the ability of firms to flexibly introduce new and specialized inputs that can be utilized by other firms. This essential feature has been almost entirely overlooked in the empirical work, with its focus on macroeconomic variables. But to us, this description of the interrelationships between firms is the epitome of what happens every day in Taiwan, as new products and firms are created and others shut down with apparent ease. It is not enough, however, to simply argue that "market forces" allow for flexibility in Taiwan that is not observed elsewhere, such as in Korea (Levy, 1991, Little, 1979, Myers, 1984). Rather, we believe that there is a context within which the firms operate that allows for this flexibility in one country but not another and that their economic organization is as valid a variable to study as is, say, capital accumulation in the economy and just as important for economic growth. To quote Wing Woo's (1990, p. 438) apt assessment of outward-looking policy, these "have clarified only the conditions under which growth is stimulated and not the mechanics of growth." By studying the organization of firms, we hope to uncover something of the mechanics of growth.

Returning to the microeconomic structure of these models, with the emphasis on new product creation, also raises the possibility that the long-run equilibria may not be unique. As noted by Romer (1994, p. 9):

> Once we admit that there is room for newness – that there are vastly more conceivable possibilities than realized outcomes – we must confront the fact that there is no special logic behind the world we inhabit, no particular justification for why things are the way they are. Any number of arbitrarily small perturbations along the way could have made the world as we know it turn out very differently.

Even Walrasian equilibrium under perfect competition allows for multiple solutions to the determination of prices across many markets simultaneously, and this indeterminacy is enhanced when we introduce the dynamics of new product creation, as in the endogenous growth models. Identifying the "small perturbations" that can move an equilibrium in one direction or another, specifically for South Korea and Taiwan, will be our task in Part II of this book.

Economic Geography

A third area where Walrasian, general equilibrium has been extended to allow for some form of organization is in recent work dealing with economic geography (Krugman, 1991, Rauch, 1993a,b, Fujita, Krugman, and Venables, 1999, Fujita and Thisse, 2002). A common starting point for these models is again the monopolistic competition framework, where now we suppose that the differentiated outputs also serve as intermediate inputs, and firms must choose their location of production. Under the assumption of transportation costs between locations, there is an inherent advantage to have many firms situated in one location: they will each be able to purchase differentiated inputs from each other, thereby generating productivity gains. At the same time, the agglomeration of firms in one area will lead to higher land rents there, tending to limit this activity. Thus, the equilibrium organization of firms across regions results from a balancing act between the gains from agglomeration versus the costs from completing for scarce land or other resources.

When some dynamic adjustment process is added onto the economic geography models, they can very easily generate both path dependence and multiple equilibria. For example, if we assume there are just two regions, A and B, then firms in region A will have a productivity advantage whenever there are more of them located there initially (each selling differentiated inputs). The dynamic adjustment process would then allow firms to move from region B to A in response to the higher profits available in A. Thus, if region A starts with a slight head start in terms of the number of firms (or some other productivity advantage), this will escalate into a more pronounced and permanent advantage through the movement of firms. The eventual equilibrium location of firms will depend on the specifics of the model; firms might abandon region B entirely, so that all goods are imported from region A. Alternatively, the low land rents in region B might allow some economic activity to remain. The important point is that if region B instead had a slight head start, then it would become the dominant site of economic activity, rather than region A. This illustrates how multiple outcomes are possible, depending on the initial conditions faced by each region.

As useful as the economic geography models are, they deal with only one aspect of economic organization: location in geographical space. Our concern in this book is instead the organization of firms *across markets*, such as the organization of business groups, and the implications of such groups for economic performance and growth. Like the economic geography models, we will have firms purchasing differentiated inputs from each other in a monopolistic competition framework; but unlike these models, we will make the decision of whether or not to sell inputs outside the group, and at what price, a *strategic* decision. Groups will have an inherent advantage through access to their own inputs at lowest cost, but will face potentially high markups when purchasing from other groups. It is this cross-market interplay of market power that will be crucial in determining the organization of the business groups, and of the entire economy.

Reconceptualizing the Walrasian Frame

Summarizing our argument thus far, we believe that the Walrasian frame will be the most useful ground for deriving organizational features in equilibrium models. This work is already beginning in the various fields of economics that we have briefly described earlier, and our book continues in that vein. At the same time, this work is early enough that it would be worthwhile to step aside from the specifics of particular models, and ask what are the general changes that should be introduced into the Walrasian framework so that it can address economic organization. We suggest three such changes, each of which is introduced in varying extents to the model and discussion within this book.

The first alteration addresses the fact that linking producers and consumers is neither mysterious nor costless, but rather consists of a series of "market-making activities" known as intermediation (Spulber, 1996, 1998). These market-making activities play the same role as Walras' fictitious auctioneer. The processes of production, intermediation, and consumption cut across markets in many different ways. The second change to make in the Walrasian frame concerns the interconnectedness of markets that results from the ownership and direct control of, or authority over, economic assets. Related to the second, the third change incorporates the interconnected of markets that results from non-market transactions that occur between independently owned firms; these are typically contractual and quasi-contractual relationships that connect economic players within and across markets. Although intermediation, ownership, and contractual relations are discussed within a Marshallian frame (that is, transaction cost and principal agent theories), they have only begun to be incorporated in a broader analysis of economic organization as conceptualized within a Walrasian frame.

The Processes of Intermediation

The first change to make to the Walrasian frame is to recognize that those activities connecting buyers and sellers are not only real and essential aspects of all capitalist economies, but also ones that involve costs and organizational complexity. Following the term used in financial markets, Daniel Spulber (1996, 1998) labels the general set of "market-making" activities linking buyers to sellers as "intermediation" and calls the firms that fulfill these functions "intermediaries." Intermediaries, he (1996, p. 135) says, are economic agents "that purchases from suppliers for resale to buyers or that helps buyers and sellers meet and transact. Intermediaries seek out suppliers, find and encourage buyers, select buy and sell prices, define the terms of transactions, manage the payments and record keeping for transactions, and hold inventories to provide liquidity or availability of goods and services." These intermediaries are usually firms, but Spulber (1996, p. 137) notes that they can also be market institutions expressly created for the purpose of intermediation, such as the organized exchanges for securities, options, futures, and other financial assets. He (1996, p.136) also cautions that the boundaries between institutions and firms and between merchants and manufacturers are not clear-cut. "In combination with managing transactions, intermediaries often transform products to add value: transporting, storing, repackaging, assembling, preparing for final use, and adding information and guaranties. Conversely, manufactures carry out many market-making activities, intermediating between sellers of raw materials or product components, and buyers of manufactured."

The absence of clear-cut boundaries separating firms and institutions performing one or another market-making or market-taking functions is due to the actual complexities of buying and selling and to the role of intermediation in resolving some of these complexities. For example, it is well known that most buying and selling occur at intermediate stages in the production of products, rather than at the point of final sale and use. The purchase of an automobile by a final user is but one transaction in a vast number of transactions of innumerable goods and services that lead to the manufacture and then final sale of the automobile. Most exchanges occur before the final sale of a good. Likewise, most intermediation takes place before the final consumer enters the picture. To spell out the intricacies of intermediation, Spulber (1996, 1998) analytically distinguishes among four distinct types that happen at various points in the manufacture and distribution of goods: 1) price setting and marketing clearing, 2) liquidity and immediacy, 3) matching and searching, and 4) guaranteeing and monitoring. As markets develop, the different processes of intermediation may be handled by different firms or may be incorporated in the firms representing buyers or sellers. How the intermediation functions are actually handled and how buyers and sellers are actually linked depend, however, on a variety of factors that need to be spelled out in theoretical terms.

A way to begin this task is to use Gary Gereffi's work on global commodity chains to conceptualize the mediated linkages between buyers and sellers. In ideal terms, commodity chains represent the organization of all steps in production and distribution of a product before final consumption. Gereffi (1994, p. 219) views commodity chains in terms of three main dimensions: "(1) an input-out structure (i.e., a set of products and services linked together in a sequence of value-adding economic activities); (2) a territoriality (i.e., spatial dispersion or concentration of production and marketing networks, comprised of enterprises of different sizes and types); and (3) [coordination procedures] that determine how financial, material, and human resources are allocated and flow within a chain."[14] Using these three dimensions in his empirical examination of many commodity chains in different product areas, Gereffi observes that the interfirm transactions in commodity chains seldom represent simple "arm's length" market exchanges, but rather are "organized" exchanges in that they are repetitive, coordinated, or even aggressively controlled by firms occupying key locations in a chain.

---

[14] Gereffi (1994) uses the term "governance structure" instead of "coordination procedures." We, however, want to theorize authority and power relationships in a more complex way. Therefore, we incorporate the meaning of governance structure in our discussion of the organization of ownership and control, leaving coordination procedures as an essential aspect of commodity chains, without however predefining the exact nature of those procedures.

Based on this observation, Gereffi (1994) argues that the sequencing of intermediate producers and consumers in commodity chains typically is structured around critical barriers to entry, which we conceptualize in this book (and formalize in Chapter 3) as a form of market power. We think of these critical barriers to entry in terms of what firms are most crucial to and can control marketing-making activities that are essential in linking buyers and sellers. In ideal terms, different barriers to entry result in different configurations. For goods that are difficult to produce (for example, capital or technology intensive products, such as automobiles, aircraft, electrical machinery), the economically most powerful firms in the chain are typically those closest to the final assembly of the product. For example, for the airline industry, the airline assembly firms, such as Boeing, and manufacturers of the jet engines, such as Rolls Royce, control or attempt to control the entire chain, backward to the suppliers of initial inputs (for example, specifying standards for aluminum) and components, and forward to the final consumers (the airline companies). Gereffi (1994) calls these chains "producer-driven chains." In producer-driven chains, the large firms will also internalize most aspects of intermediation. They will establish prices and clear inventory; they will supply capital (for example, in the form of credit) to ensure purchases occur; they will search out uses and users for their products; and they will guarantee their products and monitor their performance.

However, for standardized products that are relatively easy to make, such as clothes, footwear, and household electronics, the critical point of control in the chain is not the manufacture, but rather the design, merchandising, and retailing of the products. With these kinds of products, the intermediaries control the commodity chain. Included among these intermediaries are such specialty apparel stores as The Gap and Nike, and such mass retailers as Wal-Mart, Circuit City, and Home Depot, all of which merchandise and sell products but do not actually make them. These intermediaries are what Gereffi calls "big buyers" and the chains they control, "buyer-driven" commodity chains. As we describe more fully in Chapter 6, these intermediaries create and orchestrate product demand from manufacturers (that is, intermediary demand) based largely on their ability to organize and control intermediation processes. Spulber (1996, p. 137) describes their roles as intermediaries as follows:

> Retailers include supermarkets, discount stores, department stores, general merchandise stores, specialty apparel stores, warehouse clubs, drug stores, convenience stores and variety stores.... The retail sector performs a wide variety of intermediation functions including pricing, marketing, inventory holding, selection of suppliers, setting bid prices offered to suppliers,

quality certification, and management of transactions. Retailers have enhanced their market-making activities through Electronic Data Interchange (EDI) with their suppliers, which lowers costs and increases the speed in exchanging data on sales, inventory and marketing as well as expediting billing and invoicing. Retailers are generating improved data through bar coding of merchandise, point-of-sale scanners, and computerized inventory tracking and reordering. This increases information about sales and allows a rapid response to changing market conditions.

Controlling crucial links in the long chain of buying and selling that joins many producers to the final consumer of goods provides firms with the leverage to control the entire chain. To the extent that the firms that make up the chain also command a competitive advantage vis-à-vis other chains making or selling the same or similar goods, then these same firms establish a price structure that drives competition in the entire sector. In this sense, given a specific product, intermediation processes drive pricing for that product, and, as we will suggest, competition over pricing drives economic organization.

Ownership, Control, and Authority

The processes of intermediation are powerful drivers of cross-market integration. As is apparent from the discussion above, these processes can be controlled by firms (as well as by state and industry regulations) in any number of ways. Therefore, the second change to make in the Walrasian frame is to conceptualize the cross-market integration that results from the actual ownership and direct control of, or authority over, economic assets. This change is crucial to the entire Walrasian vision of the economy as representing the interconnectedness of markets. The change is also crucial to the empirical analysis of the large Asian business groups, which consist of firms sharing various forms of ownership, management, and asset control. As we will discuss in subsequent chapters, some of these business groups (for example, the Korean *chaebol* and the Japanese *keiretsu*) are vertically integrated into "one-set production" systems. Other business groups, such as in the Chinese family-owned conglomerates, as found in Taiwan, Hong Kong, and Southeast Asia, have comparatively modest overlap among firms in terms of production but are still centrally owned and controlled.

Contrasting the degree of overlap between the cross-market organization of production and the cross-market organization of ownership, management, and asset control forces, one has to reconsider the conventional distinction between markets and hierarchies that was first made by

Coase (1937) and Williamson (1975). Transaction cost theory assumes that the organization of production (that is, market transactions) and the organization of ownership and control (that is, hierarchy) are co-determined, as being causally linked, the latter being an efficient outcome of the former. This theoretical specification makes economic organization in the form of hierarchies a dependent variable, with variation in market transactions being the independent variable. Vertical integration, says Williamson (1991) is the "paradigm problem" for transaction cost theory.

There is no reason, however, to theorize, *a priori*, as does transaction cost theory, that inter-firm authority-bearing networks (that is, ownership networks) necessarily overlap the set of firms linked together in a commodity chain. In fact, it is obvious from Gereffi's two ideal types that the degree of overlap between the organization of ownership and asset control and the organization of production will vary by the nature of the economic activity in which the firms are engaged. For example, in a producer-driven chain, the main producing firms would exert their formal control, often in the form of shared ownership, and informal controls, in the form of market power, over their intermediate suppliers in order to coordinate the output, quality, and price of their intermediate goods. In buyer-driven chains, however, big buyers do not formally control their sub-contractors. In fact, the cost structure of producing less expensive and technologically more standardized products than those produced in producer-driven chains creates an incentive in the opposite direction, away from formal ownership and formal managerial controls.

This distinction between ownership and control becomes especially important when considering business groups, where the firms within the group may be under common (for example, family) ownership, but also may not be. What is the authority exercised by a group over its firms? To answer this, it is useful to recall Weber's "sociological concept of economic action," as described by Swedberg (1998, p. 33). This concept consists of three core features: "(1) there is a peaceful attempt to gain power of control and disposal; (2) this action is directed at something that provides an opportunity for utility (either to satisfy one's wants or for profit-making); and (3) the action is oriented to the behavior of others." Of the three, Swedberg adds (Swedberg, 1998, p. 33), the first, the power to control and dispose, is the "essential" criterion of a sociological concept of economic action, because it "introduce(s) into the analysis of the economies . . . the issue of power." Weber defines power in this sense as legitimate authority or domination (*Herrschaft*), the acknowledged right, in one's economic affairs, to control and to dispose: we can take this right to be the definition of *authority*.

With this meaning, authority is analytically distinguished from market power in any of its myriad forms (Weber, [1921–2] 1978, pp. 941–55). On the one hand, authority refers to commands that solicit obedience based on their intrinsic legitimacy or on the intrinsic legitimacy of the person issuing the command. The legitimacy of the command becomes the basis for another's obedience. On the other hand, market power refers to a calculation of utilities in the context of competing interests. For example, people buy electricity from a monopoly because they want electrical power and have no choice other than getting it from the public utility. In this example, the link between the public utility and the consumers of electricity is one of the utility's market power and the people's calculation of their own interests, but it is not a situation of command and obedience.

In conceptual terms, then, the line between market power and authority is relatively clear-cut. For example, in our model, which we describe in Chapter 3, authority is defined as the ability to control the price of intermediate goods exchanged between firms within a business group. Pricing among a number of business groups and unaffiliated firms is based on considerations of market power. In the real world, however, the dividing line between authority and market power is ambiguous, often purposefully so. More often than not, this ambiguity is an essential part of how economies actually work. As economic sociologists have shown time and again, economic networks generate a normative basis for economic action, in which cooperation with some becomes an essential component of competition with others (for example, Biggart and Abolafia, 1991). In such cooperative networks, as game theorists (for example, Axelrod, 1984) and anthropologists (for example, Geertz, 1963) have shown, people routinely bracket and sometimes entirely supplant short-term means–ends calculations, taking instead a long-term view that complying with another's request is appropriate even though there is no one in a legitimate position of power commanding compliance. In the real world, therefore, the dividing line between authority and market power is never clear-cut and is always an empirical question.

From a Weberian perspective, authoritatively constituted interfirm networks are defined by the span of effective control, which would include "not only business corporations, co-operative associations, cartels, partnerships, and so on, but all permanent economic establishments which involve the activities of a plurality of persons, all the way from a workshop run by two artisans to a conceivable communistic organization of the whole world" (Weber, 1978, p. 74). The specific content of that control (including formal authority as well as informal normative controls), as well as the organizational structure that derives from this control, originates not only from historical, developmental conditions but also from economic processes themselves, the processes of controlling and disposing of goods and property in relation to others doing the same thing. As such, players in capitalist economies, regardless of the basis and origins of their authority, respond to the economic conditions encountered within the economy itself.

Economic Networks

The third change to introduce in the Walrasian framework is to conceptualize the cross-market integration that results from non-market transactions that occur among firms that are not incorporated in an authoritatively controlled group. Gereffi (1994) demonstrates that many links
in both producer-driven and buyer-driven commodity chains involve
long-term subcontracting relationships that are neither arm's-length market transactions nor intra-group exchanges. Powell (1990), Powell and
Prantley (1992), Landa (1994), Rauch (1999), and Uzzi (1996) describe
such relationships more generally as "network transactions" and see them
as occurring within the context of markets but as being fundamentally
non-market in nature.[15] Rauch (1999, p. 4) defines these economic networks as "the set of actors who know each other's relevant characteristics
or can learn them through referral." These actors engage in preferential and repeated exchanges, which allow them collectively more market
power than each possesses individually. Rauch and Trindade (2002) cite
ethnic and, in particular, Chinese business networks as one of the primary
examples of groups engaging in non-market transactions. Such networks
increase the collective market power of the ethnic group, sometimes to
the point of monopoly in a specific line of business, without any person or subset of persons being in direct control of the network. Uzzi
(1996) describes these non-market trading relationships as examples of
"embeddedness" that grows out of repetitive transactions among a subset
of market actors operating in highly competitive market contexts. Even
more generally, iterated exchanges of all types favor the emergence of
reciprocity as the operative norm within the network, which in turn max-
imizes group advantage rather than the interests of any one individual
(Axelrod, 1984, Chung and Hamilton, 2001).

The development of a variety of economic networks and the emergence
of collective norms that coordinate intra-network transactions provide a
significant source of non-market exchanges that organize the economy.
We develop this theme in Chapters 6 and 7, where we show that the
primary drivers of the South Korean and Taiwanese economies, especially
in the early years of rapid growth, are non-market transactions. These
non-market transactions mainly represent the organized and reiterated
exchanges between big buyers and the producers of goods. In short, we

---

[15] This insight is, of course, closed related to Granovetter's notion of embeddedness.

demonstrate that these economies are driven by and are organized in response to "intermediary demand."

In sum, we propose that a Walrasian framework is, in principle, the best perspective from which to conceptualize the organization of economies. The analytic additions we make to this framework are to recognize the importance, first, of intermediation processes that interconnect markets, and second, of self-conscious attempts on the part of participants to control these processes both through cross-market ownership of firms and through developing and participating in economic networks. The key feature of the Walrasian framework that we leave untouched and to which we now turn is that *price structures* drive the interconnectedness of markets. While the inclusion of prices in an economic model seems obvious enough, we have already argued that the new institutional economists have been quite happy to set aside this "preoccupation" (Demsetz, 1993, p. 159), and focus instead on bargaining problems in the firm. Economic sociologists, too, seldom incorporate prices and price structures in their analysis. They assume the presence of prices, of course, but do not conceptualize the effects of prices on organization. This omission in economic sociology is all the more surprising because one of the founders of economic sociology, the preeminent sociologist and economist Max Weber, was himself *very concerned* with price competition, and viewed it an essential component in his grand synthesis of society and economies.[16] In fact, it is Weber's conceptualization of prices that gives us a theory of agency that fits within our reconstructed Walrasian frame.

---

[16] It is important to point out that Weber was himself a practicing economist for much of his academic career. Early and late in his career, he held academic positions in economics and taught a wide range of economics courses to large classes of students. In fact, his first book to appear in English, *General Economic History (1927)*, was a set of lecture notes (prepared by students and translated by the eminent University of Chicago economist, Frank Knight) from a class in economic history that Weber had taught in the Winter term of 1919–20, the same year he died of influenza at the age of fifty-six. He closely read and largely followed the work of Carl Menger, who is regarded as one of the three founders of neoclassical economics (along with Jevons and Walras) and who became the founding theorist of what later developed into the Austrian School of Economics. Weber was deeply involved in and an important contributor to the *Methodenstreit* (the Battle of Methods) that split German economics between analytical and historical approaches. He was friends and collaborators with Joseph Schumpeter and Ludwig von Mises, and his work was well known to Freidrich von Hayek, all three of whom promoted Austrian-School economics in the United States and England after World War II. When Weber came to sociology during the last decade of his life, he did so in order to self-consciously develop an economic sociology (*Wirtschaftssoziologie*) in order "to mediate between analytical economics and historical economics, and sometimes also to go beyond them" (Swedberg, 1998, p. 187). Weber's contributions to economics should, therefore, be understood as an insider's contribution based on full knowledge of the controversies in the discipline in his time.

Prices and Competitive Struggles: Agency in a Walrasian Frame

Weber's view that competition is the key force driving modern capitalist economies was based on his expertise in economic history. According to his reading, competition has always been a feature of all types of market economies, including those existing in the very distant past. Only in the modern capitalist era, however, has competition become fixed as the integrating feature of the economic system. What allowed competition to take this central role during "the final step in the transition to capitalistic organization of production was the mechanization of the production and of transportation, and its orientation to capital accounting" (Weber, 1978, p. 148). According to Weber (1978, p. 92), even more than mechanization per se, capital accounting is the core feature of capitalism because it is required in the evaluation of profits, and an orientation to profits and to the calculability of profits is what defines and drives the modern capitalist system.[17]

With the widespread adoption and standardization of capital accounting system in modern capitalism, "money," argues Weber (1978, p. 108), "is not a mere 'voucher for unspecified utilities.'" Instead, money becomes "primarily a weapon" in the competitive struggle of "man against man," and "prices are expression of the struggle." The role of money accounting and of prices in the competitive capitalist struggle is to rationalize the "calculatory orientation of economic action" and the quantitative estimation of competitiveness. This formulation "embeds" Weber's theory of price formation in a *reflexive system* of competition.[18] Once these accounting procedures became standardized features of capitalist

---

[17] Weber (1978. p. 91) defines capital accounting as follows:

> There is a form of monetary accounting which is peculiar to relational economic profit-making; namely, "capital accounting." Capital accounting is the valuation and verification of opportunities for profit and of the success of profit-making activity by means of a valuation of the total assets (goods and money) of the enterprise at the beginning of a profit-making venture, and the comparison of this with a similar valuation of the assets still present and newly acquired, at the end of the process; in the case of a profit-making organization operating continuously, the same is done for an accounting period. In either case a balance is drawn between the initial and final states of the assets.

[18] Weber's theory of price formation implies that competition always involves active reflexive comparisons with other players. A number of economic sociologists (for example, White, 1981, 2002, Podolny, 1993, 2001, Podolny, Stuart, and Hannan, 1996, Fligstein, 2001) have insightfully equated this reflexivity (mutual signaling) with competition and have noted its relation to prices. White's formulation is particularly important, because it had a large impact on the development of economic sociology. For example, White (1981, p. 518) notes that "Markets are self-producing social structures among specific cliques of firms and other actors who evolve roles from observations of each other's

economies, they also began to feed back on and to accelerate competitive struggles. Such feedback loops makes market economies into reflexive systems. In other words, prices, as expressions of competition, serve to translate economic performance into sets of statistics (for example, P/E ratios, market shares, debt-to-equity ratios, sales and revenues figures), by which each player in the system can be "objectively" interpreted, can be rendered "transparent." Using these statistics, entrepreneurs can objectify the cost structures of their own firm's performance relative to that of all other firms (subsets of which are competitors and actual or possible transactional partners) and then can calculate ways to maintain or change or otherwise rationalize those cost structures relative to cost structures in other firms. It is this reflexivity, made possible by capital accounting, that makes competition the driving force of capitalism, a force that is activated by the entrepreneurial ability to compete against others through balancing market power and the authoritative power to control and dispose.

Weber's view of price formation in the context of competitive struggles implies a theory of agency that fits within nicely in a Walrasian frame and that is useful in conceptualizing economic organization as a spontaneous order that arises from human actions but not human designs. Using Weber's formulation, we hypothesize that economic organization is a outcome of protracted competitive struggles among economic actors, in which the exercise of authority and market power is: (1) decisive to that outcome and embedded in contexts; (2) where authority and power have institutionalized meanings; and (3) where economic measures (for example, prices, profits, assets, solvency, wealth, conspicuous display) are both expressions of the competitive struggle and the means to calculate strategy and to track the performance of relevant actors. To this hypothesis, we would add a feature that Weber did not discuss, namely that competitive struggles follow cross-market processes, such as intermediation along commodity chains, and lead to cross-market connections in the

behavior. . . . Producers watch each other within a market. . . . What a firm does in a market is to watch the competition in terms of observables."

Although some aspects of this work are close to our own analysis, their emphasis is quite different from our own and from Weber's emphasis, whose work, incidentally, they do not cite in this regard. They tend, instead, to focus on what happens in specific markets, and see each market as relatively static, as reproducing role structure among players. These players are distinguished by differences in status and by their development of distinct niches. The competitive process is conceptualized in isolation from all other markets and tends to underplay dimensions of authority and market power and to disregard organizational changes that can occur as a result of competition. Their work, therefore, tends to focus on single markets and does not link competitiveness to Weber's concern for the organizational dynamics of capitalism.

form of ownership and networks. As we will show throughout this book, this hypothesis leads to the conclusion that economies (or significant segments thereof) "self-organize" around the principal axes of competition.

Conclusions

It is our contention in this book that the primary theorists of economic organization in both economics and sociology offer a partial equilibrium solution for what is, in reality, a general equilibrium problem. The organization of economies, we theorize, arises from competitive struggles in the context of ongoing economic activity. In this sense, the economy is "self-organizing," which means that the organizational outcomes of these competitive struggles are not knowable in advance, because, as we demonstrate in a more formal way in Chapter 3, the outcomes are the results of non-lineal processes connecting firms across markets. From the viewpoint of the economic actors, we theorize that the "dispersed actions of individuals, seeking various particular ends and not any overall social result," nevertheless lead to the emergence and reproduction of an ongoing, minutely organized economy (Koppl, 1994, p. 193). Though varied and emergent, however, the outcomes are also not the result of random events or idiosyncrasies and, therefore, do not depend, strictly speaking, on proximate causes. They arise, instead, in the "normal and ordinary course" of doing business (Koppl, 1994, p. 193).

We are hardly the first to investigate the organization of economies in a Walrasian, general equilibrium frame. Indeed, the "self-organizing economy" is used as the title of the book by Paul Krugman (1996), which draws on his writings in international economics (Helpman and Krugman, 1985) and economic geography (Krugman, 1991). Krugman's work is most definitely in a Walrasian, general equilibrium frame, incorporating some aspect of competition between firms and resulting in some form of organization. Also, Schumpeter's idea of "competitive destruction" has by now been fully incorporated into formal, mathematical models of the growth process,[19] building on the writings of Krugman and other researchers (for example, Grossman and Helpman, 1991). In this chapter we have briefly reviewed recent writings in economics that apply the monopolistic competition model to a Walrasian, general equilibrium setting. Our main interest has been to understand how *economic organization* has been introduced into the models considered, and we conclude that this work is still in its infancy.

---

[19] Segerstrom, Anant, and Dinopoulos (1990) and Dinopoulos and Segerstrom (1999).

Our argument that the price system is crucial for economic organization will be accepted by most economists, but not necessarily by economic sociologists. To address this, we have described how price competition is central to the work of Max Weber. Weberian analysis would logically suggest that economies with different types of systemically interconnected economic organizations should differ fundamentally in what and how economic and social factors drive the economy. In other words, Weberian analysis would imply that there should be an economic theory that goes along with an economic sociology. Weber, however, did not pursue this line of analysis. Indeed, in the second decade of the twentieth century, Weber saw only one instance of capitalism, that which developed in Western Europe and the United States. Moreover, even for Western capitalism, Weber did not work out the implications of how an organizational view of economies should be linked to formal economic theory. That is one of the principal tasks we begin in this book.

2

Interpreting Business Groups in South Korea and Taiwan

"In many successful late-industrializing countries in the 20th century . . . business groups with operating units in technologically unrelated industries have acted as the microeconomic agent of industrial growth" (Amsden and Hikino, 1994, p. 112). This is Alice Amsden's conclusion, presented here in an article with Takashi Hikino, but also found in many of her other writings (2001, 1989, 1985). She shares this opinion with many political economists (Cumings, 1985, Wade, 1990, Fields, 1995, Evans, 1995, Woo-Cumings, 1991, 1999), who, like herself, have been instrumental in making the strong state interpretation the most prominent explanation of Asian development. A number of economists (Leff, 1976, 1978, Aoki, 1984, 1988, Jorgensen, Hafsi, and Kiggundu, 1986, Ghemawat and Kanna, 1998, Khanna and Palepu, 1999, 2000a, b, c), while willing to concede the potential role of government policy, instead list market failures and transaction cost savings as the primary reasons for the emergence of business groups. Not to be outdone, sociologists (Granovetter, forthcoming, 1995b, 1994, Chung, 2001, 2003, Whitley, 1990, 1992, Gereffi and Wyman, 1990, Orrù, Biggart, and Hamilton, 1997, Hamilton, Zeile, and Kim, 1989) see business groups as embodiments of social networks and institutions rather than as outcomes of political or economic processes. That scholars from such diverse disciplines have zeroed in on business groups from different disciplinary angles testifies not only to their actual importance in Asian economic development, but also to their theoretical ambiguity. Business groups are important phenomena, to be sure, but how they work and what they signify are less apparent.

Business groups are our empirical point of entry into the task of conceptualizing economic organization within a Walrasian framework. For us, too, they are agents of economic growth and transformation, but, in contrast to other approaches, business groups for us are parts of larger economic orders that they help produce and of which they are also a product.

50

In the last chapter, we contrasted two general frameworks within which economic organization is conceptualized: Marshallian partial equilibrium and Walrasian general equilibrium frameworks. This chapter empirically grounds this contrast in the interpretive work done on business groups in general and those in East Asia in particular. As we will show in this chapter, most analysts develop a Marshallian interpretation of business groups. Within this framework, business groups are interpreted as if they were either single units, sets of tightly interconnected firms with a centralized governance structure, or networks embedded in institutions and trustworthy relationships – each alternative or combination of alternatives arising in response to a set of constraints or incentives or opportunities in an economy that is otherwise left undefined. The central problems of the Marshallian interpretation become essentializing assessments: What is the true nature of business groups; how do we explain their origin; what is their governance structure; and are they efficient and profitable? The answers to such questions, given a disciplinary perspective, make all business groups look very much alike, differing only in degree, but not kind; they become a general phenomenon that is seemingly disconnected from the specific economies in which they are located.[1]

Business groups, however, are not Marshallian phenomena. By definition, they are groups of firms, variously organized, that cross markets and, in so doing, organize economies. This is not an elusive observation; every analyst, including Amsden, quoted above (for example, "operating units in technologically unrelated industries") begins his or her discussion of business groups with this recognition, but somehow the multiple market features of business groups are reduced in importance relative to what business groups "really" are and what they "really" do. In this book, we show that business groups are Walrasian manifestations of competitive, capitalist economies. Indeed, we suggest that they share features found in all capitalist economies throughout the world, including the United States, but we also argue that business groups cannot be reduced to single units or to single governance structures or to embedded networks, however institutionalized. Put more precisely, business groups cannot be accurately interpreted within a Marshallian framework. They are always Walrasian in the sense that they are always shaped by a larger economic environment in which they do business. To be sure, they are agents; they are groups of firms that pull different markets together within the organized boundaries of the group, and make those interconnections across markets subject to some form of authoritative control. But these groups of firms

---

[1] Some business groups are better governed than others as measured by their profitability. For a discussion of the profitability of business groups in Japan, see Lincoln, et al., 1996; in Korea, see Woo-Cumings, 1999a; in Taiwan, see Chung, 2000.

do not organize economies as they please. As we have discussed in Chapter 1, the general equilibrium framework would suggest, and we hereby hypothesize, that how one business group internally organizes its cross-market interconnections will influence how all other business groups will organize their interconnections, and vice versa, and even more generally, how business groups individually and collectively organize will influence how other unaffiliated firms in the same economy will be organized, and vice versa. Therefore, the deduction from this premise is that the cross-market organization of business groups not only will differ from each other, but also will differ from economy to economy.

We specify a model and draw out hypotheses for a Walrasian theory of business groups in the next chapter, and we empirically test these hypotheses for the South Korean and Taiwanese cases in Chapters 4 and 8. In this chapter, we show that the existing interpretations of business groups are for the most part Marshallian, including its extensions in transactions costs and the new institutional economics. This chapter also serves to prepare the reader for the presentation of this model by giving a very brief description of the South Korean and Taiwanese business groups, including their intermarket connections, as they appeared on the eve of the Plaza Accord in 1985. As we indicate later, the Plaza Accord, under which the value of Japanese, South Korean, and Taiwanese currencies was appreciated in relation to the U.S. dollar, marks the beginning period of industrial restructuring in each of these countries: so great a shift in the price structure across markets necessitated a comprehensive reorganization among firms. Chapter 7 traces the development of both economies up to 1985, and Chapter 8 examines the period after 1985. Also, although the Japanese business groups are not the focus of our book, they are the best-known examples of business groups and, therefore, provide a useful benchmark against which we can compare the South Korea and Taiwanese cases. We will begin our description with them.

Asian Business Groups: Cross-market Networks of Independently Owned Firms

Japan

In the years before the decade long downturn of the Japanese economy that began in the early 1990s, observers of the Japanese economy believed that business groups provided the Japanese economy with a virtually unstoppable industrial momentum that would transform global capitalism in the coming decades. In retrospect, we now know that those observations were wrongheaded, but in recent years the reverse trend in which all aspects of Japanese business groups are denigrated is equally misleading. Both trends of analysis focus too tightly on the business groups themselves, on their internal workings, and on their institutional environments, but not enough on the competitive and changing locations of these business groups in the Japanese, as well as the global economy. A detailed analysis of Japanese groups is beyond the scope of our book, but it is important to recognize that Japanese business groups not only have been the primary cross-market organizers of the Japanese economy, but have also played intermediary roles for other Asian economies as well, including South Korea and Taiwan, as we will discuss in Chapters 6 and 7.

In organizational terms, in the 1980s, observers saw two major types of business groups in Japan: one a horizontally and the second a vertically arranged network among firms.[2] The first type, known as "intermarket groups" or "intermarket *keiretsu*," had ownership and loan relationships that extend across seemingly unrelated industries. There were six major intermarket groups, each of which had a main bank and a principal trading company (or *sogo shosha*) at its center, and its member firms belonged to a "president's club."[3] Three of these (Mitsubishi, Mitsui, and Sumitomo) grew out of pre-war *zaibatsu*. Because banks were, and continue to be, at the center of the groups, these groups are often called "main bank groups" (Aoki and Patrick, 1994). The affiliated firms in these groups mutually own each other's shares, and the main bank also owns shares (though it is prohibited by law from owning more that 5 percent); thus, for any one firm, the controlling interest was held only by the group as a whole. Typically, individual ownership, whether through stock or through private holdings, accounted for very little of the total ownership of Japanese business groups.

The major firms in these groups, along with a set of relatively autonomous, very large firms (for example, Toyota), organized a second type of cross-market network, called "*keiretsu*" or "vertical *keiretsu*." These vertical *keiretsu* consist of linkages among many small, medium, and large independent firms that overlapped directly with production sequences, so that the entire set of firms constituted an internally integrated commodity chain. The largest firms in the network coordinate the activities of these production networks, each organizing first, second,

---

[2] There is a very large literature dealing with the structure of business groups in Japan, with a sampling of views provided by Clark (1979), Dore (1987), Aoki (1990), Gerlach (1992), Imai (1992), Itoh (1992, Chap. 7), and Orrù, Hamilton, and Suzuki (1990).

[3] The intermarket groups are as follows: Mitsubishi, Mitsui, Sumitomo, Fuyo, DKB, and Sanwa. The independent groups are as follows: Tokai Bank, IBJ, Nippon Steel, Hitachi, Nissan, Toyota, Matsushita, Toshiba-IHI, Tokyu, and Seibu. For a description of these groups, see Orrù, Hamilton, and Suzuki (1990).

Table 2.1. *President's Club Firms by Sector in Japan's Six Intermarket Groups, 1982*

Sector	Mitsubishi	Mitsui	Sumitom	Fuyo	DKB	Sanwa
Banking and insurance	****	****	****	****	*******	****
Trading and commerce	*	**	*	*	*****	****
Forestry and mining		*	**			
Construction	*	**	*	*	*	***
Food and beverages	*	*		***		**
Fibers and textiles	*	*		**	*	**
Pulp and paper	*	*		*	*	
Chemicals	*****	**	**	***	******	*******
Petroleum products	*			*	*	*
Rubber products					*	*
Glass and cement	**	*	**	*	*	*
Iron and steel	*	*	*	*	***	****
Nonferrous metals	**	*	****		***	*
Machinery – general	*		*	**	***	*
Electrical and electronics	*	*	*	***	*****	*****
Transportation machinery	**	**		*	***	***
Precision instruments	*			*	*	
Real estate	*	*	*	*		
Land transportation				**	*	**
Marine transportation	*	*		*	*	*
Warehousing	*	*	*		*	
Service industry					*	
Total number of firms	**28**	**23**	**21**	**29**	**46**	**42**

Note: Each asterisk represents one firm.
Source: Dodwell 1984: 53, 64–5, 74, 82, 91, 100.

and sometimes third tier suppliers. These vertical *keiretsu* are common in automobile manufacturing, as well as consumer electronics and other industries (Nishiguchi, 1994, Smitka, 1991).

Table 2.1 lists the number of firms and the diversity of sectors covered just by the select firms constituting the President's Club for the six intermarket groups in 1982 (Orrù, Biggart, and Hamilton, 1997). The first column of Table 2.2 summarizes the sales of the six major intermarket groups, along with ten other vertical *keiretsu*, in each major industrial sector in 1982. It is evident that they accounted for a substantial share of sales in all sectors. Perhaps more important than their total sales is the extent to which they relied on member firms for *internal sales*, that is, subcontracting within the groups. For the six intermarket groups in Japan in the 1980s, Gerlach (1992, pp. 143–9) reports that the rate of internal transactions has been variously calculated to be around 10 percent. Numbers of roughly this magnitude were also calculated by the Japanese Fair Trade Commission in a widely publicized study, finding that intermarket

Table 2.2. *Business Group Shares by Major Sector, 1983 (percent)*

Sector	Japan – Sales Share of 16 largest *keiretsu*[a]	South Korea – Sales Share of 50 largest *chaebol* (value-added share)[b]	Taiwan – Sales Share of 96 largest business groups
Mining	17.6	10.6 (4.1)	0.0
Manufacturing	33.2	45.4 (28.3)	19.0
Construction	14.7	66.0 (31.9)	5.6
Transport & Storage	22.1	23.1 (19.7)	1.8
Banking & Finance	84.6	n.a. (n.a)	5.8
Trading & Commerce	24.2	n.a. (17.0)	4.1

Notes:
[a] Figures for Japan are for fiscal year 1982. The sixteen groups include the six "intermarket groups" of Mitsubishi, Mitsui, Sumitomo, Fuyo, Ikkan, and Sanwa, and ten other "vertical *keiretsu*" which are Tokai Bank, IBJ, Nippon Steel, Hitachi, Nissan, Toyota, Matsushita, Toshiba-IHI, Yokyu, and Seiba.
[b] Figures in parentheses give value-added of all firms in business groups selling in that sector, relative to total value-added of the sector, for the year 1986.
Source: Hamilton (1988), Table 3; Hamilton, Zeile, and Kim (1991), Table 4.

groups rely on other group members for 13 percent of purchases.[4] Larger numbers, however, are obtained for the vertical *keiretsu*. The same study by the Japanese Fair Trade Commission asks groups what they buy from companies in which they have more than 10 percent equity, even when those companies do not attend the "presidential club" (that is, are not part of the same intermarket group). These responses add another 25 percent to the 13 percent rate of internal purchase, for a total internalization ratio of 38 percent.[5] Estimates this high also occur for Japanese automobile groups. Dyer (1998) cites statistics from the Ministry of International Trade and Industry showing that 31 percent of total costs are accounted for by inputs purchased internally from affiliate firms.

Both intermarket *keiretsu* and vertical *keiretsu* are cross-market networks of firms. In the mid-1980s the intermarket *keiretsu* hotly competed with each other to obtain the largest market share in selected industrial sectors. It seemed at the time that their rapid growth and global expansion would continue well into the future, so much so that each of the competing intermarket groups rapidly built sets of vertical *keiretsu* organized in its midst to manufacture electronics and automobiles, among other products. Each intermarket group had a full set of upstream firms to supply

[4] Cited in "Japan's Industrial Structure: Inside the Charmed Circle," *The Economist*, January 5, 1991, p. 54.
[5] These numbers are cited (with accompanying text of the Japanese Fair Trade Commission report) in an internal memorandum of the Department of Treasury, Embassy of the United States of America, prepared by Timothy Geithner, February 26, 1992, and also by Richard K. Nanto of the Congressional Research Service at a meeting of the Center for Asian Pacific Affairs, The Asia Foundation, on April 15, 1994.

the intermediate inputs to complete most steps in producing these goods inside the group. All the groups influenced each other, mutually shaping each other's opportunities, as well as the opportunities of firms outside the boundaries of these business groups. It is no exaggeration to say that, in 1985, Japanese business groups organized the Japanese economy, and although much has changed in the last fifteen years (Gao, 2001, Lincoln and Gerlach, 2004), they continue to do so today.

South Korea

A central feature of Korea's industrial organization is the business groups, or *chaebol.*[6] These groups, consisting of legally independent firms, are affiliated under a common group name and are centrally controlled through direct family ownership and mutual shareholding among member firms. Table 2.3 indicates the cross-market holdings of the top five chaebol in 1985. As shown in Table 2.2, the fifty largest business groups accounted for 45 percent of total sales in the manufacturing sector in 1983, and even more in other sectors. These sales figures give an inflated estimate of the importance of the *chaebol*, however, because transactions of semi-finished goods between firms within a group are included. The figures in parentheses in Table 2.2 give the *value-added* shares accounted for by the business groups within each sector, and these figures are not affected by the frequency of intra-group transactions.[7] In manufacturing the value-added share is estimated at 28 percent in 1983, while overall, the top fifty business groups accounted for one-fifth of GDP in 1983 (Zeile, 1991).

In Table 2.4, we provide more recent numbers for the top five and top thirty *chaebol*, showing their shares of sales, value-added, as well as fixed assets and employment, within mining and manufacturing. It appears that the presence of the *chaebol* in the South Korean economy has been increasing over time. Indeed, these groups were frequently implicated in the Asian financial crisis that hit Korea in 1997–98, and became a target of policies imposed on Korea by the International Monetary Fund. Although the efficacy of these policies has been called into question, the Korean government is still pursuing plans to reshape the *chaebol* in what has been labeled the "Big Deal." This is an antitrust program on a scale that dwarfs anything done historically in the United States, and illustrates both the importance of the *chaebol* in the Korean economy and the policy

---

[6] The *chaebol* are described in Amsden (1989), Biggart (1991), Hamilton and Biggart (1988), Hamilton, Zeile, and Kim (1990), Kim (1991, 1993, 1997), Orru, Biggart, and Hamilton (1991), Steers, et al. (1989), and Zeile (1991).

[7] Value-added figures were not available for the other countries in Table 2.1.

Table 2.3. *Sector Distribution of Selected Firms in Top Six Korean Chaebol*

Sector	Hyundai	Samsung	Lucky-GS	Sunkyung	Daewoo	Ssangyong
Banking and insurance	***	**	****		***	**
Trading and commerce	*	**	*	*	**	*
Forestry and mining			*			
Construction	**	***	*	*	*	*
Food and beverages		**				
Fibers and textiles	*	***		***	****	
Pulp and paper	*	***	*			*
Chemicals	*		*		**	
Petroleum products		*	*	*		****
Rubber products	*					
Glass and cement	**					*
Iron and steel	**					
Nonferrous metals	*					
Metal products	**				***	*
Machinery – general	*		***	*		*
Electrical and electronics		*****	*******	*	***	*
Transportation machinery	******	*		*	***	
Precision instruments		*	**		*	
Real estate	*	*		*	*	*
Land transportation				**		
Marine transportation	*					*
Warehousing				*		
Service industry			*			
Total number of firms	26	24	23	13	23	15

Note: Each asterisk represents one firm.
Sources: Handbook Ilbo 1985; *Daily Economic News* 1986.

Table 2.4. *Shares of the South Korean Chaebol In Mining & Manufacturing (percent)*

	Top Five				Top Thirty			
	Shipments	Value added	Fixed assets	Employment	Shipments	Value added	Fixed assets	Employment
1977	15.7	14.5	–	9.1	34.1	31.6	–	20.5
1980	16.9	–	–	9.1	36.0	–	–	22.4
1983	22.6	16.7	18.0	8.9	40.4	32.4	37.8	18.6
1986	22.0	19.2	21.6	10.2	38.2	33.2	39.9	18.5
1989	21.3	18.6	19.1	9.9	35.4	30.0	35.9	16.8
1992	23.8	21.7	25.5	10.8	39.7	35.9	44.5	17.5
1995	25.9	27.2	26.0	11.4	40.7	40.2	44.0	18.0

Source: Lee Jae-Hyung (1997); Korea Developing Institute; and National Statistical Office; cited in Yoo (1999, p. 187).

conundrum raised by these groups (as we discuss further in Chapter 4 and Appendix D).

To measure the degree of vertical integration for the Korean business groups, we rely on self-reported accounting data that were compiled for the Korean Investors Service, as described in Chapter 4. These data contain, among other things, the inter-firm transactions for all the firms within each *chaebol* in 1989. Using this, we measure the internal sales between firms within the same group, and express this as a ratio of internal sales to total sales by the firms in that group. This *internalization ratio* is a measure of the degree of vertical integration for the group. For the largest forty-four *chaebol*, the average internalization ratio is 11.3 percent, which is quite close to that obtained for internal transactions of the intermarket groups in Japan.

There is, however, is a considerable range of internalization across different groups in Korea. The largest five groups (Samsung, Hyundai, LG or Lucky-Goldstar, Daewoo, and Sunkyong) have 1989 sales between $8.9 billion and $26 billion, and together account for 60 percent of the total sales of the forty-four groups. These five groups have an average internalization ratio of 27 percent, or three times as high as the average for the remaining groups. This is comparable to or even exceeds the degree of internalization found for the vertical *keiretsu* in Japan, making the top-five *chaebol* among the most tightly integrated business organizations found in Asia.

Taiwan

As in South Korea, business groups in Taiwan are overwhelmingly family-owned and controlled, but unlike in South Korea, they are not the dominant force in the economy.[8] Table 2.5 shows that the number and diversity of firms across sectors in the top five business groups in 1983 were less than their Japanese and Korean counterparts, and the total sales of the ninety-six largest Taiwanese business groups accounted for only 19 percent of sales in the manufacturing sector (see Table 2.2), and they had only small shares of sales outside of manufacturing. The largest group, Formosa Plastics, had 1994 sales of $6.6 billion, which is considerably smaller than any of the top-five for Korea. The groups in Taiwan also are much less vertically integrated than those in Korea. Our data in Chapter 4 will show an average internalization of 7 percent for eighty groups in Taiwan in 1994, ranging from 14.3 percent for the largest five groups

---

[8] The literature on business groups in Taiwan is relatively small when compared with the literature on the Korean chaebol. However, see Chou (1985), Greenhalgh (1988), Hamilton and Biggart (1988), Hamilton and Kao (1991), Numazaki (1986, 1991), and Chung (2000, 2001, 2003).

Table 2.5. *Sector Distribution of Firms Taiwan's Top 5 Business Groups*[1]

Sect/Group	Formosa Plastics	Linden Intern.	Tainan Spinning	Yue Loong Motors	Far Eastern
Finance & Insurance		***	***		*
Trade + Commerce		**	***		****
Fishery & Forestry			***		
Mining					
Construction		**	*		*
Food & Beverage			***		
Textiles	*****		**********	**	**
Garments & Apparel	*		**		***
Leather Products	*				
Lumber & Wood Prd.	**				
Pulp & Paper					
Chemicals	**		*		
Petroleum Products	*				
Rubber Products					
Plastic Products	***				
Glass + Cement			**	*	**
Basic Metal				*	
Metal Products					
Machinery			*		
Electrical				***	
Transport. Mach					
Precision					
Other Manuf.					
Real Estate			****	***	*
Storage & Trans	*				*
Serv. Industry	**	****			
Total Number of Firms	18	12	33	11	15

[1] Compiled from China Credit Information Service (1985).

to 6.5 percent for the remaining seventy-five. Thus, the largest groups in Taiwan have a degree of vertical integration that is only one-half as much as their Korean counterparts. This reflects that fact that the Taiwanese business groups before the mid-1990s were focused much more strongly on service sectors and on the production of intermediate inputs, which are sold domestically to small and medium-size firms, which further process and export the goods.

Table 2.6 shows that both countries have an abundance of small and medium-size enterprises, so the absolute number of such firms is not the critical issue. What is important is their respective location in the economy. In Taiwan, before the late 1980s, small and medium-size firms were the primary manufacturers and exporters of goods, and Table 2.6 shows that they were even more prominent in the *export sectors* of economy than they are in the overall economy. By contrast, in Korea, small and medium-size firms specialize in making products mainly for domestic consumption,

Table 2.6. *Small and Medium-sized Enterprises in South Korea and Taiwan.* (Percent of each category accounted for by Small and Medium-sized Enterprise in Manufacturing, 1992)

	South Korea	Taiwan
Number of firms	98.6	98.0
Number of employees	65.8	76.7
Value-added	47.6	53.2
Export	40.0	57.3

Source: Lim, 1998, p. 51

and secondarily for export, and generally in product areas that do not compete with *chaebol* production, such as agricultural and food products, as well as plastic, rubber and leather products (Lim, 1998). *Chaebol* firms dominate the export sector, contributing considerably over 50 percent of all export sales. In fact, before the Plaza Accord, the relation between business groups in Korea and small and medium-size firms in Taiwan were the mirror image of each other; each of these account for somewhere between 55 percent and 65 percent of export sales in their respective economies.

Most analysts recognize that small and medium-sized firms had, and continue to have, a more prominent role in export production in Taiwan than in Korea. It is also widely recognized that business groups in Korea were, and continue to be, deeply involved in the production of products for export, whereas Taiwan's business groups often supplied intermediate goods and services. In general, however, to many analysts these differences do not appear to be nearly as important as the basic similarities they share.

Cross-Country Comparisons

When examined at the most general level and with aggregated data, the South Korean and Taiwanese economies and their organizational components appear similar. But as we progressively disaggregate the same data, sharp differences begin to appear. The first hint of these differences is found in the sales of the primary products produced by business group firms. For each country, we have classified the sales of business group firms according to the input–output sector of their primary product. These sales are then aggregated to twenty-one broad manufacturing sectors, as shown in Table 2.7, and several non-manufacturing sectors. The group sales are expressed as a percentage of total sales of all manufacturing firms in these sectors. For Korea we show values constructed for 1983 and 1989, while

Table 2.7. *Group Sales in South Korea and Taiwan*

Sector	Korea, 1983 Group Sales/ Sector Sales	Korea, 1989 Group Sales/ Sector Sales	Taiwan, 1983 Group Sales/ Sector Sales	Taiwan, 1994 Group Sales/ Sector Sales
Primary Products:				
Agriculture, Forestry, Fisheries	na	0.3	na	2.9
Mining	10.6	12.8	0.0	0.0
Manufactured Products:				
Food Products	33.7	23.8	26.3	13.9
Beverages and Tobacco	27.6	47.3	3.8	1.4
Textiles	38.4	32.5	50.7	45.3
Garments and Apparel	12.6	0.9	12.0	0.4
Leather Products	15.2	7.6	9.1	\ 1
Lumber and Wood Products	31.5	13.4	4.0	1.1
Pulp and Paper Products	6.7	15.4	20.1	20.8
Printing and Publishing	\ 2	9.2	\ 2	0.0
Chemical Materials	54.3	37.5	42.4	35.3
Chemical Products	24.0	26.9	8.4	2.2
Petroleum and Coal Products	91.9	100	0.0	4.25
Rubber Products	76.8	21.9	13.0	1.2
Plastic Products	\ 3	38.8	5.4	5.0
Non-Metallic Mineral Products	44.6	28.0	47.6	37.6
Primary Metals	28.0	34.3	7.8	2.8
Metal Products	26.7	25.8	6.0	22.5
Machinery	34.9	33.9	3.6	12.3
Electronic Products	50.9	64.3	22.7	24.4
Motor Vehicles and Shipbuilding	79.0	80.4	23.6	34.9
Precision Instruments	14.0	11.1	0.0	0.0
Misc. Industrial Products	5.2	2.88	10.7	0.12
Total Manufacturing	45.4	40.7	19.0	16.4
Non-Manufactured Products:				
Utilities	na	3.6	na	1.2
Construction	66.0	31.7	5.6	8.4
Transportation, Comm., & Storage	23.1	23.6	1.8	3.0

Notes:
1. Leather products for Taiwan are included with garments and apparel.
2. Printing and publishing is included with pulp and paper products.
3. Plastic products for Korea in 1983 are included with chemical materials.

for Taiwan we show values for 1983 and 1994. Overall, there is a substantial degree of conformity in the sales of the groups between the earlier and later years. The principal change is that groups in both countries have been moving out of several sectors, including garments and apparel, rubber, and non-metallic mineral products (that is, stone, clay, and glass items).

For South Korea, the table shows that about one-half of the sectors have business group sales that account for more than 25 percent of total sales, and in several cases the business group sales account for more than 50 percent of total sales. The *chaebol* control the production of petroleum and coal, and the manufacture of electronic products, motor vehicles and shipbuilding. The groups have a strong presence in both upstream and downstream sectors. Overall, the forty-three business groups account for nearly 41 percent of all manufacturing sales, together with 13 percent in mining, 32 percent in utilities, and 24 percent in transportation, communication and storage. Clearly the *chaebol* dominate the economic landscape of South Korea, both upstream and downstream.

In Taiwan, by contrast, the business groups lead in only a selected number of upstream sectors. Thus, in textiles the business groups account for nearly one-half of total manufacturing sales. These groups are selling downstream to the garment and apparel sector, where business groups are almost nonexistent. This pattern can also be seen from the strong group presence in pulp and paper products, chemical materials, non-metallic minerals, and metal products. In comparison, business groups have a weak presence in most downstream sectors such as wood products, chemical products, rubber and plastic products, as well as beverages and tobacco. Clear exceptions to this pattern occur in electronic products and motor vehicles, although we will show in Chapter 4 that business groups participating in these sectors have very low levels of internalization, in contrast to the groups in Korea. Even if we count the finished products from the downstream groups, the entire set of Taiwan business groups accounts for only 16 percent of total manufacturing output, along with small shares outside of manufacturing.

In nearly every sector where Taiwanese groups have a significant share of sectoral sales, the Korean groups account for even more. In addition, Korean groups are dominant in heavy industries such as petroleum and coal, basic and non-ferrous metals, and shipbuilding. With the exception of only a small number of sectors (notably, garments, and apparel), business groups in Korea spread across nearly the entire manufacturing sector, but this is not true in Taiwan, where groups are principally found in upstream and service sectors. This difference in the sectoral allocation is consistent with the higher degree of internalization found in Korean business groups, as these groups integrate forward and backwards to span the production process.

Marshallian Interpretations of Business Groups

This brief overview of business groups in East Asia is ample to show that in every case business groups represent cross-market networks of firms. As apparent as this fact is, most writers treat these business groups as, more or less, independent objects to be explained in theoretical terms. Often these explanations are then integrated in more expansive interpretations of East Asian development. These interpretations often take the following form: The writer characterizes business groups in terms of their core features (for example, a firm disciplined by the state), and then aggregates that feature to explain the economy as a whole and economic development as a process (for example, state-led development). We will discuss the three main characterizations of business groups – as arising out of market failures, as results of political actions, and as social networks. In each case, business groups are viewed as a mini-command posts, responding to political and macroeconomic incentives and constraints or to market opportunities or to issues of trust, in an economic environment that is otherwise unexamined.

As Market Failures

As noted in the preceding chapter, until very recently, economists have used a Marshallian partial equilibrium framework to explain industrial organization. Despite many insightful extensions of this framework, especially the additions provided by the "new institutional economists," this view of competitive markets derived from neoclassical economics still lies at the core of most market-oriented explanations of Asian economic structure. Arguing that rapid development arises in those countries having the fewest policy-induced distortions, market economists call for reductions in state interference and for increases in market competition. However, confronted by the scope and significance of business groups throughout Asian economies, market economists equally recognize that these economies do not fit neatly into the categories provided by Western economic theory.

The Marshallian interpretation of economic organization envisions only two categories: firms and markets. The firm ends where the market begins. Unfettered competition among numerous, autonomous firms in the same market allows for production efficiencies to determine both the size and survival of firms. Inefficient firms go bankrupt. Efficient firms expand in size to correspond to the economies of scale and the demands for goods they produce.

Asian economies, however, are filled with networks of interlinked firms that do not compete with each other within each network. Such noncompetitive relations among independent firms lies outside the normal purview of a Marshallian perspective[9] and would appear to subject

[9] These firms that do not quite conform to either market or hierarchy are sometimes conceptualized as a hybrid firm (e.g., Williamson, 1991), which to our way of thinking is a stopgap measure to preserve theory.

unaffiliated firms to overpowering economic competition that has nothing to do with market demand or production efficiencies. This premise led to complaints, most loudly voiced by U.S. trade negotiators, that East Asian economies are not "level playing fields," but rather consist of collusive inter-firm networks closed to outsiders. The language used to voice these complaints suggested strong state interference, as with the claim that Asian governments were "creating" competitive advantage, and there were also influential studies arguing that the business groups acted collusively (Fung, 1991, Lawrence, 1991).[10] During the Asian business crisis in 1997, these same accusations, then termed "crony capitalism," were turned into causes for the financial crisis.

The first job of market theorists, therefore, has been to redefine Asian business networks into concepts that have some significance in economics. Because these networks clearly are not markets, they must be firms. This is the interpretation of one of the first economists to speculate about the nature of these groups, Nathaniel Leff (1976, 1978, 1979). "The group," writes Leff (1978, p. 664), "is a multi-company firm which transacts in different markets but which does so under common entrepreneurial and financial control." These ideas are echoed by Alfred D. Chandler, a student of the American corporation, who defines the Japanese *zaibatsu* (1982, p. 22) as an "organization comparable to the M-form" – the multidivisional conglomerate that Chandler saw as originating in the United States but, he argues, has now spread throughout the capitalist world. Following Leff's and Chandler's leads, most other analysts, including strong-state theorists, endorse the idea that, despite some differences, Asian business groups are functional equivalents of autonomous firms in the West. "The diversified business group," says Alice Amsden (1989, p. 151; also 2001, pp. 190–248), "is a variant of the modern industrial enterprise that is found in every industrialized country and that is multidivisional, comprised of large-scale production units, and managed hierarchically."

Once business groups and firms are conceptually equated, then Marshallian theories of firms and market imperfections, or alternatively political economy theories of state-led development, can be applied. For most economists, including transaction-cost theorists, a market imperfection interpretation of Asian business groups seems so self-evident as to require no elaboration. The theory is simply evoked. "The group pattern of industrial organization," says Leff (1978, p. 666), "is readily understood as a microeconomic response to well-known conditions of market

---

[10] Fung (1991) and Lawrence (1991) have examined the effects of the *keiretsu* on Japanese trade, and argued that they constitute a (limited) barrier to entry. This conclusion was questioned by Bhagwati (1992) and Saxonhouse (1993), however, who argue that the changing membership of firms belonging to each *keiretsu* invalidates any conclusions about the groups as a whole.

failure in the less developed countries. In fact, the emergence of the group as an institutional mode might well have been predicted on the basis of familiar theory and a knowledge of the environment in these countries." Jorgensen, Hafsi, and Kiggundu (1986, p. 426) echo the same thesis: Economic organizations in developing economies emerge as adaptations "to politicized resource allocation and other forms of market imperfections." The various types of business organizations observed in developing economies represent specific "aberrations" of the perfect competition model.[11] Such organizational aberrations solve particular kinds of problems encountered in "imperfect" economies.

The most recent, as well as the most theoretically sophisticated, market-failure interpretations of business groups are those fashioned by Tarun Khanna and his colleagues (Khanna and Rivkin, 2001, Khanna and Palepu, 1999, 2000a, 2000b, Khanna, 2001):

> In emerging markets there are a variety of market failures, caused by information and contracting problems.... The absence of intermediaries in emerging markets makes it costly for firms to acquire necessary inputs like finance, technology, and management talent. Market imperfections also make it costly to establish quality brand images in product markets, and to establish contractual relationship with joint-venture partners. *As a result, an enterprise may be more profitably pursued as part of a large diversified business group that can act as an intermediary between individual entrepreneurs and imperfect markets.* (Khanna and Palepu, 1999, pp. 275–6, our emphasis)

As will become apparent in later chapters, the role of intermediaries in business groups, in particular trading companies, is especially important, as are cross-market connections among business group firms, but even in this interpretation the business groups remain a creation of market failure that can be solved within the firm. The natural conclusions to draw from this line of reasoning are: 1) that if these largely undefined competitive markets had been more developed, had been less imperfect, then business groups would not have developed in emerging countries as they did in fact develop; 2) that the organization and performance of such business groups arise internally to the individual groups themselves, a matter of governance and transaction costs efficiencies among aligned firms; and 3) that the organization of economies is a simple aggregation of what happens within (and not between) firms and business groups.

---

[11] Jorgensen, Hapsi, and Kiggundu (1986) list four common types of organizational "aberrations": (1) the entrepreneurial family firm, (2) the industrial cluster, (3) the multinational corporation subsidiary, and (4) the state-owned enterprise.

As we indicated briefly in the previous chapter, economic explanations for Japanese business groups generally follow a market failure interpretation. Japanese economists Goto (1982), Imai (1992), and, most influentially, Aoki (1988, 1990) develop versions of a market failure theory of Japanese business groups. An example of this can be found in the literature on the "main bank" view of Japanese *keiretsu*, where Aoki is an important contributor (Aoki and Patrick, 1994). This literature illustrates the extent to which the Japanese business groups are primarily understood as a Marshallian problem: as responses to market failure, and either collusive or not. The work of Hosi, Kashyap, and Sharfstein (1990, 1991) has shown that membership in one of the six large intermarket groups in Japan (Mitsubishi, Mitsui, Sumitomo, Fuyo, Dai-ichi Kangyo, and Sanwa) brings with it access to debt financing that leads to measurable impacts on the investments of the firms. The provision of loans from the "main banks" is seen as relaxing a liquidity constraint that the firms otherwise face, and which reflects an imperfection in the capital market. Access to bank financing does not lead to higher profits for the group, however, and overall profits of the six intermarket *keiretsu* are no higher, and possibly lower, than for non-group firms. Weinstein and Yafeh (1998) interpret this as evidence that the "main banks" exercise market power in their provision of loans to the group firms. An alternative explanation provided by Lincoln, Gerlach, and Ahmadjian (1996) is that the group is redistributing funds from profitable to unprofitable firms within the group, allowing the latter to survive. Under either explanation, the fact that the intermarket groups do not earn higher profits than other firms is seen as highly significant: Weinstein and Yafeh (1995) use this result to argue that the *keiretsu* are not collusive at all, and may even be more competitive than other firms! We think this conclusion perfectly illustrates the way that business groups have been "classified" to fit a Marshallian framework: if they do not earn high profits, then they are not collusive; and if they are not collusive, then they must be competitive! Our own view (described formally in Chapter 3) is that business groups offer a unique vehicle for cross-market interaction between firms, which need not lead to higher profits overall, but nevertheless is *far removed* from how competitive firms would interact, and has far-reaching consequences for the economy.

In his most recent work, Aoki (2000, 2001) has broadened his treatment of institutions found in Japan and elsewhere, and advocates what he, along with Avner Greif (2002), calls "comparative institutional analysis." While starting with the same assumptions used in analyzing transactions costs, namely, imperfect information and bounded rationality of participants, this perspective goes beyond anything that Williamson (1975, 1985) or other transactions-cost theorists would envisage. Indeed, to the extent that the original work of Coase (1937) and Williamson's formulation of transactions costs can be viewed as having pro-Western bias in its view of firms as hierarchies, the "comparative institutional analysis" is intentionally *cross-national* in its approach, and embraces a "diversity" of organizational structures as the likely outcome. Aoki (2000, pp. 1–3) explicitly rejects both the "Anglo-American" view of the firm, and what he views as its theoretical counterpart, the "Walrasian equilibrium model." In its place, he offers a framework that includes the following features:

1. *Institutions as equilibria*
   The fundamental nature of institutions is [to] ... approximate equilibrium strategies of a game played in the economy....
2. *Multiplicity of equilibria*
   Even for the same exogenous parameters, equilibrium of games is likely to be multiple. Thus a diversity of institutional arrangements is possible....
3. *Equilibrium selection, institutional complementarity and institutional path dependence*
   We need some exogenous factor other than technological parameters to explain the selection of an equilibrium.... Also an institution may become sustainable because of sunk costs, even if initial factor allowing for its emergence subsequently disappear....
4. *Non-optimality of institutional arrangements*
   Since exogenous parameters do not uniquely determine the selection of equilibrium (thus institutional arrangement), there is no guarantee that institutional arrangements are efficient or converge to an efficient one.... (Aoki, 2000, pp. 172–5, emphasis his)

There are some clear areas of overlap between this perspective and the model of business groups that we shall develop: most notably, in the ideas that business groups are an equilibrium phenomena, but that their organization is subject to multiple equilibria, and hence a "diversity" of organizational arrangements is possible. But there is an equally clear difference in the notion of "equilibrium" that Aoki has in mind, and what we shall use. Aoki (1998, 2000, Chap. 3) favors an evolutionary game approach, where players adopt strategies (meaning some type of skills or organizational form) that give them the highest payoff, given the strategies chosen by others. But there is a built-in friction in the ability to switch from one choice to another, so that, in Darwinian fashion, it takes time to "weed out" the less-fit players. An equilibrium of this game is established when there is no incentive for any player to switch strategies. This notion of equilibrium is very similar to that used by Arthur (1989, 1994) and other work in evolutionary economics (for example, Nelson and Winters,

1982, Fung and Friedman, 1996). As we discussed in the previous chapter, these models rarely include *price* as a strategic choice variable, and the equilibrium is most definitely not a Walrasian equilibrium. Rather than abandoning that concept, we shall instead be extending it to allow for cross-firm ownership and cross-market exercise of market power, thereby obtaining an equilibrium organization of business groups that allows for multiple equilibria, but builds on the Walrasian framework.

As Outcomes of Political Policy

Strong-state theorists have also developed interpretations of business groups. These interpretations grow naturally out of a political-economy perspective. Political economists have long emphasized the coalitional nature of the linkage between the state and the economy (for example, Block, 1987, 1990, Evans, et al., 1985), and within development studies, this coalition has been viewed as an important factor promoting and shaping economic development (Cardoso and Feleto, 1979, Evans, 1979, 1995). Business groups are equated with a business elite, which is a group not defined organizationally, but rather in terms of interests – a top-down perspective that is in tune with Marx's methodological approach that treats individuals and firms as "personifications" of economic categories and as "embodiments" of class interests. The most recent theorizing reiterates this approach, even though the organizational features of economies have become more important.

In an extensive review of the literature, Haggard, Maxfield, and Schneider (1997a) argue that there are five general ways that business–state relations are defined, all of which are "theoretically diffuse." In relations with the state, business variously represents capital, sectorial interests, collective action (via business association), trust-inducing networks, or a configuration of firms. The first three approaches are, more or less, the conventional ways to incorporate business into a political economy perspective, by viewing business primarily as a set of interests (derived from capital, sectorial location, or business association). The last two ways (that is, business as network and as configuration) are less conventional, and because they seem similar to our own, merit brief elaboration.

For Haggard, Maxfield, and Schneider (1997a), the business networks most interesting to development specialists are precisely those having some relation to the state. They begin their review of networks by citing C. Wright Mills' analysis of the power elite and with the argument that elite networks of businesses influence the state in numerous ways. Noting the new economic sociology interpretation of networks, they argue that in most of these studies, "state actors are typically excluded" (1997, p. 55), and they cite Peter Evans as the person whose work (1995, 1997) is leading "the effort to bring the state back into sociological research on networks" (1997, p. 55). The reason they approve of Evans' work is obvious enough, for he reduces business networks to sets of elite interests that are causally related to the interests of state officials, and in so doing he brings business groups, the most prominent form of business networks in developing societies, back into the sphere of the political economist.

In his own work, Evans (1997, pp. 66–7; also see 1995) elaborates his reasoning in the following four propositions. The first two propositions are designed to explain the causal direction of the influence between the state and business: 1) "Government–business relations cannot be interpreted without first specifying the internal structure of the state," and 2) "The character of the business community can be reshaped by state policy." The last two propositions then deal with the consequences of the state's success in building a economically strong and wealthy business elite: 3) "When state policies succeed in reshaping the business community, they are likely to undercut the very patterns of government–business relations that made the policies effective to begin with" and 4) "As government–business relations evolve, a more encompassing set of state–society networks that includes institutionalized ties between the state and other social groups may provide a better means of sustaining future transformation." These propositions, as well as Evans' work more generally, particularly in the context of South Korea and Taiwan, encompass business groups, and turn them into a business elite that has no intrinsic organization and very little market or, especially, cross-market dynamics. The organization of firms and business groups is analytically connected to and subsumed within the state's political umbrella.

This general political economy interpretation is applied with particular force to Asian business groups and their role in economic development (Amsden, 1989, Amsden and Hikino, 1994, Evans, 1995, Haggard, et al., 1997a, Woo-Cummings, 1991, 1999). Alice Amsden makes the clearest case for this point of view. Making the *chaebol* the centerpiece of her very influential study of South Korean economy (1989), as well as the model for her later studies of late-industrializing economies (2001), she argues that the key feature of the *chaebol* is its diversification into a range of unrelated business activities instead of its specialization in a core product area. Finding diversified business groups in such countries as Argentina, Brazil, India, Malaysia, Mexico, South Africa, Thailand, and Turkey, in addition to South Korea and Taiwan, she claims that they represent a distinct type of firm that is *not* found in the most industrially advanced economies; this type of firm is a distinct outcome of late industrialization. The reason for their development in this time and place, she argues, is that firms in late industrializing societies are essentially specialists at learning advanced technologies existing in the industrially most advanced economies, transferring these technologies (through joint ventures, licensing, acquisitions, or other means) to their own economies, and producing new products based on "learning by doing." Over time, such diversified business groups turned the ability to execute new projects into a core competency, which encourages further diversification.

This view of diversified business groups fits nicely into strong-state theories of economic development. Like the market interpretation, the reason diversified business groups arise in developing, and not developed, economies is because this type of firm is functionally the best suited to address the problems of market failure, which is, in this case, the absence of technology and necessity to transfer technology from the more to the less advanced economies. The business groups themselves, however, cannot address this problem, because they lack resources and expertise, among other things. Instead, it is the state that addresses problems of market failure. As Amsden (2001, p. 193, her emphasis) put it, diversified business groups "all share one characteristic: *They tended to be a product of government promotion ('targeting')*." The state, acting through its principal officials, selects and enhances the performance of diversified business groups, making them the state's main agent of economic development. Although all developmental states promote diversified business groups, only those states having the most capable economic planners and the most power to implement policy are those in which the business groups are the most successful (Evans, 1995).

For most strong-state theorists, Taiwan and Korea stand out as being the most advanced of all developmental states, and of the two states, Korea is where the diversified business groups reaches its highest expression: "*Where Korea differs from most other late industrializing countries*," writes Amsden (1989, p. 14, her emphasis), "*is in the discipline its state exercises over private firms. Discipline by the state over private enterprise was part and parcel of the vision that drove the state to industrialize.*" Meredith Woo-Cummings (Jung-en Woo, 1991, p. 15) makes the same point, only more emphatically. "In reality, [the *chaebol*] are creations – productions and not reproductions – of the state and the Korean financial structure. This is true to the point where one asks if there is an important distinction in Korea between public and private, between state and civil society."

For Taiwan, whose export sectors are dominated by small and medium-sized firms, no theorist goes so far as to say that the state single-handedly created the industrial structure, as they do for Korea, but all (Gold, 1988, Amsden, 1985, Wade, 1991, Pang, 1992, Evans, 1995) argue that state policies directly led to the formation of the large diversified conglomerates, which they assume promoted small-firm segments of the economy. As we discuss more fully in Chapter 5, Amsden (1991, 2001) is particularly adamant on this point. Other writers as well acknowledge differences among state-led economies, while at the same time reaffirming the general trend. As Evans (1995, p. 58) puts it, "Looking at Korea and Taiwan make it clear that the historical embodiments of the developmental state are likely to display a range of variation, but the fundamental features ... are visible underneath the variation." The diversified business groups, the key actors in creating economic development, are the key agents that carry out the state's economic policies.

An alternative version of the strong-state story comes, surprisingly enough, from an economist, Dani Rodrik (1995, 1996, 1997), also writing with Haggard and Wade (Fishlow, et al., 1994). Like Amsden and Wade, Rodrik is responding to the conventional economic view that rapid growth in South Korea and Taiwan was a product of *laissez-faire* policies, essentially allowing the market magic to work. On the contrary, he argues, there is very little empirical evidence in general that free trade promotes economic growth (Rodriguez and Rodrik, 2000), and the specific link between the export growth and sustained government incentives or profits in that sector is lacking for both Korea and Taiwan. To explain the growth in exports, Rodrik looks elsewhere – to government incentives favoring the import of capital equipment. Greater imports of capital-goods would allow for higher exports via the balance of payments for each country, and also via the efficiency-enhancing effect of machinery imports. As government policies promoting this, Rodrik (1997, pp. 21–2) cites low real interest rates, tax subsidies to investment, government direction of investment priorities, and the provision of low-priced inputs. The ability of these incentives to increase real incomes, he argues, depends on having market failure in the capital market, keeping investment too low. Thus, Rodrik arrives at a combination of the market-failure and strong-state stories, which he argues is empirically relevant for both South Korea and Taiwan.

Our own view is quite different. Without denying that capital markets may have been imperfect (or still are), our focus for export growth will be on the *increased demand* generated by "the retail revolution" in the United States. Specifically, the repeal of "fair trade laws" in the United States during the 1960s allowed for huge increase in mass-merchandising, orchestrated by the merchandisers acting as intermediaries between U.S. consumers and Asian producers. We will argue in Chapters 6 and 7 that this increase in U.S. demand occurred just as Korea and Taiwan were in a position to meet that demand; but that it was exercised in different market segments within the two countries. Big buyers began to look to Korea for the provision of long production runs of relatively standardized products, whereas Taiwan supplied shorter production runs of more specialized, niche products. Thus, the exercise of international demand interacted with the nascent business groups to mutually reinforce their organizational structure.

As Social Networks

Economic sociologists have developed the most organizational view of business groups, but even these approaches conceive of business groups in terms of their institutional origins rather than their organizational linkages. The differences between the sociological approach and the two preceding ones are, however, important. The market and state approaches generally assume that business groups in all developing economies are very much alike and that they are manifestations of core causative forces. The sociological approach, however, is sensitive to the differences among economies and sets out to explain those differences not in terms of some master variables, but rather as the result of various institutionally grounded contingencies. The organizational approach that we develop in this book is largely compatible with the sociological approach in that we seek to add an economic dimension to an interpretation of the economy that otherwise lacks one. As we demonstrate in later chapters, however, integrating an economic dimension into the sociological interpretation also fundamentally changes the interpretation.

Granovetter (1994, 1998) offers one of the clearest expositions of business groups from a sociological point of view. Granovetter notes, "in every known capitalist economy, firms do not conduct business as isolated units, but rather form cooperative relations with other firms. . . . " Stating that "business group is to firm as firm is to individual economic agent," he paraphrases the Coasian question, "Why do business groups exist?" The answer he proposes amounts to a veritable sociology of the economy. Defining business groups as "federation of firms" that are "bound together in some formal and/or informal ways," he (1994) denies that they have some sort of economic or political essence. Such interpretations are too simplistic and too functionalist. Finding that business groups are common to most capitalist and developing economies, he suggests, nonetheless, that an empirical examination based on a "reading of the literature" reveals considerable variations from place to place. The purpose of his analysis, then, is to explain the variation, which he defines in terms of six dimensions: 1) ownership relations, 2) principles or axes of solidarity, 3) vertical versus horizontal authority structures, 4) moral economy, 5) finance, capital, and the role of banks, and 6) business/state relations. Each of these six dimensions defines an institutional context that would be sufficient to cause variation in the structure of business groups in a particular economy.

Granovetter answers his question about "why do business groups exist?" in terms of the institutional contingencies that shape "the structure of all such connections in a given economy." Among his six dimensions is no hint that these connections might represent a system of firms interacting across markets. Instead, if we dig more deeply into the sociological approach, we find that business groups are not merely shaped by institutional contingencies but are assumed to be *the result* of them. In this view, the economy has very little economic content. The same six dimensions could be singled out to explain variation in the political, instead of the economic, structure of the state. Even the term "structure" connotes a view that the economy is a static set of connections instead of sets of connections that are produced in the course of economic activity. In the sociological view, business groups (which is a surrogate for economic organization) emerge, so to speak, from prior contingencies: from particular ethnic solidarities, from specific sets of authority relations that can be traced into the distant past, from historical accidents resulting in the presence or absence of sufficient capital to establish business groups. All these and other causally prior factors supposedly create an economy that is presumed to act economically without any economic content added.

We should not single Granovetter's work out for a special critique, for his explanation is very similar to most sociological interpretations of economic activity, including Whitley (1992, 1999), Hollingsworth and Boyer (1997), Fligstein (1990), Orrù, Biggart, and Hamilton (1997), and Buğra and Üsdiken (1997). All of these writers argue that institutional factors shape the organization of economies. And although their arguments contain many insights, they all equate contingent institutional origins with the actual and ongoing operation of economic activity. In other words, they provide the sociological context in which the economy developed and operates without supplying the economics for how such contingent economies actually work.

We can illustrate this with a series of articles by one of the authors of this book (Hamilton and Biggart, 1988, Hamilton, Zeile, and Kim, 1989, Orrù, Biggart, and Hamilton, 1991, 1997). In most of the articles, Hamilton (for example, Hamilton and Biggart, 1988) describes the differences among East Asian business groups and sees these differences as indicative of broader differences among Asian economies. However, when it comes to explaining these differences, he and his collaborators cite institutional differences in family institutions and inheritance patterns, in political structure, in patterns of interpersonal authority, and in historical preconditions. Their approach, like the other interpretations mentioned previously, is to pull out of a set of causally prior factors that are analytically external to economic activity a fully functioning economy, without really being able to connect the two. For example, Hamilton (Hamilton and Biggart, 1988, Hamilton, 1997), agreeing with Wong (1985), argues that partible inheritance in Chinese societies (in which all sons received an equal portion of their father's estate) militates against the development of large vertically integrated firms and favors the formation of an economy dominated in the private sector by small and medium-sized firms. Positing an institutional mechanism that would lead to such an economy, Hamilton then produces a complex economy based on such firms without actually showing how the economy works. A simple description of the network organization of the different economies substitutes for a deeper understanding of how the economy actually works as a going concern.

Conclusion: The Exteriority of Economic Organization

All of the earlier interpretations treat business groups as the chief agents of economic development and as the main organizational features of industrializing economies in East and Southeast Asia. All these interpretations also make business groups the result of factors external to "normal" functioning economies. Market failures, state policies, embedded networks, and an assortments of social, legal, and political institutions are variously presumed to be prior to, and the create the circumstances for, the development of business groups. It is important to stress here that we are not arguing that these factors are unimportant. Quite the contrary is true. In Part II, we argue that many of these factors, such as the role of the state officials and of social and political institutions, contribute to the ongoing organizational dynamics of economies. Our critique here is not with these factors themselves, but rather with how analysts use these factors to create **marketless** interpretations of economic organization, interpretations in which market economics matters less than factors external to the economy.

Although different from each other, these marketless interpretations share several features that distinguish these interpretations from our own.[12] First, each interpretation provides a developed theory of the business group, regardless of whether the group is conceptualized as a firm

---

[12] In recent years, there has been a marked and broad-based convergence of these three interpretations that makes the partial equilibrium framing of these interpretations obvious and our critique more clear. We refer here, among others, to the work, in economics, of Aoki (2001a, 2001b), Greif (forthcoming), and Furubotn and Richter (1997); in sociology, of Fligstein (2001), Quack, et al. (2000), Nee and Brinton (2001), and Hollingsworth and Boyer (1997); and in political economy, of Berger and Dore (1996).

or as network. This is equivalent to a theory of the firm, and it normally consists of two principal analytic elements: the institutional frame and the internal organization of the group. The institutional frame, such as the state or particular social institutions, is external to the firm and supposedly shapes the organization of the group and gives it a particular character. Shaped by the institutional frames, the internal organization and governance of the group bestow on the group certain competitive advantages in the economy not enjoyed by other firms. For instance, state-disciplined business groups can solve the problems faced by developing countries, such as the relative absence of technological knowledge; trusting bearing networks of firms based on social institutions can minimize transaction costs and reduce risk.

Second, each interpretation presumes some kind of institutional linkage that stabilizes the organization of the firm or group. This stability can be thought of as a state of equilibrium. This equilibrium, however, is not due to the balancing of price structures across markets, but rather to the way the firm itself is balanced relative to its institutional environment. Aoki (2001b, pp. 141–3) and Greif (forthcoming) are quite clear: Institutions create an equilibrium that regulates the activities of agents. Ever shy of the concept of equilibrium, sociologists have developed their own equivalents, such as the tendency of organizations to move towards isomorphism within organizational fields (DiMaggio and Powell, 1983), a conceptualization that has also been applied to Asian business groups (Orrù, Biggart, and Hamilton, 1997, Whitley, 1992) as well as to economies in general (Fligstein, 2001, Whitley, 1999, Hollingsworth and Boyer, 1997). The similarities between the sociological and economic interpretations are obvious to Avner Greif (2003, pp. 150–1), one of the foremost practitioners of institutional economics applied to economic history, who said the following in a review of Fligstein's *The Architecture of Markets*:

> Those who study the "institutional foundations of markets" from an equilibrium perspective and those who study the "architecture of markets" from a cultural-political perspective have much in common. Both lines of analysis emphasize the centrality of forces leading to stability or an equilibrium situation. They integrate social, political, and economic considerations in the analysis and appreciate the need to study an economy from a systemic point of view.

Third, in all these interpretations, a theory of business groups lacks a corresponding theory of the markets or cross-market environments in which business groups operate. These are "firm-loaded" interpretations, and since the primary feature of the economy is the interaction between the institutional environment and the business group/firm, the economy itself is organizationally flat and is not a causative force influencing the firm. The interpretations contain no conceptual space for competition among firms and groups. The organizational fields tend toward stability; the institutional roles structuring the economy are constantly reproducing themselves, which tends toward stability; the big firms control the little firms, which tends toward stability. Therefore, what happens in the economy is the aggregated sum of what happens in firms. There is no conception of cross-market interactions, which is the central feature of a Walrasian frame. Nothing is left over in these interpretations for price structures or for the competitive and cooperative interactions among firms and groups within and across markets and across economies.

Fourth, many of the main theorists (Aoki, 2001a, Greif, 1998, Evans, 1995, Whitley, 1999) of these interpretations call for a similar methodological approach to examine economies, an approach that they call "comparative institutional analysis." The idea is that every economy is different from every other economy, and that these differences are due to the institutional environments that shape the leading firms and structure the nation's business systems. This approach is both indicative and symptomatic. It is indicative of a Marshallian frame that we outlined in the previous chapter, a frame that, in its new institutionalist reincarnation, emphasizes the incentives, the structures, and the solidarities that agents create and act upon. It is symptomatic of a state-based bias in Marshallian analysis. National economies are perceived to be the basic units of analysis because these are the basic institutional environments that frame economic activity. Comparative institutional analysis is overwhelmingly state-based; it is an approach that, a priori, places the causes for what happens in the economy inside the state. In its economic analysis, the state becomes the partial equilibrium frame, the geographic unit where the *ceteris paribus* qualification can be invoked. This approach, therefore, is necessarily critical of explanations based on cross-market and especially cross-border trade. For example, Aoki (2001, Aoki, et al., 1997, pp. 28–9) and Rodrik (1994) criticize "export fetishism" for the explanations of the East Asian Miracle, and Fligstein (2002) and Berger and Dore (1996) criticize the literature on globalization and on global capitalism, saying that the business within countries is far more important than trade among them.

What is missing in these interpretations is not merely a theory of trade, but more accurately a theory of markets, a theory that shows how market processes themselves are organized and change over time and how entrepreneurs relate to and attempt to control those processes through developing firms, networks, and alliances. Firm-loaded theories of economic organizations do not resolve, and usually do not even examine, how firms interact in complex economic environments and with what effects. Accordingly, it is our conclusion that most analysts of business groups offer partial equilibrium solutions for what we believe is a general equilibrium problem.

3

A Model of Business Groups

The Interaction of Authority and Market Power in the Context of Competitive Economic Activity

In her book, *Regional Advantage*, AnnaLee Saxenian (1994) makes an argument for "two models of industrial systems – the decentralized regional network-based system and the independent firm-based system." The two models come out of her case studies of two regional economies in the United States, one centered on high technology industries along Route 128 in Massachusetts and the other centered on high technology industries in Silicon Valley in Northern California. An astute ethnographer and not a formal modeler, Saxenian uses these case studies inductively to make a theoretical point: Differences in economic organization create decisive differences in the course of economic development.

Generalizations reached from two contrasting ethnographic studies do not provide much evidence for a theory, but anecdotally the cases are very persuasive. In the 1960s, the East Coast region with its mammoth, vertically integrated corporations, such as IBM, RCA, Digital Equipment Corporation, Wang, Honeywell, and General Electric, pioneered the move into high technology industries and quickly built a formidable technological and corporate advantage over firms elsewhere in the rest of the country. "By 1975," says Saxenian (1994, p. 19), "the technology complex along Route 128 employed close to 100,000 workers and was poised for a decade of explosive growth."

On the other side of the country, in the area around Stanford University south of San Francisco, the 1960s had also been a decade of expansion into high technology industries. Unlike the East Coast mega-corporations, the firms in the Silicon Valley were mainly small and narrowly focused. In the 1960s, thirty-one semiconductor firms had been started in Silicon Valley, and "only five of the forty-five independent semiconductor firms started in the United States between 1959 and 1976 were located outside Silicon Valley" (Saxenian, 1994, p. 26). Small firms, as Intel was in the late 1960s, intermingled with modestly larger firms, such as Hewlett Packard, creating complex and constantly changing networks. Here too, by 1975,

78

employment in the high technology industries had surpassed 100,000 workers, and this area was also poised for a decade of extraordinary growth.

On the eve of the great high technology expansion, the aggregate similarities between the two regions were many, which led some (for example, Kenney and von Burg, 1999) to conclude, in retrospect, that the only important differences dividing the two regions at this crucial point was technology. East Coast high technology industry concentrated on the mainframes and minicomputers, whereas their West Coast counterparts focused on semiconductors. Saxenian (1994, p. 27, 1999a) maintains, "Despite the similarities, the two regions were already developing along divergent trajectories." By the early 1980s the divergence had become clear, and by 1990, there was no contest. Most of the largest corporations on the Route 128 corridor had encountered serious difficulties; a few, such as Wang Laboratories, went bankrupt, a few more, such as DEC and Honeywell, were taken over by competitors, and the rest, such as IBM and General Electric, went through gut-wrenching reorganizations. The Silicon Valley had emerged the clear winner. Riding the crest of the demand for personal computers and workstations, firms such as Intel, Hewlett Packard, Sun Microsystems, and Microsoft grew to rank among the largest and most influential firms in the industry, even as they retained a rather narrow concentration on core products.

Regional Advantage documents the divergence between the two regions and tries to explain it. According to Saxenian, the difference between the two regions lay in the differences in organization of their respective economies, one concentrated on large vertically integrated corporations and the other on decentralized networks of interacting firms. These organizational differences nurture very different environments of work and innovation that result in dramatically different reactions to the same technology. The dynamism of the Silicon Valley, she argues (1994, p. 166), "lies not in any single technology or product but in the competence of each of its constituent parts and their multiple interconnections." Reiterating her view, Saxenian (1999a, pp. 108–9) adds, "It is precisely the openness, multiplicity and diversity of interconnections in Silicon Valley that allows economic actors to continually scan the environment for new opportunities and to invest in novel technologies, markets and applications with unprecedented speed." By contrast, Route 128 firms maintained their "extreme commitment to corporate self-sufficiency and secrecy; the vertical integration of manufacturing, the unwillingness to partner or even cooperate with others, and the geographic isolation" (Saxenian, 1999a, p. 107). She concludes as follows: "organization precedes technology" (1999a, p. 108).

Despite the persuasiveness of the two cases, Saxenian's two models of industrial systems are really not models at all, but rather ethnographically supported suggestions that, if indeed systemic organizational differences lead to significant differences in economic outcomes, then there should be an economic basis for these differences. There should be a model. She documents the organizational and cultural differences, but only infers from differential performance how the two systems actually work economically.

Saxenian's conclusions have, however, not gone unchallenged. Martin Kenney and Urs von Burg (1999) lay out the most persuasive alternative hypothesis. They argue that the organizational and cultural differences between the two regions were relatively unimportant. After all, the Silicon Valley had its big firms, too, and Route 128 had small firms. The real differences, they maintain, were technological. The Silicon Valley selected the "right" technology; the future of high technology went with semiconductors and personal computers. Route 128 firms picked the "wrong" technology. The initial decisions became magnified over time, as firms began to cluster around the right choice and abandoned the alternatives. They find that "small events" led to path dependent trajectories as increasing returns created "positive feedback loops that reinforced Silicon Valley and allowed it to outstrip Route 128" (1999, p. 99). Inverting Saxenian's thesis, they imply that technology precedes organization.

Saxenian's two cases and her suggestion that these cases represent two economic models are very important for our study of the South Korean and Taiwanese economies. Kenney and von Burg's challenge to Saxenian's conclusion is also important. In the first place, the two cases parallel the two Asian economies that we analyze in this book. The large, vertically integrated *chaebol* dominate the South Korean economy in much the same way that vertically integrated corporations dominated Route 128, and in many ways the corporate cultures are similar: inward looking, self-sufficient, unwilling to cooperate, mutually isolated players in the global economy. And, like their counterparts along Route 128, these *chaebol* have encountered serious difficulties in the past decade, especially during and after the 1997–98 Asian business crisis. By contrast, Taiwan's economy is composed of constantly changing networks of small, medium-sized, and large firms that rapidly shift from one area of production to another. During the 1990s, even after the Asian crisis, Taiwan's firms went from success to even greater success. It was not until the bursting of the U.S. stock market and high-tech bubble in 2000 that both the Silicon Valley and Taiwan experienced recessionary conditions. Like Saxenian, we, too, will demonstrate divergent outcomes between these economies and will offer an organizational explanation for the differences.

Saxenian's case studies, moreover, are not entirely separate from our own. As Saxenian has shown in later studies (1999b, 2000a, 2000b, 2000c, 2001), Taiwan's technology-dominated economy is actually deeply integrated with the high-technology economy of the United States. Where Silicon Valley stops and Taiwan's Hsinchu Science Park starts is impossible to say. By nearly every measure, except for geography, they are indistinguishable; they are integrated players in the same commodity chains, designing and building components that go in the same machines.

Kenney and von Burg's challenge to Saxenian's conclusions is also very important for our study because it forms a "friendly" alternative to our explanation. It is friendly in the sense that both the organizational and the technological alternatives emphasize emergent features within economic activity and would not support either market-failure or strong-state interpretations of Asian economic organization. It is an alternative to our own interpretation because it makes technology a cause and organization a consequence. This alternative is a worthy one for it draws on a substantial and growing literature focusing on the linkage between technology and economic development. Drawing on evolutionary and increasing return economics (Nelson and Winter 1982, Dosi 1982, Arthur 1994, David 1985), Kenney and von Burg fit squarely in a tradition that emphasizes the "lock-in effects" (Arthur 1994), possibly caused by small events, resulting in "technological paradigms" that through increasing success lead to path dependent trajectories, not merely for an industry but potentially for the entire economy. From this perspective, it is clear that technology goes before organization, and organization is an efficient outcome of a technological paradigm, even though the technology itself may not be the most efficient technology available at that time (David, 1985).

Saxenian's case studies also draw on a substantial literature. In fact, one might say that her observations fit into a "genre of research" that has developed in the past two decades, a research tradition that compares networked small firm economies with large firm economies and is a tradition that typically finds the large firm economies wanting.[1] One of the earliest and still one of the clearest expositions about these two systems is Piore and Sabel's *The Second Industrial Divide* (1984). Unlike Saxenian's ethnology, Piore and Sabel argue historically that Fordist production systems, which they equate with vertically integrated corporations, are declining relative to a densely networked production system that they call "flexible specialization." A huge literature emerged debating the merits of their argument for a decline in the large manufacturing firms and

---

[1] For a summary and critique of the main features of this literature, see Vallas, 1999.

for a rise in network forms of economic organization. As the contro-
versy evolved, the disciplinary location of the debate gradually moved to
economic geography, where the participants argued about the merits of
industrial districts and agglomeration effects. Although economists have
certainly entered the debate (for example, Krugman, 1991, 1994, Rauch,
1993a,b, Feenstra, 1998), the broader literature remains descriptive and
makes assertions about inefficiencies of mass production systems and the
efficiencies of cooperative networks without actually being able to specify
them in any detail. Saxenian's research is one of the clearest and, from
the perspective of our study of Asia, the best illustration of this line of
research. Her argument, which we share with her, is that "organization
precedes technology."

Which is the correct view? As Kenney and von Burg (1999, p. 99) note,
"It is difficult to firmly establish causation." We would add that it is
especially difficult to establish causation if we rely solely on alternative
interpretations of the same history.

Modeling Theory, Disentangling Complexity

Because it is so difficult to make causal inferences in such complex and
historically unique settings, we are using a methodological approach
designed to deal with this kind of complexity, the use of "idealized mental experiments," or what Weber called "ideal types." Although not often
recognized as such, this methodological approach is common to both economics and economic sociology. Trained as an economic and legal histo-
rian, and holding a position in an economics department, Weber (1949
[1903–05]; 1975 [1903–06]; Kalberg, 1994) first developed ideal type
methodology for historical analysis. For Weber, ideal types are logically
consistent, highly stylized models of action that can be used to disentangle
the complexity of the real world. At one point, he (1949 [1903–05]) suggested that formal economic models of action could serve as ideal types
if they were not confused with the real world. The real world, with all its
twists and turns of fate and all the historical contingencies and sheer accidents, is far too complex to be captured in any model, however detailed.
In fact, complexity is the very essence of historical change and must necessarily be preserved in any kind of historical analysis. For Weber, the use
of ideal types is a way to preserve complexity in the real world, on the
one hand, and to develop theoretically informed causal explanations of
historical change, on the other hand.

The logic of analysis is to abstract some core analytical constructs that
may have causal significance in the empirical problem under scrutiny, and
then purposefully to theorize those constructs by carrying them to their

logical conclusions. Action embodied in an ideal type is propelled by rationally extending the inner logic of the construct itself, which further disassociates it from the way action actually occurs in real life. Exploring the inner logic of a construct allows theorists to pinpoint clear relationships among elements of the construct. The clear relations, in turn, become the substance for working hypotheses for mental experiments about what might be observed if the theorized construct has some causal significance in the real world. The crucial point is, however, that the ideal type should not be confused with reality. "If the ideal type [is] 'correctly' constructed," wrote Weber, then "the actual course of events [does] not correspond to that by the ideal type." Instead, the correspondence between the theorized relationship and the empirical complexity works like an analogy. Although unreal, analogies, if they are the appropriate ones, allow users to sort out "real" connections that would otherwise go unnoticed without the help of the comparison. Ideal types are purposefully constructed analogies that, when contrasted with the real world, highlight aspects of a context that are difficult to analyze otherwise.

Models used by economists have all the qualities of ideal types. They are theories on a pin, narrow slices of reality that have been abstracted, mathematized, and made to stand on their own, apart from other considerations of reality. Economists are sometimes criticized for their models because, although parsimonious and mathematically rigorous, they have no explicit or easily understood correspondence to how economies really work. From the viewpoint of ideal type methodology, the rigorousness and parsimoniousness are not a problem. The problem occurs in determining the correspondence between the ideal type and the empirical world. Economists often seem to employ them as if they were depictions of "undistorted reality," the sort of situation that would occur if an imperfect world approached the reality expressed in the model. Making an abstraction more real than the world from which it is drawn is what Whitehead (1929, p. 11) called the "fallacy of misplaced concreteness." Weber (1949 [1903–05], p. 103) concurs: The danger of using such models "is an almost irresistible temptation to do violence to reality in order to prove the real validity of the construct."

The methodology of using economic models to make causal inferences about the real world rests on three steps, which we employ in this and the following chapters. First, the model needs to be sufficiently narrow and systematically defined to draw out the implications of the theory being examined. This rigorousness is required in order to develop hypotheses that flow strictly from the model. This is the task for the rest of this chapter. Second, the plausibility of the causal inferences rests on examining the correspondence between an idealized theory and empirical data. Do empirical tests based on the hypotheses suggest that the causal connections pinpointed in the model have an "objective probability" (Ringer, 1997) of occurring in the empirical world under scrutiny? We examine data on the business groups in South Korea and Taiwan in Chapter 4, and demonstrate that these data fit predictions of the model. Third, if there is some confidence that causal inferences are plausible, as they are in our case, then how do these connections work out in the complexity of a given case? Showing the interrelationships among economic organization and other aspects of the economy is the task for Part II of the book.

Modeling Economic Organization: Prices versus Transactions Costs

We hypothesize that the cross-market interconnectedness of firms in the context of a price structure has independent effects on the organization and economic performance of economies. As discussed in Chapter 1, we conceptualize the interconnections among firms in terms of the relationship in an organized setting between market power and authority. To clarify this point, let us consider the two models of industrial systems that Saxenian proposed. In one model, there are very large vertically integrated corporations, and in the other model, decentralized networks of firms in which different firms individually handle different aspects of production. Entrants into either setting would face a very different lineup of authority and market power and would need to adapt their own strategy of action accordingly. In the first setting, the large vertically integrated corporations individually want to enhance their own market power by internalizing (that is, exercising the use of authority over) the intermediate steps of production, thereby giving their competitors no advantages. Entrants in this setting would be forced either to vertically integrate themselves in order to compete with other firms or enter a line of business in which the large firms have no interest. In the second setting, entrants would be ill advised to vertically integrate in the same sectors where other firms are trying to carve out niches within cooperative networks of production. Here market power is achieved through establishing monopolistic control over a single link in the commodity chain, but not through integrating across all the links. To attempt to integrate across the chain at the expense of other firms in the chain would undercut the cooperation among firms and lead to tactics that would exclude the expansionary firm, possibly leading to ruin.

Let us theorize this situation in more formal terms, adding at the same time a broader notion of authority in the form of decisions made and enforced within a business group. A business group is one example of a "network" structure between firms, and in general, networks can affect production and trade in a number of ways.[2] For the purpose of our model, we will focus on just one feature: *the preferential access to intermediate inputs sold by member firms to other firms in the group.* This obviously abstracts from many actual features of business groups in South Korea and Taiwan, thereby allowing us to theorize the interactions between authority and market power in buying and selling intermediate inputs. A mathematical model along these lines is developed in Feenstra, Huang, and Hamilton (2003) and described in Appendix A, and here we summarize the essential features and results from that model.

In this stylized setting, let us divide the economy into two sectors: an upstream sector producing intermediate inputs from some primary factors and a downstream sector using these intermediate inputs (along with primary factors) to produce final consumer goods. Suppose that both the sectors are characterized by product differentiation, so that each firm retains some limited monopoly power (that is, market power) by virtue of the uniqueness of its product and, therefore, charges a price that is above its marginal cost of production. As usual under monopolistic competition, we will allow for the free entry of firms in both the upstream and downstream sectors to the point where economic profits are driven to zero. (By zero economic profits, we mean that the groups are just earning a "normal" rate of return on capital.) Thus, the profits earned by firms through charging prices above marginal cost go to cover their fixed costs of production where these fixed costs represent those of research, development, marketing, or any other fixed costs associated with having a differentiated product.

In contrast to conventional treatments of monopolistic competition, we will also allow firms to *integrate across markets* when this is advantageous. In particular, there will be an incentive to integrate both upstream and downstream, because in the absence of any such integration the market prices for intermediate inputs are above the marginal cost, which is a sure sign that agents could do better by internalizing the sale and pricing the input at exactly its marginal cost of production. By internalizing the sale in this manner, the groups located in both upstream and downstream markets will be obtaining higher joint profits than unaffiliated firms just trading the intermediate input at its market price.

The economy we have in mind is pictured in Figure 3.1. The upstream sector produces a range of products indicated by the dots at the top of

---

[2] The advantages to being within a network potentially include the following: information flows between firms and customers (Egan and Mody, 1992, Rauch, 1997); information flows on production techniques between firms and suppliers (Aoki, 1990); financial insurance provided by a bank within a group (Aoki and Patrick, 1994, Hoshi, Kashyap, and Sharfstein, 1990, 1991, Lincoln, Gerlach, and Ahmadjian, 1996); and other positive externalities between firms that reduce costs within the group (Friedman and Fung, 1996).

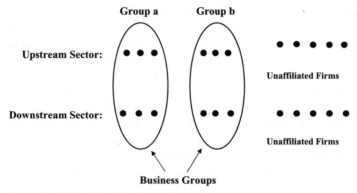

Figure 3.1. Model of Business Groups.

the diagram. These are used in the production of downstream products, which are indicated by the dots in the bottom of the diagram. A group will produce a range of both upstream products and downstream products, where it chooses the number of each and their prices as to maximize group profits. Unaffiliated firms can produce individual upstream and downstream products, as well as choose the price to maximize profits. We should stress that while profits are maximized for a group, they need not be larger than for unaffiliated firms. In the same way that we allow for the free entry of individual firms, we will also allow for the free entry of business groups. This means that competition *between the groups* will lead them to earn zero profits (that is, a "normal" rate of return on capital), as for unaffiliated firms.

Market Power and Authority in the Pricing of Intermediate Inputs

Given the importance that we place on the pricing of inputs for vertical integration, which we suppose occurs within business groups, it is useful to carefully review discussion of this point in the economics literature. Stigler (1966, p. 237) lists this as one of three reasons for vertical integration: "The third noncompetitive reason for vertical integration is to eliminate monopoly: if a cartel set noncompetitive prices on supplies, backward integration by buyers would be a suitable way to get the supplies cheaper." In his famous paper "The Division of Labor Is Limited by the Extent of the Market," Stigler (1951) describes an example of this in a coal cartel at the end of the nineteenth century, when steel companies kept acquiring mines to avoid paying the cartel's prices. That paper is primary devoted to discussing a theorem of Adam Smith, whose statement is used as the title, that firms will become less integrated (spinning off specialized activities) as the market grows. The example of backwards integration by the steel companies is used as an "important" instance where vertical integration is caused by a failure of the competitive price system rather than by the extent of the market.

The example that Stigler provides of the coal mine and steel company was subsequently formalized in simple models that consider an upstream and downstream firm, both of whom are monopolies.[3] In this situation, the upstream firm would charge a markup over its marginal cost, so the price at which the downstream firm buys the input is artificially high. As a result, the downstream firm uses too little of the input (an efficiency loss), but also charges a higher price to consumers (reflecting the high cost of materials). This is referred to as the problem of "double marginalization" of prices (that is, having markups on both the intermediate input and the final good, which leads to high consumer prices). Because of "double marginalization," both firms and consumers are worse off. Instead, by vertically integrating, the two firms can efficiently utilize the intermediate input, achieve higher profits, and even charge a lower price to consumers. Vertical integration in this case – creating one combined monopoly rather than two – is good for both firms and consumers!

At the same time, it was recognized that the benefits of vertical integration that the simple models demonstrated could be *equivalently achieved* without integration, but instead by arranging better contracts between firms. In particular, the upstream firm could charge the marginal cost for the input and also charge a fixed lump-sum fee (which is sometimes thought of as a franchise fee). By charging marginal cost for the input, it will ensure that the downstream utilizes it efficiently and, therefore, achieves the highest possible downstream profits; the fixed lump-sum fee is a way to transfer some of these profits back upstream. This type of contract is known as "two-part pricing" and is an example of what are more generally called "vertical restraints": actions taken by the upstream firm to affect the usage of its input and competition downstream (for example, franchise fees, resale price maintenance, and exclusive territories for the downstream firms). The belief is that by the use of two-part pricing and

---

[3] The earliest examination of this model was Machlup and Taber (1960), while McKenzie (1951) and Burnstein (1960) and Vernon and Graham (1971) considered a related case where the upstream firm is a monopolist but the downstream industry is competitive. In that case, forward integration from the monopolist into the downstream industry might very well raise consumer price and therefore reduce welfare, as demonstrated by Hay (1973), Schmalansee (1973), and Warren-Boulton (1974), though this result is not guaranteed. Subsequent literature emphasized that the downstream prices could either rise or fall.

other vertical restraints, the *benefits* of vertical integration (for both the firms and for consumers) can be achieved *even without* formal ownership between the firms.

To emphasize this point, we cite an early paper by Oliver Williamson (1971), which appears prior to his two books (1975, 1985) on transactions costs and, therefore, can be taken as an indication of his formative thinking on that subject. Williamson discusses reasons for vertical integration associated with market failure and deals first with the failure of competitive pricing, so that the price of a specialized input exceeds its marginal cost. In order to offset this failure, he distinguishes vertical integration versus contracts between firms:

> One possible adaptation is to internalize the transaction through vertical integration; but a once-for-all contract might also be negotiated. In a perfectly static environment (one that is free of disturbances of all kinds), these may be regarded with indifference: the former involves settlement on component supply price while merger requires agreement on asset valuation ... joint profit considerations dictate that the affected parties reach an accommodation, *but integration holds no advantage over once-for-all contracts in a perfectly static environment.* (p. 115, italics added)

In other words, there is no reason to vertically integrate if contracts between firms can be used instead. Williamson (1971) then goes on to consider environments of incomplete contracts, where the two firms are not able to specify all the contingencies that might arise in the production and sale of an input between them, nor commit to how these will be resolved. This is the starting point, of course, for the transactions cost approach: when the incompleteness of contracts imposes sufficient costs on the firms involved, it is better to integrate.

At the risk of oversimplification, we might view this article by Williamson (1971) as a seminal point in his, and others', thinking on the subject. Earlier literature such as Stigler (1951, 1966) explicitly recognized that monopolistic pricing of inputs was an "important" reason for vertical integration.[4] But subsequent literature has presumed that, in the absence of transactions costs, the effects of vertical integration could be *equivalently achieved* through contracts or "vertical controls" (for example, Warren-Boulton, 1974, who cites Williamson). Some writers have sought to establish this as a theorem (Dixit, 1983, Perry and Groff, 1985). The strong implication is that vertical integration should *not* be

---

[4] Remarkably, in the original version Stigler (1951) did not reference Coase (1937), but that reference was added when the article was reprinted in Stigler (1968).

understood as a response to monopolistic pricing of inputs, but rather as a response to transactions costs. This seems to be the prevailing view in economics, despite the fact that once we move outside the simplest of models, it is not at all obvious that vertical restraints are equivalent to integration.[5] Dixit (1983), for example, considers a model with a single upstream firm selling to multiple downstream firms, and no transactions costs. He finds that vertical restraints can achieve "perfect or near-perfect replication of the outcome under full vertical integration" (p. 63). But he goes on to emphasize the limitations of his analysis:

> Most important, it was assumed that the upstream firm was a monopolist. In most actual contexts, there are several such firms, and strategic interactions between them will be important. Questions of whether each downstream firm will be tied to one upstream firm or can diversity across them make the analysis difficult. (p. 78)

The model that we develop of business groups, illustrated in Figure 3.1, has just the feature that Dixit identifies as difficult: multiple groups, each of which are selling in both the upstream and downstream markets. We will be assuming that *within* a group, inputs can be effectively sold at marginal cost. This might be achieved through explicit "two-part pricing" or by some other arrangement that allows a transfer of profits back to the upstream firms to cover their fixed costs of product development. That is, even though the upstream and downstream firms are not fully or necessarily owned by a single company, we suppose that their membership within a business group confers the communication and authority necessary to achieve marginal-cost pricing for internal sales. This authority takes two forms: there must be a financial transfer back to the upstream firms; and in addition, the group must have the ability to control the prices charged by its downstream firms. Having the authority to achieve these outcomes, and therefore maximize joint profits, amounts to our definition of a business group in the narrow sense we are employing in this model.

However, for sales *outside* of a group, we will suppose that contracts of this type *cannot* be developed and instead will have the group charge monopolistic prices for external sales. We are, therefore, going back to Stigler (1951, 1966) and arguing that the ability to achieve marginal-cost pricing of inputs is an "important" reason for vertical integration, by which we mean membership in a business group. Because this goes against the prevailing view that vertical integration is due to transactions costs, it obviously needs careful justification both theoretically and empirically.

---

[5] See the models developed in Katz (1989) and Tirole (1989, Chap. 4), for example.

Theoretically, there is a very important reason why marginal-cost pricing of inputs, as part of a "two-part" pricing scheme, would not occur outside of business groups. By definition, a group in our model is producing differentiated goods both upstream and downstream. Consider a group making a decision to sell an input to an outside firm. By selling this input at marginal cost and charging a lump-sum fee, the group can obtain the highest profits in the upstream market. But selling this input will also have consequences in the downstream market. In purchasing the differentiated input from a business group, the outside firm will obtain some reduction in costs, and can therefore compete more effectively in downstream markets. So this will *lower* the downstream profits of the business group. In the coal-steel example of Stigler (1951), we can think of two steel companies, both of whom own their own mines and produce coal of different qualities. If company A with the higher quality coal sells this to its competitor B, this will certainly lower the profits earned by A in the downstream steel market. For this reason, it would want to charge a particularly high price for the coal and possibly withhold it from its competitor entirely. This is true even if company A attempts to use a "two-part" pricing scheme, both selling the coal per ton and charging a lump-sum fee. There may very well be no fee high enough to compensate company A for the loss in its downstream steel profits and that the competitor B would be willing to pay.[6]

Of course, if the company selling the coal could also *control the price of steel* charged by its competitor, then the situation is completely different; the downstream competition could be controlled, and the two companies could surely agree on a contract for coal. The authority to control both upstream and downstream prices is exactly what we shall give to a business group. But we feel that it is entirely implausible (that is, noncontractible) for a large business group to control the prices charged by downstream firms *outside* the group that are using its inputs: since it cannot prevent resale of these inputs, it would not even know exactly which downstream products make use of them! It follows *that the group will generally want to charge prices above marginal costs for external sale of its inputs, so as to limit downstream competition.* This is why marginal cost pricing for inputs will, in principle, never occur outside of business groups.

Stated more generally, the reason that business groups will be reluctant to sell inputs to each other is because they are engaged in "multimarket

---

[6] This assertion is easy to prove. Suppose that by selling its coal to a competitor, the *combined* profits of the two companies fall due to the enhanced competition in the downstream steel market. Then it is clear that there is no lump-sum transfer between the firms that can leave them both better off than before.

contact," competing with each other both upstream and downstream. This is recognized as possibly having significant anti-competitive effects. Bernhein and Whinston (1990) attribute this point to Corwin Edwards (1951): "When one large conglomerate enterprise competes with another, the two are likely to encounter each other in a considerable number of markets. The multiplicity of their contact may blunt the edge of their competition."[7] We will find that this holds in our model: because of their downstream competition, groups will charge unusually high prices to each other upstream or even refuse to sell to each other entirely. Ghemawat and Khanna (1998) identify the collusion over "multiple markets" as one reason for the formation of business groups, and this takes on particular force when the markets are both upstream and downstream.

Empirically, there is a good deal of evidence supporting our assumption that business groups charge lower prices for internal sales – approximating marginal costs – than for sales to unaffiliated firms. An interesting example is provided by Holmström and Roberts (1998), in their discussion of subcontracting within the Japanese automobile industry. They contrast the traditional U.S. practice in which the automaker designs the final product (including component parts) and manages all aspects of the manufacturing process through either internal procurement or short-term contracting with the system in Japan:

> In stark contrast, it is normal practice for Japanese auto firms to rely on their suppliers to do the actual design of the products supplied. The design costs are then to be recovered through the sale price of the part, with the understanding that this price will be adjusted in light of realized volumes. (p. 80)

This description applies to the vertical-oriented *keiretsu* in Japan, such as Toyota, for example. Under the scheme that Holmström and Roberts have in mind, total sales revenue consists of a fixed fee covering the design costs, and another portion that varies with the amount sold which reflects their marginal cost. This type of scheme is described in greater detail by Nishiguchi (1994, pp. 126–7):

> Along with the target cost method of new product development that emerged in Japan in the 1950s came "profit sharing rules: for purchaser and supplier. If, for example, the price for an instrument cluster (in the dashboard) was agreed on as 120 points for the first car-model year, during which time 110 points, the target price for the second year, was in fact achieved by the "joint" efforts, then the assembler would pay the supplier 115 points,

---

[7] Corwin Edwards, as quoted by Scherer (1980, p. 340).

thus sharing the profit evenly. If, however, the cost was further reduced during that period, say, down to 108 points, then the balance would go to the supplier. In other words, the assembler did not ask for a cheaper price than the second-year target price. In the second year, the assembler paid either 109 pints or 110 points net, and lower costs were continuously sought by encouraging more from the suppliers. This rule setting was a significant departure from the traditional practice in which the suppliers' incentives for improvement were frequently negated by the purchaser's attempts to try to monopolize the benefit of its supplier's new ideas. In contrast, the new arrangements inspired supplier entrepreneurship and led to a circle of purchase-supplier competition and cooperation.

This example of "two-part pricing" shows how this activity occurs *within* the vertical *keiretsu* in Japan. Nishiguchi (1994, pp. 126–7, note 41) goes on to contrast this "profit-sharing" Japanese system with the prevailing attitude in the United States: "when newly opened Japanese assembly transplants in the United States asked for proposals from local suppliers, the latter reacted extremely cautiously, and many either rejected or asked for written agreements on proprietary knowledge, initially, at least." In other words, the U.S. system relies on "written contracts" and the attendant hazards of incomplete enforcement, whereas the Japanese group system encourages "profit sharing" within the vertical groups without relying on contracts. This contrast between the U.S. and Japanese systems neatly illustrates the distinction we are making between competition and imperfect contracts *outside* of business groups, but cooperation *within* business groups.

Other recent evidence comes from South Korea. Since 1992, regulations on "undue transactions" within business groups have existed, and the Korea Fair Trade Commission is called upon investigate these cases and possibly levy surcharges on the business groups. We have examined evidence from three such cases in 1993–94, summarized in Appendix B. In the first, Goldstar Cable, an affiliate of Lucky-Goldstar group, was found to favor its affiliates over non-affiliate firms in trading various commodities, which were otherwise identical in terms of their specifications. It *sold* its products to affiliate buyers at much lower prices than to non-affiliate buyers, and also *purchased* their products at significantly higher prices than from other firms. The sales from Goldstar Cable to affiliate firms at below-market prices creates an efficiency gain within the group, whereas the purchases at above market may serve as a device to transfer profits within the group. A second case concerns Asia Automobile, an affiliate of Kia group, which purchased specific automobile parts from Kia Precision

Table 3.1. *Undue Intra-Group Transactions, Top Five* Chaebol

	No. of Subsidizing Companies	No. of Subsidized Companies	Transactions With Subsidy (billion *won*)	Surcharges Imposed (billion *won*)
Hyundai	35 (13)	11 (7)	771 (349)	22.6 (9.1)
Samsung	7 (2)	9 (3)	720 (200)	11.4 (3.0)
Daewoo	6 (11)	7 (3)	423 (42)	8.9 (4.5)
Lucky Goldstar	20 (3)	6 (2)	1,057 (68)	10.2 (2.2)
Sunkyong	12 (4)	2 (6)	1,056 (835)	19.1 (3.1)
TOTAL	80 (33)	35 (21)	4,026 (1,493)	72.2 (20.9)

Notes: The first set of numbers is from the investigation carried out during May–June 1998, and published on July 30, 1998. Numbers in parentheses are from the second round of investigations in July 1998, published November 13, 1998. Surcharges were imposed on the business groups by the Korean Fair Trade Commission.

Source: Korean Fair Trade Commission, as cited in Yoo (1999, 197).

Machinery at prices higher than from other non-group firms. A third case dealt with Hyundai Electronics Ltd, which preferentially treated its affiliate buyers over non-affiliates when selling a whole range of electronic products.

Since 1998, the Korea Fair Trade Commission has accelerated its investigations, and found that all of the top-five *chaebol* have engaged in "undue intra-group transactions." The results of these investigations are summarized in Table 3.1, drawn from Yoo (1999, 197). The first set of numbers is from investigations carried out during May–June 1998, whereas the numbers in parentheses are from the second round of investigations in July 1998. In the first investigations, internal transactions at below-market prices totaling some 4 trillion *won* (over $3 billion) were identified, between eighty subsidizing companies and thirty-five subsidized companies. Surcharges were imposed on these firms. This was promptly followed by a second round of investigations, finding another 1.5 trillion *won* (over $1 billion) of subsidized internal transactions, between another thirty-three subsidizing companies and twenty-one subsidized companies. These are only the transactions for which the Korean Fair Trade Commission found evidence of subsidy, and many others presumably occur. Based on this evidence, we believe our assumption of below-market prices being charged within business groups has substantial empirical validity, and we will rely on it heavily in our theoretical model.

Reflexivity and Nash Equilibrium

The reason that we have stressed the difference between transactions costs and our own approach is that they have profoundly different implications.

Under transactions costs, the integration of activities into a firm is effi-cient,[8] and in this sense, functionalist. Williamson recognized, of course, that the ability of a firm to effectively handle any transaction will depend on the details of the legal and social structure; on this point he cites both Mark Granovetter and Kenneth Arrow.[9] Nevertheless, when it comes time to say which activities will be undertaken inside a firm and which are done on the market, the discussion ends up being in terms of "asset specificity," which incorporates technological features such as site specificity, physi-cal asset specificity, human asset specificity, and dedicated assets (1985, p. 137).[10] Furthermore, he refers to a "fundamental transformation" (1985, Chap. 2), under which *ex ante* competition due to large num-bers is transformed into *ex post* bargaining between two parties. Thus, what begins as a story that might include social aspects, ends up reducing to bilateral bargaining between two parties depending on specific details of the "asset" in question. There is just nothing social left at the end of the day.

Let us contrast this with the economy we have pictured in Figure 3.1. To continue with our earlier example, think of each group as an inte-grated coal and steel company, where we assume that these companies each have access to a unique grade of coal that would be of value to the others. The question is the following: Would each company be willing to sell its coal to others, and at what price? Stripped of transactions costs, this is not a problem that reduces to bilateral bargaining. Rather, each company would need to consider its actions in relation to what others are doing. If there are only a *small* number of integrated companies (say, two), and company A sells coal to B, then this would create rather intense competition between the two downstream companies, because they are the only producers there. Each company would therefore be reluctant to sell coal, either charging a very high price or not selling at all. But if there are a *large* number of companies, so that each has but a small share of

---

[8] "Transactions costs are *economized* by assigning transactions (which differ in their attributes) to governance structures (the adaptive capacities and associated costs of which differ) in a discriminating way" (Williamson, 1985, p. 18, emphasis added).

[9] Citing a draft of Granovetter's 1985 article, Williamson (1985, p. 22) states, "The social context in which transactions are embedded – the customs, mores, habits and so on – have a bearing, and therefore have to be taken into account, when moving from one culture to another," and citing Arrow (1969, 1974), Williamson (1985, p. 9) remarks, "Arrow insisted that the problem of economic organization be located in a larger context in which the integrity of trading parties is expressly considered (1974). The efficacy of alternative modes of contracting will thus vary among cultures because of differences in trust (Arrow, 1969, p. 62)."

[10] This could not be stated more plainly than by Alchian (1984, pp. 38–9), cited by Williamson, "the whole rational for the employer–employee status, and even for the existence of firms, rest on [asset specificity]; without it, there is no known reason for firms to exist."

the steel market, then they would be less concerned about the effects of selling coal on their profits downstream. In that case, we would expect to see coal sold between the companies.

In other words, each company can decide on its appropriate actions only by objectifying what it is doing in relation to what others are doing. This is what sociologists call "reflexivity," and economists call "Nash equilibrium." The calculations made by each company are fully economic (profit maximizing), but they are also fully social, since they depend on the actions of others. On the social side, it would be very natural to expect the organization of the company-groups to become codified into norms and institutions. This is the "capital accounting" and the "economically regulative organizations" of Weber (1978) that we referred to in Chapter 1. But at the same time, not just any norms and institutions will arise. The mutual and simultaneous rational calculations of businesses can be expected to restrict the scope of outcomes that are observed, into a possibly small number of feasible types of economic organization.

This is where the contrast between transactions costs and our own approach becomes most acute: whereas the outcomes under transactions costs are efficient, we make no such claim; rather, we expect to observe a range of possible organizational structures, where the choices of businesses in each will depend on what others are doing. As we shall see, this leads very naturally to the result of "multiple equilibria." Examples of multiple equilibria in organizational structure include the work of Greif, Milgrom, and Weingast (1994) and Greif (1994) on the organization of trade in the Middle Ages; and Kranton (1996) on reciprocal exchange. To this work we will be adding an additional element of *general equilibrium* by simultaneously solving for both the prices of products and number of business groups and unaffiliated firms. In that way the number of groups, and so the economic organization, becomes "endogenous" to the model.[11]

Thus far in the chapter, we have exhaustively motivated our approach and discussed its relation to that of transactions costs. We have also tried to explain why it is very likely to see multiple forms of economic organization arising in equilibrium. To proceed further, we really need to demonstrate that these multiple equilibria are an outcome of the model. This is what the remainder of the chapter is devoted to. All readers should, at a minimum, be familiar with the next section, where we offer a typology of business groups that will be used throughout the rest of the book. Readers who are prepared to accept that the different configurations of groups in this typology can arise in equilibrium could jump to the next chapter

---

[11] Casella and Rauch (1997), Rauch and Casella (1998), and Kali (1998) are other examples of where business networks are determined in a general equilibrium model.

without much loss of continuity. There we compare the actual groups in South Korea and Taiwan with the simulated results from our model.

Typology of Business Groups

Business groups in the model sell intermediate inputs to their own firms at marginal cost, while these products are sold to unaffiliated firms at their marginal cost plus a markup. These conditions mean that business groups are inherently more efficient in their production than a combination of upstream and downstream unaffiliated firms, creating an incentive for these groups to form.[12] Before describing the possible equilibria, we need to ask what prevents business groups from being so efficient that they dominate the economy entirely?

We introduce into the model "governance costs," which represent the costs of monitoring and coordinating the activities of firms within the group. These costs are borne only by groups, and not by the unaffiliated firms. There is a special reason within the model for such agency costs to arise. Because the inputs produced within a group are sold internally at marginal cost, these firms would not be covering their fixed costs of production and would, therefore, need to receive a financial transfer from the rest of the group. The size of this transfer depends on the extent of fixed costs (such as research and development) that is devoted to the creation of new product varieties. Because this would normally be private information of the firm involved, it would be difficult to implement this financial transfer without leading to some inefficiency. For example, the guarantee of the group to cover the fixed costs of the upstream firms could lead to less effort expended by the managers of these firms. We do not model these agency costs in any detail, but simply assume that the groups have a fixed governance cost, over and above the costs of unaffiliated firms.[13]

---

[12] Efficiency within a group, however, does *not* necessarily translate into efficiency for the economy overall. Business groups will have an incentive to withhold their intermediate inputs from other groups, because they do not want the competing groups to enjoy the same production-efficiency that comes from having access to the specialized intermediate inputs. The withholding of intermediate inputs comes about by charging high prices for these, and possibly even an infinite price, meaning that the intermediate inputs are not sold to competing groups at all. This is a clear sign of *inefficiency* for the economy overall, because groups will not be sharing access to their proprietary input with other firms. We will have to investigate the extent to which this occurs in equilibrium.

[13] Theoretical models of financially interlinked groups include Kim (1999) and Ghatak and Kali (2001). In empirical work, Hoshi, Kashyap, and Scharfstein (1990b) investigate firms that *left* bank-centered groups following deregulation in 1983 and suggest that one reason this may have occurred was due to conflicting objectives of the banks and shareholders, where the banks are too conservative. Along different lines, Khanna and

While these governance costs act as a check on the business groups, we think it is realistic to assume that these costs are small. This has strong implications for the ability of unaffiliated firms to enter. Because a business group is otherwise more efficient than a set of unaffiliated upstream and downstream firms, when free entry drives the profits of the groups down to zero, it must be that the profits of some unaffiliated firms are even lower. This means that a zero-profit equilibrium involving the business groups, as well as the upstream and downstream firms, cannot occur; either the upstream or the downstream unaffiliated firms (or both) will be driven out of existence by the free entry of business groups.

Thus, for sufficiently small governance costs, the equilibrium organization of this stylized economy can only have three possible configurations: (1) business groups dominate in the upstream sector (called *U-groups*) and are vertically integrated downstream, but also compete with some unaffiliated downstream firms; (2) business groups dominate in the downstream sector (called *D-groups*), while purchasing some inputs internally and others from unaffiliated upstream firms; and (3) business groups drive out unaffiliated producers in both the upstream and downstream sectors and are, therefore, strongly vertically integrated (called *V-groups*). These three configurations are illustrated in Figure 3.2. The first panel shows a U-group selling to unaffiliated firms and the second shows a D-group buying from unaffiliated firms.[14] In the final panel, we display two V-groups that can choose whether to sell inputs to each other or not.

The purpose of the mathematical model is to determine which of the configurations shown in Figure 3.2 can arise in equilibrium; that is, in a situation where all firms are maximizing profits, there is free entry of both groups and firms, and there is full employment of the economy's resources (for simplicity, our model has just a single resource, called labor). Before describing the results, it is worth outlining how the model is solved. Our key simplifying assumption is that *all groups are the same size* (this also holds for unaffiliated firms in each of the upstream and downstream sectors). Thus, when a business group determines its optimal strategy, it does so knowing that all *other* groups have the same number of firms producing inputs, and the same number of firms producing final goods, with like prices in each sector. Each group must then determine whether it is profitable to *deviate* from these choice made by other groups. The economy will be in equilibrium when *no group* has any incentive to deviate

Palepu (2000b) investigate Indian groups, and find that groups with greater internal financial transfers (and therefore less transparency) are less attractive targets for foreign investment.

[14] Illustrating a *single* business group is just for convenience in the drawing, and in equilibrium there will generally be a number of groups, which we assume are all of the same size.

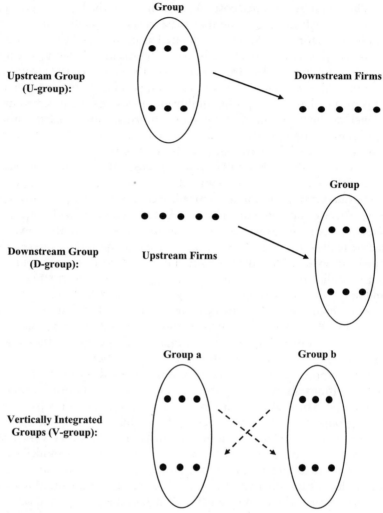

Figure 3.2. Types of Business Groups.

from the like choices made by others (and similarly for unaffiliated firms). We use the model to determine what the number and size of groups in the economy must be in equilibrium, allowing for the possibility that *more than one* configuration of groups might be consistent with no single group wanting to deviate from the common pattern.[15]

---

[15] Our assumption of "symmetry" in the calculation of equilibria is a simplifying device that rules out having large and small groups co-exist. It would be preferable, of course,

When Will Groups Sell Inputs to Each Other?

We first address the question of when the groups will sell inputs to each other. For convenience, we will focus initially on just the V-groups, supposing that any unaffiliated firms find it unprofitable to enter. A key choice variable of the business groups is the *price that groups charge for the intermediate inputs sold to other groups*. This reflects the competition that groups perceive that they face with each other. If a group A believes that selling an input to group B confers a substantial advantage to that group, in the sense that group B can produce the downstream good at lower cost and therefore compete more aggressively downstream, then group A could decide *not* to sell this input even at a very high price. We are interested in knowing when this type of outcome will occur.

To begin, we review some well-known results from economics. An *unaffiliated* firm will find most it most profitable to set the price for a good it is selling in *inverse relation* to its "elasticity" of demand: this is called the Lerner pricing rule. The "elasticity" measures the extent to which buyers can substitute away from a good if its price goes up. A good with high elasticity (many substitutes) should therefore be priced close to marginal cost; a good with low elasticity (few substitutes) can be priced much higher than marginal cost, earning substantial profits. When the elasticity approaches unity, then a firm does not lose any sales revenue at all from increasing its price, so it will set its price arbitrarily high. Since infinite prices do not make any sense, this leads to the well-known result that the elasticity of demand for any firm with some ability to set its price (that is, some market power) must be *greater than unity*.

Now consider how this Lerner pricing rule changes when a *group* is selling the intermediate input to another group. We expect that the competition in the downstream market will lead the group to set a price *higher* than would an unaffiliated firm. That is, the group not only wants to maximize its profits from selling the intermediate input (as would an unaffiliated firm), but it *also* wants to ensure that it does not give a cost-advantage to the purchasing group from having that input available, since these groups compete in the downstream market. How intense is this competition? That would depend on how many groups are in the economy. If there are only a small number, say two, then each group will be supplying one-half of the entire downstream market (since we are assuming there are no unaffiliated firms). Each group is therefore a large player

to use a model that allowed for different-sized groups even in a single equilibrium, but this task we leave to future research; the theoretical results of this chapter are enough to make a thorough comparison with the groups in South Korea and Taiwan, as in the next chapter.

in this market, and would be concerned about protecting its profits downstream. For this reason, we expect to find that the *smaller* the number of business groups competing "head to head" downstream, then the *higher* prices of the intermediate inputs become.

We can now answer the question of when a group would want to sell to other groups at all. Sales will *not occur* if the optimal price for the intermediate input is arbitrarily high, approaching infinity. In conventional models, infinite prices do not make any sense, but in our model these prices only apply to *external* sales, while the *internal* sales still occur at marginal cost. We find that the external prices are infinite – so that the groups do not sell to each other – whenever the elasticity of demand is less than or equal to $G/(G-1)$, where G is the number of business groups. For example, with just two groups, the groups will not sell to each other for any elasticities less than two; with three groups, this occurs for elasticities less than 1.5, and so forth. We will still suppose that the elasticity is greater than unity, so that for elasticities in the range *between* unity and $G/(G-1)$, sales of the inputs will be *only* internal.

These results are illustrated in Figure 3.3, where we show the number of groups G on the vertical axis and the elasticity of demand E (exceeding unity) on the horizontal axis. The dashed line along which the elasticity E equals $G/(G-1)$ is labeled as such. Whenever the number of groups or elasticity lie *below* this line, there will be no external sales: each group will be entirely self-sufficient, in an extreme form of the "one-setism" that characterizes the *chaebol* in South Korean, whereby they expand into any and all lines of business that serve their member firms. In contrast, when either the number of groups or elasticity lies *above* the line $E = G/(G-1)$, then

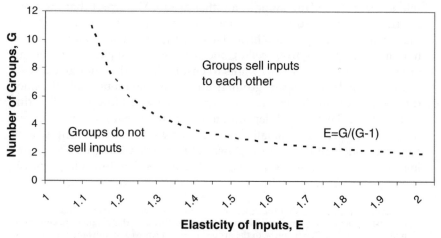

Figure 3.3. Regions Where Groups Sell Inputs or Not.

the groups will be willing to sell their inputs to each other (or unaffiliated firms). This is more characteristic of the vertically oriented *keiretsu* in Japan, for example, where a supplier to Toyota may also sell its products to other automobile groups.

Our goal now is to "fill in" the regions of Figure 3.3 with equilibria from the theoretical model. To do so, we pick a value for the elasticity of demand for inputs, E. In our model, we suppose that this same value applies to all possible inputs in the economy (another value of the elasticity applies to all final goods).[16] We then solve for an equilibrium, satisfying profit-maximization and free entry of all business groups (later we also add unaffiliated firms), and full-employment of resources in the economy. This allows us to determine the number of groups, G, in equilibrium, and that will be plotted in Figure 3.3 above the elasticity we started with. This exercise is then repeated for *every other value of the elasticity*: in each case, we find the number of groups, and their prices charged for inputs and final goods. In this way, we will obtain a plot of various equilibria of the economy, depending on the value of the elasticity. Obviously, the precise position of this plot will depend on details of the model, such as consumer tastes and resource endowments. We will be choosing representative values for these other parameters in the mode and then keep them fixed in the simulations.[17] Our interest will be in the more general features of the equilibria obtained, and in particular, whether for each elasticity there is a *unique* number of groups or *several* group configurations that are consistent with equilibrium.

---

[16] Initially, we used an elasticity of demand for final goods equal to 5. While we found both V-group and U-group equilibria at this value, it was difficult to find D-group equilibria in which the unaffiliated downstream firms had no incentive to enter. To limit this incentive, it was necessary to use lower values for the final demand elasticity, especially when the elasticity of demand for inputs itself was low. Accordingly, all our equilibria are computed with an elasticity of demand for final goods equal to 5 for $E \geq 2.65$, and equal to $1.9\,E$ for $E \leq 2.60$.

[17] The elasticity of demand used for final goods is discussed in the previous note. Labor is the only factor of production in the model, so the size of the labor force, L, determines overall demand and the size of the economy. We initially choose $L = 1000$ to obtain the equilibria shown in Figures 3.4–3.8, along with the other parameters: governance costs equal to 0.2, elasticity of demand for final goods equal to 5, labor share in costs equal to 0.5, fixed costs for business groups of creating a new intermediate input or final good equal to 5. These parameter values are also used for Figures 3.13–3.15. Then, to plot the "high concentration" equilibria in Figures 3.9 and 3.11, we change the size of the labor force so that the average sales of V-groups in the simulations equal the average sales of the "top five" *chaebol* in South Korea in 1989. However, for the "low concentration" equilibria shown in Figures 3.10 and 3.12, we use a value of L that is 25 percent lower than its value in the "high concentration" equilibria, reflecting the smaller overall size of the Taiwanese economy. Another parameter of importance is the amount of internal sales within groups that are channeled through trading companies or retail firms in the model. This parameter, denoted by r in note 24, is set at 0.15.

Equilibria with Vertically Integrated Groups

We have found so far that an equilibrium of the economy with only V-groups can take one of two forms: either the groups do not sell to each other, or they choose to do so at some optimal price. Let us focus initially on the case where *no sales* occur between the groups. The question then is: how many groups will choose to enter, so that the profits of each are bid down to zero? This will clearly depend on how large the economy is, as measured by its resource endowments. For a given size, however, we find that with no sales between the business groups then the number of such groups is *uniquely determined*. That is, with all groups choosing to expand into as many upstream and downstream products as they find optimal, and free entry of groups of this same size, none of whom are selling to each other, there will only be room for a certain number of groups in the economy.

This result is illustrated in Figure 3.4, where, like Figure 3.3, we show the number of groups G on the vertical axis, and the elasticity of demand E for the intermediate inputs on the horizontal axis. The line along which $E = G/(G-1)$ is shown. For each value of the elasticity, we solve for the number of groups consistent with equilibrium, and this value of G is plotted as a triangle. We see that for elasticities less than about 2.5, the equilibrium number of groups is small enough so that the plotted

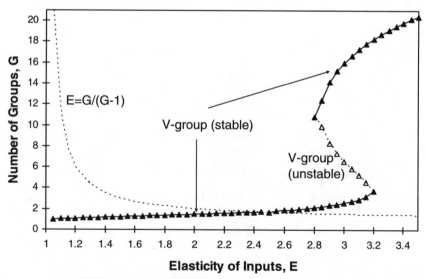

Figure 3.4. Number of V-Groups.

points lie *below* the line $E = G/(G-1)$, meaning that the groups do not sell any intermediate inputs to each other. Furthermore, in this region the equilibrium number of groups is *uniquely* determined once we specify the elasticity and other parameters of the economy (such as its size): for each elasticity, there is a certain number of V-groups consistent with equilibrium.

Now consider values of the elasticity exceeding 2.5. This moves us into the region *above* the line $E = G/(G-1)$, so that groups begin selling inputs to each other. What then, is the equilibrium number of groups in the economy? It would appear that this depends on the price charged for the intermediate inputs: if this price is high, it would prevent business groups (and unaffiliated firms) from entering; while if this price is low, then more groups would want to enter. But we have already argued that the equilibrium price of the intermediate inputs *depends* on the number of business groups: when there are fewer groups, they each have a larger share of the downstream market, and would want to charge a higher price for the intermediate inputs used by their rivals. So now there is a circularity in the argument: the equilibrium number of groups will depend on the price of the intermediate inputs, but the price charged for these inputs will depend on the number of groups. This kind of circular reasoning is precisely what gives rise to *multiple equilibria* in any economic model, and our stylized economy is no exception. We, therefore, expect to observe two types of equilibria: those with a small number of business groups and a high price for the intermediate inputs; and those with a large number of groups and a lower price of the intermediate input.

This line of reasoning is confirmed when we actually solve for the equilibria. For elasticities just slightly greater than 2.5, there is a still a unique number of groups G consistent with equilibrium. However, for elasticities between about 2.8 and 3.2 we find that there are three equilibria, giving the "S-shaped" curve shown in Figure 3.4. The idea that equilibria come in odd numbers is a characteristic feature of many economic and physical models. Like an egg standing upright either just balances where it is, or falls to the left or right with the slightest bump, the "middle" equilibrium is often unstable, while those on either side are stable. We have checked the stability of the V-group equilibria by slightly increasing the number of groups beyond the equilibrium number and computing whether profits of the groups rise or fall. If profits fall, then the number of groups will return to its equilibrium number, so the equilibrium is stable. If the profits rise, then even more groups would be induced to enter and the equilibrium is unstable.

The *stable* V-group equilibria are illustrated with solid triangles in Figure 3.4, and the *unstable* are illustrated with open triangles. To further

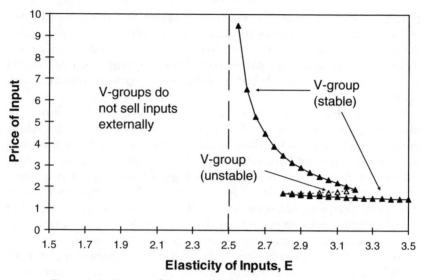

Figure 3.5. Pricing of Inputs with V-groups.

understand how these multiple equilibria arise, in Figure 3.5 we plot the optimal price for the intermediate input.[18] For values of the elasticity less than 2.5, the business groups do not sell to each other, that is, the price of the inputs is infinite. For slightly higher values of the elasticity, the price begins to fall, and when the elasticity reaches 2.8 there appear *multiple* equilibria, with high and low prices. The high-priced equilibria support a small number of business groups, and the low-priced equilibria support a larger number of groups, with an intermediate case in-between these two. The intermediate case is unstable, while both the high-price and low-priced equilibria are stable.

To summarize our results thus far, computing the equilibria of our stylized model with V-groups confirms our expectation that *multiple equilibria* can arise. The price system itself imposes some structure on the organization of the economy, but equally important, does not fully determine which of these equilibria will arise: in principle, an economy with the same underlying conditions (such as resource endowments and consumer tastes) could give rise to more than one possible equilibrium organization. We have confirmed these multiple equilibria are stable, meaning that once they are established there is no reason for them to change, even as the economy experiences some degree of change in underlying conditions.

[18] Note that the marginal cost of intermediate inputs has been set at unity in the model, which equals the internal price within a group.

Upstream and Downstream Business Groups

We now add the possibility of unaffiliated firms locating in the upstream or downstream markets. Because there is free entry of these firms, they will choose to enter whenever the profits available cover the fixed costs of entry; entry will continue until profits are driven down to zero. While we shall allow entry into both the upstream and downstream markets, we do not expect both to occur simultaneously, since the business groups in the model are more inherently more efficient than a like-sized combination of upstream and downstream firms. Recall that we have offset the efficiency advantage of the groups by giving them small "governance" costs, which are an additional fixed cost that each group bears. In our model, we adjust this "governance cost" so that upstream or downstream firms are profitable in at least some equilibria. That is, we intentionally choose the "governance cost" to obtain a *wide range* of possible equilibrium configurations.[19]

To determine whether the unaffiliated firms enter, we first need to check the V-group equilibria illustrated in Figure 3.4. For many of these equilibria, we find that the profits that could be earned by either unaffiliated upstream or downstream firms are not sufficient to cover their fixed costs, so entry would not occur. This is not the case, however, for the low-priced equilibria with a correspondingly large number of V-groups that occur at the top of the "S-shape" in Figure 3.4. For values of the elasticity exceeding 2.8, these equilibria allow for profitable entry of *downstream* unaffiliated firms. Accordingly, we allow these firms to enter until profitable opportunities are exhausted, and re-compute the number of business groups in the equilibrium. Because these groups compete with the downstream firms, they are dominant only in the upstream market and are, therefore, referred to as U-groups.

In Figure 3.6, we show the equilibrium number of U-groups as squares, for elasticities exceeding 2.8. We have confirmed that these equilibria are stable in the sense that a small increase in the number of business groups

---

[19] Actually, we introduce two types of "governance costs" into the model: the first is a fixed cost carried by each group; and the second is a fixed cost for each new input or final good developed (due to research and development, and marketing, for example). The latter fixed cost is carried by both unaffiliated firms and groups, but we assume it is *slightly higher* for the groups. In other words, the *unaffiliated* firms are assumed to be slightly better at creating new products, in either the upstream or downstream market. This assumption is needed to help offset the efficiency advantage that the business groups have. In addition, this assumption helps limit the incentive of the business groups to *take over* the unaffiliated firms. We suppose that if such takeover occurs, then the fixed costs of product creation are raised slightly when the unaffiliated firm is merged with the group, so the group will not necessarily want to pursue such a takeover, even if the unaffiliated firm is profitable.

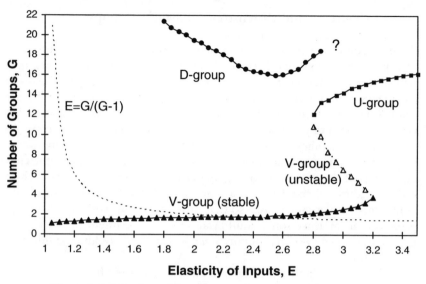

Figure 3.6. Number of Business Groups.

will lead to lower profits for all of them; therefore, some groups will exit to restore the zero-profit equilibrium. The U-groups charge low prices for the intermediate inputs, which is optimal because each individual group has only a small share of the downstream market, and because it is not that concerned over the cost-advantage it gives to rivals by selling them inputs. This configuration of the economy can be thought of as analogous to Taiwan, where business groups dominate in the upstream markets, such as chemicals, but supply these inputs at competitive prices to a great number of downstream firms.

Next, we check for the equilibrium configuration in which there are unaffiliated upstream firms, so the business groups dominate in the downstream market, and are called D-groups. For example, D-groups can be conceived of as primarily assembly firms in downstream markets, which produce some of their own intermediate inputs. Automobile manufacturers in Japan such as Toyota seem to fit this description, and GM and Ford in the United States are moving in that direction, both of whom have split off their parts production into separate companies (Delphi for GM and Visteon for Ford). Other example include Dell Computers or any number of footwear and garment brand name manufacturers (for example, Nike or The Gap) that purchase inputs from various affiliate and non-affiliated suppliers, and then assemble and market the final products. D-groups are plotted as circles at the top of Figure 3.6, for elasticities between 1.8 and 2.8. These equilibria are all stable, though there are also *other unstable*

D-group equilibria that we have not plotted.[20] The prices charged by the D-groups for sale of the intermediate inputs are low, despite the fact that most of these equilibria occur in the range of elasticities where the V-groups would not sell the inputs externally. The D-groups charge a low price for inputs partly because there are many of them in the downstream market, so that each group has only a small fraction of the market, but also because they face competition from other unaffiliated upstream producers. Thus, in the same way that we have *multiple* stable equilibria for elasticities exceeding 2.8, with the U-groups pricing low and the V-groups pricing high, we also have multiple stable equilibria for elasticities in the range from 1.8 to 2.6, with the D-groups pricing low and the V-groups pricing high (often at infinity).

At the top of Figure 3.6, we show a final area of equilibria labeled with a question mark. These are initially solved as D-group equilibria, allowing for the entry of upstream, unaffiliated firms. However, when we check for the profitability of downstream unaffiliated firms, it turns out that they would also want to enter. Therefore, in this range we evidently have an equilibrium configuration with business groups, upstream and downstream firms. The same situation applies at the other end of the D-group equilibria, for elasticities below 1.8. We have not fully explored this case in our model, but logic certainly suggests that it is a plausible outcome; the difficulty of solving for this equilibrium prevents us from analyzing it further.

High Concentration and Low Concentration Equilibria

Given the complexity of the equilibria in Figure 3.6, it is useful to pause and summarize the general features of this diagram. Recall that our method of solving for the equilibria has been to pick each value of the elasticity, and then determine the equilibrium number of groups and their prices; this is repeated for all other elasticities. For many of the elasticities, we have found *two* stable equilibria. For example, for elasticities between 1.8 and 2.6, we have either the D-groups or the tightly integrated V-groups, who do not sell inputs to each other. For elasticities between about 2.8 and 3.2, we have either U-groups or V-groups. Beyond

---

[20] These appear below the stable D-group equilibria in the upper-portion of Figure 3.6, and for elasticities below about 2.6, create an unstable equilibrium between each pair of stable D-group and stable V-group equilibria (for a given elasticity). The presence of these unstable D-group equilibria confirms that, for given parameters, equilibria come in odd numbers: if the equilibrium is not unique, then there should be 3, with one being unstable, or 5, with two being unstable, etc.

elasticities of 3.2, there is a unique type of equilibrium, with U-groups.[21] These unique equilibria extend beyond the elasticity of 3.5 that are shown in Figure 3.6, up to an elasticity of about 6.6, after which we no longer find profitable business groups for the "governance costs" we have assumed in the model.

We will be arguing that some of the equilibria we have found bear a resemblance to the group structure in Korea, and other equilibria resemble that found in Taiwan. To make this precise, we will have to have some criterion for selecting between equilibria. Since we think of different elasticities as applying to different types of goods, it would not make any sense to say, for example, that Korea has low elasticities while Taiwan has high elasticities. On the contrary, we will suppose that *any* value of the elasticity can apply in either country, and we shall focus on all values between 1.8 and 6.6 (at intervals of 0.05).[22] Then, for each elasticity, we will choose the equilibrium with the *large* number of business groups, and say that it belongs to the *low concentration* set, while we will choose the equilibrium with the *small* number of business groups and say that it below to the *high concentration* set. In this way, we will be identifying two generic types of equilibria, distinguished by the degree of concentration of the business groups, over the whole range of elasticities being considered.

To further illustrate this division into two equilibrium sets, let us return to Saxenian's two case studies. Along Route 128, only a few very large vertically integrated corporations dominated the economy. Within the high technology sector, the corporations specialized in proprietary products, which meant low elasticities for their intermediate inputs as well as final products, and few sales among corporations. Other intermediate inputs were standardized, leading to higher elasticities, and were provided by other firms. Nevertheless, the large corporations dominated the economic landscape to the point of marginalizing other types of activities. In the Silicon Valley, by contrast, a full range of elasticities occurred in the same industry, which in turn supported many different types of firms in the same sector. For example, corporations with upstream niches, such

---

[21] Beyond elasticities of 3.2, there is a unique U-group equilibrium shown in Figure 3.6. Recall from our previous discussion, however, that there is another type of equilibrium in which all three types of firms enter (unaffiliated upstream, unaffiliated downstream, and business groups); this was indicated by the question mark at the top of Figure 3.6. So there might be multiple equilibria even for elasticities exceeding 3.2: an equilibrium of the U-group type and another with all three types of firms. Because we did not solve for this equilibrium, we cannot include it in our analysis.

[22] Below elasticities of 1.8, we show only a single equilibrium in Figure 3.6 with the tightly integrated V-groups. However, we have also found that for elasticities in this range there is likely to be an *alternative* equilibrium, involving the simultaneous entry of business groups, upstream and downstream firms. Because we have not been able to solve for this equilibrium in detail, we do not consider elasticities below 1.8.

as Intel, could cooperate with other small and large upstream suppliers producing more standardized components (for example, monitors and peripherals), all of which could then be assembled by downstream corporations, such as Dell or Gateway, into final products. In the first case, the economy would support only a limited number of big groups, but in the second the economy would support a full range of firms.

Figure 3.6 formalizes this difference into two equilibria sets. The *high concentration* equilibria include the stable V-group at the bottom of the figure, for all elasticities up to 3.2, followed by the stable U-group equilibria for elasticities above 3.2. For completeness, we will also include the *unstable* V-group equilibria when graphing this path, as a reminder of what lies in-between the V-group and U-group equilibria. The *high concentration* equilibria, using all elasticities from 1.8 to 6.6, are again illustrated in Figure 3.7. In brief, these equilibria include the V-groups, which we will show are very big, and the U-groups, which are considerably smaller in their sales.

The *low concentration* equilibria form a path at the top of Figure 3.6, and include the D-group for elasticities up to 2.8, followed by the U-group equilibria for elasticities above 2.8. When there is a unique equilibrium, as for the U-groups with elasticities above 3.2, then it belongs to *both* the high-concentration and low-concentration set. The *low concentration* equilibria, using all elasticities from 1.8 to 6.6, are again illustrated in Figure 3.8. It is obvious that there is a considerable overlap of the equilibria between Figure 3.7 and 3.8: all U-groups for elasticities above 3.2

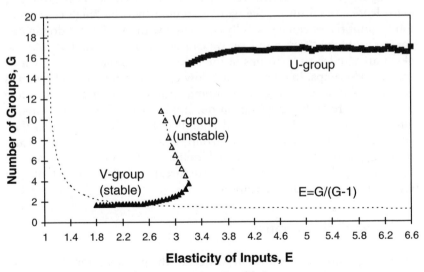

Figure 3.7. *High Concentration* Equilibria.

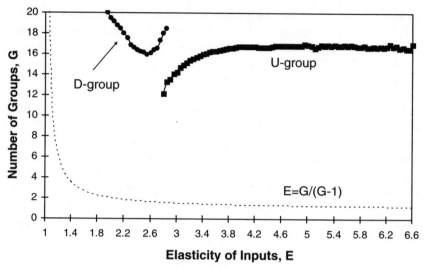

Figure 3.8. *Low Concentration* Equilibria.

belong to both sets. In addition, the low concentration equilibria includes U-groups for elasticities between 2.8 and 3.2, and D-groups for elasticities between 1.8 and 2.8.

Our goal for the rest of the chapter is to characterize the high-concentration and low-concentration equilibria in terms of some variables that can be measured in practice, and then in the next chapter, to compare these theoretical results with the actual business groups in South Korea and Taiwan. We will be arguing that the "high concentration" equilibria set can be usefully compared with the *chaebol*-dominated Korean economy. Within this set we can distinguish the largest *chaebol*, which are similar to V-groups in the model, from other *chaebol*, which resemble U-groups. In contrast, the "low concentration" equilibria set is more useful in interpreting the economic organization of Taiwan, where most groups resemble U-groups in our model. We will obtain economic outcomes based on the simulated equilibria from the model, and then compare these to actual business group data, using both diagrams and simple summary statistics. The variables that we focus on to compare the simulated equilibria and actual data are threefold: sales, vertical integration, and horizontal diversification.

Vertical Integration

We will measure the *vertical integration* of the groups using the ratio of their *internal sales to total sales*. Recall that the internal sales of inputs

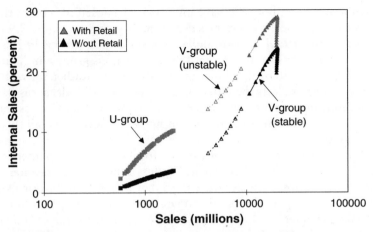

Figure 3.9. Internal Sales in *High Concentration* Equilibria.

occur at marginal cost, while total sales are measured as internal plus external sales of inputs, plus external sales of the final goods. These can be quite readily constructed in each of the simulated equilibria. In Figures 3.9 and 3.10, we plot the internal sales ratio against the sales of the business group, for the high concentration and low concentration equilibria, respectively. Notice that the sales axis is plotted as a logarithmic scale, and we have deliberately kept this scale the same in each graph, to emphasize that the high-concentration V-groups are so much bigger. In fact, the largest V-group plotted in Figure 3.9 has sales of nearly 24 billion, whereas the smallest U-group in either Figure 3.9 or 3.10 has sales

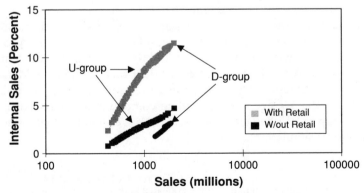

Figure 3.10. Internal Sales in *Low Concentration* Equilibria.

of about 500 million. We have intentionally chosen the size of the labor force in the model so that the sales of the V-groups in Figure 3.9 roughly matches the *actual sales* (in dollars) of the largest groups in Korea, but the *relative size* of the different types of business groups in the model is not affected at all by the choice of the labor force. Rather, the *relative size* of the groups reflects the different outcomes of the model across the high-concentration versus low-concentration equilibria, and across the range of elasticities for the intermediate input being considered (all those from 1.8 to 6.6).

The internal sales ratio constructed from the model is plotted in black, and labeled "Without Retail Sales."[23] It is apparent that the internal sales of the V-groups is much larger than that of the U-groups or D-groups. When we compare the simulated equilibria to the actual group data, in the next chapter, we shall compute the internal sales ratios over all firms in the group, both *including* and *excluding* the internal purchases of trading companies and of other wholesale and retail firms. The reason for doing so is that, in the actual group data, including the transactions of trading companies will give an upward bias to the internal sales ratios. Our model does not incorporate any of the informational considerations that would give rise to trading companies, but it does contain a rudimentary distinction between manufacturing and retailing activities. The upstream sector in the model produces and sells intermediate inputs, while the downstream sector assembles and sells the final products. We can conceptually split the downstream sector into its two parts – assembly and retail sales – and treat these as distinct activities. If we suppose that the sales are done by firms other than those engaged in assembly activity, but belonging to the same group, then the purchases of the retail firms can be either included within the internal sales ratio or excluded. These two calculations differ only in an accounting sense in the model, and will correspond to how the internal sales ratios will be computed for the actual group data.

To introduce retail firms into the model in an accounting sense, we assume that a fraction of a business group's final sales are first sold within the group, from an assembler to a retail firm. In our business group data (discussed in the next chapter), we find that the largest *chaebol* in South Korea have as much as 25 percent of their final sales first sold internally within the group. For all groups in Korea for which we have data, we find that the average sales to trading companies and retail firms within the group are 15 percent of final sales, so we shall use that value within the model simulations.

---

[23] Specifically, the internal sales ratio *excluding* retail sales equals $A/(A + B + C)$, where: A = sales of inputs within the group, evaluated at their marginal cost; B = group sales of inputs to other groups or unaffiliated firms; C = group sales of final goods.

In Figures 3.9 and 3.10, the gray points indicate internal sales ratios that are computed *inclusive* of the retailing activity of each group and are labeled "With Retail Sales."[24] Naturally, the internal sales ratios are higher when the retail purchases are included. We see in Figure 3.9 that the internal sales ratios for the V-groups are still higher than that for the U-groups, whether retail sales are included or not. In Figure 3.10, where we plot the low concentration path, the D-groups have internal sales of around 40 percent and the largest U-groups slightly less than this, when retail sales are included. This is still less than the large V-groups in Figure 3.9, where the internal sales are between 45 and 50 percent when retail sales are included. Thus, we conclude that whether retail sales are included or not, the large V-groups have internal sales that exceed the remaining U-groups in the high concentration equilibria and also exceed any of the groups found in the low concentration equilibria.

Horizontal Diversification

A second way that we contrast the high-concentration and low-concentration equilibria is in the range of varieties of the intermediate input, and the final good, that each group produces. A conventional measure of horizontal diversification is the Herfindahl index. Defined over the share of sales s_i that the group makes in different sectors i, the Herfindahl index equals $1 - \sum_i s_i^2$, where a value closer to unity indicates *greater product diversification*. In our model, and when we look at the actual groups in Korea and Taiwan, we can measure the Herfindahl index over all sales of a group or just internal sales, and over all products sold or just intermediate inputs. We shall report the results from two alternatives: the broadest case, where the Herfindahl index is defined over all sales and products; and the narrowest case, where the Herfindahl index is defined over just intermediate inputs sold internally to the group.[25]

---

[24] The internal sales ratio *including* retail sales equals $(A + r D)/(A + B + C + r D)$, where: A, B, C are defined in the previous footnote, D = group sales of final goods evaluated at their marginal cost, and r is the fraction of internal sales that go through a trading company or retail firm. We have set $r = 0.15$, which is a representative value for the groups in South Korea. We imagine that the transactions rD are made to a group trading company, which then sell the goods to consumers for the amount C. For clarity in Figures 3.9 and 3.10, both internal sales ratios are plotted against total sales measured as $(A + B + C + D)$.

[25] In our model, each group sells internally the same amount of each input variety produced, so the narrow measure of the Herfindahl index becomes $[1 - (1/\text{the number of input varieties})]$. The broad measure of the Herfindahl index combines both the input varieties and output varieties, and measures the sales of each relative to total sales $(A + B + C + D)$ defined in the previous footnote. Using rD rather than D in this calculation would have only a very minor effect on the results.

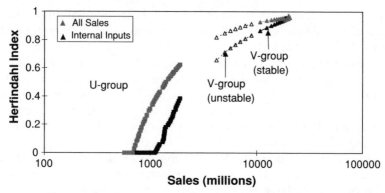

Figure 3.11. Variety per Group in *High Concentration* Equilibria.

In Figures 3.11 and 3.12, we plot the two Herfindahl indexes for the high concentration and low concentration equilibria, respectively. The sales axis is again measured logarithmically. In Figure 3.11, the Herfindahl indexes for either all sales (in gray) or just internal inputs (in black) approach unity for the largest V-groups. In contrast, the highest value of the Herfindahl index for the U-groups in the high concentration equilibrium is about 0.6 for all sales, and 0.4 for internal inputs, indicating much less product variety; these indexes fall to zero for the smallest U-groups.[26] The low concentration equilibria, shown in Figure 3.10, include both the D-groups and U-groups. When the Herfindahl index is computed over all sales, the D-groups have product diversity between 0.6 and 0.7, whereas the U-group index ranges from zero to 0.7. Product variety is somewhat less when measured for just internal inputs, where the D-group index ranges from 0.1 to 0.4, while the U-group index ranges from zero to 0.6.

Economy-Wide Product Variety

We conclude that the V-groups in the high-concentration equilibria have the greatest product variety, exceeding that of U-groups and D-groups regardless of how the index is measured. This reflects in part their very large size and also the economies of scope that come with size. Because any new input will be sold to a large number of downstream firms within the V-group, there is a strong incentive to develop more input varieties. From this result we *should not* conclude, however, that the high-concentration

---

[26] Because our model allows the number of varieties produced to be less than unity, the Herfindahl index can become negative. We plot these observations as zero values.

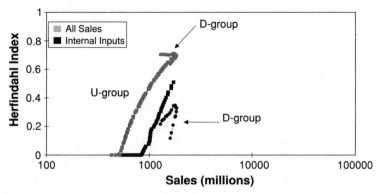

Figure 3.12. Variety per Group in *Low Concentration* Equilibria.

equilibria will have greater product variety for the economy overall. On the contrary, our model predicts that a high concentration equilibrium with V-groups will have *less variety of final products* in the economy *overall* than a low-concentration equilibria evaluated at the same elasticity (and for like values of the other parameters, such as the size of the labor force). This is shown in Figure 3.13, where we graph the economy-wide number of final goods; the number of final goods is lower in the V-group equilibria than that obtained with either D-groups or U-groups.[27] Thus, despite the horizontal diversification of the large V-groups, these equilibria display the feature that the *economy overall* is more specialized. We think that this fits the anecdotal characterization of many South Korean groups as wanting to become "world leaders" in specific products, such as cars (the Hyundai), microwave ovens, or dynamic random-access memory chips, so that the economy becomes quite specialized in these products. In contrast, Taiwan supplies a vast array of differentiated products to retailers in the United States and elsewhere, customizing each product to the buyers' specification.

To understand why the economy-wide variety of final products is reduced by V-groups, note that the large input variety of *each* group, combined with marginal-cost pricing of inputs internally, results in low downstream costs. This gives the V-groups an incentive to produce a higher *quantity* of any final product than would other types of groups or unaffiliated firms, with corresponding higher sales. But now we need to appeal to the resource constraint for the economy. With the V-groups

---

[27] Product variety is higher in the D-group equilibria than the U-group equilibria in Figure 3.13 because the former is computed for smaller values of the elasticity of demand for final goods. Aside from this feature, product variety would be quite comparable across the D-group and U-group equilibria.

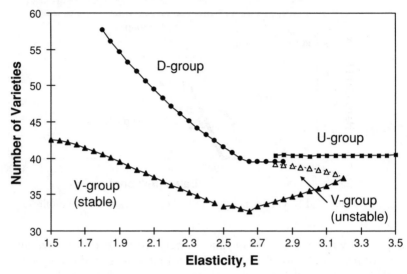

Figure 3.13. Economy-Wide Variety of Final Goods.

selling more of *each* final good variety than would other types of groups, it is impossible for the economy to *also produce* more final varieties; on the contrary, with the same labor force available, a low-concentration equilibrium with either U-groups or D-groups must have *higher variety of the final goods* than a high-concentration equilibrium with V-groups. Put simply, the focus of the V-groups on high sales for each final product rules out the possibility that the economy also produces a wide range of final consumer goods.

What about the economy-wide variety of intermediate inputs? We do not derive any prediction about this from our model, but we might conjecture that the huge size of the V-groups will lead them to produce a wide range of inputs. This is confirmed in Figure 3.14, where we graph the economy-wide number of intermediate inputs. The fact that this is highest for the V-group equilibria means that these groups enjoy some efficiencies in production, as a wide variety of differentiated inputs lead to lower costs. But are these lower costs passed onto consumers? Not necessarily, because the V-groups also have the higher market-shares in both upstream and downstream markets, leading to high markups over marginal costs. So to determine the impact on consumers, we need to compare the prices charged by groups for final goods. This is done in Figure 3.15, where we graph the prices of final goods at various values of the elasticity of demand for inputs, E. Except for a small range around $1.8 \leq E \leq 2$, the prices charged by V-groups groups are slightly higher

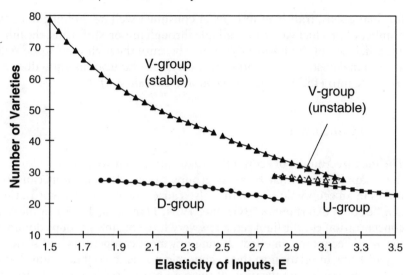

Figure 3.14. Economy-Wide Variety of Inputs.

than for D-groups or U-groups, despite the fact that their marginal costs are lower.

Thus, we find that the *combined* vertical and horizontal integration of the V-groups leads to higher prices for final goods. The reduced variety of the final goods in the V-group equilibria, combined with higher prices

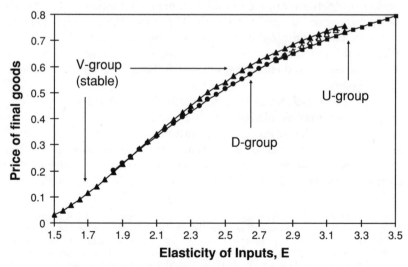

Figure 3.15. Price of Final Goods.

for final goods, translates into lower consumer welfare (holding fixed the number of product varieties available through imports).[28] Thus, the inherent efficiency of the business groups – because they sell inputs internally at marginal cost, and also produce a very wide range of inputs – does not translate into efficiency for the economy overall.

Conclusion

The idealized model of economic organization that we have developed in this chapter shows that business groups can be thought of as causative forces in an economic system that also causes them; in other words, there is a "double determinacy" (Greene, 1974, Hamilton, 1984). In the high concentration equilibrium set, a few very large business groups dominate the whole economy, in effect driving out most competitors and structuring all firms in relation to their economic power, a configuration that in turn reinforces internalization of the core businesses in the large groups, making them even larger. By contrast, in the low concentration equilibrium set, the presence of numerous players in the economy push groups towards concentrating on and deepening niches where they have relative advantage. A few groups (the D-type groups) in the context will specialize in downstream final manufacturing and assembly, and many other groups (the U-type groups) will be upstream suppliers of core intermediate goods for firms downstream. The economics of this equilibrium suggest that it is to the advantage of both D- and U-groups to encourage market competition among unaffiliated firms that either supply goods to the D-groups or buy goods from the U-groups, thereby increasing their economic power within the respective commodity chains. This configuration, in turn, militates against vertical integration as a strategy to increase economic power and encourages, instead, the proliferation of niches and niche players.

Using this model, let us now return to the two models that Saxenian proposes and that we discussed in the first part of this chapter. Her two models – vertically integrated corporations and network forms of organization – are somewhat different than our own. Her models, of course, are not about business groups or, ostensibly, about the relation between economic power and authority in different kinds of economies. As do

---

[28] We confirmed in our calculations that with the rise in prices and fall in product variety due to V-groups, then welfare also falls (holding fixed the range of imported final goods). This result will be sensitive, however, to the CES specification of product variety, which means that unaffiliated firms produce the socially optimal variety. In an alternative "address" specification, Dixit (1983) and Mathewson and Winter (1983) find that vertical integration raises welfare, despite the fall in product variety.

most scholars in this research tradition, Saxenian pits independent firms against networks of firms and argues that networks are "better" than autonomy. Our multiple equilibria model of business groups adds several new dimensions to this discussion, which we will, in turn, explore empirically in the following chapters.

Specifically, the model implies that networks can be present in *both* equilibria sets. In the high concentration set, business groups are types of networks. As illustrated by the *chaebol* in South Korea and the *keiretsu* in Japan, these large business groups spawn networks of firms, some core firms tied by authority (by virtue of partial ownership) and other firms pulled into "less-than-arm's-length" and potentially coercive dealings by the sheer economic power of the big groups. In the low concentration set, business groups are constituted in a very different way. As they are in Taiwan, they themselves may be networks of firms that concentrate tightly on a niche or that diversify across many unrelated niches. As we will see, Taiwanese business groups usually represent some combination of the two. Outside the business groups, however, networks can also emerge among firms that are not affiliated with either upstream or downstream business groups. Because our model suggests that both upstream and downstream business groups maximize their profits by encouraging competition among, respectively, suppliers or purchasers of intermediate goods, then the model would also imply that unaffiliated firms might counteract that advantage by organizing linkages among themselves. In other words, the low equilibrium set is not only compatible with Saxenian's network model, but also might even explain it more fully, as simultaneous interaction of different kinds of firms in the same setting, as the interaction of power and authority in the context of a price structure.

4

Economic Organization in South Korea and Taiwan

A First Test of the Model

If our Walrasian view of economic organization is correct, then business groups can be thought of as causative forces in economic systems that also cause them. Before testing this idea empirically, we needed first to develop a theory of business groups. To this end, in the last chapter, we constructed a highly stylized economic model consisting of upstream sectors producing intermediate inputs and downstream sectors using those inputs to produce final consumer goods. In the model, manufacturing firms decide whether to buy intermediate products at zero markups from a firm within a group, or at full markups from unaffiliated firms. Solving this model based on pricing decisions of firms in general equilibrium reveals *multiple equilibria* in the form of two distinct and economically stable solutions to business group integration in an organized economy: a high and a low concentration set of groups.

We can think of these two stylized economies as both consisting of interconnected networks of firms where authority and economic power interact in the context of a price structure. In one solution, the few very large business groups organize an economy in which they remain the stable elements, pushing other groups and independent firms into niches that the large groups do not dominate. In the other solution, many business groups coexist by occupying different distinct upstream or downstream niches and by trading with unaffiliated firms. The idealized model, therefore, predicts that business groups, which represent concentrated and authoritatively held assets, organize themselves quite differently across economies. In other words, business groups reflect the economy in which they are embedded and in which they are instrumental in maintaining themselves as going concerns.

The task of this chapter is to determine to what extent this stylized depiction helps us to interpret the organization of the South Korean and Taiwanese economies. We focus, in particular, on business groups as they are configured in their respective economies. We hypothesize that the high

120

concentration equilibrium set is analogous to what we empirically observe in South Korea and the low concentration set is analogous to what we empirically observe in Taiwan.

To facilitate the comparison between the theoretical model and the actual economies, we have created a database of the top business groups in both countries, forty-four business groups for South Korea in 1989, and eighty groups for Taiwan in 1994. For both countries we are able to construct a *transaction matrix* for the major business groups. This matrix specifies the sales to other member firms within the group, as well as total sales and other information for each firm. Thus, the transaction matrices can be used to construct measures of the vertical integration for each business group. We shall first report detailed results for the Korean groups, and then describe the Taiwanese groups. The contrast between the two sets of groups vividly illustrates both the differences in their size and vertical integration. The largest groups in Korea are huge by comparison with other groups found in Korea or Taiwan; in each group, they are vertically integrated within production chains and broadly diversified across industrial sectors. By contrast, business groups in Taiwan are niche players in a diversified economy.

Korean Business Groups, 1989

The primary source for the 1989 Korean data is the volume *1990 Chaebol Analysis Report* (*Chaebol Boon Suk Bo Go Seo* in Korean) published by Korea Investors Service, Inc. This volume provides information on the fifty largest business groups (measured in terms of assets) in South Korea, but for six of these groups the data on internal transactions within the groups are missing. Thus, the 1989 database for Korea includes only forty-four groups, with 499 firms. Data on financial and insurance companies belonging to the groups are excluded from the database, because their sales cannot be accurately measured. In Table 4.1, we show summary information for each of these forty-four groups: their 1989 sales; number of firms (where * indicates that this number includes a trading company); and other variables as discussed later.

The business groups are sorted according to their primary sector of external sales. By examining their external sales, we are asking, in effect, what goods and services provide these groups with their primary sources of revenue. Groups are classified either as 1) a manufacturer of final consumer products, 2) a manufacturer of industrial products, 3) a provider of services, or 4) a construction company. To obtain the category of each group, we totaled the external sales for each firm in a business group according to the above four categories. We then totaled the sales in each

Table 4.1. *Business Groups in Korea, 1989*

Group Name	1989 Sales ($ mill.)	Number of Firms (* TC)	Internal Sales Ratio (%)	Internal Sales (%, no Retail)	Herfindahl Index (all sales)	Herfindahl Index (internal manufact.)	Type of Group
Majority of Sales in Final Consumer Products							
Samsung	26,175	32*	31.9	18.9	0.70	0.35	V
Hyundai	25,500	30*	33	19.8	0.80	0.78	V
Lucky-Goldstar	18,807	46*	26	12.6	0.74	0.46	V
Daewoo	13,835	23*	23.5	9.7	0.68	0.66	V
Lotte	3,900	24*	9.2	7.7	0.80	0.64	V
Doosan	2,576	19*	12.5	10.8	0.84	0.77	V
Kia	4,602	9*	25.6	6.6	0.20	0.04	D
Miwon	1,295	13*	12.5	6.4	0.65	0.26	D
Taejon Leather	627	7	1.6	1.6	0.61	0.11	D
Anam Industrial	537	5	8.7	8.7	0.28	0.00	D
Jinro	490	10	2.6	2.6	0.63	0.14	D
Majority of Sales in Industrial Products, Services, or Construction							
Sunkyong	8,910	16*	20.6	10.3	0.69	0.42	U
Ssangyong	5,777	15*	14.8	11.6	0.75	0.63	U
Han Jin	3,895	11*	2.7	2.2	0.25	0.12	U
Hyosung	3,473	12*	9.7	4.3	0.63	0.43	U
Hanwha	3,172	19*	7.7	4.7	0.80	0.58	U
Kolon	2,218	14*	10.6	4.0	0.65	0.00	U
Dongbu	1,978	7*	26.1	17.3	0.50	0.12	U
Daelim	1,951	12*	4.4	0.6	0.38	0.27	U
Dongkuk Steel Mill	1,886	10*	5.4	3.4	0.27	0.01	U
Dong Ah Construction	1,866	12*	1.1	0.7	0.39	0.00	U

Sammi	1,696	5*	36.7	27	0.51	0.00	U
Kumho	1,430	8*	3.3	0.4	0.64	0.00	U
Hanil	1,296	12*	7.1	7.1	0.61	0.39	U
Halla	1,262	7	10.2	10.2	0.62	0.51	U
Kangwon Industries	1,256	12*	33.5	11.4	0.74	0.31	U
Samyang	1,038	5	1.6	1.6	0.41	0.63	U
Kohap	1,016	6*	18.2	12.5	0.53	0.37	U
Poongsan	941	6	3.3	3.3	0.36	0.08	U
Woosung Construction	834	6	2	2	0.47	0.00	U
Kukdong Oil	812	3	19.3	0	0.39	0.00	U
Dongkuk Corporation	689	7*	11.3	1.1	0.55	0.00	U
Tongil	687	11	4.4	4.4	0.74	0.08	U
Tong Yang	672	5*	9.3	9.3	0.49	0.33	U
Byucksan	672	18	0.6	0.6	0.75	0.50	U
Daesung Industries	589	8	2	2	0.55	0.55	U
Oriental Chemical	528	9	8.9	8.9	0.40	0.48	U
Taihan Electric Wire	490	3	3	3	0.12	0.00	U
Kyesung Paper	437	5	17.3	17.3	0.28	0.00	U
Han Yang	436	4*	6.6	0.7	0.22	0.00	U
Hanbo	420	3	2.6	2.6	0.35	0.44	U
You One Construction	281	2*	0.3	0	0.41	0.00	U
Kuk Dong Construction	247	4	0.1	0.1	0.10	0.00	U
Life Construction	211	4	3.5	3.5	0.48	0.00	U
Mean	3,441	11.3	11.3	6.7	0.52	0.26	
Weighted Mean		23.9	22.1	12.2	0.66	0.45	

category and classified the business groups according to that category representing the majority of its external sales. The groups selling primarily final consumer products appear at the top of Table 4.1 and the groups selling industrial products, services, or construction are listed in the lower portion of the table.

The largest of the Korean groups have become well-known names in the United States, such as Samsung and Hyundai, both of which have the majority of their sales in final consumer products. These two groups each had total sales exceeding $25 billion in 1989, while the forty-four groups together had sales of $152.5 billion.[1] This magnitude is sometimes compared to the Korean GDP ($219.5 billion in 1989) to conclude that the business groups control the majority of the domestic economy. Such a comparison is incorrect, of course, because the GDP is a value-added concept, reflecting the contribution made by each firm over and above its cost of materials and labor. The *1990 Chaebol Analysis Report* included the value-added calculations for each group, which are included in the database, and these total $32.2 billion over the forty-four groups. Thus, these groups account for about 15 percent of the Korean GDP in 1989.

Of principal interest is the extent to which business groups' sales go to other firms in the group, or equivalently, the extent to which the group relies on its own firms for intermediate inputs. We will refer to this as the "internalization" of a group, and it can be measured by the ratio of the sales to other firms in each group relative to total group sales.[2] The internal sales ratio for each group is shown in the fourth column of Table 4.1. It is apparent that larger groups have rather high internalization, exceeding 30 percent in several cases, and that internalization is correlated with the size of each group. This can be observed in the simple and weighted averages reported at the bottom of Table 4.1; the simple average of the internal sales ratio is 11.3 percent, but the sales-weighted average is about twice as large, at 22.1 percent. Nevertheless, there are still some smaller groups that have very high internalization, such as the Sammi steel group, with an internal sales ratio of 36.6 percent.

There is one feature of the internalization ratio that is somewhat misleading and that is the fact that it includes the *trading companies* of most groups. These are companies that act as intermediaries in transactions between firms in the group and that also sell to and buy from firms outside the group. Including these firms can artificially increase the internalization ratio, when, for example, the trading companies are simply transferring

[1] The dollar values for Korea have been converted from the Korean won using the exchange rate of 679.6 won per dollar at the end of 1989.

[2] That is, the internalization ratio is calculated as (internal sales within a group)/(internal sales within a group plus all external sales to other firms or consumers).

products between firms in the group. Twenty-seven out of the forty-four groups in Korea – or about 60 percent – have trading companies, and these are indicated by an asterisk in column three of Table 4.1.

In order to correct for the presence of the trading companies, two questions need to be addressed. The first is how to distinguish trading companies. In the Korean database, we relied on three criteria. First, telephone surveys to the forty-four Korean business groups were made to find out if each group had a trading company. Second, company descriptions in the *Yearbook on the Korean Economy and Business, 1991/92*, published by Business Korea were used. If a company was described as a trading arm of their business group, it was included as a trading company. Third, along with the company description, if a company was largely involved in the group's internal transactions, it was counted as a trading company. Most of the trading companies are classified in wholesale and retail trade, although only a subset of firms in that sector are designated as trading companies.

The second question is how to correct for the presence of these companies when measuring the degree of internalization. Consider a trading company that purchases from firm A and sells that product to firm B, both in the same business group. Because this firm is simply acting as an intermediary in the transactions, it would be double counting to include both the purchase and sale. But since the product was transferred from A to B, it would be incorrect to exclude both transactions as well. Instead, we should ignore either the purchase or the sale by the trading company. We decided to ignore the *purchases* of the trading companies from other firms within the group.[3] This means that when a trading company buys from an outside firm and sells to another firm within the group, the sale will be counted as an internal transaction. But when a group firm sells to a trading company that then sells outside the group, no internal transaction is counted at all. We use the phrase "without trading companies" (or, "no TC") to mean that we are consistently ignoring the purchases of trading companies from within the group. We have re-computed the internal sales ratio for each of the business groups without trading companies.[4] This reduces the average internalization of all forty-four groups from 11.3 percent to 8.2 percent, and the weighted average from 22.1 percent to 13.8 percent.

---

[3] All of the trading companies made purchases from other firms in their group and most also made sales.

[4] The purchases of the trading companies are excluded from both the numerator and denominator of the internal sales ratio. Thus, the internal sales ratio calculated without the trading companies equals (all internal sales within a group, except those made to trading companies)/(all internal sales within a group, except those made to trading companies, plus all external sales to other firms or consumers).

Because most of trading companies are engaged in wholesale and retail trade, by excluding their purchases we are moving towards a measure of groups' vertical integration within just manufacturing activities. To properly measure manufacturing integration, we also need to exclude the purchases of *all other* firms within each group that are classified within wholesale and retailing. There are some differences between the trading companies and other firms classified in that sector. Many of the trading companies are actively involved in seeking overseas customers, and therefore play an informational role within the business group. In contrast, the other wholesale and retailing firms are engaged in marketing the products domestically, through establishments owned by the group. This distinction is not hard-and-fast, however, and there is considerable overlap in their activities.

As a natural extension to omitting the purchases of trading companies, in the fifth column of Table 4.1 we report the internal sales ratio while omitting both the purchases of trading companies and *all other* firms in the wholesale and retail sector within each group.[5] As compared to the original calculation, omitting trading companies and other wholesale and retailing firms reduces the average internalization ratio from 11.3 percent to 6.7 percent, and reduced the weighted average from 22.1 percent to 12.2 percent. The internalization of the some of the largest business groups is reduced by roughly *one-half* through avoiding the double counting of goods transferred between firms within a group by a trading company and other wholesale and retail trades. We regard this as a conservative and more accurate measure of vertical integration than the first calculation.

Turning to horizontal diversification, the *chaebol* in Korea are sometimes criticized for spanning so many activities in different sectors; the desire to grow ever larger, expanding into the whole range of upstream and downstream products, is sometimes called "one-setism." We can measure the diversification of the groups across different sectors using the Herfindahl index, defined as $1 - \sum_i s_i^2$, where s_i is the share of total sales in each sector i. To implement this index, we divided the entire economy into thirty-one sectors.[6] Each firm in a group is identified as selling in one of these sectors by its major product category, and then the Herfindahl index is computed for each group. We considered four different calculations:

---

[5] This internal sales ratio is calculated as (all internal sales within a group, except those made to trading companies or other wholesale/retail firms)/(all internal sales within a group, except those made to trading companies or other wholesale/retail firms, plus all group sales to external firms or consumers).

[6] Motor vehicles and shipbuilding are separated in this classification, so there are twenty-two manufacturing sectors, two primary products, three non-manufacturing products as shown in Table 2.7 of Chapter 2, plus wholesale and retail trade, finance and insurance, real estate and business services, and other services, for a total of thirty-one sectors.

using all sales or just internal sales; and using all products or just manufacturing. In the next columns of Table 4.1 we report the results from two alternatives: the broadest case, where the Herfindahl index is defined over all sales and all products; and the narrowest case, where the Herfindahl index is defined over just manufacturing inputs sold internally to the group.

The simple average of the Herfindahl index over all sales is 0.52, and the weighted average is 0.66, indicating that the larger groups are more diverse in their sectoral sales. This remains true if instead we consider the internal sales of manufacturing goods, where the simple average is 0.26 and the weighted average is 0.45. Focusing on manufacturing sales in the top five groups, Hyundai has multiple firms producing in primary metals, metal products, machinery, electronic equipment, shipbuilding, and motor vehicles. These firms are supplying their products to the other firms located downstream, and ultimately marketing the finished goods to consumers using their trading companies. Samsung reveals an even greater diversification of firms, including textile-producing firms supplying firms making garments; pulp and paper processing firms supplying printing and publishing firms; firms producing chemical materials that supply firms making plastic products; and firms manufacturing machinery and electronic equipment that supply firms making motor vehicles. Lucky-Goldstar reveals a dominant concentration within electronic products, with nearly half of its firms in that sector, but still maintains a presence in chemical and plastics, metals, and other sectors. The smallest of the top four *chaebol*, the Daewoo group, has a similar range of activities as Hyundai, but is much less densely interconnected than the top three. Daewoo is also the only one of the top four *chaebol* to go bankrupt during the Asian business crisis, as we will discuss later in the chapter. All these examples, however, serve to illustrate the "one-setism" that characterizes the largest groups. Some of the smaller groups also have a high degree of product diversification, but as we discuss below, these groups are producing intermediate products, final products, or services, all of which are aimed primarily for the domestic market.

Classification of Korean Business Groups

The Walrasian model we proposed in Chapter 2 predicts that business groups will vary within economies, as well as between them. The *high concentration* equilibria predict that business groups in the economy will appear as two distinct types: 1) a relatively small set of very large vertically integrated groups (V-groups), a subset of which consists of smaller and comparatively less vertically integrated and hence more unstable groups;

and 2) a larger set of business groups producing substitutable (high elasticity) intermediate goods and services (U-groups) (see Figures 3.7 and 3.9). In contrast, the *low concentration* equilibria predict that the two types of business groups occurring in this configuration are 1) an extensive set of upstream business groups (U-groups) producing specialized, although relatively undifferentiated intermediate goods and services; and 2) an extensive set of downstream business groups (D-groups) making specialized and more differentiated products, the intermediate goods for which are purchased from outside the group. In this section, we propose a simple classification of the business groups in Korea to distinguish V-groups, U-groups and D-groups, and we shall apply the same classification to Taiwan.

First, the business groups whose majority of sales are in industrial products, services, or construction are classified as U-groups. These appear in the lower portion of Table 4.1. In the upper part of the table we list those groups whose majority of sales are in final consumer goods, and we need to have a criterion for classifying these as either V-groups or D-groups. In earlier work (Feenstra, Hamilton, and Huang, 2001), we had compared the "top five" *chaebol* found in Korea to the V-groups in our model. Although this classification was simple, it suffers from a number of drawbacks. It uses sales as the only criterion for being a V-group; the Korean groups included among the top five can change over time; and this rule offers little guidance about how to classify the business groups in Taiwan. So we now adopt an alternative classification for the V-groups in Korea that does not rely on only their size and that can be applied equally well to Taiwan.

Within the model, V-groups appear in the high concentration equilibria as vertically integrated producers of final consumer products. The high concentration equilibria also reveal that the internalization ratio will directly vary among V-groups: those groups having the highest level of total sales will also have the highest level of internalization, but the ratio will decline as the level of V-group sales declines. According to the model (see Figure 3.9), the internalization ratio for the stable V-groups is uniformly above 10 percent, but the unstable groups may go below this. In the model, D-groups produce final consumer products, but because they purchase their intermediate inputs from unaffiliated firms and other groups, their internalization ratios (without retail) are generally less than 5 percent (see Figure 3.10).

The classification rules we follow, therefore, are as follows: Any group whose majority of sales are in industrial products, services, or construction is classified as a U-group. Any group producing mainly final products whose internalization ratio is above 10 percent is classified as a V-group, and any group producing a final product whose internalization

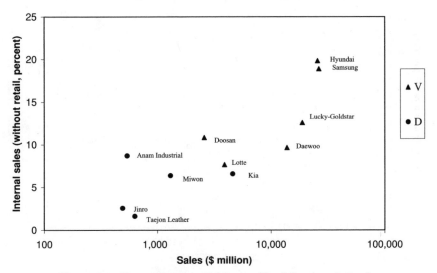

Figure 4.1. Korean Groups Producing Final Consumer Products.

ratio is below 5 percent is classified as a D-group. The internal sales simulations (Figure 3.9 and 3.10) do not provide a clear way to distinguish between V-groups and D-groups when the internalization ratios are between 5 percent and 10 percent. However, the simulations based on the Herfindahl index of internal manufacturing allow us to predict that V-groups will have a Herfindahl index on internal manufacturing diversification of above 0.5 and D-groups will have a score of 0.5 or below. Therefore, those groups producing a final product falling within this intermediate range of internalization are classified as V-groups if they have a Herfindahl index for internal manufacturing above 0.5 and as D-groups if they have a score of 0.5 or below. The results from this classification scheme applied to Korea are shown in the last column of Table 4.1, and graphed in Figures 4.1 and 4.2.

V-Groups: In Figure 4.1, we show the sales and internalization ratios (without retail) for those groups whose predominant revenues come from producing final consumer products. The four largest *chaebol* (that is, Samsung, Hyundai, Lucky-Goldstar, and Daewoo) have sales much larger than the rest of the groups. In fact, the combined total sales of just these four groups are considerably larger than the combined total sales for all the remaining forty *chaebol* in our dataset. These four groups all specialized in producing consumer products for export, as well as for the domestic economy, and as predicted by the model, there is a clear and direct relationship between level of internalization and total sales in Figure 4.1. This relationship is less apparent when the U-groups are also

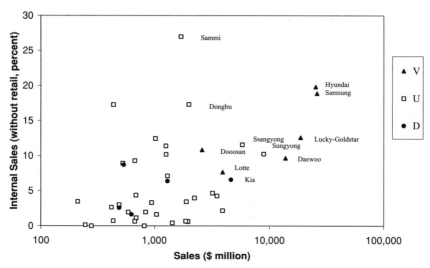

Figure 4.2. Types of Korean Groups.

included, in Figure 4.2. But with one exception for a U-group (Sammi, see subsequently), the two largest *chaebol* (Hyundai and Samsung) have the highest internalization ratios in the entire economy, and for other V-groups the level of internalization declines as total sales decline.

Our classification of the V-groups for Korea also includes two other groups – Lotte and Doosan – which specialize in food products for the domestic economy. There are some peculiarities to domestic food industries, both in South Korea and Taiwan, that set business groups specializing in food products apart from other groups, as discussed below. Even including these two conglomerates, all of the V-groups exhibit one-setism, with vertically integrated production networks centered around the final products they produce. Using the internal transaction data, we diagram these networks in Figure 4.3. Each point in these diagrams corresponds to a firm belonging to the group, and a line between two points indicates that there are internal transactions between the firms recorded in our database. As these diagrams show, the vertically integrated production networks are unmistakable and are particularly dense in the top three business groups (that is, Hyundai, Samsung, and Lucky-Goldstar), but are somewhat less dense in Daewoo, Lotte, and Doosan.

D-Groups: While the model also predicts that there should be no D-groups in Korea, on the basis of our classification five of the forty-four groups are listed as D-groups (that is, Kia, Miwon, Taejon Leather, Anam Industrial, and Jino). Two of these groups (Miwon and Jinro) also produce food products for the domestic market. The four food-producing

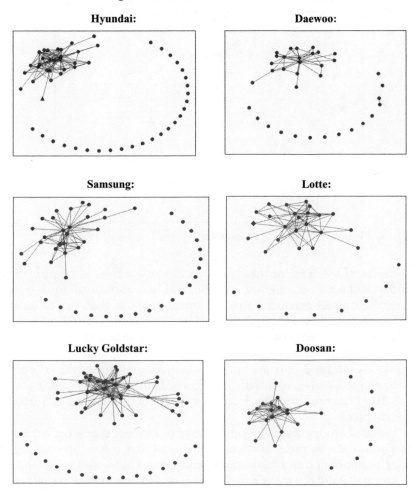

Figure 4.3. Internal Transactions in Korean V-Goups, 1989.

groups taken together (Lotte, Doosan, Miwon, and Jinro) form a separate set of business groups specializing in the same domestic sector, a sector in which they generally do not compete head-on with the largest *chaebol*. Food groups are generally vertically integrated in some respects, typically by having centrally owned shipping, bottling, and packaging firms. However, since individual firms typically produce specific food products (such as beverages, livestock, and canned goods), there is limited upstream and downstream differentiation among firms in the group, and thus group organization tends to be flatter and the level of internationalization is often lower than occurs in groups producing other types of consumer

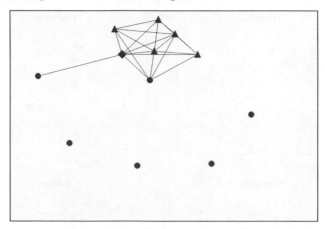

Figure 4.4. Internal Transactions in Kia D-Group, 1989.

products. If we examine these food groups as a whole, comparing them within and across economies, it is apparent that the Korean food groups resemble one-set production systems much more so than the Taiwanese food groups, which we will discuss below. Also within South Korea, there is considerable variation among these four conglomerates. As Figure 4.3 shows, both Lotte and Doosan contain dense vertically integrated networks. Miwon and Jinro are much less vertically integrated than the other two, and less stable, too; with Jinro going bankrupt in 1997 just before the Asian financial crisis hit Korea, as we describe in more detail later in the chapter.

Included among the D-groups is another *chaebol* that went bankrupt just before the financial crisis hit Korea, and that is Kia. Specializing in steel, automobiles, and related products, Kia can be viewed as an aspiring V-group that did not make it in the end. The diagram of the internal transactions of Kia, in Figure 4.4, is clearly less dense than for the V-groups, and its extent of diversification across intermediate and final products is much lower than for the V-groups. Indeed, it is the low value of its Herfindahl indexes that have led us to classify Kia as a D-group, but we would suggest that it could equally well be classified as an *unstable* V-group. Its bankruptcy in 1997 was precipitated by falling sales in the Korean domestic car market and also an overcapacity in the steel industry that led to the largest losses by Kia Steel. Kia was in fact an attractive asset for the other two, larger automobile groups, Hyundai and Daewoo, and in addition, the Samsung group had previously attempted to take it over to expand its own presence in autos. All three groups expressed an interest in acquiring Kia's two automobile units – Kia Motors and Asia Motors. Ultimately, Kia Motors was sold to Hyundai late in 1997.

The final two groups that we have classified as D-groups for Korea are Anam Industrial and Taejon Leather. They produce final products. Anam Industrial makes watches and other types of inexpensive precision products, and Taejon Leather makes leather products as well as some automobile parts. Both have very low levels of internalization and internal manufacturing diversification, and hence clearly fall into the D-group classification. They are, however, quite small as *chaebol* go, and they produce goods that are marginal to the main economy, indicating the relative unimportance of D-groups in Korea.

U-Groups: Figure 4.2 shows the location of those *chaebol* classified as U-groups relative to that of the V-groups. With a couple of exceptions, the U-groups have lower levels of internalization than the largest V-groups. Of the thirty-three firms classified as U-groups, twenty-two of them have internalization ratios below 5 percent. Most of these twenty-two business groups have relatively few firms in their groups and those few firms only have a limited range of intra-group transactions. This same general configuration is found in the two U-groups having exceptionally high internalization ratios, Sammi and Dongbu. These two groups serve as a clear contrast to the general V-groups described earlier. Both Sammi and Dongbu were, in 1989, specialty steel producers (Sammi was another of the *chaebol* declaring bankruptcy just before the Asian financial crisis struck Korea). Figure 4.5 shows the network of transacting firms for Sammi. The very high levels of internalization are due to steps required to process the metal to make primary metal products, such as steel girders for construction and an assortment of standardized metal parts, each major step of which is encompassed by a separate firm. In Taiwan, Formosa Plastics reveals a similar pattern of separate steps in processing

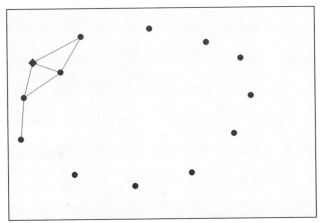

Figure 4.5. Internal Transactions in Sammi U-Group, 1989.

intermediate products being differentiated into separate firms. Most upstream suppliers of intermediate industrial products in both Korea and Taiwan do not require so many separate steps, and hence have lower levels of internalization.

For Korea, there are a number of exceptions to these general patterns. Several of the largest *chaebol* classified here as U-groups have substantial sales in final products, so much so that they straddle the U- and V-group divide. We should note that the largest *chaebol*, here classified as V-groups, also sell intermediate products, even though the bulk of their sales are in final consumer products, and so the classificatory distinction between the groups can be somewhat ambiguous. This ambiguity, however, only shows up in the case of Korea, and is particularly evident in two groups, Sungyong and Ssangyong, the latter of which failed during the Asian financial crisis. Both *chaebol* were heavily involved in petroleum and chemical material derived from petroleum. Although most of their revenues came from these upstream industries, both *chaebol* also produced an array of final products. The principal networking patterns for both *chaebol* are centered on the petroleum processing firms, which appear in the core cluster of firms shown in Figure 4.6 for Sunkyung. The U-group classification is, therefore, appropriate for both groups, despite the clear tendency in both cases to expand into final consumer products.

One other notable feature of Korean U-groups is the relative absence, when compared with U-groups in Taiwan, of groups specializing in services. Only one group in Table 4.1 is classified as a service-oriented conglomerate, and that is Han Jin, the operator of Korea's major airline

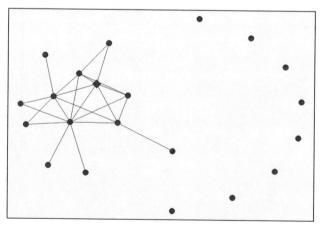

Figure 4.6. Internal Transactions in Sunkyung U-Groups, 1989.

(Korean Air). The reason for the relative absence of groups in Korea whose major revenues derive from services is explained by the fact that all of the largest *chaebol* also contain firms specializing in various services, ranging from retail outlets and financial services to transportation and shipping, but revenues derived from these service firms are dwarfed by revenues from consumer products. In addition, six of the thirty-three U-groups in Korea are groups specializing in construction. The groups are typically small with very low levels of internalization. These groups compete with construction companies in most of the largest *chaebol*, and as a consequence, many of them went bankrupt during or immediately before the Asian financial crisis.

On the basis of the previous analysis, we can conclude that business groups in the Korean economy can be divided into two basic types and that these two types correspond roughly to those predicted to emerge in the high concentration equilibria. On the one hand, all of the largest *chaebol* are organized as vertically integrated conglomerates. This is particularly apparent in those *chaebol* producing final products for export and domestic markets, but the same trend shows up in large groups producing intermediate and final products for the domestic market only, such as petroleum products produced by Sungyong and Ssangyong and food products produced by Lotte and Doosan. On the other hand, most of the remaining *chaebol* produce standardized intermediate products aimed at the domestic economy or are construction companies. These groups have a narrow range of mostly standardized industrial products (or services) and a limited number of firms with internal transactions. As we will show in the next section, these smaller groups specializing in intermediate inputs share many features with Taiwanese business groups that occupy a similar location in Taiwan.

Taiwanese Business Groups, 1994

We used three primary sources to collect the 1994 Taiwan data: *Business Groups in Taiwan, 1996/1997*, published by the China Credit Information Service (CCIS), which is based on 1994 information; company annual reports for 1994 filed with the Taiwan stock exchange, which detailed their intra-group transactions; and when that information was incomplete, additional information on intra-group transactions collected by having CCIS contact the groups. *Business Groups in Taiwan, 1996/1997* provides information on 115 business groups in Taiwan. For the largest eighty of these groups, data on sales to and purchases from other firms in the groups were collected from their annual reports. As with the Korean database, the sales of firms in some service sectors are incomplete. This means that one of the largest Taiwanese groups, the Linden group (which owns Cathay Insurance), is not included in the database, and this is also the case for the Evergreen group (a group specializing in sea and air shipping). Using the information available, the 1994 database for Taiwan includes eighty groups, with 797 firms, as listed in Table 4.2. As for Korea, we separate the groups into those whose majority of sales are in final consumer products (at the top of the table) and those selling industrial products, services, or construction (at the bottom of the table).

The largest groups in Taiwan are considerably smaller than their counterparts in Korea and the total sales of the Taiwanese groups are $76.3 billion, or about half as much as the Korean groups.[7] In order to do a comparison with the Taiwanese GDP, which was $241 billion in 1994, we need to have a value-added figure for the groups. This was not provided in any of the source materials, but a rough estimate can be obtained by noting that the ratio of value-added to total sales for all the Korean groups is 21.2 percent. If we apply this same ratio to the total sales of the Taiwanese group, we obtain an estimated value-added of $16.2 billion, so that the eighty groups account for 6.7 percent of the Taiwan GDP. The average number of firms in each group, shown at the bottom of column three, is also smaller than for Korea.

In the fourth column of Table 4.2, we report the internal sales ratio for the Taiwanese groups. In contrast to the Korean groups, it does not appear that the internalization ratios for Taiwan are significantly correlated with the size of the groups. Thus, the largest group – Formosa Plastics – has an internalization ratio of 15.8 percent, which is no larger than that which occurs for a number of other groups of varying size. This can also be seen from the averages reported at the bottom of Table 4.2. The average for the internal sales ratio is 7.0 percent and 9.5 percent, computed as simple and weighted, respectively. Both the size and difference between these are much smaller than for the Korean groups. Thus, the groups in Taiwan have less vertical integration on average than occurs in Korea and also less difference between groups of various sizes.

We have corrected for the presence of trading companies in the business groups of Taiwan. Two criteria were used to select trading companies: if the name of the firm from *Business Groups in Taiwan, 1996/1997* included the words "trading company" or if the description of products from that source indicated "buying and selling" as a primary activity, then the firm was counted as a trading company. Trading companies

---

[7] The U.S. dollar values for Taiwan have been converted from the New Taiwan dollar using the exchange rate of 26.24 NT$ per US$ at the end of 1994.

Table 4.2. *Business Groups in Taiwan, 1994*

Group Name	1994 Sales ($ mill.)	Number of Firms (* TC)	Internal Sales Ratio (%)	Internal Sales (%, no Retail)	Herfindahl Index (all sales)	Herfindahl Index (internal manufact.)	Type of Group
Majority of Sales in Final Consumer Products							
Yulon	4,264	23*	26.6	5.2	0.77	0.26	D
President	3,932	31*	6.4	4.5	0.70	0.29	D
Tatung	3,634	36	8.3	6.3	0.38	0.18	D
Acer	3,243	9*	3.5	2.4	0.62	0.01	D
Chinfon	2,986	16*	24.1	1.1	0.19	0.00	D
Rebar	1,221	9*	1.4	0.9	0.72	0.00	D
Lien Hwa Mitac	900	12*	2.8	2.7	0.53	0.00	D
Walsin Lihwa	881	8	0.1	0.1	0.02	0.06	D
Lite-On	875	10	0.5	0.5	0.71	0.50	D
Kwang Yang	855	7*	6.3	6.3	0.20	0.18	D
United Microelectronics	673	4	8.5	8.5	0.00	0.00	D
Shinlee	456	12*	0.4	0.4	0.52	0.00	D
Umax Elitegroup	436	8*	7.2	7.2	0.00	0.00	D
Aurora	406	7*	17.5	8.6	0.09	0.00	D
Ase	404	5*	10.5	1.3	0.35	0.00	D
Vedan	327	8*	8.1	7.5	0.04	0.00	D
Chicony Electronics	217	3	4.3	4.3	0.00	0.00	D
Kenda Industrial	211	8	0.5	0.5	0.49	0.00	D
Fwu Sow Industrial	200	7*	7.1	7.0	0.01	0.00	D
Ve Wong	161	3	10.0	10.0	0.00	0.00	D
Bomy	116	9	29.5	0.0	0.48	0.00	D
Ren Hou (Chih Lien)	83	10*	0.0	0.0	0.51	0.00	D
Yung Shin Pharmaceutical	78	8*	2.7	1.8	0.05	0.00	D
Tong Hsing	35	4*	2.8	2.0	0.57	0.00	D
Sampo	1,096	11	12.5	12.5	0.26	0.00	V
Great Wall	375	12	21.1	20.7	0.31	0.17	V
Ching Kuang Chemical	104	3	10.6	10.6	0.26	0.00	V

(*continued*)

137

Table 4.2 (continued)

Group Name	1994 Sales ($ mill.)	Number of Firms (* TC)	Internal Sales Ratio (%)	Internal Sales (%, no Retail)	Herfindahl Index (all sales)	Herfindahl Index (internal manufact.)	Type of Group
Majority of Sales in Industrial Products, Services, or Construction							
Formosa Plastics	6,654	16	15.8	15.8	0.54	0.58	U
Shin Kong	5,724	25*	0.4	0.4	0.40	0.22	U
Wei Chuan Ho Tai	4,889	23*	28.1	0.4	0.55	0.02	U
Far Eastern	4,291	26	0.7	0.5	0.53	0.05	U
Hualon	2,517	9*	16.4	4.7	0.70	0.00	U
Ho Hsin	2,104	15*	0.2	0.2	0.50		U
Tuntex	1,831	16*	8.1	7.9	0.78	0.38	U
Teco Electric & Machinery	1,474	17*	2.6	2.6	0.60	0.15	U
Chi Mei	1,268	6*	0.3	0.3	0.25	0.09	U
Pacific Cable	1,214	26	3.2	3.2	0.54	0.05	U
Tainan Spining	1,075	17	2.1	2.1	0.71	0.00	U
Pacific Construction	1,032	15	2.8	2.7	0.63	0.46	U
Yuen Foong Yu	1,000	8*	18.5	4.5	0.46	0.13	U
Ruentex	997	25*	0.7	0.0	0.51	0.00	U
Taiwan Cement	997	16	3.6	3.6	0.48	0.39	U
Cheng Loong	823	7*	16.3	16.2	0.08	0.00	U
Shih Lin Paper	766	5	0.1	0.1	0.20	0.00	U
Chung Shing Textile	668	5	6.6	6.1	0.50	0.00	U
Yeang Der	618	14	1.0	0.1	0.37	0.02	U
China General Plastics	598	5	12.6	12.6	0.67	0.00	U
Chun Yuan Steel	528	5	4.7	4.7	0.36	0.00	U
Adi	484	9	0.7	0.3	0.22	0.00	U
Pou Chen Industrial	434	3	4.5	4.5	0.49	0.00	U
Ho Cheng	375	8*	14.5	14.5	0.26	0.50	U
Taiwan Glass	350	9*	2.6	0.6	0.00	0.00	U

Company							
Tung Ho Steel	350	4	0.6	0.6	0.25	0.09	U
Lealea	335	7	9.4	9.4	0.17	0.00	U
Chia Hsin Cement	303	7*	7.0	7.0	0.00	0.00	U
Hwa Eng Cable	303	3	8.9	8.9	0.51	0.00	U
Lily Textile	301	7	0.7	0.7	0.04	0.00	U
Chia Her	293	5	1.6	1.6	0.38	0.00	U
Sun Moon Star	287	5*	7.1	3.8	0.49	0.00	U
Ta Ya Cable	276	6	4.0	4.0	0.10	0.21	U
Shing Nung	256	13*	6.2	5.9	0.42	0.22	U
Tah Tong Textile	235	13*	4.5	0.7	0.55	0.39	U
Dahin	231	5*	12.3	9.9	0.51	0.21	U
Lee Tah Farm Industrial	204	5	11.6	11.6	0.19	0.50	U
Asia Chemical	180	13*	4.6	2.7	0.10	0.00	U
Men Yi	170	4	1.0	1.0	0.00	0.00	U
China Unique	166	4	2.8	2.8	0.22	0.00	U
Hong Ho Precision Textile	159	6*	3.4	3.4	0.10	0.00	U
Chun Yu	158	7*	6.1	5.3	0.45	0.50	U
Ability	157	11	2.2	2.2	0.26	0.38	U
Far Eastern Machinery	156	7	0.3	0.3	0.20	0.00	U
UB	139	8	7.4	7.4	0.48	0.00	U
Chien Shing Stainless Steel	137	6	8.4	8.4	0.17	0.00	U
South East Cement	134	5	8.0	8.0	0.12	0.46	U
Taiwan Everlight Chemical	104	5*	14.2	3.5	0.30	0.00	U
Nan Pao Resins	104	3	8.4	8.4	0.22	0.00	U
Victor Machinery	101	12*	1.2	1.2	0.16	0.00	U
Fu I Industrial	77	5*	5.1	5.1	0.30	0.00	U
San Wu Textile	53	3	2.7	2.7	0.57	0.05	U
Fong Kuo	48	4	6.5	6.5	0.34	0.10	U
Mean	954	10.0	7.0	4.7	0.35	0.10	
Weighted Mean		16.9	9.5	4.5	0.48	0.16	

140   *Emergent Economies, Divergent Paths*

in most cases belong to the input–output sectors called domestic wholesale trade, domestic retail trade, or import and export trade, although only a subset of the firms with these sector classifications are designated as trading companies. Groups in which trading companies exist are denoted by an asterisk in column three of Table 4.2, along with the total number of firms in the group.

Of the eighty business groups, thirty-nine or roughly one-half were found to have trading companies, but only twenty-three of these have any recorded purchases between that company and other firms in the group.[8] The extent to which the Taiwan trading companies are involved in the internal transactions of their groups is considerably less than in Korea. When the trading companies are excluded from the calculation of the internal sales ratio, then average internalization falls from 7 percent to 6 percent or from 9.5 percent to 8.5 percent calculated as a weighted average. This is much smaller than the corresponding reduction for Korea. One reason for this is that there are a number of groups with high internalization (over 15 percent) that do not have trading companies but still have high domestic retail sales. Two of these groups are very large producers of motor vehicles: Yulon with sales of $4.3 billion, and Chinfon, with sales of $3.0 billion; whereas a third group, Wei Chuan Ho Tai with sales of $4.9 billion, produces autos and a wide range of services. These groups sell to a domestic automobile market that was at the time protected by tariffs and domestic content requirements.[9] The fourth group, Bomy, is a smaller producer of fruit and vegetable juices, which also sells domestically.

To determine the impact of excluding these wholesale and retail sales from the groups' internalization, in the fifth column of Table 4.2 we recompute the internal sales ratio while omitting the purchases of trading companies and all other firms classified in the sectors of domestic wholesale trade, domestic retail trade, or import and export trade. The internalization of the three large groups (Yulon, Chinfon, and Wei Chuan Ho Tai) and the smaller Bomy group falls dramatically, although the internalization of Formosa does not change at all. The average internal sales ratio now becomes 4.7 percent, while the weighted average is 4.5 percent. There is evidently no relation between sales and internalization once the retail sales of the three large, automotive groups are excluded.

[8] There might be some other cases of internal purchases that we are not aware of due to missing data.
[9] Taiwan has had a 30 percent tariff on imported autos and also a domestic content requirement that 50 percent of parts and components for sedans be made in Taiwan. Up until 1994, it also banned imports from Japan. Despite these restrictions, imports accounted for one-third of the total sales in 1994, with the largest sales coming from Japanese automobiles produced in the United States.

The corresponding internalization rates computed without retail sales for Korea are 6.7 percent (simple average) and 12.2 percent (weighted average). The weighted average in particular is considerably higher than that for Taiwan, indicating the tendency of the largest groups in Korea to have high vertical integration, even after trading companies and other retail firms are excluded.

There is also a difference between groups in the two countries in their extent of horizontal diversification, as measured by the Herfindahl indexes. In the final columns of Table 4.2, we report the Herfindahl indexes for Taiwan, in the broad case, which are defined over all sales and all products; and the narrow case, which are defined over just manufacturing inputs sold internally to the group. The simple average of the Herfindahl index over all sales is 0.35, and the weighted average is 0.48, as compared to 0.52 and 0.66 for Korea. Thus, the Korean groups have greater product diversity, though in both countries there is some tendency for larger groups to be more diverse in their sectoral sales. When we consider the internal sales of manufacturing goods, the Herfindahl indexes fall substantially to 0.10 (simple average) and 0.16 (weighted average), as compared to 0.26 and 0.45 for Korea. The largest group, Formosa Plastics, still has a high value of 0.58 for the Herfindahl index, which was comparable to the level of the largest groups in Korea. However, as we will describe in more detail later, there are important differences in the diversification of Formosa Plastics and the Korean groups, in that Formosa has its largest sales in just a few upstream sectors – chemical and plastics, and heavy machinery – with high internal sales between them, and a smaller presence in synthetic textiles, which is also an intermediate product. Generally, the Taiwanese groups tend to be focused on a narrower range of activities, diversifying across one or two areas in addition to their major sector. As examples among the top five business groups in Taiwan, Shin King and Far Eastern both have their major presence in textiles, with diversification to chemicals, plastics and non-metallic minerals. In these cases, the dominant sector is located upstream, but there are very limited linkages between that sector and others where the group has diversified. Clearly, one-setism is not present in these cases. This pattern is typical of the Taiwanese business groups and contrasts with the much larger and more diversified groups at the top of the business-group hierarchy in Korea.

Classification of Taiwan Business Groups

To what extent does the configuration of business groups in Taiwan match the low concentration equilibria? To answer this, we make use of our

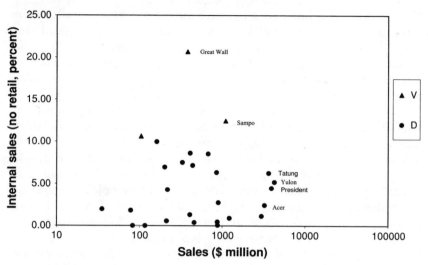

Figure 4.7. Taiwanese Groups Producing Final Consumer Products.

earlier rules for classifying the groups as V-groups, D-groups, or U-groups and summarize the results in Table 4.2 and Figures 4.7 and 4.8.

From Table 4.2, we see that, among the eighty Taiwanese business groups for which we have internal transaction data, twenty-three are classified as D-groups, fifty-four as U-groups, and only three as V-groups.

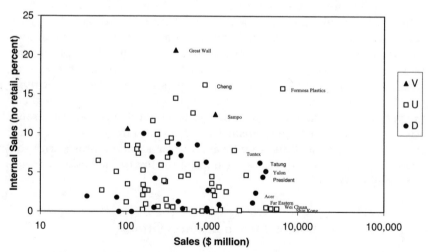

Figure 4.8. Types of Taiwanese Groups.

These three V-groups are so classified because they have high internalization ratios, but as we will show later, that classification is suspect when
we examine each of these cases more closely. Of these eighty groups, only
10 percent (eight) have internalization ratios (without retail) above 10,
whereas 27 percent (twelve) of the Korean dataset have internalization
ratio (without retail) above the same level. In sharp contrast with Korea,
and with the notable exception of Formosa Plastics, the groups with the
largest total sales in 1989 have modest to low levels of internalization.
Another striking contrast with Korea is the fact that, of the ten largest
business groups in our Taiwanese database, two groups (that is, Shin
Kong and Wei Chuan Ho Hai) are primarily providers of services;[10] five
groups (that is, Yulon, President, Tatung, Acer, and Chinfon) are oriented
primarily toward the domestic market or are downstream assemblers of
final products, most parts for which are purchased from unaffiliated firms;
and three groups (that is, Formosa Plastics, Far Eastern, and Hualon) are
manufacturers of intermediate industrial products that are sold at market
rates to other firms. No business group in the top ten or, for that matter, anywhere in the Taiwanese economy resembles Korea's top-ranked,
vertically integrated *chaebol*.

   D-Groups: Figure 4.7 shows those groups producing final goods for
sale to consumers. Unlike in Korea, where eleven groups are classified
as specializing in producing final products, there are twenty-seven such
groups in Taiwan. With three exceptions, however, all of these groups are
classified as D-groups. The two D-groups with the highest sales (that is,
Yulon and President) make products for the domestic market. Yulon is
primarily an automobile and automobile parts manufacturer, and President is primarily a manufacturer of food products. Figure 4.9 shows the
internal transaction networks in a number of D-groups, including Yulon
and President. Both groups reveal some vertical integration even though
the measured levels of internalization and manufacturing diversification
are quite low, especially for the type of manufacturing done by Yulon.
The internal transaction network of the President group resembles the
food-producing groups in Korea, particularly Lotte. However, close comparisons of the diagram for Yulon with those for Hyundai and Daewoo,
and of the diagram for the President group with those for Lotte and
Doosan, reveal a single-core "hub and spoke" pattern in Taiwan as compared to a much denser set of interlocks with multiple cores in Korea.

---

[10] The number would be four were the Linden and Evergreen groups included in our
database. Both would rank among the top ten and both primarily provide services. The
Linden group specializes in financial services and the Evergreen group provides shipping
and transportation services.

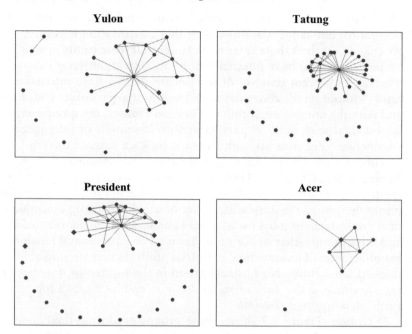

Figure 4.9. Internal Transactions in Selected Taiwanese D-Groups, 1994.

This "hub and spoke" pattern is a characteristic of Taiwanese business groups, indicating the presence of core firms in a group that coordinates the business of the group and minimal vertical integration among other firms in the group. By contrast, the diagrams of Korea's business group reveal dense networks of transactions among many core firms in a group.

The next two largest firms are Tatung and Acer. Both groups are manufacturers of high technology products, particularly computers, computer parts, and peripherals. These two groups are prototypical D-groups. Although there is some vertical integration, it is minimal as measured by both internal transaction and manufacturing diversification. Also, for Tatung, the "hub and spoke pattern" is particularly pronounced. From these measures, as well as from detailed descriptions (China Credit Information Services, 1990–91, pp. 145–60, 501–11) and interviews, it is clear that Acer and Tatung buy most of their intermediate inputs from non-affiliated firms that go into their final products.

V-Groups: The only three groups (that is, Sampo, Great Wall, and Ching Kuang) shown as V-groups in Figure 4.7 received this classification simply because they produce final products and have high internalization scores. All three of these groups, however, could be more properly listed as

Sampo:

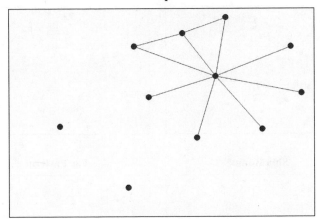

Great Wall:

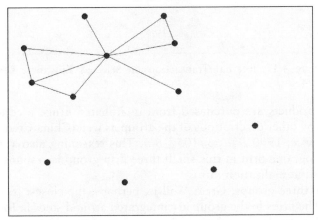

Figure 4.10. Internal Transactions in Selected Taiwanese V-Groups, 1994.

D-groups. Sampo and Ching Kuang make electrical and electronic products and Great Wall food products. The diagram of Sampo's internal transaction (Figure 4.10), a clear "hub and spoke" pattern, suggests limited vertical integration. An inspection of the actual transactions reveals that only one firm in the group has a high level of intra-group transactions, high enough to give the entire group a high internalization ratio. Because there are few other internal transactions within Sampo, the group has no measurable diversification in manufacturing. Also, since other firms in Sampo have substantial external sales, it is very likely that the inputs

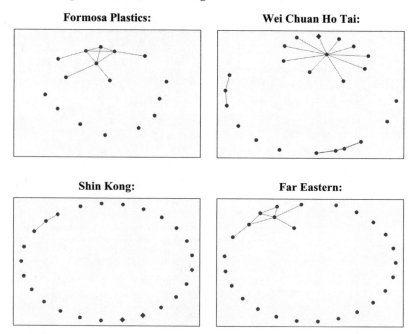

Figure 4.11. Internal Transactions in Selected Taiwanese U-Groups, 1994.

for these products are purchased from unaffiliated firms, a conclusion supported by other descriptions of the group as well (China Credit Information Service, 1990–91, pp. 1057–66). This reasoning also applies to Ching Kuang; one firm in this small three-firm group is responsible for the group's internalization ratio.

Of these three groups, Great Wall is, perhaps, the closest to being a V-group. The firms in the group are integrated around steps in food production. But the "hub and spoke" pattern is obvious here as well, as Figure 4.10 shows, and examining the internal transactions shows that they are highly concentrated in only two of the group's firms. Still, Great Wall resembles other food groups, such as Doosan in Korea, even if it is, in reality, much less vertically integrated than the Korean food groups.

U-Groups: Figure 4.8 shows the relation of U-groups in Taiwan's economy to D-groups. By a small margin, the three largest groups in our Taiwanese dataset are classified as U-groups; they are primarily suppliers of upstream industrial products and services. The largest business group in Taiwan by total sales, Formosa Plastics, also ranks among the highest in Taiwan in its level of internalization. As the diagram of these internal transactions shows (Figure 4.11), however, there are relatively few connections between firms and the high internalization ratio is almost entirely due to the steps needed to process petroleum into plastic, and to manufacture various types of synthetic materials.

The next three largest U-groups in Taiwan (that is, Shin Kong, Wei Chuan Ho Tai, and Far Eastern) have extraordinarily low internalization ratios. On the basis of their external sales, Shin Kong and Wei Chuan Ho Tai are classified as service groups and Far Eastern, as an industrial group. These classifications do not do justice to the complexity and diversity of the businesses in which these groups are engaged. In fact, these three groups are prototypical examples of the diversity of intermarket niches that is characteristic of most of Taiwan's largest business groups. We should emphasize that, in Korea, the top *chaebol* also show great diversity in the services that they provide, at market rates, to all buyers. The difference between Korean and Taiwanese business groups in this regard is that the vertically integrated manufacturing core so prominent in the top *chaebol* is absence or severely attenuated in Taiwanese business groups.

As shown in Figure 4.11, Shin Kong has a few internal transactions within a small set of firms, making textiles from synthetic fibers, but other than that there are no internal manufacturing transactions. The Wei Chuan Ho Tai group is a diversified conglomerate with a prominent food production specialty and a modest automobile and auto parts manufacturing business, but most revenues for the group come from a range of financial and retail services businesses. Much the same configuration is found in the Far Eastern group. However, despite prominent businesses in retail and other service industries, the prominence of upstream industrial products, primarily in the manufacturing of textiles, tips the balance of revenues toward industrial products.

In sum, this analysis of business groups in Taiwan demonstrates that the predictions based on the low concentration equilibria are very close to what we actually find in Taiwan. There are no business groups in Taiwan that resemble the largest *chaebol* with their dense networks of internal transactions centered around the production of final products. Instead, what we find in Taiwan is a sizeable set of groups that assemble products for both the export and domestic markets and that buy most of the component parts from unaffiliated firms. Among these consumer-oriented groups, the ones having among the highest level of integration are the groups producing for the domestic economy, such as the protected (in 1989) domestic auto market (for example, Yulon) and the local market in processed foods (President and Great Wall). Groups producing products for overseas buyers, which form the majority of the D-groups in Taiwan, differ somewhat in their levels of integration, but they are uniformly low

Table 4.3. *Comparison of Korean Groups with Simulated* High Concentration *Equilibria*

Included Groups	Statistic	Sales ($ mill.)	Internal Sales Ratio (percent)[1]	Internal Sales Ratio (no retail)[2]	Herfindahl Index (all sales)[3]	Herfindahl Index (internal inputs)[4]
(a) Korean Groups, 1989						
All 44	Mean	3,441	11.3	6.7	0.52	0.26
	St.Dev./$\sqrt{N}$	917	1.6	1.0	0.03	0.04
V-groups[5]	Mean	15,132	22.7	13.3	0.76	0.61
	St.Dev./$\sqrt{N}$	4,197	4.0	2.0	0.03	0.07
U-groups[6]	Mean	1,608	9.3	5.7	0.49	0.22
	St.Dev./$\sqrt{N}$	311	1.6	1.1	0.03	0.04
D-groups[7]	Mean	1,510	10.2	5.2	0.47	0.11
	St.Dev./$\sqrt{N}$	787	4.3	1.3	0.10	0.05
(b) Simulated *High Concentration* Stable Equilibria						
All	Mean	6,236	12.9	8.1	0.51	0.34
	Stan. Dev.	8,072	9.4	9.0	0.34	0.41
V-groups[8]	Mean	18,412	26.9	21.7	0.96	0.95
	Stan. Dev.	2,704	1.7	1.8	0.01	0.03
U-groups[9]	Mean	1,119	6.9	2.3	0.32	0.08
	Stan. Dev.	365	2.1	0.8	0.20	0.12
(c) Hypothesis Tests for Actual versus Simulated Means[10]						
All group mean same as simulated mean	(Yes)	Yes	Yes	Yes	Yes	
V-group mean same as simulated mean	Yes	Yes	No	No	No	
U-group mean same as simulated mean	Yes	Yes	No	Yes	(Yes)	

Notes

[1] Computed as the ratio of sales between firms in each group to total sales of the group.

[2] "No retail" means that the internal sales ratio is calculated without including the purchases of any trading companies or other wholesale or retail firms from within the group.

[3] The Herfindahl index equals $1 - \sum_i s_i^2$, where s_i is the share of total sales in each sector i.

[4] The Herfindahl index is computed over just internal sales of manufacturing inputs.

[5] There are six V-groups as listed in Table 4.1.

[6] There are thirty-three U-groups as listed in Table 4.1.

[7] There are five D-groups as listed in Table 4.1.

[8] The V-groups occur for twenty-nine equilibria with elasticities between 1.8 and 3.2, as shown in Figures 3.9 and 3.11.

[9] The U-groups occur for sixty-nine equilibria with elasticities between 3.2 and 6.6, as shown in Figures 3.9 and 3.11.

[10] The hypotheses tests are described in Appendix C.

in diversification of their manufacturing, which indicates a reliance on other firms for intermediate parts. The rest of the business groups in the Taiwanese economy, the U-groups, engage in a range of services and in producing upstream inputs, such as fabric and plastics. These groups support the production of final goods without producing those goods themselves. Business groups in Taiwan are part of an interdependent economy, in which the goods and services essential for business group revenues are supplied by unaffiliated firms and other business groups. By contrast, in Korea, many of the goods and services for the *chaebol*, and especially the largest *chaebol*, are supplied internally, through intra-group transactions.

Comparison of Actual and Simulated Business Groups

Summarizing our results so far, we have found that the business groups found in Korea and Taiwan are different – both across and within the economies. The very large V-groups found in Korea fit the high concentration equilibria of our theoretical model, whereas the more prevalent D-groups found in Taiwan fit the low concentration equilibria. Both economies have U-groups, as also predicted by the model. Our arguments have been based on diagrams and descriptions of business groups, focusing on their size, internal transactions, location in the upstream and downstream sectors, and diversification across products. To make this comparison of the actual business group data with our model simulations more precise, we turn now to a statistical comparison of the actual and simulated data. Our goal it to test the hypothesis that the mean values of the Korean business groups' data – in size, internalization, and diversification – fit the mean values of the simulated high concentration equilibria, and likewise, that the mean values of the Taiwanese business groups' data fit the low concentration equilibria. We perform these statistical tests with the help of Tables 4.3 and 4.4.

Korean Business Groups and High Concentration Equilibria

Part (a) of Table 4.3 lists the mean values of characteristics for the forty-four Korean business groups: their sales, internalization ratios, and Herfindahl indexes of diversification. In addition, we provide the same information for the Korean groups that we have classified as V-groups, as U-groups, and as D-groups. In part (b), we list the mean values for the *simulated* data in the stable, high concentration equilibria. We will be testing whether the actual means in part (a) are statistically different or not from the simulated means in part (b), with the results of these hypotheses test shown in part (c).

Let us begin with the sales of the groups. The Korean groups classified as V-groups have average sales of $15,132 million in 1989. This compares with average sales of the simulated V-groups of $18,412 million. Recall from Chapter 3 that we have chosen the size of the labor force in the model so that the average sales of the simulated V-groups equals the average sales of the "top five" *chaebol* in Korea. It is therefore no surprise that the average simulated sales is close to that of the Korean groups classified as V-groups (which include four out of the top five *chaebol*, along with two smaller groups). To formally test whether these mean values are different, we note that average sales of $15,132 million has a standard deviation of $4,197, so its 95 percent confidence interval is approximately $15,132 ± 2 · 4,197 million. This range easily includes the simulated mean sales of $18,412 million, so we accept the hypothesis that the actual and simulated mean sales of the V-groups are the same, which is recorded as a "yes" in part (c) of Table 4.3.

Our choice of the labor force in the model ensures that the V-group sales match the "top five" groups in Korea, but once the labor force is fixed, the size of other groups in the model is determined by the equilibrium conditions – without regard to their actual size. Therefore, comparing the simulated with the actual size of U-groups amounts to a test of the model. For the U-groups, the simulated data have a mean of $1,119 million. This compares with the average sales for Korean *chaebol* classified as U-groups of $1,608 million, with a standard deviation of $311. Once again, we formally test whether the mean of the actual data is the same as the simulation by constructing the 95 percent confidence interval $1,608 ± 2 · 311 million. This interval includes the simulated mean of $1,119 million, so we can accept the hypothesis that the actual and simulated mean are the same, again recorded as a "yes" in part (c) of the table. The fact that the V-groups and U-groups differ so much in size – in both the model and the actual data for Korea – demonstrates a remarkable conformity between the high concentration equilibria and the Korean *chaebol*. We interpret this outcome as strong confirmation that the Korean groups fit the high concentration equilibria.

We proceed in a similar fashion for the other variables listed in Table 4.3: their internal sales ratios (with or without retail), and Herfindahl indexes of diversification (computed over all sales, or just over internal sales manufacturing inputs). In each case, we test the hypothesis that the mean of the actual Korea data equals the mean of the simulated data. Generally, we perform two versions of the hypothesis test. The first is a simple construction of the confidence interval for the actual data, as above, and comparing this with the simulated mean. This test is taking the simulated mean as a fixed, non-stochastic value, and asking whether it lies within the confidence interval of the sample mean. In the second test, we treat the simulated mean as itself stochastic, reflecting the fact that our simulations are performed over multiple values of the elasticity E between inputs (shown on the horizontal axis of Figures 3.3–3.8). The details of this test are described in Appendix C. The second test is generally easier to accept than the first, though in practice, they usually give the same results. In the few instances where the second test allows us to conclude that the actual and simulated means are the same, but not the first test, the outcome is indicated in parentheses as "(yes)" in part (c).

Looking over the results in part (c), in nearly all cases we can accept the hypothesis that the actual means of the Korean *chaebol* and simulated means from the high concentration equilibria are equal. There are two exceptions to this outcome, however. Both of these concern the comparison of the simulated V-groups with the Korean *chaebol* classified as such. For the internal sales ratios, we can accept the hypothesis that the simulated and actual Korean mean are the same for the broad measure (including trading companies), but not for the narrow measure (excluding trading companies and other wholesale and retail firms). More importantly, for the Herfindahl indexes of diversification, both the broad and narrow measures show differing means in the actual and simulated data. In particular, the simulated V-groups show *greater* diversification than do the actual Korea groups: the simulated equilibria have Herfindahl indexes above 0.95, whereas the actual data for V-groups have values of 0.76 or lower. This finding that the simulated V-groups show greater diversification than in the Korean data means that – in this respect – our model does not exactly mirror the actual business groups. We think that there are several good reasons for this finding, however, which indicate the limitations of our stylized model.

First, the V-group equilibria in our model occur when there are no unaffiliated firms at all competing with the business groups. This type of equilibria tends to increase the range of goods produced by the business groups in the model. The absence of unaffiliated firms is a theoretical outcome that occurs for a range of elasticities in the simulations, but in practice, we rarely if ever see the Korean *chaebol* competing with no other firms at all. The existing competition facing the *chaebol* will limit their expansion into all other lines of products, and for this reason, we should not be surprised that the simulated equilibria have greater diversification. Second, each of our simulated equilibrium have been computed under the "symmetry" assumption that all groups are the same size, and all final products are demanded in the same amounts. Having identical demand across final products in the model tends to increase the Herfindahl index, as compared to the disparate demands across products that we expect in reality. Third, our model has assumed a particular value of the elasticity of demand for final products, which was 5 in most simulated equilibria.[11] We have not experimented with alternative value of this elasticity, but it can be expected that higher values would reduce the markups and profits on final goods, and therefore reduce the extent of diversification across products in the simulation.

For all these reasons, when comparing the Herfindahl indexes of diversification, we do not expect the stylized model to match the actual economies precisely. Nevertheless, the fact remains that both the model and the actual V-group data for Korea display *high values* for diversification – much higher than for the *chaebol* we have classified as U-groups or D-groups, for example. In this sense, there is conformity between the simulated and actual values for the diversification of groups. For the other variables we have examined – sales and internalization – the high concentration equilibria from the model show a remarkable similarity to the actual Korean data. These comparisons increase our confidence that there is an "objective probability" (Ringer, 1997) that our Walrasian interpretation of the organization of the South Korean economy is a correct interpretation. Our confidence is further reinforced when we compare groups in the Taiwan economy with the low concentration equilibria, as we turn to next.

Taiwanese Business Groups and Low Concentration Equilibria

In part (a) of Table 4.4, we show the mean values of characteristics for the eighty Taiwanese business groups, as well as breaking down the sample into those we have classified as V-groups, D-groups, and U-groups. In part (b), we list the mean values for the *simulated* data in the stable, low concentration equilibria. Once again, we test whether the actual means in part (a) are statistically different or not from the simulated means in part (b), and show the results of these tests in part (c).

With only a couple of exceptions, we again find strong conformity between the low concentration equilibria from the model and the actual Taiwanese data. Looking at sales, for example, the actual D-groups sell more on average that the actual U-groups: $1,108 million versus $908 million. In the simulated low concentration equilibria, the sales of the D-groups and U-group are $1,648 million and $899 million, respectively,

---

[11] As described in the notes to Chapter 3, initially we used an elasticity of demand for final goods equal to 5. Although we found both V-group and U-group equilibria at this value, it was difficult to find D-group equilibria in which the unaffiliated downstream firms had no incentive to enter. To limit this incentive, it was necessary to use lower values for the final demand elasticity, especially when the elasticity of demand for inputs itself was low. Accordingly, all our equilibria are computed with an elasticity of demand for final goods equal to 5 for $E \geq 2.65$ and equal to $1.9 \cdot E$ for $E \leq 2.60$.

Table 4.4. *Comparison of Taiwan Groups with Simulated* Low Concentration *Equilibria*

Included Groups	Statistic	Sales ($ mill.)	Internal Sales Ratio (percent)[1]	Internal Sales Ratio (no retail)[2]	Herfindahl Index (all sales)[3]	Herfindahl Index (internal inputs)[4]
(a) Taiwan Groups, 1994						
All 80	Mean	954	7.0	4.7	0.35	0.10
	St.Dev./$\sqrt{N}$	154	0.8	0.5	0.03	0.02
D-groups[5]	Mean	1,108	7.9	3.7	0.33	0.06
	St.Dev./$\sqrt{N}$	279	1.7	0.7	0.06	0.03
U-groups[6]	Mean	908	6.1	4.6	0.36	0.12
	St.Dev./$\sqrt{N}$	195	0.8	0.6	0.03	0.02
V-groups[7]	Mean	525	14.7	14.6	0.25	0.00
	St.Dev./$\sqrt{N}$	296	3.2	3.1	0.01	0.00
(b) Simulated *Low Concentration* Stable Equilibria						
All	Mean	1,069	7.9	2.5	0.42	0.15
	Stan. Dev.	432	2.5	0.8	0.24	0.15
D-group[8]	Mean	1,648	10.5	2.6	0.70	0.28
	Stan. Dev.	171	0.6	0.5	0.02	0.05
U-group[9]	Mean	899	7.2	2.5	0.35	0.11
	Stan. Dev.	333	2.3	0.8	0.21	0.15
(c) Hypothesis Tests for Actual versus Simulated Means[10]						
All group mean same as simulated mean	Yes	Yes	No[11]	(Yes)	(Yes)
D-group mean same as simulated mean	Yes	Yes	Yes	No	No
U-group mean same as simulated mean	Yes	Yes	(Yes)	Yes	Yes

Notes:

[1] Computed as the ratio of sales between firms in each group to total sales of the group.

[2] "No retail" means that the internal sales ratio is calculated without including the purchases of any trading companies or other wholesale or retail firms from within the group.

[3] The Herfindahl index equals $1 - \sum_i s_i^2$, where s_i is the share of total sales in each sector i.

[4] The Herfindahl index is computed over just internal sales of manufacturing inputs.

[5] There are thirty-four D-groups as listed in Table 4.2.

[6] There are fifty-three U-groups as listed in Table 4.2.

[7] There are three V-groups as listed in Table 4.2.

[8] The D-groups occur for nineteen equilibria with elasticities between 1.8 and 2.8, as shown in Figures 3.10 and 3.12.

[9] The U-groups occur for seventy-seven equilibria with elasticities between 2.8 and 6.6, as shown in Figures 3.10 and 3.12.

[10] The hypotheses tests are described in Appendix C.

[11] This hypothesis test is accepted as "(yes)" if the three V-groups in the Taiwan sample are excluded.

so the D-groups are again larger on average. Taking into account the standard deviation of these estimates, we readily accept the hypotheses that the mean sales in the actual data equals that in the simulated data for each type of group. That conclusion holds equally well for the internal sales ratios, too. The internal sales are higher for the D-groups than the U-groups when computed with trading companies, indicating that some downstream groups (like Yulon and Chinfon) are relying on their own marketing arms. The same is true in the simulated D-groups. But when the activities of the trading companies and other wholesale and retail firms are excluded, then the internal sales ratios are nearly the same for the D-groups and U-groups, in both the actual and simulated data.

The most important exception to the similarity of means occurs for the Herfindahl indexes of diversification, when comparing the simulated and actual D-groups.[12] The Herfindahl indexes are more than twice as high in the simulated equilibria (0.70 and 0.28) than for the actual Taiwan D-groups (0.33 and 0.06). This is very similar to our finding for the comparison of the simulated and actual V-groups in Korea, and for similar reasons. Our stylized model can easily overstate the degree of diversification of the simulated groups by focusing on "symmetric" equilibria, and considering only one value for the downstream elasticity between products. Despite this theoretical limitation, we interpret the results in Table 4.4 as providing strong support for the low concentration equilibria as a stylized description of the business groups in Taiwan. The characteristics of the actual D-groups and U-groups are reproduced in our model simulations, just as many characteristics of the V-groups and U-groups in Korea were reproduced in the high concentration equilibria.

There are other hypotheses tests that can be performed, where rather than comparing the actual and simulated means, we instead compare the actual mean characteristics of different types of business groups in one country or the other. For brevity we do not record these results in detail, but they are reported in Appendix C. It is of interest to know, for example, whether the actual V-groups in Korea are statistically different from the U-groups or D-groups found there. That hypothesis is readily confirmed, and we find that the V-groups are larger in terms of sales, internalization, and

---

[12] The other exception occurs for the comparison of the overall Taiwan mean for the internal sales ratio (no retail) with the mean of the same variable for the overall low concentration equilibria. The equality of these means is rejected, as shown by the "no" in the first line of part (c) in Table 4.4. However, because this test is performed on the overall sample mean, the internal sales ratio is pulled up by the presence of the three V-groups in our Taiwan sample. If these three groups are excluded, then using the second version of the hypothesis test we obtain equality of the seventy-seven group mean with the simulated low concentration mean for the internal sales ratio (with or without retail), as indicated in the notes to Table 4.4.

diversification. On the other hand, it is hard to distinguish the D-groups from the U-groups in Korea or in Taiwan, in the sense that the mean values of their characteristics are not significantly different. Obviously, though, the D-groups and U-groups are selling in different sectors, downstream and upstream. For Taiwan, where the D-groups are most prevalent, the differences we find between them and the U-groups (D-groups are larger, with higher internal sales from trading companies) are mimicked in the simulations, even though these differences are not statistically significant. Finally, we can compare the small number of V-groups classified as such in Taiwan (contrary to our model) to the other Taiwanese groups. The V-groups in Taiwan are selling downstream, like the D-groups, but do not differ from them in the mean value of their characteristics (except in their internal sales). This reinforces our earlier observation that the V-groups in Taiwan could just as well be classified at D-groups, so that Taiwan just does not have anything similar to the very large, vertically integrated *chaebol* of South Korea.

Unstable Equilibria

Our discussion so far in the chapter has focused on the *stable* equilibria of our model, but the simulations of our model also admit a range of *unstable* equilibria, for the V-groups in particular (see Figures 3.6, 3.7, 3.9, and 3.11).[13] In the remainder of the chapter we will explore the meaning of these unstable equilibria, and hypothesize that there is a link between these and the bankruptcies that occurred in Korea prior to and during the Asian financial crisis. We have made this argument at length elsewhere (Feenstra, Hamilton, and Lim, 2002), and focus here on just two questions: namely, how the unstable equilibria can lead to bankruptcies in the model, and how this theoretical phenomena – what we shall call "catastrophes" – compares with the actual experience in Korea during 1997–98. Because the catastrophes offer a theoretically consistent explanation for the bankruptcies leading up to the crisis in Korea, and this explanation is consistent with the evidence we consider, we take this narrative to provide further support for our Walrasian model as a description of the Korean economy.

---

[13] Recall from Chapter 3 that there are also unstable D-group equilibria that we have not plotted. These appear below the stable D-group equilibria in the upper-portion of Figure 3.6, and for elasticities below about 2.6, create an unstable equilibrium between each pair of stable D-group and stable V-group equilibria (for a given elasticity). However, these unstable D-group equilibria are fundamentally different than the unstable V-group equilibria, in that they do not create the kind of "catastrophe" that we investigate below, in Figures 4.13 and 4.14.

The Financial Crisis and Bankruptcies in South Korea

There are several different stories told for why the financial crisis hit Korea in 1997. According to one version, this was a case of "contagion" from the crisis that first hit Thailand, and was precipitated by the excessive inflows of short-term foreign loans into both those countries. This arose in part due to low interest rates in creditor countries, especially Japan, but also due to financial liberalization in some of the East Asian countries.[14] Both Thailand and Korea, for example, allowed unregulated financial companies – the so-called "merchant banks" in Korea – to borrow short-term offshore, and then re-lend these funds domestically (World Bank, 2000, pp. 21–4). Short-term external debt in Korea peaked at $75 billion in 1996, which was 15 percent of the GDP and twice the level of foreign exchange reserves. The situation was even worse in Thailand, where the short-term debt exceeded 25 percent of the GDP and was nearly twice as high as reserves in 1997.

There are some interesting organizational features to this financial story, whereby the merchant banks in Korea acted as financial intermediaries by borrowing short-term abroad and lending long-term to the business groups. The resulting imbalance in the balance sheets of the merchant banks – in terms of the maturity and the currency-denomination of their assets – certainly contributed to the financial distress, as we discuss in Appendix D. But we feel that the underlying cause of the crisis in Korea was not a financial or "contagion" story, but rather, was linked to the prior fall in demand for its exports.

The annual growth rate of Korean exports, which exceeded 30 percent by the end of 1995, plunged to negative values during 1996, along with a substantial fall in export prices. This can be seen from Figure 4.12, where we graph the change in dollar export values and prices for Korea, over the months September 1994–September 1997 as compared to one year earlier.[15] To give one important example, the price of 16 megabyte DRAM chips plunged from $54 at the end of 1995 to $13 by the middle of 1996, and $3 by the end of 1997 (World Bank, 2000, p. 49). Korea relied on semiconductors for much of its exports: some $16 billion in exports sales in 1997 and 1998, or 12 percent of its total exports, so the fall in prices for this commodity had a dramatic impact on the economy.

---

[14] There may be some truth to the argument by Bhagwati (1998) that the inflow of foreign capital to the Asian countries resulted from financial market liberalizations foisted on these countries by the "Wall Street-Treasury complex" (see also Wade and Veneroso, 1998), but this alone cannot explain the financial panic in Korea. Rather, any explanation of the crisis in Korea must begin by explaining the unprecedented bankruptcies that occurred from early 1997, before the exchange rate and banking crisis there.

[15] Figure 4.12 is constructed from data from the International Financial Statistics, International Monetary Fund.

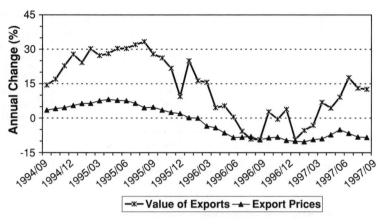

Figure 4.12. Change in Korean Exports ($).

Despite the fact that Korean exports began to grow again in 1997, so that the current account was in balance by November 1997, the overhang of the external debt remained. Many observers believe that created a crisis of confidence in the ability of private firms to repay the debt, particularly if the Korean won were to devalue. At that time, the won was on an adjustable peg, with the daily change in the exchange rate limited to a 2.5 percent band around the previous day's average (Kim, 1999a, p. 72). The anticipation that the won might be allowed to float and depreciate led to an enormous flight out of the currency and into dollars, draining the foreign exchange reserves of the central bank. The central bank devoted some $25 billion to the defense of the won during November, until its foreign exchange reserves reached a low of $6 billion,[16] which was perhaps one-tenth of the short-term foreign debt. This was far too low to support the existing peg, so the won was allowed to float in November 17, 1997, and depreciated by 50 percent by the end of the year.

Following the depreciation was a period of financial distress in Korea: a number of other business groups declared bankruptcy, and some of the merchant banks were shut down under the direction of the International Monetary Fund. We show in Appendix D how the bankruptcies of the groups *after* November 17, 1997, are linked more to their short-term debt than to their long-term viability, suggesting that the bankruptcies resulted from a financial panic. But our interest here is in the bankruptcies that occurred *prior* to November 17, and that precipitated the financial crisis. In Table 4.5, we list all cases of bankruptcy among the top sixty

---

[16] These values are obtained from Kim (1998, p. 35). Shim (2000, Table 1) reports "usable" foreign exchange reserves of $7.3 billion in November 1997.

Table 4.5. *Bankruptcies in the Korean* Chaebol, *1996–98*

Name of Group	Major Products	Date Bankrupt
Wooseong	Construction	96-01-19
Hanbo	Construction, steel	97-01-23
Sammi	Steel	97-03-19
Jinro	Liquor, foods	97-04-21
Hanshin	Construction	97-05-31
Kia Auto	Automobiles, steel	97-07-18
Dae-Nong	Textiles, retail	97-09-11
Ssang-Bang-Ul	Apparel, construction	97-10-20
Haitai	Confectionary, beverages	97-11-03
Newcore	Retail	97-11-04
Floating of the Korean won on November 17, 1997		
Su-san	Machinery	97-11-18
Tae-Il	Hard disk drive	97-11-18
Sin-Ho	Paper	97-11-28
Halla	Auto parts, construction	97-12-08
Hanwha	Explosives, chemicals	97-12-16
Jin-Do	Fur coats, containers	97-12-16
Ssangyong	Cement, construction	98-01-10
Dong-Ah	Construction	98-01-10
Hanil	Cement, construction	98-01-15
Nasan	Textiles	98-01-15
Kukdong	Construction	98-01-20
Kohap	Textiles, plastics, chemicals	98-01-30
Chung-Gu	Construction	98-04-23
Keopyung	Chemicals, retailing	98-05-20

Note: All firms belong to the top sixty largest conglomerates in terms of the asset values as of the end of 1996, which were assessed by the Bank Supervision Authority of Korea.
Source: Revised from Lee (1999).

chaebol during 1996–98, taken from Lee (1999).[17] These started in the construction sectors, where 189 construction companies went bankrupt in 1996 (that is, one in every other day), many of which were large construction firms (*Maeil Kyongje* 96/12/24).[18] The steel industry suffered as the construction sector dwindled, while the decrease in exports of automobiles, machinery, electronics, and ships also contributed to the fall in steel consumption. With the slump in the steel industry, the

[17] Note that these bankruptcies do not include the "workouts" experienced by a number of groups after the exchange rate devaluation of November 17, 1997.
[18] The increase in the number of bankrupt construction firms is astonishing. In 1990, three firms went bankrupt while fifty firms in 1994, 145 firms in 1995, and 189 firms in 1996 went bankrupt.

chaebol specializing in steel (Hanbo, Sammi, and Kia[19]) began to fall in 1997.

The next *chaebol* that went bankrupt in 1997 were domestically oriented midsize groups (Haitai, New Core, Dae-Nong, Jinro, Hanshin, etc.). These *chaebol* had also expanded considerably during the economic boom in 1994–95, with capital borrowed primarily from domestic creditors. The industrial sectors in which these *chaebol* engaged were mainly domestic consumer products like food, apparel, retail, and housing building. In addition to the domestic economic slump, wage increases also negatively affected the financial performance of these firms. By and large, the burden of financial service that resulted from the massive expansions on debts and the downturn of domestic economy pushed those *chaebol* into bankruptcy. Late in 1999, Daewoo became the first instance of a top five *chaebol* that was forced into bankruptcy. Since that time, individual firms within other top five *chaebol* have gone bankrupt (such as Samsung Motors in 1999, bought by Renault the next year, and a bailout of Hyundai Engineering and Construction in 2001), but without bringing down the entire business group.

Adding the Daewoo to the list of bankrupt groups in Table 4.5, it is remarkable that fully 40 percent of these (ten out of twenty-five) went bankrupt *before* the exchange rate crisis of November 17, 1997. Furthermore, most of these groups are of an intermediate size. Thirteen of the cases in Table 4.5 are among the top six to thirty ranked *chaebol* in 1996 in terms of their assets (see Appendix D), so that *one-half* of these have gone bankrupt. The remaining ten cases are from the next thirty-one to sixty ranked *chaebol*, so that *one-third* of these have gone bankrupt. Of these, several of the groups appear in the list of top six to thirty groups in 1997 or 1998. Thus, there is some indication that bankruptcies are concentrated among the intermediate-size (top six to thirty) *chaebol*, though Daewoo is an exception to this.

Furthermore, the groups that went bankrupt prior to November 17, 1997 were not the groups most heavily invested in the electronics industry – Hyundai, Samsung, Lucky-Goldstar, and Daewoo – despite the fact that semiconductors suffered the sharpest decline in prices. The subsequent bankruptcy of Daewoo is attributed more to excess capacity in automobiles, and fraudulent financial practices by its management, rather than losses in its electronics firms; so too, the bankruptcy of Samsung Motors in 1999 was not due to losses in electronics. The question then arises as to how these groups avoided bankruptcy at the time of the

---

[19] Kia produced cars, too, but the first bankrupt firm of the group was its steel-producing firm.

fall in semiconductor prices, and why the economic decline fueled the bankruptcy of the smaller and midsize groups.

A clue towards answering the first question comes from a company review of Samsung conducted at the end of 1996 – after the fall in semiconductor prices, but before the Asia crisis:[20]

> When semiconductor earning began sagging, Samsung managers say they redoubled their efforts towards making and marketing such consumer items as TVs, refrigerators and cellular phones. Sale of non-semiconductor products jumped 31% to $15 billion, more than enough to make up for the 17% decline in semiconductor sales to $8 billion. "We have succeeded in changing our product portfolio," says Noh Geun Sik, executive vice-president in charge of Samsung Electronics' global operations. "In the past, we were too dependent on one product. But when things are going well in semiconductors, we made bold investment in other areas. Now, that's helping us to cover the slump in semiconductors."

In fact, Samsung had 1996 sales exceeding those in 1995, despite the fall in semiconductor prices. The explanation given by its managers is the diversification of this group across product categories. We find it plausible that the largest groups can achieve this diversification, effectively insulating them from large falls in export prices. But the same would not be true for smaller groups, whether they are focused in the export or domestic market. Thus, the *chaebol* that obtain a majority of revenues from autos, steel, construction, or retailing would be hit particularly hard by the general slowdown caused by a fall in exports, and this is exactly what happened to second-tier groups such as Hanbo, Sammi, Kia, Haitai, and others.

It may appear paradoxical that a fall in exports could impact smaller groups oriented towards the domestic market even more than the large, export-oriented groups. But this observation is consistent with our theoretical model. We have found that the high concentration equilibria that describe Korea include both large, vertically integrated groups (V-groups) and smaller groups focused on upstream production (U-groups), both of which are stable. In between these is a range of midsize vertically integrated groups that are *unstable*, meaning that with any shock to the system these groups would disappear, either downsizing into the smaller groups or being absorbed into the larger groups. Both of these events happened in Korea, as Kia was absorbed upwards into the larger Hyundai, and many

---

[20] Quotation from Charles S. Lee, "The Chips Are Down," *Far Eastern Economic Review*, December 26, 1996 and January 2, 1997, p. 90.

others groups were downsized. In contrast, the larger V-groups are stable, as are the smaller U-groups; small shocks should therefore not have a large impact on their structure. The stable V-groups in the high concentration equilibria, like the largest business groups in Korea, have greater diversity across product varieties than smaller groups. Thus, these groups are better insulated from price shocks. The Asian crisis was certainly a shock to the economic system, and at a stylized level, our model helps us understand why the top five *chaebol* were not unduly affected by the fall in export demand and prices, even though the midsize and smaller groups in Korea were.

Catastrophe in the Model

Our model of Chapter 3 can in fact be used to demonstrate these ideas more formally. Let us consider a fall in overall demand, as was experienced for Korean exports. Total demand in our general equilibrium model is measured by the size of the labor force, L (which is the only factor of production). Recall that we chose the labor force so that the average size of the V-groups in the high concentration equilibria was approximately equal to the average size of the top-five *chaebol* in Korea. Let us call this starting point $L = 100$ (or 100 percent of its initial value). Then to explore the consequences of a fall in demand, we simply lower L from its initial value. To simplify the exercise, let us focus only on the V-group configuration, as was graphed in Figure 3.4 for a wide range of the elasticity of inputs, E. We are most interested in those elasticities that lead to *multiple equilibria*, which occurred between $E = 2.8$ and $E = 3.2$ in Figure 3.4. For concreteness, let us choose a particular value of the elasticity, say $E = 3$.

At the elasticity of 3, there are two stable V-group equilibria: a low concentration equilibria that allows for a large number of business groups and a high concentration equilibria that only allows for a smaller number of groups. Although we have argued that the Korean *chaebol* typically display the characteristics of *high concentration* equilibria, we now want to discuss the dynamics of how this organizational structure can come about. To this end, suppose that through past entry some Korean industry finds itself with a larger number of business groups in the *low concentration* equilibria. In Figure 4.13, this occurs at point A with the initial income of $L = 100$. What happens now as the total demand, measured by L, decreases?

As demand falls in Figure 4.13, the equilibrium number of groups also falls, to the left of point A. Under the conditions of free entry and exit in our model, a smaller market will imply a smaller number of business

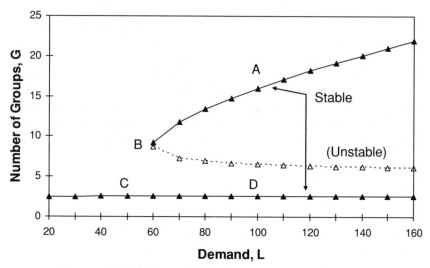

Figure 4.13. V-Groups (Elasticity = 3).

groups. This process is "continuous," so that a small change in demand would lead to a correspondingly small change in the structure of the business groups. However, when we reach the point B at about L = 70 (or 70 percent of its initial value), the nature of the organizational change suddenly changes. For any further fall in demand, the equilibrium will drop *discontinuously* from B to C and the number of groups is reduced suddenly to restore a zero-profit equilibrium at C. This requires the bankruptcy of many of the groups at B, which leads to a drastic change in the organizational structure of the industry.

The process of moving from B to C is called a "catastrophe" in mathematical language (Woodcock and Davis, 1978), and it is well known that this type of discontinuity is a generic feature of many nonlinear systems, including those in economics (Rosser, 1991). It has even been suggested that such catastrophe might apply to monopoly equilibria (Bonanno, 1987). In our model, such catastrophic changes in organization are a characteristic feature of the V-group equilibria. This is shown by Figure 4.14, which expands Figure 4.13 by graphing the V-group equilibria over a wide range of elasticities, E, and values of demand, L. Whenever demand falls (moving backwards in Figure 4.14), there is a range of industries (that is, values of the elasticity E) for which the low concentration equilibria will no longer exist, and the industry must, therefore, be reorganized toward *increasing concentration*. In less formal language, the industry will fall off the cliff illustrated in Figure 4.14. But as demand grows again, the reverse

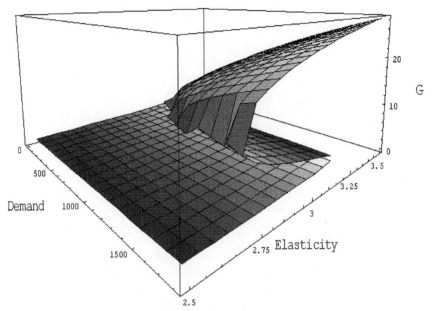

Figure 4.14. V-Group Equilibria.

change *does not necessarily happen*. Returning to Figure 4.13, as demand grows, the equilibria would most plausibly move from C to D, thereby remaining on the high concentration path. It would take some significant shock to move the equilibria back to the less-concentrated point A. Without such a deliberate push, the process of a fall in demand and subsequent recovery could plausibly move the equilibrium from a less-concentrated position toward greater concentration.

It seems to us that these theoretical results provide an apt description of the process of bankruptcies in the Korean *chaebol* during the first three quarters of 1997. The groups that went bankrupt often had some firms absorbed by other business groups (such as with Kia being absorbed by Hyundai), so that the resulting equilibria became more concentrated. According to Beck (2000, p. 19) and data from the Korean Fair Trade Commission, nearly all of the top ten *chaebol* increased their assets from 1996 to 1999, and the top four's share of total assets among the top thirty rose from 48 percent to 58 percent over this period. This trend toward increasing concentration was *not* automatically reversed by the economic recovery of 1999. Rather, the bankruptcies and reorganizations that occurred during 1997–98 became an "embedded" feature of the economic organization, so that the Korean economy ended the twentieth century with groups that were as large or even larger than before.[21]

Conclusions

Using the Walrasian model we specified in Chapter 3, we have shown here that the business group data from South Korea and Taiwan matches the predictions of simulations based on the model. This correspondence between predictions and data allows us to conclude that a Walrasian view of business groups is, at a very minimum, an appropriate way to interpret the formation and configuration of business groups in both countries. We should, perhaps, phrase this conclusion even more strongly; cross-market organization of competitive capitalist economies shapes the location and performance of firms and groups of firms that constitute those economies. The Walrasian model of business groups that we have proposed and for which we offer a first test in this chapter is derived from this general proposition.

Both the strong and the weak versions of the conclusion suggest several implications that we should mention here and address in later chapters. First, the test substantiates our contention that business groups should be interpreted more broadly as aspects of "normal" economies and as emergent results of competitive economic processes. They should not be interpreted solely as the results of market failure or of state policies. Nor should they be seen as simply the product of trust-bearing social networks. We should emphasize that market institutions, state policies, and social networks have considerable impacts on economic organization, but, in the first instance, what shapes capitalist economic organizations are the competitive interactions among firms, groups, and other direct actors in the economy.

Second, our analysis also suggests that business groups are not only found in developing economies, as Amsden (2001) has suggested. Rather, business groups should appear in all capitalist economies and, therefore, they should not disappear as developing economies mature. Business

---

[21] Since then, there has been some further reorganization of the groups. The leading example is the Hyundai group, where divisions among the sons of founder Chung Ju-yung have led to a breakup of the group: into Hyundai Motor Co. (split from Hyundai in September 2000); Hyundai Construction (split off in August 2001); Hyundai Heavy Industries (split off in February 2002); and a possible split of Hyundai Investment and Hyundai Securities. Prior to these, LG Semiconductor was merged with Hyundai Electronics in May 1999 as part of the government's "Big Deal" policies, and then was renamed Hynix Semiconductor in March 2001 and split off from Hyundai in August 2001. Despite these various splits, the individual Hyundai groups are still very large, with Hyundai Automobiles listed as the fifth-ranked *chaebol* in terms of assets in 2001.

groups are simply an emergent aspect of competitive economic processes. We will address this issue in the conclusion to this book, but for now we should note that in the United States, antitrust laws mask and, to some extent, attenuate, but do not disallow the formation of an American equivalent of business groups, which usually occur in the form of the multidivisional corporations.

Third, our test also suggests that a Marshallian partial equilibrium frame is insufficient to interpret business groups and, more broadly, the organization of economies. Analyses done within a Marshallian frame do not incorporate the competitive intermarket dimensions, particularly cross-market price structures, that our model suggests are instrumental in the self-organization of economies. Therefore, these analyses entirely miss the variation that exists among business groups both within and between economies.

Fourth, to the extent that business groups do differ within and between economies, then we should ask, what is the extent of these differences? Clearly, the management structure and the research and development efforts of Korea's largest *chaebol* not only differ qualitatively from those found in Taiwanese business groups, but also from those found in Korea's smaller *chaebol*. The analysis also implies that the organizational skills needed to run Taiwan's D-groups extend beyond the boundaries of groups themselves, because a large part of the business is organized through interactions with unaffiliated firms. If these differences among business groups in the same economy are differences that make a difference, then an institutional argument based on an institutionally based "organizational logic" or on some common set of institutions becomes increasingly difficult to make.

Fifth, and finally, if there are multiple and equally valid (in economic terms) configurations by which economies can be organized, then why are some economies organized in one way and other economies in another way? More concretely, why did South Korea and Taiwan start down such different paths? That is the core question we address in Part II.

Part II

*Emergence and Divergence
of the Economies*

5

The Origins of Capitalist Economic Organization

Why do business groups in South Korea and Taiwan, as well as the organization of economies in which they are embedded, differ from each other? Why should Korea have moved along a path toward an economy where so much production, especially in the export sectors, is concentrated in only a small number of vertically integrated *chaebol*? Why should Taiwan have taken a very different path, one where business groups firms assemble parts made by unaffiliated firms or where they occupy upstream and service niches in an economy pulled along by downstream demand, mainly from small and medium-sized firms? In the language of our model, why was the "high concentration" equilibrium set selected in Korea and the "low concentration" set selected in Taiwan? The answers to these questions are the subject of Part II.

In the opening chapters of this book, we covered a number of answers that various writers have given to explain the **presence** of business groups, rather than the **differences** among them. These answers usually represent one or a combination of either strong-state, market-failure, or institutional explanations. Although we do not deny the importance of political policies or of problems with capital markets in developing economies, we believe that such factors should be seen as proximate causes, as occurrences or events that trigger economic changes, often extremely important ones, without actually dictating the organizational medium of that change. Moreover, we believe that the organizational medium, and not proximate causes, determines the trajectory of economic development in the long run. But the issues here are complicated ones, which deserve a clear framing before we dive into our answers to the questions posed earlier.

In the initial decades after World War II and the Korean War, the modern capitalist economies of South Korea and Taiwan began to take shape. Although this formative period, roughly between the years of 1955 and 1975, is undoubtedly important in shaping the organization of each of

169

these capitalist economies and in starting the divergence between them, how do we explain what happened in this formative period that leads, causally speaking, to what we observe four decades later? Here we are examining two cases, South Korea and Taiwan, which logically, in these two decades of initial development, may or may not have the same causative factors at work. Because of the interconnectedness of potentially significant factors, causal attribution in historical analysis is difficult because, although quantification may be brought to bear on the issues, the process of attributing adequate causation to any set or sets of factors necessarily rests on qualitative judgments.

The typical explanations of economic development, in general, and of these two cases, in particular, emphasize historically prior events and conditions of the sort that border on accident and happenstance. For example, in this formative period, who could deny the importance of war and the threat of war? In the late 1950s and early 1960s, South Korea was just in the process of reconstruction after a disastrous war with its northern counterpart, and Taiwan, under martial law until July 1987, braced for embargos and, at worst, invasion from the People's Republic of China (PRC). On a per capita basis, in the 1960s, both countries had among the largest standing armies in the world, and four decades later the problems with their socialist alter egos still have not been resolved. As important as these "eventful conditions" are, do they determine, in a causative way, the organizational configuration of the economy? We can say for certain, in the 1960s, that the organization of the socialist economies of North Korea and the PRC were mightily shaped by government command, but can we say the same about South Korea and Taiwan?

As we will describe more fully below, the strong-state theorists make a persuasive case for the role, in the formative decades, of decisive political events in creating the organizational matrix of these economies. Market theorists are typically critical of purely political explanations. Although they recognize the importance of state support for capitalist development, the actual organization of Asian economies, they argue, results from problems in the marketplace, such as an absence of adequate capital markets to build an industrial base (Leff, 1977) and of sufficient information to make and market products in a global economy (Khanna and Palepu, 2000a,b). Business groups, and hence the organization of these economies, they surmise, arise from these market failures.

Although they certainly differ in emphasis, the strong-state and market-failure explanations share many of the same logical features. As we will describe more fully in the next chapter, both sets of explanations create "supply-side narratives" to explain the rapid economic growth that started in the 1960s. These supply-side narratives load all the necessary and sufficient causes both for growth and for divergence into the same gun. Both interpretations argue that unique historical conditions set the initial conditions, from which subsequent patterns emerge. This emphasis on proximate causes works in a very similar way to the technological explanation, drawn from evolutionary economics, that Kenney and von Berg (1999) advanced and that we contrasted with Saxenian's organizational explanation in the first pages of Chapter 3. Seminal events establish a pattern of interaction among key actors. Early successes lock in that pattern, creating an institutionalized system of interdependence that leads to a path-dependent trajectory of development. If one accepts the primacy of proximate causes, then all one needs to do in order to explain the differences in economic organization between South Korea and Taiwan is to demonstrate different sets of immediate forces that pushed each economy in different directions.

This approach is decidedly historicist, concentrating as it does on a narrow set of near-term conditions and ignoring the background factors that shape events without actually causing their occurrence. Our approach, by contrast, suggests that these background factors play decisive roles in how competitive economies (as opposed to command economies) come to be organized, including the decisive reasons that South Korean and Taiwanese economies took divergent organizational paths. The analysis in this chapter concentrates on disentangling proximate causes from background factors, which we identify as institutional and sociological. We argue that institutional and sociological factors present at the time rapid industrialization began were decisive in determining the direction of development.

To repeat a point we made in Chapter 1, it is our view is that economic organization in capitalist economies does not arise from either historical happenstance or historical inevitability. Instead, we see **economic organization as a historical outcome of protracted competitive struggles among economic actors, in which the exercise of authority and market power is: (1) decisive to that outcome and embedded in contexts; (2) where authority and power have institutionalized meanings; and (3) where economic measures (for example, prices, profits, assets, solvency, wealth, conspicuous display) can be used to calculate strategy and to track the performance of relevant actors.** In the last chapter, we demonstrated that our highly stylized model of competitive struggle that we presented has clear relevance to what is found empirically in South Korea and Taiwan. This correspondence between the model and empirical data from the two economies does not, however, indicate that the model is, in any way, the "correct" depiction of the organization of these two economies. Because we are using the model as an ideal type, our successful test of the model merely indicates that there is an "objective probability" that the causal mechanisms we isolated and modeled do, in fact, have explanatory significance in these two cases.[1]

Accordingly, in Part II we analytically untangle these causal factors from other factors in these two economies in order to ascertain whether or not they have actual historical significance. In this chapter, we focus on the structural conditions present at the outset of rapid growth and show that these conditions differed markedly between South Korea and Taiwan. We also note that neither set of structural conditions was sufficient, in and of itself, to generate the rapid economic growth that began in the middle part of the 1960s or to sustain the divergent trajectories of growth that became apparent in the 1970s. In the next chapters, we spell out the conditions that led to the rapid emergence of both economies, namely the retail revolution in the United States and the backward organizational linkages between American retailers and Asian manufacturers. Then in Chapter 7, we demonstrate that the matching process linking Western and Asian firms interacted with the initial conditions to produce different organizational dynamics in the two economies and, subsequently, different paths of development.

Authority and Market Power

As we discussed in Chapter 1, the core features of the economic model in Chapter 3 contain the three elements of Weber's "sociological concept of economic action" (Swedberg, 1998, p. 33): "(1) there is a peaceful attempt to gain power of control and disposal; (2) this action is directed at something that provides an opportunity for utility (either to satisfy one's wants or for profit-making); and (3) the action is oriented to the behavior of others." Of the three, the power to control and dispose, is the "essential" criterion of a sociological concept of economic action, because it "introduce(s) into the analysis of the economies ... the issue of power" (Swedberg, 1998, p. 33). The meaning of power in this sense is legitimate authority or domination (*Herrschaft*), the acknowledged right, in one's economic affairs, to control and to dispose. In this context, authority refers to the right, the legitimate power, of a person to control and dispose of his or her own property and to manage people who have the obligation to obey that person. Within the framework of Weber's discussion of this issue, it is clear that the authority of the *state* is relevant only insofar as the state has property rights (broadly defined) over the economy, allowing it directly to control and dispose of the economy or some

---

[1] For a discussion of "objective probability" in historical analysis, see Ringer's (1997, pp. 63–72) interesting discussion of Weber's use of ideal types.

parts thereof, as well as to manage people within it. Again, it is an empirical question as to whether and to what degree the state has these rights as
matter of course in either South Korea or Taiwan. As we will discuss later
in Chapter 7, the state, in both locations, is certainly not a disinterested
observer. In fact, the state is an active participant in shaping the economy,
but the empirical question concerns the nature of this participation. However, within the model, as well as within Weber's analytic framework, the
power to control and dispose refers to direct control. Insofar as the economy is privately owned, as are large segments of both the South Korean
and Taiwanese economies, then the state is an "economically regulative
organization" and has indirect rather than direct control (Weber, 1978,
pp. 74–5). Simply put, our model purposefully does not include the state
and does not incorporate state power as a distinguishable element. Therefore, in order to test the causal adequacy of the model, the question we
are asking of the historical material is to what extent can South Korea's
and Taiwan's economic organizations be explained as an outcome of a
competitive struggle among non-state economic actors? Insofar as we can
reasonably do so, then we need to rethink the role of the state in developing and developed economies. As we will argue, the state only indirectly
triggers development and reinforces existing patterns of economic organization, often unintentionally, but the state does not directly create the
patterns themselves.

Before we present our case, however, it is essential to have the alternative
explanations clearly in mind. It is essential because these explanations are
persuasive, especially in the Korean case. Therefore, in order for our thesis
to be equally persuasive, we need to show not only the relevance of the
non-state based authority for the formation of business groups in the
immediate post-war period, but also that alternative explanations can be
understood in the same terms.

Proximate Causes

If we just concentrate on the first two decades of post-war economic
growth, roughly from 1950–70, it is very difficult to distinguish between
strong-state and market-failure explanations, so much are they part of
the same story. The story begins with politics.

Both countries began as legitimate, free-standing political units only
at the end of their respective wars; for South Korea, with the end of the
Korea War in 1953 and, for Taiwan, with the defeat of Chiang Kai-shek
and his Kuomintang forces in the Chinese Revolution, their escape from
Mainland China, and the establishment of the Republic of China on
Taiwanese soil in 1949 and 1950. For the next two decades, both sets

of combatants stood armed and ready to resume battle, and even today, nearly five decades later, the possibility of war has not disappeared. This ever-present militancy was especially important in the formative years because the political goals of both countries were definitely not on economic development. Rather, in the early years both controlling regimes concentrated on the immediate problems they faced: creating a "legitimate" basis for rule, rebuilding the economic infrastructure, and reconstructing the agricultural economy to maximize self-sufficiency in food production and reduce rural dissent. By 1955 comprehensive land reform in both countries had made landowners of those who worked the soil. Also, in both countries, the state took over the Japanese-owned businesses, a legacy from the colonial era before World War II, and made some initial and important decisions on the allocation of these assets. In Korea, the Syngman Rhee regime (1953–60) sold most of these businesses for a fraction of their worth to businessmen who were well connected and supportive of his government (E. M. Kim, 1997, Woo-Cumings, 1991). In Taiwan, antagonism between local Taiwanese, who controlled most of the post-war economy, and the Mainlanders, who migrated to Taiwan with Chiang Kai-shek and who controlled the government and military, prompted the state to keep the former Japanese holdings under the control of state officials and party bureaucrats (Gold, 1986).

Apart from these few first steps, which all agree laid an important foundation for later changes, most analysts concentrate on the 1960s as the actual turning point, as the formative period of industrialization. Many writers (Haggard and Moon, 1993, p. 66, Clifford, 1994, p. 39, Fields, 1995, pp. 51–3, E. M. Kim, 1997) examining Korean industrialization give this moment of takeoff a precise time and place. On May 16, 1961, Park Chung Hee, a general in the South Korean Army, led a coup d'etat that seized power from a short-lived democratic government that had been elected into office after Rhee had been forced out. Not long after the coup, as Woo (Woo-Cummings, 1991, p. 84) reports,

> General Park summoned the ten major business leaders and struck a deal with them. In exchange for exempting businessmen from criminal prosecution and respecting their properties whether ill or well gotten, businessmen "paid" fines levied on them by establishing industrial firms and then donating shares to the government. In retrospect, this deal had the quality of an historical compromise; in any case, it occasioned the launching of "Korea Inc." Henceforth, state and big business would share the same destiny: prosper or perish.

Park's regime backed up this "historical moment" by creating what Evans (1995, p. 52) calls a "superagency," the Economic Planning Board, to develop and implement economic policy, and staffed it with U.S.-trained economists. Park also quickly nationalized the Korean banking system and centralized executive control over it. Exerting control over the flow of capital and over would-be capitalists, Park's officials then developed a series of five-year development plans that set national goals and rationalized the effort to become a strong country. In the first five-year plan, Clifford (1994, p. 54) argues, "the state's decision to adopt an export-oriented strategy came about almost by accident" and was strictly a way to redress the lopsided imports and dwindling foreign exchange holdings. But initial successes and, more importantly, Park's recognition that national strength could be equated with industrial might, which in turn could be measured by the world's willingness to buy Korean-made products, increasingly made the government's export exhortations into virtual commands. Park's administration converted "exporting into a national campaign, almost a patriotic duty. Export producers were given priority in investment decisions, credit allocations, and other benefits. Each province set its own export target. And each year the administration's year-end targets became an object of watchful waiting and, when made, the subject of widespread public discussion" (Cole and Lyman, 1971, p. 90; cited by Clifford, 1994, p. 55).

Development theorists further argue that, although these initial steps created the direction and supplied the will to proceed with economic development, much of the credit for development goes to the corps of government officials who did the day-to-day work of implementing policy, monitoring performance, and planning the next steps along the road to industrialization. For Peter Evans (1995), these officials formed a "Weberian bureaucracy" capable of the dispassionate calculation and faithful service needed to do this day-to-day work efficiently.[2] Although

---

[2] From the viewpoint of Weber's sociology, Evans' concept of Weberian bureaucracy is misleading and, as applied to Korea, inaccurate. In the first place, Weber's concept of bureaucracy (1978, pp. 941–1005) is an ideal typical depiction of the organization of officials (the "specific way of distributing the powers of command." Weber, 1978, p. 953) where the legitimate principle of domination is obedience to a system of rational laws (legal rational domination). Evans divorces the apparatus of rule from the principles of domination, and makes all bureaucracy into rational bureaucracy, which may vary in effectiveness. Weber, however, is quite clear when he shows that bureaucracy does not need to arise only from a system of domination based upon legal principles. Instead, until the modern era, bureaucracies were widespread historically in regimes organized on patrimonial principles, which, as this chapter makes clear, is the extension of patriarchal principles beyond the ruler's household. Weber (1978, pp. 1028–31) carefully contrasts patrimonial and legal rational bureaucracies and cites the officialdom in imperial China (Weber, 1978, pp. 1047–51) as the best example of a patrimonial bureaucracy. Imperial Korea could also have been given as an example. The ruling apparatus in modern Korea, especially in the early years after the Korean War, was certainly not organized as a legal rational bureaucracy. This fact has been noted by a number of Weberian scholars (Eisenstadt, 1973, N. Jacobs, 1985, and Biggart, 1990), all of whom characterize the state

recognizing its bureaucratic elements, other writers particularly stress the government's authoritarian control of the economy (Cumings, 1985, Lie, 1998). Either way, the strong-state perspective emphasizes the "primacy of politics" (Pempel, 1999b) and the rigidly bureaucratic means by which politically made economic goals were imposed on a compliant, if not always enthusiastic society. One of the consequences of this "disciplinary mechanism" (Amsden, 1989, pp. 145–7) is that the state was the "visible hand" controlling the economy and creating its industrial structure, particularly the preeminence of the *chaebol*.

Although market-oriented theorists (for example, Lal, 1985, Lau, 1986, Scitovsky, 1986) do not deny the importance of the Korean government's decisions to support economic development, their interpretations are quite different. They see the state's actions as getting the Korean economy in a position to respond freely to economic forces in the global economy, that is, in a position to engage in "free trade." Opening the economy to global forces allowed international trade to become the avenue for Korea's rapid expansion, which in turn allowed particular types of market failures to have decisive roles in shaping Korea's economic structure, sector by sector (Levy, 1991). In fact, several economists, most notably Lal (1983, p. 47), remarked that during the critical growth periods in the 1960s and 1970s, "Far from confuting the liberal case for free trade, Korea provides one example of how periods of virtual free trade have been accompanied by a high rate of income growth which has been lowered whenever that policy has been departed from." Korea's economic success, says Lal (1983, p. 46), "has been achieved *despite* intervention" from the state.

Although strong-state theorists (Amsden, 1989, Wade, 1990, Woo-Cumings, 1999) argue vehemently against this kind of market interpretation, there cannot be much doubt that both political and economic conditions in the formative period greatly influenced Korea's takeoff and subsequent development. If we were just considering the Korean case, then it would be easy to argue that this combination of eventful conditions was a sufficient cause for the formation of Korea's concentrated form of economic organization. But we are not considering Korea in isolation, and our contrast between South Korea and Taiwan does not make this attribution so obvious after all.

Although Taiwan's economic development did not have such a dramatic beginning as did South Korea's, both strong-state and market theorists use

and business as being organized according to the principles of patrimonial bureaucracy. Given the predominance of personal rule in South Korea, both in the government from 1950 on and in the business empires created by the *chaebol*, there can be no doubt that patrimonial features had to persist into the modern era, which is a point developed in this chapter. Driven to prove his strong-state theory, however, Evans has persistently overstated the role of rational bureaucracy, in particular, and the role of the rational state, in general, as an explanatory variable in the process of economic development.

the same set of forces to account for the growth: For Taiwan, too, strong-state theorists (Amsden, 1985, Gold, 1986, Winckler and Greenhalgh, 1988, Pang, 1992, Wade, 1991, Haggard and Pang, 1994, Evans, 1995) emphasize strong government, economic policy agencies staffed with U.S.-trained economists, a series of four-year plans, centralized control of a state-owned banking system, and ownership of substantial and crucial portions of industrial production. While not denying the state's role, market theorists (Myers, 1984, Levy, 1991, Dollar and Sokoloff, 1994, Lau, 1986) argue that export-oriented manufacturing under conditions of a liberal trade regime fueled Taiwan's high growth even more than it did for South Korea.

Although both sets of theorists stress the similarities, they also see some important differences between South Korea and Taiwan, differences that contribute to divergence in economic outcomes. Unlike the political turmoil that occurred in South Korea, in Taiwan, the government was stable and centralized throughout the entire formative period. As Wade (1991, p. 71) remarks:

> The positions of president of the Republic, chairman of the party, and commander-in-chief of the armed forces have been held by only two individuals, Chiang Kai-shek up to 1975, and his son, Chiang Ching-kuo thereafter (to his death in 1988). The legislature has been kept ineffectual by the powerful executive branch of government. All civil associations are controlled by the state or the party; labor unions, particularly, are kept inactive and dependent.

Most strong-state analysts (Amsden, 1985, Gold, 1986, Winckler and Greenhalgh, 1988, Pang, 1992, Wade, 1991, Haggard and Pang, 1994, Evans, 1995) cite this coercive stability as evidence that the Taiwanese government was more authoritarian and more in control of the economy than was the case in Korea. Economic development in Taiwan during this period was viewed as "a textbook case of elite-led revolutionary social transformation" (Gold, 1986, p. 64). The leading indicator of this top-down transformation was the state's direct ownership of around 50 percent of Taiwan's total industrial production for most of the 1950s. Even through the 1960s, state and party ownership of the economy remained substantial, averaging about 43 percent, a figure much higher than was the case in South Korea or Japan. Controlling the "heights of the economy" (Gold, 1986, p. 75), the government also encouraged the formation of large business groups in sectors that the government targeted for growth, such as in textiles and plastics. "These biggest groups, combined with state monopolies and foreign investors," concludes Amsden (1991, p. 1124), "may have accounted for a higher degree of market concentration in 'upstream' industries than in South Korea."

If Taiwan's economy were shaped by very similar forces as South Korea's, except for the fact that Taiwan's state was supposedly more powerful and in better control of the economy, then, all other things being equal, one might predict that Taiwan's economic organization would have remained highly concentrated in the formative period and might have become even more concentrated in subsequent decades. Of course, this outcome did not occur, and, moreover, the trajectory went decisively in the opposite direction. By the 1980s, it was clear that small, medium-sized, and modestly large firms had become export motors propelling the economic transformation. If there was ever a case of bottom-up industrialization, then Taiwan's industrialization would be that case. How did the Taiwan government lose control on what it supposedly had such a firm grasp?

From the viewpoint of strong-state theory, the emergence and increasing importance of Taiwan's small and medium-sized firms presents an interpretive problem, a paradigmatic anomaly if you will, that needs to be explained. A number of strong-state theorists, including Evans (1995, pp. 55–60), note some differences between Taiwan and South Korea, including the fact that Taiwan's state apparatus intervened less in the economy than did the Korean state, but contend, nonetheless, that state-owned industries and the large business groups continued to control the rest of the economy through their extensive networks. Acknowledging the interpretive problem more clearly, Shafer (1997, pp. 115–16, our emphasis) states, "There is an easy explanation for this divergence (in firm size and degree of concentration). . . . *Korea and Taiwan diverged because their leaders chose different policies to effect restructuring.*" Whereas the Korean state "chose to restructure by building national champions through the use of policies that encouraged economic concentration," the Kuomintang regime chose not to enrich and thereby to empower the native Taiwanese. They instead chose policies that "avert(ed) the growth of economically and politically powerful large firms and reinforce(d) barriers to collective action by business and labor." This statement echoes Wade's (1990, p. 325) earlier conclusion that the difference in firm concentration reflects a "difference in government strategy."

Although he is clear about the direction of causation, with state policy causing business organization, Wade (1990, p. 328) in his actual discussion of Taiwan's development implies that the organization of the economy leads the government to act in particular ways, which in turn reinforce that organization:

> Taiwan's small and nimble firms were quite responsive to profit opportunities opened by the public investments; while Korea's concentrated structure allowed the government to target its

industry-specific policies at a small number of firms each capable of a substantial response. Moreover, Korea's big firms, undertaking more head-on challenges to multinationals in high-volume, low-profit markets, needed direct assistance to surmount the high entry barriers. Taiwan's niche-seeking firms needed less firm-specific help (which would in any case have been more expensive to deliver, because of numbers), but had relatively more need for stable prices and real exchange rates, being more vulnerable in export markets to price and exchange rate instability than the risk-spreading Korean business groups.

Statements like this one might have prompted Wade to ask which comes first, economic organization or economic policy? But no such issue was raised.

This same ambiguity is found in Alice Amsden's (1991) well-argued effort to account for the anomaly. She begins by stating, for the decades of the 1950s and 1960s, that big firms in Taiwan (including the large state-owned sector) controlled a larger portion of production than was the case in any other developed or developing country. She (1991, p. 1124) says that, in the absence of a convincing theory of changes or firm size during economic development, "intuition and the law of comparative advantage suggest that typically firms will start small and grow larger." This shift toward larger firms should accelerate, she adds, when "capital-intensive industries emerge and scale economies become more important." In Taiwan, however, by the late 1980s, the total contribution of large firms had declined and the contribution of small and medium-sized firms had increased, a trend that accelerated as Taiwan's exports increased rapidly and as Taiwan's industry upgraded from labor- to capital-intensive manufacturing. She (1991, pp. 1124–5) argues that the decisive factor in explaining Taiwan's firm structure is the fact that "state enterprises and multinational corporations have tended to be more important in Taiwan than in some other late-industrializing countries, certainly Japan and South Korea. The reasons for this are primarily political (reflecting) a bias against big private business, which was exacerbated by the ethnic differences between the Taiwanese business community and the Mandarin-dominated Kuomintang political elite."

Although Amsden stresses the decisive importance of politics in creating this bias, as well as in moving the center of industrialization to the rural countryside, she also recognizes large firms continued to exist in this climate and that what seemed most important for these large firms was precisely the emergence of small firms. Unlike in Korea and Japan, she (1991, p. 1129) observes, "subcontracting in Taiwan is characterized by a highly developed division of labor.... In general, firms are relatively less vertically integrated." Not knowing quite how to interpret the facts, she (1991, p. 1129) notes that the big firms primarily make intermediate inputs, but these "'up-stream' producers of heavy capital goods and chemicals apparently do not export directly but instead supply inputs to smaller domestic firms.... The obvious conclusion is that big and small business need each other." She does not push these observations further. Instead, she (1991, p. 1133) concludes by returning to her main thesis, namely that "it is necessary ... to recognize the power that the state has wielded over both industry and agriculture and, consequently, its ability to arrange a marriage of convenience between the two."

Although both Wade and Amsden seem to recognize that economic organization has an existence apart from the state and that the state is a regulator of this interaction among firms, they do not examine these features in depth. Instead, both writers conclude that the immediate consequence of government policies was to organize the economy in specific ways and, moreover, that these policies and the officials who enforced them directly controlled the trajectory of development.

In general terms, then, strong-state and market-failure interpretations for South Korea and Taiwan focus on precise policies and particular people, all serving as "real and sufficient" causes both for the organization of firms in the economy and for the trajectory of economic development in the formative period and in the decades that follow. Both sets of interpretations locate these causes endogenously, internal to the societies in question, making the explanations for the rapid growth strictly production-based interpretations, the essence of a supply-side narratives, as we term them in the next chapter. It is our contention, that, although these endogenous proximate causes are very important, their causal effects cannot be understood unless these immediate causes – the people and events – are framed within social, institutional, and long-term historical contexts. To paraphrase Max Weber (1958, p. 280), although these social, institutional, and historical patterns do not actually "cause" industrialization, they nonetheless provide a path of least resistance along which people, driven by their economic interests, can travel.

We now begin our own explanation.

The Structural Origins of Capitalist Economic Organization

We narrow our focus to the precise features represented in our model: competitive struggle in the context where economic actors have the authority to control and dispose of economic activity. We will examine three aspects of this competitive struggle: In this chapter, we show, first, the institutional meaning of authority in relation to control of economic assets and rights over property and, second, the lineup of economically active participants actually capable of exercising their authority and market power in the economy in the years immediately after World War II. In Chapters 6 and 7, we look at the third key factor, the presence of global economic opportunities that economically active participants could respond to and take advantage of, and the interaction between these opportunities and an array of the available responses, the paths of least resistance alluded to above. In this chapter, by contrasting the background conditions in South Korea and Taiwan, we show that the two economies had very different starting points that led, under conditions of rapid growth, to divergent paths of development.

Succession and Control

It is easy to demonstrate substantial differences between Korean and Chinese societies in people's ability routinely to control and dispose of economic assets. The place to begin this comparison is one of the key points of economic control in family-based societies, namely the ability to transfer assets across generations. Historically, inheritance patterns between Korean and Chinese societies differ dramatically. Throughout the last period of agrarian rule in Korea, the Chosen dynasty (1392–1910), Koreans practiced a form of primogeniture, in which the eldest sons preferentially received the lion's share of their fathers' estates. During the same period in late imperial China, which covers the last two dynasties, the Ming (1368–1644) and the Qing (1644–1911), the Chinese practiced partible inheritance or multigeniture, in which all sons received equal shares of their fathers' estates. This seemingly small difference in normative practice points to substantial differences in economic organization between the two societies, especially differences in landowning, the foundation of agrarian economies. In this section, we will examine these historical patterns and argue that, although much has changed in recent times, the structural underpinnings for these patterns remain in effect in the post–World War II era, especially in the formative years before 1985.

In the Choson dynasty, up through the middle of the nineteenth century, landholding in Korea was highly concentrated, organized in large estates, and controlled by elite families, who collectively constituted the *yangban* class. It was the elite *yangban* families that institutionalized primogeniture as the normative pattern to pass down their privileges and economic resources to succeeding generations. "The Korean *yangban*," according to Martina Deuchler (1992, p. 12), "showed the characteristics of a hereditary aristocracy that effectively controlled access to political power by

defining eligibility for the examinations and occupied the upper eche-
lons in government, possessed large landed wealth, and generally enjoyed
the prestige and culture Confucian education conferred upon them."
Deuchler (1992, p. 45) explains that, before the *yangban* elite rose to
prominence in the early years in the Chosen dynasty, the inheritance system had been bilateral in which both male and female lines of descent
"enjoyed equal rights and duties," and in principle sons and daughters
received equal shares of inherited property. But as the *yangban* elites grew
politically more powerful as a landowning status group, they adopted neo-
Confucianism (a reinterpretation of Confucianism developed in China
during the Song dynasty, 960–1280 A.D.) as a means to legitimate and to
consolidate their control within the agrarian empire.

The details of this adoption are important, because they pinpoint differences between the Korean and Chinese cases. As Deuchler convincingly
argues (1992), the Confucianization of the elite legitimized the formation
of patrilineages, which distinguished between male and female lines of
descent and, among males, differentiated senior and junior branches of the
patriline (that is, between older and younger brothers and their subsequent
descent lines). Progressively, the senior branch of the patriline, which had
ritual authority over other branches, also claimed economic superiority.
The result was the formation of a type of primogeniture (Deuchler, 1992,
pp. 223–30). The eldest sons of elite families retained the largest share
of the inheritance, usually about two-thirds of the fathers' estates. More
importantly, the senior patriline of the lineage also claimed the right to
hold and control the corporate property of the lineage itself. This practice
meant that entire estates could be passed intact from generation to generation. Over time, control of landed resources became highly concentrated
in the hands of privileged landowners who were able to shape political
institutions to substantiate and legitimate their privileges.

By contrast in Chinese society, which includes Taiwan, the landholding
patterns were very different. China covers a very large and geographically
very diverse area. It is, therefore, not surprising that China did not have
a uniform agrarian system, even though partible inheritance was the rule
throughout all of late imperial China (Shiga, 1978). Nevertheless, none of
the regional variations in landholding that existed in late imperial times
resembled that of Korea in the same period.

In northern China, which is the area adjacent to the present-day North
Korea, where maize and wheat were staples, tenancy rates were very low.
The families who tiled the soil owned most land. Rowe (1985, p. 248)
calls this pattern of landholding the "yeoman farmer" type, and notes that
there was very little concentration of landholding. In Central and South
China, where rice was the staple and where double and triple cropping
was common, rates of tenancy were much higher. In some places, up to

90 percent of all peasants were tenants (Rowe, 1985, p. 249). But in all these same locations, the peasant tenants were the ones who made their own economic decisions. In fact, the economic power of tenants was formalized through a system of divided ownership that was common throughout most of the rice-growing regions, a system known as the "one-field, two lords" (*yitian liangzhu*) (Rawski, 1972, Palmer, 1987, Eastman, 1988). The landlord owned the subsoil; the tenant owned the topsoil. Not only could tenants sell topsoil rights to others, but they could also sublet the land on a permanent basis, giving rise to a "one-field, three lords" system. "Whether with three lords or two," comments Eastman (1988, p. 77), "the position of the first lord, the so-called landlord, was usually unenviable. He not only found it difficult to evict the topsoil owner, even if payment of the rent was in arrears, but also as *de jure* owner, had to pay the taxes. In most areas, therefore, ownership of the topsoil rights was highly attractive, often selling for considerably more than the subsoil rights." Where the two- and three-lord system prevailed, as it did throughout South China, including Taiwan, subsoil owners were reduced to absentee landlords with very little power to retrieve the land or to control its utilization. Small landowners, sharecropper, and even tenants exerted greater control over agricultural decision making than did larger landowners – the exact opposite outcome that occurred in the Korean case.

Partible inheritance and the separation of topsoil and subsoil rights led to the fragmentation and diversification of landholding through a constant process of subdivision and re-accumulation. Both tenant and rentier lands were continually being subdivided among sons. Successful sons would buy or rent more land, but the land they accumulated would consist of small, scattered plots, rather than large, contiguous fields. Such dispersed plots could not be farmed through efficient economy of scale techniques, but rather perpetuated the tenancy system, for as soon as more land was accumulated than a household could easily farm, then the owner of topsoil or subsoil rights would sell or sublet the parcel. In such circumstances, land ownership for both subsoil and topsoil owners became widely commercialized. As Huang (1990, p. 330) notes, "a peasant economy under partible inheritance requires a land market to reproduce itself: a peasant inheriting less land than his household can survive on has to be able to purchase or rent land." Land, therefore, became owned as much for speculation and investment as for production and subsistence.

Like primogeniture in Korea, the practice of partible inheritance in late imperial China was reinforced by neo-Confucian reforms implemented during the sixteenth century, when the principle of patrilineage (*tsung*) was renewed and lineage halls were built throughout China (Chow, 1994). However, instead of emphasizing inequality among patrilines, as the

Koreans did, Chinese continued to stress the importance of the household (*jia*) as the basic unit of economic control. At least from Song times on, Chinese thinkers understood the contradiction between authority vested in patrilines as opposed to authority vested in households. During the resurgence of neo-Confucianism in the Song dynasty, some writers advocated rebuilding society on the basis of patrilines, and had they been successful, observed Denis Twitchett (1959, p. 132), "it might well have had the revolutionary effect of enabling the new landowning class that arose in Song time to establish themselves as a separate and permanent hereditary 'gentry' of landowners. But, as it happened, the division of inheritance continued, and (the patrilineage became) a ritual group" (Twitchett, 1959).[3] In the Chinese case, therefore, the patrilineage served as a ritualized group structured through authoritative households, instead of, as in the Korean case, a system of authoritative patrilineages that politically and economically structured subordinate households.

In summary, then, both the Korean and the Chinese systems of family-based controls over economic resources are based on shared Confucian ideals, but the two societies institutionalized opposing principles embedded in the doctrines. Whereas the Korean system allows for intergenerational concentration of economic resources within families, the Chinese system requires egalitarian distribution of resources within families across generations. These inheritance practices continue today with some important variations. As we will discuss in Chapter 7, primogeniture among *chaebol* owners is the preferred practice. *Chaebol* founders have ability to pick their own successor, which is preferably, but not always their eldest son, and thereby to pass the entire *chaebol* organization intact to the next generation. By contrast, in Taiwan, as well as in other Chinese societies, the owners of large firms and business groups almost universally practice multigeniture, in which the father's estate is divided among sons (and now sometimes among daughters as well) at the time of the father's choosing or after his death. So much is this a practice that Wong Siu-lun (1985) has shown that the Chinese family firm in modern times has a three-generational pattern that is an artifact of these inheritance practices.[4]

---

[3] In their rejection of the concentrating authority in the patriline, the Chinese continued to stress the centrality of the household as the unit controlling economic resources (Shiga, 1978, Watson, 1982, Ebrey, 1984, Chow, 1994, Fei, 1992). In China, therefore, the conception of patriline, concludes Ebrey (1984, p. 232), "developed as a compromise between classical *tsung* (clan) principles and the imperatives of the contemporary institution of the *jia*. The notion of patriline implicit in many legal decisions is that of a descent line with a focus not on a distant ancestor (as in the *tsung* model) but on each individual adult. Just as brothers were potential heads of separate *jia*, they would each also continue a separate line."

[4] Wong's model is as follows: In the first generation of the three-generation cycle, the father founds and successfully expands his business, and he brings his sons into the business

These very different principles governing inheritance do not occur in an institutional vacuum, but rather exist as a part of a cluster of factors that represent very distinctive economic systems in pre-modern as well as modern times. We should emphasize that we are not stressing cultural, as much as we are stressing structural, differences between Korea and China. We further note that such structural differences between culturally very similar societies are not unusual. For example, the American colonies, which shared the same English culture, differed dramatically in inheritance practices. As Walton and Rockoff (1994, p. 59) report, primogeniture was the law in the Southern colonies where wealthy plantation owners were "loathe to divide the plantations into smaller units" and where "legislative power – rested in (their) hands." By contrast, multigeniture was the law throughout New England and the middle colonies. Free-holding family farmers "had a keen vested interest in multigeniture. By this legal form of inheritance, each son was motivated to stay at home (or nearby) longer and work (with less supervision) more diligently to maintain and expand the family farm." Similarly, in medieval Europe, different estate groups followed different marriage and inheritance practices simultaneously, the aristocracy preserving their patrimony by means of arranged marriages and primogeniture and other estate groups using different principles for marriage and inheritance (Duby, 1981). As these examples show, the different inheritance practices in Korea and China point to their being embedded in very different economic and political systems, a difference captured, in Weber's terminology (1978), in the opposition between "patrimonialism," on the one hand, and "patriarchy," on the other hand.

Patrimonialism and Patriarchy

Max Weber used to the concept of "patrimonialism" to define a situation in which patriarchy (that is, the right of the male head of household to rule over the household) is extended beyond the household as a principle of domination to rule over a more extensive population. Although the concept does not quite fit Asian societies (Hamilton, 1984a, 1990), the concept is still useful to contrast the situation in Korea with that in China. In Chosen Korea, elite authority over land and people rested on kinship

to help him run it. At the time of the father's death, the second generation, that of the sons, takes over, and if they get along well, they share the business. If they do not, then they each take an equal share. If they do stay together, however, the third generation will almost invariably divide the assets, because now the sons of the sons (the cousins) have to cooperate in running the business. The cousins, however, are seldom able to overcome the inherent inequality that will have emerged: Some of the sons of the second generation will likely have more sons than others. The conflict in interest among cousins can only be resolved by splitting the father's estate equally along the lines of the sons in the second generation.

principles. The eldest male in the senior patriline extended his authority over his junior kinsmen and their households and lines of descent, over his own and his lineage properties, and, most importantly, over his slaves and later his tenants on the basis of his patriarchal position as head of household in the senior patriline. The principles embodied in his rule were the dependencies established through his relationships with others and their obedience to the demands of these relationships, backed up by his own ability (including relying on the state) to enforce that obedience. Patrimonialism is, therefore, a system of control that exaggerates patriarchy in one social location and negates it in other locations. The institutionalization of slavery in Korea is a clear indication of this imbalance.

In Chosen, Korea, the *yangban* families were geographically so extensive and socially and politically so powerful that they were also able to bind peasant agriculturists to the soil through developing what Palais (1996, p. 225) calls "a closed hereditary system of slavery." Noting differences between Western and Korean forms of slavery, Palais (1996, pp. 210–11) remarks that Korean slavery was like other forms of slavery in that "Slaves could be bought and sold, given as gifts, or inherited. They conformed to the definition of chattel property and were referred to as such." The actual proportion of the total population classified as slaves was huge. During most of the Choson period before the middle of the eighteenth century, the percentage of slaves in Korea's total population is estimated to range from 30 to 50 percent (Palais, 1996, pp. 251–2). As Deuchler (1992, p. 206) makes clear, Korea's system of slavery was directly related to the elite's near monopoly on landowning:

> The land and slaves that constituted most private property were linked in close economic interdependence: the cultivation of land demanded a labor force of slaves; the slaves sustained themselves by land. The slaves not only worked the fields, they were also indispensable domestic servants. In short, slaves were the "hands and feet" of the elite, and their numbers indicated the degree of their master's prosperity.

The elite families, however, were not the only slave owners. The largest slave owner was the royal household. Palais (1966, p. 217) estimates that "the system of servile state labor...at its height numbered over 350,000 slaves and was not brought to an end until 1801."

Slavery was not officially abolished in Korea until 1894. However, beginning in the seventeenth century and continuing through the eighteenth century, a series of political reforms defined the distinction between slaves and commoners, allowing many slaves to convert their status into that of tax-paying commoners (Palais, 1996, p. 270). As a consequence of these reforms, the numbers of slaves declined greatly in the eighteenth century, with most slaves becoming tenants, not unlike what occurred in the American South. By the nineteenth century, tenancy rates had mushroomed, approaching those in South China. Unlike in South China, however, tenants throughout the nineteenth century had no subsoil rights; landholding still consisted of owning large, contiguous estates; and the landowner maintained economic control over decisions involving the utilization of the land directly or more often through an intermediary class of rural agents (*tosaum and saum*), essentially bailiffs, whom the landlord used to control rural populations (Shin, 1978).

As the institution of slavery shows, in Korea household-based authority of the senior patriline extended as far as ties of dependency could reach, up to the level of the state and down to the lowliest slave and tenant. This is what patrimonialism means: it is a way of organizing a system of control through extending principles of authority vested in the family beyond the family itself. As we will show in Chapter 7, in the early years of industrialization before 1985, *chaebol* owners used analogous techniques to manage their business groups, techniques that center on the patriarchal authority of the owner and that draw on ties of dependency to extend that control beyond the owner's family to encompass the entire *chaebol*.

As a general rule, and with the important exception of the Chinese imperial household,[5] patrimonialism is not a concept that applies to household authority either in late imperial China or modern Chinese societies, including Taiwan. For Chinese societies, it is apparent that a very different system of control was institutionalized and that this system had very different consequences for the allocations of economic resources than that which occurred in Korea. The Chinese system centers on what is known as "common living, common budget" (*tongju gongcai*). The phrase defined, and to some extent continues to define, in China and Taiwan, what constitutes a household (*jia*): All those who live together hold their economic resources in common.

"Common living, common budget" said the great Japanese scholar of Chinese law, Shuzo Shiga (1978, p. 114), denotes "a joint account relationship that covered all the aspects of consumption and the maintenance of wealth; the fruits of labor of all the members and the profits accruing from commonly owned wealth were treated as income, and all the members' living expenses . . . were paid out of it." The counterpart to this system in the United States is the pooling of husband's and wife's incomes in a common account, out of which all expenses are paid. In China, though, this system extended across generations. All those individuals defined as

---

[5] The imperial household was clearly organized on the basis of patrimonial logic. The core officials were eunuchs and bondservants who served in high positions at the pleasure of the imperial ruler. See, for instance, Tsai (1996) and Wu (1970, pp. 38–51).

being within a joint account relationship "legally" constitute a household.[6] The property of a household (*jiachan*) is, says Shuzo (1978, p. 114), "nothing other than a designation of wealth managed by such a joint account." In other words, the concept of "household property" does not imply that such property "should remain intact for generations." Quite the opposite, household property, including land, "could, depending on the household income and expenditures, be bought and sold with comparative nonchalance." "What this means," Shuzo concludes, "was that household property was, in essence, a fluid value that could be grasped quantitatively and that (in traditional times) land was the safest accumulation device into which to convert it. Consequently, every time the joint account relationship itself was broken up, the land too could be parceled up in any way whatever." In modern terms, and often in modern practice as well, the concept of household property means nothing more than a portfolio of assets.

As a principle of economic action, the "common living, common budget" system leads to three consequences. First, the norms of familial authority also double as the norms of authority for making economic decisions. Roughly speaking, these norms can be characterized as "patriarchal," in the sense that everyone in the household owes their final obedience (*xiao*) to the male head of household, and as "patrilineal" in the sense that the descent line and moral ordering within the family follow the relationship between father and son (Bellah, 1970, Fei, 1992).[7] Even though, in normative terms, the male head of household can be said to control the economic behavior of household members, he does not actually own the assets of the household, but rather he holds them as a custodian for the whole household during his lifetime and has a moral obligation to grow and pass on these assets to his sons and their sons' sons (Baker, 1979). This linkage between father and son also implies a fundamental equality among sons/brothers. As long as there is one household, what belongs to the father belongs equally and collectively to all the sons as well. It is in this sense that Shuzo (1978, 119) concludes that "there is no conceptual contradiction in the notion of 'common living, common budget' under conditions of a single person's ownership." Everything owned individually is in the portfolio of household assets.

The second consequence is that the collectivity that constitutes the household can expand only so far before it must divide into multiple households (*fenjia*), each adopting their own version of "common-living,

---

[6] Chinese law can be conceived of as moral law, as opposed to legal-rational law. For a good analysis of the absence of Western style law in China, see Ruskola, 2000.

[7] For analyses of the normative foundations of patriarchal authority in Chinese families, see Baker, 1979 and Fei, 1992.

common budget." In practice, even in pre-modern China, it was rare for a household to contain more than three generations – parents, sons and unmarried daughters, and sons' wives and children (Baker, 1979). (Married daughters and their children leave their natal household and become members of their husband's household.) In fact, Shuzo (1978, p. 116) cites a number of studies covering the period from the Han dynasty to modern times showing the size of a typical household to be five or six people. This figure no doubt masks considerable regional and historical variation, but the general point is correct: In late imperial times, Chinese households tended to be relatively small and, from an economic perspective, centralized, internally cooperative, accumulative, and flexible. And we should add, they embodied a gender division of labor, with work clearly divided between men and women of the household (Fei, 1992, Baker, 1979).

There are several reasons for the persistence of such relatively small and economic active households in China, but certainly two of the most important are, first, the difficulty, after the father dies, of centralizing control over household assets among brothers who each have a right to an equal share of the estate, and, second, the impossibility, after the brothers die, to centralize control among cousins who do not have an equal share of household properties.[8] Therefore, households typically divide assets after the death of every previous generation and sometimes before; for example, during their own lifetimes, parents can decide to divide the household.[9] Whenever household assets are divided, however, it is a serious matter:

> Division of household property . . . means a legal act whereby the actual wealth of the household is calculated, omitting no sum whether great or small, and divided among all; the joint account relationship that hitherto governed both income and expenditure is severed. Consequently, even in households having virtually no wealth to distribute, "division of household property" has great significance in the sense that it severs the joint account relationship. (Shuzo, 1978, p. 116)

---

[8] An estate is divided equally among the sons of the household founder, but not equally among the sons' sons.

[9] Shuzo (1978, p. 116) writes as follows:

> The precise point in time when division of the household's property takes place is not fixed and has no direct connection with the death of the father of the household. It may be provided for by the parents during their own lifetime, or it may be attended to some time after their deaths. However, whenever the deed is done, it must be done simultaneously for all the brothers, or if the brothers are all dead, for all the cousins. This applies even in cases in which there are brothers who are too young to be independent. At such times the parents, if they are alive, or if not, one of the brothers, will take the youngsters in charge and rear them, managing their respective shares of the property in the role of guardian.

The very success of the "common living, common budget" system depends on the frequency, fairness, and finality of household division.

The third and, for our contrast with Korea, the most important consequence of the "common living, common budget" system is what we might call the "all men are brothers" complex.[10] Patriarchal authority, as a rule, does not extend beyond the household. Everyone is a member of some household, and is subject to the constraints of authority and obedience that is defined within that household. Strictly in normative terms, therefore, the patriarchal authority lodged in any one household should not reach beyond the boundaries of that household because it butts up against the patriarchal authority in someone else's household. This fact is even, or we should say, especially, true for brothers. Once a household is divided, brothers become independent and no longer form a cooperative unit as they necessarily did before the household split. In fact, they become competitors, each trying to expand the resources of his own household, often at the expense of his brother's (Baker, 1979). Because there was no legitimate way around this fact, there was also no institutionalized mechanism in pre-modern Chinese society that allowed household patriarchy to be turned into patrimonial authority. Therefore, in normative terms, each household was viewed as being equivalent, that is, equally legitimate as a locus of authority and equally autonomous in terms of its decision-making powers. This equivalence among households led to the development in late imperial China of formally egalitarian relationships among household heads, which is captured in the phrase "All men are brothers."

The "all men are brothers" complex in China, of course, never led to economic equality among households, although in the long run it may have reduced the level of inequality by narrowing extremes between the very rich and very poor (Brandt and Sands, 1990). Nevertheless, this condition of household equivalence did structure, and even today continues to structure, the economic and political relationships among households. This is not the place for an extended discussion of how household equivalence institutionally plays out in modern as well as late imperial China. Here it is important only to describe these manifestations in analytical terms so that we can understand the organizational dynamics among entrepreneurial households in Taiwan after World War II.

From late imperial times up to the present day, there has been widespread use of organizational devices balancing the ability to maintain

---

[10] "All Men Are Brothers" is the English title of a famous Chinese novel, *Shui Hu Chuan*, from the Ming dynasty. The title refers to the ties of fictive kinship that join an association of bandits in common endeavors. The presence of such associations evoking ties of fictive kinship were exceedingly common in all sorts of legitimate, as well illegitimate groups.

the authority, prerogatives, and autonomy of individual households, on the one hand, and the necessity to establish alliances beyond the household in order to take advantage of economic opportunities and grow household assets, on the other hand. These organizational devices are voluntary on the part of participants and can be thought of as institutionalized "locations" or "occasions" for building and maintaining relationships based on the principle of reciprocity that, in turn, might lead to mutual advantage vis-à-vis others not party to the relationship. We should think of these alliances for the purpose of mutual advantage as creating horizontally based "patronage networks" (Faure, 1989), essentially fluid and flexible networks designed to build positions of economic power (that is, market power) held collectively (if not always equally) by insiders in relation to others who are not a part of the alliance. Furthermore, we should emphasize that once these networks are going concerns, they represent collective monopolies that effectively counter the building of individually owned monopolies (Hamilton, 1985).

"The proliferations of patronage networks," observes Faure (1989), "was the mainstream in the development of economic institutions in the Ming and Qing." For example in late imperial times, regional associations (*huiguan*) and trade associations (*gungzuo*), which were the medium through which almost all commerce and most non-rural occupations were organized, were voluntary patronage networks that effectively controlled all aspects of business (Hamilton, 1985, Faure, 1989, Hamilton and Chang, 2003).[11] Similar network-based associations were widespread in rural society, including various forms of religious organizations, irrigation societies, literary clubs, and surname associations. Most importantly, as Faure (1989; see also Ruskola, 2000) clearly demonstrates, higher order kinship associations (the so-called clan or *tsung*) were also patronage networks, voluntary associations of people with the same surname who used ritual worship of a distant, common ancestor as the location (ancestral

---

[11] These associations were locations where merchants and artisans from the same region met, where each group of traders collectively decided on the standards of their business, and where individuals made deals with one another. We should note that the commercial world in late imperial China was huge, the largest in the world up until the eighteenth century, and that the late imperial state did not regulate any aspect of this world – did not standardize weights and measure, did not guarantee a medium of exchange, played no role in credit institutions, and did not back up its own paper currency. Regional and trade associations created and maintained all aspects of business and they did so in a way that allowed fellow regionals access to economic opportunities and at the same time coercively regulated their activities, forcing them to conform to group standards. These regional associations continued in force until 1949, when the Communist revolution closed down all privately owned firms. *Huiguan* reemerged after 1978 economic reforms, when rural to urban migration again became common and when private ownership began to spread. Outside the Mainland, these and other similar associations proliferated wherever the Chinese migrated – mainly Southeast Asia and North America.

hall) and the occasion (periodic observance of ritual) to form networks to control economic activities in the countryside. In all such networks, including clan associations, positions of greatest influence did not follow from ascribed but rather from achieved positions, for the simple reason that those individuals having the highest level of achievement (for example, degree holders, literati, landownership, and commercial wealth) typically had the most connections to outsiders, and thus could serve as the best patrons for others in the network.

Structurally similar networks of mutual advantage are commonplace in modern Chinese societies as well,[12] and there is a large literature describing how they work in contemporary Taiwan.[13] In order not to confuse the cause and the consequence of rapid economic development in Taiwan, we merely want to show, at this point in our explanation, that in the immediate post-war years in Taiwan the background conditions structuring authority and control over economic assets set the stage, as it were. Competing patriarchal households, a propensity and strategies for creating horizontal networks among these households, and a willingness to use these as a way to gain economic power – all these factors formed the institutional backdrop that was in place in Taiwan in the post–World War II era. None of these factors actually caused the rapid growth that Taiwan would undergo in the late 1960s and 1970s, but they did provide the medium of economic development, the organization through which growth occurred.

In conclusion, the background of economic institutions and family practices dramatically differed between Korean and Chinese societies. In South Korea, on the eve of industrialization, past history and then current family practices made an economy organized through large, centrally controlled firms a likely possibility, a path of least resistance. By equal measure, in Taiwan, on the eve of industrialization, past history and then current family practices made an interlinked small-firm economy also a likely possibility. Both paths mirrored a pre-industrial past and rested on reproduced patterns of household and inter-household authority. Whatever their potential, however, in the years immediately after World War II, these institutionally framed paths represent one among many trajectories that might have occurred. We need look only across the 38th Parallel at

---

[12] A brief survey of this literature is found in the introduction to Fei (1992) and in King (1991, 1985). More recent works include Yan (1996), Yang (1994), Kipnis (1997), Landa (1994), Yao (1987), Tong and Yee (1998), Menkhoff (1993), Luo (1997), Lui (2001), and Chung and Hamilton (2001).

[13] There is no general survey of this literature relative to Taiwan, but in relation to business practices see Chen (1994, 1995), Shieh (1992), Hamilton (1997), Kao (1991, 1999), and Hsing (1997). In relation to politics and social institutions, see Jacobs (1979), Cohen (1976), and Hwang (1987).

North Korea, or across the Taiwan Straits at the People's Republic of China, to see alternative outcomes. That capitalist economic growth did occur is to be explained by other factors rather than these institutional ones described. For these factors, we need to look at the individuals who actually had a hand in building the new economy.

The Entrepreneurial Potential

About twenty year separates the end of World War II in 1945, which also marked the end of Japanese colonialism in South Korea and Taiwan, from the beginnings of rapid industrialization in the late 1960s and early 1970s. In these twenty years, South Korea and Taiwan encountered many similar situations that helped fix the course of economic development that would follow. Civil war tore both Korean and Chinese societies apart, leading to new governments being established in Taiwan (1949) and South Korea (1951). Both new governments were militarist regimes that ruled through martial law and that maintained among the largest standing armies in the world. Both governments were initially more concerned with being ready for war and with their political longevity and legitimacy than with economic development and industrialization. The two countries were beneficiaries of a great deal of foreign aid from the United States, and additional monies flowed into South Korea from the garrison of Untied Nations troops, mostly from the United States, that guarded the uneasy truce. In the first instance, the regimes in both countries focused their economic policies on rebuilding the agrarian economy, and both implemented extensive agricultural reforms that put land in the hands of those who tilled the soil. In many respects, the immediate economic and political conditions in South Korea and Taiwan were quite similar, but they differed in at least one major way: the composition of the group of individuals who would become the entrepreneurial force creating the capitalist momentum in the late 1960s and 1970s.

On the eve of industrialization, the entrepreneurial potentials in South Korea and Taiwan were poles apart. In South Korea, the individuals who were able to take advantage of such economic opportunities as were available were overwhelmingly clustered in Seoul, the capital of South Korea, which was many times larger than South Korea's next largest city, Pusan. The concentration of entrepreneurial talent in this one location, under conditions where businessmen competed for patronage from the state and for contracts from the United Nations and U.S. Armed Forces, led to a situation, well before the outset of industrialization, where a few big winners emerged from a crowd of would-be entrepreneurs. It was these few big winners who competed with each other using their authority within their enterprises and their economic power vis-à-vis other enterprises to create the biggest and best *chaebol* in the country.

By contrast, in Taiwan, the individuals who were eager and able to grasp opportunities were socially diverse and geographically scattered throughout the island – in different urban areas and, especially, in the rural countryside. The social and geographical dispersion of these would-be businessmen and women led to a diversity of entrepreneurial efforts, some failing, some succeeding, but many leading in different directions. This very diversity of efforts led to multiple successful outcomes, which in turn stimulated Taiwan's decentralized and largely rural-centered indus-trialization.

To understand these fundamental differences in entrepreneurial poten-tial between the two countries is to see both as part of evolving century-long trends in urban and rural development and not merely as a proximate cause. Because these trends are reasonably clear and well documented, the only requirement here is briefly to describe them and to show their influ-ence on the patterns of early industrialization in both countries.

A Few Big Winners

In South Korea, the period from the middle of the nineteenth to early twentieth centuries was a time of fundamental change in the economic foundations of Korean society. During this period, the locus of the Korean economy shifted from a system of landed wealth, with revenues from agriculture providing the elites with most of their revenues, to a system of commercial and industrial wealth, with urban-based economic activ-ity as the mainstay of national as well as elite revenues. At the core of this transformation was the changing relationship between the *yangban* elite and peasant farmers. In the eighteenth century, reforms redefined the ties between the aristocratic landowners and slaves, and as a consequence many slaves became reclassified as tenants who sharecropped or who paid a fixed rent to the landlords. This quasi-contractual relationship deterio-rated in the nineteenth century, as "the growth of landlordism, tenancy, usury, and indebtedness" further undermined the conditions of peasants and caused them to revolt (Palais, 1996, pp. 367–8). One peasant protest after another occurred from the 1812 Hong Kyongnae Rebellion (Palais, 1996) to peasant uprisings in 1946 (Shin, 1994, 1996, 1998). Peasants directed most of their discontent at landowners, the wealthiest of whom, by the time of the end of the nineteenth century, had begun to retreat permanently from the countryside and to become absentee landlords and urban residents.

The rural exodus of elites was further encouraged by the onset of Japanese colonialism. Beginning in the closing years of the nineteenth century, the Meiji government in Japan, following the lead of Western powers, began actively to seek colonial possessions. The Sino-Japanese War of 1894–95 led to Japan's annexation of Taiwan and increased interest in Korea. By 1895, Japanese businessmen began actively to invest in the Korean economy, particularly in the agricultural sector, first in the rice trade between Japan and Korea and then directly in the purchase of land, which large Japanese enterprises bought and then rented to Korean farmers (Duus, 1984). After Japan's formal takeover of Korea in 1910, the colonial government conducted a cadastral land survey of all lands and allocated secure land titles, along with the requirement for the owners of the land to pay land tax (Cumings, 1984, Meyer and Yamada, 1984, Eckert, 1991). As a consequence, those remaining *yangban* landlords received "formal title to their land, but in exchange they had to develop that land to pay the new land tax. The land-tax reform, then, at least forced those landowners to make their land produce wealth, and in case they could not, to sell it to other parties who could" (Meyer and Yamada, 1984, p. 430). Korean landlords, however, often did not upgrade agriculture on their lands, but instead continued to rely on "maximization of rents through pressure on tenants" (Eckert, 1991, p. 22). A continuation of peasant unrest prompted the colonial government to further standardize relations between landlord and tenant farmers, giving the farmers more leeway to resist landlord exploitation. The colonial government also took over "all the land which belonged to the Yi royal family, Yi government officials, schools, and temples," and then sold much of it "to Japanese investment companies" (Myers and Yamada, 1984, p. 429). By the 1930s, owning "20 percent or more of the total arable land" (Ho, 1984, p. 373), the Japanese were the largest and the most progressive block of landowners in Korea.[14]

Pressured on all sides, the Korean elite began to withdraw from the countryside and began actively to pursue opportunities that started to appear in urban areas as a direct consequence of colonial industrial and commercial policies. "With regard to colonial industrialization," concludes Shin (1998, p. 1316), "a key focus is the historical process of capital movement from landed to commercial and industrial areas by Korean landlords." In the urban areas, Japanese *zaibatsu* (a word written with the same characters as *chaebol*, meaning money clique) had invested heavily in industry and mining and had opened the way for a lively import/export trade. By 1945, "about a quarter of Japan's industrial base" was in its

---

[14] Despite Japanese intensive efforts to improve agricultural production in Korea, the rate of agricultural growth was slower than what occurred in Taiwan and even began to decline after 1927, "falling from an annual compound rate of 1.85 percent in 1912–1927 to 1.3 percent in 1927–37" (Ho, 1984, p. 360).

colonies and much of that in Korea (Cumings, 1984, p. 487). These largely urban investments opened many opportunities for enterprising Koreans with some capital in hand, so much so that a number of scholars trace the origins of Korean capitalism to the colonial period (Eckert, 1991, McNamara, 1990, 1996, Shin, 1998, Kohli, 1994, 1997).

Many other scholars, however, argue that the new capitalist class emerged during the 1950s and not in the colonial period (Haggard, Kang, and Moon, 1997b, Kong, 1993, Jones and Sakong, 1980). Although urban investments grew quickly before the outbreak of World War II, the disruptions caused by the colonial dissolution and especially the Korean War broke the hold of the old elite in the rising urban economy. Moreover, rural land reform ended any possibility of the elite's reestablishing a base of power in the countryside. In 1946, in response to renewed peasant uprisings, the post-war government began to institute land reforms that finally put an end to landlordism in Korea. The post-war government of Sygman Rhee confiscated all Japanese-owned properties, rural as well as industrial.[15] The regime, then, gave the land held by the remaining Korean landlords, in plots no larger than three hectares, to those who cultivated the soil, and in addition made actual cultivation a condition for ownership rights to agricultural lands (Burmeister, 1994). Former landlords received land bonds from the government in exchange for their land. In principle, they could use these bonds to purchase, among other things, the industrial assets previously owned by Japanese. Most landlords, however, were unable to buy much of this property because, by end of the war, the majority of the Korean landowners actually owned relatively little land, and post-war inflation rapidly eroded the value of the bonds. "The effort at converting landlords into capitalists," concludes Jones and Sakong (1980, p. 35), "is generally held to have been a failure." By the time the land bonds could be cashed in, the former landlords were simply too poor to become capitalists. The land reforms, however, finally destroyed any possibility of a rural elite capable of mobilizing resources for industrialization. The government not only fragmented the ownership of rural land, but also passed additional measures restricting the development of a land market (Burmeister, 1994). Tenancy was banned; farmers could only own a maximum of three hectares; and because of strict zoning, rural land could not be used for non-agricultural purposes. Therefore, in the run-up to industrialization, as well as in the period of early rapid growth in the late 1960s and early 1970s, Korea's rural population, concentrating mainly on farming small plots, made few contributions to Korea's new industrial economy.

---

[15] Local governments often took Japanese-owned land at the end of World War II and simply gave it to those tilling the soil (Burmeister, 1994).

Table 5.1. *Number of Firms in Major Korean Cities After Independence*

Industry	Seoul (A)	Inchon	Pusan	Taeku	Mokpo	Kwangju	Taejon	Kunsan	Total (B)	Ratio (A/B)
Mining	335	1	16	6	2	3	3	2	368	91.0
Agriculture	171	3	5	5	5	10		8	207	82.6
Fishery	53	2	8	1	1	1		7	73	72.6
Machinery	285	8	7	18	3	1	6	9	337	84.6
Metal	28	3	14	1	2	1		1	50	56.0
Electric	109		11	5		1	1	3	130	83.8
Chemical	287	7	11	12	1	9		10	337	85.2
Pottery	27	8	19	5	2	5	3	1	70	38.6
Food	157	8	27	20	3	6	3	9	233	67.4
Furniture	117	2	18	2	1	8	2	4	154	76.0
Textile	146	4	31	22	3	4	6	6	222	65.8
Gen. Mfg	521	32	63	29	4	19	14	12	694	75.1
Construction	324	6	38	29	2	10	16	8	433	74.8
Printing	110	3	10	4	2	10	3	1	143	76.9
Finance	189	6	8	16	1	3	4	1	228	82.9
Transportation	124	17	36	3	9	6	6	12	213	58.2
Trading	218	14	12	1	5	2	1	9	262	83.2
Other	887	34	157	61	4	29	30	71	1273	69.7
TOTAL	4088	158	491	240	50	128	98	174	5427	75.3

Kong, J., B. Choe, Y. Oh, 1998, 1950- Yundae Seoul Ui Chabonga.
Sources: Economic Yearbook, 1949, IV. pp. 136–53.

The entrepreneurial potential realized in the period after the Korean War, instead, came out of an urban-based, post-war reconstruction and was overwhelmingly based in one city, in Seoul, and to a much smaller extent in Pusan. In 1948, before the outbreak of the Korean War, as Table 5.1 shows, Seoul was the headquarters for 75 percent of all the major firms in Korea (Kong, Choe, and Oh, 1998, p. 35). After the war, the lopsided urban concentration continued with Seoul becoming the hub for reconstruction and the location of the command headquarters for the United Nations troops. In the 1950s, Seoul was the center of politics, the center of business, and the center of Korean social life. Beginning in the 1950s, people from all over South Korea began to pour into what has been called Korea's "city of hope." By 1960, one in ten South Koreans lived in Seoul and by 1985, one in four.

In the 1950s, the concentration of businesses, capital, and opportunity in Seoul created the entrepreneurial foundations for South Korean industrialization. The concentration of commercial and industrial investments in one location nurtured, even before 1961, the formation of an elite group of capitalists, a group close to the patronage offered by the Rhee regime, to plentiful and cheap labor from migrants moving into the

Table 5.2. *Korea's 23 Largest Capitalists in 1961*

Rank	# of firms owned	# of firms and year of establishment (or take over)			Top 30 group in 1997 (sales rank)[2]	Top 30 group in 1989 (sales rank)[3]	Arrested by Park's gov't[4]
		After 9/15/45[1]	Before 9/15/45[1]	Not known			
1	14	13	1		Samsung (2)	Samsung (1)	Yes
2	11	9	2				Yes
3	8	6	1	1			Yes
4	6	6					Yes
5	4	4			LG (3)	LG (3)	
6	4	3		1	Dongyang (24)	Dongyang (34)	Yes
7	4	4					Yes
8	4	4					Yes
9	4	4					Yes
10	11	6	2	3			
11	6	6					Yes
12	9	8	1		Ssangyong (6)	Ssanyoung (6)	
13	2	2					Yes
14	2	1	1				Yes
15	12	10	2				Yes
16	6	4	2				Yes
17	10	4	6			Samyangsa (26)	
18	4	3	1				
19	2	2			Hyundai (1)	Hyundai (2)	
20	2	2			Doosan (15)	Doosan (12)	
21	4	4					
22	4	4					
23	1	1			Hanwha (7)	Hanwha (11)	
TOTAL	134	110	19	5			

[1] Independence Day: August 15, 1945.
[2] Source: Sin Sanop Kyongyongwon. 1998. *1999 Hanguk 30-tae chaebol chaemu punsok* (1999 Korea's top 30 chaebol financial analysis), Soul: Sin Sanop Kyongyongwon.
[3] Source: Hanguk Sinyong pyongga 1990. *1990 Chaebol punsok pogosuh (1990 Chaebol Analysis Report)*, Soul: Hanguk Sinyong pyongga (Korea Investors Service).
[4] Source: Lee, Jong-Jae. 1993. *Chaebol Iryoksuh (Chaebol Resume)*, Soul: Hangukilbo, pp. 127–38.
Notes: This table was reconstructed from data in Kong, Che-uk. 1993. *1950 yon dae hankook eui chabonga yonku (An analysis of Korean Capitalists in 1950s)* pp. 185–6.
(Kong's source is: Bujeong Chookjae Chosadan (*Illicit Wealth Accumulation Investigation Committee*), 1991, Sanup Eunhang Daebu Myongse (*The Bank of Industry Loans Lists*)).

city, and to the economic opportunities arising from the presence of foreign troops. As Table 5.2 shows, over 80 percent of the firms started by these top entrepreneurs date from the late 1940s and 1950s. By 1961, these businessmen had already expanded their enterprises into multiple-firm business groups.[16] These business groups of the 1950s are clearly

[16] Of the 100 largest firms in 1955, seventy were started after 1945; 11 were started before 1945; and for 19 firms the starting date is unknown (Daehan Kyongje Yongam Sa, 1995).

forerunners of the *chaebol*. As Table 5.2 also shows, the owners of these business groups were the ones who were originally charged with corruption in the Chang regime, immediately after the student uprising in 1960, and who were later imprisoned by Park, after his coup d'état in 1961. The number of businessmen arrested varies somewhat by the source, but it is clear that thirteen of those arrested founded an association of the top businessmen in Seoul shortly after being released from prison on July 14, 1961. These thirteen were soon joined by Lee Byung Chul, the founder of Samsung, who had waited out the difficult times in Japan and who became the first chairman of the association. By October 1961, the association had accepted seven more members, including Chung Ju Yung, the founder of Hyundai, and took the name of Federation of Korean Industries, a name they still have today. After a number of businessmen protested the exclusivity of the Federation membership, the Federation added more members, so that by the end of 1962 the number of members came to forty.

These forty businessmen composed the capitalist elite that arose in the 1950s in South Korea. They knew each other well. They were competitors, as well as collaborators. They formed a tight, but rarely harmonious group, were most able to take advantage of and nearly to monopolize the rapid number of opportunities that began to arise after 1962, and played a major role in the government's economic development projects initiated in the 1960s. It would be a mistake, however, to see this group as a small, protected minority whose success was sponsored and guaranteed by the Park regime. Such a protected status would lend support to a strong-state interpretation of Korea's economic development. The truth is quite otherwise. Of the top twenty-three capitalists listed in Table 5.2, only eight are listed in the top fifty *chaebol* in 1989. Most of these business groups did not survive, and if they did, they did not grow large. Some went bankrupt in the late 1960s; others were edged out of the main competition and, remaining modest in size, fell into niches in an economy that was increasingly dominated by just a few big *chaebol*.

The most important point for our purposes is the fact that, at the outset of rapid industrialization, there already was a small group of capitalist winners who were hotly competing with each other. These capitalists knew that they could diversify their holdings, knew that they could legitimately manage them in a centralized fashion, and knew that they could pass everything intact to succeeding generations. With this knowledge, they were already building, relative to the economy at the time, industrial empires, internally integrated economic systems that concentrated capital and economic resources. The Park regime further encouraged this group of businessmen. By pitting one enterprise group against another and by selectively channeling additional opportunities their way, the government

made an already select group even more exclusive. It should be no surprise, therefore, that these entrepreneurs, rationally understanding the
economic world in which they lived and struggling to maximize their
own economic power vis-à-vis one another, led the entire economy along
a developmental trajectory toward higher levels of concentrations. They
created, in other words, a lived-in version of what we call in this book "a
high concentration equilibrium."

Many Players and Many Winners

Taiwan's entrepreneurial potential and early period of industrialization
differ from what occurred in South Korea. Stepping back in time, to the
early years after World War II, no one could have anticipated what important roles small and medium-sized firms would play in Taiwan's industrialization. First of all, no one anticipated Taiwan's industrialization, and
second, in those countries around the world that had industrialized by
that time, large firms and groups of large firms led the industrialization
process, and not small firms (Chandler, 1977, 1990). The production
strategies for small and medium-sized firms that proved so successful in
many places from the 1970s on could not be imagined in the 1950s, and
certainly no governmental planning agency anywhere in the 1950s would
have had the foresight to develop plans for industrialization based on
a foundation of small firms. And yet, it was the very success of small
and medium-size firms in Taiwan that shaped the process of industrialization and set this economy on a trajectory of development that continues
today.

The success of small and medium-sized firms did not occur in a vacuum,
however. In fact, in looking at Taiwan's industrial economy in full bloom,
as we will do in more detail in Chapter 7, we can see that the success of
these firms ultimately depends on three sets of linkages, each of which is
configured differently. First, small and medium-sized firms are linked **forward, principally through contracts, to intermediary buyers of products,**
mostly large retailers and brand-name merchandisers in the United States
and Europe; second, they are linked **backward, through market transactions, to the suppliers of intermediate good and services,** such as the
makers of textiles and plastics, the shippers, and the insurers, almost all
of which are provided domestically by large Taiwan conglomerates; and
third, they are linked **horizontally, through non-contractual and quasi-
contractual relationships, to other small, medium, and modestly large
firms that form production networks,** sometimes called satellite assembly
systems. With this line-up of firms, forming a diverse and yet strongly
integrated economy, there are many players and many winners. Moreover, in this economy, the entrepreneurial potential is spread throughout

the economically engaged population, and is not concentrated in any one sector or any one type of firm.

In retrospect, however, this extremely diverse, yet integrated economy is impossible to locate in the 1950s and early 1960s. Of course, with the advantage of hindsight, we can easily construct a presentist interpretation by tracing the important factors in the present back to their historical roots, and making those historical roots the first cause for what becomes an inevitable outcome. The fallacy of this type of explanation is clear enough.[17] With such an interpretation, we peer into the past and pick out only those economic factors that allowed, in Taiwan's case, the small firms to succeed, ignoring everything else in the process. Adopting this explanatory strategy would make the initial conditions into necessary and sufficient causes for what appeared to come later, resulting in a linear causal explanation.

As we showed earlier in this chapter and as we will further elaborate in Chapter 7, in the Korean case, a few big winners had already emerged in the 1950s. That was the initial starting point in Korea, a pre-condition, but not a necessary or sufficient cause for the rapid growth that came later. Nonetheless, there is a structural continuity in Korea that links the more or less static economy in the 1950s to the rapidly growing economy that emerged in the 1960s and 1970s. But Taiwan's economy in the 1950s and early 1960s bears little resemblance to Taiwan's economy in the 1970s and 1980s. In fact, there is no structural continuity of the sort found in Korea. Strong-state and market theorists recognize this sudden transformation, which they see as the period of industrial take-off and as proof for their respective explanations. But none of their explanations for industrial take-off demonstrates much of an understanding of the integrated nature of Taiwan's economy by the 1980s or of the crucial role that small and medium-sized firms played as the driving force behind that integration.

Rather than being present before the outset of rapid growth, both the driving role of small and medium-sized firms and the economy's remarkable integration emerged **during** the process of industrialization, after growth had already begun in the late 1960s. Taiwan's economic growth, therefore, cannot be explained in a linear fashion, as a gradual accumulation or even rapid growth of previously existing conditions. Instead, this growth has the unmistakable features of being truly emergent, of diverse parts suddenly coming together, leading to an unexpected synergy, and

---

[17] See David Hackett Fischer's (1970, pp. 135–40) classic description of this fallacy, "the fallacy of presentism," about which he says, "it is the mistaken idea that the proper way to do history is to prune away the dead branches of the past, and to preserve the green buds and twigs which have grown into the dark forest of our contemporary world."

resulting in an economic organization that became more than the sum of its parts.

We should examine these parts on the eve of industrialization, even if they do not adequately explain the industrial growth that came in the late 1960s and early 1970s. The first and most striking point of difference between Taiwan and South Korea in the 1950s and 1960s is the role of the agrarian countryside in the early periods of economic growth. Unlike the rural transformation that occurred in Korea, rural Taiwan showed considerable continuity throughout the nineteenth century and early twentieth century. During the nineteenth century, until the Japanese colonized it in 1895, Taiwan remained an expanding frontier region attracting many migrants from Fujian, the mainland province directly across the Taiwan Straits. Early in the period, many landowners bought or claimed substantial tracts of land from aboriginal inhabitants (Wang, 1980), and then rented these lands, usually on a permanent basis, to immigrant farmers coming from the Mainland who cleared the land and made it arable (Knapp, 1980, Hsu, 1980). These immigrants were, moreover, actively recruited by the promise of new lands to farm, lands on which they could live permanently. But once these new residents became established, they in turn often sublet all or a portion of the land they rented, usually for the reasons mentioned in the previous section. As on the Mainland, a three-tier system of land ownership and control soon emerged: cultivators (the subtenants), the *hsiao-tsu hu* (the tenant-landlords), and the *ta-tsu hu* (the great landlords) (Knapp, 1980, Hsu, 1980). From the outset and despite high rates of tenancy, the peasant cultivator and not the landlords had decision-making power over the use of the land.

Colonizing Taiwan in 1895, the Japanese government began quickly to make Taiwan "an agricultural appendage of Japan" (Ho, 1978, p. 29) through a strategy of agricultural commercialization. The key target of the government's policy was the peasant cultivators and their utilization of the soil. By 1896, the colonial government had begun to establish experimental stations to promote agricultural innovations, such as higher-yield varieties of rice and the increased use of fertilizer. By 1900, a consortium of Japanese businessmen, which included the Japanese imperial household and the Mitsui family, built the first modern sugar mills in Taiwan to replace small traditional mills operated by peasants. The consortium actively promoted, through a contracting system that guaranteed prices, the widespread cultivation of sugar cane (Williams, 1980). By 1910 there were ten modern sugar mills in operation and by 1940 there were fifty, all Japanese owned (Isett, 1995, p. 254, Williams, 1980, p. 231). As the sugar cane system evolved, these mills relied heavily on Taiwanese cultivators for the cane. This reliance is clearly revealed by the fact that Japanese owned farmlands, which at its peak amounted to about 10 percent of all farmland in Taiwan, only contributed about 20 percent of the cane for the mills. "The remaining 80 percent was grown in a typical year by about 130,000 small Taiwanese farmers, each growing an average of only one-half hectare" (Williams, 1980, p. 234).

Also in 1900, the colonial government started to encourage the formation of farmer associations to disseminate agricultural innovations and to increase the market awareness of producing cash crops, initially rice and sugar (Myers and Saburo, 1984, p. 432). In 1904, the government completed a cadastral survey and in 1905 instituted land reforms that clarified property rights, increased land taxes, and bought out the great landlords, making the tenant-landlords the legal owners and, in effect, restarting the three-tiered landholding system with a new subsoil owner.[18] By 1906, the Japanese had completed the first step in Taiwan's modern transportation infrastructure, building a railway system and a network of roads going north–south along the fertile western side of the island (Hsu, Pannell, and Wheeler, 1980). Although the Japanese invested in Korean agriculture as well, Myers and Saburo (1984, p. 439) conclude that throughout the colonial period, "the Japanese made greater capital investment for agriculture in Taiwan than in Korea" and as a result, they further argue that Taiwanese peasant farmer became much more productive than their Korean counterparts.

We would add to Myers and Saburo's conclusion that Taiwanese farmers also became more entrepreneurial than Korean farmers, more able rapidly to change their economic behavior to capitalize on new market opportunities. As Table 5.3 shows, Taiwanese crops increasingly became export commodities, and Taiwan's peasants, oriented to market exchange, became the chief generators of export surplus (Ho, 1978, pp. 25–40), even though most agricultural profits from the export trade were systematically siphoned off by Japanese industrialist and middlemen (Ho, 1984). Between 1897 and 1905, agricultural exports to Japan increased sixfold (Myer and Saburo, 1982, p. 432), and, according to Ho's calculations (1978, p. 45), from 1906 until 1940, agricultural production increased on average 3.4 percent a year. Ho (1978, p. 47) further shows that during this interval, of all food crops, rice and sweet potatoes (staples in the local diet) increased the least and "minor food crops, which includes fruits and vegetables, both easily spoiled cash crops, experienced the most rapid growth." Now open to distant markets,

---

[18] The removal of the great landlords, however, as Samuel Ho (1978, p. 44) notes, "was not a change as radical as it may seem, for by the end of the nineteenth century the *ta-tsu-hu*'s power over the land had already diminished considerably." Moreover, removing the great landlord did not fundamentally change the three-tier system, but merely changed the owner of the subsoil.

Table 5.3. *Growth and Composition of Colonial Exports of Korea and Taiwan*

Period	Index of export volume	Exports to Japan as% of total exports	% of total Manufacturing Exports			
			Foodstuffs[a]	Consumer goods[b]	Producer goods[c]	Industrial Raw materials[d]
KOREA						
1911–15	100	78	72	5	1	22
1916–20	456	83	68	5	1	26
1921–25	640	92	68	4	2	26
1926–29	735	91	67	6	2	25
1930–35	956	90	61	8	2	29
1936–38	1,688	84	49	15	3	32
TAIWAN						
1906–10	74	66	80	15	6	5
1911–15	100	75	77	13	<0.5	10
1916–20	148	73	78	8	1	13
1921–25	189	77	85	7	2	8
1926–29	284	78	85	7	2	7
1930–35	381	87	87	5	1	7
1936–38[e]	526	90	89	5	1	5

Notes: The volume indexes of imports and exports for Korea are constructed by deflating the values of imports and exports by, respectively, price indexes of imports and exports. The price indexes are those constructed by Toshiyuki Mizoguchi and can be found in his "Foreign Trade in Taiwan and Korea under Japanese Rule," *Hitotsubashi Journal of Economics*, 14 (February 1974). The volume indexes for Taiwan are from Samuel P. S. Ho, *Economic Development of Taiwan 1860–1970*, New Haven: Yale University Press, 1978, Table A49. These are Laspeyres indexes with 1925 value weights.
[a] Food and raw materials for processed food.
[b] Clothing, apparel, consumer durables, printed matters, charcoal, and miscellaneous goods.
[c] Timber, metals, glass, cement and stone products, machinery and equipment, and transport equipment.
[d] Fiber, leather, rubber, chemical products (including fertilizers), oil (excluding edible oil), coal, and minerals.
[e] Average of 1936 and 1939.
Source: Samuel Pao-San Ho (1984)

self-directed peasant farmers became increasingly oriented toward market production.

At the same time that the Japanese colonial government encouraged agriculture, it also discouraged industrial and commercial endeavors. Unlike the colonial period in Korea, where Korean elite became increasingly urban and engaged in commerce and industry, in Taiwan, the government prohibited, until 1924, the Taiwanese from organizing or operating corporations without Japanese participation, and as a result Japanese-owned businesses dominated Taiwan's commercial and industrial landscape. Even so, most of the firms the Japanese established in Taiwan, such as the *zaibatsu*-owned sugar mills (Williams, 1980), were aimed to increase Taiwan's agricultural role in the Japanese colonial empire rather than to create new industries. "In 1936," reports Ho (1978, p. 77), "the six largest industrial firms accounted for nearly 80 percent of the paid-up corporate capital in the factory enclave, and of the six, five were sugar companies.... Eighty-five of the 107 factories that employed more than 100 workers (in 1933) were in food processing, of which 37 were sugar refineries," all of which were Japanese owned. By the end of World War II, therefore, the Taiwanese had a very limited role in their own economy and, by far, the most economically engaged group was agricultural cultivators.

This general trend accelerated in the first two decades after World War II. The four-year period, between the Japanese defeat in 1945 and the sudden arrival of Chiang Kai-shek's fleeing military and government forces in 1949, was marked by considerable unrest, violence, and repression resulting from Kuomintang's attempt to reestablish Chinese rule in Taiwan after a break of over fifty years. This process culminated in February 28, 1947, when Taiwanese staged mass protests against the Nationalist government after the police beat and killed several people. The Kuomintang government responded to these protests by sending thousands of troops to "pacify" the Taiwanese, resulting in deaths of between 10,000 and 20,000 Taiwanese and the elimination of Taiwan's "intellectual and social elite" (Gold, 1986, p. 53). Three years later, the remnants of Chiang Kai-shek's Nationalist government and military fled to Taiwan, adding in the course of less than two years "between one and two million civilian and military refugees" to a population in 1945 that was "only six million" (Gold, 1986, p. 55).

In 1950, Taiwan, in essence, became a new nation (Tsang, 1993). The first priorities for this new nation were political and not economic: stability, legitimacy, and war readiness. Chiang rebuilt his army and navy and established military garrisons on a number of offshore islands close to the Mainland, particularly Quemoy and Matsu, where offshore bombardments and the threat of Communist invasion continued through 1958. These expensive and ongoing military projects further reduced the amount of resources that the Nationalist government could use for the development of the domestic economy. With import substitution policies in full force in the 1950s, manufacturing exports were minimal.

The main substantive economic goal in the 1950s was to create a self-sustaining rice-based system of agriculture, which would be needed in the event of war and blockades. To facilitate the growth of agriculture, the Nationalist government embarked on land reform, reallocating land to those who actually tilled the soil. Similar to the land reforms in Korea, tenant farmers assumed subsoil ownership of their land to a maximum of 2.9 hectares per family. The government claimed all excess land and sold it to farmers and would-be farmers with less or no land. In exchange, the former landlords were given ten-year bonds and received stock in some government-owned enterprises.

   Although the details of the land reform in Taiwan are similar to what had occurred in Korea (in part, no doubt, because the same set of American advisors counseled both countries), the conditions in the countryside were quite different. Whereas in Korea, land reform arose as a response to rural protests, in Taiwan it addressed the issue of property rights in what was otherwise a peaceful society. As Ho (1987, p. 240) notes:

> Because of the stability and agricultural growth it enjoyed during the colonial period, rural Taiwan in 1945 was a relatively well ordered society, with fewer signs of social unrest or disintegration than any other of the political units then governed by the Chinese Nationalist Government. The decision to implement land reform in Taiwan was therefore more in response to the crisis on the mainland than to rural problems in Taiwan itself.

The land reforms, moreover, had the unintended consequence of invigorating an already economically active countryside. An aspect of the government's agricultural policy was to squeeze revenues out of agriculture to finance other areas by distorting the price the government sold fertilizer to farmers in exchange for the rice that the government bought from the farmers. This policy, however, encouraged farmers to grow other crops with higher returns (Fu and Shei, 1999). Between 1952 and 1968, Taiwan's agriculture grew at over 5 percent per year (Ho, 1978, p. 147), and became increasingly oriented to export cash crops. In 1948, nearly 70 percent of the total output consisted of rice and sweet potatoes; ten years later these two crops totaled 55 percent; by 1975, they were only 40 percent. "Sugar cane, tea, peanuts, and a variety of fruits and vegetables, many produced for export, supplanted the basic food crops" (Galenson, 1981, p. 75). In the late 1950s and early 1960s, Taiwan became "the world's largest exporter of canned mushrooms and canned asparagus and one of the world's largest exporters of bananas and canned pineapple" (Ho, 1978, p. 150). And in the late 1960s and early 1970s, Taiwan's farmers became one of the primary suppliers of fresh produce for the Vietnam War. In 1955, nearly 90 percent of Taiwan's exports were agricultural or processed agricultural products. As late as 1965, these categories, still increasing in absolute terms, continued to provide well over 50 percent of Taiwan's exports (Taiwan Statistical Data Book, 1994, p. 194).

   Even more important, as agriculture grew, so too did the income of farmers. Yearly studies of farmers undertaken by the Taiwan Provincial Department of Agriculture and Forestry show that in the 1960s farmers' disposal income rose steadily, with cash and bank savings each up over 200 percent in the decade (Tuan, 1976, p. 15). In the same period, loans to farmers through formal institutions, such as credit agencies and banks, increased by over 400 percent (Tuan, 1976, p. 16). In addition, surveys of farmers found that over 40 percent of all loans came through informal channels, such as rotating credit associations and family and friends, and these loans also showed a rapid increase in the late 1960s and early 1970s (Tuan, 1976, p. 21). A number of other studies revealed that this rural income, not surprisingly considering Taiwan's small freeholder rural economy, was evenly distributed throughout the countryside (Thorbecke, 1979). In retrospect, it is clear that the availability of capital resources at the rural level directly fed the next phase of Taiwan's economic growth, a phase that we will describe in Chapter 7, but before this phase began, there was no way to have forecast the tremendous growth and economic transformation in rural society that was just around the corner. Equally, in 1965, there was no way to have predicted that the rural sector would serve as "the foundation for (Taiwan's) development" (Fu and Shei, 1999).

At the same time as the government used land reform to stabilize the countryside, to increase agriculture production, and to squeeze needed revenues out of the farmers, the government also tried to develop local manufacturing industries by promoting a large firm sector of the economy. Many large firms and business groups were established well before the industrialization began. In the 1950s, at the same time that agriculture exports were expanding, Taiwan's nationalist government began to establish large firms in selected manufacturing sectors in order to reduce imports and thereby to preserve foreign exchange. Immediately after World War II, the government took control of the former Japanese-owned agricultural enterprises, and consolidated them into large sugar, fertilizer, and machinery manufacturing companies and established a broad range of large firms supplying basic infrastructure and upstream products. These companies assumed major control of telecommunication, electrical power, petroleum, steel making, shipbuilding, and petrochemical production. In the 1950s, these state-owned enterprises accounted for nearly 50 percent of the valued added in the manufacturing sectors, but beginning in the 1960s, this proportion declined relative to the rest of the economy until 1971, when it leveled out at an average for the next fifteen years of 14 percent (Council for Economic Planning and Development, 1987, p. 89).

Also in the 1950s, the state began to sponsor a few privately owned enterprises in an attempt to make Taiwan more self-sufficient from foreign imports. These firms all occupied basic upstream and midstream sectors important in local consumption, such as textiles, synthetic fibers, cement, and plastic. Many of the entrepreneurs getting their start this way were Mainland businessmen who had moved to Taiwan with Chiang Kai-shek

(Gold, 1986, p. 70), but a few Taiwanese also established businesses this way, the most important of which was Wang Yong-qing, the founder of Formosa Plastics, which, as we discussed in Chapter 4, founded the largest and among the most vertically integrated business groups in Taiwan.

The evolution of Formosa Plastics nicely illustrates what happened in the economy more generally. When the state and the selected owners of large firms started their businesses, they did not have an export market in mind. These firms were designed to satisfy and perhaps even to expand local demand slightly. For instance, in 1954, when Wang built his first production facility to manufacture PVC powder to make plastics, the domestic demand for PVC was around 15 tons per month, but the plant he built had a capacity of 120 tons per month. When a large amount of the initial production runs of 100 tons per month could not find any market "and wound up in large piles sitting in the company's warehouses" (Taniura, 1989, pp. 67–8), Wang decided to vertically integrate and to expand his operation to be sufficiently efficient to be internationally competitive and thus able to export the PVC powder and other related products. To solve the lack of domestic demand, he established several additional firms to begin manufacturing intermediate and finished plastic products. In 1958, he started the Nan Ya Plastics Corporation to make film, sheets, and vinyl leather. These upstream products could be turned more easily into finished goods. Then he started two additional firms, Qiaka Lin Plastics Corporation and Xindong Plastics Corporation, to make final products (such as raincoats, shower curtains, and diapers) with the intermediate goods that his upstream firms produced. These final products were intended for both the domestic and export markets. By the early 1970s, however, the demand for intermediate plastic products from small and medium-sized firms in Taiwan grew so quickly and was so large that Wang dropped his plans to vertically integrate down to final products and concentrated instead on making his upstream production of immediate plastic products more efficient.

As will become clear from our discussion in Chapter 7, the reason for Wang's decision was the bifurcation of Taiwan's economic organization that occurred in the late 1960s and 1970s, and that created what Chou Tein-chen (1985) has called a "dichotomous market structure." In this period, the private (not state-owned) sectors of the economy split between midstream and downstream production. For instance, in the petrochemical industry:

> ... two strata [formed] consisting of the midstream, which is controlled oligopolistically by larger business enterprises, and the downstream, a production sector in which a great number of very small manufacturers are caught up in an atmosphere of

friction-filled competition. The finished product sector first rose in connection with exports, and on the basis of this sector the midstream materials sector and then the petrochemical industry grew and developed. The level of competition becomes fiercer and fiercer and profit margins become thinner and thinner as processing proceeds downstream. (Taniura, 1989, p. 72)

Early in the 1970s, Wong Yong-qing found himself in a situation where he no longer wanted to compete with small and medium-sized firms in the downstream markets. Being wise enough to know his markets and his firms' relative advantages, he refocused his factories on the upstream and intermediate levels. In his analysis of Formosa Plastics, Taniura (1989, p. 72) concludes "having been able to make it back upstream has enabled the Formosa Plastics Group as a private group to grow as it has." As small and medium-sized firms began to enter export production, most owners of other large firms came to the same realization to retreat into less competitive upstream niches. Once this realization occurred, Taiwan's economy became integrated across markets and increasingly driven by the manufacture and export of finished goods, most of which were produced by small and medium-sized firms.

Now we can restate the main conclusion of our analysis of Taiwan's economy on the eve of its industrialization. Taiwan's economy lacked integration and dynamism. Only in the 1970s did Taiwan's economy become internally integrated, organizationally interdependent across upstream, intermediate, and downstream markets, and set on a trajectory of development. In the earlier period, the economy was lopsided with a huge, slow growing, and basically inefficient government sector supplying basic services and with a much smaller but more dynamic rural sector just beginning at the margins to engage in export production. Integration came only after the emergence of industrialization. The best indication of this integrated, interdependent economic organization is, during the period of rapid growth from the early 1970s through the 1990s, the consistent and relatively stable tripartite division of labor between the far upstream state-owned sector, the large business groups supplying intermediate goods and services, and the small and medium-sized firms. The relative percentage of the total output for the state, big business, and small and medium-sized firm sectors has remained fairly constant during the 1970s and 1980s, a time when Taiwan's output, mostly export production, and pre-capita income soared. The large business portion of this output remained fairly constant, with perhaps a slight decline in recent years, despite considerable variations in the internal mix in the groups listed among the top 100 business groups (Chou, 1985, p. 46) and considerable changes in the composition of Taiwan's exports.

The continuity of the overall division of labor suggests that the export sector of the economy, consisting primarily of the output of modestly sized firms, created the demand for intermediate goods and services that allowed the large business groups and state-owned enterprises to grow at roughly the same rates as the export sector. The changes in the mix of the big business groups on top, however, reflect changes in the demands for intermediate goods and service as the composition of Taiwan's exports change over time (moving largely from textiles, footwear, and household electrical appliances to high technology products). As the demand for specific intermediate goods and services declined, the group or groups supplying those goods declined in importance as well. As one group falls, however, its position among biggest groups is given over to another group supplying a good whose demand has risen. Business groups of all sizes rise and decline for other reasons as well, but in terms of creating market institutions and controlling economic forces, the data are clear that the state-owned sector and the largest business groups are not the main organizational forces propelling the Taiwan economy, as is the case in the South Korean economies. Instead, Taiwan's business groups are themselves the creation of other market forces, in particular of the export sector. In short, the small firm tail of Taiwan's economic organization wags the entire economy. It is, therefore, essential to examine the forces shaping this sector in order to understand the organization of the entire economic, which is the task we take up in the next chapter.

Conclusion

In this chapter, we have outlined the structural origins of the divergent paths of economic development that occurred as rapid industrialization proceeded. In South Korea, at the onset of economic growth after World War II, institutionalized patterns of authority and social conditions favored an economic competition among a few big players who were centrally located in Seoul, who were known to each other, and whose intergroup competition state officials encouraged. Given conditions of rising global demand for finished goods that existed worldwide in the late 1960s and early 1970s, conditions which we will discuss in the next chapter, the stage was set in Korea for an economic organization that moved toward vertical integration and high concentration in a few major enterprises, whether or not government officials supported the trends. That President Park did support the trends – that his government did reaffirm big business concentrations and their entry into the global economy – undoubtedly propelled the process of *chaebol* consolidation forward at a much faster rate than otherwise would have occurred without his assistance. In this context, rapid corporate expansion and one-setism pushed the entire economy toward a highly concentrated economy centered on relatively few very large enterprise groups.

By contrast, very different patterns of authority and related social conditions created in Taiwan an economic organization that contained, in the years just before rapid growth, many economically engaged and geographically dispersed entrepreneurs. Most of these were petty entrepreneurs, mainly farmers growing cash crops for local and exports markets and small-time craftsmen of one sort or another. A few entrepreneurs, through political connections and good fortune, headed large firms and large groups of firms, but before the middle 1960s these firms struggled along with the general economy. The economy itself was neither integrated nor internally interdependent. However, increasing demand in the late 1960s invigorated this entrepreneurial landscape. Rather suddenly, many people in different economic locations eagerly became players and many of these players became winners. In Korea, during roughly the same period of time, a few economically powerful and politically well-connected businessmen were in place at the outset of industrialization. These individuals and their large conglomerate holdings were able to lay claim to, and push competitors out of, the upstream, intermediate, and downstream sectors of the economically most lucrative areas of production, and thus create industrial empires rivaling any business group or corporation in the world.

6

The Rise of Intermediary Demand

A Reassessment of the "Asian Miracle"

For most analysts, it is an unexamined article of faith that the so-called "Asian miracle" is a push rather than a pull story, a supply-side narrative in which the administrative efficiency, entrepreneurial energy, and productive capacity of a select group of Asian economies created rapid economic growth. Drawing on new data that allow us to examine disaggregated trade data as if they are historical documents, we find clear evidence that pull factors relating to the organization of **intermediary demand** and the **demand responsiveness** of Asian manufacturers must be counted among the most important causes of growth in, and divergence among, Asian economies beginning in the initial period of industrialization and continuing through today. A level of economic activity that we call "intermediary demand" (by which we mean a range of market-making activities that include, among other things, merchandising, retailing, and the infrastructure of product procurement) had, and continues to have, a major impact on the organization of Asian economies and has, in interaction with local conditions, decisively shaped the different rates and divergent trajectories of growth throughout the region.*

Using our revised Walrasian framework to conceptualize Asian firms, we not only need to examine the interconnectedness of markets **within** countries, as we did in Chapters 3 and 4, but we also need to examine the interconnectedness of markets **between** countries. Part I shows that differences in the interconnectedness of markets within countries had systemic repercussions for the organization of those economies. In this and the next chapter, we extend the previous analysis to show that the interconnectedness of markets among economies, as signified by the

---

* Because retail is an ambiguous term, we use the term "intermediary," following Spulber (1996, 1999), to identify those categories of economic actors that come between the manufacturers of products and the final consumer of those products. Intermediary demand is, therefore, the demand generated by the major buyers, but not the final consumers, of Asian products.

212

organization of international trade, directly energizes the competitive dynamics among firms within economies engaging in that export trade. Therefore, we hypothesize that export demand generated by intermediaries is a potential driver of both the emergence and divergence among economies.

In this and the next chapter, we present evidence in support of this hypothesis. Specifically, we will show that the organization of intermediary demand shapes the organization of production, including the institutional environment in which production occurs. Conversely, we will also suggest that the demand responsiveness of export-oriented manufacturers drives the development, globalization, and consolidation of intermediaries. We further hypothesize that these buyer-driven and demand-responsive factors interact with the two sets of causal forces – institutionalized authority in relation to economic action and the lineup of economic players on the eve of industrialization – that we examined in Chapter 5. We consider these previously discussed factors to be "necessary but not sufficient causes" for the capitalist economic organizations that emerged in South Korea and Taiwan. In other words, the particular family-based authority systems and the particular lineup of entrepreneurs on the eve of industrialization, in and of themselves, can explain neither the fact of economic growth nor the emergent and distinctive economic organizations that suddenly took shape in South Korea and Taiwan between 1960 and 1985. However, when we add the demand-side factors to the previous two sets, then we have the necessary and sufficient conditions for both the emergent economies and the divergent trajectories. The authority/ market power dimensions of the model that we presented in Chapter 3 are crucial in explaining the extraordinary process of growth and divergence that occurred in the 1960s and 1970s. This explanatory power, in turn, increases our confidence that the model accurately stylizes a process that actually occurred in these two economies.

In this and the following chapter, we lay out the evidence for an explanation of Asian industrialization that incorporates demand-side or "buyer-driven" factors. At first glance, it might seem that supply-side and demand-side explanations are merely two sides of the same coin. However, as we demonstrate in the next section of this chapter, all conventional explanations of Asia's industrialization miss a primary driver of growth – intermediary demand – and therefore miss the processes by which these economies became organized as they are. Instead of looking at the processes of organizing, most analysts simply assume the adequacy of a producer-driven, supply-side narrative, not only for Asian industrialization, but also for economic growth and change in general. The reason for this assumption stems from the fact that the debates among analyst typically have a producer bias; typically analysts debate over which sets of supply-side causes are more important for economic growth – the state or the market. These debates largely consist of an interdisciplinary struggle between economists and political economists (mostly political scientists and a number of sociologists) that no amount of evidence and demonstration can resolve, principally because the debate is over which independent variable represents the "true cause" in the absence of clearly specified dependent variables.

By contrast, the demand-responsive alternative that we offer is an organizational view that defies simple reduction into tidy sets of first causes from which definite and singular outcomes emerge. In this context, rising demand is not a first cause from which everything else flows, but rather is an empirical condition that elicits responses from multiple actors in differently organized settings that in turn lead to divergent, emergent outcomes. These outcomes cannot be reduced to a single simple lineal causal model. What we do in our analysis is to follow the empirical trail (that is, the evidence) and to demonstrate how different outcomes flows from similar empirical conditions. Although this approach is inductive, it is, in addition, an approach directed by and interpreted through our theoretical view of economic organization, in general, and the ideal-typical model of authority and economic power, in particular, which we have provided in Chapter 1.

Our first step, then, is to summarize the underlying assumptions of "supply-side" narratives for Asia's economic growth. Although varied, most of these Asia-centric accounts are familiar and well worked, and we outlined the most prominent version, the strong-state version, at the start of the previous chapter. Therefore, our presentation of these accounts in this location will be brief. We will emphasize, however, that the causal connections between state policies and macro-economic environments, on the one hand, and economic organization, economic performance, and the trajectories of development, on the other hand, are merely assumed to hold and are not actually explained or even seriously examined.

Our second step is to lay out in greater detail the main lines of a demand-side explanation. First, we show that beginning in the 1950s a fundamental reorganization has occurred in the retail sector in the United States, a reorganization that grew more pervasive and, after 1965, more global throughout the rest of the century. Led by brand-name merchandisers and specialty and discount retailers, the retail sector of the American economy both expanded and grew more concentrated as it began to target niche markets by offering American consumers differentiated goods that matched their emerging life-style choices. The demand for these goods grew at an extraordinary rate from the 1960s on and continues, albeit less hectically, to the present day. Most of the brand-name merchandisers and discount retailers that grew the fastest and that held the largest market share in their respective sectors by the 1990s only started their businesses or converted to discount retailing in the late 1960s and 1970s. Rarely owning their own factories, these firms relied almost entirely on various types of product sourcing and contract manufacturing, much of which was initially centered in East Asia.

The core empirical point of this chapter is, therefore, to describe the global importance of changes in the organization of retailing (and of market intermediaries more generally) on shaping systems of production in Asia. To make this point more emphatic, we ask whether and how the increasing market power of the steadily concentrating global retail sector (now featuring such discount stores as Wal-Mart, Target, Best Buy, and Costco, and global merchandisers such as Nike, The Gap, and Dell, all of which have been established or started discount retailing since 1960) has direct and lasting impacts on the development and organization of local economies in Asia. The significant point here is not that there are intermediaries that order goods, but rather that the economic power of these intermediaries (in terms of their share of their respective markets) has allowed them in less than forty years, increasingly, to make manufacturing into **price-sensitive, organizational extensions of retailing**.

The third step in our argument examines the export patterns of South Korea and Taiwan to the United States, using highly disaggregated data. We show through "trade data archeology" that, in the first twenty years of rapid growth, roughly from 1965 to 1985, the exports were heavily concentrated in only a few categories of highly differentiated goods, most of which were the result of product sourcing and OEM (original equipment manufacturing) production. More importantly, despite some very important similarities, the trade data also reveal some striking differences between the two economies, differences that correspond to the increasing organizational divergence between the two economies, with Korea's export sector being increasingly dominated by large vertically integrated business groups (the *chaebol*) and Taiwan's export sector being increasingly dominated by small and medium-sized firms.

Supply-Side Narratives: In Search of an Asian Model of Development

Beginning in the 1970s and continuing through today, a huge literature has emerged analyzing and attempting to locate the causes for Asia's post-war industrial transformation. Even after the heady days of rapid growth in Asia have ended, stopped dead in its tracks by the Asian financial crisis followed by a global recession, the debate about the East Asian Miracle continues (Stiglitz and Yusuf, 2001, Woo-Cumings, 2001,

Amsden, 2001, Woo, Sachs, and Schwab, 2000, Haggard, 2004). In such books as Stiglitz and Yusuf's *Rethinking the East Asian Miracle* (2001) and Woo-Cumings's *The Developmental State* (1999), theorists rework the same three sets of causes that first appeared in the late 1970s and 1980s: 1) the macro-economic environment (that is, market fundamentalism), 2) the centrality of the state, and 3) the importance of non-state institutions, such as the family and authority systems, and related cultural factors. Since the publication of the World Bank's *The East Asian Miracle* (1993), there has been more willingness among all participants in the debate to combine these sets, rather than to pit them against each other, in order to fashion a more comprehensive explanation of the rapid growth.[1] Moreover, the critiques of this literature that have appeared in recent years and that gained prominence during the Asian business crisis (Young, 1992, 1993, 1995, Krugman, 1994a and 1994b) also disparaged one or more of these sets of causes without introducing new factors.[2] The pros and cons of the debate, however, continue to be important because, say analysts, if a more balanced assessments of causes can be formulated, then these assessments will lead to policies allowing countries to "achieve sustainable high growth rates again" (Ito, 2001, p. 91) without repeating the mistakes leading up to the Asian financial crisis.

Throughout this debate, there is an unexamined assumption that the causes for Asian economic growth (or the lack thereof) are to be found solely in Asia, and that the story of Asian industrialization is strictly a "supply-side narrative." The underlying assumption made by nearly all participants in the debate is that the Asian Miracle is an Asian product. Their theories are country-centered, producer driven accounts of how this Asian product was created in situ. As we explained in earlier chapters, most of the recent interpretations also use these theories, or some variant thereof, to provide an explanation of the lineup of firms and business groups in all these countries: the *keiretsu* in Japan (Gerlach, 1992, Lincoln and Gerlach, 2004), the *chaebol* in Korea (Amsdem, 1989, Kim, 1997, Woo-Cumings, 1991, 1999), and the family-owned conglomerates in Taiwan, Hong Kong, and Southeast Asia (Hamilton, 1997, Redding, 1990, 1991, Yeung and Olds, 2000). The market fundamentalist theories (Khanna and Rivkin, 2001, Khanna and Pelepu, 2000a, 2000b, Leff, 1977, 1978) argue that business groups result from market failures; the developmental state theories (Amsden, 1989, 2001, Kim, 1997, Evans,

---

[1] Although recognizing some points of the opposing sides, the theorists still remain partisan advocates of their own points of view (Stiglitz and Yusuf, 2001, Woo-Cummings, 1999).

[2] These critiques claimed instead that there was no real growth in productivity beyond the capital inputs, a finding (later questioned by others, such as Pack, 2001) that fueled the post-crisis charge that the Asian states' economic policies rested on cronyism and created conditions of moral hazard instead of being based on dispassionate economic analysis.

1995, 1997, Gold, 1986, Woo-Cumings, 1999), from state policies and bureaucratic supervision; and the sociological theories (Hamilton and Biggart, 1988, Whitley, 1992, 1999, Granovetter, 1994, 1995b, Orrù, Biggart, and Hamilton, 1997, Biggart and Guillen, 1999, and Guillen, 2001), from socially embedded networks and institutional environments.

In each interpretation, the presumed set of causes (for example, market failure, macroeconomic management, state policy, institutional environment) forms a structure of constraints, incentives, and "organizing logics" (Biggart and Guillen, 1999) that are external and temporally prior to economic activity that, in turn, produces a specific set of organizational and performance outcomes within the economy. Although the interpretations usually are couched in causal terms, often with a forceful stimulus/response phrasing in the form of "if this, then that," the actual connection between cause and effect is usually assumed rather than examined and explained.[3] In addition, although many of these standard explanations acknowledge the importance of what is ambiguously described as "globalization" or "global capitalism" or the "world economy," very few theorists of whatever bent incorporate such globally significant economic or organizational factors in their causal explanations of local and national economic development.

The extraordinary thing about all of these interpretative accounts is how rarely any of them ever mention the demand-side of Asia's export orientation. To be sure, theorists frequently cite export trade as "the engine of growth" in East Asia and a few emphasize the bilateral trade with the United States as being particularly significant for Asian economic growth (for example, Chow and Kellman, 1993). But then, when they give causal explanations for these observations, they examine the producers of goods and, more frequently, the circumstances of production, rather than the buyers of goods and the circumstances relating to consumption. In fact, those market economists most ardently advocating export trade as an explanation of Asian growth have not only developed explanations of what they call "export push" (Bradford, 1994, Page, 1994), but also have conspicuously neglected to mention "export pull." On the other side of the Asian Miracle debate, even those strong-state theorists, such as Amsden (1989, 2001), Wade (1990), and Evans (1995, 1997), who are most critical of market explanations, simply assume that market processes prevail at the demand end: Somehow all those manufactured and exported products find overseas buyers. Robert Wade (1990, p. 148), who discusses the Taiwanese government's economic policies in meticulous detail, seems to speak for most theorists when he writes that the "marketing side of Taiwan's export growth" "remains a mystery."

---

[3] For more discussion on this point, see Hamilton, et al., 2000.

Aside from a Wallersteinian world system perspective, whose predictions are at odds with what is observed in the East Asia economies,[4] the only concerted effort to analyze pull factors has been the global commodity chain approach, first developed by Gary Gereffi (1994, Gereffi and Korzeniewicz, 1994) and elaborated by others (Appelbaum and Smith, 1996, Bonanich, et al., 1994). This approach, however, has been used primarily to examine specific industrial sectors, such as garments and footwear, without at the same time linking what is happening in these sectors to changing economic phenomenon, including Asian industrialization. Put more precisely, the global commodity chain approach misses both ends of the phenomena in question: it neither examines changes in the organization of demand nor the consequences of global commodity chains on the organization of production. It is focused on industries rather than economies. The demand-driven explanation offered here does not challenge Gereffi's approach, but rather incorporates it at more general levels of empirical and theoretical analysis.

The Retail Revolution and the Development of Intermediary Demand for Asian Products

Most studies of modern capitalist economies are analyses of production. Chandler (1977, 1990), Piore and Sabel (1984), Williamson (1975, 1985) Hollingsworth and Boyer (1997), Whitley (1999), Fligstein (1990, 2001), Burawoy (1985), and Saxenian (1994) – in these and many other works, scholars emphasize, in widely varying ways, systems of business and institutions relating to the manufacture of goods. Similarly, studies of capitalism in Asia also have the same focus (for example, Hamilton and Biggart, 1988, Aoki, 1988, Amsden, 1989, Gerlach, 1992, Whitley, 1992, Kim, 1997, Evans, 1995). Even the Marxist and world systems perspectives have a decided bias toward manufacturing as the core activities of capitalist economies. Whatever the perspective, these studies share a recognition that the organization of production is a decisive factor in the development of capitalism. It is, therefore, very unusual for any of these studies to examine distribution and consumption in the same light as production, if these activities are mentioned at all.

---

[4] Wallersteinian world system perspective suggests that core capitalist countries manufacture products for distribution around the world. Peripheral countries supply primary material, and not manufactured goods (Wallerstein, 1974, 1984). See Frank, 1998 and Arrighi, et al., 2003 for an updating and reevaluation of this perspective in reference to Asia.

There are, however, a few notable exceptions, such as Gereffi's work mentioned earlier, as well as others (Porter, 1990, Dicken, 1998). Although these works remain focused on understanding production, and on conceptualizing production in terms of commodity chains, value chains, and globalized networks, they nonetheless recognize that retailing is an important activity organizationally linked to manufacturing. Other scholars, more often than not located in business schools (Bluestone, et al., 1981, Abernathy, et al., 1999, Spulber, 1996, 1998, Brown, 1997, Dunlop and Rivkin, 1997, Reardon, et al., 2004), have examined the retail sector more directly, and have begun to realize that an extraordinary transformation in retailing is well underway and that this transformation, in turn, affects production. Except for extensive studies on apparel manufacturing, however, the connections between retail and manufacturing have not been extensively examined and linked to the industrialization of developing countries.

Despite the lack of a fully developed analysis of retailing and its connections to manufacturing, it is our conclusion, based on an analysis of trade data, that the retail revolution in the United States must be counted among the primary causes of the initial industrialization of East Asia. A full analysis of this transformation in retailing is, however, beyond the scope of this chapter and will be addressed in other locations (Petrovic, Hamilton, and Kotha, 2004, Petrovic and Hamilton, forthcoming). The task here is to convince the reader that a transformation has, in fact, occurred and that, whatever else occurred as a consequence of the transformation, it was the driving force behind South Korea's and Taiwan's initial industrialization.

In a 1981 publication, Bluestone and his colleagues (1981) used the term "The Retail Revolution" to describe what, in retrospect, has turned out to be merely an initial phase in the latest round of growth in the sector. They argue that consolidation and concentration in retailing in the United States occurred at different times and for different reasons than had occurred in manufacturing. In the decades before World War II, the manufacturing sectors of the American economy had already gone through several periods of mergers and massive consolidations that not only resulted in vertical and horizontal control over processes of production, but, by virtue of the economic power of manufacturing firms, also allowed them to control the distribution and retailing of their products as well (Chandler, 1979). For example, the automobile manufacturers developed franchised retail outlets, as did some consumer appliances makers (for example, RCA and GE). More often, manufacturers dealt directly with wholesalers that in turn distributed products to many small retail stores, most of which were independently owned. These changes in American manufacturing are nicely described and much debated in a series of books and articles starting with Chandler (1977, 1990) and proceeding on to Fligstein (1990), Lazonick (1991), Roy (1997), Prechel (2000), Perrow (2002), and Langlois (2003).

Despite the preponderance of small independently owned retailers, there were a number of large retail chains that began to emerge before World War II. The mail-order mass retailers, such as Sears and Roebuck and Montgomery Ward, were very prominent before World War I, and in the 1920s, with the growth of cities and the decline of rural America, these same firms began to establish chain stores in urban cores throughout the United States. Also, the largest retailer before World War II was A & P (Atlantic and Pacific), which had established a national chain of grocery stores early in the twentieth century. These chain stores, however, were important exceptions to the rule, as most retail firms, whatever the type of product they sold, continued to be small, regionally concentrated and privately owned. Clothing, shoes, groceries, hardware and building supplies, household appliances, as well as most other consumer products were sold through such locally or regionally owned stores, and these stores obtained their goods through supply lines that they neither directly controlled nor could indirectly influence through their buying power. Therefore, with only a few exceptions before World War II, there was a stark contrast between the relative concentration of manufacturers in their respective sectors (Chandler, 1990) and the relative lack of concentration of retailers in their respective sectors (Bluestone, et al., 1981).

The divergence between manufacturers and retailers was exacerbated by state and federal legislation known as "fair trade laws." Mostly passed during the Great Depression, these laws "(technically Resale Price Maintenance statutes) were the legal mechanism that permitted manufacturing firms to set a minimum price that retailers (and wholesalers) could charge for the products they produced" (Bluestone, et al., 1981, pp. 124–5). Although these laws were not well enforced or very effective in maintaining price levels for most products (Petrovic, Hamilton, and Kotha, 2004), they nonetheless reduced the enthusiasm and probably the capacity within the retail sector for widespread expansion and consolidation.

Immediately after World War II, therefore, the large-firm model of corporate capitalism predominated (Prechel, 2000). In the United States, the position of General Motors, Ford, IBM, General Electric, Westinghouse, Boeing, and a long list of other large corporations in nearly every economic sector seems unassailable (Chandler, 1990, pp. 638–732). Likewise, in the early post-war years, mammoth business groups in Europe and Japan, such as Daimler-Benz, Volkswagen, Mitsubishi, and Mitsui, re-emerged and gradually grew stronger than they were before the war, and new giants, such Toyota and Sony, entered the scene.

While manufacturing firms had built dominant positions in their respective industries before and immediately after World War II, retail firms (for example, departments stores and supermarkets) only started the process of concentration in earnest in the 1950s (Bluestone, et al., 1981). Although fair trade laws continued to favor manufacturers over retailers, such large chain retailers as Sears, J.C. Penney, Bon Marche, and Montgomery Ward went through a period of rapid expansion and began to dominate department store retailing. These national chains became so dominant, in fact, that many small, independently owned department stores simply went out of business in the face of the centralized buying power of these national stores.

One of the great advantages of the large department store chains was their ability "to escape price-maintenance regulations by selling private-label products, such as Sears's Kenmore line produced by Whirlpool." In fact, "the proliferation of private labels reduced the efficacy of fair trade laws to the point where active support almost disappeared" (Bluestone, et al., 1981, p. 126). By the mid-1960s, most states no longer actively enforced these laws, and by the mid-1970s the laws had been repealed throughout most of the United States. In 1981, when Bluestone and his colleagues examined the retail structure of the United States, the retail revolution was in full swing. "Repeal (of fair trade laws)," they (1981, p. 126) concluded, "precipitated a virtually total restructuring of the retail sector."

The initial set of changes, occurring in the late 1950s and 1960s, were, in large part, a consequence of three interrelated factors: tax policies on commercial construction, the construction of interstate highways, and suburbanization. First, in 1954, the U.S. Congress passed, and President Eisenhower signed into law, the Internal Revenue Code of 1954. These tax laws provided for accelerated depreciation of commercial buildings, among other business investments. This loophole in tax laws allowed investors to make much higher returns on commercial construction than on equities, and so the shopping-center construction boom began, stimulated not from the demand of consumers for convenient shopping locations, but rather from money of speculators (Hanshett, 1996). At the end of 1953, there were about ten major shopping centers in the country, but beginning immediately in 1954, there was a surge not only in the more common strip malls, of which there were about 500 in 1954, but also more importantly in the construction of large shopping centers. "In 1964, ten years after the initial surge of the shopping center development, there were 7,600 shopping centers in the United States, including nearly 400 large regional shopping malls, and accounting for almost 30 percent of total retail sales" (Petrovic, et al., 2004; also see Bucklin, 1972, Cohen, 2002). All of these shopping centers not only needed anchor stores, which were usually general retailers such as Sears and Macy's, but also specialty stores that could bring in niche consumers.[5] Most major retail chains of this period expanded rapidly in size, especially those that were already large and well capitalized. Sears, J.C. Penney, and Federated Stores (Macy's) were among the clear winners in the contest to become the standard anchor stores in the new malls being built.

By the 1960s, however, the supply of available additional retail space created opportunities for a whole new lineup of specialty retailers, retailers that began to appeal to the main currents of the Vietnam and post–Vietnam War era: a growing youth and sports subcultures fed by television programs and advertising, the rapid increase in women working in professional jobs, counterculture movements that led to alternative lifestyles and niche fashions. These new specialty retailers, such as The Gap and The Limited, started operation in the 1960s, expanded rapidly and went public in the 1970s, and joined the exclusive Fortune 500 group of leading U.S. companies in the 1980s.

The second major driver of the retail revolution was another act of government, the Federal Highway Act of 1956, which established the interstate highway system, including ring roads around major American cities. By the 1960s, high-speed interstate highways connected all major urban areas in the country. These highways facilitated not only suburbanization, which is our third factor, but also the ability of firms efficiently to use trucking as their primary form of product distribution, which in turn led to more developed logistical systems of distribution.

A closely related third driver was suburbanization of America's urban population. The mass migration to the suburbs that started in the late 1950s and continued through the 1980s led to massive home construction and to widespread home and automobile ownership. It also supplied consumers for shopping centers that had been built around every major urban area. These consumers increasingly became able to choose among the niche-market lifestyles that specialty retailers began to target. Each enhanced the other. By the late 1970s, in response to the boom in home construction and the rise in home ownership, Home Depot, among other similar firms, started business, quickly expanded, and soon dominated the retail sector in hardware and home building supplies.

These three drivers of the initial phase of the retail revolution paved the way for two sets of changes, both occurring in the 1960s and 1970s: the emergence and rapid widespread adoption of value merchandizing and, at nearly the same moment, the split in value merchandising between general merchandisers and specialty retailers. As Table 6.1 shows, it was during

---

[5] From the late 1950s through the 1980s, investment in retailing grew at a faster rate than the growth of sales or the GDP (Regan, 1999, p. 399).

Table 6.1. *U.S. Retail Firms With Revenues over $5 Billion, 2001, Ordered by the Founding Year*

Name	Industry	Fortune Rank	Revenues 2001	Founded		Web Site
Sonic Automotive	Automotive	288	6,337	1997		http://corp.autonation.com/about/mile.asp
AutoNation	Automotive	101	19,989	1996	As a division of Republic, in 1999 fully independent	
United Auto Group	Automotive	292	6,221	1990		http://www.unitedauto.com/corpinfo.htm
Office Depot	Office Products	173	11,154	1986		http://www.officedepot.com/CompanyInfo/
Staples	Office Products	178	10,744	1986		http://www.staples.com/about/default.asp?HPR=152
BJ's Wholesale Club	Warehouse Club	331	5,280	1984		
Best Buy	Electronics	131	15,327	1983	Originally founded in 1966, changed the name and concept in 1983	http://media.corporate-ir.net/media_files/nsd/cost/cost.time.pdf
Costco Wholesale	Warehouse Club	44	34,797	1983		
Home Depot	Home Improvement	18	53,553	1978		
Toys 'R' Us	Toys	175	11,019	1978	1958 as a discount toy retailer: Children's Supermart	www.gap.com/
TJX	Apparel	179	10,709	1977	As T. J. Maxx, a division of Zayre	
Nike	Apparel Marketer	204	9,489	1972		
Gap	Apparel	149	13,848	1969		
Circuit City Stores	Electronics	157	12,959	1968	Originally in 1949, expanded and changed name in 1968	
Rite Aid	Food and Drug	132	15,297	1968	Under current name, founded in 1962 as Thrif D Discount Center	
CVS	Food and Drug	93	22,241	1963		
Limited	Apparel	208	9,363	1963		
Kmart	General Merchandisers	40	36,910	1962	A division of Kresge	http://www.kohls.com/
Kohl's	General Merchandisers	253	7,489	1962	First department store, grocery business since 1920	http://www.lowes.com/lkn?action=pg&p=AboutLowes/CompanyInfo

(continued)

Table 6.1 (continued)

Name	Industry	Fortune rank	Revenues 2001	Founded	Web Site
Target	General Merchandisers	34	39,888	1962 A division of Dayton Hudson	
Wal-Mart	General Merchandisers	1	219,812	1962	http://www.dollargeneral.com/
Dollar General	General Merchandisers	326	5,323	1956	
Dillard's	General Merchandisers	230	8,388	1949	
Albertson's	Food and Drug	38	37,931	1939	http://www1.albertsons.com/corporate/
Publix Super Markets	Food and Drug	133	15,284	1930	http://www.dillards.com/info/company.index.jsp
Federated Dept. Stores	General Merchandisers	118	16,895	1929	http://www.publix.com/
Winn-Dixie Stores	Food and Drug	160	12,903	1928 As Winn&Lovett Grocery Co., a supermarket company, changed name to Winn-Dixie in 1955	http://www.federated-fds.com/company/his_1.7.asp
Saks	General Merchandisers	297	6,071	1924	
Lowe's	Home Improvement	94	22,111	1921	
Vanity Fair (VF Corp.)	Apparel Marketer	320	5,519	1919 Founded in 1899, from 191 as a textile compnay under the present name, in 1969 it intergated into jeans business	
Safeway	Food and Drug	45	34,301	1914	http://about.nordstrom.com/aboutus/?origin=hp-lefnav
J. C. Penney	General Merchandisers	50	32,004	1902	http://www.saksincorporated.com/our_stores/histories.html
Nordstrom	General Merchandisers	314	5,634	1901	http://www.vfc.com/pages/history.asp
Walgreen	Food and Drug	78	24,623	1901	
Sears Roebuck	General Merchandisers	32	41,078	1893	http://www.kroger.com/corpnewsinfo-history.htm
Kroger	Food and Drug	22	50,098	1883	
May Dept. Stores	General Merchandisers	143	14,175	1877	http://www2.mayco.com/common/annual_report.jsp

this period that most of the now prominent stores in both categories began operations or converted to value merchandising. In one year alone, 1962, only months apart from each other, Wal-Mart, Kmart, Kohl's, and Target first began operations as self-service discount department stores.[6] Specialty retailers, as we indicated earlier, date from this period as well. Both categories of value merchandisers, as well as the national department store chains, would increasingly source the goods they sold from Asian manufacturers.

It was the national department store chains that first opened the path to Asia in the early 1960s. The initial orders were very small and occurred at a time when international trade was, proportionally, near its all-time low (Feenstra, 1998). Beginning with the Great Depression, and continuing through World War II, the level of imports into the United States had fallen from its highs at the turn of century to its low points during and immediately after World War II. The post–World War II consumer boom of the 1950s and early 1960s was fueled, almost entirely, with products produced by American manufacturers. However, by the early 1960s, the economies of Europe and Japan had been largely rebuilt, and with sudden expansion of retail outlets in the late 1950s and 1960s and the fierce competition among them for consumers, some of the largest retailers began sourcing a few products from foreign manufacturers. Although only a few primary references are available on overseas sourcing (for example, Stores of the World Directory 1970–71), it seems likely that the first retailers to source overseas were those seeking high-fashion apparel (mainly from Europe), and those developing in-house brands for apparel, a wide variety of toys for children, and cheap consumer electronics, especially transistor radios. Most all of the later categories came from Japan and

---

[6] Leading the fight against fair trade laws (Bluestone, et al., 1981, p. 125), discount retailers began to compete directly with full-service department stores by sourcing items that they regularly stocked and that were not necessarily branded (for example, children's clothes, toys, tools, and kitchenware) and by working closely with brand-name merchandisers to sell products that were branded (for example, household electronic products, such as televisions and stereos). Kmart opened its first discount store in 1962, in 1976 changed its name from Kresge to Kmart, and rapidly expanded after that. In 1969, according to Kresge's Annual Report (1969, p. 6), only 5 percent of the company's sales was from imported items, but they planned to expand "imported merchandise from the Orient" in the "near future." Kmart established buying offices in Taiwan in 1971 and by 1992 had placed over 500 million US$ worth of orders from Taiwan alone, where approximately 40 percent of their foreign orders were placed (Gereffi and Pan, 1994, p. 137). Toys-R-Us started as a toy supermarket in 1957, adopted discount methods in the 1960s, became a publicly listed firm in 1970, and grew quickly to be the dominant retailer of toys in the United States; many of their lines of toys were sourced in East Asia. Wal-Mart opened its first discount store in 1962, its first distribution center in 1970, and went public in 1979 with one billion dollars worth of sales. By 1990, both Wal-Mart and Kmart had replaced Sears and J. C. Penney as the top U.S. retailers. Home Depot, now the world's largest home improvement retailer, started in 1978.

Hong Kong, locations where a reasonable quality and quantity of goods could be obtained less expensively than they could in the United States or Europe.

Garments were among the first goods to be sourced in Asia. The initial group of American textile and apparel manufacturing firms to develop contract manufacturing in Asia were known as the "big five" (that is, Regal Accessories [Irving Alpert], Republic Cellini [Hy Katz], Marlene, Spartan Mayro, and CBS [Jack Clark]), all major manufacturing firms located in the South and all producing in-store brands for major department stores (Bonacich and Waller, 1994, pp. 81–2). As orders expanded and the value of maintaining low prices increased, these firms began to contract an increasing proportion of their garments from Asia. In order to arrange contract manufacturing relationships, these firms "worked almost exclusively with the large Japanese trading companies, especially Mitsui" (Bonacich and Waller, 1994, p. 81). The trading company served as the go-between – contracting with the manufacturing firms, arranging for inputs, supervising the quality, and delivering the product.

It quickly became apparent, however, that neither the Southern textile and apparel firms nor the Japanese trading companies were needed to match retailers to manufacturer. The general department stores and, more importantly, the new generation of discount and specialty retailers, especially those specializing in fashion apparels, eliminated the middlemen and began directly to arrange their own contracting relationships in Asia. This was so much the case that "the big five all died in the 1970s" (Bonacich and Waller, 1994, p. 83). As we demonstrate in the next chapter, the role of Japanese trading companies diminished as well. Gary Gereffi (Gereffi and Pan, 1994, p. 137) shows that most of the major department stores opened buying offices in Taiwan in the early 1970s, and soon began to buy large quantities of a limited range of items.[7] The same firms also established offices in South Korea in the same period (Jung, 1984, pp. 109–10). For instance, The Limited opened its first store in Kingsdale Mall in Columbus, Ohio, in 1963; offered its first public stock in 1969; and began purchasing goods in Asia in 1971 from Mast Industries, a Hong Kong-based importing firm that has served since that time as its principal intermediary buyer in Asia. Mast Industries, which became a wholly owned subsidiary of The Limited in 1978, opened its buying offices in Taiwan in 1973 and its buying offices in South Korea in 1976. According to Gary Gereffi's interviews with Mast Industries (Gereffi and Pan, 1994, pp. 139–40), for many years The Limited "placed 100 percent of its apparel orders with Taiwanese factories." By the late 1980s, The Limited had become the world's largest retailer of women's apparel. Not coincidentally, most other specialty retailers and brand-name apparel merchandisers – The

[7] See Table 7.1.

Gap, Calvin Klein, Esprit, Ann Taylor, Polo/Ralph Lauren, and Yves St. Laurent – started their companies in the late 1960s and early 1970s, and all of them followed a similar model, initially arranging for a portion and sometimes all of their manufacturing in Asia, and only later expanding to other locations besides Asia.

Niche-market footwear soon followed the same model developed by fashion apparel manufacturers. The founder of Nike designed a specialized running shoe and started contract manufacturing in Japan in 1971, and founded the Nike Company in 1972. By 1979, Nike, which owned not a single factory, claimed 50 percent of the running shoe market in the United States and ordered millions of shoes at a time from Korean and Taiwanese factories. Other footwear makers – Reebok, Timberland, Clark, and many more – followed suit, so much so that by 1985, Taiwan and South Korea manufactured over 50 percent of all footwear imported into the United States (U.S. Customs Trade Data 1972–2002).

From the beginnings of large-scale global buying in 1965, sourcing certain kinds of items (which we will describe later) in Asia worked very well. Contract manufacturing spawned an alternative relationship between retailers and manufacturers, a relationship that greatly privileged retailers: Beginning on a small scale in the early 1960s, but then accelerating rapidly after that, retailers started directly to source batches of differentiated goods specially ordered for sale in niche markets. The standard reason given for the early contract manufacturing in East Asia is the cheap labor, which of course was a factor. But even more important was that American-based retailers, engaged in hot competition in their home markets, began to develop and organize manufacturing directly without owning factories and without the corporate and labor negotiations that would be involved in subcontracting with American-based firms. This model of merchandising blurred the distinction between retailing and manufacturing, so much so that many manufacturing firms, such as Nike and later Dell Computers, began to appear that did not actually manufacture anything, but rather focused almost entirely on building and assessing consumer demand, designing products for consumer niches, and merchandising those products to the targeted markets.

Unlike most other manufacturing firms of the day, these merchandisers sourced their products from specialized manufacturing firms that could produce the desired goods on demand at the right prices and quality. It is important to note that many of these specialty retailers and brand-name merchandisers created markets for distinct products where no differentiated markets had existed before. Manufacturers that no longer had to worry about factories, labor, assembly lines, and long production runs focused all their attention on the products themselves – on making those products and their consumption extraordinary and widely desired and on assessing consumer demand. Merchandising, including establishing a brand name, was crucial, and a part of the merchandising and branding process was to transform the products into a way of living, into an object of necessary consumption given a style of life. Nike did not simply sell shoes in competition with every other footwear company, but rather sold a way of life that went with the shoes, high-performance shoes that were different for, and that maximized the wearer's performance in, every activity. By emphasizing the specialized setting where the product is worn or the special person who wears it, the brand-name merchandisers tried to reduce in the mind of consumers the substitutability of the product. Their success in identifying niche markets and making products for those niches had the effect of reducing competition with other manufacturers making the same general category of products. Paradoxically, by narrowing the range of targeted consumers, brand-name merchandisers actually greatly increased their market share, as well as their market power, in and beyond those segments. Running shoes were no longer worn just for running or denim jeans just for outdoor wear.

These manufacturers without factories initially specialized in selling fashion goods and goods with rapidly changing product cycles. For example, The Limited "is reputed to have the fastest turn around time for garment sourcing in the business (thirty to forty days from order to shipment)" (Gereffi and Pan, 1994, p. 140). Although well suited to fads and fashions, this method of manufacturing soon became a model of production that both would-be merchandisers and would-be manufacturers could emulate and that quickly spread to include household appliances, consumer electronics, and nearly very other easily manufactured consumer product.

The initial rounds of changes in the retail revolution created entrepreneurial space for even more substantial changes. These changes occurred in the late 1970s and early 1980s, a time when the American economy had entered a severe downturn. The end of the Vietnam conflict and the disruption caused by the second oil shock produced a recession. The recession, in turn, led many American consumers to economize by shopping where they could find the lowest prices. It was in this period that competition between the new discount and specialty retailers, on the one hand, and the older, more traditional retailers, on the other hand, came to a head, and set off a wave of mergers and acquisitions, causing even greater consolidation within the sector. Figure 6.1 traces this consolidation of chain stores across the entire retail sector from the 1960s to the 1990s. From Figure 6.2 we can see that this consolidation was striking in certain core segments of the retail sector. The number of mass discounters reduced from over ten to four major chains. Moreover, the major department stores, such as Macy's and Bon Marche, curtailed their in-store brands and began to build mini-boutiques within their stores, featuring such brand-name apparel manufacturers as Polo and Anne Klein.

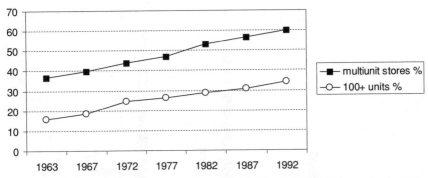

Figure 6.1. The Revenue Share of Multiunit (Chain) Stores in the U.S. Retail Sector, 1963–92. *Source:* BEA, Economic Census, 1963–92.

In addition, many of the same brand-name manufacturers began to open factory outlet stores in scattered locations around the United States and elsewhere.

The rise of the new retailers stocked with items manufactured in Asia contributed to a reorganization of U.S. manufacturing that occurred in the late 1970s and early 1980s. Many analysts of the period (for example, Bluestone and Harrison, 1982) began to worry that American firms were

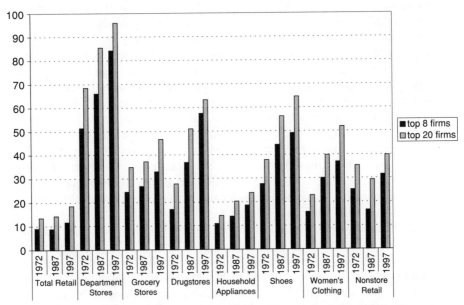

Figure 6.2. The Revenue Share of Top Twenty and Top Eight Firms in Selected Retail Sectors, U.S. *Source:* BEA, Economic Census, 1972–97.

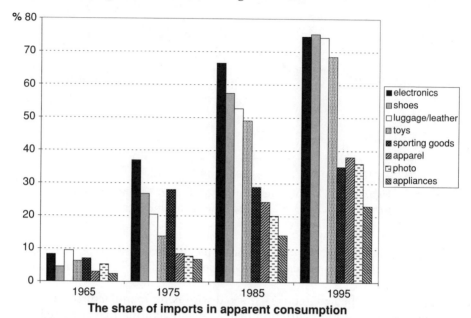

Figure 6.3. Import Penetration in Consumer Goods.

no longer competitive. Many older and well-established manufacturing firms were forced into bankruptcy and many survivors had to restructure, including IBM, among many others. The Upper Midwest, formerly renowned as the industrial heartland of America, became widely known as the "Rustbelt" (Bluestone and Harrison, 1982, Harrison and Bluestone, 1988). A fundamental cause of this crisis in American manufacturing was that the traditional retailers maintained their American-based supply lines and stocked their shelves with more traditional types of products, but as these retailers lost customers, because of their competitors' low prices and the availability of new products carried by other retailers, the orders with American manufacturers declined as the imports of foreign products surged. As Figure 6.3 shows, the percentage of imports in relation to total American consumption of major categories of consumer goods doubled or nearly doubled every decade between 1965 and 1985, and grew substantially after that time as well.

By the middle 1980s, this competition among retailers was exacerbated by the necessity to adopt the techniques of "lean retailing" (Abernathy, et al., 1999). The initial elements allowing for the formulation of lean retailing began obscurely in the 1970s with the development of the Uniform Product Code (UPC), barcodes, and scanning devices. A group of food manufacturers (including Heinz, General Mills, and General Foods) and grocery store owners (including Kroger, A&P Tea Company, and First National Stores) first met in 1969 to discuss the development of products codes to make the management of grocery store inventories more efficient. The committee completed their work in 1974, the same year the first item bearing a UPC symbol, a package of Wrigley's gum, "crossed the scanner at Marsh's Supermarket in Troy, Ohio" (Brown, 1997, p. 5). The UPC committee anticipated that "there would never be more than 6,000 registrations," but the registrations soared, numbering over 110,000 distinct UPC symbols by 1994, the twentieth anniversary of the beginning. By 2002, the figure had doubled again.

Barcodes, scanners, and more generally "electronic data interchange" (EDI) became the medium to continue the trend towards the globalization of supply lines that was already well begun in the late 1960s and 1970s.[8] A core principle of value merchandising – for discount retailers, brand-name merchandisers, and specialty retailers – is to match as closely as possible the number and types of goods on hand to the number and types of goods that consumers will actually buy. This involves a precise calculation of consumer demand. In the 1960s and 1970s, however, value merchandisers and department stores could only anticipate consumer demand, and to hedge their risks they would buy limited quantities of a limited range of each type of differentiated good – so many in extra large sizes, so many in pink.

The development of high-powered mainframe computers and database software suitable for inventory control, both of which became widely available until the 1980s, made barcodes and scanners the instruments of assessing consumer choice at the place and time of purchase. By the late 1980s, these innovations allowed retailers and merchandisers to rationalize their supply chains. Abernathy and his colleagues (Abernathy, et al., 1999) describe the "four building blocks" of this effort to rationalize supply chains, the total configuration of which they call "lean retailing." As already discussed, the first building block of lean retailing is standardized product codes, barcodes, and scanning technology. Second, based on UPC and barcodes, merchandisers and retailers quickly developed computerized inventory management systems. "Mass merchants have 150,000 SKU (stockkeeping units) and department stores may have over a million, indicating the variety of styles, colors, fabrics, sizes, and products that constitute ... sales. Bar codes permit organizations to handle effectively the kind of vast product differentiation that would have been prohibitively expensive in an earlier era" (Abernathy, et al., 1999, p. 61). Computerized

---

[8] EDI is "A standard format for computer-to-computer transmission of business information and transactions between trading partners, such as invoices and purchase orders." Uniform Code Council: http://www.uc-council.org/.

inventory systems facilitated the development of electronic data interchange, which allowed retailers and suppliers to communicate in a
common, standardized way. Using a common communication interface,
contract manufacturers obtained real-time information about how products were selling and which items needed to be reordered, thereby
expediting "purchase orders, shipping invoices, and funds transfer"
(Abernathy, 1999, p. 62).

Third, merchandisers and retailers adopted state-of-the-art distribution
centers, which rely on "sophisticated equipment like scanners and automated conveyer systems" to manage the flow of goods (Abernathy, et al.,
1999, p. 64). These modern distribution centers are the retailers' equivalent of the just-in-time inventory systems pioneered by Toyota and other
Japanese manufacturers in the 1970s. Applied to retailing, they are basically transfer points, instead of the traditional warehouses that national
department stores had depended on in earlier years.

Fourth, lean retailing relies on enforcing "standards across firms"
(Abernathy, et at., 1999, pp. 69–70). Standardization across firms and
across networks of firms in such things as sizes, colors, weights and
measures, operating systems, communication devices, and any number
of other matters allows multiple firms and multiple networks of firms to
work together in a seamless way. Standardization creates a common world
of work processes, or what Abernathy and his colleagues call "packages,"
within and between industries, permitting firms in different sectors of the
economy (such as manufacturing, retailing, and shipping) and whose personnel never meet face-to-face to coordinate their joint endeavors. For
example, by adopting standardized packages, retailers supply manufacturers with all the necessary information to make the product "floor-ready."
Packaged in the right box, affixed with the correct retail price for a given
location and with the right barcode and tracking information, the product
can be shipped from the manufacturing site, tracked along the way, delivered to a distribution center and then to the specific store where the item is
needed ready for display, with no further effort on the part of the retailer.

Other types of retailers now commandeered the innovations first
designed for grocery stores. At first, however, the adoption of UPC codes
was uneven. Many of the older retail firms, such as Sears, not only had
predominantly American supply-lines, but also had already made large
capital investments in developing proprietary, automated inventory systems, and were reluctant to make additional and even larger investments
to adopt universal product codes and standardized scanning devices. But
after Kmart and Wal-Mart both adopted the technology in the early
1980s and "began to demand that their vendors adopt the U.P.C." as
well (Dunlop and Rivkin, 1997, p. 5), most other retailers not only had
to adopt the new technology, but had to start sourcing products in Asia
as well.

The need to cut costs and to restructure led once powerful manufacturers to join the ranks of the factory-less brand-name merchandisers. Beginning in late 1970s and continuing through the 1990s, such firms as Schwinn (bicycles), Eddie Bauer (specialty outdoor clothing), General Electric and Westinghouse (household appliances), and Compaq (computers) closed all or most of their consumer product factories in the United States and began to contract all or a large part of their products overseas, mostly in East Asia. In the same period, the last surviving manufacturer of televisions and radios, Zenith, gave up its American factories in favor of Asian contractors. For a time, in the 1980s and early 1990s, even automobile makers, such as Chrysler and General Motors, sourced entire lines of automobiles from Japan and South Korea.

In making the move to Asia, some American firms actually invested in and helped to organize the Asian production of their branded goods. Others played a more passive role, letting the Asian manufacturers perform the primary entrepreneurial roles. In both regards, these businesses simply followed in the footsteps of the earlier firms, copying the first-comers' techniques of contract manufacturing and direct sourcing of component parts and finished goods. What started in textiles had by the late 1980s spread to almost very category of consumer goods, including computers and the full range of high technology products, most of which were never mass produced in the United States. Dell Computer Corporation and Gateway, like many other high technology firms, owe their successes entirely to contract manufacturing, much of which is centered in Taiwan; they started their businesses, respectively, in 1984 and 1985.

By the beginning of the 1990s, the widespread adoption of lean retailing by American retailers (and increasingly European retailers as well) created **price-sensitive networks of firms that turned manufacturing into organizational extensions of retailing products.** All the steps in manufacturing, distributing, and selling goods came increasingly to be organized backwards from "consumer choice." Consumer choice, however, was increasingly less about consumption and a theory of consumer preferences than about actual sales information and the development of complex organizational capabilities to analyze and react to any purchase that is made for whatever reason at the time and the place the purchase is made. When retailers have instantaneous information at the point of sale about what product was bought and increasingly who bought it, then they no longer need to posit a psychological or sociological theory of why people buy what they do in order to put together an inventory of products to sell. Instead, retailers and brand-name merchandisers merely have to analyze actual choices and, as quickly as possible, give buyers more and a greater selection of what they are already buying. For rapid response to demand, these sellers of goods needed to be organizationally linked to the makers of goods, and they needed to control these production networks so that

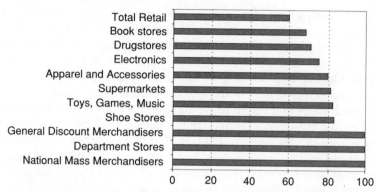

Figure 6.4. Revenue Share of Multiunit (Chain) Stores in Selected Retail Sectors, United States, 1997. *Source:* BEA, Economic Census Data, 1997.

they could obtain the goods they wanted to sell, at the price they wanted to pay, and delivered at the time and place they specified. Their backward linkages organized and predictable, merchandisers and retailers were free to focus on assessing and massaging consumer choice. A Wal-Mart executive made this point very succinctly: "We don't *sell* stuff," he said, "we *buy* stuff for consumers" (Quoted by Blackwell, 1997, p. xv, our emphasis). To paraphrase Gereffi (1994), the retail revolution turned retailers and brand-name manufacturers into buyers, "big buyers."

Wal-Mart is now the world's largest company, ranking first in the Fortune's list of the top 500 global companies. Together with a relatively small number of other chain stores, Wal-Mart has led the consolidation of the retail sector. Figure 6.4 shows the share of total revenues of chain stores in selected retail sectors in 1997. There is no question that a retail revolution has occurred, and, as we will demonstrate, there is no question that it had tremendous effects on the growth of East Asian economies.

Intermediation and the Organization of Intermediary Demand

The development and rationalization of organizational linkages between big buyers and manufacturers emerged into a sector of economic activity that Daniel Spulber (1996, 1998) has identified as "intermediation," and the demand generated by this sector is what we call "intermediary demand." In economic terms, intermediation involves market-making processes linking buyers and sellers, and intermediaries are the agents that carry out these process. These agents "seek out suppliers, find and encourage buyers, select buy and sell prices, define the terms of transactions, manage the payments and record keeping for transactions, and hold inventories to provide liquidity or availability of goods and services." In addition, "intermediaries often transform products to add value: transporting, storing, repackaging, assembling, preparing for final use, and adding information and guaranties" (Spulber, 1996, pp. 135–6). According to Spulber's "conservative" calculations (1996, p. 141), "intermediation contributes about 28 percent of the GDP (of the U.S. economy)."

A raw estimate of this sort does not do justice to the roles that intermediaries play. Although they represent a significant portion of the U.S. economy, the significance of American-based intermediaries lies in the fact that they do not merely "make markets," do not simply link preexisting consumers to preexisting manufacturers, thereby providing some efficiencies and reduced transaction costs, which is the implication of Spulber's analysis. Instead, based on our analysis, it is abundantly clear that intermediaries play a pivotal role in creating markets in first place. In so doing, they contribute to the restructuring of entire economies, both in the United States and overseas. On the consumer side, they create new types of buyers – discount shoppers, lifestyle enthusiasts. They supply differentiated goods for differentiated people. Because every purchase is tabulated and analyzed and made part of a computerized feedback loop that connects final demand to manufacturing, the gap between the final consumer and the big buyers is small and continually growing smaller.

On the manufacturing side, as portrayed in Figure 6.5, the same outcome occurs. The tighter the linkages with the final consumer, the tighter the linkages have to be to the manufacturers as well. In competition with others in their own sector, intermediaries strive to reduce risk on both sides in both consumer and manufacturing markets. To create these tight linkages with manufacturers, intermediaries attempt to organize their linkages backwards to the manufacture from point-of-sale information. The new retailers are able to organize these backward linkages because they have great and increasingly exclusive access to final consumers, which creates huge barriers to entry for any would-be manufacturers of consumer goods, and because they develop long-term manufacturing relations with producers who have (at least initially) limited or no access to these markets except through the big buyers. These are manufacturers that are entirely dependent on the big buyers for their business. This exclusivity, therefore, allows the new retailers to exert great market power "backwards" over the manufacturing process itself and *to organize* manufacturing process to reflect their needs based on a "real-time" analysis of consumer choice. Although a great and mainly laudatory literature has grown up about "flexible specialization,"[9] what the concept really means is an arrangement to induce *dependent manufacturing*.

---

[9] For a comprehensive review of this literature, see Vallas (1999).

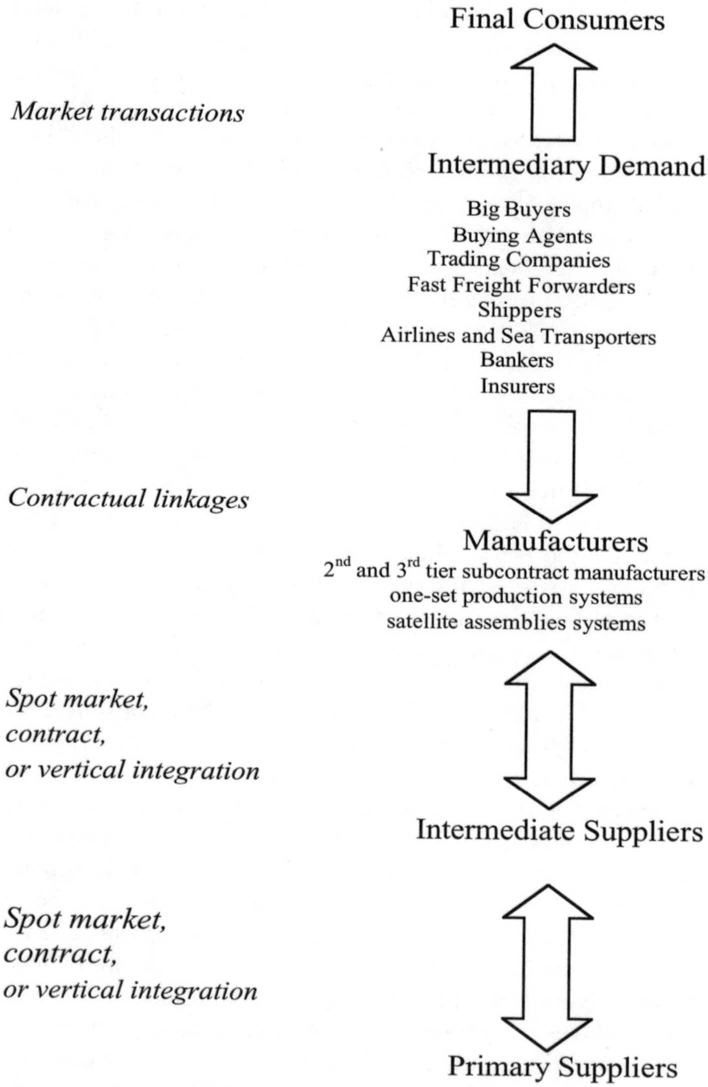

Final Consumers

Market transactions

Intermediary Demand

Big Buyers
Buying Agents
Trading Companies
Fast Freight Forwarders
Shippers
Airlines and Sea Transporters
Bankers
Insurers

Contractual linkages

Manufacturers

2nd and 3rd tier subcontract manufacturers
one-set production systems
satellite assemblies systems

Spot market,
contract,
or vertical integration

Intermediate Suppliers

Spot market,
contract,
or vertical integration

Primary Suppliers

Figure 6.5. The Emergent Economic Organization of the Global Economy.

The intermediation that emerged in the course of the retail revolution, therefore, is not a benign process, but is rather one that redefines the linkages across markets and opens all of these linkages to competitive struggles for dominance. Entrepreneurial discovery of new opportunities has led to innovations – new niches, new technologies, new organizational combinations of firms that transform market competition at local, national, and global levels.

The extraordinary development of the Asian economies was an outcome of intermediary demand generated during the first great waves of the retail revolution occurring in the United States after World War II. Beginning in the 1960s and 1970s, and then rapidly accelerating after 1975, intermediaries made Asian manufacturers an integral part of the retail revolution that occurred in the United States. Big buyers were not the only intermediaries involved. In fact, establishing the connections between the big buyers and the Asian manufacturers became the work of many types of people and firms. The big buyers themselves employed jobbers, who directly ordered and supervised the manufacturing; they went through brokers, who bought goods for them; they worked directly with Asian manufacturers, who often came to their headquarters in the United States; they made deals with Asian trading companies, which in turn arranged for the manufacturing to be done. However the actual connections between manufacturers and buyers were established and maintained, there was, in addition, a large number of firms, trade associations, and government and privately sponsored councils and institutes that helped to arrange these connections. Trade fairs, international expositions, chambers of commerce, development councils, and trade associations – all focused on matching foreign buyers to Asian manufacturers. Cities and national governments spent millions to build huge complexes, such as the World Trade Centers in Taipei and in Seoul, to house the expositions, to maintain lists and provide permanent exhibits of products made by local firms, and to facilitate the matching process through providing an assortment of services. Furthermore, entire industries arose to service these connections: banking, insurance, shipping, fast-freight forwarders, air freighters, communication equipment, and many others.

All these various connections between the manufacturers and the retailers, as well as the supporting infrastructure and service providers, developed and accelerated the growth of intermediary demand. At the time, in the late 1960s, when big buyers first began to order manufactured Korean- and Taiwanese-made goods through Japanese trading companies, there were few institutions and services supporting this intermediary level of economic activity. But by the 1980s, everything was in place – the supporting institutions and service firms and, most of all, the linkages between retailers and manufacturers. As the organizations of intermediary demand and the routines of lean retailing became established, the economic activity funneled through this level simply exploded, so much so that it is not too far-fetched to say that buyers and sellers became tied to each other's success. The development of quality contract manufacturing in Asia allowed new types of consumer products and new types of firms selling those products to emerge in the United States, and the rapid and overwhelming success of merchandising and retailing in the United States and elsewhere encouraged Asian entrepreneurs rapidly to expand, to diversify, and to upgrade their manufacture of export products. The early and continuing successes in making products designed for and often ordered by merchandisers and mass retailers in the United States and Europe fed back on the Asian economies, promoting rapid growth and the emergence of complex economic organizations. In retrospect, we can see that these Asian connections also helped to accelerate the retail revolution in the United States.

The evidence for this demand-driven explosion of manufactured goods exported to the United States from Asia is found in the trade data, and in supplementary material that helps to explain the data. It is to this evidence we now turn.

Trade-Data Archeology

A large part of the difficulty in systematically analyzing factors relating to demand has been the lack of trade data sufficiently detailed to connect manufacturing activities in Asia with merchandising and retailing activities in export markets. Previously, the best export data available were trade statistics, supplied by exporting countries, which are aggregated into major product categories, such as textiles and garments. These aggregated classifications allowed few, if any, distinctions within categories or between countries producing the same range of products.

Working under the auspices of the International Trade and Investment Program at the National Bureau of Economic Research, Feenstra (1996) recently compiled a comprehensive database of all U.S. imports from 1972–94, and even more recently has updated the database to the year 2001.[10] This database contains the most disaggregated trade data available. Collected by the U.S. Customs Service, the data report the country of origin for U.S. imports at a 7-digit level known as the Tariff Schedule of the United States Annotated (TSUSA) from 1972–88, and at the 10-digit Harmonized System (HS) level from 1989 on. Both of these are fine enough to distinguish between four-wheeled and three-wheeled baby carriages, or between bicycles having wheel sizes between 55 and 63.5 centimeters and those having wheel sizes 63.5 centimeters and larger, or between parts of almost any export product and the whole product itself. For example, in 1985, listed among Taiwan's 6,257 categories of export products sold to the United States were 1,691 distinct types of garments and 127 distinct types of footwear. Although these data are

---

[10] These data are available at www.internationaldata.org.

only for imports into one country, albeit by far the most important trading partner for both South Korea and Taiwan, they are still an invaluable source of data for making inferences about Asia's contribution to the retail revolution, as well as about the organization of Asian economies.

These trade data are, in fact, so disaggregated that they serves as historical records of East Asian economic development. They are the footprints left behind on the path to industrialization. They indicate the real record of growth, the best remaining record of the items that firms actually made and sold overseas and whose sales provided revenues that could be reinvested, pocketed, or otherwise used. Because trade data record the products exported, trade data permit us to track the changes in the products being produced for export. The more disaggregated the data are, the more the data reflect actual items being produced. The closer we get to the actual products, the better we can make inferences about the main drivers pushing these products, as well as the firms and the economy producing those items. Of course, as for any historical study, different types of documents and records need to be triangulated in order to interpret and to be confident in the findings, and accordingly we do not rely on trade data alone. Nonetheless, the careful use of trade data provides one of the best ways to examine the path of development and, by inference, the organization of economies proceeding along this path.

We should point out, however, some limitations to our use of these data. Systematically reported trade data are a fairly recent development (Morgenstern, 1963, pp. 167–8). Standardized import/export data were only developed after the United Nations established standardized national economic statistics in the 1950s, and most developing nations only established an adequate customs accounting system in the 1960s. (For political reasons, the UN still does not report the trade statistics for Taiwan.) Therefore, we do not have access to highly disaggregated trade data for Taiwan and South Korea before 1972, after which we rely on the U.S. import statistics.[11] For the 1960s, we rely on aggregated trade data based on different classificatory systems reported in the statistics given by each country. Although the comparison are not as exact or as fine-grained as we would wish, they still give us sufficient information to infer that the products manufactured for export from the late 1960s were similar to those in 1972 when standardized reporting begins.

---

[11] Worldwide bilateral import and export data for most countries, from 1970–92, are available from Feenstra, Bowen, and Lipsey (1997), based on data from Statistics Canada; this has been updated to 1997 by Feenstra (2000), and both databases are described as www.internationaldata.org. However, those data are available at the 4-digit Standard International Trade Classification, which is considerably more aggregated than the 7-digit TSUSA data for the United States from 1972–89, or the 10-digit HS classification for 1989–2001, both of which we use.

Just concentrating on the U.S. imports from South Korea and Taiwan, we can infer from the initial period of industrialization, from 1965 to 1985, that the primary goods produced were mostly the result of contract manufacturing. Before summarizing these findings, it is well to keep two facts in mind: First, in the initial decade of rapid economic growth, roughly from 1965 to 1975, most of the growth in both countries is accounted for by growth in the export sector of these economies. This is particularly true for Taiwan, whose population and total economy were roughly half the size of South Korea's, but whose export totals to the United States exceeded Korea's every year from 1965 to 2000. Second, in the mid-1960s, exports to the United States suddenly leaped forward, making the United States by far the largest single market for exports from South Korea and Taiwan. Moreover, unlike their exports to other countries such as Japan, which included many agricultural products, the exports to the United States overwhelmingly consisted of manufactured, differentiated goods (that is, goods that have no set prices and no established market in which prices are set [Rauch, 1999]). In fact, in the twenty years from 1965 to 1985, nearly 45 percent of the value for all manufactured goods exported from Taiwan and 35 percent from Korea went to the United States. In a nutshell, then, the initial period of growth of South Korean and Taiwanese economies primarily resulted from manufactured exports to the United States.

A detailed analysis of these exports into the United States from 1972 until 1985 shows two sets of trends. One set of trends shows basic similarities between South Korea and Taiwan in their pattern of exports to the United States, and the second set reveals that underlying these similarities are basic and increasingly apparent differences between the two economies. The similarities between the two countries reflect similarities in the demand from intermediaries, and the differences grow out of the divergence in economic organization between the two countries that was present at the outset of industrialization and that increased as time went on.

Similarities in Trade Patterns

To give a sense of the similar patterns in export growth, Figure 6.6 shows, especially in the early years, the tremendous increase in the value of exports to the United States, and Figure 6.7 shows the ratio of exports to the United States in relation to the total exports. Clearly, the exports to the United States account for much of the increase in total exports until the 1980s. Figure 6.8 gives some depth to this pattern. In the early years of industrialization, until 1985, there was in both countries a rapid

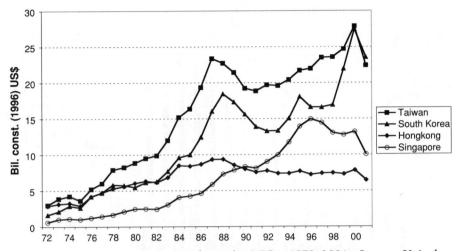

Figure 6.6. U.S. Imports from the NICs, 1972–2001. *Source:* United States, Import Data 1972–2001.

proliferation of the categories of goods (at a 7-digit level) exported to the United States and a less spectacular but still substantial growth in the number of categories of garments and footwear in that total. Nothing so far is surprising, but in Figure 6.9 we see that, despite the fact that both South Korea and Taiwan exported thousands of different categories of products to the United States, the total value of the exports is highly

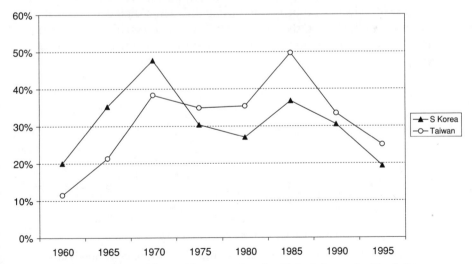

Figure 6.7. The Share of Exports to the United States in Total Exports from South Korea and Taiwan, 1960–95

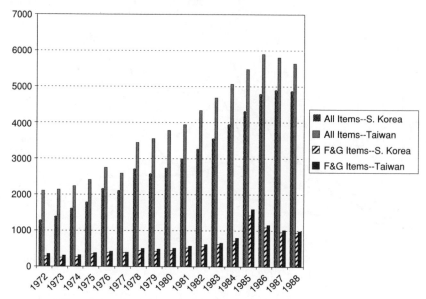

Figure 6.8. Number of 7-digit TSUSA Categories of Imports: Total and Footwear+Garment Combined, 1972–88.
Source: NBER, TSUSA U.S. Import Data, 1972–85.

concentrated in only a few product categories. The highest concentration for both countries occurs in the earliest period with nearly 50 percent of the value of Korea's exports going to the United States and 25 percent of the value of Taiwan's exports contained in only ten 7-digit categories. The concentration lessens in the early 1980s, but then increases again in the late l980s and throughout the 1990s, so that by 2000, the top ten 10-digit

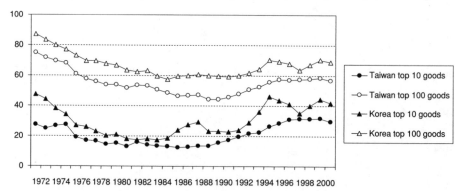

Figure 6.9. The Share of Top Ten and Top 100 Categories of Goods in Total Export Value, South Korea and Taiwan, 1972–2001.
Note: 1972–88 Based on the 7-digit TSUSA; 1989–2001 Based on the 10-digit HS. *Source:* U.S Import Data, 1972–2001.

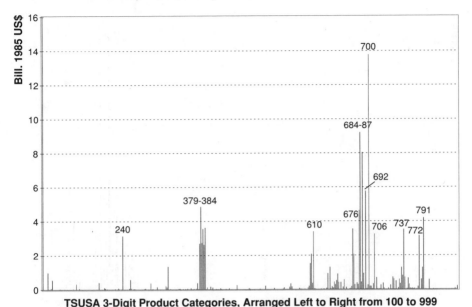

TSUSA 3-Digit Product Categories, Arranged Left to Right from 100 to 999

Figure 6.10. South Korea Exports to the United States, 1972–88 ($ mill).

items in both economies accounted for over 30 percent of the total value of exports to the United States, while the top 100 categories account for over 60 percent of all exports. We should note a difference here as well; throughout the entire period, Korea's exports are consistently more concentrated in only a few product categories than are Taiwan's exports.

Exactly what were the top categories of exports and what were the patterns of change over time? Aggregating the TSUSA categories at the 3-digit level for the period from 1972 to 1988, which is the entire period this classification system was used, we can see, in Figures 6.10 and 6.11, that during this fifteen-year period most imports from South Korea and Taiwan occurred in only a few general product categories and that, at the 3-digit level, the export landscapes of both countries look very similar. Going from the left to right, the peak categories above two billion U.S. dollars in one or both export landscapes are plywood (TSUSA 240), garments (381–4), steel (610), machinery and component parts of machinery (646), (653), (661), (676), electrical appliances (684), electronic products (television and radio) (685), (687), transportation vehicles and parts (692), footwear (700), luggage and related products (706), furniture (727), bicycles (734), (737), rubber and plastic products (772), and leather products (791).

All these figures in this section show similarities in patterns of export trade between South Korea and Taiwan. As we will spell out more fully later, these similarities primarily reflect export pull, that is, the demand

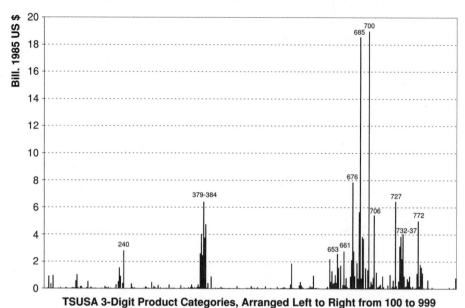

TSUSA 3-Digit Product Categories, Arranged Left to Right from 100 to 999

Figure 6.11. Taiwan Exports to the United States, 1972–88 ($ mill).

from big buyers choosing what categories of goods to buy from South Korean and Taiwanese manufacturers. Within these categories, there is a huge range of very different sorts of products, and it is in the manufacture of these products that systematic differences between South Korea and Taiwan emerge.

Differences in the Patterns of Goods Produced for Export

If we examine inside the main 3-digit categories that are so prominent in the export landscape, we find that the similarities mostly disappear and that the differences emerge and become increasingly obvious over time. Several trends are apparent in this regard. The first trend is that, in the earliest period of import data from 1972 to 1976, the export profile of both countries contained very similar and often identical products, and that most of the value of each broad category was highly concentrated in only a few products within that category. Remember this is the period before specialized buying strategies and specialized manufacturing strategies had emerged, a period when buyers were making their first big orders and when local manufacturers were engaged in intense competition to obtain these orders. In these years, for example, garments exports were among the highest categories of exports from both countries, with garments providing about a third of the total value of Korea's exports to the United States and a quarter of Taiwan's. Among the 263 and 345 types of garments that South Korea and Taiwan, respectively, exported to the United States in 1972, the top five items provided 42 percent of the total value of garments from Korea and 39 percent from Taiwan. Three of the top five garment items are the same for both countries, namely specific types of sweaters, knit shirts, and trousers, all for women and girls.

The second trend emerged between 1975 and 1985, when intermediary demand for Asian goods dramatically increased and when buyers and manufacturers began to figure out their respective strategies to fill that demand. In this period, as orders began to pour in, the composition of products in each category begins to change, and the product mix of exports from each country in each category increases dramatically. This trend is true for both countries, but especially so for Taiwan. This second trend merges with a third trend: Very quickly a division of labor emerged between South Korea and Taiwan, with each country beginning to specialize in particular products within each category. In some cases, such as footwear, specialization appeared very early in the process, as is clear from Figure 6.12.[12] This figure shows that, even from the very first period of our data in 1972, Taiwanese and South Korean footwear exports were producing somewhat different types of footwear, even though they shared some of the same products (a type of soft-sole vinyl shoe for women). However, as new categories emerged by the middle 1970s, a clear division of labor between Taiwan and South Korea footwear manufacturers was established and continued to grow throughout the entire period, with Taiwan specializing in rubber and plastic shoes and South Korea in leather shoes.

Rubber and plastic products, which are important export items for both countries throughout the period, show another variation of these two trends. Before 1975, both countries predominately exported rubber and plastic wearing apparel to the United States, but as Figure 6.13 shows, after 1975, Korea increasingly specialized in exporting various kinds of tires – tires for cars, trucks, buses, and bicycles – while during the same interval, Taiwan's exports in this category expanded to include an array of products in addition to plastic wearing apparel: religious articles, household furnishings, curtains, Christmas tree ornaments, as well as some bicycle tires.

Fourth, during this fifteen-year period leading up to 1987, products within categories gradually begin to segment, with South Korean exports

---

[12] In order to depict this trend graphically, we included all 7-digit categories of footwear whose total value exceeded $10,000,000 U.S. in any year period between 1972 and 1985.

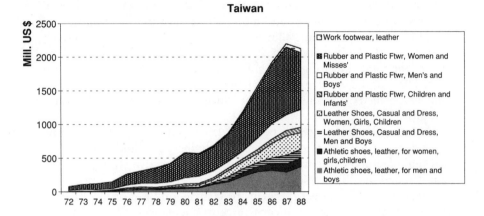

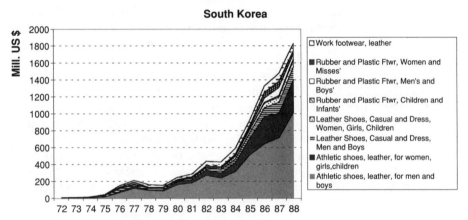

Figure 6.12. Footwear, 1972–88.

in most categories increasingly consisting of products that could be mass-produced (for example, in garments: men's shirts, as opposed to women's fashion), and often, but not always, were final products ready for consumer use, such as microwave ovens, video machines (VCRs), tires, and automobiles. In contrast, within the same 3-digit product categories, Taiwanese exports tended to be component parts, goods having short product cycles (for example, in garments: women's clothes), and some fairly complex final products that can be assembled from standardized components (for example, computers, TVs, and bicycles), this in addition to a considerable range of relatively inexpensive, simply made consumer products (for example, luggage, household products made of plastic). Figures 6.14 and 6.15 depict the clearest examples of this trend: household appliances and transportation parts and equipment, including bicycles and bicycle parts.

Taiwan

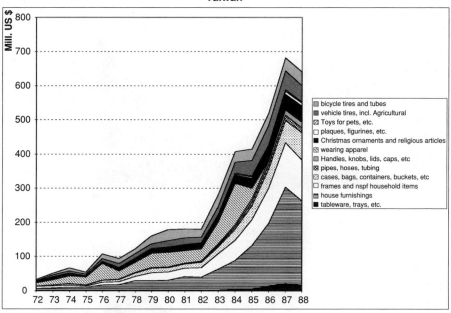

South Korea

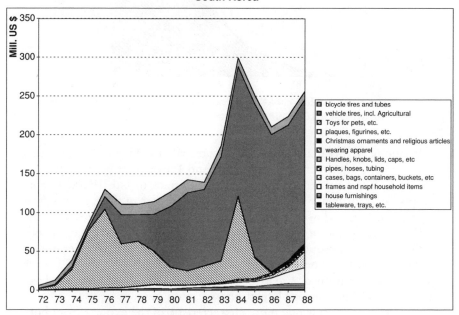

Figure 6.13. Rubber And Plastic Products, 1972–88.
Source: NBER, HS U.S. Import Data.

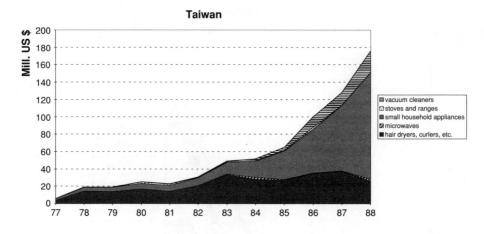

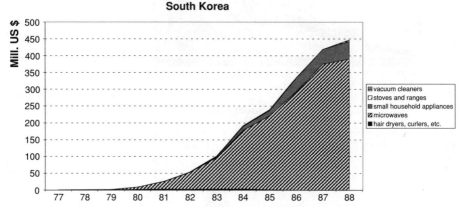

Figure 6.14. Household Appliances, 1972–88. *Source:* NBER, HS U.S. Import Data, 1972–2001.

In summary, this analysis of trade data reveals a sudden and accelerating expansion of exports from South Korea and Taiwan that began in the late 1960s and that does not level off until the mid- to late 1980s, twenty years of extraordinary growth. The rapid emergence of these exports was highly concentrated in only a few product categories. As Figures 6.16 and 6.17 show, demand in these categories grew rapidly, so that many goods continued to be produced in common, but within these categories during this twenty-year period export products began clearly to diverge, as each economy began to specialize in particular types of production capabilities and the products compatible with those capabilities.

Our analysis reveals one more characteristic of the exports from both countries that we have not yet discussed. Examining the trends over this twenty-year period, we have been struck by the sudden oscillations in

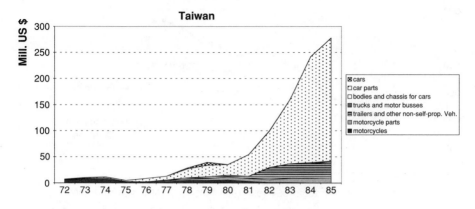

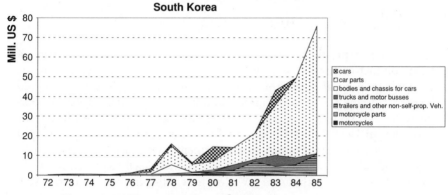

Figure 6.15. Transportation, 1972–85.
Source: NBER, HS U.S. Import Data, 1972–2001.

products in nearly every major category of exports to the United States. Many product lines, particularly those with less total value, expand rapidly for a few years and then go into an equally rapid decline, seemingly being replaced by a score of nearly equivalent goods. Some of these shifts are due to changes in classification between years, but the oscillations also come from changes in the demand, or more precisely abrupt changes in the orders for goods as buyers seek out new product styles and the lowest-cost suppliers. It is difficult, if not impossible, to explain these oscillations only from the producer side. These are clearly demand-driven changes.

Linking Exports to Intermediary Demand

The principal exports from both South Korea and Taiwan are exactly those products that fueled the retail revolution in the United States: garments, footwear, bicycles, toys, televisions, microwaves, computers,

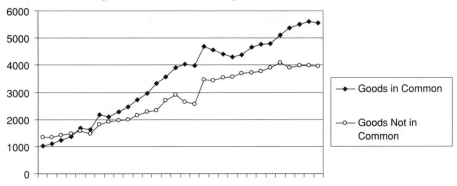

Figure 6.16. Similarity Between South Korea and Taiwan's Export Landscapes.
Source: U.S. Import Data, 1972–2001.

thousands of plastic household and office items, and a large array of semiconductors that have in turn become the core components in a vast and growing number of other products, such as cell phones and digital cameras. Using the data on imports collected by the U.S. Customs Service, we can be precise about these imports. For instance, we know for sure that in 1985, South Korea and Taiwan were two of the three largest importers into United States of all garments with nearly 28 percent of the total value (along with Hong Kong, which itself exported an additional 24 percent of the total). Within that total, the two countries sent

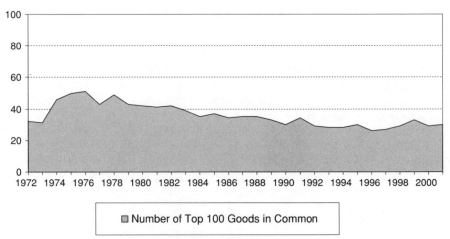

Figure 6.17. Divergence between South Korea and Taiwan's Top Export Goods. *Source:* U.S. Import Data, 1972–2001.

26 percent of the value of all imported women's garments and 60 percent of the value of all imported men's shirts. Also in 1985, Taiwan imported into the United States 57 percent of total value of all imported bicycles, and Korea 28 percent of all imported microwaves. In the same year, the two countries imported into the United States 54 percent of all handbags and luggage, 40 percent of all toys and games, 36 percent of all television sets, 24 percent of a huge category of miscellaneous rubber and plastic products, and a whopping 50 percent of imported footwear of all types. If we go to the 7-digit level, then in 1985, Taiwan supplied 100 percent of fifty-five different categories, and South Korea 100 percent in twenty-four different categories of products, most of which for both countries were categories of textiles and clothing.

If we survey the main items of exports throughout the period from 1972 to 1985, it becomes clear that products secured through contract manufacturing forms an extremely high percentage of the total exports. For instance, according to a report on the Korean garment industry (cited by Lee and Song, 1994, p. 148), "Until 1988, approximately 95 percent of garment exports were produced under contract to foreign firms, rather than under Korean-owned labels." According to Levy's analysis of the footwear industry in South Korea and Taiwan (1988, p. 46), "(I)n the initial phases of export expansion," Levy notes, "export business in both nations was based overwhelmingly on the fulfillment of orders placed by Japanese trading companies, and designed for the U.S. market." Japanese trading companies were soon supplanted as Western firms began to place their orders directly. In both countries, Western brand-name merchandisers, such as Nike and Reebok, controlled export footwear industry (Levy, 1988, 1990). Also in his case study of the manufacture of personal computers in the two countries, Levy (1988) cites figures from the trade associations for electronic appliances that 84 percent of Korean-made personal computers and 72 percent of Taiwan-made computers were sold under non-local brand names. The world's largest exporter of bicycles during the 1980s and early 1990s, Taiwan's export industry until the late 1980s was largely OEM manufacturing (Cheng, 1998). At one point in the late 1970s, Schwinn placed an order of 100 million bicycles with Giant, "which was then only a small factory" (Cheng, 1998, p. 7).

Examining the lists of exported finished manufactured products in those early years of economic growth, it is difficult to find any major product category that was not dominated by contract manufacturing or any major retailers that were not involved in contract manufacturing in East Asia. Garments, household appliances, electronic products, toys, and bicycles – the majority of all of these finished exports were sold under foreign-owned brand names and product labels. Many manufactured exports from both countries, but especially from Taiwan, were component parts, and other types of intermediate goods, such as textiles. A sizeable amount of other manufactured exports were inexpensive unbranded products, such as kitchen items and tools of various kinds, which were sold in a range of retail outlets, often in discount stores, such as Kmart and Wal-Mart. As long as they were purchased from South Korean and Taiwanese firms in contracted batches for assembly or sale elsewhere, however, even the simplest and least expensive items were driven by intermediary demand.

Conclusion

From the perspective of America's total imports in the late 1960s and 1970s, those imports from East Asia represented only a modest but steadily increasing percentage, especially in comparison with imports of oil from the Middle East and manufactured and agricultural products from Europe. But from the perspective of Asia's industrial expansion, these U.S.-bound exports accounted for a huge percentage of the total output of these Asian economies and drove these economies forward into capitalism. Ironically, the very success of these Asian connections also helped to transform the retail and manufacturing structure of the United States.

What made East Asian countries, and specially Taiwan and South Korea, such good places to arrange buyer-driven manufacturing? Gary Gereffi (1994), whose work has consistently informed our own, argues that the greatest advantage of doing business in South Korea and Taiwan is the capability of firms there to act as "full-package providers," able to execute every step in the manufacturing, packaging, and delivery processes, and, remarkably, they were able to be full-package providers from the very first. In other words, the reason these economies became so crucial to American retailers and mass-market merchandisers is that they adapted to and were instrumental in the construction of intermediary demand. Their advantage was their demand-responsiveness.

This conclusion, of course, begs the question: What is the nature of this demand-responsiveness? The next step, therefore, is to examine the "backward effects" of this increasingly organized demand structure on the organization of manufacturing in South Korea and Taiwan.

7

Global Matching, Demand Responsiveness, and the Emergence of Divergent Economies

In the last chapter, we offer what we believe is a new hypothesis for the industrialization of South Korea and Taiwan: A primary force driving not only the emergence, but also the divergence of these two economies is the development of intermediary demand growing out of the U.S. retail revolution, to which Korean and Taiwanese firms were able to respond successfully, but in different ways. This claim will certainly be controversial because the existing explanations for East Asian industrialization consistently ignore factors relating to demand. To be more specific, existing explanations do not consider the interconnectedness of global markets in explaining industrialization. They do not consider how changes in the growth and organization of one economy, the U.S. economy, can shape the growth and organization of other economies, the Asian economies. The possibility of this proposition is implicit in our revised Walrasian perspective that we outlined in Chapter 1. Insofar as markets are interconnected, then a change in one market should result in changes in other markets. Within this perspective, theoretically speaking, markets should not be confined artificially to only markets within a national economy. Rather, the test of the extent of interconnectedness is empirical: Are markets actually linked in fact, and if so, with what consequence for all markets so linked?

We demonstrated in the last chapter that changes in the organization of retailing in the United States is directly related to changes in the composition of international trade between the United States, on the one hand, and South Korea and Taiwan, on the other. This demonstration is the first step in supporting our initial hypothesis: Consumer markets in the United States and the supplier markets in East Asia are definitely interconnected.

Now in this chapter we proceed with the second step; given that markets in the United States and East Asian are interconnected, then how should we hypothesize the consequences of this interconnectedness? Should we hypothesize, for example, that the growth of exports from South Korea

253

and Taiwan would have been qualitatively similar to their actual pattern if the retail revolution in the United States had not occurred, but would have occurred at a significantly slower pace? This is to say that East Asian industrialization would have occurred anyway without trade from the United States, but just at a slower pace because manufacturers could not have marketed their products as successfully without expanding consumer markets in the United States. This hypothesis retains many of the elements of the supply-side narratives that we described in the last chapter, but adds demand as the factor that stimulates an existing or nascent or even (given an organizational logic) potentially existing structure of production.

Our revised Walrasian perspective, however, suggests that the earlier hypothesis would be incorrect. We argue in Part I that the **organization** of economies is directly shaped by the interconnectedness of markets. Therefore, in line with our perspective, we should hypothesize that South Korea and Taiwan would not have industrialized the way they did, and with the kind of economic organization that emerged in each economy, without the linkages with U.S. retailers. A corollary to this hypothesis is that without these linkages, the South Korean and Taiwanese manufacturers would not have had the same types of exportable products as they did in fact develop, and therefore the course of development would have proceeded very differently. In this chapter, we will offer support for this part of our hypothesis.

Our task in this chapter, therefore, is to describe how the changes in U.S. retailing that we described in the last chapter are directly connected with the processes of organizing the rapidly industrializing South Korean and Taiwanese economies. We propose that the main actors organizing these economies are the owners and managers of firms directly involved in the ongoing economic competition within these two economies. Following the main outlines of our model, we further propose that state officials are only indirectly involved in the organizing process.

In Part II of this book, we will have presented sufficient evidence for our readers to evaluate the two most prominent alternative hypotheses for our explanations. In the final chapter, we will address these alternatives, but the reader now should be aware of the arguments that are coming and of the evidence being presented in relation to them. The first counterfactual poses the question: Assuming the U.S. retail revolution occurred as we described, but assuming also that the supportive economic policies of South Korean and Taiwanese governments were absent, can we envision that South Korea and Taiwan would have developed along the organizational and product lines that actually emerged? Second, absent the U.S. retail revolution, can we assume that the South Korean and Taiwanese economies would have generated the same types of exportable products and the same patterns of economic organization as they did in fact develop? These two counterfactuals are, of course, another way to ask which factor is the more decisive in the organizational development of these economies: factors relating to the state or factors relating to demand.

Global Matching

To examine the backward effects for retailer on manufacturers, we need to set the process of rapid industrialization in motion, by describing, first, how the process got going and, second, how the divergence of these two very distinct economies became outcomes of the same "searching and matching" aspect of the intermediation process (Spulber, 1996, 2001), which following the terminology of James Rauch (1996, 1999) we call "global matching."

Going into this discussion, we need to reemphasize two aspects of the retail revolution. First, in the initial years of industrialization, foreign retailers and merchandisers, mostly based in the United States, accounted for much of the rapidly increasing demand for export products from Taiwan and South Korea. Second, in order to obtain these products in rapid, reliable, and predictable ways, most retailers and merchandisers had to enter into price sensitive contractual or quasi-contractual relationships with those South Korean and Taiwanese manufacturers that they thought could best deliver their orders. These relationships established **price-sensitive networks of firms that turned these manufacturing sites into organizational extensions of merchandising and retailing and that produced a kind of commercial capitalism, a capitalism tied directly to processes of selling, rather than the processes of making products.** To enter into such relationships required American and, just as importantly as we will see, Japanese firms to engage in a search and selection process to find suitable manufacturers in South Korea and Taiwan.

Moreover, as the organizations and processes of intermediary demand were instituted on both sides of the Pacific, Asian entrepreneurs also began to search both for products that retailers would want to sell and for retailers that would actually place orders. In the early years of rapid growth, this mutual search for suitable partners was a scramble, a "gold-rush" environment, in which deals were made and remade with great speed. These ongoing, constantly readjusting, but gradually stabilizing efforts to find maintain partnerships, where all sides were searching for the best matches, produced backward effects (that is, from retailing to manufacturing) that led to divergent trajectories of rapid growth between South Korea and Taiwan. By the time that the full effects of the Plaza Accord of 1985 were felt in the economies of East Asia, in the late 1980s and early 1990s, the divergent trajectories were organizationally in place and, within the normal course of events, were irreversible. Our concern here, then, is to trace these emergent trajectories in the initial years of industrialization, up to the time of the Plaza Accord. In Chapter 8, we will examine the development of these economies in the years after 1985.

The Three Dimensions of Global Matching

The process of mutual selection between Western and Japanese buyers and Asian manufacturers occurs simultaneously along three interrelated dimensions. First, the selection process involves what Mortensen (1988, p. 216) calls a "voluntary pairing under competitive conditions." The process of firms pairing off with each other is analytically similar to workers with specific skills being matched with a job that requires a certain set of skills, and to people trying to locate a marriage partner where both individuals mutually try to find a mate with the qualities that each most desires. Researchers have shown that actual or perceived competition for mates or for workers encourages an early selection, but such a selection, though stable in the short run, does not necessarily lead to a stable match over the long term. "When matching requires time, is costly, and takes place under conditions of uncertainty both because it is not rational to wait indefinitely for the perfect partner and because experience is required to discover the value of a specific partnership," then subsequent searches are likely in order to find better matches (Mortensen, 1988, p. 238). Even when subsequent matching occurs, however, inertia, propinquity, and satisficing (that is, making less than optimal choices) remain an integral part of the selection process.

Because the matching process is crucial to good outcomes, it is commonplace in such a context to employ a middleman to arrange the match. What matchmakers (including families and friends) do for marriages and what headhunters and employment agencies do for finding the right person for the right job, a range of brokers and trading companies do for linking retailers and merchandisers with the appropriate manufacturing firms. Although little studied, these "international trade intermediaries," as Rauch (2001) calls them, are a ubiquitous aspect of the matching process in South Korea and Taiwan, especially in the earlier years of industrialization.

The second dimension, an outcome of global matching, is spatial. The matching process linking two or more firms together results in the selection of a geographical space where the agreed upon economic activity occurs. This link between individual choice and geographical location has been the subject of a number of important theoretical discussions, all of which demonstrate that individual choices made locally and sequentially for whatever reason (that is, micromotives) have systemic and emergent (that is, non-linear and transformative) organizational effects on a much wider geographical location. This discussion began with Thomas Schelling's famous game-theoretic experiment (1978, pp. 135–66), in which he showed how individual housing choices made sequentially by racially tolerant people, who choose locations where they would not be "too much" in the minority, will result in widespread patterns of segregation over time.

Drawing not only on the work of Schelling, but also on Arthur (1994, Arthur, Durlauf, and Lane, 1997) and Arrow (Arrow, Anderson, and Pines, 1988), Paul Krugman and his colleagues (Krugman, 1994a, 1996, 1997, Fujita, Krugman, and Venables, 1999) expanded on these basic ideas to establish what they call the "new economic geography." Krugman (1997, p. 240) describes the basic theme underlying this new branch of economics as follows:

> The spatial economy is, self-evidently, a self-organizing system characterized by path dependence; it is a domain in which the interaction of individual decisions produces unexpected emergent behavior at the aggregate level; its dynamic landscapes are typically rugged, and the evolution of the spatial economy typically involves "punctuated equilibria," in which gradual change in the driving variables leads to occasional discontinuous change in the resulting behavior.

Among the examples that the new economic geographers (for example, Fujita, Krugman, and Venables, 1999, Pohl, 2001) cite are urban hierarchies, city location, the appearance of industrial clusters and agglomerations, economic development, and patterns of international trade. Sudden transformations occasionally occur across all of these examples. For example, a new type of industrial cluster – Silicon Valley – may suddenly appear that transforms not only the spatial dimensions of that region, but also possibly the spatial dimensions of the national or even the global economy (Saxenian, 1994). All such economic transformations are the result of "emergent self-organizing systems" that lead to rapidly increasing returns in one or more locations.[1] These are "systems that form

---

[1] To the readers unfamiliar with the literature on complexity and self-organization, we need to emphasize that the term "self-organization," as it is generally used and as we use it here, refers to the outcome of a process of interaction among participants, in this case, an interaction among economic actors. Under conditions of continued competitive activity, what starts out as random, chaotic, or disorganized quickly becomes organized and interdependent. Even though individual decisions may be calculated and are even "rational" from the actors' point of view, they do not aggregate to become an organization that can be predicted based on individual intentions. As Rosser (1999, p. 182) notes, "Probably the most obvious implication of the study of complexity in its various forms is that a general assumption of rational expectations is very unlikely to hold."

structures not merely in response to inputs from outside but also, indeed primarily, in response *to their own internal logic*" (Krugman, 1966, p. 99, our emphasis). These systems are what Friedrich Hayek (1967) called "spontaneous orders," which are the "results of human action but not of human design."

The third dimension of global matching involves the selections not only of partners in a geographical place, but also of an economic space within which the specific relationships between two firms is defined. By economic space, we mean the competitive environments in which the relative locations and the relative leverage of the two firms along a commodity chain are negotiated. In the earlier years of matchmaking among firms, the economic relationship was often narrowly defined in terms of the task to be performed and was distant in terms of trust and predictability; more often than not the relationship was brokered through third-party firms, initially Japanese trading companies. However, as experience in working with subcontract manufacturers increased and trust developed (or failed to develop) among the participants, as the infrastructure for the activity encompassing intermediary demand became increasingly institutionalized, and as the economies within which global matching predominated grew more complex and sophisticated, then the firms involved typically relocated themselves relative to each other, even when the firms remained the same.

As we will show subsequently, this dimension of global matching is very important in our understanding of the demand responsiveness of these economies. The negotiation process not only establishes a division of labor between two firms linked together in a chain of production and distribution, but also a balance of economic power among interlinked firms, including their relative ability to control (via authority or economic power) different areas of economic activity and to establish prices and profit margins within those areas. Such negotiations are not easy or necessarily straightforward even in stable economies in the best of times, but during conditions of rapid economic change, as occurred in the early days of industrialization in East Asia, they were tumultuous and drove the process of economic self-organization forward.

For example, as Gereffi (1994, Gereffi and Pan, 1994) has documented, what began as narrowly defined relationships between the big buyer and the sub-contract manufacturer soon developed into "triangle manufacturing" systems in which the Asian manufacturer would begin to subcontract parts (and sometimes all) of the manufacturing jobs out to other firms. This turned the subcontractor into a middleman in an increasingly complex network of firms, many of which in the 1990s were moved from Taiwan and South Korea to other countries, such as China and Indonesia. "Since the buyer has no direct production experience," explains Gereffi

(1994, p. 224), "it prefers to rely on the East Asian NIC manufacturers it has done business with in the past to ensure that the buyer's standards in terms of price, quality, and delivery schedules will be met by new contractors in other . . . locations." Industrial upgrading is another way for Asian manufacturers to relocate their economic position relative to the same or different buyers (Kao and Hamilton, 2000, Ernst, 2001, Gereffi, 1999).

We will now examine each of these dimensions in turn.

Voluntary Pairing in a Competitive Environment

From our interviews,[2] we have learned that for most Asian manufacturers, there is a sharp difference between customers and consumers. Especially in the earliest years of rapid growth, Asian manufacturers knew who their customers were and the importance of their orders. These customers were not the distant masses of consumers in the United States or Europe, but rather the handful of buyers or their agents who usually came directly to their factories to order and to inspect the final goods.

The interest in customers is apparent everywhere one looks – trade shows, English-language phone books, world trade centers, billboards and displays lining airport corridors, promotional literature in hotel rooms, and the ubiquitous factory showrooms. The showrooms are especially indicative. Whatever the size of their firm or whatever product they make, most manufacturers have a showroom in or near their factory. The showroom is usually the best room in the building, and it is there, on the walls or in display cabinets of this showroom, that the factory owners proudly show off their wares. In Taiwan, many of these goods are recognizable, for they bear an array of American and European brand names. Hamilton recalls one Taiwanese manufacturer, in the midst of describing the array of hydraulic jacks he produced, all bearing different brand names and all with distinctive colors and styles, proudly proclaim that the only way you can identify his jacks in American stores is the "k" imprinted on the bottom. By contrast in South Korea, in the late 1980s, the showrooms in Samsung and Hyundai had begun to display products with the Samsung or Hyundai brand name proudly affixed. Whatever the company's strategy, however, these showrooms are important, because this is where the customers, the big buyers, are greeted and hopefully impressed.

---

[2] These interviews have been done in collaboration with Cheng-shu Kao, whose research team at the Institute for Society and Economy at Tunghai University in Taiwan has conducted extensive interviews with nearly 1,000 Taiwanese firms from 1985 to the present day, both in Taiwan and China. See Kao and Hamilton, 2000, 2004, and forthcoming.

One of the most striking examples of such showroom behavior that either of us has witnessed comes from a particularly wealthy Taiwanese entrepreneur living in the countryside in south central Taiwan. For his showroom, he constructed a five-story hotel-like facility. The first two floors housed his display area for the current year's product lines; the third floor included offices, a dining room, and an entertainment area complete with karaoke; and the top two floors were divided into palatial suites, decorated with leather-covered furniture and gold-plated bathroom fixtures, to accommodate his buyers at a level of luxury far exceeding that of any hotel in the region. Like other factory owners, this person had only a few customers, five at the time of the last interview in 1992, and he knew all five well. Representatives of these customers visited only once or twice a year, usually at different times, but their rooms were ready whenever they came. Among his five customers were Wal-Mart and Kmart, from whom he had multimillion-dollar contracts to make most of the plastic lawn furniture that these retailers sold. To these manufacturers, consumers and final consumption are distant, but customers and demand are very near.

In the search to explain the sudden and extraordinary success of Asian economies, most analyses have overlooked the real customers for Asian manufacturers and have underestimated what we are calling intermediary, as opposed to final, demand. However, once we focus empirically on intermediary demand, then it is obvious that the processes of intermediation, and in particular "matching and searching" and "guaranteeing and monitoring" (Spulber, 1996), are intrinsic aspects of the organization of intermediary demand. Finding buyers and keeping them happy, locating manufacturers and keeping them busy, working out all the details of making and packaging and shipping the products ordered – these have been prominent and economically transformative activities from the beginning and certainly remain the core concerns of the main players, including a subset of state officials.

From our point of view, the biggest mysteries are not about marketing or intermediary demand per se, but rather about how the whole process got started in the first place and about what the effects of this demand are on the organization of these economies. Because no one has examined these points in any detail, the origins and consequences of global matching in both South Korea and Taiwan are obscure. In trying to account for the origins of global matching, we do find, however, in the most detailed accounts (Fields, 1995, Rhee, et al., 1985, Jung, 1984, Levy, 1990) of the earliest decade of industrialization, from 1965 to 1975, that we could locate (and there are surprisingly few of these), that Japanese trading companies most likely brokered a substantial portion of the initial orders, played a prominent role throughout the formative period, and were instrumental in getting the process of global matching started in both locations. In retrospect, their prominence in South Korea and Taiwan should not be surprising.

Japanese Trading Companies as the Initial Matchmakers

Japanese trading companies, known as *sogo shosha,* were extremely important in facilitating the re-industrialization of Japan after World War II. The nine top trading companies, generally one for each of Japan's largest business groups, handled most of the trade into and out of Japan ever since the early 1950s (Yoshino and Lifson, 1986, Tsurumi, 1984, Kojima and Ozawa, 1984). These same companies also served an identical role within the domestic economy where they brokered trade among firms both within and between business groups. Okumura Hiroshi, one of the leading specialists on Japanese business groups, notes that even the largest Japanese corporations trade "only with a few, specified partners." The trading companies "serve as intermediaries for intercorporate trading" throughout the Japanese economy, and handled most exchanges among firms of all sizes. This use of trading intermediaries, says Okumura (1991, p. 222), created "a very large web of reciprocal dealings in Japan" and thus a dense networks of cooperating firms. Because these companies played such a large role domestically, when Japanese economy expanded in the 1950s and early 1960s, Japanese trading companies became an important vehicle of that expansion, integrating the manufacturing foundation of the Japanese economy with the global distribution of Japanese products, as well as the buyers of needed primary and intermediate inputs.

In the 1960s, just as the retail revolution was occurring in the United States, Japanese trading companies also began to expand their operations outside of Japan. Partly in response to opportunities presented by U.S. retail firms, these firms began to establish manufacturing firms for the specific purpose of making products for export. Eighty percent of these firms were located in developing countries, mostly other countries in Asia (Kojima and Ozawa, 1984). These manufacturing firms were usually organized as joint ventures, which represented some combination of a Japanese firm, a local firm, and the trading company. According to Kojima and Ozawa (1984, p. 43),

> This geographical concentration reflects the fact that most of these ventures produce standardized products in highly labour-intensive operations, both for local markets and for export, by capitalizing on low-cost labour in Third World countries. It is also in the developing countries that the trading companies' ability to provide business-infrastructural services is in great demand and can create profitable opportunities for direct investment.

The first areas of industrial expansion and direct foreign investments for Japanese businesses in the post-war years were, quite naturally, two former colonies, Taiwan and South Korea. This expansion came in the context of the Vietnam War, when orders for Japanese exports were directly influenced by the presence of U.S. military forces in East Asia,[3] and the Cold War, when American economic policies treated imports from Asian nations more favorably than imports from most other developed and developing countries. Japanese investments in Japan's former colonies came as a result of the sudden expansion of Japanese production driven largely by a sudden expansion in U.S. demand for a narrow range of products.

The matchmaking started first in Taiwan, where the presence of Japanese trading companies dates from the colonial period, when Mitsui's trading company was the principal broker in the sugar exports to Japan. After World War II, the trading groups reestablished their role in agricultural exports to Japan, in large part because the two countries and their people remained on cordial terms, some preferring Japanese colonial rule to the harshness of the early KMT regime. In the 1960s, when the Japanese economy itself was rapidly expanding and the competition among the largest Japanese business groups was intense (Patrick and Rosovsky, 1976), many large groups began to look for new opportunities and cheaper labor in areas outside of Japan.[4] Already established in Taiwan, the Japanese trading companies led the way for firms aligned with their group to extend their businesses beyond Japan.

At first, in the early 1960s, a trickle of Japanese manufacturing companies established branches and joint ventures in Taiwan in order to evade Taiwan's high tariff barriers (The Economist Intelligence Unit, 1983). But beginning in 1966, a flood of investment began, making Taiwan in the 1960s the largest recipient of overseas Japanese investment. In fact, according to our calculations based on the records of Japanese foreign investment in Taiwan (The Oriental Economist, 1984), 50 percent of Japanese firms and Japanese/Taiwanese joint ventures that were in

---

[3] For instance, hundreds of thousands of U.S. soldiers and their family stationed in Vietnam as well as other places around the world were introduced to Japanese products in the PX, the commissary, where they bought high-quality, Japanese-made tape decks, radios, watches, and array of other products at prices that seemed very cheap in comparison with U.S. prices.

[4] We should note that in the late 1950s and early 1960s, exports from Japan to the United States were very modest. In this period, the largest two sectors of exports to the United States were consumer electronics (mostly transistor radios) and steel, both constituting around 5 percent of total U.S. consumption in these sectors. Rather suddenly after 1965, however, Japanese exports to the United States rapidly increases in most product categories, so that by 1970 the categories of exports doubled, tripled, and sometimes quadrupled the 1965 level.

existence in 1983 started in the six years between 1966 and 1971. Of the ninety-four firms established in Taiwan by the Japanese before 1984, 87 percent were joint ventures between Japanese and Taiwanese firms. Most of the Japanese firms initiating these joint ventures were affiliated with Japanese business groups. Also, most Japanese firms establishing a presence in Taiwan were in manufacturing, over 60 percent of which involved precision metalworking and electrical products (The Oriental Economist, 1984). As Gold (1986, pp. 82–4) observed, several of Taiwan's largest electronics manufacturers in the 1980s (for example, Tatung and Sampo) got their start in the 1960s as joint ventures with a Japanese firm. Knowing what we know about Japanese firms, it is almost certain that Japanese trading companies handled most of the import and export needs of those firms in which Japanese firms were involved.

In the late 1960s, according to one report (Olson, 1970, p. 173), Japanese trading companies handled "more than half of Taiwan's exports to third countries." If we would add in Taiwan's export trade to Japan, then the total amount of trade handled by these companies would exceed 60 percent. During these same years, Taiwan's exports to the United States dramatically increased. Therefore, it is very likely that Japanese trading companies served as intermediaries for a significant portion of this export trade with the United States.

This conclusion is supported by other sources. For example, we also know that Japanese trading companies handled large initial orders for shoes (Levy, 1990) and garments (Bonacich and Waller, 1994). There is also evidence that Japanese trading companies continued to play matchmaker throughout the 1970s and 1980s. Based on a variety of Taiwanese sources, Karl Fields (1995, pp. 221, 225) estimates that Japanese trading companies brokered 50 percent of Taiwan's total export trade in the early 1980s. Using other sources, Wade (1990, p. 147) comes up with several similar estimates. All these figures, however, are largely conjecture. As Fields (1995, p. 221) notes, "accurate figures on the extent of the Japanese trading ... are virtually impossible to obtain." However, even if we do not know their exact level of involvement, we have still sufficient information to suggest that their role in matching American buyers with Taiwanese manufacturers was extremely important in the late 1960s and early 1970s.

The same Japanese trading companies appear to have played a very similar role in South Korea's initial economic growth, at least before 1975 (Jung, 1984). Evidence about their role in South Korea, however, is even more fragmentary than their role in Taiwan, but it appears that their influence grew more slowly and then faded more quickly than was the case in Taiwan. After the Korean War, South Korea continued to have strained relations with its former and hated colonial master. Full diplomatic relations with Japan were not restored until 1965. Despite the lack of diplomatic relations, Japanese trading companies began to open offices as early as 1960, and by 1965 "some sixty major Japanese trading and industrial companies established offices in Seoul" (Fields, 1995, p. 204). After 1965, a few major Japanese firms began to establish new firms in South Korea, but then in the 1970s, a rapid expansion occurred, when South Korea replaced Taiwan as the leading destination of overseas Japanese investments, most of which went into joint ventures. The 146 Japanese firms and joint ventures present in South Korea in 1984 were mostly involved in manufacturing and were divided among electronic products (28 percent), machinery and metal products (25 percent), chemical products (19 percent), and textiles and garments (13 percent). Of these 146 firms, over 64 percent were started in the six years from 1971 to 1976 (The Economist Intelligence Unit, 1983). As occurred in Taiwan, most of the Japanese firms in South Korea were affiliated with one of the large Japanese business groups and very likely used Japanese trading companies as intermediaries. We also know that a number of American shoe and garment firms used Japanese trading companies to place orders in South Korea (Jung, 1984, p. 108, Lee and Song, 1994, Levy, 1990).

The first estimate for the percentage of Korea's export trade handled by Japanese trading companies that we could find is for 1976 and places the total at 15.6 percent (Jung, 1984). A survey of a small but significant sample (ninety-five respondents) of large firms in the previous year showed that 25 percent used Japanese trading companies (Rhee, et al., 1985, p. 114). It seems likely that in the late 1960s and early 1970s their role was larger than these percentages indicate. The reason for our assessment is that even in the earliest years of industrialization, export trade was highly concentrated in the largest firms (as we will describe later). Japanese trading companies were likely the first and most important agents matching Korea's large manufacturing firms with American buyers. Obtaining experience with foreign partners, however, these large firms soon took control of their own marketing.

This shift began abruptly in 1975. In that year, recognizing the importance of Japanese trading companies in Korea's export economy (Jung, 1984), the Park regime issued a directive giving lucrative incentives for the largest *chaebol* to establish *sogo shosha*-style trading companies to serve as the marketing arm for member firms and to serve as intermediaries between non-member firms and foreign partners (Fields, 1995, pp. 183–208). The very next year, in 1976, analysts estimate that the *chaebol* handled nearly 20 percent of Korea's export trade, nearly 5 percent more than Japanese trading companies did in the same year (Jung, 1984, p. 114; also cited by Fields, 1995, p. 204). After 1976, the percentage of Japanese involvement in Korea's export trade further declined, falling below 8 percent by 1982. This sudden decline is explained entirely by the fact that the *chaebol*, already by far the largest exporters in the early 1970s, rapidly took over the marketing of their own products.

Before 1975, therefore, Japanese trading companies handled the lion's share of exports from Taiwan, South Korea, and probably Hong Kong as well. They were able to accomplish this feat by developing vast communication networks that allowed them to match orders on the one side of the Pacific Ocean with manufacturing capabilities on the other side. In the 1970s, Mitsui and Co., for example, had established "the most comprehensive sophisticated system, called a 'global on-line network system'; telex-com-computers are strategically installed in five key cities around the world. The daily volume of telex communication can amount to as many as 80,000 dispatches and receipts" (Kojima and Ozawa, 1984, p. 25).

In both South Korea and Taiwan, the same Japanese trading companies were the first matchmakers linking local manufacturing and global retailing. More research on this topic would be very useful. However, assuming that Japanese trading companies were the early intermediaries, we can then extrapolate from the trade statistics cited in Chapter 6 that the Japanese trading companies were placing similar orders in both places, primarily for specific types of garments, plywood, simple electrical products, and shoes. If that is in fact the case, then we should conclude that the export trade they brokered in the late 1960s and early 1970s accounted for a substantial percentage of the increase in exports that occurred during these years. With exports starting from such a low base, it is likely that just the output of the joint ventures themselves contributed significantly to total exports. It would be nice to know these details for sure, but as important as these trading companies and the joint ventures might have been in these early years, they did not remain so for long. By the middle 1970s, the situation had changed in both countries.

Direct Buying and Local Trading Companies

By the early 1970s, local manufacturing in both countries had begun to boom. These rapid increases can be traced to the dramatic expansion in linkages between foreign buyers and local manufacturers. By the mid-1970s, the largest American retailers had established their own buying offices in South Korea and Taiwan, thereby eliminating many of the largest transactions handled by the Japanese intermediaries (Gereffi and Pan, 1994, p. 137, Jung, 1984, p. 110). According to records of the Korean Federation of National Economic Associations (Rhee, et al., 1984, p. 56), by 1975, "364 foreign companies had branches or representative offices in Korea. Of these, 267 were from the United States, forty from

Table 7.1. *Top Ten Retail Buying Offices in Taiwan, 1992*

Company	Year Established	Value of Orders Placed in Taiwan (US$ millions)	Sourcing Channels[a]		Types of Merchandise	
			Taiwan (%)	Offshore (%)	Soft Goods[b] (%)	Hard Goods (%)
Kmart	1971	500	40	60	45	55
Wal-Mart[c]	1981	300	55	45	30	70
J.C. Penney	1971	200	70	30	50	50
Associated Merchandising Corp. (AMC)[d]	1973	180	60	40	65	35
Mast Industries[e]	1973	140	100	0	100	0
Montgomery Ward	1983	135	77	23	35	65
Woolworth	1975	110	80	20	46	54
Sears	1967	75	98	2	40	60
May Department Stores	1974[f]	70	78	22	65	35
R. H. Macy & Co.	1986[f]	50	80	20	73	27

[a] Combined total for soft goods and hard goods.
[b] The soft goods percentages are exclusively apparel, with the following exceptions: Kmart – apparel, handbags, and home fashions; Wal-Mart – apparel (70 percent) and footwear (30 percent); and Montgomery Ward – apparel and footwear (minimal).
[c] Wal-Mart's sole sourcing agent in Taiwan, and much of the rest of Asia as well, is Pacific Resources Export Limited (PREL). Although registered as a Hong Kong trading company, PREL is owned by Indonesia's Salim Group, one of the biggest industrial conglomerates in Asia.
[d] Associated Merchandising Corporation is a group buying office that serves about forty different stores in the United States, including Dayton-Hudson, Federated Department Stores, Target, and Bradlees.
[e] Mast Industries is the main overseas sourcing arm and a wholly owned subsidiary of The Limited.
[f] R. H. Macy and the May Company bought jointly in Asia from 1960 to 1973. The following year, May Company set up its own buying office; Macy purchased through Linmark Services, an independent buying agent, until 1986, when Macy established a separate buying office.
Source: Gereffi and Pan (1994, p. 137), based on interviews in Taiwan by Gary Gereffi.

Japan, and thirty-six from other countries," and among these were Kmart, Sears, Associated Merchandising, and J.C. Penney (Jung, 1984, p. 110). In Taiwan, according to the excellent work done by Gary Gereffi and his colleague Pan Mei-lin (1994), reproduced in Table 7.1, most of the main big buyers had established their direct buying offices in the early 1970s. In both countries, the retailers proceeded to order huge quantities of goods in the succeeding years. Also, by the mid-1970s, shipping lines had established container ports; fast freight forwarders had opened their offices; and banks had begun offering financing services, such as letters of credit. In short, by the 1970s, global matching and all the associated services to support these linkages had become sufficiently well developed to propel industrialization to new levels.

Although very few analysts have commented on these trans-Pacific linkages, it is apparent that all the participants, including government officials, understood that economic development involved a matching game. Manufacturers (usually led by the most prominent ones) in both South Korea and Taiwan, often assisted by their respective national governments, began to organize associations (or re-activate existing associations) of manufacturers designed to promote trade. The three primary strategies of these groups were to facilitate matches (by providing lists and samples of products and assorted information on firms), to solve actual and potential problems with international exchanges (providing cultural, legal, financial, and infrastructural services), and to negotiate with the local government regarding economic policies.

The Korea Traders Association was established in 1946, but "did not really get underway until . . . the 1960s and 1970s." By 1984, the Association had 3,000 members (Rhee, et al., 1984, p. 52). Linked to this association were more than thirty groups of manufacturers specializing in specific exports, such as The Korean Knitted Goods Exporters Association, the Korea Electronic Products Exporters Association, and the Korea Footwear Exporters, most of which were housed in the World Trade Center in Seoul (Rhee, et al., 1984, 52). The World Trade Center itself was build as a project of the Korea Trade Promotion Corporation (KOTRA). As a part of the Park's initiative to promote exports, the Korean government founded and financed the Korea Trade Promotion Corporation in 1962, and by the 1980s had established nearly 100 information showrooms around the world "to provide information about Korean importers and exporters, the commodities they buy and sell, and the services they need and provide in foreign investment and construction" (Rhee, et al., 1984, p. 52).

Manufacturers from Taiwan also organized a similar range of trade associations to promote exports, although these associations were never as centralized or as effective as their counterparts in South Korea. Several associations of importers, exporters, and manufacturers began in a small way in the 1940s, but did not become active until the 1960s and 1970s (Kuo, 1995). Sponsored by the government, the China External Trade Development Council started in 1970; organized its first trade delegation in 1972; sponsored the first trade fair in Taiwan in 1973, which was for garments; and began worldwide promotions of Taiwanese products in 1973 and 1974 (Wade, 1990, pp. 145–6). The Taiwan Textile Federation, however, did not start until 1975; the World Trade Center did not officially open until 1986, and the Taiwan Bicycle Exporters' Association did not organize until 1992. For Taiwan, and perhaps for Korea as well, many of these attempts to create associations were less efforts to match foreign buyers with a select group of manufacturers than it was for a select group of manufacturers that were already matched with foreign buyers to negotiate trade policies with the Taiwanese (and Korean) government, which was quite explicitly the only stated mission of the Taiwan Bicycle Exporters' Association (www.tbea.org).

Although associational and governmental efforts to match foreign buyers to local manufacturers have been consistently important in the development of both countries, these efforts have generally lagged the growth of export trade and the interfirm linkages that this trade implies. Therefore, we are inclined to view governmental and associational activities as merely an aspect of the emergence and rationalization of these two economies, instead of being a primary cause of matching in the first place. Perhaps the clearest indication of their secondary role is the sudden and extraordinary expansion of local trading companies in both countries.

Like icebergs floating in the ocean, local trading companies sit on top of and organize a vast body of firms producing for export. How these local trading companies are organized themselves, and how they in turn reflect the organization of manufacturers (which they in turn have helped create), gives us a good picture about how the larger economies themselves are organized, as well as how these economies grow and change. Local trading companies were extremely important in both locations, but the differences between their organization in South Korea and Taiwan could not be more dramatic and indicative of both the emergence and divergence in these two industrializing economies.

As we stated earlier, in South Korea in 1975, the Park regime issued a directive enabling the largest *chaebol* to establish their own trading companies. This directive should be understood against the backdrop of the economic growth that was occurring in the previous decade, from approximately 1965 onward. During this period, the *chaebol* began to compete among each other for the increasing orders being placed by foreign buyers, and a few of these *chaebol* were able quickly to consolidate their position at the very top of the Korean economy. Although Korea's general trading companies were established after the process of *chaebol* consolidation was already well underway, the extraordinary growth of these companies still captures a significant portion of this consolidation as it was occurring.

In 1975, five *chaebol* received licenses to establish their own Japanese-style general trading companies. Five more *chaebol* received licenses in 1976, and three more in 1977. Collectively the trading companies grew at an extraordinary rate of over 50 percent per year from the date of establishment for the next eight years. However, as Table 7.2 shows, even as export trade handled by general trading companies was growing exponentially, some *chaebol* were already beginning to lose out in the competition. The government revoked the licenses of the general trading companies for five *chaebol* whose trade volumes fell below that of the previous year. By 1985, only seven *chaebol*-owned trading companies had licenses, and

Table 7.2. *Exports of Korean Trading Companies (US$ million)*

	1975	1976	1977	1978	1979	1980	1981	1982	1983	1984	1985
Company:											
Samsung	223	355	507	493	767	1,237	1,608	1,836	2,199	2,754	3,017
Ssangyong	125	141	176	265	420	642	754	956	1,033	1,239	1,262
Daewoo	161	301	501	709	1,119	1,415	1,895	1,958	2,490	2,576	2,990
Kukje	64	197	328	472	564	744	849	934	0	0	0
Hanil	37	218	127	188	0	0	0	0	0	0	0
Hyo Sung	0	113	199	338	583	764	784	598	682	749	897
Bando/LG	0	134	212	330	467	493	611	688	1,059	1,440	1,443
Sunkyong	0	114	247	283	320	430	578	600	653	846	940
Samwha	0	0	167	260	0	0	0	0	0	0	0
Kum Ho	0	99	204	256	305	356	185	166	0	0	0
Hyundai	0	0	320	260	450	1,028	1,721	2,632	3,138	3,334	3,969
Yulsan	0	0	91	151	0	0	0	0	0	0	0
Korea Trade[a]	0	18	25	24	51	67	84	75			
TOTAL	610	1,690	3,104	4,029	5,046	7,176	9,069	10,443	12,376	13,995	15,144
% share of Korea's exports	12	21.9	30.9	31.7	33.5	41	42.7	47.8	50.6	47.9	50

Notes: Zero indicates zero or no data available.
[a] Korea Trade is an exporting agent for small and medium-scale producers.
Sources: For years from 1975 to 1980, Rhee, et al., 1984, pp. 148–9, using data from Korean Traders Association, 1981. For years from 1981 to 1985, Fields, 1995, p. 193, using data from Business Korea 4/93.

these seven handled over 50 percent of Korea's total exports. Moreover, three of these seven handled nearly 33 percent of the total. Clearly, even as Korea's export economy was booming, some *chaebol* had lost out in the competition for export growth. The separation between the top *chaebol* and all the rest, as predicted in the model presented in Chapter 3, is plainly borne out in the evidence even from this early date.

As high as it seems, the *chaebol's* 50 percent concentration actually understates the *chaebol's* growing control of export trade. According to Jung's calculations, the *chaebol's* general trading companies only handled 26.5 percent of Korean exports to the United States. The "low share of the exports," he (1984, p. 116) argues, "reflects the fact that there were already established trade channels such as American retailers and importers, and to a less extent, other foreign trading companies," mostly Japanese. The largest exporters to the United States, Jung (1984, p. 116) further states, are those with large manufacturing firms that have established trading subsidiaries in the United States outside of the *chaebol's* main general trading company to work more closely with retailers and merchandisers, such as "textiles in the case of Daewoo and Samsung and footwear in the case of Kukje."

The largest *chaebol*'s general trading companies used their exclusive licenses and other government bestowed privileges to build positions of economic power vis-à-vis other *chaebol*, as well as small and medium-sized firms. In some sectors where the largest *chaebol* did not have big firms or could not exploit Fordist production techniques, such as the labor-intensive manufacture of wearing apparel, the *chaebol* nonetheless integrated export production by being in a position, first, to obtain and then maintain large orders from American retailers and, then, to organize sub-contracting networks around the *chaebol*'s integrated cotton and synthetic production and export capabilities (Lim, 1998, pp. 69–70, Lee and Song, 1994). In other sectors where the largest *chaebol* initially had limited capabilities, such as in electronics, the *chaebol* quickly built their own internal vertically integrated production facilities by taking over small and medium-sized firms with expertise in the area, by starting joint ventures with Japanese firms (as Goldstar did in 1970 and Samsung did in 1973), and by importing components (usually from Japan) that could not be obtained internally (Lim, 1998, p. 116). This same process was repeated when the top *chaebol* began to manufacture automobiles for export. In those instances when they did obtain standardized parts from suppliers, the top *chaebol* would obtain the part from a great many suppliers, thereby being able to push the costs down to the lowest possible level. By concentrating on building vertically integrated production systems and by controlling export channels, the top *chaebol* increased their economic power over other firms and other *chaebol* in the economy. These competitive tactics of the top *chaebol*, concludes Haeran Lim (1998, p. 118), caused the "development of subcontracting relationships, and the development of SMEs more generally (to be) very slow during the 1970s."

The exact opposite result occurred in Taiwan. At the same time that this dramatic concentration of the top *chaebol*'s hold over export production was occurring in South Korea, an equally dramatic expansion of local trading companies was occurring in Taiwan. This expansion took a very different path, however. In the late 1960s and early 1970s, the number of trading companies in Taiwan began rapidly to grow. The expansion reflects the growth of small and medium-sized firms, whose exports by this early date had already begun to drive the process of industrialization. According to Levy, the number of trading companies in Taiwan grew from an already substantial number of 2,777 in 1973 to 20,597 in 1984. According to Fields (1995, p. 211), this figure should be even higher: "By 1986, Taiwan had over 60,000 firms involved in foreign trade, and over 40,000 of these were designated as 'exclusive' trading firms, not engaged in manufacturing." Liu reports a yet higher number of trading companies, 65,000, which "was about half of the total number of manufacturing companies in Taiwan" (cited by Hsing, 1999, p. 105).

The share of Taiwan's total export trade attributed to these trading companies varies, but it is certain that Levy's figure is too high and Fields' figure is too low. Levy (1991, p. 157) calculates that in 1984, on average, 20,597 trading firms each export $1,400,000 US worth of goods. That makes the total exports attributed to these trading firms nearly equal to Taiwan's total exports. Fields (1995, p. 225), however, estimates local trading companies only handled 20 percent of Taiwan total export trade, which is certainly too low for the simple reason that small and medium-sized firms contributed around 65 percent of Taiwan's exports, most of which went through the hands of local trading companies even though Japanese or American buyers or trade intermediaries handled the shipment to retail outlets in the United States. An accurate figure is impossible to come by because most estimates assume that the export trading pie is divided among distinct groups (for example, Japanese *sogo shosha*, American and European buyers, local manufacturers, government agencies and trade associations, and local trading companies), when in fact Taiwanese trading companies worked with foreign buyers all the time, thereby distorting the percentages.

Moreover, our interviews have revealed that many of the "exclusive trading companies" are merely small firms that are independently owned by entrepreneurs who also own one or more manufacturing firms. These trading companies may deal in a variety of export goods beside the ones produced by the entrepreneurs. As Hsing (1999), Chen (1994), and others have shown, Taiwanese trading companies are not so much instruments of individual firms as they are both organizers and embodiments of production networks. Nearly all production networks of small, medium-sized, and modestly large firms, which the Taiwanese call "satellite assembly systems," are represented by one or more trading companies, whose chief task is to find and manage orders that keep the network of firms employed and profitable.

Most of Taiwan's trading companies are very small, with an average of seven employees (Hsing 1999, p. 105), and they work with a relatively small set of manufacturing firms, usually ten or more, all of which are independently owned (Hsing, 1999). Collectively, these firms establish a production network capable of filling orders the trading companies generate (Shieh, 1992, Hsing, 1999, Kao and Hamilton, 2000). These trading companies are often called *pibao gungsi*, "suitcase companies," because the owners typically travel in the United States and Europe, with their sample suitcase in hand, going from one buyer to another in hopes of finding matches between the buyers and the manufacturing networks they represent. On their travels, the owners collect information about their particular industry and samples that may serve as models for new products.

When orders have been received, the owner of the trading company helps put together a production network to fill the specific orders, and may even loan money to assist manufacturers in buying the needed manufacturing equipment to set up the satellite assembly system (Chen, 1994, Shieh, 1992, Hamilton, 1997). If the orders are large or numerous, then each of the independent firms in the assembly network will expand somewhat and, more importantly, will subcontract a portion of their work to other firms, thereby extending the network beyond the original set of firms. When orders are small and few, the original set of manufacturers may reduce the number of subcontractors, and some of the firms in the set may begin searching for other products that can be easily manufactured, the production of which may lead to the formation of one, and sometimes several, new production networks, along with new trading companies to promote the new products. It is for this reason that, during the early years of industrialization, the number of Taiwanese firms and trading companies each grew at about the same pace and at about the same rate as the overall economy grew.

In trying to explain the reasons that Korean and Taiwan economies differ, a number of analysts (Amsden, 1989, Wade, 1990, Shafer, 1997, Rodirk, 1994) cite differences in government policies. It is, therefore, worthwhile to note that both governments also **tried and failed** to promote countervailing trends in their respective economies. It is certain that both governments had significant roles to play in the overall development process. When governments enacted policies that conformed to the existing momentum, their policies were usually successful, sometimes wildly so, as is the case with industrial targeting in South Korea. However, when governmental actions ran counter to the organizational momentum of the economy, they were almost always unsuccessful. For instance, the South Korean government has a long history of trying to stem the growth of the *chaebol* and to stimulate small and medium-sized firms, and the Taiwanese government has tried to encourage the formation of large firms and branded exports, but both sets of policies have been to no avail. As Dollar and Sokoloff (1994, p. 11) concluded, "One general lesson from the experiences of South Korea and Taiwan is that it is difficult to implement an industrial targeting policy that is not basically in line with where the private sectors are planning to go anyway."

This same pattern of governmental failure also happened in both countries in their dealings with local trading companies. During the period when *chaebol* consolidation occurred, the trading arm of Korea's small and medium-sized firms, Korea Trade International, also received a license to operate as a general trading company. This trading group, however, never handled more than 1 percent of the total export trade. Besides the eight licensed general trading companies (including the Korea Trade International), the government also permitted individual trading companies to export goods. Although, the number of these companies grew over four-fold, from 1,200 firms in 1973 to 5,300 in 1984, the value of exports these firms handled remained very small, except of course for the seven main trading companies of the *chaebol*.[5] In the Korean case, governmental incentives could not help small firms or their trading arm to succeed in an economy dominated by a few corporate octopi (a term that Koreans often used to describe the large *chaebol*) that also had ample governmental incentives to operate and that grabbed every profitable thing in sight.

In Taiwan, the opposite governmental policy failed. This was a government program to establish and give incentives to large trading companies. Being aware of the proliferation of small and medium-sized firms and being equally aware of the Korean government's support for Japanese-style general trading companies, the Taiwanese government became concerned that the Taiwanese economy was losing its competitive advantage and that the overall economy needed to be upgraded. Heavy industries needed to be developed and sponsored, brand names needed to be established, and large trading companies were needed to handle and promote export products (Dollar and Sokoloff, 1994, Fields, 1995). In a worried mood, the government passed legislation in 1978 to create large trading companies. Eight large trading companies eventually formed and all eventually failed (Fields, 1995, pp. 209–37). The reason they failed is because small and medium-sized firms, Taiwan's export engine, did not need the promotional services of these large trading companies. These small and medium-sized manufacturing firms were best served by the local entrepreneurs who helped to put together the production networks and who vigorously promoted their products, both in Taiwan to buyers and overseas at the headquarters of merchandising and retail firms.

In summary, then, in both South Korea and Taiwan, local trading companies served as important intermediaries matching foreign buyers with local manufacturing firms, and in both cases, they were partly reflections and partly creators of the emerging organization of these two industrializing economies. It is our thesis that, under conditions of increasing intermediary demand, the economic interaction (for example, the competitive struggle as well as selective cooperation) among firms created an organizational momentum that shaped the economic trajectory of development

---

[5] Brian Levy (1994) cites these figures from the Korea Traders Association, but his calculations for the "average value of industrial exports per trader" of $5,200,000 per each of the 5,300 traders must include the exports from eight trading companies, as the total value of these exports nearly equals the total value of Korean exports in 1984. In fact, Jung (1984, p. 107) notes that in the early 1980s there were about 4,500 trading companies in Korea and this classification includes general trading companies as well as other large manufacturing firms that have trading subsidiaries in the United States, most of which would be members of the largest *chaebol*.

and that was difficult to change once the organizational parameters of the economy are apparent to the main participants.

The Spatial Dimensions of Global Matching

Global matching involved repeated voluntary pairings of firms in conditions where both sides of the match were involved in highly competitive environments. Aware that the retail revolution was underway and increasingly using advanced technology to track consumer choices, merchandisers and retailers in the United States (and later Europe and Japan) hotly competed with one another, and, as a consequence of this competition, fundamentally reshaped the organization of the entire retail sector, if not the entire American economy. An important aspect of this competition, especially in fashion products that characterized the earliest exports to the United States from East Asia, was organizationally to decouple the manufacture from the design and merchandising of goods, while keeping the linkages tight enough to control the quality, quantity, delivery schedule, and price of the final products. This system of retailing produced at the manufacturing end of the commodity chain a requirement to produce specified goods in batches, in other words, a batch-production, as opposed to a mass-production system. Retailers ordered goods in batches of various sizes, at a specified price and level of quality; manufacturers had to set their profits at the time, and according to the size of the order, instead of estimating profits over the lifetime of a long but indeterminate production run, which is the case in mass-production systems.

This system of batch-production put considerable pressure on manufacturers, **wherever they were located,** to streamline their manufacturing processes to control the quality of production (so they would not have to absorb the cost of shoddy products that big buyers would not accept) and to control their costs so that they could increase or at least maintain their profit margins. In the late 1960s and 1970s, Asian manufacturers used their low labor costs to give themselves an initial price advantage and therefore to begin receiving sizeable orders. But once these orders began to come, the manufacturers had to work hard to have them continue and to work even more diligently to establish a more lasting relationship that reflected trust and performance from both parties to a match. This desire to work with merchandisers and retailers meant that Asian manufacturers had to be open to the capriciousness of fad and fashion-driven markets in the United States and elsewhere, and to be amenable to the price, quality, and scheduling demands of the big buyers. In other words, these manufacturers had to act as loosely coupled organizational extensions of retail and merchandising firms.

Very quickly, in this increasingly rationalized context of repeating batch orders, American big buyers began to increase the number of their suppliers and to differentiate among suppliers, judging which ones could best fill which orders. At the same time, Asian manufacturers began to specialize in certain types of production and in certain types of products that corresponded to that type of production. Although previous research on this topic is surprisingly sparse and firsthand information sketchy, we can still follow this process of repeated orders by drawing inferences from the agglomeration process that was occurring simultaneously.

Seoul-Centered Agglomerations

As we have described in Chapter 5, on the eve of industrialization, a few big winners had already emerged within South Korea's economy. We can now piece together the story of these big winners as the process of industrialization unfolds. In 1962, just before rapid industrialization begins, a survey of the manufacturing sector of the Korean economy reports that the most concentrated, as well as the most developed, industry in South Korea at the time was cotton textile manufacturing and the "most under-developed" and least concentrated was electrical equipment (Economic Research Center of Korea, 1962, pp. 107, 342). In the cotton textile industry, the largest fifteen mills (ten of which were spinning mills and five weaving) were owned by fourteen companies that had organized themselves into an exclusive group called the Spinners and Weavers Association of Korea (SWAK). Of these fifteen mills, six were owned by the members of the even more exclusive Federation of Korean Industries, five of which were among the "big eight" (Lim, 1998, p. 69, Economic Research Center of Korea, 1962, p. 109), and out of a total of forty-four cotton-spinning mills and 604 cotton-weaving mills, these fifteen mills, each employing over 500 people, controlled 80 percent of Korea's total production (Economic Research Center of Korea, 1962, pp. 107–9). Most of the production from these mills was for the domestic market, although a small portion ($860,000 U.S.) was exported.

In 1960, in the electrical equipment sector, there were 614 firms registered in South Korea (Institute of Developing Economies, 1975, p. 102), only one of which employed over 200 workers, and only seventeen out of the 129 employed fifty or more workers. The industry suffered, concluded the economic analysts, from a "shortage of capital, inadequate technology, and lack of supporting industries" (Economic Research Center of Korea, 1962, p. 342). In 1962, none of these firms were owned by Federation members, and none were engaged in export production.

Ten years later, in 1971, textile production, including cotton textiles, had increased 440 percent (from 35,284 to 190,401 million won in 1965 constant prices), and electrical equipment had jumped nearly 2,300 percent (from 1,723 to 40,965 million won, in 1965 constant prices) (Institute of Developing Economies, 1975, pp. 98–9). Despite this rapid increase and although the number of workers jumped dramatically (textiles: from 81,649 to 202,660 workers; electrical machinery: from 4,458 to 42,172 workers), the number of manufacturing firms in these two sectors increased very little. In textiles, the total number of firms grew by only 8 percent (from 2,493 to 2,696) and in electrical machinery only 45 percent (from 614 to 890) (Institute of Developing Economies, 1975, pp. 102–3). It is obvious, and substantiated by our disaggregating these statistics, that the large firms in textiles grew much larger, and a few large firms emerged in electrical equipment. Predominately owned by the rising *chaebol*, often in cooperation with Japanese and American firms, which made sizeable investments, these large firms accounted for almost all of the increases in production in both sectors.[6] Moreover, looking at this buildup, researchers from the Tokyo-based Institute of Developing Economies (1975, p. 20) concluded that the main products from these factories (for example, textiles, plywood, wigs, and electronic parts) "are exported exclusively to the American market."

During this same decade, another important shift occurred: The growth of large firms mainly occurred in one urban area: Seoul (Meyer and Min, 1988). In 1960, manufacturing was already concentrated in South Korea, primarily in the three largest cities (that is, Seoul, Pusan, and Taegu), as well as Seoul's three industrial suburbs: Incheon, Suweon, and Euijeongbu. These six urban areas accounted for over 67 percent of the total urban population of South Korea and over 71 percent of its total manufacturing. By 1970, population and manufacturing were even more concentrated, with nearly 73 percent of the total population and nearly 80 percent of the total manufacturing being located in these six areas. Breaking these totals down, however, we see that in almost every manufacturing sector Pusan's and Daegu's percentages declined and Seoul's increased, often dramatically. For instance in 1960, only three of the fifteen largest textile companies were located in Seoul (Economic Research Center of Korea 1962, p. 109). At the time, Seoul accounted for only 8 percent of textile production and about 32 percent of garment manufacture. By 1970, however, most of the state-of-the-art textile factories had been built in Seoul, and Seoul accounted for nearly 36 percent of total textile production and about 46 percent of garment manufacture. The concentration of the electrical machinery and footwear sectors in Seoul grew even more dramatically during the ten-year period, jumping respectively from 31.8

---

[6] In 1969, the Korea Development Bank reported "the share of exports (in electrical machinery) held by foreign-invested firms (was) 75.8 percent" (The Korea Development Bank, 1970, p. 107).

to 62.8 percent and 22.7 to 63.4 percent during the decade. Not coincidentally, in the 1960s, the largest *chaebol* (Samsung, Hyundai, Daewoo, and Lucky-Gold Star) all established their headquarters and a significant portion of their manufacturing plants in Seoul.

It is important to note that this concentration in the greater Seoul region occurred despite strenuous and growing government efforts to encourage industrial growth in other areas, including the development and promotion of nine industrial parks for heavy industry and twenty-four regionally based industrial parks to spur decentralization. During the 1970s and 1980s, Seoul continued to grow in both population and manufacturing, although Seoul's relative proportion of total manufacturing began to decline as heavy industries began to pick up in the late 1970s and 1980s, much of which came to be located outside of Seoul proper (Cho and Kim, 1991, pp. 349–70).

Rural Agglomerations in Taiwan

At the same time that manufacturing concentrated in the Seoul region, export-oriented manufacturing in Taiwan decentralized and increasingly became located in rural areas outside of the largest cities of Taipei and Kaohsiung, which were also the locations of most state-owned enterprises, as well as the headquarters of some of Taiwan's largest business groups. One gets a sense of this spatially decentralized industrialization from Samuel Ho's pioneering studies (1978, 1982). Writing in the middle 1970s, Ho (1978) initially did not notice the significant rural component of Taiwan's industrialization. In fact, working within the conventional paradigm of urban-based industrialization, Ho pointed to the significant rural-to-urban migration that occurred in the 1960s as evidence that industrialization was underway. By the early 1980s, however, the decentralized pattern of Taiwan's industrialization had become obvious. Surprised by the presence of rural industrialization in Taiwan, Ho took a closer look at Taiwan's unusual industrial foundation through a revealing comparison with the concurrent industrialization process in South Korea. Defining "rural Taiwan" as "Taiwan minus the five major cities (Taipei, Keelung, Taichung, Tainan and Kaohsiung) and the most industrial prefecture (Taipei prefecture)," Ho (1982, p. 981), using data from the government's 1971 census of manufacturing establishments, found that 52 percent of small factories (five to forty-nine employees), 49 percent of medium-sized factories (fifty to ninety-nine), 49 percent of medium to large factories (100 to 499), and 46 percent of large factories (500+) were located in rural areas. By contrast, in Korea in 1975, 50 percent of small factories, 28 percent of medium-sized factories, 26 percent of medium to large factories, and 19 percent of large factories were located in rural areas, which Ho (1982, p. 981) defined as "Korea minus Seoul, Pusan and the two most industrial provinces (Gyeonggi Do and Gyeongsangnam Do)." Taiwan's spatial patterns of industrialization continued to become more decentralized as Taiwan's industrialization continued, a pattern lasting until around the 1990s, when many small and medium-sized firms moved to Mainland China.

As revealing as they are, these statistics really do not portray what happened in the countryside between 1965 and 1975. In the late 1960s, the rate of Taiwan's agricultural growth suddenly declined. Many areas of agricultural production declined in absolute terms, including rice, soybeans, peanuts, bananas, pineapples, asparagus, and mushrooms, all of which were important export and domestic cash crops during the late 1950s and 1960s (Taiwan Statistical Data Book, 1994, pp. 69–73). This sudden decline can be traced to the equally sudden growth in industrial production. Unlike in Korea, where industrial production was concentrated in the Seoul region, in Taiwan, industrial production was widely dispersed throughout the island, in the countryside as well as in the cities. No single city in Taiwan stood out as the center of industrial production as Seoul did in Korea. In fact, the fastest growing locations for manufacturing were small towns and villages. Factories even began to spring up in the middle of rice fields, the very property owned by the rural entrepreneurs themselves.

The government unintentionally helped to nurture this rural industrialization. In addition to land reform, the Nationalist agricultural policies in the 1950s had encouraged local networks by establishing rural cooperatives and local party organizations, associations in which many people living in small towns and villages participated. At the same time, the Nationalists removed the former landlords from economic as well as political power (Ho, 1978). This reform was a move to consolidate their power at the local level, but the reform actually encouraged considerable local networking resulting in intra-party factionalism (Jacobs, 1979). Although the Kuomintang encouraged local networks, the state gave no direct support for non-agricultural economic pursuits. Nonetheless, people in rural areas began to explore others ways to expand their ability to make money beyond farming. Through extensive interviews, Kao (1999) and his collaborators (Chen, 1994, 1995, 1997) learned that many of the earliest entrepreneurs, often sons of farmers, had migrated for a time to nearby cities to learn skills that later became instrumental in starting their own businesses in the countryside. The capital used to start these new businesses usually came from their savings and from family members or friends and friends of friends, many of whom engaged in part-time farming. These interviews correspond to Tai-li Hu's account (1984) of her mother-in-law's rural village, Liu Ts'o, where no factories were started during the 1960s, but where a few villagers had gained sufficient skill in nearby Taichung City to return to Liu Ts'o in the early 1970s to establish, "all of a sudden" (Hu, 1984, 2), twenty small-scale factories. As in Hu's account, many firm owners relied heavily on raising capital and recruiting labor from the social networks that developed in the aftermath of land reform (Ho, 1982, Speare, 1992, Liao and Huang, 1994).[7] This "all-men-are-brothers" type of network, initially based on locale and kinship, enabled the agriculturally based rural society to generate enough resources for a few entrepreneurs to start modest businesses in the late 1960s. By the mid-1970s, however, these early beginnings mushroomed into a full-scale manufacturing boom, a boom that would transform Taiwan's local society (Fu and Shei, 1999).

The boom occurred in many different sectors, but the primary growth occurred initially in garments, footwear, miscellaneous plastic products, and household electrical appliances, all of which used labor-intensive manufacturing techniques and all of which were linked to retailers and merchandisers in the United States. The manufacture of these exports concentrated in particular rural areas, so that different areas specialized in making different goods. For example, three of Taiwan's primary export products in the early years of industrialization – cotton textiles and garments, footwear, and bicycles – were primarily produced in the rural areas of two districts in central Taiwan: Changhwa and Taichung districts.

Hemei, a small town straddling the border between Changhwa and Taichung districts, became the production center for cotton textile and garments, with several thousand firms, many of which were unregistered, suddenly springing up in the vicinity of the town in a matter of ten years (Chen, 1997). Hemei was the site of a traditional cotton industry that in the Japanese colonial period had produced, among other things, narrow width cotton cloth used for foot binding. By the late 1960s, firms around Hemei, linking up with Western buyers, began to make cloth and garments for export, and soon the number of firms and the amount of production exploded. The 1981 Industrial and Commercial Census (pp. 456–8), a survey of all firms in Taiwan, shows that 28 percent of all textile factories (synthetic fiber as well as cotton factories) in Taiwan were located in the area around Hemei. (We should note that these statistics for these two districts exclude the area of Taichung City, which is the principal urban area in the region.) Disaggregating cotton textiles from textiles

---

[7] Hu (1984, 212) argues, however, that in her case study "the capital accumulated for the development of rural small-scale industry was not mainly from agriculture." Our interviews indicate that, although rural-based capital accumulation might have been modest, the use of rural resources, including the land and labor of those living in the countryside, was substantial and facilitated the rapid growth of industries that occurred in the 1970s and early 1980s.

made from synthetic fabrics, we further see that nearly 50 percent (48.5) of all cotton textile factories in Taiwan (677) were located in these two rural districts.

By 1980, the center of footwear production was located a little to the northwest of Hemei, in the rural areas around Lukang. Thousands of footwear firms were established in this area in the 1970s and early 1980s, many of which were too small to register (Hsing, 1998). Of the registered firms making plastic footwear in the 1981 census (1,444), 55 percent were located in the rural areas of Changhwa and Taichung districts, and another 8 percent in the metropolitan area of Taichung City (Industrial and Commercial Census, 1983). The same pattern recurs for bicycle production. The rural areas of the two districts contained 60 percent of all registered factories (329/549) producing bicycles and bicycle parts, with Taichung City adding almost another 10 percent (52) (Industrial and Commercial Census, 1983).

These and many other examples that could be given show a similar pattern. Small, medium, and some modestly large firms, primarily located outside of the major metropolitan areas, produced finished goods for export. The firms producing the intermediate goods needed to produce these products – the plastics, the steel, the chemicals – were often located in or near the largest metropolitan regions, especially in the vicinity of Taipei and Kaohsiung. The sudden boom in the establishment of small firms was closely linked to the ready availability of intermediate goods, but large firms not only did not supervise the production activities of small firms, but also mostly withdrew from trying to produce final goods themselves (for example, Taniura, 1989, p. 72, Chou Tein-Chen, 1985). Instead, throughout the 1970s and 1980s, the integration between the large firms supplying intermediate goods and the smaller firms making export products occurred as a result of the responsiveness of small and medium-sized firms to intermediary demand. In other words, the drivers of Taiwan's economic integration were the small rather than the large firms.

In summary, although agglomerations emerged in both countries during the early years of industrialization, the spatial dimensions of these agglomerations were strikingly different. South Korea's industries concentrated in the Seoul region, while Taiwan's factories dispersed throughout the countryside – in large, small, and medium-sized towns and cities. Although these agglomerations sprang up in a context of rapidly increasing orders from Western buyers, the agglomerations themselves are manifestations of underlying organizational processes, or what Krugman (1996) identifies as "self-organization."[8]

---

[8] By the term "self-organization," Krugman wants to convey, first, that economic order (by which he means an organized economy) emerges out of instability ("the principle

Self-organization, that is the dynamic by which an emergent economy (or some segment thereof) becomes internally organized, should not be seen as a mysterious process. Remember in Schelling's example (1978) that sequential decisions made by proactive people in regard to their personal desires about where to live end up having broad systemic consequences for urban space. We are making an analogous argument, namely that entrepreneurs, recognizing their authority to command and their market power to persuade, make sequential competitive decisions regarding their businesses in relation to other businesses in the same economic environment that are also making similar decisions. Although these decisions may be firm specific (for example, firm owners may decide not to sell intermediate inputs to other firms), collectively and sequentially over time these decisions have profound and emergent effects on the organization of entire economies.

More specifically, in the cases of South Korea and Taiwan, the divergent patterns of economic organization were the consequences of proactive sequential efforts on the part of South Korean and Taiwan manufacturers to continue and to further extend connections with intermediary demand though the use of whatever leverage and combination of authority and market power that was available to these manufacturers. The collective effects of those decisions, especially those in the early years of industrialization, became "locked-in" (a term used to indicate systemic integration, which makes going concerns difficult to change without changing the entire system) and set on a path of development. Certainly, the balance of power and authority among firms at the outset of economic growth that we described in Chapter 5 had continuing and decisive effects on attempts to create successful firms, but it was the repeated matches between big buyers and Asian manufacturers, with each hotly competing with other firms in their own respective economic environments, that pushed these two Asian economies along very different trajectories of development.

of order from instability") and, second, that the emergent order is shaped by random endogenous factors (the principle of order from random growth). In thinking through our two cases, we would agree with Krugman that the divergent economic orders that were firmly in place by 1985 in South Korea and Taiwan emerged from earlier periods of economic instability and uncertainty, which arose from civil wars, martial law, poverty, and mixed policies from governments that were unsure how to proceed economically. (We might note, moreover, that government policy in retrospect seems a lot more rational and more export growth-oriented than it actually was at the time.) However, the second principle does not square with what happened. Although the factors determining these emergent organizations were certainly endogenous, they were hardly random. Indeed, the endogenous factors shaping self-organization within these economies were institutionally in place before the period of growth began and continually worked to structure the process of growth as demand-driven industrialization accelerated.

Matching in Economic Space

The final dimension of global matching that we have identified is the selection of partners in economic space, by which we mean the competitive environment in which relative location and relative leverage of two firms linked in a commodity chain are negotiated and resolved. One of the most significant aspects of economic development in both countries was the ability of South Korean and Taiwanese manufacturers to upgrade their location in economic space, often while maintaining their ties with the same intermediary buyers. These initial efforts to create more secure linkages with the big buyers, which occurred in the late 1970s and 1980s, happened at the same time that the retail sector in the United States was in the midst of the remarkable consolidation that made such discount retailers as Wal-Mart, Kmart, and Home Depot the largest retailers in the world and the biggest of big buyers in East Asia. Therefore, the expansion and upgrading of manufacturing capabilities in South Korea and Taiwan occurred, not at the expense of their American buyers, but rather in conjunction with their overwhelming successes.

In the early years of industrialization, both Korea and Taiwan produced very similar products. As we showed in Chapter 6, these similarities, mostly specific types of textiles, clothes and shoes, show up at the 7-digit level of classification. Although they were often identical, these products were not manufactured in the same way. Brian Levy's comparisons (1988, 1990) of the footwear and electronic appliance industries between both countries provide particularly good illustrations of these differences. As Levy (1988) shows, the total values and the rates of growth of footwear exports from Korea and Taiwan were very similar between 1970 and 1985, but the average export value per manufacturer was very different. The big buyers of these shoes (Levy mentions Nike and Reebok, but they were soon joined by many others), at least initially working with Japanese trading companies, developed subcontracted manufacturing in both countries simultaneously, but with different results.

As demand for running shoes surged in the United States, observed Levy (1988, p. 47), both Nike and Reebok "turned to the giant Korean footwear factories, which had in-house operations in excess of forty production lines." In these factories, 50,000 to 60,000 pairs of shoes per month could be produced on a single footwear production line. In order to be able to produce such quantities, Korea footwear manufacturer firms vertically integrated, "stitching in-house the uppers for footwear, and manufacturing in-house rubber soles, as well as assembling complete shoes" (Levy 1988, p. 44). These very large firms were very good at economy-of-scale production, at manufacturing many copies of the same item, so good, in fact, Levy (1988, p. 47) notes, that 71.3 percent of the entire Korean footwear exports in 1985 was accounted for by "a single footwear item – non-rubber athletic shoes," a percentage that is in line with our calculations based on U.S. trade statistics as well (see Figure 6.11).

By contrast, in Taiwan, footwear manufacturers responded to increasing orders from the same American big buyers, not by building larger factories, but rather by extending their subcontracting networks. "Taiwanese producers," observed Levy (1988, p. 44), "specialized in footwear assembly, and subcontracted the task of upper stitching and sole manufacture to independent vendors."[9] As a consequence of these subcontracting networks, footwear manufacturers were able to diversify their footwear exports over time, and were able to move up the value chain and "increasingly compete in the high fashion end of the world market for footwear" (Levy, 1988, p. 47). The Taiwanese advantage in the footwear market was their ability "to fill rapidly shifting niches for small volume fashion items" (Levy, 1988, p. 47).

Besides footwear, Levy also shows that the production of keyboards as a single item, as well as the production of finished personal computers, followed the same pattern, vertical integration in large firms in Korea and diversified networks of independently owned small and medium-sized firms in Taiwan. Moreover, the general pattern – of Korean enterprises growing larger and internally more diversified and of Taiwan enterprises linking with other firms and diversifying their products over time – that we have theorized in Chapter 3 and observed in Chapter 4 – is found in the initial years of industrial growth. The same pattern shows up again in the 1990s in the automotive and electronic industries, which we will describe in Chapter 8.

These illustrations show that in Korea, on the one hand, large firms, many of which were affiliated with the *chaebol*, developed economy-of-scale productions systems. These firms internalized the manufacture and assembly of most components that went into final products. In Taiwan, on the other hand, the same or similar products were made by small and medium-sized firms arranged in satellite assembly systems, each firm of which would make different components that would later be assembled into the finished good. As both economies become more intensively organized as export-driven economies – with exported goods organized in Korea through *chaebol* and in Taiwan through small and medium-sized firms – the mode of production and many of the actual products being produced increasingly diverged.

Although upgrading and divergence in products were driven by intermediary demand, one of the main reasons that demand kept rising was

---

[9] We should add here, that these manufacturers obtained their intermediate inputs from local and international suppliers, from whom they maintained impersonal market-based connections.

the ability of manufacturers to respond to this demand by building what amounts to systems of production, that is, a cross-market organization of production that extends beyond individual firms and individual business groups to incorporate entire sectors and, in our cases, entire economies. As we theorized in Part I, the core features of these systems of production are not externally imposed by macroeconomic incentives or policy directives, but rather arise internally, as intrinsic aspects of competitive activities themselves where economic players endeavor to position themselves relative to others by exercising authority within firms and groups of firms and by exercising market power over other firms beyond their actual authority to control. More specifically, in terms of our two cases, it was the ability of the manufacturers in both locations to put together internally competitive networks of production that not only responded to initial orders from big buyers, but also soon created demand-responsive systems of production that, in turn, shaped the emerging retail revolution in the United States and elsewhere. Put simply, the firms in the export sectors of both economies specialized not so much in products *per se*, as in a way of organizing production that had affinities to an array of different products for which big buyers would place orders. This point returns to the hypothesis we made in the opening section in Chapter 3, where we argued that the organization of economies precedes and largely shapes not only the technology used to manufacture products and the upgrading of that technology, but also the products actually produced. Further evidence for this and related hypotheses regarding the divergent performances of these economies is the topic of the next chapter. For now, however, it is enough to document the emergent systems of production, systems that centered on the use of authority and market power.

The Use of Authority and Market Power in South Korea

The *chaebol* powered their way to prominence by specializing in supplying mass-produced consumer goods for intermediary buyers. Their initial successes in manufacturing large runs of the same goods led to product upgrading strategies that created Korea's "one-set" production systems. These upgrading strategies received a strong early boost from the Korean government, after President Park and a small coterie of loyal assistants announced in 1973 a plan to develop heavy and chemical industries (Woo, 1991, p 129). The plan called for the rapid development of heavy and chemical industries (HCI), the intermediate products of which were not ideally suited for export. Aimed in part to fortify the nation against what was perceived to be a growing threat from North Korea and from being resource-dependent in a time of oil shortages, the plan, which was at first rejected by the *chaebol*, gained support as the largest *chaebol* owners realized that embracing the plan would be a low-cost way to upgrade and internalize the *chaebol*'s production capacities. Moreover, since size and resources were among HCI's criteria, this became a plan to which the largest *chaebol* alone had nearly exclusive access (Kim, 1997, pp. 140–66). In fact, as Eun Mee Kim (1997, pp. 148–9) suggests, the major features of this plan were worked out "without much consultation with the technocrats in the Economic Planning Board" in order to coincide with the interests of the largest *chaebol*.

As the policies for HCI developed in the first few years, one of the key features of the "Big Push," as the plan became known, was industrial targeting. Ideally the goal of industrial targeting was to strengthen those currently weak industrial sectors whose output was deemed essential for a strong national economy. The targeted industries were iron and steel, nonferrous metal, machinery, shipbuilding, electrical appliances and electronics, and petrochemicals. Although weak, most of these targeted industries were already present in the largest *chaebol*. Therefore, working in close coordination with government officials, *chaebol* owners used the Big Push initiative to formulate a policy that would advance and rationalize the plans that were already present (Kim, 1997, p. 143–66).

The key feature of the policy, which strong-state theorist Jung-en Woo (1991, p. 130) called "truly breathtaking," required that "the production of producer goods had to substitute for imports and simultaneously (or with as little lag as possible) to be good for export." In essence, this policy allowed the largest *chaebol* to receive ample government support, usually in the form of low-cost loans, for deepening their one-set production systems. They accomplished this goal by creating production facilities (usually by starting independent firms within the *chaebol*) to manufacture those intermediate inputs that they had been previously imported (most often from Japan) and that were essential components in products that they manufactured largely for export. In fact, as our colleague E. M. Lim (2002) shows, most of the internal buying within the top five *chaebol* that we reported in Chapter 4 comes from firms started during the 1970s and early 1980s and that were largely financed through the low-cost loans provided by the government. Haggard, Kim, and Moon (1991, p. 866) conclude, "The target-setting exercise became a way to identity policy barriers to expanded exports and the firms began to set their own targets." Far from creating an oligopolistic industrial structure via policy directive, the government's plan for HCI merely gave a "big push" to the internalization processes that was already well underway in the *chaebol*.

Underlying the very rapid expansion of the *chaebol*, in general, and especially of the top five, in particular, was the centralization of authority and the development of a system of control within the *chaebol* by which all the activities of the independent firms in the group were coordinated. We need to emphasize this point, because it is often ignored in otherwise insightful examinations of the *chaebol*.[10] The chief vehicle of *chaebol* expansion was the system of control that allowed the activities of these firms to be coordinated within groups. As we described in Chapter 5, Koreans did have access to such a system of authority, a system of power that centered on the head of a family, but that could extend well beyond the boundaries of the family itself. In short, Koreans could legitimately and did draw upon a patrimonial model of authority to link together and centralize control over what was, essentially, a group of independent family-owned enterprises.

In the early years of industrialization, this is exactly what occurred, the use of patrimonial logic to develop a system of enterprise control. We should underscore the point that we are discussing the period of before 1985, the period during which the top *chaebol* consolidated their control over the Korean economy. In recent years, many elements of patrimonial control have been criticized as being outmoded and not in Korea's best interests, and as a consequence the *chaebol*'s managerial structures become increasingly professionalized (more bureaucratic and technically proficient), even though family dynamics still continue to play important roles (Chang, 1999). Before 1985, however, it was the patrimonial controls that facilitated the extraordinary growth of the *chaebol* in the first place, which in turn set off the fierce competition among the largest groups, a competition that was as much among families as it was among firms (Biggart, 1990). This competition among the "big horses" (Lim, 2002), in turn, drove Korea along its particular path of development.

The general outlines of this system of control are not well-known and so bear repeating, if only briefly, in this context (also see Biggart, 1990, Kim, 1997, Kim, 1995, Chang, 1999, Lim, 2002). We can describe the system of control within the *chaebol* as following along two lines of authority: control through ownership and control through management.[11] In the period before the Korea government began to cajole the *chaebol* to list their biggest companies on the Korean stock exchange, the head of the *chaebol* and his family owned the majority of the shares in all member firms. After the *chaebol* heads began to list their largest companies on the stock market, the *chaebol* all developed elaborate ways to control

---

[10] The prevailing interpretation of the *chaebol* has been that of Alice Amsden (1989, see especially pp. 154–88, 2001). This interpretation draws heavily on Alfred Chandler's work on American multi-division firms (1977, 1990). Long a student of Chandler's work, Amsden makes the Korean *chaebol* into a bureaucratic corporation in a late-industrializing society that learns well the industrial lessons of the late twentieth century. Amsden persistently ignores the patrimonial side of the *chaebol*, rarely mentions the family dynamics that are so much a part of the *chaebol*'s origin and growth, and does not cite those who offer alternative interpretations.

[11] For a parallel treatment of control in Chinese-owned conglomerates, see Hamilton, 2000.

the firms through various patterns of cross-shareholding, so that the owners continued to control around 50 percent of the shares, even though they personally owned only a relatively small portion of the actual shares themselves (Kim, 1995, Chang, 1999, pp. 132–43). Based on a quantitative analysis of equity holdings, Chang (1999, p. 142) concludes, "all forty-nine *chaebol* business groups share the isomorphic pattern of nested hierarchy in their equity holding network." He isolates two main influences in force before 1985 that allowed this form of control through ownership to develop. First, "the credit-based financial market so organized by the state allowed the *chaebol* privileged access to cheap credit, and thus facilitated the use of crossholdings." Second, "strong familism ... generated powerful motives to keep equity control within the family boundary." Interestingly, the owners of the top five *chaebol* controlled, on average, a higher percentage of total shares than did the owners of the smaller *chaebol*, even though that control was harder to achieve because the assets and number of shareholder were larger and the number of listed firms was greater (Kim, 1995, p. 42).

Although *chaebol* owners maintained their control of the *chaebol* through centralizing ownership within the family, their ability to coordinate the activities of the business depended on their ability to extend that authority beyond the boundaries of the family by creating a centralized management structure under the control of the *chaebol* heads themselves. Although technical proficiency was important, the managerial structure itself was founded on a system of personal relationships that tied managers directly to the owners. Lim (2002, pp. 173–230; also see Biggart, 1990 and Kim, 1997) shows that *chaebol* owners systematically employed four types of relationships to extend their authority beyond the family in order to control their network of firms. These four types of relationships are patrilineal ties dominated by males in the immediate family, affinal ties through marriage, classmate ties, and fellow-regional ties. Before 1990, most managers in the largest *chaebol* were tied to the owners by one or more of these ties.[12]

The vertical hierarchy created through these relationships is arranged differently in different *chaebol*, but all of them use, especially in the early period of industrialization, some combination of dependent ties to accentuate the loyalty of subordinates to the *chaebol* head. At the top of most hierarchies are those who owe the most obedience to the *chaebol* head, the patrilineal relatives of the owners, particularly their sons, brothers, and nephews, in descending order of preference. The most centrally located

---

[12] We should note here, as we will describe later, that the same four types of relationships also show up in the formation of Taiwan manufacturing networks. However, in Taiwan, these relationships help cement household-centered horizontal networks.

of these would normally be the son selected to succeed his father as the head of the *chaebol* (Chang, 1999, pp. 33–46).

There are, however, only so many sons, brothers, and nephews to fill an expanding number of managerial positions that developed as the *chaebol* rapidly grew in size and complexity. Moreover, not every son or brother had equal interest or ability. Therefore, many other managers at the top and especially in the second tier of positions were filled by classmates of the *chaebol* head. Some of these were college classmates, but in a number of prominent cases, most notably in Daewoo, they were high school classmates (Lim, 2002). Although Daewoo is notable in this regard, the use of school ties are very common in most *chaebol*, in part because these ties directly and personally link the *chaebol* heads with their top managers, making these managers dependent on their classmate/*chaebol* head for their success.

Lower tiers of management were often recruited from the same hometown or same province as the *chaebol* founder (Biggart, 1990). Such fellow-regional ties are very important types of relationships in Asian societies in general and in Korean and Chinese societies in particular. These ties presume special and reciprocal loyalties (Hamilton, 1985, Biggart, 1990, Fei, 1992, Lim, 2002). In the context of the *chaebol*, however, regional ties created a managerial network resting on normative ties of loyalty that centralized the power of the *chaebol* heads. Because many *chaebol* founders come from Seoul and Kyongsang provinces, it is difficult to distinguish among *chaebol* on this score, even though Lim (2002, p. 207) reports that over 73 percent of all managers in the top ten *chaebol* come from these two provinces. For those *chaebol* founders coming from other provinces, such as the Kumho group, nearly 64 percent of the managers from the chairman to director positions in 1990 came from the Chollar region, the same region as the founder.

The fourth type of relationships is affinal ties, normally based on the marriage of the founders' daughters. These ties are primarily used to link the *chaebol* family with powerful political and economic connections. According to a study by the *Seoul Economic News* in 1991, 33.1 percent of the top thirty *chaebol* had developed governmental connections through marriages of the daughters of *chaebol* owners with high-ranking officials (Lim, 2002, p. 202). The report notes that most *chaebol* keep "systematic data on marriage networks of group owners. Particularly in those *chaebol* where family power is predominant, their planning and coordination offices keep the data" (*Seoul Economic News*, 1991, p. 438, cited by Lim, 2002, p. 202). Lim (2002, p. 203) concludes that the "wide web of marriages ties among *chaebol* and the top government officials implies that marriage ties provide important connections that are effective in running *chaebol* business."

The four sets of relationships arising from these ties were, and to some extent still are, used to create a management structure centered on the *chaebol* heads. Management structure developed through these dependent relationships suggests a system of control that is distinctly non-bureaucratic, a system that emphasizes the personal control of the *chaebol*. Unlike the portraits painted by Evans (1995) and Amsden (1989, 2001), the *chaebol*'s emergence was not based on the technical proficiency of a rational bureaucracy, but rather on the personal authority of the *chaebol* head wielded within what Weber (1978, pp. 1006–69) called a "patrimonial bureaucracy."

Also, as Weber noted in the case of other patrimonial bureaucracies, dependent ties work in conjunction with an administrative structure that reinforces them. As the *chaebol* began to grow in complexity in the late 1960s and 1970s, the *chaebol*'s organizational structure also began to centralize decision making in the office of *chaebol* heads (Kim, 1995). In many *chaebol*, the chairman initially kept an office in the main firm, but soon *chaebol* organization began to distinguish between day-to-day managerial control over what was happening within individual firms and the overall direction and coordination of the group. Samsung was the first to develop a headquarters office, called a secretariat, in the late 1950s, but soon most other *chaebol* had a secretariat or an equivalent, where the *chaebol* head and personal staff managed the activities of the entire enterprise group. The founders normally entrusted a line manager with whom he had a close relationship with the responsibility of overseeing the activities of individual firms, but even that responsibility was closely supervised by the chairman's office. All of the main decisions regarding budget and personnel for the entire group were typically made in the founder's office.

The centralization of ownership and managerial control allowed the *chaebol* to be personal vehicles of the owners and their heirs. Succession and inheritance helped to ensure that this personal control was to be maintained over time. Like the inheritance rules for the great estates in pre-capitalistic times, which we outlined in Chapter 5, succession of control within the *chaebol* has been based, until very recently, on primogeniture, on passing the *chaebol* intact from father to the one son whom the father picked as his chief heir (Kim, 1997, Chang, 1999). Typically, the founder selected the eldest son, but not always (Chang, 1999, p. 43), as was the case with Samsung, among others. Based on his analysis, Chang concludes that in ownership, control, and succession "the existing evidence predominantly suggests that the *chaebol* closely follow rules prescribed by the Korean family dynamics." In the context of elite holding, such family dynamics also imply intense competition among families. The fact that Koreans practice a form of primogeniture meant that family-owned conglomerates could grow into industrial empires and be passed on intact to the next generations. In the context of Korea's early industrialization, this is exactly what happened.

The Use of Authority and Market Power in Taiwan[13]

At the same time that largest *chaebol* were consolidating their control over the Korean economy, manufacturing networks in Taiwan became less concentrated and geographically more dispersed. These trends began as small and medium-sized firms started to grow in number and to lead the export sector. According to the calculations of Biggs (1988a, pp. 3–4), who expanded on earlier findings by Scitovsky (1986, p. 146), in Taiwan, in the twenty years between 1966 and 1986, "the number of reported firms increased by 315 percent and the average firm size expanded 15 percent." During the same years, the opposite process occurred in South Korea, where "average firm size jumped by 300 percent and its firms grew in number by only 10 percent." In fact, so many firms sprang up in Taiwan in these years that the number of registered firms reached a total of 700,000, which works out to be one firm for every fifteen persons in Taiwan, or if we count only adults, then one firm for every eight persons (Chang, 1988, p. 10).

The two remarkable aspects of this extraordinary growth in the number of small and medium-sized firms are, first, that Taiwan's KMT government neither sponsored nor financed this expansion, and, second, that these small and medium-sized firms could actually manufacture, with great flexibility, large quantities of diverse and often very complex products. Underlying both the financial structure and production wizardry of these small and medium-sized firms was a system of authority that allowed Taiwanese manufacturers to form cohesive inter-personal and inter-firm networks and to direct them for the purpose of making money.

Small, medium-sized, and even large firms raised most of their investment and operating capital from reinvested profits and from investment networks composed of family, friends, and colleagues. Because the economic organization between the two economies was so different, the level of investment and operational capital needed by Taiwanese manufacturers was much lower than that required by Korean manufacturers. As in South Korea, in Taiwan, until the 1990s, the stock market was not used as a source of investment capital for firms of whatever size. Even among the top 100 business groups, in 1985, only a few had even one listed firm. Unlike South Korea, however, Taiwan firms, even large ones, were not heavily financed through loans from government-owned banking system

---

[13] This section draws on Hamilton (1997).

or from international sources, such as the World Bank or multi-national corporations. Instead, according to Biggs (1988b, pp. 26–9) and confirmed by other analysts (Chen, 1994, 1995, Lee, 1990, Fields, 1995, Semkow, 1994, Winn, 1991, 1994), in the years before 1985, capital investments for the manufacturing firms in the private sector came from two main sources. First, the largest portion, about 45 percent to 55 percent, came from accumulated profits that were then reinvested to expand existing firms and to start new firms. The smaller the firms, the more likely it was that the owners supplied the capital themselves. Second, the next largest portion, about 30 percent of the total investment capital, came from the unregulated curb market, that is, from family, friends, and personal associates. Again the smaller the firm, the more likely it was that the owners obtained their investment capital from informal money markets.[14]

By all accounts, a very large portion of firms of all sizes obtained their capital outside of formal channels throughout the industrializing period. "In theory," notes Lee Sheng-Yi (1990, p. 36), "as the money and capital markets become more developed, the informal money market should lose its significance. However, in spite of the falling interest rates [in the formal money markets in 1986 and 1987], the share of the informal money market was no lower." Taiwan's informal money market was, in fact, so large that it accounted, according to Lee's (1990, pp. 36–7) analysis of Taiwan's financial system in 1986, for about 20 percent of the money flow for the entire country. And it was also large enough that over time it became a well-institutionalized source of investment and operating capital. The Central Bank of Taiwan even compiled and published the prevailing interest rates, including regional differences within Taiwan, for three categories of informal money markets: loans against post-dated checks, unsecured loans, and deposits with firms (Lee, 1990, p. 34).

The major source of investment capital in the informal market, especially for small firms, was unsecured loans. These loans were, and continue to be, made through various types of savings clubs and mutual aid associations (*hui*), some of which are organized on a temporary and others on a more permanent basis.[15] "The basic condition for each of these

---

[14] According to Lee (1990, p. 36), "Some small enterprises, which do not yet have a properly audited account and cannot offer adequate collateral to banks, cannot borrow effectively from banks, and therefore have to borrow from the informal money market at a high rate of interest. There are about 70,000 exporting and importing firms, big and small, competing in the market. Moreover, there is a considerable number of small trading and manufacturing firms which are not registered at all, with the convenience of tax-evasion and freedom from all sorts of government regulations with respect to pollution control, fire precaution and other considerations. Naturally, an unregistered firm has to resort to the informal money market." Also see Biggs, 1988a, Semkow 1994.

[15] For a recent explanation of rotating credit associations, see Biggart, et al. (1994).

associations," says Lin Pao-an (1991, p. 106), "is its constituted base – a group of people joined by personal trust. The members may be one's relatives, friends, neighbors, or colleagues. For strangers to be included is rather rare. The rights and duties of *hui* members are based on personal trust. There are no formal laws and no administrative agencies to enforce the obligations of *hui* members."

Large businesses used bank loans much more frequently than small businesses, especially for operating expenses (Fields, 1995, Semkow, 1994, Lin, 1991). But even the large business groups, notes Kao Cheng-shu (1991, p. 71), could not deal extensively with state-owned banks and so came to "rely heavily upon the private sector, which includes family members, friends, and business partners." "The private sector," he continues, "is the most important sources of funds for businesses. . . . [I]n capital formation or in investment, businessmen always have to build a back-up system that can support them at the right time and in the right place. In [Taiwan] a personal network based upon 'personal trust' is the foundation of this back-up system."

This "back-up system" consists of personal networks that operate according to the norms of reciprocity, that lie beyond the control of any one family, and that join willing participants in a pact of open-ended cooperation. Such "all men are brothers" types of networks, or what are sometimes known as *guanxi* networks (Hamilton, 1997), formed the organizational backbone of the manufacturing sectors of the economy throughout the early period of industrialization, and continue to do so after the Plaza Accord, although to a much lesser degree today (Kao and Hamilton, 2000). Although these networks are often portrayed as benign and as quintessentially Chinese forms of cooperation, they are, in fact, organizations that exert strong controls over their participants and that work according to clearly understood rules (Chung and Hamilton, 2001). It is the coerciveness of these networks over individual members that make them, from the participants' point of view, a useful tool to organize certain types of economic activities, particularly those requiring a lot of flexibility and responsiveness to factors of demand and risk that are beyond the manufacturers' ability to control.

The coerciveness rests on a dual axis of control that binds everyone into a cooperative network. The first axis of control is the patriarchal family. *Guanxi* networks are built on the assumptions that each player is an independent *laoban*, a boss who has the final, if not the sole responsibility for the decisions made regarding family property and that the each *laoban*'s span of authority, although very strong within its own familial sphere, does not and, in principle, cannot extend beyond it. This creates a situation in which no one person has the **authority** to dominate the network.

The second axis of control is the associations of equals, in this case the association of *laoban*, who are tied together by strong norms of reciprocation and trust. These norms are described in other locations (Hamilton and Wang, 1992, Hamilton, 2000, Chung and Hamilton, 2001, Lui, 2001, Kao and Hamilton, 2004), but in general these norms should be seen as "a clearly developed inter-subjective set of 'tit-for-tat' rules that greatly enhance the level of co-operation in Chinese society. The logic of co-operation is similar to that found in a great many locations. But Chinese practices differ from those in other societies in the extent to which these 'tit-for-tat' rules provide the institutional foundation for everyday interaction" (Chung and Hamilton, 2001, p. 335).[16] As the most noted theorist of Chinese society, Fei Xiaotong (1992, p. 28; see also pp. 94–113), concluded, the coerciveness of these rules is due to the fact that "the unit of control is the dyadic relationship, and not the individual, as is the case with the rule of law. Therefore, the entire network of people joined through a set of relationships is implicated in any one person's failure to perform appropriately.... (C)ontrol in this system is a shared responsibility, in that everyone supervises the actions of others."

From the individual's point of view, then, the crucial decision is whether to participate in a specific *guanxi* network or not. That decision rests on whether the economic activities of the network will succeed over the long term (for example, the size of the order and the possibility of new ones) or perhaps how important this set of partners is to one's long-term plans. Once the decision is made to participate, then the rules of reciprocation come into play. As Chung and Hamilton (2001, p. 337) note, however, "This social dimension does not make an economic decision less 'economic.' Rather, the social logic (of *guanxi*) adds another level and more complexity to economic calculation."

Especially in the early years, *guanxi* networks provided small and medium-size businesses with the resources by which to organize export-oriented commodity chains (for example, Chen, 1994). These networks were organized on the basic of some relationship held in common, and often employed the same types of ties found in Korea, namely kinship, school, and locality. Unlike in Korea, however, these relationships provided an additional source of trust (and added coercion) that the rules of reciprocation would be obeyed.

When used to raise investment capital for manufacturing, personal networks of *guanxi* owners gave entrepreneurs many advantages that a

---

16 Chung and Hamilton (2001) note that as Axlerod shows in the outcomes of the "prisoner's dilemma" game. "The most successful solution to an iterated game in which one can choose either to maximize one's gain at the expense of another or to co-operate and share gains is always co-operation." The tit-for-tat rules are an institutionalization of that outcome in the context of Chinese society.

formal banking system would not. It gave them a ready source of capital that could be used as they wished. Should an area of manufacturing prove successful, it gave them a potential set of partners in manufacturing and distributing products that could be rapidly increased to the level of the demand. Equally important, it gave them a low-cost source of information about what to produce, how to improve production, and where and how to sell their products. Some researchers (Chen, 1994, 1995, Hamilton, 1997) have shown that the denser and more extensive the *guanxi* networks, the more that production information, including research and development and product innovations, actually become a function of the networks themselves. Without the *guanxi* networks, small and medium-sized networks could not shift product lines and could not produce the array of products that they have, in fact, produced. But with the assistance of their *guanxi* "back-up system," entrepreneurs can rationally calculate their speculative investments and, as Kao (1991) stated, be "in the right place at the right time."

Although *guanxi* ties served as the medium to create production networks, the networks themselves normally took the form of what is called a "satellite assembly system" (*weixing gongchang*) (Shieh, 1992, Hsing, 1992, Kao and Hamilton, 2000). Satellite assembly systems varied in terms of the relative sizes of the firms directly involved. In general, a group of small, medium, and sometime large independently owned firms joined together to produce a product that has been ordered, via a trading company, by an overseas buyer. Each firm produced one part or one set of parts of the final product. Depending upon the size of the order and the complexity of the part, that firm would organize a secondary satellite assembly system to make that part. All the parts were then delivered to an assembly firm that assembled, painted, packaged, and shipped the final product.

In some satellite assembly systems, the assembly firm was the largest firm in the group and was basically an end producer that subcontracted a portion, sometimes a very large portion, of the final product to small independent firms. In other assembly systems, some of the component parts would be manufactured by firms much larger than the final assembly firm, such as a large metalworking firm producing a component for a small bicycle assembly firm. In yet other production networks, the assembly system was not localized. Rather, the product was moved from plant to plant and only completed at the final stop (Hamilton, 1997).

One other aspect found in many cases of established subcontracting networks and satellite assembly systems was that some, and often the majority, of the firms in a network were initially started by employees in one firm who created their own independent firms and developed subcontracting relations with their former bosses (Shieh, 1992). Employers would often encourage such departures and even invest in firms started by their best and most capable employees in order to develop the subcontracting network. Although it is counterintuitive, such encouragement of and investments in potentially competing firms created a satellite assembly system capable of achieving economies of scale on a temporary basis without enlarging the size of existing firms and without making large capital investments in labor and machines that might not produce at capacity or that might not produce very long. Investment capital was put into people who would repay at a premium and who would likely remain morally bound to their former bosses and economically anchored in their satellite assembly systems, at least as long as the business orders held out.

However arranged, all these manufacturing networks worked fundamentally alike. First, relationships among owners and among firms were not regulated through contracts having legal standing. Although agreements might be written out so that no one forgets the details, agreements were based on trust, backed up, of course, with the collective force of the network participants themselves. Second, there was formal equality among independent entrepreneurs, although participants would defer to the firm owner who has obtained the order. And third, participants universally engaged in similar celebratory reciprocations of food and drink and gifts. In fact, as Kao and Hamilton (2004) note, within each satellite assembly system, all the participants metaphorically and literally sat at the same round table and observed the same social etiquette of differentiating between guest and host, an exercise in differentiation, cooperation, and equality – all at the same time. Utilizing these networks, Taiwan manufacturers have created a system of production that turned out products of amazing complexity, ranging today from household appliances to laptop computers.

Conclusion: Networks and Global Matching

In the twenty-five years between 1960 and 1985, both South Korean and Taiwanese manufacturers responded aggressively to the rising demand from intermediary buyers by creating manufacturing networks to produce goods. Both sets of manufacturers, however, responded differently. In Korea, the largest *chaebol* developed networks of firms over which the *chaebol* heads had authority, and as a consequence of this control, these *chaebol* were able successfully to consolidate their hold over the export sector and ultimately over the entire economy. In Taiwan, by contrast, faced with the competition offered by the many and constantly emerging networks of small and medium-sized firms, the largest business groups retreated from or never even entered the export sector in consumer products. As a consequence of the proliferation of these networks, organized as they were around satellite assembly systems, Taiwan's export sector grew increasingly diverse – in ownership, in geographical locations, and in the products produced.

In this and the previous chapter, we have spelled our reinterpretation of industrialization in South Korea and Taiwan. In Chapter 6, we argued that rapidly increasing intermediary demand, the result of the retail revolution in the United States, is a primary driver of Asia's economic transformation. In this chapter, we show in organizational terms how the formation of distinctive trajectories of growth grew out of the competitive struggle among local Asian manufacturers to respond to this increasing demand. It is our observation that the repeated and emergent process of global matching corresponds to the equally emergent patterns seen in the export trade statistics analyzed in the previous chapter. We would like more research on this topic, but it seems very likely that the actual process of matching buyers to manufacturers involved not only the selection of products being purchased, but also the selection of a system of production by which the products were manufactured. Big orders of the same product were more likely to go to those locations specializing in producing big orders, regardless of the exact product being ordered. Likewise, smaller batch orders were more likely to end up with firms that did not need large orders to survive and that were flexible enough to produce many different small lots effectively and efficiently. This iterated matching process led to economies that became more specialized in their style of production and, accordingly, in the types of products they produced with that style of production. This divergent outcome, as we will see in the next chapter, has global consequences in the 1990s and 2000s, as Taiwan becomes more integrated in the global productions led by U.S. firms, and South Korea becomes less so.

This path towards greater divergence started in the 1970s, when, under conditions of rapidly increasing demand from big buyers, the activity of responding to orders (that is, keeping orders coming in from previous buyers and finding new buyers, possibly for new types of products) prompted owners constantly to enlarge, upgrade, or otherwise enhance their production capacity. For *chaebol* owners, this necessity, brought on by the intense competition from only a handful of other *chaebol*, led to aggressive internalization strategies, strategies to enlarge production in existing firms, to establish new firms, to create a mechanism for internal financing, and to develop greater internal self-sufficiencies, all of which denied competitors any access to internal resources. These internalization strategies began very early in the period of rapid growth and encouraged owners to follow "a path of least resistance" in creating inter-firm networks over which they would have personal control, namely networks of firms owned by *chaebol* heads and their families and managed by people personally dependent on, and loyal to, these owners. Through such patrimonial systems of control, a few owners and their personal staffs were able to control vast resources within their respective groups and to chart the direction of group expansion. In a relatively short period of time, this centralized control of *chaebol* owners and the competition among these relatively few large players pushed the entire South Korean economy along a trajectory of development toward oligopoly. By the early 1980s, this trajectory of development was in place and, for all practical purposes, could not be changed, short of a total catastrophe, which, as we explain in Chapter 4, occurred during the 1997 Asian financial crisis when about half of the top fifty *chaebol* went into bankruptcy or otherwise dissolved, including one of the top four *chaebol*, Daewoo.

In Taiwan, the activity of responding to big-buyer orders led to an equally rapid buildup of production networks. Even in the early days of growth, these networks were widely dispersed in rural as well as urban areas, and involved many relatively small and medium-sized firms. In enlarging their production capacity, firm owners, here too, followed the path of least resistance. Instead of trying to expand the size of their firms, they expanded their subcontracting networks. That path was so much easier than trying to obtain large amounts of capital needed for large firms from recalcitrant state-owned banks or to fight the competition from others that would surely arise if individual entrepreneurs tried to go it alone. Building cooperative *guanxi* networks was a tried-and-true method to accomplish risky tasks and a method that could also be highly predictable. Once these production networks began and turned out to be successful in getting and keeping orders, they quickly proliferated. Organizing such production networks became a clear strategy to get rich, and an astounding percentage of Taiwanese households pooled their resources, started their own firms, and, through their connections, joined one and sometime several production networks. The outcome of these crescendoing activities was for entrepreneurs to search frantically for production and service niches in which they might have some relative advantage over others, and, finding such a location, then to organize networks of colleagues to create a position of economic power that would discourage others from entering the same pursuit. In this competitive environment, almost any attempt to upgrade a family owned business into a self-sufficient *chaebol*-like production system manufacturing goods for export would be doomed, because such an export strategy, if momentarily successful, would be quickly undermined by the aggressiveness and cheaper cost structures of satellite assembly systems.

In summary, both the South Korean and the Taiwanese cases suggest that explicit networks do not precede the activity that sets them in motion.

Although the social potential for patterns of inter-firm networks may exist in a society's cultural repertoire (Swidler, 1986), we would have to argue that networks are a reflexive consequence of the activities themselves. Actual and potential economic players gauge the competitive environment in which they do business. Different environments give rise to different strategies to make money and ultimately to different economic organizations. Neither South Korean nor Chinese firms are invariably embedded in the same, or even similar, network organizations. Instead, relative to a specific competitive environment, firm owners plan their own goals and assess alternative possibilities for achieving them. Whatever those goals and alternatives are, economic players typically follow paths of least resistance. In the initial years of industrialization, they did not try to create sets of new rules and new institutions to further their material and ideal goals. Rather they accepted, as given, the existing rules and institutions, and used them as points of leverage to elevate their own ambitions. They objectify themselves relative to that context and **power** their way forward. There are always many possibilities that remain untapped; many opportunities that are left unanswered; and many indeterminacies, accidents, and unforeseen events that give an edge to this or that outcome. But out of this mix, when economic players, step by step, make their decisions and undertake activities simultaneously and in the same economic environment, they conjointly create an economic organization in which they themselves become fully embedded and of which they are primary products.

Although we cannot demonstrate quantitatively many of the more qualitative conclusions about the divergence that we have reached in Part II, we can test some of the implications of these conclusions, namely that such different systems of production as are represented by South Korea and Taiwan produce different kinds of products, and that these differences arise early, persist over time, and carry across categories of products. It is to this test we now turn.

8

Trade Performance of South Korea and Taiwan

A Second Test of the Model

In his review of the book *Trust: The Social Virtues and the Creation of Prosperity*, by Francis Fukuyama, Robert Solow makes the following remarkably candid comment:

> ... I, for various reasons, would like him to be right. Academic economics likes to pretend that economic behavior is pretty much the same, always and everywhere, almost uninfluenced by socially conditioned perceptions and norms. If Fukuyama's thesis could be proved to be right, it might help to loosen up the profession's view in other contexts as well. (*The New Republic*, September 11, 1995, p. 37)

Unfortunately, the book does not meet Solow's criterion of proof, and he concludes:

> I believe that the sorts of things that Fukuyama wants to talk about are more important than my colleagues in economics are willing to admit. I would rather they are talked about imprecisely than not discussed at all. But imprecision is not a virtue, and "for example" is not an argument. (p. 39)

To convince economists that organizational structure matters, it is necessary to point to objective measures of economic performance that are affected. We have argued at length that the business groups in South Korea and Taiwan are different, and that these differences are rooted in the exercise of authority and market power in the two countries. We have also shown that the predictions of the authority/market power model – in terms of the size, vertical integration, and horizontal diversification of business groups – match up remarkably well with contrasting structure of the groups in South Korea and Taiwan: this was our first test of the model, in Chapter 4. But do these differences in the business groups really matter? Beyond looking at the structure of the groups themselves, are there

299

some testable hypotheses arising from our model that can be accepted or rejected from other data on the two countries, and which do not have obvious alternative explanations?

One such hypothesis has already been suggested from our detailed look at disaggregate exports from these countries in the previous chapters: namely, that Taiwan exports a *greater variety of goods* than does South Korea. This is a simple way to capture the idea the Taiwan is exporting in a multitude of niche markets, customizing its products to the specific needs of intermediary buyers in the United States and elsewhere. In contrast, by focusing on large batches of more standardized products, becoming "world leaders" in products such a microwave ovens and automobiles, South Korea is necessarily exporting a smaller range of products than Taiwan. This hypothesis was a prediction from our theoretical model of Chapter 3, where the product variety of exported products in the "high concentration" equilibria (similar to Korea) is less than the product variety of exports in the "low concentration" equilibria (similar to Taiwan). These theoretical results are reviewed below, and the first goal of this chapter is to statistically test this hypothesis using the detailed export data from these countries to the United States.

A second hypothesis that we shall test concerns the product quality or "mix" coming from these two countries. Current empirical research in international trade has observed that countries at differing stages of development tend to produce goods of correspondingly different qualities: plastic sandals giving way to cloth sneakers, followed by leather footwear, etc. Even at the most disaggregate 10-digit classification used for imports by the U.S. Customs, a single product will sell a quite different prices from various countries, which must reflect differences in product quality (Schott, 2004). Focusing on just South Korea and Taiwan, we can similarly measure the degree to which exports of these countries occur in higher- or lower-priced categories of a good, and attribute these patterns to differential product quality or "mix." A hypothesis advanced by Rodrik (1993) is that the large *chaebol* in Korea will focus on selling high-quality products, because the reputational advantage so gained will then lead to enhanced demand for its other products.[1] We generalize this hypothesis to state that the largest business groups in either South Korea or Taiwan can be expected to provide the highest-quality products, and find empirical support for this second hypothesis.

Thus, the differences in export variety that we have already begun to describe in the previous chapters can be statistically tested, and we shall find that the results strongly support our theoretical model. But again we ask: do these differences matter? They do, for several reasons. First, a

---

[1] Product reputation also plays a role in the business group model of Wan and Weisman (1999).

recent line of research in economics has argued that product variety – especially the variety of intermediate inputs – can be expected to enhance *productivity* in the downstream industries using these inputs. This research comes under the name of "endogenous" growth theory, as described by Romer (1990) and Grossman and Helpman (1991), among others. We will argue that the differing product variety of exports from South Korean and Taiwan is indeed linked to the productivity of downstream industries in these countries, providing a direct confirmation of "endogenous" growth theory.

But more important to the subject of this book, we will argue that the differing export orientations of South Korea and Taiwan also affects their response to *cyclical fluctuations in the global economy*. In other words, the fortunes of these countries become *tied to the foreign buyers of their products*, so that when export prices or demand falls significantly, then so too will the production in the export sectors and overall GDP of these economies. This is illustrated most dramatically by the financial crisis that struck South Korean in 1997–98. As we argue in Chapter 4 and Appendix D, the export orientation of that economy – particularly towards semiconductors and certain other products whose prices fell dramatically prior to the crisis – was the root cause of the bankruptcies that occurred there. These bankruptcies, in turn, precipitated the banking crisis and ultimately currency crisis and devaluation of the Korean won in late 1997. Taiwan was largely immune from the Asian financial crisis because of its greater export variety – so that the prices and volume of its exports did not fall nearly as much – but this broad orientation did not help it several years later, when demand for the entire range of semiconductors and related products fell with the bursting of the "high-tech bubble" in the United States. The logical consequence of our "demand side" interpretation of Asian growth is that the economies become tightly linked to economic fluctuations in their export partners, and this is well illustrated by the recessions that have hit both South Korean and Taiwan – each in their own unique way – in recent years.

Divergence in Export Variety of South Korea and Taiwan

As we have described in the previous chapters, both Korea and Taiwan began by producing very similar products, such as textiles, clothes, and shoes. But the same goods were produced in very different ways between the two economies. In Korea, large firms, some of which were affiliated with the *chaebol*, developed "one-set" productions systems. These firms internalized the manufacture and assembly of most components that went into final products. By contrast, in Taiwan, the same product was made by small and medium-sized firms arranged in a satellite assembly systems, each firm of which would make different components that would later be assembled into the finished good. As both economies become more intensively organized as export-driven economies – with exported goods organized in Korea through *chaebol* and in Taiwan through small and medium-sized firms – the mode of production and the actual products being produced increasingly diverged.

In Chapter 6 we discussed the export patterns from these countries up to the late 1980s, when there was a dramatic re-alignment of exchange rates. On September 22, 1985, at the Plaza Hotel in New York City, after years of running trade deficits with South Korea, Japan, and Taiwan, the United States completed negotiations on a currency reform measure that all parties signed. The Plaza Accord, as this currency reform became known, removed the pegged trading range of East Asian currencies with the U.S. dollar and allowed the Asian currencies to appreciate. Within two years, Taiwan's currency moved from forty to thirty New Taiwan dollars to one U.S. dollar, while Korea's currency appreciated more moderately. In the span of just a few years, the Japanese, Taiwan, and, to a lesser degree, South Korean economies went through a momentary period of jubilation, a period when everyone felt much richer and many began to make extravagant purchases at home and abroad. The period of jubilation ended quickly, however, when domestic manufacturers realized that they could not longer meet the price points that the U.S. retailers and merchandisers required.

Based on interviews made in Taiwan at the time (Kao and Hamilton, 2000, 2004), leading manufacturers lowered their own profit margins to the point of breaking even, and had to relentlessly squeeze other firms in their production networks. They complained of working harder for longer hours and for less pay than they did in the early 1980s, when it seemed like everyone was getting rich. By 1990, in both Taiwan and Japan, the property and stock market bubble collapsed. Japan entered a long, deflationary recession, from which, in the year 2005, it has yet fully to emerge.

The currency revaluation stopped the Japanese economy in its tracks, but not its main exporting firms. By the late 1980s, Japanese industries were major OEM suppliers in only just a few products (for example, microwaves, computers). Instead, many of the largest Japanese business groups had gone to considerable effort to build their own globally recognized brand names (for example, Sony, Panasonic, Toyota) or to use their technology to develop upstream products, such as Toshiba's LCD panels and Shimano's bicycle gears, that they then could sell to all makers of the respective products. In order to remain competitive in terms of price and quality, the major Japanese companies transferred their final assembly sites, along with some production, to other countries. The automobile makers went to the United States to achieve cheaper costs and avoid tariff barriers (Kenney and Florida, 1993), and also invested heavily in Southeast Asia, especially in Thailand (Doner, 1991). The huge consumer electronic conglomerate, Matsushita, transferred much of its manufacturing and assembly to Malaysia, where it contributed about 5 percent of Malaysia's GDP. The effect of these foreign direct investments on the domestic economy was widely reported as the "hollowing out" of the Japanese economy.

Unlike Japan, South Korea and Taiwan were able to escape severe recessions, and they even were able to increase their exports, but they did so in characteristically different ways. By 1985, the four largest South Korean chaebol (that is, Hyundai, Samsung, Lucky-Goldstar, and Daewoo) dwarfed all the other business groups in South Korea in size and sales, and virtually monopolized exports from South Korea. After the currency evaluations, these behemoths began to follow the precedent set by the largest Japanese business groups, establishing global brand names and developing higher quality, up-market products. They extended the scope and scale of their enterprise groups in Korea, and they began to systematically globalize their business. They built manufacturing plants in cheap labor areas, such as Indonesia and Central America for shoe and garments, as well as in locations near their target markets, such as in Eastern Europe. They established an array of differentiated products – Samsung and LG in consumer electronics, Hyundai and Daewoo in automobiles – that undercut the prices of their Japanese competitors. This strategy led these business groups to disengage from U.S. branded products, but still allowed them to market their products with American retailers, in competition with all other brands (Lew and Park, 2000).

In the wake of the Plaza Accord, many of Taiwan's export manufacturers faced a serious dilemma (Kao and Hamilton, 2000, Hsing, 1998). They had OEM contracts for goods that they needed to deliver to U.S. retailers, but they could not produce those goods profitably. If they failed to honor their contracts, the retailers and brand-name merchandisers would easily find other manufacturers to make the products. If they stayed in Taiwan and honored their contracts, they would likely go bankrupt, and lose the contract anyway. After several years of hesitation, those small and medium-sized firms making garments, bicycles, footwear, and other types of similar consumer goods moved their manufacturing operations to China. The move occurred suddenly, like a stampede, in a matter of just a couple of years. The abrupt departure of so many exporters shows up clearly in the trade statistics. In some industries, such as bicycles, most of the production networks moved to China when the lead firm moved, but in other industries, such as footwear, toys, furniture, and garments, only the lead firm moved, and once in China, they vertically integrated their production, producing most component parts of their products in-house. Many firms producing for export, however, split their operations, with low-end mass production going to China and the high-end batch production staying in Taiwan.

In the late 1980s and early 1990s, at the same time when Taiwan's most successful export manufacturers were contemplating moves to China, or perhaps to Southeast Asia, the high technology boom occurred in Silicon Valley. Taiwan's high technology industry was closely linked to Silicon Valley through multiple connections (Saxenian, 1999). Early on, Taiwanese manufacturers were leading producers of PC peripherals and component parts, but as the boom in the United States continued, Taiwanese manufacturers, in their own Silicon Valley outside of Hsin Chu in north central Taiwan, began to make more and more of the standardized PC components and founded a number of leading PC firms, most notably Acer Computers. Along with several other firms, Acer became one of the world's leading OEM producers of inexpensive PCs. The high technology in Taiwan was also fed by the establishment of semiconductors foundries, which are upstream firms that made semiconductor chips to order for any downstream firm that designs and wants to use those chips in dedicated products. The first and most important of these foundries was the government-sponsored Taiwan Semiconductor Manufacturing Association (TSMC).

Major retailers and brand-name merchandisers, such as Dell Computers, Hewlett Packard, and Gateway, were primary drivers of Taiwan's high technology industry. As the demand for these American branded products rose, so too did the productive capacity of Taiwan's high technology manufacturers. The success of these firms was not based on, and did not lead to, the efforts to develop their own brand names; rather they continued to upgrade their capabilities as high-level contract manufacturers deeply integrated in industries led by U.S. retailers and merchandisers.

It is against this background that we shall begin the chapter, then, by examining the overall pattern of exports from South Korea and Taiwan to the United States after 1989, and then discuss the trends in particular industries. The Plaza Accord immediately made the export goods from both economies more expensive abroad, and accelerated the shift out of labor-intensive products towards more high-skilled and capital-intensive exports in both Taiwan and South Korea. This shift corresponds in time with a change in our U.S. import data in 1989, from the Tariff Schedule of the USA (TSUSA) to the Harmonized System (HS).

Export Landscapes

The broadest pictures of exports from the two countries can be obtained by aggregating the HS system to 3-digit categories of goods and summing exports over 1989–2000. The resulting "export landscapes" are plotted

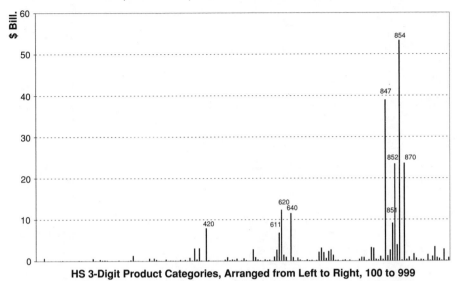

Figure 8.1. South Korea Exports to the United States, 1989–2000 ($ mill).

in Figures 8.1 and 8.2, and we have labeled those 3-digit categories with cumulative exports exceeding $5 billion. The dominant export industries in both countries are those within the HS 800 category, which includes various types of machinery and mechanical appliances, electrical equipment, and parts thereof. The largest exports from Korea are from two categories of high-technology equipment: semiconductors and integrated circuits (854), with cumulative exports exceeding $50 billion over 1989–2000, and office machines and parts (847) with cumulative exports of about $40 billion. The relative ranking of these industries is reversed for Taiwan, where cumulative exports within office machines and parts (847) exceed $80 billion, which is more than twice as much as that exported within semiconductors and integrated circuits (854). This reversal reflects a rather profound difference in the export orientations of the two countries, whereby Korea has focused on DRAMs within semiconductors, which is a large-volume but highly competitive product, whose price fluctuates a great deal with changes in global capacity and demand. Taiwan, by contrast, has focused on the assembly of personal computers and their components, and within the semiconductor category, has specialized in smaller-volume chips that are customized to the needs of buyers. These products are less prone to price fluctuations.

The next largest cumulative exports from Korea are close to $25 billion for both video, radio, and TV equipment (852) and motor vehicles and parts (870). Taiwan exports about half as much within the former

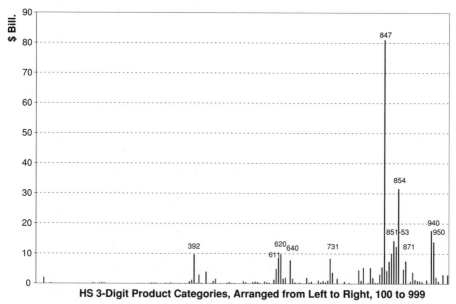

Figure 8.2. Taiwan Exports to the United States, 1989–2000 ($ mill).

industry, though it also has cumulative exports exceeding $10 billion in the related industries of electric motors, generators, and appliances (850) and electronic devices for cars, lighting, and communication (851). It exports almost no motor vehicles at all, though it does have substantial exports of their parts. The other industries that show up in the export landscape for Taiwan include certain plastic products (392), outer garments (611 and 620), footwear (640), wires, nails and screws (731), motorcycles, bicycles and parts (871), household furniture (940) and toys (950). Korea has cumulative exports exceeding $5 billion in many of the same industries, and in addition, trunks and bags (420).

Of these items with the highest cumulative exports over 1989–2000, some are declining in importance over time. In particular, the less technologically sophisticated products (plastic products, trunks and bags, and footwear) are no longer among the top exports from either country in 2000. Rather, the exports for both countries become concentrated in a fairly narrow range of knowledge and capital-intensive products, and this concentration is greater in Korea and than in Taiwan. There are eighteen 3-digit HS categories where the exports from Taiwan to the United States exceed $500 million in 2000, and only nine such categories for Korea. The single 3-digit industry with the greatest exports from both countries is office machines and parts. For the "top nine" industries for

Table 8.1. *Korean and Taiwan Exports to the United States, in 3-digit HS Categories ($ million)*

	1995	1996	1997	1998	1999	2000	2001
A: With exports from Korea or Taiwan exceeding $2 billion in 2000							
HS 847 – Office Machines and Parts							
South Korea	3,879	3,921	4,238	3,474	5,548	7,885	4,711
Taiwan	7,426	8,289	9,914	9,625	9,697	10,667	8,849
HS 852 – Video, Radio, and TV equipment							
South Korea	1,717	1,110	990	1,517	2,892	4,601	5,915
Taiwan	824	889	1,102	1,309	1,872	2,554	2,129
HS 854 – Semiconductors and Integrated Circuits							
South Korea	7,140	6,274	6,037	5,295	6,715	7,683	3,814
Taiwan	3,333	3,277	3,488	3,330	4,044	5,507	3,723
HS 870 – Motor Vehicles and Parts							
South Korea	1,795	2,009	2,080	1,891	3,223	5,175	6,760
Taiwan	383	422	461	495	598	632	647
B: With exports from Korea or Taiwan exceeding $500 million in 2000[a]							
South Korea	18,204	16,807	16,937	16,251	23,232	30,921	26,422
Taiwan	19,597	20,812	23,352	23,541	25,207	29,829	23,871
C: Total exports from Korea or Taiwan to the United States.							
South Korea	24,026	22,532	22,939	23,701	31,152	39,829	34,915
Taiwan	28,876	29,797	32,474	32,985	35,057	40,384	33,262

Note:
[a] This includes eighteen 3-digit HS categories (as detailed in notes 2 and 3).

Korea,[2] average exports to the United States in 2000 are $3.3 billion, or $2.7 billion if we exclude office machines and parts. In comparison, average exports from Taiwan in its "top nine" exporting industries is $2.9 billion, or $1.9 billion with office machines and parts excluded.[3] Thus, with the exception of office machines and parts, Korean exports are more concentrated in a narrower range of industries than are Taiwanese exports to the United States.

There is an important difference in exports over time among these major industries, as shown in Table 8.1. In Part A of Table 8.1 we report the

[2] The nine 3-digit HS categories with Korean exports to the U.S. exceeding $500 million in 2000 are outer garments (611,620), compressors, air conditioners and refrigerators (841), office machines and parts (847), electronic devices for cars, lighting and communication (851), video, radio and TV equipment (852), electric circuits and other apparatus (853), semiconductors and integrated circuits (854), and motor vehicles and parts (870).
[3] Within the entire group of eighteen industries where Taiwanese exports exceeding $500 million in 2000, average exports are $1.8 billion. In addition to the nine 3-digit HS categories detailed in the previous footnote, the other nine industries with Taiwanese exports to the U.S. exceeding $500 million in 2000 are certain plastic products (392), wires, nails and screws (731), fasteners (830), machine tools (846), molds and fittings (848), electric motors and devices (850), motorcycles, bicycles and parts (871), household furniture (940), and toys (950).

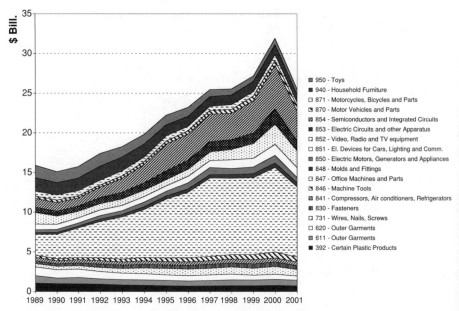

Figure 8.3. South Korea Exports of "Top Eighteen" Industries.

3-digit HS categories whose recent annual exports from Korea or Taiwan exceed $2 billion; in Part B we include the "top eighteen" industries whose exports exceed $500 million in 2000; and in Part C we include all exports to the United States. The "top eighteen" industries are also graphed in Figures 8.3 and 8.4.

Korean exports of semiconductors to the United States reached a peak of about $7 billion in 1995, but declined in the years immediately thereafter due to falling prices (Table 8.1 and Figure 8.3). Exports in 1998, for example, were nearly $2 billion below their 1995 peak. Much smaller declines in Korean exports also occurred within office machines, and video, radio, and TV equipment. Taiwanese exports within these industries, by contrast, declined slightly or not at all over the year 1995–2000 (Table 8.1 and Figure 8.4). This reflects differences in the composition of exports within these broad industries, as we will examine in detail later in the chapter.

Notice that over 2000–01, however, high-technology exports from both countries to the United States experienced a marked decline, which was due to the U.S. recession and reduction in business investment. But Korean exports of motor vehicles remained high, held up by strong consumer demand for durables in the United States. So while reduced exports of high-technology equipment from Korea were partially offset by growing export of motor vehicles, this did not occur for Taiwan, where the U.S.

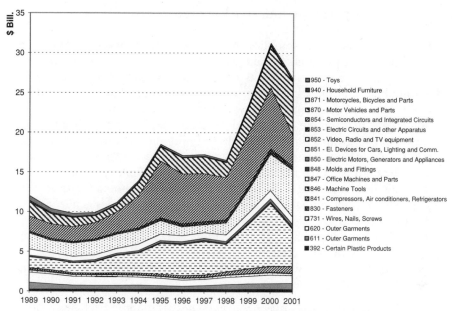

Figure 8.4. Taiwan Exports of "Top Eighteen" Industries.

recession hit squarely its dominant high-tech exports with little or no offset in other industries. These trends are also evident if we look at the eighteen industries exporting more than $500 million from either country to the United States in 2000 (part B of Table 8.1), or more broadly at total exports (part C). The total Korean exports from the "top eighteen" industries experienced a pronounced fall in the years 1995–98, then rise to 2000, and fall by about 14 percent from 2000 to 2001. In contrast, the Taiwanese exports in the "top eighteen" industries rise continuously from 1995 to 2000, and then fall by 20 percent to 2001. Taiwan managed to escape the softening in export demand that hit Korea prior to the 1997–98 financial crisis, but was impacted more strongly by the 2000–01 U.S. recession.

These differences in the time-path of exports from the two countries feed back on their economies, and offer an explanation for why Korea suffered most during the financial crisis, whereas Taiwan has experienced a slowdown more recently. To convincingly make this argument will occupy much of our attention later in this chapter, and is intimately tied, we believe, to the different structure of the high-tech industries across the two countries. We begin by examining the somewhat simpler case of the transportation industry, which includes both motor vehicles and parts (HS 870) and motorcycles, bicycles, and parts (871). This industry will be used to motivate our measurement of product variety and "mix."

Transportation Industry Exports

Korean exports of automobiles, from Hyundai, Daewoo and Kia, are well known to consumers in America and worldwide. In 1997, on the eve of its financial crisis, Korea was the world's fourth largest producer of automobiles and the sixth largest exporter of automobiles (Kim, 2000a, p. 60, note 1). What is most exceptional about the automobile industry in Korea is that, unlike other developing and newly industrialized countries, Korean groups have been able to build and export the entire car, while establishing brand-name recognition and dealerships on a global scale. In contrast, Taiwan produces finished automobiles primarily for its domestic market, while exporting a plethora of automobile parts as well as being a leading global producer and exporter of bicycles. Thus, Korea has intentionally transformed its automobile industry into a "producer-driven" commodity chain, whereas Taiwan has continued to export as part of "buyer-driven" commodity chains.

The distinction between these two types of commodity chains is described by Gereffi and Korzeniewicz (1994, p. 7):

> The difference between the two types of commodity chains resides in the location of their key barriers to entry. Producer-driven commodity chains are those in which large, usually transnational, corporations play the central roles in coordinating production network (including backwards and forwards linkages). This is most characteristic of capital- and technology-intensive commodities such as automobiles, aircraft, semiconductors, and electrical machinery. Buyer-driven commodity chains, on the other hand, are those in which large retailers, brand-named merchandisers, and trading companies play the central role in shaping decentralized production networks in a variety of exporting countries, frequently located in the periphery. This pattern of industrialization is typical in relatively labor-intensive consumer goods such as garments, footwear, toys, and housewares.

In producer-driven chains, the producers themselves decide what models to push onto the market; but in buyer-driven chains, the retailers and merchandisers perform the design and marketing functions, and have these orders filled through their network of suppliers. The characterization of the automobile industry as a "producer-driven" chain applies mainly to the production of finished vehicles in industrialized countries, as well as in Korea. Outside of the industrialized countries, assembly may occur simply through "knock-down" sets or the production of labor-intensive component parts. Taiwan has focused on the production of high-quality aftermarket components such as brakes, mufflers, and other auto supplies, which are retailed through Grand Auto, Wal-Mart, Sears, and other distributors in the United States (Biggart and Guillén, 1999, p. 735).

Both South Korea and Taiwan started at about the same place in the automobile industry: in 1972. Taiwan manufactured twice as many vehicles as South Korea – 22,000 as compared to 9,500.[4] In the years that followed, however, these industries followed quite different paths. By 1987, Korea had reached the production of nearly a million vehicles, over four times as many as Taiwan.[5] While most cars were still for the domestic market, it then turned towards the huge international market. Hyundai exported its first car to the United States in 1986, and by 1995, slightly more than half of production was for export (Kim, 2000a, p. 64). Notice that Hyundai's success occurred despite the appreciation of the Korean won following the Plaza Accord. In contrast, the larger appreciation of the New Taiwan dollar after 1986 effectively foreclosed Taiwan's entry into the export market for finished vehicles: the government had attempted to attract foreign producers to Taiwan, but a deal with Toyota fell through in 1984, and after 1986 the Japanese producers looked towards the lower wages found elsewhere in Southeast Asia.[6]

Interestingly, the very policies that encouraged the Korean *chaebol* to become major exporters of motor vehicles appear to have hindered Korean firms from producing automobile components. Initially, programs such as the Automobile Industry Protection Law (1962) and Automobile Industry Basic Promotion Plan (1969) prohibited imports of assembled cars but allowed for tariff-free imports of components.[7] Later, the Korean government tried to encourage more local production of components by raising local content requirements in the late 1970s, but this only created a protected local market for component producers, and they never achieved the quality levels required for mass export. Of one recent poll conducted with Korean parts producers, two-thirds reported that they did not export at all, and of those that do export, the share of exports in often quite small.[8] On the import side, some of the most technologically advanced components of the automobiles – such as the power transmission – continue to be imported into Korea from Japanese producers (Kim, 2000a, p. 68).

While the impact of exchange rate changes as well as government policies are no doubt important in shaping the industry across the two

[4] Biggart and Guillén (1999), p. 733.
[5] Biggart and Guillén (1997), p. 207.
[6] Biggart and Guillén (1999), p. 734. According to Biggart and Guillén (1997, p. 208), Taiwan has a small export market to Canada through the sales of Mercury Tracer cars, built by Ford Lio Ho Motors.
[7] Biggart and Guillén (1999), p. 731.
[8] Kim (2000a), p. 68, citing Park, Jung-hu and Hong-eyn Kim, 1997, *Globalization Strategies of the Korean Automobile Industry*, Seoul: Korea Institute for Industrial Economics and Trade.

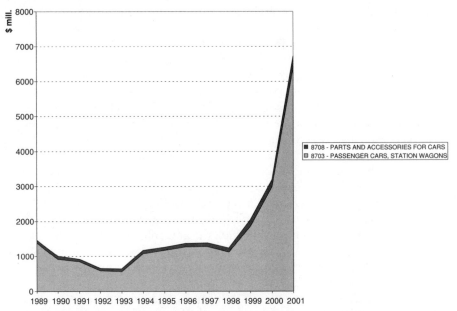

Figure 8.5. South Korea Exports of Transportation Products.

countries, Biggart and Guillén (1999) argue that the key difference is the organizational capacity of the *chaebol* to harness the resources needed to design, produce, and market finished vehicles. Acting through a combination of low-interest funds from the state, vertical links to suppliers, and fierce competition between each other, the largest *chaebol* were able to overcome the barriers to entry inherent in auto manufacturing, and produce cars that were second in quality but among the lowest in price. In contrast, the economic organization of Taiwan, with the business groups located upstream and many small and medium-sized firms downstream, never would have supported global production and exports from this capital-intensive industry: "The economy of densely networked family firms is ill suited to a capital-intensive enterprise such as auto assembly. It is ideal, however, for producing capital-light but knowledge-intensive products."[9]

The differences in the exports from this industry to the United States are illustrated in Figures 8.5 and 8.6, which use the principal products from the HS categories 870 and 871. Korean exports are focused predominantly on the passenger car (Figure 8.5). While these exports experienced a significant decline from 1989 to 1993, they began to grow again in 1994

[9] Biggart and Guillén (1999), p. 735.

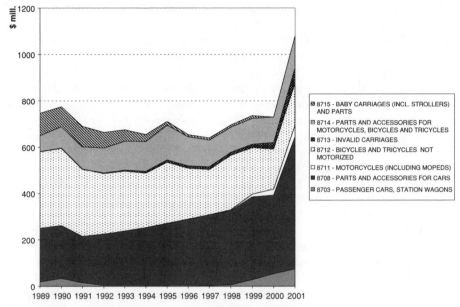

Figure 8.6. Taiwan Exports of Transportation Products.

and nearly recovered to their former values by 1997, just prior to the Asian crisis. There was fall in exports to 1998 due to the crisis, and then a rapid rise again through 2001, by which time exports of automobiles and parts to the United States exceeded $6 billion. Taiwanese exports, by contrast, remained much more stable over the 1989–2000 period and are spread across a much wider range of products (Figure 8.6): in addition to a very small number of cars, there are substantial exports of automobile parts, bicycles, parts for bicycles, trailers and parts, and even wheelchairs and baby carriages! There is an increase in exports of some $300 million over 2000–01, but the magnitude of exports remains small in comparison to Korea.

Predictions from the Model of Business Groups

With this example from the transportation industry, we need to formulate a specific hypothesis that would allow us to distinguish these exports from Korea and Taiwan and that can be applied across other industries. We are not attempting here to capture the rich dynamics of specific industries, nor the details of their institutional differences. Rather, we are looking for a key difference between the exports of these countries that would show up in any year, and would allow us to evaluate the role that economic organization plays in their export patterns.

At the end of Chapter 3, we described an important hypothesis arising from the model of business groups: an economy dominated by strongly vertically integrated groups (V-groups), as we have argued characterizes Korea, will have *less product variety* of final goods than a like-sized economy where the business groups are primary located in the upstream or downstream sectors, as characterizes Taiwan (with its U-groups and some D-groups). This holds even though the *individual* V-groups are actually diversified across a very wide range of final goods, as applies to the large *chaebol* in Korea, especially. Thus, despite the diversification across products and markets of the *chaebol*, we predict less product variety for the entire economy than obtained from the smaller and more dispersed groups in Taiwan.

This seemingly paradoxical conclusion comes from the overall resource constraints for the economy, that is, the limits on what can be produced given the labor, capital, and natural resources. The V-groups in our model, like the largest *chaebol* in Korea, benefit from access to a wide range of differentiated intermediate inputs from the group firms, sold at marginal cost. The production costs of final goods are therefore low, and so the V-groups find it most profitable to produce a higher quantity of *each* final good than would other types of groups, or unaffiliated firms. This fits, for example, the often reported desire of the top *chaebol* to become "world leaders" in specific commodities, such as cars, microwave ovens, or semiconductors. But with the V-groups producing a high quantity of each final good, it is impossible for the economy to also produce *more product varieties*, given its resources. On the contrary, an economy with groups primarily in the upstream sectors (U-groups), like Taiwan, actively selling goods downstream to unaffiliated firms, will have higher product variety than would the like-sized economy that is organized with V-groups.

This theoretical conclusion is illustrated in Figure 8.7, where we plot the total number of final goods produced, or product variety, in each of the equilibria. On the horizontal axis we measure the elasticity of demand for differentiated inputs, which takes on a single value in each equilibrium. For each value of the elasticity, we solve for one or more equilibria, and then compute the economy-wide level of product variety. As in Chapter 3, we distinguish several types of equilibria: those without any unaffiliated firms, but just strongly vertically integrated group (V-groups); those with downstream firms, receiving inputs from the less vertically integrated business groups upstream (U-groups); and those with upstream firms, selling inputs to the business groups located downstream (D-groups). Each of these are labeled as such.

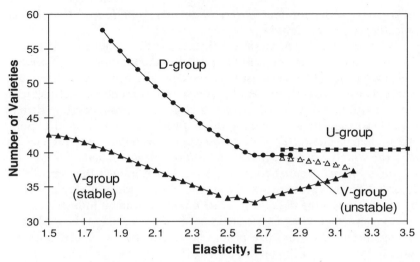

Figure 8.7. Economy-Wide Variety of Final Goods.

From Figure 8.7, we see that the extent of product variety in the V-group equilibria is *always less* than the product variety in either the D-group or the U-group equilibria. Thus, when the business groups sell to downstream unaffiliated firms, as in the U-group configuration, the economy will achieve a greater variety of the final product than in an equilibrium consisting of vertically integrated groups. The U-group configuration is how we have characterized many of the business groups in Taiwan, while the V-groups describe the largest *chaebol* in Korea. Given that the size of these economies is similar,[10] this leads to our first testable hypothesis: that Taiwan will exhibit *greater product variety of final goods* than South Korea. Because the final goods are also exported in our model (whereas the intermediate inputs are not),[11] we restate this hypothesis

[10] From the Penn World Tables, version 5.6, Korean per capita income in 1990 was $6,673, and its population was 42.9 million, giving a GDP of $286 billion. Per capita income in Taiwan in 1990 was $8,063 and its population was 20.4 million, giving a GDP of $164 billion; Korea had this level of GDP some five years earlier. Since Korea is larger than Taiwan in terms of GDP, this factor alone would lead to greater product variety in Korea from our model of Chapter 3. Therefore, our finding in this chapter that Taiwan actually has higher product variety, despite the size advantage of Korea, reinforces the conclusion that the differing economic organization of the two countries must account for this.

[11] In Figure 3.14 of Chapter 3, we show the economy's product variety of intermediate inputs as simulated from our model, and it has just the "reverse" pattern as found for final goods: equilibria with just V-groups have the greatest variety of intermediate inputs, and equilibria with D-groups or U-groups have the least. This result was already hinted at earlier, when we noted that the V-groups in our model, like the largest *chaebol* in Korea, benefit from access to a wide range of differentiated intermediate inputs from

as: there is *greater product variety* **of exports** *from Taiwan than Korea, reflecting its less integrated group structure.*

A second, related hypothesis is that the *most diversified* groups in either country will have greater incentive to develop a reputation in *high-quality,* which would lead to an increase in demand for all its products. That is, any action that shifts out the demand curves for all its products, such as building reputation, will more valuable to a large multi-product group than to a smaller group or to a single-product firm. Thus, the second hypothesis is that in *market dominated by large, diversified business groups, we expect higher product quality than if the market is served by smaller groups or single-product firms.* This result is obtained theoretically by Rodrik (1993), who supposes that the level of product quality perceived by buyers equals the *average* product quality within an industry. In that case, groups that have a high share of sales within the industry have a greater incentive to improve product quality. The hypothesis does not directly follow from the model we described in Chapter 3, because of a simplifying assumption we used there: that all groups were "symmetric" in equilibrium, producing the same quantity and charging the same price for each good (this rules out any differences in product quality). We introduce this second hypothesis, however, because it is a natural extension of our model and it turns out to be easy to test empirically using the same data used to measure product variety.

Product Variety and Quality Indexes

Product Variety

Returning now to the example of the transportation industry, we shall use this to explain our measure of product variety and product quality. In addition to using the disaggregate HS data, it will be useful to classify the products in this industry according to the Standard Industrial Classification (SIC). The transportation equipment industry is labeled 37 in the SIC, and contains roughly twenty 4-digit industries, ranging from bicycles to guided missiles. Those industries with the highest value of exports from Korea and Taiwan to the United States are shown in Table 8.2: motor vehicles and passenger car bodies (SIC 3711); motor vehicle parts and

---

the group firms. The reason these specialized inputs are developed is to lower their costs of final goods, so that the *wide range* of inputs and *narrow range* of final goods for the V-group equilibria go hand-in-hand. The key distinction in our model between final goods and intermediate inputs is that the former are *traded internationally*, whereas the latter are *not traded*. In other words, what we have called "final goods" can represent products sold to consumers or to firms, provided that they can be exported; in contrast, the "intermediate inputs" are not traded internationally.

Table 8.2. *Transportation Industry Exports from South Korea and Taiwan to the U.S. (Values and number of HS categories)*

Year	Variable	Korea Total	Taiwan Total	Korea, Taiwan Common		Korea, Unique	Taiwan, Unique	Variety Index[1]
SIC 3711 – Motor vehicles and passenger car bodies								
1992	Value ($mill)	1,205	4.3	5.1	4.2	1,200	0.06	−5.45
	Number HS	9	2		1	8	1	
1993	Value ($mill)	750	5.0	6.3	5.0	743	0	−4.78
	Number HS	15	2		2	13		
1994	Value ($mill)	1,262	4.7	7.2	4.7	1,255	0.03	−5.16
	Number HS	20	4		2	18	1	
SIC 3714 – Motor vehicle parts and accessories								
1992	Value ($mill)	150	309	149	306	0.7	3.2	0.006
	Number HS	52	59		46	6	13	
1993	Value ($mill)	154	325	154	325	0.6	0.5	−0.002
	Number HS	54	63		51	3	12	
1994	Value ($mill)	188	373	187	372	0.8	0.8	−0.002
	Number HS	71	78		66	5	12	
SIC 3751 – Motorcycles, bicycles, and parts								
1992	Value ($mill)	11	476		410	0	66	0.15
	Number HS	11	38	11	11		27	
1993	Value ($mill)	3.2	506	302	11	159	0	347	1.16
	Number HS	11	37		11		26	
1994	Value ($mill)	2.0	492	2.0	337	0	155	0.38
	Number HS	7	36		7		29	

Note:
[1] This index measures the product variety of Taiwan relative to Korea, so a positive (negative) value indicates the Taiwan (Korea) has greater product quality. The formula used is shown in (8.1) and discussed in the main text.

accessories (SIC 3714); and motorcycles, bicycles, and parts (SIC 3751). For each of the years 1992–94, we show the *value of exports* from Korea and Taiwan to the United States (in millions of dollars), and the *number of HS products* that each country is exporting.

For example, during this period Korea sold between $750 million and $1,262 million of motor vehicles and car bodies to the United States, in up to twenty HS products; most of these sales were in finished autos. In contrast, Taiwan sold only between $4.3 and $5.0 million in up to four product categories. Most of these detailed products overlapped with categories in which Korea also sold, as shown by the column labeled "common" in Table 8.2.[12] At the same time, there are numerous HS categories that

[12] Thus, in 1993, both of the HS products that Taiwan sold in the United States were also exported by Korea, and in 1994, two out of the four HS products that Taiwan sold also had Korean sales.

were *unique to Korea*, that is, products that Korea exported to the United States but Taiwan did not. Furthermore, these unique products accounted for the vast majority of Korean sales: $1,255 million out of the total $1,262 in sales in 1994. A similar pattern is shown in the 1992 and 1993, with Korea having most of its sales in product categories which Taiwan does not export to the United States at all.

It is quite clear within this SIC industry of "motor vehicles and passenger car bodies," that Korea has much greater product variety than Taiwan in its sales to the United States, which is *contrary* to our first hypothesis. But as we look more closely, the reasons for this become clear. Nearly all of Korean sales in this industry are accounted for by finished autos, or more precisely, HS categories that are further subdivisions of "passenger motor vehicles with a spark ignition engine capacity of over 1000CC" – in other words, the family car, all of which were produced by four of the top ten *chaebol*. By contrast, Taiwan's exports are nearly all in just one single category – a "passenger motor vehicle with a spark ignition engine capacity of *under* 1000CC." Just what is this product? It turns out to be *all terrain vehicles (ATV)*, which are used recreationally and in some construction sights, and which both countries sell to the United States. So while the huge productive capacity of the Korean *chaebol* are harnessed around worldwide exports by massive groups like Hyundai, Daewoo, and Kia, the Taiwanese are mainly exporting dune buggies!

The fact that Korea sells many more "unique" products in this industry – not sold by Taiwan at all – is an appropriate way to establish that Korea has higher product variety. To make this more precise, we would like to have a measure of product variety that reflects not only the number of HS categories, but also the sales in each, and especially the sales in the unique products that one country sells but the other does not. This can be developed as follows:

The total sales of motor vehicles and bodies from Korea to the United States in 1994 was $1,262 million, and from Taiwan was $4.7 million, so the ratio of these is $4.7/1,262 = 0.0037$. In comparison, for the common product categories imported from both countries (which are the ATV and their bodies), Korea sold $7.2 million and Taiwan sold $4.7 million, giving the ratio $4.7/7.2 = 0.65$. Taiwan is selling about one-third less of these *common* products, but we would associate this with their *volume* of trade rather than product *variety*. To correct for this, we deflate the first ratio by the second, and take the natural logarithm, obtain a measure of product variety, $\ln(0.0037/0.65) = -5.16$. This is reported in the final column of Table 8.2 for 1994, and for the other years we obtain similarly large negative values. Computing the mean and standard deviation of the product variety indexes for motor vehicles and bodies over the three years, we easily conclude that the mean is significantly less than zero,[13] so that Korea has *greater product variety* than Taiwan in this industry.

To summarize, our method for computing product variety of Taiwan relative to Korea is to construct the index,

Product Variety Index

$$= \ln \left[\frac{\text{(Taiwan Sales/Korean Sales) of all products}}{\text{(Taiwan Sales/Korean Sales) of common products}} \right]$$

(8.1)

Clearly, this index will be higher when Taiwan is selling more unique products, and smaller when Korea is selling more unique products. If both countries are selling in exactly the same disaggregate HS categories, then product variety (measured as a logarithm) is zero, indicating that there is no difference at all between the countries. In this case, there still might still be a difference in the *distribution* of sales across the common product categories, but this is not what the product variety index measures. Rather, the product variety index depends on having *some but not complete* overlap in the product categories of the two countries, so there are both common and unique products. This index is given a more formal economic justification in Appendix C.

Looking at the other industries in Table 8.2, the results for "motor vehicle parts and accessories" (SIC 3714) are in marked contrast to those for finished vehicles. In this case Korea and Taiwan both sell in a large number of product categories, and many of these (over fifty) are common to the two countries. Taiwan sells about twice as much as Korea in total, but we view this as an indication of the volume of trade rather than product variety. Notice that the value of sales from each country in unique product categories is very small – less than $1 million in most years. Accordingly, when we calculate the product variety index, we obtain values that are small in magnitude and that vary in sign over the years (see the last column of Table 8.2). Taking the sample mean and standard deviation of the variety index for motor vehicle parts over 1992–94, we cannot reject the hypothesis that the mean value is zero: in this industry, there is no systematic difference in product variety across the countries.

Finally, turning the motorcycles, bicycles and parts (SIC 3714), the results are quite different again. Now it is Taiwan that sells a great deal to

---

[13] The sample mean of the product variety indexes for motor vehicles and bodies is −4.92, and the standard deviation is 0.43. The standard deviation of the mean is constructed as $0.43/\sqrt{3} = 0.25$. The ratio of the mean and its standard deviation equals $-4.92/0.25 = 19.68$, which has a t-distribution under the null hypothesis that the population mean is zero. The lower 5% value of the t-distribution (with 2 degrees of freedom) is −2.92, and since $-19.68 > -2.92$ we easily reject the hypothesis that the population mean is greater than or equal to zero.

the United States, some $500 million, in a large number of product categories. Notice that in every product category where Korea sells, Taiwan also does, and considerably more. The difference in sales values for these *common* products is very dramatic, but again, this represents a difference in the volume of trade rather than product variety. When the variety index is calculated, we consistently obtain positive values, indicating that Taiwan has greater product variety than Korea (see the last column). This is the reverse of what we found for finished automobiles. Furthermore, computing the sample mean and standard deviation of product variety index for motorcycles and bicycles over the three years, we conclude that the mean is significantly greater than zero at nearly the 90 percent level of significance,[14] so that Taiwan has greater product variety.

In these three industries within transportation equipment, we have therefore found a rich array of outcomes. In finished motor vehicles, which require highly capital-intensive and large-scale production, Korea has much greater sales values and product variety than Taiwan. This is also an industry in which the largest *chaebol* dominate. In automobile parts, the two countries cannot be ranked in their product variety of automobile parts, though Taiwan sells about twice as much. Motorcycles, bicycles, and their parts can be produced at a much smaller scale than autos, and in this industry Taiwan has both higher export value and product variety than Korea. Taiwanese production in this industry is dispersed over many small firms, woven into a tight and highly efficient network. The contrast between automobiles and bicycles perfectly captures the difference in the economic organization of the two countries, and in their trade patterns.

Product Quality or "Mix"

Next, we turn to a measure of product quality. We cannot hope to assess the underlying quality for each and every product. Instead, we can measure the extent to which one economy or the other is focused on more "high-end" products, in each industry. In other words, what is the "mix" of products sold from each economy: are they mostly inexpensive, easily manufactured products; or complex products that sell for a higher price? We will essentially rely on the price of each disaggregate category to

---

[14] The sample mean of the product variety indexes for motorcycles, bicycles, and parts is 0.56, and the standard deviation is 0.53. The standard deviation of the mean is constructed as $0.53/\sqrt{3} = 0.305$. The ratio of the mean and its standard deviation equals $0.56/0.305 = 1.84$, which has a t-distribution under the null hypothesis that the population mean is zero. The lower 10% value of the t-distribution (with 2 degrees of freedom) is 1.89, and since $1.84 < 1.89$ we cannot reject the hypothesis that the population mean is zero at the 90% level. However, at a slightly lower level of significance, this hypothesis can be rejected.

Table 8.3. *Transportation Industry Exports from South Korea and Taiwan to the United States (Unit-values and indexes)*

Year	Variable	Korea	Taiwan	Taiwan/Korea Unit-Value Ratio	Taiwan/Korea Price Index	Mix Index[1]
SIC 3711 – Motor vehicles and passenger car bodies						
1992	Unit-Value ($/unit)	6,216	793	0.13	0.63	−1.60
1993	Unit-Value ($/unit)	5,920	1,048	0.18	0.63	−1.27
1994	Unit-Value ($/unit)	6,598	1,131	0.17	0.65	−1.33
SIC 3714 – Motor vehicle parts and accessories						
1992	Unit-Value ($/unit)	18	7	0.39	0.36	0.09
1993	Unit-Value ($/unit)	18	8	0.44	0.51	−0.07
1994	Unit-Value ($/unit)	22	7	0.32	0.46	−0.28
SIC 3751 – Motorcycles, bicycles, and parts						
1992	Unit-Value ($/unit)	39	21	0.53	1.39	−0.97
1993	Unit-Value ($/unit)	8	20	2.50	0.55	1.57
1994	Unit-Value ($/unit)	3	18	6.0	1.45	1.44

Note:
[1] This index measures the product mix of Taiwan relative to Korea, so a positive (negative) value indicates that Taiwan (Korea) has greater product mix. The formula used is shown in (8.2) and discussed in the main text.

measure the technological sophistication of that product, at least as compared to other products within a narrowly defined industry. Accordingly, we will call this a measure of "product mix," and it will still give us additional insight into the different production and trade patterns of the two countries.

Beginning with motor vehicles and passenger car bodies, we first calculate the unit-value (or average price) of these products from each country. For Korean exports which are mostly finished autos, the unit-values are about $6,000, but for the Taiwanese ATV (that is, the dune buggies), the unit-values are closer to $1,000. These are shown is the third and fourth columns of Table 8.3, and their ratio is shown in the fifth column. The fact that the unit-value is so much higher in Korea reflects the type of product that each country is exporting, and we interpret the higher Korean unit-values as an indication of higher "product mix" or "quality." However, the comparison of unit-value is also affected by pure price differences between the countries *for the same product*. In particular, the ATV exported from Taiwan sell for about two-thirds the price of the ATV exported from Korea, as is shown in the sixth column labeled "price index." Price differences across countries for the same product reflect a host of factors such as exchange rates, wages, cost of materials, market competition, etc. In our measure of product mix, we would like to control for these price differences for common products, so we *divide* the ratio of unit-values by the price index, and take the natural logarithm. The index of product mix in 1994 is therefore obtained as $\ln(0.17/0.65) = -1.33$. In the other years we also obtain negative values, and we can easily accept the hypothesis that the mean is significantly less than zero. This indicates that Korea has *higher product mix* than Taiwan, that is, Korea is exporting relatively more higher-price items.

To summarize, our method for computing product mix of Taiwan relative to Korea is to construct the index,

$$\text{Product Mix Index} = \ln\left[\frac{\text{(Taiwan/Korean) Unit Values}}{\text{(Taiwan/Korean) Price Index}}\right] \quad (8.2)$$

The unit-values that appear in the numerator are straightforward to compute: they are total sales value divided by total quantity sold within each product category. In added up the quantity sold, we obviously want to have goods that are similar, that is, we do not want to add apples and oranges. This means that the industries chosen to assess product mix should be as narrow as possible. In Table 8.3, we have been using each 4-digit SIC category as an industry, but even this may be too broad (within industry 3711, for example, we are adding up units of finished vehicles and their bodies). When looking across other years, we will be able to use the 5-digit SIC as the industry level for 1978–88, but only have the 4-digit SIC available in 1989–94. A more formal economic interpretation of this product mix index is provided in Appendix C.[15]

---

[15] The price index that appears in the denominator of the previous formula requires some explanation. Essentially, this compares the prices of *common products* between the two countries. If there is only a single common product, we would use its price ratio; with several common products, we need to take an average of their price ratios. Many formulas are available to compute the average of the price ratios, or price index. The formula we have used first takes the natural log of the price ratios for individual products, which we write as $\ln(p_{it}/p_{ik})$, where i denotes the individual products, exported from $t = $ Taiwan or $k = $ Korea. Note that the price index is computed only over a common product, which is available from both countries. Then we average these using the export shares from Taiwan and Korea, which we denote s_{it} and s_{ik}. These sales shares must sum to unity for each country, over the common products sold by both. For SIC 3711 in 1994, for example, there are two common products: the all terrain vehicles and their bodies. Taiwan sells \$4.6 million of the first, and \$20,000 of the second, so the sales share of the first is 0.996 and of the second is 0.004. Similarly, Korea sells \$7.2 million of the ATV and \$25,000 of their bodies, so the sales share of the ATV is 0.997 and of the bodies is 0.003. The price index, measured as a natural log, is then obtained as:

$$\ln[\text{(Taiwan/Korea) Price Index}] = \sum_i \frac{1}{2}(S_{it} + S_{ik})\ln(p_{it}/p_{ik}).$$

This price index is used in the denominator of the product "mix" index, to "deflate" the ratio of unit-values and therefore obtain the product mix index. Finally, note that since the price index is written in natural logs, we would take the exponential before using it in the denominator of the product "mix" index. Alternatively, we can rewrite the product "mix" index as equal to Product Mix Index = $\ln[\text{(Taiwan/Korea) Unit Values}]$ − $\ln[\text{(Taiwan/Korea) Price Index}]$, and then directly use the log price index computed as above.

Turning to the other industries in Table 8.3, the average price of motor vehicle parts and accessories from Korea is about $20 per unit, while those products from Taiwan have an average price of $7 or $8 per unit. It would appear to indicate that Korea has more sophisticated items in its product mix, but we need to correct for the price differences of common products. As we see from the price index reported in the middle of Table 8.3, Taiwanese products sell for 36 percent to 51 percent of the comparable Korean products exported to the United States. Adjusting the ratio of unit-values for this price difference, we obtain the product mix index reported in the final column, which fluctuates between positive and negative. Thus, there is no consistent comparison of the countries in product mix, as we also found for product variety in this industry.

Finally, turning to motorcycles, bicycles, and parts, there has been an interesting change over the three years shown. In 1992, Korea sold products with an average price of $39, but by 1994 this had fallen to $3. Over this period, Korea was actually exiting from the most expensive category of bicycles, that is, "bicycles with both wheels exceed 65 cm diameter," or full-size adult bikes. This is where Taiwan has about half of its sales, exceeding $200 million per year, but Korea dropped from sales of $2 million in 1992 to just $30,000 in 1994. Korea's largest sales in 1994 actually occurred in *seats* for motorcycles and bicycles, which explains why its unit-value dropped to $3! Corresponding to this shift in product composition, the product mix index in Table 8.3 changes from negative in 1992 to positive and large in 1993–94, indicating that Taiwan is exporting substantially more expensive products than Korea, and has higher product mix in at least the later years.

This evidence from the product mix index reinforces what we have already found from product variety: these two very successful economies are organized so differently, and with such different productive capabilities, that it shows up very clearly in their trade with the United States The huge productive capacity of *chaebol* could not be harnessed around dune buggies or bicycles! Capital intensive, high-value products are the principal, if not the only kinds of products that can sustain the "one-set" production systems that the *chaebol* have perfected. By contrast, there is no way that Taiwan's small and medium-sized firms could produce an automobile that could compete worldwide like those that Korea produces. The options that have been chosen by one would have been folly for the other.

Taiwan–Korea Comparison of Product Variety

We now turn to a more general evaluation of the product variety in exports for Korea and Taiwan, across a broader range of industries and years. For this purpose, we have constructed the product variety and mix indexes within *each* 4- or 5-digit SIC industry, over the years 1978–94.[16] These years were divided into three sub-periods, 1978–82, 1983–88, and 1989–94 to check for changes in product variety and mix that may have occurred. One difference from the detailed example we just gave for transportation equipment is that we include only those 4- or 5-digit industries that have at least *three common products* in both countries, over some sub-period. This would exclude, for instance, the "motor vehicles and passenger car bodies" industry given at the top of Table 8.2, where the countries have only *two* common products in some years. By excluding these cases, we are therefore focusing on industries where both countries have significant common presence in the U.S. market. To determine which country dominates in product variety or mix, we compute the *mean* of each index over the years within each period. We first report results at the 4- or 5-digit level, testing whether the means of the indexes are significantly positive or negative. We then test the joint hypothesis that all *5-digit industries within a 2-digit category* have greater product variety in one country or the other (see Appendix C for the formal derivation of this test).

Looking first at the disaggregate results in Table 8.4, the divergence of the two economies is clear. We find that about 40 percent of the categories of manufactured goods, Taiwan produces a greater variety of products than Korea, a trend that increased to 67 percent by the 1989–94 period (see the last line of Table 8.4). Thus, Taiwan has gone from having a greater product variety in less than half the disaggregate industry, to more than two-thirds. Taiwanese manufacturers had especially diverse products in final goods categories, but were also more diverse in most intermediate goods as well. In comparison, Korea shows greater diversity in only about 5 percent of categories in the early years, though rising to 20 percent by 1989–94. All of these industries were "high-end" final products. For the rest of the categories, mostly intermediate goods such as chemical products and primary metals, production is sufficiently similar across countries that there are no statistically significant results.

In Table 8.5, we report the results of the testing the joint hypothesis that all 4- or 5-digit industries *within* a two-digit class have higher product variety from one country or the other. If the hypothesis that *Korea has greater variety* in all industries is *rejected* at the 10 percent level, and that *Taiwan has greater variety* in all the industries is *not rejected* at the 25 percent level, then we conclude that Taiwan has higher product variety, which is denoted by T. If the opposite case holds, this is denoted

---

[16] Five-digit industries were used for 1978–88, while 4-digit industries were used for 1989–94.

Table 8.4. *Hypothesis Tests for 4- or 5-digit SIC: Taiwan versus Korea*

Industry (SIC)	Variety Index									Product Mix Index								
	1978–82			1983–88			1989–94			1978–82			1983–88			1989–94		
	T>K	K>T	U	T>K	K>T	U	T>K	K>T	U	T>K	K>T	U	T>K	K>T	U	T>K	K>T	U
Intermediate Products																		
Textile Mill Products (22)	2	0	4	5	3	3	3	5	2	2	2	2	3	3	5	4	4	2
Lumber & Wood Products (24)	2	0	0	2	0	1	1	0	0	2	0	0	1	0	2	1	0	0
Pulp & Paper Products (26)	0	0	2	1	0	3	4	0	1	1	1	0	1	1	2	2	3	0
Chemical Products (28)	0	0	2	2	0	3	7	2	1	1	0	1	2	0	3	6	2	2
Stone, Clay, & Glass (32)	3	1	3	6	0	4	6	3	0	2	2	3	4	3	3	4	2	3
Primary Metal (33)	1	1	3	2	3	2	3	1	1	4	1	0	1	4	2	3	1	1
Fabricated Metal (34)	8	0	3	9	1	7	12	0	2	6	1	4	7	3	7	10	4	0
SUBTOTAL	16	2	17	27	7	23	36	11	7	18	7	10	19	14	24	30	16	8
Final Products																		
Food Products (20)	4	1	1	6	1	0	6	3	1	2	1	3	2	3	2	6	4	0
Apparel & Textile Prod. (23)	8	0	8	9	1	13	11	9	1	4	9	3	4	13	6	5	14	2
Furniture (25)	–	0	0	0	0	1	1	0	0	–	1	0	0	1	0	0	1	0
Printing & Publishing (27)	2	0	2	1	0	3	2	1	1	1	3	0	3	1	0	3	3	0
Rubber & Plastic Prods. (30)	1	0	2	2	1	7	5	0	1	2	1	0	2	7	1	4	4	0
Leather Products (31)	3	1	4	4	0	5	5	2	1	2	3	3	3	3	4	0	9	0
Industrial Machinery (35)	1	0	3	5	1	5	21	2	5	0	2	3	3	5	3	6	11	6
Electrical Equipment (36)	4	1	9	11	1	12	20	3	3	3	8	3	7	10	7	8	16	3
Transportation Equip. (37)	1	0	0	1	0	1	1	0	1	1	1	0	0	2	0	0	1	1
Precision Instruments (38)	2	0	4	3	0	3	5	2	2	1	3	2	4	4	1	5	4	0
Misc. Manufacturing (39)	4	0	9	5	1	9	8	1	3	2	6	5	6	6	3	4	7	3
SUBTOTAL	30	3	42	47	6	59	85	24	19	17	37	21	28	57	27	41	74	13
TOTAL																		
Industries by Test	46	5	59	74	13	82	121	35	26	35	44	31	47	71	51	71	90	21
Number of industries		110			169			182			110			169			182	
Percentage	42	5	54	44	8	49	67	19	14	32	40	28	28	42	30	39	49	12

Notes: T > K (K > T) means the hypothesis that the Taiwan index is less (greater) than the Korean index at the 5-digit level was rejected at the 10 percent level; U means that both these hypotheses could not be rejected. 5-digit SIC industries are used for the years 1978–88, while 4-digit SIC industries are used for 1989–94.

325

Table 8.5. *Hypothesis Tests for 2-digit SIC: Taiwan versus Korea*

Industry (SIC)	Number of Common Goods			Variety Index			Product Mix Index		
	1980	1985	1992	78–82	83–88	89–94	78–82	83–88	89–94
Intermediate Products									
Textile Mill Products (22)	44	157	274	U(T)	U	T	U(K)	U	U
Lumber & Wood Products (24)	14	18	15	T	T	T	T	T	T
Pulp & Paper Products (26)	7	16	54	U	U	T	T	U(T)	U
Chemical Products (28)	9	39	108	U	U(T)	U(T)	U(T)	T	T
Stone, Clay, & Glass Prod. (32)	51	72	104	T	T	T	U	U	U(T)
Primary Metal (33)	35	74	116	U	K	U	T	K	U
Fabricated Metal (34)	151	222	274	T	T	T	T	T	U
SUBTOTAL	311	598	945	T–3	T–3	T–5	T–4	T–3	T–2
				K–0	K–1	K–0	K–0	K–1	K–0
				U–4	U–3	U–2	U–3	U–3	U–5
Final Products									
Food Products (20)	58	67	118	T	T	U	U(T)	U	U(T)
Apparel & Textile Prods. (23)	376	1170	649	T	T	U	U	U	U
Furniture (25)	–	15	29	–	U	T	–	K	U(K)
Printing & Publishing (27)	19	25	40	T	U(T)	U(T)	K	K	K
Rubber & Plastic Prods. (30)	29	76	192	U(T)	U(T)	T	U	U	U
Leather Products (31)	93	159	192	T	T	U	K	U	K
Industrial Machinery (35)	17	62	279	U(T)	T	T	K	U(K)	U
Electrical Equipment (36)	191	236	464	U(T)	T	T	U	U	U
Transportation Equipment (37)	10	22	44	T	T	U	K	K	K
Precision Instruments (38)	71	68	178	U(T)	T	T	U	K	U
Misc. Manufacturing (39)	94	132	165	T	T	T	K	U	U
SUBTOTAL	1269	2630	3295	T–6	T–8	T–6	T–0	T–0	T–0
				K–0	K–0	K–0	K–5	K–4	K–3
				U–4	U–3	U–5	U–5	U–7	U–8
TOTAL				T–10	T–12	T–11	T–4	T–3	T–2
				K–0	K–0	K–0	K–5	K–5	K–3
				U–7	U–6	U–7	U–10	U–10	U–13

Note: T (K) means the hypothesis that the Taiwan index is less (greater) than the Korean index for all 4- or 5-digit industries within each 2-digit group was rejected at the 10 percent level; U means that these two hypotheses were both accepted or both rejected; U(T) and U(K) are borderline cases. Five-digit SIC industries are used for the years 1978–88, whereas 4-digit SIC industries are used for 1989–94.

by K. Borderline cases occur when first hypothesis is not rejected at the 10 percent level, but is rejected at the 25 percent level; or when the second hypothesis is not rejected at the 25 percent level, but is rejected at the 10 percent level; and these are denoted by U (for uncertain) followed by the letter of the country that has the higher index at the weaker significance level. Cases where both of these hypotheses are both rejected or both accepted are denoted by U, indicating that the conclusion is entirely uncertain.

Looking at the summary at the bottom of Table 8.5, Taiwan is found to have greater product variety in ten to twelve 2-digit industries across the three sub-periods, while Korea did not show greater diversity in any of the industries during all periods. A closer inspection of these results shows that the Taiwanese advantage in product variety holds more strongly in *final goods* than in *intermediate inputs*. This is consistent with our first hypothesis, since the business groups in Taiwan are mainly focused in the upstream sector, and the economies of scale within these groups can *offset* the tendency of the small and medium-sized enterprises to proliferate across varieties. Thus, in textile mill products and pulp and paper, Taiwan has a share of business groups that exceeds that for Korea (as reported in Chapter 4), and in both these sectors the product variety ranking in Table 8.5 is uncertain. For chemical products and primary metal, the share of groups (including the state) in Taiwan and Korea is roughly comparable, and in these cases the product variety ranking in Table 8.5 is again uncertain (though in favor of Korea for 1983–88 in primary metals). In contrast, for all other intermediate sectors and final goods we find higher product variety in Taiwan, at least by the weak hypothesis test.

Summing up, in the upstream sectors where the groups in Taiwan are strong, their presence offsets the tendency to find higher product variety as compared to Korea. The only exception to this is stone, clay and glass, where Taiwan has higher product variety despite having about the same share of business groups as in Korea. But in those sectors where the presence of business groups are markedly less in Taiwan than in Korea, which includes all the final goods sectors, we still find markedly higher product variety from Taiwan. This provides robust support for our first hypothesis, that Taiwan has greater product variety in its exports than Korea, especially for final goods.[17]

Taiwan–Korea Comparison of Product Mix

Turning next to a comparison of product mix indexes, these are also reported in Tables 8.4 and 8.5. We find that Korea specializes in

---

[17] This hypothesis is also confirmed by Martins (1992).

higher-value *final products* (both consumption and capital goods), while Taiwan specializes in higher-value *intermediate goods*. In other words, Korea has higher product mix in final products, whereas Taiwan has higher product mix in intermediate products. This is consistent with the business groups in each countries developing a reputation for high-quality products in their respective markets.

The detailed evidence for differences in the product mix can be found within the textile, wood, paper, and metal products industries. Looking first at textile mill products, Korea and Taiwan had their own specializations in different 5-digit industries, which made the 2-digit category "uncertain"; but Korea had a clear lead in the apparel category, which uses textiles as the intermediate input and creates the final products. The small and medium-sized firms creating apparel products in Taiwan, by contrast, would have no incentive to market higher-priced apparel products, but simply produce whatever is demanded by the large retailers in the United States and abroad. Turning next to the lumber and wood industry, Taiwan had higher product mix in lumber and wood products (intermediate inputs) for both periods, while Korea was specialized in higher-end furniture (a final product) during the second period. The third example is paper products. Korea and Taiwan had their own strength in particular types of paper products, but Korea clearly had higher product mix relative to Taiwan in the printing and publishing industry, which is again a final product. The last example is from the metal products sector. Taiwan had higher product mix in fabricated metal for both periods, and in primary metal during the first, both of which are intermediate inputs, while Korea led in industrial machinery, which is a final capital good sold to firms.

By dividing the industries into intermediate and final products, and looking at the 2-digit level, the respective specializations of the two countries becomes even more evident. All of the 2-digit categories in which Taiwan had higher product mix are *intermediate inputs* (with the exception of a weak result in food products), for all three sub-periods. In contrast, Korea has higher product mix in nearly one-half of the 2-digit *final goods*, with the other final goods categories being uncertain. These results from the product mix index bear a close relation to the business groups shares in reported in Chapter 4. After adding up Taiwanese business group and state-owned shares, there are six industries whose shares are greater than 30 percent of the total sales: food, textile mill products, chemical materials, stone, clay and glass products, and primary metal and transportation equipment. Except for food and transportation equipment,[18]

---

[18] In the food industry, Taiwan has higher product mix despite being classified as a final good. As we have noted earlier, this industry also includes animal feeds, which are

these are all intermediate inputs and we have found that Taiwan has higher product mix than Korea. Taiwan's lead in some cases was overtaken by Korea in the second period, particularly in primary metals, where Korea had *chaebol* shares that exceed the Taiwanese business group shares. Similarly, Korea has *chaebol* share in nearly all final industries that exceed Taiwan, and also has higher product mix.

Summarizing, the sectors in which Taiwan maintains a lead in product mix are nearly all intermediate inputs, where it also has high business group shares. In contrast, Korea has higher product mix in many final products, where it also has high *chaebol* shares. Thus, the presence of business groups in either case appear to be closely related to the production of high-value product varieties, consistent with our second hypothesis. Together with our finding on product variety, this again demonstrates the importance of economic organization in affecting the export patterns of the countries.

Product Variety and Productivity

This chapter has focused on the product variety of exports from South Korea and Taiwan, but why is this important? From the point of view of consumers, having more product varieties available brings a welfare gain, so that buyers in the United States and worldwide benefit from access to the wide range of inexpensive products exported by both countries. From the point of view of Korea and Taiwan themselves, the access to differentiated *intermediate* products provides a particular benefit to firms in these countries: the product variety of inputs can be plausibly linked to *productivity* in the downstream industries. Establishing this link in theory has been the focus of much research in economics during the past decade, under the name of "endogenous" growth theory. Adding a dynamic element to the models of monopolistic competition, a rich set of predictions concerning research and development, trade, and productivity growth has been developed (see Romer, 1990 and Grossman and Helpman, 1991). As we discussed in Chapter 1, however, nearly all empirical tests of these models have dealt with macroeconomic variables: aggregate investment, GDP growth, R&D spending, etc. This empirical work does not do justice to the underlying microeconomic structure, which stresses the incentives faced by producers to innovate new product varieties and to imitate existing ones. An economy whose organization allows for greater flexibility

---

intermediate inputs. The transportation industry is a special case in which Taiwanese business groups' production is concentrated in automobile manufacturing and state-owned in shipbuilding, most of which is for domestic consumption rather than export.

in this innovation process can be expected to display higher productivity growth.

Our finding that the product variety of exports from Taiwan exceeds that of Korea suggests that the productivity of those downstream industries in Taiwan that use these exported varieties would be enhanced. For example, think of the extensive range of chemical and plastic products that are manufactured by Formosa Plastics. We have already argued that these are provided to many small and medium-sized firms downstream, who are themselves engaged in production and export of other products. The productivity of this downstream network is surely enhanced by having access to the inputs provided by Formosa Plastics. Of course, since Formosa also *exports* many of its products, firms in Korea and elsewhere can also have access to these unique product varieties, and may likewise experience some degree of productivity gain. But we would expect that the beneficial effects of the Formosa products accrue most fully to those firms with easiest access to these products, that is, to the downstream firms in Taiwan. In the same way, business groups in Korea that are successful in developing unique intermediate inputs would confer a productivity advantage on their own downstream firms, in addition to other Korean firms who purchase these inputs.[19]

This link between product variety and productivity is confirmed in the empirical work of Feenstra, Madani, Yang, and Liang (1999). The data

---

[19] This hypothesis is complicated by other aspects of our theoretical model of Chapter 3 that we discussed in note 11. In addition to the *traded goods*, where the product variety is greater in the in the D-group and U-group equilibria (see Figure 8.7), there are also *non-traded intermediate inputs* in the model. The product variety of these are shown in Figure 3.14, where the equilibria with the strongly vertically integrated V-groups has more variety of intermediate inputs. Normally, the increased variety of intermediate inputs would translate into productivity gains, and hence lower costs of production for the final goods, as in endogenous growth theory. However, the V-group equilibria also have the special feature that the groups are withholding their inputs from others, through charging high prices to non-group firms (possibly even infinite prices). This exercise of market power will lead to inefficiency in the economy, so the question arises as to which effect will dominate: the efficiency gain of having more intermediate inputs, or the efficiency loss of high prices for these? This question is resolved in Figure 3.15, where we graph the marginal cost of producing a final good, depending on the elasticity of demand for inputs. The V-group equilibria prove to have lower costs of production, so that the efficiency gain of input variety more than offsets the efficiency loss of monopolistic pricing for the inputs. Nevertheless, the efficiency gains are not as great as might be expected given the difference in the range of intermediate inputs. At the lowest elasticity values, around 1.8, the V-groups have costs 33 percent lower than the D-groups, despite the fact that the V-groups are producing an a range of intermediate inputs that is about *three times* that produced in the D-group equilibria. Like the criticism often heard against the *chaebol* in Korea, the V-groups are duplicating activities across industrial sectors – producing all their own steel, chemicals, construction, etc. – but are dissipating the efficiency gains by not trading the inputs with others.

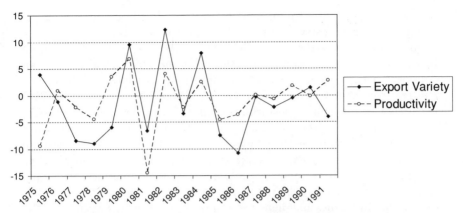

Figure 8.8. Change in Export Variety and Productivity (Percent) (Taiwan relative to Korea).

they use to measure product variety are the disaggregate exports of South Korea and Taiwan to the United States, as in this chapter. They analyze the relationship between changes in export variety and the productivity in these countries for sixteen sectors, over 1975–91. The results lend support to the "endogenous growth" model. They find that changes in relative export variety have a positive and significant effect on productivity in nine of the sixteen sectors, which are: food products; beverages and tobacco; apparel; chemicals and plastics; rubber products; stone, clay, and glass products; fabricated metal products; machinery; and instruments. Most of these sectors are can be classified as "secondary" industries, in that they rely on as well as produce differentiated manufactures, and therefore seem to fit the idea of endogenous growth. In Figure 8.8, we graph the annual *change in export variety* and the annual *change in productivity*, computed as averages over the nine industries. These year-to-year changes are measured in Taiwan relative to Korea. For example, in the years 1980, 1982 and 1984, there is a rise in the product variety of exports in Taiwan relative to Korea, and a corresponding rise in the productivity of these nine industries in Taiwan relative to Korea. Generally, Figure 8.8 confirms that there is a close connection between changes in export variety and productivity, and these have a correlation coefficient of 0.49 over 1975–91.[20] Beyond a visual correlation, we would like to suggest that there is a *causation* at work: industries with greater product variety in their outputs or input are inherently more productive. That is the message

[20] The correlation rise to 0.64 when computed over 1976–91, excluding 1975.

of the "endogenous" growth models, and it is neatly confirmed in this examination of industry data for Taiwan and South Korea.[21]

Funke and Ruhwedel (2001a,b, 2002) have applied this idea more broadly to analyze economic growth across the OECD and East Asian countries. Using panel datasets, they find that a country's export variety (relative to the United States) is a significant determinant of its GDP per-capita and its export performance. In addition, Feenstra, Markusen, and Zeile (1992) look at productivity within the Korean *chaebol*, and find that those groups with the greatest *entry* of new firms also had the highest productivity. This also supports that link between product variety and productivity if the new entrants are producing intermediate inputs that are preferentially sold with the group. Taken together, these various empirical studies highlight the importance of export variety to the economic performance of Korea and Taiwan.

High Technology Exports

We conclude this chapter by looking in detail at the high technology industry – including office machines and semiconductors – where the differences in production and exports between Korea and Taiwan are especially important. As we found for automobiles, Korea was the fourth largest producer and sixth largest exporter of electronic components in 1996 (Lew and Park, 2000, p. 48). This is another case where Korea has successfully transformed its industry into a "producer driven" commodity chain, whereby some of the largest *chaebol* have achieved global scale in products such as dynamic random access memories. These products compete with those from Japan, Singapore, and the United States, for the mass market available through sales of personal computers. Taiwan, by contrast, has specialized in "designer chips," and its upstream foundries such as Taiwan Semiconductor Manufacturing Company (TSMC) work cooperatively with small chip design firms to create special purpose chips that go into export products. These are purchased by firms worldwide as part of "buyer-driven" commodity chains, and need not be at the high-end of the market: they are used in simple toys, for example, and put the "bark" into electronic dogs.[22] We begin by reviewing how the differing structure of these industries came about.

---

[21] Among the primary industries, which rely more heavily on natural resources, the authors find mixed evidence: the correlation between export variety and productivity can be positive, negative, or insignificant. In addition, the authors also find evidence of a positive and significant correlation between *upstream* export variety and productivity in six sectors, five of which are secondary industries.

[22] Emily Thornton, "Bowing to Designers: Taiwan chip makers compete for contracts," *Far Eastern Economic Review*, April 3, 1997, p. 54.

Beginning from the production of radios in the 1960s, Korea moved up the ladder of products to cassette tape recorders and black and white televisions in the 1970s, color televisions and VCRs in the 1980s, and then to camcorders, CD/DVD players and digital televisions today.[23] In percentage terms, however, consumer electronics has declined in importance (falling from 33 percent of production in 1985 to 22 percent in 1996), while electronic parts and components has risen (from 46 percent in 1985 to 54 percent in 1996).[24] Chief among these components is semiconductors, which accounted for over 40 percent of total electronic exports in 1997 and 1998.[25] To produce these the Korean industry relies on imports of capital equipment, plants and core components, mainly from Japan.[26] In turn, it relies on exports of semiconductors and other final products to the United States and worldwide.

Production of semiconductors is concentrated among the largest *chaebol*: Samsung, Lucky-Goldstar, Hyundai, Daewoo, and Korea Electronics. While these groups were supported by cheap government credit in the 1960s and 1970s, as well as by various five-year plans to develop the industry, their investment and business decisions sometimes diverged from government interests. As described by Lew and Park (2000, pp. 54–5):

> In the early 1980s, the Korean government conducted a promotion plan for the semiconductor industry. The plan's main strategy was import-substitution of semiconductors. But the *chaebol* did not follow this directive, and instead made large-scale investments for the international market. However, this conflict was resolved very quickly through an altered strategy in the mid-1980s, in which the government began to support local firms' R&D in semiconductors for the sake of exports.

This telling example shows that the *chaebol* were quite capable of moving in directions not suggested by the government, and which required enormous investments to achieve global scale. Similar to autos, semiconductors is again a case where the Korean industry has intentionally transformed itself into a "producer-driven" commodity chain, marketing products such as dynamic-random access memories (DRAMs) under their own brand names, to become one the world's leading suppliers of this commodity.

The organization of the Taiwanese industry is completely different. As described by Kao and Hamilton (2000), the development of the

---

[23] Lew and Park (2000), pp. 49–50.
[24] Lew and Park (2000), p. 51, Table 3.
[25] Lew and Park (2000), p. 51.
[26] Lew and Park (2000), p. 51.

high-technology industry in Taiwan dates from the early 1990s, and in particular, the Plaza Accord of 1985 and subsequent appreciation of the New Taiwan dollar. This revaluation had an immediate effect on the cross-market price structure within Taiwan's economy. Momentarily everyone was much richer as computed in U.S. dollars. The price of imports fell considerably, and local consumption and styles of life rose quickly. Real estate prices, which had been rising, now took off, and money poured into property construction. Stock market speculation also increased.

After a short lag time, however, the cost of labor in Taiwan grew prohibitively high and accordingly Taiwan exports became more expensive on world markets. By the late 1980s, the real estate bubble burst, the stock market collapsed from a high of about 14,000 to a little over 2,000, and rising exports began to taper off. Beginning in 1988, Taiwan's outward investment surged. In a two-year period, 1988–90, some of Taiwan's most profitable manufacturers – those specializing in footwear, textiles, and garments – were out of business or moved the site of their assembly operations to China and Southeast Asia. Those entrepreneurs who stayed in Taiwan began to look for new products to manufacture, including high-tech products. These entrepreneurs were highly educated, many receiving their education in Taiwan, but an important few had gone to school in the United States, had worked in Western high technology firms, and then had moved back to Taiwan to start businesses or manage existing ones.

This new set of entrepreneurs built on a previous high technology industry that had arisen in Taiwan in the early 1980s, but that had remained small and relatively unsophisticated. According to interviews with these entrepreneurs conducted by Kao and Hamilton (2000), the personal computer (PC) industry in Taiwan developed accidentally and with no direct assistance from the government. The government indirectly helped, however, by banning the manufacture of gambling machines. With the government prohibition, those firms that had been making these machines needed to find something else for its production network to manufacture. Drawing on their expertise, they decided to make PC clones and copies of Apple II. When asked how he could make a computer from scratch, one entrepreneur replied with the Chinese saying, "We have no experience with horses, but we have ridden a donkey." From this beginning, the PC factories in Taiwan grew to become the main OEM suppliers for such American PC computer companies as Compaq and Dell. By 1999, Taiwan was the third largest manufacturer of PC-related products, behind the United States and Japan.

The new beginning for the high technology firms occurred in the early 1990s. Demand in the United States for computer components and peripherals was high, and many U.S. firms were in hot competition with each other to offer the latest PCs to consumers who were just developing an appetite for fast computers with lots of memory. The area of deepest concentration of software and hardware producers was in Silicon Valley. Saxenian (1994, 1998) shows these producers were highly networked, and from the beginning Taiwanese and Chinese-American entrepreneurs had an important presence among Silicon Valley firms. Many of the hardware firms were eager to locate high-quality and low-cost OEM producers for components that had very rapid product cycles. Drawing on their connections in both California and Taiwan, a number of Chinese high technology engineers started manufacturing firms in Taiwan, many adjacent to one another in the Hsinchu Science-Based Industrial Park.

At this time, in the late 1980s, Taiwan had no silicon wafer semiconductor factory. The Taiwan government decided Taiwan's economy needed to be competitive in high technology industries, but did not want to compete head on with firms in the United States and Japan. Private entrepreneurs (Morris Chang, a former executive at Texas Instrument, being the most prominent one) persuaded government officials to follow the pattern of other large firms in Taiwan, namely to be upstream providers of intermediate inputs that SMEs could then use to manufacture exports. Joining with Philips Electronics, the government established Taiwan Semiconductor Manufacturing Company (TSMC), the world's first dedicated independent semiconductor manufacturing foundry. A semiconductor foundry is simply an OEM manufacturer of semiconductor chips designed and merchandised by other firms, in much the same way that garments and footwear had been in Taiwan. In fact, TSMC's charter prevents the company "from designing or making our own brand-name IC products. TSMC therefore is a partner, not a competitor with other semiconductor companies" (TSMC Annual Report 1998, p. 7).

TSMC's success epitomizes Taiwan's new surge in what Kao and Hamilton (2000) call "reflexive manufacturing." From the beginning, TSMC began to work cooperatively with small chip design firms that would create special purpose chip sets that would go into export products. The design firms, in turn, worked with export manufacturing firms, some located in Taiwan and some elsewhere. The key feature of the semiconductor foundry business is its integration into a manufacturing system whose foremost characteristic is its quick response to external demand, the essence of reflexive manufacturing. The approach proved successful, and soon other entrepreneurs started foundries in competition with TSMC. The foundry business took off. Today, semiconductor foundries form an extremely important segment in the global high technology development, and Taiwanese foundries have a commanding lead, producing over 80 percent of the global demand in foundry-made chips. With foundries, every high technology firm can have their own "virtual fab." They can be designers and merchandisers of products that they do not produce. Increasingly

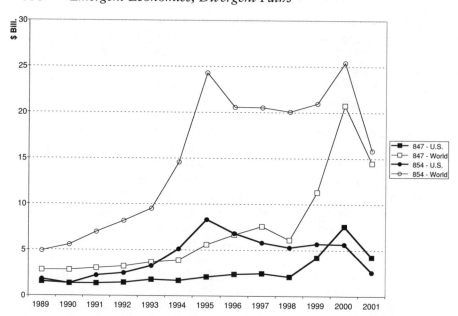

Figure 8.9. South Korea Exports of Office Equipment (847) and Semi-conductors (854).

the global high technology industries are becoming "buyer driven chains," and increasingly Taiwan's organizational capacity for reflexive manufac-turing has pushed the global high technology in this direction.

Exports of Office Machines and Semiconductors

With this description of the high technology industry in the two countries, we return to the question of how their organizational differences show up in the export patterns of South Korea and Taiwan. We expand our earlier discussion of their exports to the United States to now also include their worldwide exports.

In Figures 8.9 and 8.10, we show the exports from Korea and Taiwan in office machines and parts (HS 847) and semiconductors and integrated circuits (HS 854) – both the United States and worldwide. It is evident that Korean exports in both categories of goods are more volatile than those from Taiwan. Thus, for office machines (847) Korean exports drop in 1998, during the financial crisis, but this drop is barely apparent for Tai-wan worldwide exports, and does not occur at all for their exports to the United States. In semiconductors (854), exports from Korea peak in 1995, and then display a sharp decline through 1998, which illustrates global glut in semiconductors. In contrast, worldwide exports from Taiwan

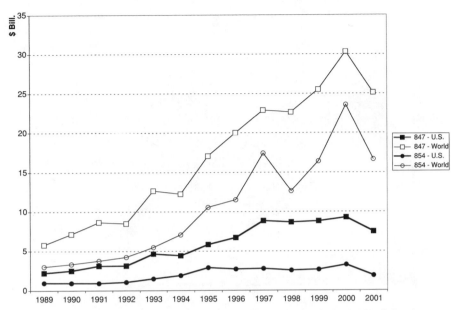

Figure 8.10. Taiwan Exports of Office Equipment (847) and Semiconductors (854).

experience a one-year drop in 1998, but once again, this decline does not occur for their sales to the United States.

What has protected Taiwan from the market fluctuations in these industries that are so apparent for Korea? We would argue that the much greater fall in exports from Korea than Taiwan was due to the different composition of export goods, and especially the heavy reliance of Korea on dynamic random access memory (DRAM) chips. To verify that semiconductors are an important part of the fall in export demand from Korea, we have examined these sales from each of Korea and Taiwan to the United States, and their prices. In Figures 8.11 and 8.12, we show the sales of the principal semiconductor chips sold by each country to the United States, over the years 1994–2001. There are three categories of DRAMs, distinguished by their size, all of which are shown in the legend of each graph. Sales of these DRAMs from Korea to the United States exceeded $4 billion in 1995, but plunged to less than $2 billion by 1998. These export sales were made in part by other types of semiconductors, but Korea remains heavily reliant on the DRAMs in its export sales. By contrast, a glance at Figure 8.12 shows that Taiwan spreads its export sales more evenly over multiple categories of semiconductors, and its sales of DRAMs to the United States did not reach even $0.5 billion until 2000. It is evident

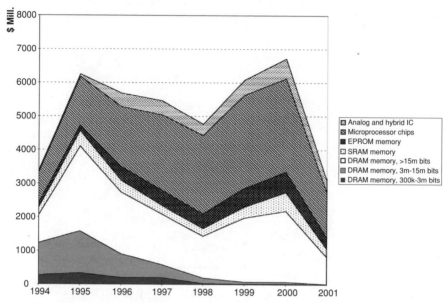

Figure 8.11. South Korean Exports of Semiconductor Products.

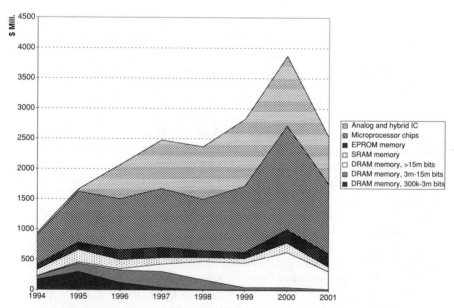

Figure 8.12. Taiwan Exports of Semiconductor Products.

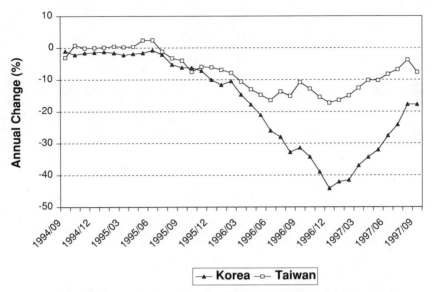

Figure 8.13. Semiconductor Export Prices to the United States ($).

that overall sales of semiconductors from Taiwan did not suffer the fall over 1995–98 that is so apparent for South Korea, though they did fall over 2000–01.

The same contrast between the countries shows up in the price indexes of semiconductor products sold from Korea and Taiwan to the United States, as shown in Figure 8.13, where we graph the annual change in prices over the months September 1994–September 1997 as compared to one year earlier.[27] It can be seen that semiconductor export prices from Korea declined by nearly 45 percent at the end of 1996, while those from Taiwan declined by less than 20 percent. We stress that the differences in the Korean and Taiwanese export prices shown in Figure 8.13 come entirely from the *composition* of their respective exports. The price of sixteen megabyte DRAM chips dropped from $54 at the end of 1995 to $13 by the middle of 1996, and $3 by the end of 1997 (World Bank, 2000, p. 49), and this applies to any country exporting that commodity. But Korea relied on DRAMS for much more of its exports, so the fall in

---

[27] Figures 8.13 and 8.14 are constructed from survey data on import prices into the United States from the Bureau of Labor Statistics (BLS), as described in Alterman, Diewert, and Feenstra (1999). Specifically, the price index used is the Törnqvist formula using prices collected by the BLS and current annual export values from Korea and Taiwan in their sales to the United States . Because the Törnqvist formula uses current rather than lagged export values, it gives a more accurate measure of export prices than other indexes.

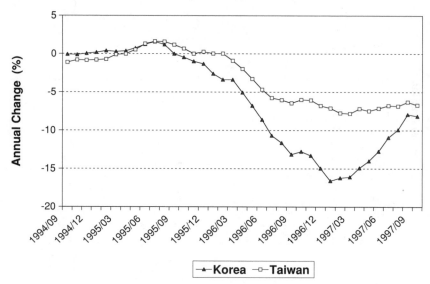

Figure 8.14. Aggregate Export Prices to the United States ($).

prices for this commodity had a much greater impact on the economy. Indeed, semiconductors are important enough in Korean exports to the United States that the fall in their prices had a substantial impact the overall export price index, as shown in Figure 8.14. Thus, the focus of the largest *chaebol* on becoming "world leaders" in DRAMs led to a dramatic fall in overall export prices, whereas Taiwan was insulated from this by its differing export composition.

In Chapter 4, we argued that the fall in exports for Korea, as illustrated most aptly by its semiconductor exports, played a key role in the bankruptcies of the *chaebol*, which precipitated the financial crisis that occurred in that country in 1997–98. Taiwan was largely immune from that crisis due to its greater diversity of exports. But this diversity did serve to insulate Taiwan during the U.S. recession of 2000–01. The fortunes of Taiwanese exporters are sufficiently integrated with the fortunes of Silicon Valley that the bursting of the "high tech bubble" in the United States had a pronounced impact of Taiwanese exports, as well as those from South Korea. The drop is evident in Figures 8.9 and 8.10, and hit Taiwan just as hard as Korea. Indeed, as we suggested earlier in the chapter, the Korean economy was somewhat better positioned to withstand this high-tech demand shock because of its exports of alternative products to the United States and world market, such as automobiles, which continued to grow in 2001. So in contrast to the 1997–98 crisis, which hit Korea especially hard, the 2000–01 U.S. recession has had the greatest impact on Taiwan.

Conclusions

Our objective in this chapter has been to provide a more formal, statistical test of the differences in export structure of South Korea and Taiwan, and in particular, their differences in export variety. Consistent with the theoretical model of Chapter 3, we have confirmed that Taiwan has greater variety in its exports to the United States for nearly all industries. We attribute this difference to the alternative organization of business groups found in the two countries. In addition, we have found that Taiwan exports higher-priced goods in many intermediate industries, whereas Korea exports higher-priced goods in many final industries. That hypothesis goes beyond our theoretical model of Chapter 3, but is consistent with the reasoning of Rodrik (1993), whereby multi-product groups will be more interested in maintaining a reputation for product quality.

The results on product variety reported in this chapter confirm the importance of economic organization in determining trade patterns and also demonstrate the usefulness of using business groups as a measure of economic organization. While we have found evidence that economic organization matters, we do not make any claim that one system of organization is "better." There are tradeoffs: the strongly vertically integrated groups have lowest costs, resulting from a wide range of differentiated inputs; but these benefits are not passed through to consumers because of monopolistic pricing and reduced variety of final goods.[28] In normal time periods, we would expect these contrasting patterns of product variety and productivity to show up differently in various industries. But in exceptional periods, such as the Asian crisis of 1997–98, we make a stronger claim: that the particular structure of the Korea economy, with the vertically integrated *chaebol*, make it more susceptible to downturns caused by the collapse of export markets on which it depends for sales. In these exceptional periods, we believe that the differing economic organization of Korea and Taiwan shows up even in their aggregate growth rates and macroeconomic performance.

[28] See the discussion in Chapter 3.

Conclusions

Local Economies in an Age of Global Capitalism

In his new and very thoughtful book, *Principles of Economic Sociology*, Richard Swedberg (2003, p. 54, his emphasis) makes the following point: "It seems clear that economic sociology should set capitalism at the very center of its analysis since this is *the* dominant way of organizing the economy – legally, politically, and socially – in today's world." Although the point may be obvious, Swedberg (2003, pp. 63–5) notes that very few sociologists actually build an economic sociology on this fact:

> Today's economic sociologists have often taken capitalism for granted and have failed to develop a sociology of capitalism. On the whole, they have preferred to deal with middle-range phenomena, such as firms and networks of various kinds. . . . When it comes to the discussion of capitalism among contemporary sociologists . . . the desire to show that social relations and institutions matter is often so strong that the key mechanism in capitalism – the generation of profit and its reinvestment in production – is hardly ever mentioned, and rarely theorized. This leads to a flawed view of capitalism, and a failure to understand its dynamics as well as its capacity to mobilize people and resources for its purposes.

Although Swedberg singles out economic sociologists, we would add that many economists are guilty of the same oversight: The narrowed concentration on the firm and equating the firm with economic organization in general obscures the very workings of capitalism. As we argue in Chapter 1, this oversight results in large part from conceptualizing economic organization within a Marshallian frame.

342

Recapitulation

Throughout this book, we have adopted a different perspective, a reconstructed Walrasian perspective, in which the economies become organized through very real struggles among firms and networks of firms competing for profit and market power. We argue that this competition among players is inherently reflexive; it is based on an objectification of one's position relative to ongoing assessments of what others are doing simultaneously in the same competitive market environment. At least in part, the competitive struggle is driven by the ability to influence relative prices within such environments. This is done through the use of authority to internalize supply chains inside the firm or business group and through the use of market power to force others to accept one's own terms. The ongoing struggle results in continuous efforts to develop advantageous cross-market organizations.

In Chapter 3, we develop a formal model to test the plausibility of these ideas. We start with nearly the same question that Oliver Williamson (1975, 1985) asks, the question of whether a firm or business group should make or buy an intermediate input or needed service. However, our hypothesis, unlike Williamson's transaction cost solution, is that the "make or buy" decision is made in light of what other firms in the economy are or might be doing at the same time. The mathematical solution to the model (see Appendix A) reveals multiple equilibria. When there are only a few head-on competitors, then the rational solution to the question is to internalize. In other words, the solution is to make the input or provide the service internally. But when there are many players and many potential competitors, then the rational solution is to buy more of the input or service from others. The multiple solutions seem logical and obvious from the outset and, within the mathematical formulations of the model, are clearly evident and provide an economic foundation for predicting multiple stable outcomes for the organization of capitalist economies. The model, however, does not clarify why economies come to adopt one organizational equilibrium as opposed to another one.

In developing this model, we go beyond what is normally thought of as Walrasian economics. The Walrasian frame lacks a clear theory of the firm and of the agency of firms relative to other firms. Instead, it assumes an equilibrated price structure where all players in the economy are simply price-takers. We go one step, *one big step*, further. Our model adds to the Walrasian frame a theory of reflexive agency in the context of competitive struggles where price is an "expression" of that struggle (Weber, 1978, p. 108). The implication of the model is that competitive struggles create an equilibrated organizational structure for the economy as a whole. Another way to phrase this equilibrating process is that competitive struggles create self-organizing economic systems around the principal axes of competition. Modeling this self-organizing process shows that the number of stable outcomes are actually quite few. For this book, we identity only two outcomes: high and low concentration equilibria. A further implication of such self-organizing economies is that the fate and fortunes of individual firms and business groups are directly related to (and are not independent from) the fate and fortunes of others in the same competitive environment.

Although the ideas motivating the model seem obvious enough and although the implications of the model are straightforward, they fly in the face of most writings in institutional economics and economic sociology. Entire economies, or major subsections thereof, are rarely the object of analysis (Swedberg, 2003, pp. 53–73), and when they are, they are normally viewed as more or less stable institutional structures (for example, Fligstein, 2001) rather than dynamic economic organizations systemically interconnected through prices and competition. As we discussed in Chapter 1, institutional economics, especially transaction cost theory, focuses on the dyadic relationships between transacting firms, while placing the ongoing competitive capitalist environment within and among markets in suspended animation, as it were. The dyadic relationship is scrutinized, problematized, and at times, through aggregation, made to stand for the entire economy. The dynamic economic world outside this narrow frame becomes an object of investigation only insofar as it impacts the dyadic relationship. When this outside world does become an object of analysis, the dynamism is lost. The exterior frame becomes a more or less stable institutional environment that impinges on the transaction and can be a constraint, an irritant, a facilitator, or even a source of market failure. Such is the partial equilibrium bias in institutional economics. When a general equilibrium approach is taken, as in the recent comparative institutional analysis of Aoki (2000, 2001) discussed in Chapter 2, then the notion of Walrasian equilibrium is abandoned in favor of game-theoretic solutions, so that prices play a minor role at best.

As Swedberg (2003, pp. 63–5) points out in the previous passage, economic sociology also makes many of the same mistakes. The focus is often on showing the social underpinnings of the same "middle-range" phenomena that institutional economists find so interesting: firms, inter-firm networks, and governance structures. And, like institutional economists, when economic sociologists examine whole economies, the temptation "to show that social relations and institutions matter is so strong" that the dynamics of capitalism is often ignored.

In fact, when reading the economic and sociological literatures on the workings of modern economies, it would seem that our price-driven organizational perspective is well outside the normal range of debate. It is for this reason that we have gone to such lengths in this book to demonstrate the plausibility of our perspective. Asian business groups, those vast cross-market organizational behemoths of Asian economies, are our point of entry. As described in Chapter 2, the prevailing economic and sociological interpretations of Asian business groups are all narrowly focused and organizationally flat. They are outcomes of market failures or the economic embodiments of social networks or the direct results of policy directives. In none of these explanations is the patterning of business groups within and across economies the result of competitive capitalist processes that have organizational consequences. Set against these interpretations, we argue that business groups (or at least business groupings) are organizational features common in all competitive capitalist economies.

To test our ideas, we focus on two highly successful, yet quite differently organized economies, South Korea and Taiwan. Of all the countries in Asia, South Korea and Taiwan have been the sites most often selected for testing these theories about economic development. Hong Kong and Singapore are more like city-states than nations with much of their productive capacity located in other countries (Chiu, Ho, and Lui, 1996). By contrast, South Korea and Taiwan can be viewed holistically; they are "complete" in the sense that they have all the domestic and international dimensions of complex economies. Japan's economy is also complete, but relative to the other developed economies in the region, it is so huge, developed so early, and is industrially so advanced that to compare it to other economies in the region seems like comparing apples to oranges. Therefore, the economies of Taiwan and South Korea have become the prime locations for testing alternative theories of economic development and economic organization.

There are other reasons that they make a good pair for testing theories. They are geographically close to each other, although historically speaking interaction between them has been limited.[1] People of both locations share much of the same culture, which is broadly Confucian and Buddhist, and is oriented at a personal level to family and kinship norms and to advancement through education and hard work. Both countries were Japanese colonies, and both economies were largely destroyed in World War II and, for Korea, in the Korean War as well. Both economies are about the same size; both started rebuilding through import-substitution

---

[1] Put somewhat differently, the countries are clearly two cases of development and not a product of diffusion caused by prolonged interaction. There is, however, some merit to Bruce Cumings' point that Japan and their two former colonies, Taiwan and Korea, form a region, Northeast Asian capitalism. While this point is true, it is also the case that we want to explain the differences between Taiwan and Korea rather than the similarities. A similarity cannot be used to explain differences.

policies in the 1950s and then became aggressively export oriented at about the same time, in the 1960s and early 1970s; and both grew very rapidly at roughly the same rates thereafter. In the post-war period, both countries maintained large standing armies to confront communist neighbors with whom they continue to this day to maintain a cautious, though no longer belligerent, stance. During all of this post-war period until the last decade, the politics in both countries were decidedly one-party, authoritarian systems, but in the late 1980s, both countries created democratic institutions and by the century's end became among the most democratic countries in Asia. All these and other similarities make Taiwan and South Korea as close to naturally occurring experimental groups as exists in the world today, and therefore they are nearly everyone's favorite choice for applying their own particular perspectives on capitalist development.

We selected these two economies, however, not because they were so much alike, but rather because, despite their many similarities, they are also profoundly different exactly along the dimensions of our study: economic organization. The differences in organization between these two very advanced capitalist economies are, in fact, so pronounced and lead to such contrasting economic outcomes that they provide "natural" cases to examine the organizational processes that we hypothesize are decisive in shaping economies and their diverging performances in the global arena.

The book represents a series of tests of our principal ideas. We draw several sets of hypotheses from our model presented in Chapter 3. The first test of the model comes in Chapter 4. Using comparative data on internal transactions among firms within the top business groups in both countries, we show that the model's predictions for economic organization come very close to the actual configuration of business groups in both economies with South Korea resembling a "high concentration" economy and Taiwan a "low concentration" economy. Furthermore, if economic organization represents self-organizing economic systems equilibrated through prices, then we should expect that radical changes in market conditions should have systemic organizational outcomes. We test this idea in Chapter 4 by showing that changes in the demand for Korean exports just prior to the Asian financial crisis of 1997 explain at least in part the profound effects that Korea suffered during the period of the financial crisis: what we call a "catastrophe" in South Korea's economic organization.

We then ask the following: If the model reveals objectively plausible causal connections in the organization of both economies, then are these causal connections empirically and historically present, and how do they arise and actually work out in practice? The answers to these questions form our discussion in Part II. Here we demonstrate that the same competitive processes are responsible for both the emergence and divergence of these two economies. Specifically, in Chapter 5, we show decisive differences between the two societies at the outset of industrialization that pushed each economy towards a different equilibrium. Then, in Chapters 6 and 7, we argue that rapidly increasing external demand, orchestrated by intermediaries linked to the American economy, fueled internal competition in response to that demand in both economies. We judge these conditions fulfill the requirement of the model and are sufficient, in and of themselves, to explain the emergence and the divergence of these two economies during the initial phase of industrialization from the 1960s to the 1980s.

In Chapter 8, we carry this analysis forward in the second test of the model and use the model's prediction for measuring the performance of entire economies – the variety of goods produced and traded. Here, too, the empirical data drawn from disaggregated exports to the United States strongly support the predictions of the model through the entire period from the early 1970s to the end of the century.

Throughout these demonstrations, our thesis that economies self-organize around the principal axes of competition has not only been sustained, but also has provided more predictive "punch" than any of the alternative explanations for the patterns and trajectories of economic development of Korea and Taiwan. Now in the final sections of the conclusion we want, first, to discuss the reasons that our explanation, including the use of our model, has more explanatory power than the alternative explanations. Then, second, we want to speculate where these theoretical and empirical conclusions take us for countries beyond South Korea and Taiwan.

Alternative Explanations

Consider the four major alternatives to our interpretation: first, that state officials and their economic policies proved decisive in creating Asia's industrial transformation; second, that market fundamentals were themselves sufficient to produce the observed outcomes; third, that social institutions and embedded networks best explain the economic organization and economic performance; and fourth, that without the U.S. retail revolution, Asian economies would have developed as they did anyway, only perhaps more slowly. For the first three alternatives, we will show our explanation offers a fuller and more nuanced understanding of how these particular factors work – the state, macroeconomic incentives, and social networks – than is developed in the alternative explanations themselves. For the fourth alternative, we will explain the primary reasons that none of the first three alternatives would even be an issue had the retail revolution in the United States not occurred.

The Role of the Developmental State

It is our view that the state officials always perceive economies on which they are trying to develop policies as going concerns. For the most part, they tacitly accept and take for granted the cultural milieu as well as the organizational features of the societies and economies of which they are a part. Perceiving economies as complex objects in motion, even the most supportive state planners spend most of their time trying to figure out what is going on. They collect statistics, they consult experts, they read world economic trends to see which industrial sectors are worthy of support and which ones are not. They also listen to local businessmen, some in official gatherings and others in private within their circle of families, friends, and colleagues. Although their world of activity is as complex and as confusing as any other world of activity, state planners also have an added dimension of needing to plan and to take some sort of action. In essence, they, too, need a product that is reasonable and has some chance of being accomplished. If politics is the art of the possible, then politicians need to define what is possible. In practical terms, this means politicians typically refine what is already present and cultivate what is already growing. And for the most part that is precisely what we believe state planners in South Korea and Taiwan did.

Our analysis, therefore, convinces us that much of the literature on the developmental state overstates the rationality and expertise of government officials and exaggerates the "accuracy" and impact of their policies. Although state policies and programs may enhance an economy's ability to grow and change, the effects of state actions are often very limited.

In fact, the position that politicians and state planners occupy in regard to the economic policy in those early years of economic growth is very much like that outlined by Cohen, March, and Olsen (1972) in the "garbage can" theory of organizational choice. In contexts "where goals and technology are hazy and participation is fluid," solutions, problems, and participants all become at least partially uncoupled. Solutions go in search of problems; only so many solutions to problems are available at any one point in time; and these solutions depend more on who is participating at the moment than on what problems are being addressed at the same time. In terms of our cases, it is clear that decisions made in reference to the economy were, in fact, often solutions to non-economic problems (for example, nationalism in a time of martial law) that were made after it was apparent that intended goals of the policies would be reached without the actual policies being implemented.

The five-year plans developed in both South Korea and Taiwan are cases in point.

That state officials use a "garbage can" approach to make their decisions is not to say that the state has no role in economic development. Quite the contrary, we believe that state actions, while not a leading cause of economic transformation, do serve to rationalize existing trends. Capitalist economic organization involves complex interdependent cross-market economic activities linking an array of firms engaged in related endeavors. Such interdependent linkages generate an internal momentum that is difficult for any single actor to alter, however well placed. Howard Becker (1995) calls this momentum the "power of inertia." The details of the activity are means of integration and interdependency: the product standards, the requirements of importing and exporting, the rules for accounting, the sizes of containers for container ships, the barcodes on nearly every component, the modes of communication, the means of finance – all these and ten thousand other trivial and nontrivial details combine to interlink the actors and activities, and make any attempt to change the direction of the whole such a difficult, if not impossible, thing to do.

Insofar as politicians and state planners develop policies that complement the existing organization of the economy, such as industrial targeting in South Korea, then the role of the government will be to push the economy in the direction that it is already going. Such policies could and often do have strong effects. In Korea's case, state policies undoubtedly favored some *chaebol* over others, which hastened the dominance of the top four or five *chaebol* over other business groups. In Taiwan's case, the development of government-sponsored initiatives in the computer industry to finance factories, such as Taiwan Semiconductor Manufacturing Corporation, to supply intermediate inputs for smaller firms downstream was not only tremendously successful in helping Taiwan build a viable high technology sector, but also purposefully built on existing patterns: allowing the exports manufactured by smaller firms to drive the demand for the intermediate inputs manufactured by larger upstream firms.

By contrast, on many occasions when state planners wanted to alter the direction of development, their attempts failed. In South Korea, the government often tried and always failed to curb the growth and economic concentration of the *chaebol*. The first round of initiatives to limit *chaebol* growth occurred in the 1970s; another attempt was made in the early 1980s and another in the 1990s. By far the largest attempt was made in the aftermath of the Asian financial crisis. But each time the government's efforts failed, and after each of the government's attempts, the *chaebol* reached yet higher levels of concentration (Lim, 2002). An equal, if not greater, failure was the Korean government's attempt to encourage the growth of small and medium-sized firms (Lim, 1998).

In Taiwan's case, it took many years for state officials to understand Taiwan's intimate connection to intermediary buyers and the deep integration of Taiwan's manufacturers in the global economy. If K. T. Li's account (1988) of Taiwan's industrialization is any indication, even the leading planners did not know what they were doing until it was apparent that development had already started. It was only then that they had sufficient information and sufficient wherewithal to use the power of the state to develop economic and social institutions that might (but often did not) lead to further development.

In the early years of industrialization, state officials in Taiwan worried about the small size and the obscurity of most firms, and tried occasionally to "upgrade" some aspects of the economy. As we already discussed in Chapter 7, they tried to create large trading companies by emulating the Japanese model, but these attempts were unsuccessful because most production networks grew from orders from overseas buyers that originated with or was handled by brokers in Taiwan who had their own, very small trading firms. Accordingly, while these small trading firms proliferated, the government-sponsored trading firms languished (Fields, 1995). The state planners also supported the formation of integrated, more or less permanent subcontracting systems, again based upon the Japanese model, but these also failed (Lorch and Biggs, 1989). The state also started special banks to increase the size of small and medium-sized firms through special financing, but the results were disappointing, because businessmen did not want to take loans from state sources. State planners tried to build an export-oriented transportation industry, so that Taiwan could begin exporting automobiles and trucks. But Taiwan, a country that had in 1985 one of the highest ratios of manufactured exports to total output of any country in the world and a country that had twenty-seven automobile firms in the same period (all for the domestic market), exported very few automobiles (Biggart and Guillén, 1999). Finally, state officials have repeatedly prohibited Taiwan's businesses from investing in Mainland China, but to no avail. Today, billions of Taiwanese dollars have already been invested in businesses on the Mainland, and around 500,000 Taiwanese business people have invested and now live in the area around Shanghai alone.

All these examples indicate that state policy does not lead to accomplished fact. State planners in both countries have had to contend with and ultimately to accept that economic organization generates its own momentum and produces effects that are independent of state officials and macroeconomic factors. There is obviously a relation among all of these factors, but the role of economic organization is independent from

both and, in turn, influences both. Rather than being autonomous and separate from the economy, state officials, as well as entrepreneurs, become
encased in an increasingly institutionalized and increasingly rationalized
system of firms, creating a distinct economic world, which government
officials can neither ignore nor easily reform. Once the emergent economic
organization becomes a going concern, the viable options for the state's
economic policies become progressively narrowed. For state officials and
entrepreneurs alike, once economic organization develops its own internal momentum, it is like the proverbial tiger: once you begin riding it,
you cannot get off.

The Role of Macroeconomic Incentives

Starting with Chalmers Johnson (1982), developmental state theorists
(for example, Amsden, 1989, Wade, 1990) have viewed their interpretation as an alternative to neoclassical economic explanations. The contrast
between the two sets of explanations is over the nature of the state's role
in economic development. The neoclassical account also contends that
the state needs to play a role in economic development, but the role is a
supporting one: the state is to establish economic institutions (for example, banking, equity, and currency markets), infrastructure (for example,
roads, railways, ports, and telecommunications), and geopolitical stability so that markets are free and open to all comers. Additionally, the
state needs to monitor the economy for price distortions, to provide a
regulatory framework to assure compliance to contracts and guarantee
the rights to private property, and to supply education and other welfare
functions so that the right human capital is available at the right time in
the right quantities. In general, developmental state theorists would not
disagree with this list, but unlike developmental state theorists, neoclassical economists further submit that once the state performs its supporting
roles, the state must not intervene further to cause market failures of any
kind. If the state does intervene and market failures do occur, then economic development is distorted. As we explained in Chapter 2, market
failure is the explanation that most economists offer for business groups in
East Asia; they are distortions arising from market failures, most often the
result of state policy regarding capital markets and resource allocations.

As is clear from the World Bank's analysis of *The East Asian Miracle*
(1993), the neoclassical economic explanation for East Asian industrialization is every bit as supply-side, producer-driven as the developmental
state explanations. The World Bank's message is that East Asian states
practiced market fundamentalism, and were good at creating a macroeconomic climate (for example, high savings rates, high levels of education,
high investment rates, and good labor markets) that led to rapid growth.

Because they "got the fundamentals right," argues the World Bank (1993, pp. 347–52), industrialization occurred rapidly. The ensuing financial crisis in Asia led to a re-evaluation of the role of the state versus markets, and while a more nuanced view is provided by Stiglitz and Yusuf (2001), those contributions still emphasize the supply-side of the growth equation.

What is missing in all these descriptions of East Asian growth is a role for *demand*. We have argued in Part II that the export growth from South Korea and Taiwan was at least in part the result of *increased demand* generated by the retail revolution in the United States. Specifically, the repeal of "fair trade laws" in the United States during the 1960s allowed for huge increases in mass-merchandising, orchestrated by the merchandisers acting as intermediaries between U.S. consumers and Asian producers. This increase in U.S. demand occurred just as Korea and Taiwan, encouraged by Japanese trading companies, were in a position to meet that demand. However, their response was exercised in different market segments within the two countries. Big buyers began to look to Korea for the provision of long production runs of relatively standardized products, whereas Taiwan supplied shorter production runs of more specialized, niche products. Thus, the exercise of intermediary demand resulted in quite different product varieties from each country. As evidence for the importance of demand, in Chapter 7 we point to the work of sociologist Gary Gereffi (1994, 1999), who has documented the process by which U.S. retailers went about ordering goods from Asia. Statistically, it can be clearly demonstrated that Taiwan exports a greater variety of products to the United States than South Korea in nearly every industry (Chapter 8).

There are some hints about the importance of demand for trade and growth elsewhere in the economics literature, and we hope that our detailed examination of South Korean and Taiwan will help bring this topic squarely to the forefront of inquiry. The consequences of *not* clearly distinguishing demand from supply-side factors can be seen from the debate concerning the importance of "openness" to growth. Consistent with the neoclassical views, many economists would like to believe that more open economies (as measured by the share of overall trade in GDP) grow faster than those less open. The empirical evidence on this topic, however, is far from conclusive: see Rodriguez and Rodrik (2000). One of the pervasive problems in this debate is that the openess of an economy is fundamentally *endogeneous*: it is determined in general equilibrium, reflecting both supply and demand-side factors. For example, higher productivity of a country could lead to greater exports along with faster growth (the supply-side view). Or an increase in demand could lead to more exports and faster growth (a demand-side view) or any combination of these could still lead to a correlation between exports and growth. The problem is that such a correlation – to the extent that it exists – does not establish causality.

One approach to deal with this ambuguity is to introduce statistical instruments that both explain openess and that are arguably *exogenous*. An example is the distance from a country to its trading partners, with closer countries trading more with each other. Frankel and Romer (1999) first estimate a "gravity equation," whereby trade depends on distances and the GDP of trading partners, and then demonstrate that the predicted trade shares from this equation are indeed significant in explaining per-capita income and growth. In other words, countries that are close to large and wealthy partners can be expected to grow faster as a result. This approach is implicitly introducing a role for demand, since the proximity to large partners leads to more trade in part because of demand factors. But there is still a supply-side element in the equation, since large trading partners will not only buy more, but they will also sell more. So the use of the "gravity equation" alone does not adequately distinguish demand from supply-side factors, and this can be interpreted as one reason for the ongoing debate on this topic.[2]

More direct evidence on the importance of demand from international trade comes from the work of James Rauch and colleagues. The idea that selling goods on international markets requires a "match" between buyers and sellers is explored empirically by Rauch and Trindade (2002). Earlier work by Gould (1994) for the United States and Head and Ries (1998) for Canada had confirmed the importance of immigrant networks in promoting trade with their home countries. Rauch and Trindade (2002) expand this to consider global bilateral trade, and show the importance of Chinese ethnic networks in enhancing trade. These networks are measured by the level or fraction of the population in a country that is of Chinese ethnic background, which is entered along with other typical variables in a gravity equation. It is found that the variable measuring Chinese networks enhances trade, and particularly trade in differentiated goods, where there is more informational difficulty in assessing their value. These results support the idea that Chinese entrepreneurs are acting as interme-diaries, taking advantage of the production networks throughout Asia to increase demand for those goods.

These examples from the economics literature are meant to illustrate how demand factors have just begun to be considered as determinants of trade and growth. The retail revolution in the United States is an especially important case of institutional and policy changes that had

---

[2] See the recent contribution by Rigobon and Rodrik (2004).

widespread consequences for the American markets and its suppliers – South Korea and Taiwan, as we have focused on here, although there is no doubt that many other Asian countries were also affected. The current-day fascination with China, with Wal-Mart as the "big buyer," is yet another example of how demand is channeled through intermediaries to such an extent that it profoundly affects the global structure of production and export sales as occurred earlier for South Korea and Taiwan.

The Role of Social and Political Institutions

As we noted in Chapter 2, one of the goals of writing this book is to add an economic dimension to economic sociology. The importance of a sociological view of the economy has always been to show, as Granovetter (1985) correctly saw, that economies cannot be explained by economic factors alone, but rather that economic activities are powerfully shaped by social relations, networks, and institutional environments. But the acuteness of this insight has created its own problems. As Swedberg (2003) noted at the beginning of this chapter, economic sociologists have been so eager to declare the relevance of social relations and institutions for economic activity that they have neglected to show how these elements fit into a theory of capitalism. Moreover, in doing so, they have also proclaimed the sociological view of the economy superior to an economic view. Economists, of course, are not blameless in preferring their own points of view and have been known openly to slight neighboring disciplines, sociology being their favorite.

This eagerness to argue that sociological and economic perspectives are fundamentally at odds with each other is, we firmly believe, a wrongheaded approach. Throughout this book, we do not make a distinction between what is economic and what is sociological because all the main objects of our analysis (for example, economic organization, competition, business groups) are, simultaneously, both. Economic phenomena necessarily combine both economic and sociological aspects. Accordingly, our purpose has not been to preserve or to weigh the worth of each perspective, one against the other, but rather to combine both perspectives fully in a theory of how economies become going concerns and change over time. Either perspective without the other is diminished.

Based on our analysis in this book, therefore, we conclude that the desire to separate the two disciplines has the consequence of making economic sociology less important than it should be. There are at least three areas of our research where economic sociology makes a greater contribution if an economic dimension is added to the analysis: economic reflexivity, business groups, and a market-based approach that joins both supply- and demand-side phenomena. All of the main components of these three areas have been developed elsewhere in the sociological literature, but adding an economic component to each, substantially augments the persuasiveness of the explanations.

First, the cornerstone of the model that we develop in Chapter 3 is the reflexivity of economic actors in which participants constantly objectify their own positions relative to others in that setting and take actions based on those comparisons. The works of Harrison White (1981, 1992, 2002) develop this perspective in some detail. Early on, he (1981, pp. 543–4) said, "Markets are tangible cliques of producers watching each other. Pressure from the buyer side creates a mirror in which producers see themselves, not consumers." Although White's insightful work is among the most economic of the economic sociologists, he still largely restricts his analysis to single "producer" markets. In his most recent work (2002), he links producer markets to upstream suppliers and downstream buyers, but his analysis remains fixed on specific markets, largely ignores prices, and does not reveal systematic differences in the configuration of these linkages in different competitive environments. Taking their clues from White, others writers (for example, Podolny, 1993, 2001, Podolny, Stuart, and Hannan, 1996, Fligstein, 2001) have also developed the idea of economic reflexivity, but also remain wedded to a market-by-market Marshallian frame to interpret issues about industries, as well as about national and global economies.

The core ideas we add to these previous works is the Walrasian framework, which includes prices struggles in competitive cross-market activities, and, of course, the goal of explaining the organization of economies. These additions change the structure of the reflexivity argument. Unlike in White (1981), Podolny (1993) and Fligstein (2001), reflexivity does not lead to a stable hierarchy of roles within a producer market, but rather to a dynamic and ever changing cross-market configuration of large and small firms and business groups that could, and did in both Taiwan and South Korea, experience sharp disruptions. In general, the message of general equilibrium analysis is this: The interconnectedness of markets undermines stability in any one market. To paraphrase a point we made earlier (Chapter 1, p. 20), the organizing forces leading to stability in n markets does not account for, or work out the consequences of, the dynamism that occurs when n markets in a whole economy are interconnected. Capitalist markets are always interconnected. Therefore, it would give economic sociology greater explanatory power if these competition- and price-based interconnections are examined and incorporated within an economic sociological framework.

Second, our entry point into the analysis of the South Korean and Taiwanese economies is the business groups in those two countries.

Economic sociologists (Hamilton and Biggart, 1988, Kim, 1991, 1997, Gerlach, 1992, Whitley, 1992, Kim, 1993, 1994, Lincoln, et al., 1996, Granovetter, 1994, Orru, et al., 1997) have consistently done very penetrating work on business groups. They have demonstrated that there are difference among these groups from country to country and have explained these differences in terms of social relationships and social institutions. The differences they point to – to such things as governance or authority structures, inheritance patterns, and industrial diversification – are ones that we point to as well.

By adding an economic dimension to these analyses, we obtain a more unified perspective that contributes to the sociological literature on business groups is three ways. First, adding an economic dimension shifts the focus from organization per se to organizing processes. Our analysis suggests that social and institutional factors become germane through the economic activities that underlie competitive struggles; they are emergent features of economic organization that only become salient in the course of pursuing economic goals.[3] Second, these social relations and institutions serve as points of leverage in how entrepreneurs organize economic activities and that the same relations and institutions can be used in different locations or in different times to build very differently organized economies. In other words, it is not the institutions or social relationships that determine the organization, but rather it is the competitive contexts in which those social relations and institutions become useful that do. Third, the lineup of business groups in an economy is an outcome of the competitive struggles, of which price competition is a one of the chief expressions of that struggle. In sum, without integrating the economics into a sociological perspective, business groups become more or less static manifestations of social and institutional differences among countries. Integrating the economics and the sociological perspective allows one to interpret and compare the organizing processes, the performance, and the trajectories of change in and between complex economies.

Third, the Walrasian framework that we presented in Chapter 1, with its emphasis on cross-market connections, is anchored in the analysis of markets. Drawing on the earlier work of Karl Polanyi (1957), economic sociologists (for example, Zelizer, 1979, 1985, White, 1981, Baker, 1984, Granovetter, 1985, Swedberg, 1994, 2003, Abolafia, 1996, Lie, 1997, Fligstein, 2001) have studied and theorized markets for some time. Although some emphasize the social construction and cultural

---

[3] This same point, although in a very different context, has been made by Howard Becker (1995), who shows that the music industry is integrated through standardized ways of performing that activity, and by Weber, who wrote (1958, p. 280) that the train of economic interest is propelled along tracks laid down by cultural and social ideals and institutions.

underpinning of markets (for example, Abolafia, 1996, Zelizer, 1979, 1985), most economic sociologists (Granovetter, 1995a [1974], White, 1981, 2002, Baker, 1984, Swedberg, 1994, 2003, Fligstein, 2001) conceive of markets as "social structures." As Granovetter (1995a [1974]) and White (1981, 2002) argued early on, such structures often take the form of networks of social relations, which become institutionalized as self-reproducing sets of roles (Fligstein, 2001).

Despite their insightful work on market structure, economic sociologists have consistently ignored two aspects of markets that we emphasize with our approach: price competition and demand. Swedberg (2003, p. 129) generally acknowledges that "economic sociologists have on the whole paid little attention . . . to prices and their determination." But were they to include prices in the role Weber (1978) suggested (see Chapter 1), then their analysis would concentrate less on the stability among competitors in the same producer market and more on the active struggle and interconnectedness among competitors in all markets, including the varied use of authority and market power to achieve participants' economic interests. Our research shows that the outcomes of competition in one markets (for example, discount retailers in the United States) has direct impacts on organization and competition in other markets (for example, supplier markets in Asia). Prices are not only the tools to carry out competition, but they are also integral part of the process by which economies become organized and reorganized. Therefore, to ignore price competition is to miss one of the principal organizing processes of capitalist economies. That said however, considering only prices, without also considering the sociological context in which price struggles are manifest, is equally naive. Both sociology and economics are needed to develop a theory of capitalist markets.

Within a Walrasian framework, such a theory of capitalist markets necessarily emphasizes both supply and demand. As we noted in Chapter 6, economic sociologists typically look at the producer-side of capitalist economies, and generally assume that the consumer side takes care of itself. Less frequently, although often with great insight, economic sociologists (Hirsch, 1972, Bell, 1976, Hamilton, 1978, Bourdieu, 1984, Granovetter and Soong, 1986, Frenzen, et al., 1994) examine consumption, but when they do so they typically follow Veblen (1899) with a theory of consumption and consumer behavior. Less frequently, they emphasize the intermediaries that "make" the consumer markets. As we have noted throughout this book, Gary Gereffi (1994a, 1994b, 1994c, 1999, Gereffi, et al., 2005), and a number of close colleagues (Bonacich, et al., 1994, Appelbaum and Smith, 1996) have conceptualized "global commodity chains," and distinguish between commodity chains controlled by producer and those controlled by big buyers, who we define as intermediaries. Although enormously helpful in their ethnographic detail, Gereffi and the handful of others who work on global commodity chains (for example, Gereffi, et al., 2002, Gereffi, et al., forthcoming) primarily focus on the lineally conceived production networks and on whether the producer or the retail/merchandisers ends of the chains controls the chain. Until recently, they did not conceptualize the economic organization at either end of the chain, either the organization of producer economies or the organization of consumer economies. Also, they neither examined the causal linkages between the two types of economies nor the price competition that shaped the commodity chains themselves. In sum, adding price and economic organizational dimensions to the global commodity chain approach would, we believe, enhance the approach, producing in the end a more sociological view of how commodity chains are embedded, simultaneously, in multiple institutional environments.

In summary, the previous three explanations for East Asian economic development – the development state, the free market, and social and cultural institutions – aim, more or less, at a generalized theory of how global development occurs. The generalizability of the so-called Asian model of development has been discussed and variously criticized for years. Although we offer our own interpretation as an alternative to these explanations, we do not want to argue that ours is a generalized theory of development. Quite the contrary, ours is a historical explanation that is illuminated by economic and sociological theories. This point is clear from the key role played by the retail revolution in the United States.

The Role of the Retail Revolution

Our interpretation suggests that, even if the states' economic policies had been neutral with respect to economic organization, the two economies would still have emerged and diverged in ways similar to what actually happened, although different sets of actors would likely have won the competitive struggles in both locations. The same cannot, however, be said for the retail revolution. Our analysis strongly indicates that without the U.S. retail revolution, the pattern of Asian economic growth would have been very different. Without repeating the details of the demand-side narrative that we presented in Chapters 6 and 7, we conclude that there are four reasons that a counterfactual hypothesis would not hold. Specially, without the U.S. retail revolution, can we assume that the South Korean and Taiwanese economies would have generated the same types of exportable products and the same patterns of economic organization as they did in fact develop?

First, our analysis suggests the structural changes in the competitive environment of retailing in the United States directly contributed to rising demand for products supplied by Asian manufacturers. It was the sudden and dramatic increase in demand for a few products that gave the initial sets of Taiwanese and South Korean entrepreneurs their first successes and their capital to expand into new product lines, and that brought other businesspeople into competition with the first set of entrepreneurs. Without this export pull, there would have been limited incentives and limited resources to develop production networks.

Second, we have shown that many initial products ordered from Asia were made directly and exclusively for specific retailers or brand-name merchandisers in the United States. Considering the rapid increase in the amount and variety of differentiated products ordered throughout the 1970s and 1980s, we believe it is impossible for Asian manufacturers to have searched the markets for the right products to make for the U.S. consumer. Instead, the process almost always worked the other way around: Foreign buyers would contract with South Korean and Taiwanese manufacturers and tell them what to make and often how to make it. Therefore, it is our conclusion that, before the 1990s, South Korean and, particularly, Taiwanese businessmen were integrated in the "products worlds" created by U.S. retailing through their contractual relations with retailers. Without the retail revolution, and without the specific linkages between U.S. and Asian firms, South Korean and Taiwanese manufacturers would not have developed the products that they did in fact develop.

Third, we have hypothesized and presented confirming evidence to show that the patterns of economic organization derive directly from a combination of two processes. (1) The evolving ordering strategies of U.S. retailers and merchandisers rationalized the type of product with the type of production system. Large volume orders of complex products requiring capital intensive techniques of production (that is, televisions, microwaves, and automobiles) went to firms and business groups capable of producing those products. Small to large batch orders of standardized products requiring short turnaround times and low prices went to other firms and business groups capable of producing those products. The retail ordering strategies, therefore, were selection devices that promoted a geographical division of labor with different self-organizing systems of production emerging in different locations. (2) These ordering strategies, coupled with rapidly expanding orders, promoted distinctly different competitive environments. We argue that these different environments can be theoretically understood through the model that we presented in Part I and for which we have given confirming evidence. Without the retail ordering and without the specific competition the orders generated, the patterns of economic organization would not have emerged as they did.

We should qualify this conclusion with the caveat that the propensity for large firms and business groups would have been present in South

Korea, and small and medium-sized firms in Taiwan, even had the retail revolution not occurred. This conclusion derives from the evidence that we present in Chapter 5. But propensity does not lead to accomplished fact. As we noted earlier, Korean business networks in the United States are overwhelmingly small and medium-sized firm networks. Moreover, when many Taiwanese businesspeople moved their manufacturing operations to China, they left their satellite assembly systems behind, and vertically integrated their factories. As a consequence, the Taiwanese business networks in China in the first years of the twenty-first century are beginning to look a lot different than they looked in Taiwan in the 1980s (Kao and Hamilton, 2001, forthcoming). This observation corresponds, of course, to our principal hypothesis, namely that in a capitalist market economy, the competitive environment shapes economic organization more than political institutions, and economic organization, in turn, shapes the trajectories of economic change.

Fourth, our analysis strongly implies that the industrialization of East Asia should be viewed analytically as a onetime only event, rather than as a model of development that other societies might emulate. We demonstrate in this book that the historical transformations occurring on both sides of the Pacific are empirically part of the same phenomena, a phenomenon that can be understood theoretically in both economic and sociological terms, but that remains quintessentially historical in nature: a onetime only occurrence. We demonstrate also that this historical conjuncture has real causes and multiple outcomes flowing from it. Concurrent export-oriented industrialization in Japan, Hong Kong, and Singapore had similar causes, and subsequent rounds of industrialization in the 1990s in Southeast Asia, in China, and in India can be demonstrated to be historically and directly linked (for example, through direct foreign investment made by Asian manufacturers and global retailing strategies by U.S., European, and Japanese firms) to the first round of Asian industrialization. These cases argue for the diffusion, and not for the independent invention, of Asian capitalism. Of course, we cannot argue that, without the U.S. retail revolution, there would have been no economic development in Asia. Some types of development obviously would have occurred, but how it actually did occur can only be causally explained and analyzed rigorously by demonstrating the inseparability between the U.S. retail revolution and the so-called Asian Miracle.

Further Tests and Implications of the Model

Having concluded that our explanations for East Asia's capitalist expansion is an historical one, we now need to ask to what extent are our findings generalizable beyond the cases of South Korea and Taiwan. Although our explanation of East Asian industrialization emphasizes its rootedness in time and place, the theories we use to substantiate this claim are general and, we believe, can be used across a variety of settings.

The most obvious level to test the generalizability of the model is at the level of national economies. Although we suspect that the main European cases used in the emerging sociological literature on national business systems (Whitley, 1999) and national diversity in global capitalism (Berger and Dore, 1996, Hollingsworth, 1997, Quack, Morgan, and Whitley, 2000) could be usefully conceptualized through the approach we outline in this book, we also think there is a danger in equating national economies with the boundaries of competition, especially in an age of increasingly complex global interconnections. Even for South Korea and Taiwan at the early stages of their trade (before 1985, as we examined in Chapters 6 and 7), a crucial factor leading to the emergence and divergence of these economies was their linkages to global intermediaries, which in turn created the conditions for competition at the national level. Our conclusion is that the economic organization in either country would not have emerged as it did without the rapidly increasing global demand being channeled through these intermediaries. Therefore, one of the principal insights to be gained at the level of national economies is that cross-market global connections (or the absence thereof) in any one segment of a nationally organized economy may have profound effects on how that economy is organized locally. National economies matter, but it is an empirical questions whether the boundaries of reflexive competition is coterminous with the boundaries of the state.

Despite our own use of national economies to test our theories, we believe that the most promising level of analysis will likely not be at the national level, but rather at highly competitive, inter-market segments that occur within and often across national economies. Perhaps the best example of such an inter-market segment is the high technology sector in the United States. As we suggest in Chapter 3, AnnaLee Saxenian's analysis (1994) of "two models of industrial systems" reveals similar dynamics that we describe for South Korea and Taiwan. Adding our conclusions to her analysis, we would hypothesize that the configurations of firms along the East and West Coasts each initially reflected the competitive environment in that setting. On the East Coast, along Route 128, high technology firms initially saw their chief competition to be other firms in the same location. Competition was localized among a few big firms, and they internalized accordingly. IBM steadily emerged as the giant, like Hyundai and Samsung in Korea, and others in the same region were correspondingly diminished as IBM grew more prominent. On the West Coast, in the Silicon Valley, the presence of many players encouraged a division of labor. Standardization across firms encouraged all firms to organize their activities around upstream suppliers, principally Intel's microprocessors and Microsoft's operating systems, and downstream assemblers, initially dominated by such firms as Hewlett Packard, which owned some dedicated manufacturing facilities, but soon was joined by Dell and Gateway, which are pure assembly firms not engaged in any manufacturing themselves. Many small, medium, and large firms began to supply components for an increasingly networked system of manufacturing, a system resembling and actually linked to Taiwan's satellite assembly systems.

As IBM's organization grew internally vaster, the Silicon Valley's networked system of manufacture developed more standardized parts and procedures and widened geographically. The firms in each area specialized in very different types of products, with the Route 128 firms having generally higher value and less variety than Silicon Valley firms. The balance between the two areas tipped when the development of personal computers began to substitute for minicomputers and mainframes, a development that eventually collapsed the price structure for the latter products and ultimately pushed most of these firms into bankruptcy and forced buyouts. In the Silicon Valley, however, the rising demand for personal computers, along with the increasing standardization of hardware components and operating software, propelled a modular form of manufacturing, in which many different cross-market combinations of inter-firm alliances became possible and profitable in many different geographical locations. In large part facilitated by the development of large downstream assemblers, merchandisers, and discount retailers (all of whom began offering a wide variety of differentiated products in response to consumer demand), this modularity encouraged ever greater demand-responsiveness and organizational variety across increasingly globalized networks of production. Taiwan's success in high technology industries relative to that in South Korea is due to its greater integration in these inter-firm networks that were integral to and grew out of Silicon Valley firms. In the case of Silicon Valley, then, the local high technology sectors are a part of an emergent global system in which competition at the global level influences organizational patterns at the local level.

The same level of analysis and similar conclusions apply to other economic segments that cut across national economies and that consist of multiple markets. Automobile and automobile parts manufacturing is another good example, and an example that organizationally leads to different organizational outcomes than the Silicon Valley case. For automobile manufacturing, the more traditional, vertically integrated corporations and business groups (for example, General Motors, Toyota, Daimler Chrysler, Volkswagen, and Hyundai) have maintained their hold on the industry, even though they have had to reorganize their supply lines, and in the process becoming less vertically integrated while at the same time becoming globally more horizontally integrated. In this example, South Korean *chaebol* are important players in the global automobile competition. As with electronics, competition at the global level shapes local economic organization in direct and profound ways.

These examples illustrate the potential application of our model to other scenarios beyond South Korea and Taiwan. But beyond the specific examples, we hope this book has raised some a number of questions for further research. Among the most important of these is the historicity of East Asian development. We have argued that a fundamental cause of the so-called Asian Miracle was the retail revolution that began in the United States in the 1960s and 1970s and that continues today on a worldwide basis. A crucial aspect of this revolution is the rise of global intermediaries that join globally based manufacturers to final consumers. Abernathy et al. (1999) have explained some of the more recent drivers of this retail revolution (for example, lean retailing) as it pertains to the garments, but the main features of this retail revolution, and especially its specific links to Asian industrialization, have not been examined.

It is evident that our study – which began as an inquiry into the differences between business groups in South Korea and Taiwan – has grown into something much more. Our conclusion that business group configurations grow out of capitalist competition leads us to the conclusion that business groups are not transitory phenomena that will disappear as economies become more industrialized. They are not "caused" by some form of market failure or social network. Instead, business groupings, if not business groups themselves, are widespread, occurring wherever capitalist competition occurs. Such groupings should occur even in the United States, where mergers, acquisitions, and expansions have been effectively channeled but not negated by anti-trust legislation. The divergent structure of business groups depends, furthermore, on the demand factors facing economies, as expressed through global intermediaries. During the initial period of industrialization (1965–85), Asian manufacturers increasingly became **organizational extensions** of U.S.-based retailers and mass merchandisers, a trend that goes across nearly all industries, including most prominently high technology and automotive industries and that, in many respects and with some important exceptions, continues today. We also conclude that the reciprocal linkages between U.S.-based retailers and merchandisers, on the one hand, and Asian manufacturers, on the other hand, became important drivers of both the retail revolution and of the Asian industrialization. Each relied on the other. Relative to competitors in their local economies, the Asian manufacturing and supply chains gave a competitive advantage to those U.S.-based retailers and merchandisers that used them, and the contractual linkages to Western retailers gave a competitive advantage to those Asian firms that were able to obtain and maintain the contract.

These findings lead us towards an analysis of the organization of local economies in an age of global capitalism. The economic organization of South Korea and Taiwan cannot be understood without reference to the demand-pull of the United States, just as the same is true for the tremendous growth in China today. W. B. Yeats famously concluded one of his poems with the line, "How do we know the dancer from the dance?" This question goes to the heart of our inquiry. Many economists and sociologists focus on the dancer without seeing the dance. They equate the dancer, stopped still in her motion, with the dance. For us the key questions are not whether institutions and firms and networks matter, or whether transaction costs are important. We know all these are crucial to the ongoing economic activities. Rather, the key question is how these relate to and become manifestations of the processes of capitalism.

Appendix A

Mathematical Model of Business Groups

The model of business groups described in Chapters 3 and 4 is formally developed in Feenstra, Huang, and Hamilton (2003), which is reproduced in part here, along with the mathematical Appendix from that paper.

The business groups model is a natural extension of the monopolistic competition framework used in industrial organization (Dixit and Stiglitz, 1977, Spence, 1976) and international trade (Helpman and Krugman, 1985). In this framework there are large numbers of firms, each producing a unique product. Although it is normally assumed that the firms operate independently, we shall allow groups of firms to *jointly maximize profits*, and such a group of firms is called a "business group." Equivalently, we can think of a business group as a multi-product company, that chooses both the range of upstream and downstream goods to produce, and their optimal prices. Helpman and Krugman (1985, pp. 220–2) recognized that the monopolistic competition model had the potential to include economic organization in their discussion of "industrial complexes," but this idea was not pursued further in the trade context; instead, the upstream and downstream linkages between firms became a building block of the new models in economic geography (Krugman, 1991, 1996). The equilibrium concept we use is closest in spirit to the work in industrial organization by Perry (1989, pp. 229–35), though also anticipated by the early work of Caves (1974).

A Model of Business Groups

We will consider an economy divided into two sectors: an upstream sector producing intermediate inputs from labor and a downstream sector using these intermediate inputs (and additional labor) to produce a final good. The final good could be sold to firms (as a capital good) or to consumers, but for concreteness, we will consider only the latter case. The

365

intermediate inputs are not be traded internationally, but the final good is traded. Suppose that both the sectors are characterized by product differentiation, so that each firm charges a price that is above its marginal cost of production. As usual under monopolistic competition, we will allow for the free entry of firms in both the upstream and downstream sectors, to the point where profits are driven to zero.

In contrast to conventional treatments of monopolistic competition, we will also allow groups to produce *multiple varieties* of inputs and outputs. In particular, there will be an incentive to produce both upstream and downstream products to take advantage of the efficiencies from marginal cost pricing of the intermediate input. The running of a group can be expected to have some costs of bargaining and agency, associated with distributing the group's profits among affiliate firms. This is very much in the spirit of the diseconomies of size discussed by Williamson (1975, Chap. 7, 1985, Chap. 6), and some kind of diseconomy of firm or group size must be present in any organizational model. Modeling these "governance costs" in any detail would lead us into financial details about the relationship between groups and banks, which is well beyond the scope of our market-power based model.[1] So we will simply assume that they take the form of a *fixed cost* α associated with the running of a business group, and in addition, *additional costs* associated with each intermediate and final product produced by the group (over and above the research and development costs that an unaffiliated firm would incur for such products). In the same way that we allow for the free entry of individual firms, we will also allow for the free entry of business groups.

It will be important to specify the sequence of decisions in this model. One possibility is to consider a three-stage game, where the price and number of *final goods* for groups, (q_{bi}, N_{bi}), $i = 1, \ldots, G$, and the *price* for unaffiliated downstream firms, q_{cj}, $j = 1, \ldots, N_c$, are determined in the *third stage*; the price and number of *intermediate inputs*, (p_{bi}, M_{bi}), $i = 1, \ldots, G$, and the *price* of unaffiliated upstream firms, p_{cj}, $j = 1, \ldots, M_c$, are determined in the *second stage*; and the *number of groups and unaffiliated firms* G, M_c, and N_c are determined in the *first stage* to ensure non-positive profits. This formulation would ensure that when group i sells its intermediate inputs externally at the price of p_{bi}, it will take

---

[1] Theoretical models of financially interlinked groups include Kim (2004), Fung (2002) and Ghatak and Kali (2001). In empirical work, Hoshi, Kashyap and Scharfstein (1990b) investigate firms that *left* bank-centered groups following deregulation in 1983, and suggest that one reason this may have occurred was due to conflicting objectives of the banks and shareholders, where the banks are too conservative. Along different lines, Khanna and Palepu (2000b) investigate Indian groups, and find that groups with greater internal financial transfers (and, therefore, less transparency) are less attractive targets for foreign investment.

into account the effect of this on the final goods price q_{bj} of all other groups, $j \neq i$, since these are chosen at a later stage. But this formulation leaves out the possibility that a group can exercise some vertical restraint over its downstream firms, such as resale price maintenance, and thereby *commit* to certain prices for final goods. Since resale price maintenance is an assumption sometimes used in models of wholesalers-retailers (see Ordover, et al., 1990, 1992, Chen, 1999, 2001), we will want to give the same degree of control to business groups, and shall incorporate it into our model.

Rather than considering a resale price ceiling or floor, we will instead allow for a *pricing rule*, whereby business group i commits to price its final goods at the markup μ_{bi} over marginal cost. Denoting marginal costs by ϕ_{bi}, the final goods prices are then $q_{bi} = \mu_{bi}\phi_{bi}$, where μ_{bi} is chosen optimally at the *second stage* of the game (given the choices of the other groups). There is now little reason to distinguish the second and third stage, and we will collapse these decisions into a *single stage*, where the strategies chosen are $(p_{bi}, M_{bi}, \mu_{bi}, N_{bi})$ for each business group $i = 1, \ldots, G$, the prices $p_{cj}, j = 1, \ldots, M_c$ for upstream unaffiliated firms, and the markups μ_{cj} for downstream unaffiliated firms, $j = 1, \ldots, N_c$. Given these optimal strategies, the number of groups and unaffiliated firms are determined at a prior stage to ensure non-positive profits.

Making this setup explicit, the business groups $i = 1, \ldots, G$ each maximize joint profits,

$$\max_{\{p_{bi}, M_{bi}, \mu_{bi}, N_{bi}\}} \Pi_{bi} = N_{bi}[y_{bi}(\mu_{bi} - 1)\phi_{bi} - k_{yb}] + M_{bi}[\tilde{x}_{bi}(p_{bi} - 1) - k_{xb}] - \alpha, \tag{1}$$

where: N_{bi} is the number of final goods, produced with fixed costs k_{yb}; y_{bi} is the output of each final good, produced with marginal cost ϕ_{bi} and sold at the price $q_{bi} = \mu_{bi}\phi_{bi}$; M_{bi} is the number of intermediate inputs, produced with fixed costs of k_{xb}; $\tilde{x}_{bi}$ is the quantity sold *outside* the group of each intermediate input, at the price p_{bi} and produced with marginal costs of unity; and α is the level of fixed "governance costs" associated with the running of a business group. Governance costs may also depend on the size of the group, measured by the numbers of products N_{bi} and M_{bi}, and to allow for this we permit the fixed costs k_{yb} and k_{xb} for business groups to *exceed* those for unaffiliated firms.

In addition to the external sales of inputs at the price p_{bi}, the group will sell its inputs internally at marginal costs of unity, and we will denote the *internal* quantity sold by x_{bi}. It is quite possible that the profits earned by the upstream firms, which is the second bracketed term on the right of (1), are negative because these inputs are sold internally at marginal cost. Thus, we would expect some transfer from the downstream to the upstream firms to cover these losses. Our key simplifying assumption on the "governance costs" is that *they do not depend on the amount on the amount of the transfer*, though they can depend on the numbers of upstream and downstream firms, as noted previously. It is this simplifying assumption that allows us to ignore the transfer in the specification of (1).[2]

The marginal cost of producing each output variety for the group $j = 1, \ldots, G$ is assumed to be given by the CES function:

$$\phi_{bj} = w^{\beta} \left(M_{bj} + \sum_{i=1, i \neq j}^{G} M_{bi} \, p_{bi}^{1-\sigma} + \sum_{i=1}^{M_c} p_{ci}^{1-\sigma} \right)^{\left(\frac{1-\beta}{1-\sigma} \right)}, \tag{2}$$

where: w is the wage rate, and labor is a proportion β of marginal costs; M_{bj} inputs are purchased internally at the price of unity; M_{bi} inputs are purchased from the other $i = 1, \ldots, G, i \neq j$ groups, at the price of p_{bi}; and M_c inputs are purchased from unaffiliated upstream firms at the price of $p_{ci}, i = 1, \ldots, M_c$. We will set $w = 1$ by choice of numeraire, and suppress it in all that follows. The elasticity of substitution σ is assumed to exceed unity, so that it is meaningful to think of changes in the number of inputs available from each source.

Turning to the unaffiliated firms, the upstream firms $j = 1, \ldots, M_c$ each choose their price to maximize profits:

$$\max_{p_{cj}} x_{cj}(p_{cj} - 1) - k_{xc}, \tag{3}$$

where: x_{cj} is the output of each intermediate input, sold at price p_{cj} and produced with marginal cost of unity and fixed costs k_{xc}. Similarly, the unaffiliated downstream firms $j = 1, \ldots, N_c$ each choose their markup μ_{cj} to maximize profits:

$$\max_{\mu_{cj}} y_{cj}(\mu_{cj} - 1)\phi_c - k_{yc}, \tag{4}$$

where: y_{cj} is the output of each final good, produced with marginal cost ϕ_c and fixed costs k_{yc} and sold at price $q_{cj} = \mu_{cj}\phi_c$. The marginal cost of producing each output variety is:

$$\phi_c = \left(\sum_{i=1}^{G} M_{bi} \, p_{bi}^{1-\sigma} + \sum_{j=1}^{M_c} p_{cj}^{1-\sigma} \right)^{\left(\frac{1-\beta}{1-\sigma} \right)}, \tag{5}$$

---

[2] Indeed, given this assumption, we can provide for weaker group incentives, such as Nash bargaining between the upstream and downstream firms over profits (Pepall and Norman, 2001). This would still imply the maximization of groups profits overall, with the bargaining strength of individual firms then affecting their share of profits.

where: M_{bi} are inputs purchased from $i = 1, \ldots, G$ business groups at the price of p_{bi}, and M_c inputs are purchased from unaffiliated upstream firms $j = 1, \ldots, M_c$ at the price of p_{cj}. Recalling that we have normalized $w = 1$, it is apparent that the marginal costs for a business group in (2) are *less than* those for an unaffiliated firm in (5), because the business groups are able to purchase their own inputs at the cost of unity.

Using the cost functions, we can also define the external sales of each intermediate input, $\tilde{x}_{bi}$, which appears in (1). Specifically, we differentiate (2) and (5) with respect to the price p_{bi}, multiply these by the outputs $N_{bj} y_{bj}$ and y_{cj}, respectively, and sum these to obtain:

$$\tilde{x}_{bi} = \frac{1}{M_{bi}} \left[\sum_{j=1, j \neq i}^{G} N_{bj} y_{bj} \left(\frac{\partial \phi_{bj}}{\partial p_{bi}} \right) + \sum_{j=1}^{N_c} y_{cj} \left(\frac{\partial \phi_c}{\partial p_{bi}} \right) \right]. \tag{6}$$

The term $(1/M_{bi})$ appears because $\tilde{x}_{bi}$ refers to the external demand for *each* intermediate input sold group i, of which there are M_{bi} in total. Substituting (6) into (1) gives the complete expression for profits of a business group.

With profits maximized as in (1), (3), and (4), we will restrict our attention to *symmetric* equilibria, where each business group produces the same number M_b of intermediate inputs and N_b of final goods, sold at prices p_b and markups μ_b, respectively. Similarly, unaffiliated upstream and downstream firms each have the same prices, denoted by p_c and $q_c = \mu_c \phi_c$, respectively. Then we choose the total number of business groups G, as well as the number of upstream and downstream products from unaffiliated firms, M_c and N_c final goods, such that profits for all these groups are non-positive. A key question of interest will be whether the solutions for G, M_c and N_c are unique or not: is there more than one configuration of groups and unaffiliated firms that are consistent with equilibrium?

The possibility of multiple equilibria will depend on the optimal prices, of course, and we shall solve for these in the next section. But even before this, it useful to consider the possible configurations of groups and unaffiliated firms that can arise in equilibrium. This will depend very much on the level of "governance costs" within the groups. If these costs were zero, then a group would be more efficient than a like-number of unaffiliated upstream and downstream firms (due to its internal marginal cost pricing of inputs). Then in a zero-profit equilibrium for groups, the profits of unaffiliated firms would be negative, and they would never enter. Focusing on this equilibrium alone would be uninteresting from an organizational point of view. Conversely, if the governance costs are large then both upstream and downstream unaffiliated firms, together with groups, could very well occur in a zero-profit equilibrium. This is probably realistic, but having all types of firms makes the computation of equilibria intractable. Accordingly, we take a "middle of the road" approach, and will assume that the governance costs are large enough to allow the possibility that either upstream or downstream unaffiliated firms to enter, but small enough to prevent entry of both types.

With these assumptions, the equilibria that we consider will have one of three possible configurations: (1) *V-groups* – the business groups prevent the entry of unaffiliated producers in both the upstream and downstream sectors ($M_c = N_c = 0$), and are therefore strongly vertically integrated; (2) *D-groups* – business groups are the only firms in the downstream sector ($N_c = 0$) and are vertically integrated upstream, while purchasing inputs from some unaffiliated upstream firms ($M_c > 0$); (3) *U-groups* – business groups are the only firms in the upstream sector ($M_c = 0$) and are vertically integrated downstream, but also compete with some unaffiliated downstream firms ($N_c > 0$). We stress that this terminology does not make any presumption about the *horizontal integration* of the various types of groups: this is something that we will have to determine in equilibrium. In fact, it will turn out that the largest V-groups are also spread horizontally over a wide range of products, much like the largest *chaebol* in Korea.

In order to observe a U-group or D-group equilibrium, we further need to rule out the possibility that all unaffiliated firms would want to *merge* with a business group. This is ruled out by supposing that unaffiliated firms have lower fixed costs associated with each product, which are automatically increased if that firm is part of a group: that is, we will assume that $k_{yb} \geq k_{yc}$ and $k_{xb} \geq k_{xc}$, with these inequalities holding as strict when needed to make merger unprofitable. These extra fixed costs associated with the business group should be interpreted as governance costs that are *additional to* the fixed costs of α. The precise specification of fixed costs that will rule out merger will depend on the equilibrium. Despite the somewhat *ad hoc* nature of this assumption, we emphasize that it is made as a compromise between tractability (preventing all firms from entering) and interest (having the possibility that some unaffiliated firms will enter, and not merge). This still leaves the possibility of mergers across groups. In order to rule out this activity we need to appeal to some extra costs associated with governing a group of increasing size, that lie outside the notation of our model. With this list of assumptions, we can turn to the solution of the model.

Prices and Output of the Business Groups

We assume that demand for the differentiated final products arises from a CES demand system with elasticity η and that the final products are traded internationally. It follows that the demand for a single output variety from a business group can be written as:

$$y_{bi} = \frac{q_{bi}^{-\eta}(L + w^* L^*)}{\left[\sum_{j=1}^{G} N_{bj} q_{bj}^{1-\eta} + \sum_{j=1}^{N_c} q_{cj}^{1-\eta} + N^*(q^*)^{1-\eta}\right]}, \tag{7}$$

where $w^* L^*$ in the numerator is foreign income, and N^* in the denominator is the range of foreign varieties, sold at the price of q^*. Because the intermediate inputs are not traded, trade is balanced in the final goods sector. Due to trade-balance, the foreign wage and price in (7) are endogenous, and if we solve for their equilibrium values, the demand expression is simplified as,[3]

$$y_{bi} = \frac{q_{bi}^{-\eta} L}{\left[\sum_{j=1}^{G} N_{bj} q_{bj}^{1-\eta} + \sum_{j=1}^{N_c} q_{cj}^{1-\eta}\right]}. \tag{7'}$$

This is identical to the expression for demand in a closed economy. That is, making use of the trade-balance condition, the total (domestic plus foreign) demand for each final product with trade in (7) is identical to the domestic demand in the absence of trade in (7'): while trade benefits consumers through increased product variety, it does not affect the pricing decisions of firms. It follows that the equilibria that we shall compute are equally valid in an open or a closed economy: the assumption of trade balance has eliminated any difference between these from the firms' point of view.

We shall use this demand system to compute optimal markups on final goods, and for convenience, express these in the *symmetric* equilibrium (dropping the subscripts distinguishing each group and unaffiliated firms). Given the CES demand function in (7), the optimal markup for each unaffiliated downstream firm equals:

$$\mu_c - 1 = \left(\frac{1}{\eta - 1}\right). \tag{8}$$

Substituting (8) into (4), profits become $[y_c/(\eta - 1)] - k_{yc}$ and setting these equal to zero we obtain the level of output:

$$y_c = (\eta - 1)k_{yc}/\phi_c. \tag{9}$$

---

[3] Trade balance in final goods means that home import expenditure equals home exports. Denoting the denominator of (7) by D, trade balance is expressed as: $LN^*(q^*)^{1-\eta}/D = w^* L^*(\sum_{j=1}^{G} N_{bj} q_{bj}^{1-\eta} + \sum_{j=1}^{N_c} q_{cj}^{1-\eta})/D$. Using this equality in (7), we immediately obtain (7').

While this expression for output under monopolistic competition is not that familiar, it follows directly from the markups in (8), and will be useful in computing equilibria.

Turning to the business groups, we solve for the number of final goods N_b, and the optimal markup μ_b for each group. Note that there is a natural limit on the range of varieties that any group will want to produce. Starting with a group of some size, if it were to develop another differentiated final product for sale to consumers, then this would involve the usual fixed costs, but the revenue received from the sale of the good would in part come by drawing demand away from other products sold by the same group. Thus, after it has reached some size a group would no longer find it profitable to expand its range of final goods, even though an unaffiliated firm might choose to enter the market.

Each business groups sells a positive range N_b of final products, and it follows from (7) that the elasticity of demand with respect to a change in the price of its products is,

$$\frac{\partial y_{bi}}{\partial q_{bi}} \frac{q_{bi}}{y_{bi}} = -[\eta + s_{ybi}(1 - \eta)], \tag{10}$$

where s_{ybi} denotes the market share of its products:

$$s_{ybi} = \frac{N_{bi} q_{bi}^{1-\eta}}{\left(\sum_{j=1}^{G} N_{bj} q_{bj}^{1-\eta} + \sum_{j=1}^{N_c} q_{cj}^{1-\eta}\right)}. \tag{11}$$

Using symmetry, the optimal markup of price over marginal cost therefore equals,

$$\mu_b - 1 = \frac{1}{[\eta + s_{yb}(1 - \eta) - 1]}. \tag{12}$$

To determine the optimal number of output varieties, we can differentiate (1) with respect to the number of varieties sold by a single group, and set this equal to zero, obtaining:[4]

$$y_b(\mu_b - 1)\phi_b - k_{yb} - s_{yb}y_b(q_b - \phi_b) = 0. \tag{13}$$

The first terms on the right of (13) are the direct gain in profits from selling another output variety, less the fixed costs of production. However, expanding product variety will also have the effect of reducing the demand for other varieties sold by the same group, which is the last term on the

---

[4] To derive (13), we differentiate (7′) with respect to the number of varieties sold by a single group, obtaining $dy_{bi}/dN_{bi} = -y_{bi} q_{bi}^{1-\eta}/(\sum_{j=1}^{G} N_{bj} q_{bj}^{1-\eta} + \sum_{j=1}^{N_c} q_{cj}^{1-\eta}) = -s_{ybi} y_{bi}/N_{bi}$. Using this and symmetry, we readily obtain (13) by differentiating (1).

right of (13). The optimal choice for the number of product varieties will just balance these two effects.

Notice that combining (12) and (13) we obtain, $[y_b \phi_b / (\eta - 1)] - k_{yb} = 0$. Therefore, we obtain the final output of a downstream group firm:

$$y_b = (\eta - 1)k_{yb}/\phi_b. \tag{14}$$

Thus, we obtain the same general formula for output for the business groups in (14) and unaffiliated downstream firms in (9), though with the business group having lower marginal costs ($\phi_b < \phi_c$) and higher fixed costs ($k_{yb} \geq k_{yc}$), their output is correspondingly *higher*. Intuitively, the economies of scale inherent in a vertically integrated group lead it to produce longer production runs.

While business groups sell a higher quantity of each final good, it is also the case that their *sales revenue* from each final variety exceeds that of an unaffiliated downstream firm. This can be seen by comparing (9) and (14), obtaining $\phi_b y_b = (\eta - 1)k_{yb} \geq (\eta - 1)k_{yc} = \phi_c y_c$. With the markup over marginal costs higher for the group than an unaffiliated firm [compare (8) and (12)], it immediately follows that $q_b y_b > q_c y_c$, so that the *sales revenue* from each downstream product produced by a business group exceeds that for an unaffiliated downstream firm. This result has important implications for *total variety* of final goods in the economy.

To determine downstream variety, we close the model with the full employment condition. There are several ways to write this, but one that will be convenient is the equality of national product measured by the value of final goods, and total wage income received. The latter is just L, or the labor supply. The former is the total value of final goods produced by business groups and any nonaffiliated downstream firms, so that,

$$L = G N_b q_b y_b + N_c q_c y_c. \tag{15}$$

If there are only business groups in equilibrium, then product variety is $G N_b = L/q_b y_b$, whereas if there are only unaffiliated firms then product variety is $N_c = L/q_c y_c$. With $q_b y_b > q_c y_c$ as shown previously, it follows immediately that *an economy that includes business groups will have a lower variety of final goods than an economy with the same parameters, but that is composed entirely of unaffiliated firms*. This finding generalizes the result of Perry and Groff (1985).

We next solve for the prices of the upstream unaffiliated firms. The elasticity of demand facing the upstream firms is σ, so that the markup of the optimal price over marginal costs equals:

$$p_c - 1 = \left(\frac{1}{\sigma - 1} \right). \tag{16}$$

Substituting this into (3), we see that profits equal $[x_c/(\sigma - 1)] - k_{xc}$ and setting these equal to zero we obtain the level of output in the free-entry equilibrium:

$$x_c = (\sigma - 1)k_{xc}. \tag{17}$$

Again, we obtain a simple expression for output under monopolistic competition, which will be useful in computing equilibria.

Finally, we turn to the optimal range of inputs developed by each group (M_b) and the price for external sale of these inputs (p_b). Choosing M_b to maximize profits in (1), the following result is derived in the next section:

LEMMA 1. *When the business group choose product variety optimally, then,*

$$x_b + \tilde{x}_b = (\sigma - 1)k_{xb}. \tag{18}$$

Thus, we obtain the same general formula for the sales of each input for the business groups in (18) and unaffiliated upstream firms in (7), though with the business group having higher fixed costs ($k_{xb} \geq k_{xc}$), their sales of each input can be higher. The finding that the formulas in (7) and (18) are so similar is a rather remarkable result, considering the fact that group firms charge different prices for the sales of the intermediate input to firms within and outside its own group. Indeed, there is no guarantee that group firms will find it optimal to sell to outside firms at all: the optimal price for outside sales may be $p_b = +\infty$. By definition this situation cannot arise in a *U-group* equilibrium, since in that case there are no unaffiliated upstream producers, so that if the business groups decided to not sell intermediate inputs then no unaffiliated downstream producers could survive (and the equilibrium would be one of *V-groups*). Thus, to determine whether the groups will choose to sell to other firms, we focus on the case of either *V-groups* or *D-groups*, so that $N_c = 0$:

LEMMA 2. *Suppose that* $N_c = 0$. *Then each group will sell inputs to the other groups if and only if,*

$$G > \left(\frac{\sigma}{\sigma - 1}\right), \tag{19}$$

in which case the optimal prices are given by:

$$\left(\frac{p_b - 1}{p_b}\right) = \frac{1}{[\sigma + s_{xb}(1 - \sigma)]}\left(\frac{G}{G - 1}\right). \tag{20}$$

This result is also proved in the next section. In (20), s_{xb} is the share of total sales of intermediate inputs made by each business group, given by,

$$s_{xb} = \left[\frac{M_b p_b^{1-\sigma}}{(G-1)M_b p_b^{1-\sigma} + M_b + M_c p_c^{1-\sigma}} \right]. \tag{21}$$

The term $[\sigma + s_{xb}(1 - \sigma)]$ is the elasticity of demand for input varieties from one group. Equation (20) differs from the standard Lerner formula by the extra term $G/(G-1) > 1$. This reflects the fact that when a group sells an input, it will give competing firms a cost advantage, thereby lowering profits in the final goods market. Accordingly, it will charge a higher price than usual. If G is too small, so that (19) is violated, then profits will continually increase as p_b is raised and the group optimally chooses $p_b = +\infty$. In this situation the groups sells none of their inputs externally, and $\tilde{x}_{bi} = 0$ in (6) for $i = 1, \ldots, G$.

With this description of business groups' pricing and output decisions, it becomes possible to compute equilibria for the economy. In addition to the equations shown previously, the complete model consists of a number of business groups G, and nonaffiliated firms M_c and N_c, such that the profits earned by each group are non-positive and there is full employment. In the next section, we show how a small number of (nonlinear) equations characterize equilibria in each of the three configurations: (1) *V-groups* – business groups drive out unaffiliated producers in both the upstream and downstream sectors; (2) *D-groups* – business groups are the only firms in the downstream sector; and (3) *U-groups* – business groups are the only firms in the upstream sector. We solve these equations from a wide range of starting values in order to check for possible equilibria. As noted earlier, we will chose the fixed governance costs intentionally to rule out the complex case where all types of firms coexist.

Proofs of Lemmas and Derivation of Equilibria

To solve for the equilibria, we will make use of the full-employment condition, which in written in the symmetric equilibrium as:

$$L = GN_b k_{yb} + GN_b \beta y_b \phi_b + GM_b k_{xb} + GM_b x_b$$
$$+ GM_b \tilde{x}_b + G\alpha + N_c k_{yc} + N_c \beta y_c \phi_c + M_c k_{xc} + M_c x_c.$$

Using (9), (14), (17) and (18), this is simplified as,

$$L = G\left[N_b k_{yb}(1 + \beta(\eta - 1)) + M_b k_{xb}\sigma + \alpha \right]$$
$$+ N_c k_{yc}(1 + \beta(\eta - 1)) + M_c k_{xc}\sigma. \tag{22}$$

Another useful relation is the equality of GDP as total factor income and the value of final sales,

$$L = GN_b q_b y_b + N_c q_c y_c. \tag{23}$$

Using (8), (9), (12), and (14), this is written in the symmetric equilibrium as,

$$L = GN_b k_{yb} \left[\eta + \left(\frac{s_{yb}}{1 - s_{yb}} \right) \right] + N_c k_{yc} \eta. \tag{24}$$

We should also indicate the values for internal and external sales of inputs, x_{bi} and $\tilde{x}_{bi}$. *External* sales of each input variety shown in (6) can be written as $\tilde{x}_{bi} = \tilde{x}_{bbi} + \tilde{x}_{bci}$, where $\tilde{x}_{bbi}$ is sales to other groups and $\tilde{x}_{bci}$ is sales to downstream unaffiliated firms. Computing the derivative of unit-costs, the sales to other business groups are,

$$
\begin{aligned}
\tilde{x}_{bbi} &= \sum_{j=1, j \neq i}^{G} p_{bi}^{-\sigma} \left[\frac{y_{bj} \phi_{bj} (1 - \beta) N_{bj}}{M_{bj} + \sum_{i=1, i \neq j}^{G} M_{bi} p_{bi}^{1-\sigma} + \sum_{i=1}^{M_c} p_{ci}^{1-\sigma}} \right] \\
&= p_b^{-\sigma} \left[\frac{(G-1) y_b \phi_b (1 - \beta) N_b}{M_b + (G-1) M_b p_b^{1-\sigma} + M_c p_c^{1-\sigma}} \right]
\end{aligned}
\tag{25a}
$$

where the second line applies in the symmetric equilibrium. The sales to unaffiliated firms are,

$$
\begin{aligned}
\tilde{x}_{bci} &= \sum_{j=1}^{N_c} p_{bi}^{-\sigma} \left[\frac{y_{cj} \phi_c (1 - \beta)}{\sum_{i=1}^{G} M_{bi} p_{bi}^{1-\sigma} + \sum_{i=1}^{M_c} p_{ci}^{1-\sigma}} \right] \\
&= p_b^{-\sigma} \left[\frac{y_c \phi_c (1 - \beta) N_c}{G M_b p_b^{1-\sigma} + M_c p_c^{1-\sigma}} \right]
\end{aligned}
\tag{25b}
$$

where the second line applies in the symmetric equilibrium. Similarly, *internal* sales of each product variety are,

$$
\begin{aligned}
x_{bi} &= \frac{y_{bi} \phi_{bi} (1 - \beta) N_{bi}}{\left[M_{bi} + \sum_{j=1, j \neq i}^{G} M_{bj} p_{bj}^{1-\sigma} + \sum_{j=1}^{M_c} p_{cj}^{1-\sigma} \right]} \\
&= \frac{y_b \phi_b (1 - \beta) N_b}{\left[M_b + (G-1) M_b p_b^{1-\sigma} + M_c p_c^{1-\sigma} \right]}
\end{aligned}
\tag{26}
$$

where the second line applies in the symmetric equilibrium.

LEMMA I. *When the business group choose product variety optimally, then,*

$$x_b + \tilde{x}_b = (\sigma - 1) k_{xb}. \tag{18}$$

Proof: We need to differentiate (1) with respect to M_{bi} and set this equal to zero. Since profits in (1) have been maximized with respect to the markup μ_{bi}, it is legitimate to consider a small change $d\mu_{bi}$ chosen to ensure that the change in M_{bi} has *no effect of the final-goods price* $q_{bi} = \mu_{bi}\phi_{bi}$ charged by group i. Specifically, we will choose $d\mu_{bi}$ such that:

$$dq_{bi} = \mu_{bi}d\phi_{bi} + d\mu_{bi}\phi_{bi} = 0 \quad \Rightarrow \quad d\mu_{bi}/d\phi_{bi} = -(\mu_{bi}/\phi_{bi}).$$

Suppose first that there are no external sales of the intermediate inputs by group i, $\tilde{x}_{bi} = 0$. Because the price q_{bi} is constant, it follows that the demand y_{bi} for each final good of group i is also constant, so that change in M_{bi} only affects costs. Then from (1) we have,

$$\frac{d\prod_{bi}}{dM_{bi}} = N_{bi}\left[y_{bi}(\mu_{bi} - 1) + \frac{d\mu_{bi}}{d\phi_{bi}}y_{bi}\phi_{bi}\right]\frac{\partial\phi_{bi}}{\partial M_{bi}} - k_{xb}$$

$$= -y_{bi}N_{bi}\frac{\partial\phi_{bi}}{\partial M_{bi}} - k_{xb} = \frac{x_{bi}}{(\sigma - 1)} - k_{xb}, \tag{27}$$

where the second equality follows by using $d\mu_{bi}/d\phi_{bi} = -(\mu_{bi}/\phi_{bi})$, and the final equality follows from differentiating (2) and comparing the result to (26). Then (18) follows by setting (27) equal to zero, and using symmetry.

Now suppose that there are sales of the inputs outside the group. From (2), the costs to other groups depends on $M_{bi}p_{bi}^{1-\sigma}$, chosen by group i. Since profits in (1) are maximized with respect to p_{bi}, we can consider a small change in p_{bi} designed to keep this magnitude constant,

$$dM_{bi}p_{bi}^{1-\sigma} + (1 - \sigma)M_{bi}p_{bi}^{-\sigma}dp_{bi} = 0. \tag{28}$$

We will consider the optimal choice of M_{bi} with p_{bi} adjusting as in (28), which ensures that the costs of the other groups and therefore their own final-goods prices are constant. With q_{bi} and q_{bj} all constant, then demand y_{bi} is also constant. The change in profits of group i is,

$$\left.\frac{d\prod_{bi}}{dM_{bi}}\right|_{(28)} = \frac{\partial\prod_{bi}}{\partial M_{bi}} + \left.\frac{d\prod_{bi}}{dp_{bi}}\right|_{(28)}\left.\frac{dp_{bi}}{dM_{bi}}\right|_{(28)}.$$

Using (1), the same steps as in (27), and (28) this is evaluated as,

$$\left.\frac{d\prod_{bi}}{dM_{bi}}\right|_{(28)} = \frac{x_{bi}}{(\sigma - 1)} - k_{xb} + \tilde{x}_{bi}(p_{bi} - 1)$$

$$+ \left[\tilde{x}_{bi}M_{bi} + M_{bi}(p_{bi} - 1)\left.\frac{d\tilde{x}_{bi}}{dp_{bi}}\right|_{(28)}\right]\left.\frac{dp_{bi}}{dM_{bi}}\right|_{(28)}$$

$$= \frac{x_{bi}}{(\sigma - 1)} - k_{xb} + \tilde{x}_{bi}(p_{bi} - 1)$$

$$+ \left[1 - \sigma \left(\frac{p_{bi} - 1}{p_{bi}} \right) \right] \frac{\tilde{x}_{bi} \, p_{bi}}{(\sigma - 1)}$$

$$= \frac{x_{bi}}{(\sigma - 1)} - k_{xb} + \frac{\tilde{x}_{bi}}{(\sigma - 1)}, \tag{29}$$

where the second equality follows by computing $\partial \tilde{x}_{bi}/\partial p_{bi}$ from (25a,b) while keeping $M_{bi} \, p_{bi}^{1-\sigma}$ constant in the denominator, and by computing dp_{bi}/dM_{bi} from (28). Setting (29) equal to zero and using symmetry, we obtain (18). QED

LEMMA 2. *Suppose that $N_c = 0$. Then each group will sell inputs to the other groups if and only if,*

$$G > \left(\frac{\sigma}{\sigma - 1} \right), \tag{19}$$

in which case the optimal prices are given by:

$$\left(\frac{p_b - 1}{p_b} \right) = \frac{1}{[\sigma + s_{xb}(1 - \sigma)]} \left(\frac{G}{G - 1} \right). \tag{20}$$

Proof: Let p_{bi} and q_{bi} denote the prices chosen by group i, with p_{bj} and q_{bj} the prices of the other groups $j = 1, \ldots, G$, $j \neq i$. As p_{bi} is increased, this will raise the costs to the other groups and, therefore, increase $q_{bj} = \mu_{bj}\phi_{bj}$, holding fixed the optimal markups μ_{bj}. Since profits in (1) have been maximized with respect to the markup μ_{bi}, it is legitimate to consider a small change $d\mu_{bi}$ to ensure that the *change in the prices of final goods by all groups are equal*. Specifically, we will choose $d\mu_{bi}$ such that:

$$dq_{bi} = d\mu_{bi}\phi_{bi} = dq_{bj} = \mu_{bj}(\partial \phi_{bj}/\partial p_{bi})dp_{bi}. \tag{30}$$

The left of this expression is the change in the price of final goods for group i, due to a small change in its markup, and on the right is the change in the final goods price of another group j, due to a change in the price p_{bi} of intermediate inputs sold by group i (but holding the markup of group j fixed at its optimal level). By ensuring that all final goods prices change by the same amount, this ensures that the *relative outputs and market shares of all final goods are unchanged*. This will simplify the calculation of the change in group i profits due to the combined change $(d\mu_{bi}, dp_{bi})$ satisfying (30).

Using symmetry of the initial equilibrium, we divide (30) by $q_{bi} = q_{bj} = \mu_{bj}\phi_{bj}$, and rewrite this expression as,

$$\frac{dq_{bi}}{dp_{bi}} \frac{1}{q_{bi}} = \frac{dq_{bj}}{dp_{bi}} \frac{1}{q_{bj}} = \frac{\partial \phi_{bj}}{\partial p_{bi}} \frac{1}{\phi_{bj}}. \tag{30'}$$

Thus, with a rise in p_{bi} leading to equi-proportional increases in q_{bi}, q_{bj}, and ϕ_{bj}, and total consumer expenditure fixed at L, these price increases must be matched with equi-proportional reductions in final goods output y_{bi} and y_{bj}. Thus,

$$\left.\frac{dy_{bi}}{dp_{bi}}\right|_{(30)} \frac{1}{y_{bi}} = \left.\frac{-dq_{bi}}{dp_{bi}}\right|_{(30)} \frac{1}{q_{bi}}, \quad i = 1, \dots, G. \tag{31}$$

Notice that this implies that $q_{bi}\, y_{bi}$ is constant under (30), as is $\phi_{bj}\, y_{bj}$.

The total change in profits for group i is,

$$\left.\frac{d\prod_{bi}}{dp_{bi}}\right|_{(30)} = \frac{\partial\prod_{bi}}{\partial p_{bi}} + \left.\frac{d\prod_{bi}}{dq_{bi}}\right|_{(30)} \left.\frac{dq_{bi}}{dp_{bi}}\right|_{(30)}$$

$$+ \sum_{j=1,\, j\neq i}^{G} \left.\frac{d\prod_{bi}}{dq_{bj}}\right|_{(30)} \left.\frac{dq_{bj}}{dp_{bi}}\right|_{(30)}.$$

Using (1), this is evaluated as,

$$\left.\frac{d\prod_{bi}}{dp_{bi}}\right|_{(30)} = M_{bi}\left[\tilde{x}_{bi} + (p_{bi} - 1)\frac{\partial\tilde{x}_{bi}}{\partial p_{bi}}\right] + N_{bi}\phi_{bi}\left.\frac{dy_{bi}}{dp_{bi}}\right|_{(30)}. \tag{32}$$

In the first term of (32), the elasticity $-(\partial\tilde{x}_{bi}/\partial p_{bi})(p_{bi}/\tilde{x}_{bi})$ is computed from (25a) (holding $\phi_{bj}\, y_{bj}$ constant) as $[\sigma + s_{xbi}(1 - \sigma)]$, where s_{xbi} is the intermediate market share of group i, given by:

$$s_{xbi} = \left[\frac{M_{bi}\, p_{bi}^{1-\sigma}}{M_{bi} + \sum_{j=1,\, j\neq i}^{G} M_{bj}\, p_{bj}^{1-\sigma} + \sum_{j=1}^{M_c} p_{cj}^{1-\sigma}}\right].$$

This expression appears as (21) under symmetry.

In the second term of (32), we note that equi-proportional increases in q_{bi} and reduction in y_{bi} has the effect of holding $q_{bi}\, y_{bi}$ constant in profits, and simply reducing y_{bi} by the amount given by the last term in (30'). To evaluate this term, differentiate (2) to compute,

$$\frac{\partial\phi_{bj}}{\partial p_{bi}} = p_{bi}^{-\sigma}\left[\frac{\phi_{bj}(1 - \beta)M_{bi}}{M_{bj} + \sum_{i=1,\, i\neq j}^{G} M_{bi}\, p_{bi}^{1-\sigma} + \sum_{i=1}^{M_c} p_{ci}^{1-\sigma}}\right]$$

$$= \left[\frac{\tilde{x}_b M_b}{y_b(G - 1)N_b}\right], \tag{33}$$

where the second line applies with symmetry, with $\tilde{x}_b$ given by (25a). Then combining (31)–(33) and using symmetry, we obtain,

$$\left.\frac{d\prod_{bi}}{dp_{bi}}\right|_{(30)} = M_b\tilde{x}_b\left\{1 - \left(\frac{p_b - 1}{p_b}\right)[\sigma + s_{xb}(\sigma + 1)] + \frac{1}{(G - 1)}\right\}. \tag{34}$$

Setting (34) = 0, we see that there is a finite solution for p_b if $G > \sigma/(\sigma - 1)$, and this solution is (20). Otherwise, expression (34) remains positive for all positive values of p_b, so the business group optimally chooses $p_b = +\infty$. QED

With these preliminary results, and henceforth using symmetry of the equilibrium, we have the following characterizations of the *V-group* equilibria (Proposition 1) and the *D-group* equilibria (Proposition 2):

PROPOSITION I. *Assume $N_c = 0$. Then the V-group equilibria can take one of two forms. Either:*

a. *the business groups do not sell inputs to each other ($\tilde{x}_b = 0$), and the number of groups is given by the unique positive solution to,*

$$G^2 \left(\frac{\Delta \alpha \eta}{L} \right) + G \left[1 - \frac{(\eta - 1)\Delta \alpha}{L} \right] - (1 + \Delta) = 0, \tag{35}$$

provided that $G \leq \sigma/(\sigma - 1)$, where $\Delta \equiv (\sigma - 1)/[(\eta - 1)(1 - \beta)]$; or,

b. *the business groups do sell to each other ($\tilde{x}_b > 0$), while the number of groups is given by any positive solution to,*

$$G^2 \left(\frac{\tilde{\Delta} \alpha \eta}{L} \right) + G \left[1 - \frac{(\eta - 1)\tilde{\Delta} \alpha}{L} \right] - (1 + \tilde{\Delta}) = 0, \tag{36}$$

provided that $G > \sigma/(\sigma - 1)$, where $\tilde{\Delta} \equiv [(\sigma/f(p_b)) - 1]/[(\eta - 1)(1 - \beta)]$, and,

$$f(p_b) \equiv 1 - (\sigma - 1) \left[\frac{(p_b - 1)p_b^{-\sigma}(G - 1)}{1 + (G - 1)p_b^{-\sigma}} \right]. \tag{37}$$

Proof: (a) Since $N_c = 0$ then $s_{yb} = 1/G$, so that $s_{yb}/(1 - s_{yb}) = 1/(G - 1)$. Setting $\Pi_b = 0$, and using $\tilde{x}_b = 0$ with (12) and (14) we obtain,

$$N_b k_{yb} = (G - 1)M_b k_{xb} + (G - 1)\alpha. \tag{38}$$

Using $N_c = 0$, (22) and (24) are simplified as,

$$L = G \left[N_b k_{yb} (1 + \beta (\eta - 1)) + M_b k_{xb} \sigma + \alpha \right] + M_c k_{xc} \sigma, \tag{22'}$$

$$L = G N_b k_{yb} \left[\eta + \left(\frac{1}{G - 1} \right) \right]. \tag{24'}$$

Condition (18) becomes $x_b = (\sigma - 1) k_{xb}$ since $\tilde{x}_b = 0$, so that using (14) and (26),

$$(\sigma - 1) k_{xb} = \frac{(\eta - 1)(1 - \beta) k_{yb} N_b}{\left(M_b + M_c p_c^{1-\sigma} \right)}, \tag{39}$$

where $p_c = \sigma/(\sigma - 1)$.

The previous are four equations in four unknowns – G, N_b, M_b, and M_c. Setting $(22') = (24')$ to eliminate L, and using (38) repeatedly to convert terms involving N_b to involve M_b instead, we can derive the quadratic equation,

$$G^2 - G\left[1 + \frac{(\sigma - 1)}{(1 - \beta)(\eta - 1)} \left(1 + \frac{\alpha}{M_b k_{xb}} \right)^{-1} \right]$$

$$- \left(\frac{M_c k_{xc}}{M_b k_{xb}} \right) \frac{\sigma}{(1 - \beta)(\eta - 1)} \left(1 + \frac{\alpha}{M_b k_{xb}} \right)^{-1} = 0. \tag{40}$$

Using (39) we can solve for (M_c/M_b) as,

$$1 + \left(\frac{M_c}{M_b} \right) \left(\frac{\sigma}{\sigma - 1} \right)^{1-\sigma} = \left[\frac{(\eta - 1)(1 - \beta)}{(\sigma - 1)} \right] \left(\frac{N_b k_{yb}}{M_b k_{yb}} \right)$$

$$= \left[\frac{(\eta - 1)(1 - \beta)}{(\sigma - 1)} \right] (G - 1) \left(1 + \frac{\alpha}{M_b k_{xb}} \right),$$

where the second equality follows from (38). Substituting this into (40), we obtain a rather long quadratic equation for G, which has the following two solutions:

(i) $M_c = 0$ and $G = 1 + \left[\frac{(\sigma-1)}{(1-\beta)(\eta-1)} \right](1 + \frac{\alpha}{M_b k_{xb}})^{-1}$, or,

(ii) $M_c > 0$ and $G = (\frac{k_{xc}}{k_{xb}})(\frac{\sigma}{\sigma-1})^{\sigma} > 1 + \left[\frac{(\sigma-1)}{(1-\beta)(\eta-1)} \right](1 + \frac{\alpha}{M_b k_{xb}})^{-1}$.

These solutions are viable equilibria provided that $\tilde{x}_b = 0$, so that the group finds it optimal to *not* sell its inputs externally, as assumed previously. From the previous Lemma, we know that $\tilde{x}_b = 0$ if and only if $G \leq \sigma/(\sigma - 1)$. This immediately rules out the solution in (ii) whenever k_{xc} is close to k_{xb}. The solution in (i) is viable provided that $G \leq \sigma/(\sigma - 1)$.

To simplify the expression in (i), we can substitute (38) into (24′) to solve for,

$$\frac{\alpha}{M_b k_{xb}} = \alpha \Big/ \left\{ \frac{L}{G[\eta(G-1)+1]} - \alpha \right\}. \tag{41}$$

Substituting (41) into (i), we obtain the quadratic equation in part (a). Part (b) is proved along with Proposition 2, subsequently. QED

PROPOSITION 2. *Assume* $N_c = 0$. *Then in the D-group equilibrium unaffiliated upstream firms are profitable* $(M_c > 0)$, *and the business groups also sell to each other* $(\tilde{x}_b > 0)$, *while the number of groups is given by:*

$$G = \left(\frac{k_{xc}}{k_{xb}} \right) \left(\frac{\sigma}{\sigma - 1} \right)^\sigma \left[1 + (G-1) p_b^{-\sigma} \right] \tag{42}$$

which implies,

$$G = (p_b^\sigma - 1) \Big/ \left[\left(\frac{p_b(\sigma - 1)}{\sigma} \right)^\sigma \left(\frac{k_{xb}}{k_{xc}} \right) - 1 \right]. \tag{43}$$

Proof: Now we suppose that $G > \sigma/(\sigma - 1)$ so that the group sells externally. Setting $\Pi_b = 0$ and using (14), we obtain:

$$\frac{N_b k_y}{(G-1)} + \tilde{x}_b M_b (p_b - 1) = M_b k_{xb} + \alpha. \tag{44}$$

The full-employment conditions (22′) and (24′) continue to hold. Condition (18) is $x_b + \tilde{x}_b = (\sigma - 1) k_{xb}$, so that using (26) and (25a) we obtain,

$$\tilde{x}_b = (G-1) x_b p_b^{-\sigma} \quad \Rightarrow \quad x_b = \frac{(\sigma - 1) k_{xb}}{\left[1 + (G-1) p_b^{-\sigma} \right]}.$$

Substituting this into (44) we obtain,

$$\frac{N_b k_{yb}}{(G-1)} = M_b k_{xb} f(p_b) + \alpha, \tag{44′}$$

where $f(p_b)$ is defined in (37).

Then setting (22′) and (24′) to eliminate L, and repeatedly substituting (44′) to replace terms involving N_b with those involving M_b, we obtain the quadratic equation,

$$G^2 - G \left[1 + \frac{\sigma - f(p_b)}{(1 - \beta)(\eta - 1)} \left(f(p_b) + \frac{\alpha}{M_b k_{xb}} \right)^{-1} \right]$$

$$- \left(\frac{M_c k_{xc}}{M_b k_{xb}} \right) \frac{\sigma}{(1 - \beta)(\eta - 1)} \left(f(p_b) + \frac{\alpha}{M_b k_{xb}} \right)^{-1} = 0. \tag{45}$$

When $M_c = 0$, then G is solved as:

$$G = 1 + \frac{\sigma - f(p_b)}{(1 - \beta)(\eta - 1)} \left(f(p_b) + \frac{\alpha}{M_b k_{xb}} \right)^{-1}. \qquad (45')$$

When $M_c \geq 0$, we first rewrite the expression $(\sigma - 1) k_{xb} = x_b + \tilde{x}_b$ using (26) and (25a) as,

$$(\sigma - 1) k_{xb} = \frac{k_{yb} N_b (1 - \beta)(\eta - 1)\left[(G - 1) p_b^{-\sigma} + 1 \right]}{\left[M_b + M_b(G - 1)p_b^{1-\sigma} + M_c p_c^{1-\sigma} \right]},$$

where $p_c = \sigma/(\sigma - 1)$. It follows using (44') and (37) that we can solve for M_c as,

$$\frac{M_c p_c^{1-\sigma}}{\left[1 + (G - 1)p_b^{-\sigma} \right]} = \frac{M_b}{(\sigma - 1)} \left[(G - 1)\left(f(p_b) + \frac{\alpha}{M_b k_{xb}} \right) \right.$$
$$\left. \times (\eta - 1)(1 - \beta) - \sigma + f(p_b) \right]. \qquad (46)$$

Notice that when $M_c = 0$ in (46), we again solve for G as in (45'). When $M_c > 0$, we substitute (46) into (45) to obtain a rather long quadratic equation in G. One solution (for $M_c = 0$) is (45'), and the other solution (for $M_c > 0$) is given by (43).

In order to prove part (b) of Proposition 1, we can make use of (24') together with (44') to obtain,

$$\frac{\alpha}{M_b k_{xb}} = \alpha f(p_b) \Big/ \left\{ \frac{L}{G[\eta(G - 1) + 1]} - \alpha \right\}. \qquad (47)$$

Substituting (47) into (45'), we obtain (36). To compute the D-group equilibria there are five unknowns – p_b, s_{xb}, G, M_b, and M_c – and five equations to solve for them – (20), (21), (43), (46), and (47). To compute part (b) of the V-group equilibria there are four unknowns – p_b, s_{xb}, G, and M_b, with $M_c = 0$ – and four equations to solve for them – (20), (21), (36)–(37), and (47). QED

Propositions 1 and 2 provide us with the equations used to compute the V-group and D-group equilibria. Finally, we turn to the case of *U-groups*, in which case $N_c > 0$. We first need to derive the prices charged by these groups for the external sale of intermediate inputs, assume that the business group cannot discriminate in its sales to other groups or to downstream unaffiliated firms. Then the optimal price for external sales of the intermediate input is:

LEMMA 3. *With $M_c = 0$ and $N_c \geq 0$, the optimal price p_b for U-groups will satisfy:*

$$\left(\frac{p_b - 1}{p_b}\right) = \left\{\frac{1 + \dfrac{\theta}{(G-1)}\left[1 + \left(\dfrac{s_{yc}}{1 - s_{yb}}\right)(\lambda - 1)\right]}{\sigma + (1 - \sigma)\left[\theta s_{xb} + \dfrac{(1-\theta)}{G}\right]}\right\}, \quad (48)$$

where θ is the fraction of external sales $\tilde{x}_b$ that are sold to other groups, and,

$$\lambda = \left[\frac{1 + (G-1)p_b^{1-\sigma}}{Gp_b^{1-\sigma}}\right]. \quad (49)$$

Proof: Let p_{bi} and q_{bi} denote the prices chosen by group i, with p_{bj} and q_{bj} the prices of the other groups $jc = -1, \ldots, G, j \neq i$. As p_{bi} is increased, this will raise the costs to the other groups and, therefore, increase $q_{bj} = \mu_{bj}\phi_{bj}$, holding fixed the optimal markups μ_{bj}. Since profits in (1) have been maximized with respect to the markup μ_{bi}, it is legitimate to consider a small change $d\mu_{bi}$ to ensure that the market shares of all *other* business groups are held constant. Imposing symmetry on the prices $q_{bj} = q_b$ of all other groups $j = 1, \ldots, G, j \neq i$, as well as on the number of final products $N_{bj} = N_b$ for $j = 1, \ldots, G$, and the prices of downstream unaffiliated firms $q_{cj} = q_c$ for $j = 1, \ldots, N_c$, then the market share of group $j \neq i$ is written from (11) as,

$$s_{yb} = \frac{N_b q_b^{1-\eta}}{\left[N_b q_{bi}^{1-\eta} + (G-1)N_b q_b^{1-\eta} + N_c q_c^{1-\eta}\right]} \quad (11')$$

Totally differentiating this expression, we find that s_{yb} is constant provided that,

$$\frac{d\ln q_{bi}}{d\ln p_{bi}} = \left[\left(\frac{1}{s_{yb}}\right) - (G-1)\right]\frac{d\ln q_b}{d\ln p_{bi}} - \left(\frac{s_{yc}}{s_{yb}}\right)\frac{d\ln q_c}{d\ln p_{bi}}, \quad (50)$$

where,

$$s_{yc} = \frac{N_c q_c^{1-\eta}}{\left[N_{bi} q_{bi}^{1-\eta} + (G-1)N_b q_b^{1-\eta} + N_c q_c^{1-\eta}\right]} \quad (51)$$

is the combined market share of all downstream unaffiliated firms.

Thus, we will evaluate the total change in profits for group i due to a small change dp_{bi}, assuming that the downstream prices of other groups q_b and unaffiliated firms q_c are adjusted holding their markups μ_b and μ_c fixed at their optimal level. Furthermore, we assume that the markup for group i, μ_{bi}, is adjusted so that dq_{bi} satisfies (50), i.e., the market shares of all *other* business groups $j = 1, \ldots, G$, $j \neq i$, are constant. Because total consumer expenditure equals L from (7'), when the market shares for the other groups s_{yb} are fixed, then so is expenditure on their products, so that $q_b y_b = \mu_b \phi_b y_b$ are both fixed: the increase in q_b due to the rising input price p_{bi} will be matched by an equi-proportional reduction in y_b. The same is not true for group i, however: the increase in q_{bi} satisfying (50) will be matched by an reduction in y_{bi} that need not be in the same proportion.

Then the total change in profits for group i is,

$$
\frac{d\Pi_{bi}}{d\ln p_{bi}} = \frac{\partial\Pi_{bi}}{\partial\ln p_{bi}} + q_{bi} y_{bi} N_{bi} \left.\frac{d\ln q_{bi}}{d\ln p_{bi}}\right|_{(50)} + y_{bi} N_{bi} (q_{bi} - \phi_{bi}) \left.\frac{d\ln y_{bi}}{d\ln p_{bi}}\right|_{(50)}
$$

$$
= p_{bi} \tilde{x}_{bi} M_{bi} \left[1 + \left(\frac{p_{bi} - 1}{p_{bi}} \right) \frac{\partial\ln\tilde{x}_{bi}}{\partial\ln p_{bi}} \right] + q_{bi} y_{bi} N_{bi} \left.\frac{d\ln q_{bi}}{d\ln p_{bi}}\right|_{(50)}
$$

$$
+ y_{bi} N_{bi} (q_{bi} - \phi_{bi}) \left.\frac{d\ln y_{bi}}{d\ln p_{bi}}\right|_{(50)} \tag{52}
$$

The first terms on the right are simply the partial effect on profits of changing the input price p_{bi}, which is evaluated using its elasticity of demand. The other two terms are the effect on profits of changing q_{bi} according to (50), and the induced effect of all price changes in q_{bi} and q_b on y_{bi}.

In order to evaluate the induced effect on y_{bi}, we write this from (7) as:

$$
y_{bi} = \frac{q_{bi}^{-\eta} L}{\left[N_b q_{bi}^{1-\eta} + (G-1) N_b q_b^{1-\eta} + N_c q_c^{1-\eta} \right]}, \tag{7''}
$$

where we have made use of symmetry: $q_{bj} = q_b$ for all other groups $j = 1, \ldots, G$, $j \neq i$, $N_{bj} = N_b$ for $j = 1, \ldots, G$, and $q_{cj} = q_c$ for $j = 1, \ldots, N_c$. Totally differentiating (7'') and using (50) we find that,

$$
\left.\frac{d\ln y_{bi}}{d\ln p_{bi}}\right|_{(50)} = \left.\frac{-d\ln q_b}{d\ln p_{bi}}\right|_{(50)} + \left(\frac{\eta s_{yc}}{s_{yb}} \right) \left(\left.\frac{d\ln q_c}{d\ln p_{bi}}\right|_{(50)} - \left.\frac{d\ln q_b}{d\ln p_{bi}}\right|_{(50)} \right).
$$
$$
\tag{53}
$$

From the optimal pricing rule (12), and using symmetry so $s_{ybi} = s_{yb}$, we have that,

$$\eta(q_{bi} - \phi_{bi}) = q_{bi} + \left(\frac{s_{yb}}{1 - s_{yb}}\right)\phi_{bi}. \tag{54}$$

Substituting (50) and (53) into (52), and making use of (54) along with $Gs_{yb} + s_{yc} = 1$, we obtain:

$$\frac{d\Pi_{bi}}{d\ln p_{bi}} = p_{bi}\tilde{x}_{bi}M_{bi}\left[1 + \left(\frac{p_{bi}-1}{p_{bi}}\right)\frac{\partial\ln\tilde{x}_{bi}}{\partial\ln p_{bi}}\right] + y_{bi}\phi_{bi}N_{bi}$$

$$\times\left[\left.\frac{d\ln q_b}{d\ln p_{bi}}\right|_{(50)} + \left(\frac{s_{yc}}{1-s_{yb}}\right)\left(\left.\frac{d\ln q_c}{d\ln p_{bi}}\right|_{(50)} - \left.\frac{d\ln q_b}{d\ln p_{bi}}\right|_{(50)}\right)\right].$$

$$\tag{55}$$

To simplify this expression further, use (2), (5) and the constant optimal markups, along with (25) to compute that,

$$\left.\frac{d\ln q_b}{d\ln p_{bi}}\right|_{(50)} = \frac{\partial\ln\phi_b}{\partial\ln p_{bi}} = \left[\frac{\tilde{x}_{bb}p_bM_b}{(G-1)y_b\phi_bN_b}\right], \tag{56}$$

$$\left.\frac{d\ln q_c}{d\ln p_{bi}}\right|_{(50)} = \frac{\partial\ln\phi_c}{\partial\ln p_{bi}} = \left[\frac{\tilde{x}_{bc}p_bM_b}{y_c\phi_cN_c}\right], \tag{57}$$

each of which can be substituted into (55). Finally, to compute $(\partial\ln\tilde{x}_{bi}/\partial\ln p_{bi})$ we use (25) to obtain:

$$\frac{\partial\ln\tilde{x}_{bi}}{\partial\ln p_{bi}} = -\{\sigma + (1-\sigma)[\theta s_{xb} + (1-\theta)/G]\}, \tag{58}$$

where $\theta \equiv (\tilde{x}_{bbi}/\tilde{x}_{bi})$ is the share of a business group's external sales of intermediate inputs this is sold to other groups. Notice that the derivative in (58) is computed while holding ϕ_by_b constant in the numerator of (25a), as discussed earlier. We also treat ϕ_cy_c constant in the numerator of (25b) when computing this elasticity.

Substituting (56)–(58) into (55), and setting the latter equal to zero, we obtain:

$$\left(\frac{p_{bi}-1}{p_{bi}}\right) = \left\{\frac{1 + \frac{\theta}{(G-1)}\left[1 - \left(\frac{s_{yc}}{1-s_{yb}}\right)\right] + (1-\theta)\left(\frac{N_bk_{yb}}{N_ck_{yc}}\right)\left(\frac{s_{yc}}{1-s_{yb}}\right)}{\sigma + (1-\sigma)\left[\theta s_{xb} + \frac{(1-\theta)}{G}\right]}\right\}.$$

$$\tag{59}$$

To simplify this further, note that $(1-\theta)/\theta$ is the *supply* from each business group to all downstream unaffiliated firms, relative to all other business groups. This must equal the *demand* from downstream unaffiliated firms relative to that from business groups, given by $(\tilde{x}_{bc}/\tilde{x}_{bb}) = \lambda(N_c k_{yc}/N_b k_{yb})$, using (25), (9), (14) and (49). Thus,

$$\left(\frac{1-\theta}{\theta}\right) = \frac{\lambda N_c k_{yc}}{(G-1)N_b k_{yb}}. \tag{60}$$

Substituting (60) into (59), we obtain (48). QED

In the denominator of (48), s_{xb} is still given by (21) but with $M_c = 0$, and is interpreted as the share of total demand for intermediates by a group (including internal demand) coming from *one* other group. We could analogously define the share of total demand for intermediates by a unaffiliated downstream firm supplied by *one* group, which is simply $(1/G)$. Thus, the weighted average $[\theta s_{xb} + (1 - \theta)/G]$ appearing in the denominator of (48) can be interpreted as the share of total demand for intermediates supplied by one group, so that the entire denominator is simply the elasticity of demand for the inputs of a group. If the numerator were unity, then (48) would be a conventional Lerner pricing formula. Instead the numerator exceeds unity, reflecting the fact that when a group sells an input, it will give competing firms a cost advantage, thereby lowering profits in the final goods market. Accordingly, the business group charges a higher price for its inputs than would a firm that is not vertically integrated across both markets.

With the prices given by (48), the *U-group* equilibrium is characterized by:

PROPOSITION 3 (U-GROUP EQUILIBRIA). *Assume $M_c = 0$. Then in the U-group equilibrium the business groups sell inputs to unaffiliated downstream firms ($N_c > 0$) and to each other ($\tilde{x}_b > 0$), while the number of groups is given by any positive solution to:*

$$\frac{\alpha \tilde{\Delta} G^2}{L}\left[\left(\frac{s_{yb}}{1-s_{yb}}\right) + \eta\right] + G\left[1 - \left(\frac{s_{yb}}{1-s_{yb}}\right)\right]\tilde{\Delta}$$

$$+ \frac{\alpha \tilde{\Delta} \eta}{L}\left(\frac{N_c k_{yc}}{N_b k_{yb}}\right)\right] + \left(\frac{N_c k_{yc}}{N_b k_{yb}}\right) = 0, \tag{61}$$

provided that $G > \sigma/(\sigma - 1)$, where $\tilde{\Delta} \equiv [(\sigma/g(p_b)) - 1]/[(\eta - 1)(1 - \beta)]$ and,

$$g(p_b) = 1 - (\sigma - 1)(p_b - 1)\left\{\frac{p_b^{-\sigma}[(G-1) + \lambda(N_c k_{yc}/N_b k_{yb})]}{1 + p_b^{-\sigma}[(G-1) + \lambda(N_c k_{yc}/N_b k_{yb})]}\right\}. \tag{62}$$

Proof: Using $\Pi_b = 0$ and (12), we obtain:

$$\left(\frac{s_{yb}}{1 - s_{yb}}\right) N_b k_{yb} + \tilde{x}_b M_b (p_b - 1) = M_b k_{xb} + \alpha. \tag{63}$$

Using $\tilde{x}_b = \tilde{x}_{bb} + \tilde{x}_{bc}$ from (25) with $M_c = 0$, along with x_b from (26) and $x_b + \tilde{x}_b = (\sigma - 1)k_{xb}$ from (18), we can derive,

$$M_b \tilde{x}_b (p_b - 1) = M_b k_{xb} [1 - g(p_b)],$$

where $g(p_b)$ is defined in (62). Substituting this into (63) we obtain,

$$\left(\frac{s_{yb}}{1 - s_{yb}}\right) N_b k_{yb} = M_b k_{xb} g(p_b) + \alpha. \tag{63'}$$

Setting (22) = (24) with $M_c = 0$, and substituting (63') to replace terms involving M_b with those involving N_b, to obtain:

$$G = G \left[\left(\frac{s_{yb}}{1 - s_{yb}}\right) - \left(\frac{\alpha}{N_b k_{yb}}\right) \right] \left[\frac{(\sigma/g(p_b)) - 1}{(\eta - 1)(1 - \beta)} \right] - \left(\frac{N_c k_{yc}}{N_b k_{yb}}\right). \tag{64}$$

In order to fully determine the equilibrium, we also need to solve for (N_c/N_b). We will make use of the relations,

$$\left(\frac{\phi_c k_{yb}}{\phi_b k_{yc}}\right) = \left(\frac{y_b}{y_c}\right) = \left(\frac{q_b}{q_c}\right)^{-\eta} = \left\{ \left(\frac{\phi_b}{\phi_c}\right) \left[1 + \frac{1}{\eta} \left(\frac{s_{yb}}{1 - s_{yb}}\right) \right] \right\}^{-\eta}. \tag{65}$$

The first equality of (65) follows from (9) and (14); the second equality from the CES demand system; and the third equality from the pricing formulas (8) and (12). Making use of the first and last expressions we obtain,

$$\left(\frac{\phi_c}{\phi_b}\right) = \left[1 + \frac{1}{\eta} \left(\frac{s_{yb}}{1 - s_{yb}}\right) \right]^{\eta/(\eta - 1)} \left(\frac{k_{yb}}{k_{yc}}\right)^{1/(\eta - 1)} \tag{66}$$

and substituting this into the last equality of (65) we have,

$$\left(\frac{q_c}{q_b}\right) = \left[1 + \frac{1}{\eta} \left(\frac{s_{yb}}{1 - s_{yb}}\right) \right]^{1/(\eta - 1)} \left(\frac{k_{yb}}{k_{yc}}\right)^{1/(\eta - 1)}. \tag{67}$$

The shares s_{yb} and s_{yc} of one business group and all unaffiliated firms are related by $G s_{yb} + s_{yc} = 1$. It follows that (s_{yb}/s_{yc}) equals,

$$\left(\frac{s_{yb}}{1 - G s_{yb}}\right) = \frac{N_b q_b^{1 - \eta}}{N_c q_c^{1 - \eta}} = \left(\frac{N_b}{N_c}\right) \left[1 + \frac{1}{\eta} \left(\frac{s_{yb}}{1 - s_{yb}}\right) \right], \tag{68}$$

where the first equality follows from the CES demand system, and the second from (67). Rewriting (68) we obtain,

$$\left(\frac{N_c k_{yc}}{N_b k_{yb}}\right) = \left[\left(\frac{1-s_{yb}}{s_{yb}}\right) - (G-1)\right]\left[1 + \frac{1}{\eta}\left(\frac{s_{yb}}{1-s_{yb}}\right)\right]. \quad (69)$$

To simplify this further, note that λ in (49) equals $(\phi_c/\phi_b)^{(\sigma-1)/(1-\beta)}$, using (2) and (5) with $M_c = 0$. It follows from (66) that,

$$\left(\frac{s_{yb}}{1-s_{yb}}\right) = \eta\left[\lambda^\delta (k_{yc}/k_{yb})^{1/\eta} - 1\right], \quad (70a)$$

where,

$$\delta = \frac{(1-\beta)(\eta-1)}{\eta(\sigma-1)}. \quad (70b)$$

Substituting (70) into (69), we obtain,

$$\left(\frac{N_c k_{yc}}{N_b k_{yc}}\right) = \lambda^\delta (k_{yc}/k_{yc})^{1/\eta}\left[\frac{1}{\eta}\left(\lambda^\delta (k_{yc}/k_{yc})^{1/\eta} - 1\right)^{-1} - (G-1)\right]. \quad (71)$$

To solve for the level of N_b and M_b, we can make use of the full-employment conditions (22) and (24) together with (9) and (14) to derive,

$$N_b = \left(\frac{L}{k_{yb}}\right) \bigg/ \left\{G\left[\eta + \left(\frac{s_{yb}}{1-s_{yb}}\right)\right] + \eta\left(\frac{N_c k_{yc}}{N_b k_{yb}}\right)\right\}, \quad (72)$$

and,

$$M_b = \left(\frac{L}{Gk_{xb}\sigma}\right)\left\{1 - \left[\frac{(1+\beta(\eta-1))(G+(N_c k_{yc}/N_b k_{yb}))}{G\eta + G(s_{yb}/(1-s_{yb})) + \eta(N_c k_{yc}/N_b k_{yb})}\right]\right\} - \left(\frac{\alpha}{k_{xb}\sigma}\right). \quad (73)$$

Substituting (72) into (64) we obtain the quadratic equation (61). The equilibrium is now defined by six variables – G, p_b, s_{xb}, θ, λ and (N_c/N_b) – with six equations given by (21), (48), (49), (60), (61)–(62), and (71). QED

Parameter Values: Initially, equilibria were computed with the parameter values: governance costs $\alpha = 0.2$, elasticity of substitution for final goods $\eta = 5$, labor share $\beta = 0.5$, labor force $L = 1000$, fixed costs for business groups $k_{xb} = k_{yb} = 5$. While we found both V-group and U-group equilibria at this values, it was difficult to find D-group equilibria in which the unaffiliated downstream firms had no incentive to enter. To limit this incentive, it was necessary to use lower values for the final demand elasticity, especially when the elasticity of substitution σ for inputs was low. Accordingly, all our equilibria are computed with an elasticity of substitution for final goods of $\eta = 5$ for $\sigma > 2.65$, and $\eta = 1.9\sigma$ for $\sigma < 2.60$. The fixed costs for unaffiliated firms were initially set equal to $k_{xc} = k_{yc} = 5$, but then lowered slightly if needed to allow them to enter in the equilibria being considered. For example, the U-group equilibria illustrated in Figure 3.6 are calculated for values for k_{yc} ranging from 4.73 to 4.82, which allow downstream unaffiliated firms to enter. We have also confirmed that the profits of the upstream unaffiliated firms are strictly negative along the U-group equilibria in Figure 3.6, and likewise, the profits of downstream unaffiliated firms are strictly negative along the D-group equilibria, and the profits of all unaffiliated firms are strictly negative in the V-group equilibria.

These parameter values described earlier are used for Figures 3.4–3.8 and 3.13–3.15. Then to plot the high concentration equilibria in Figures 3.9, and 3.11, we change the size of the labor force L so that the average sales of V-groups in the simulations equal the average sales of the "top five" *chaebol* in South Korea in 1989. However, for the low concentration equilibria shown in Figures 3.10 and 3.12, we use a value of L that is 25% lower than its value in the high concentration equilibria, reflecting the smaller overall size of the Taiwanese economy.

Appendix B

Examples of Differential Pricing Practices of Korean Groups

In Chapter 3, we refer to investigations by the Korea Fair Trade Commission dealing with differential pricing practices within Korean *chaebol*. Several such cases are summarized subsequently.

Case 1. Goldstar Cable Ltd.[1]

Source: The Korea Fair Trade Commission (1994), "A Case on the Illegal Internal Transactions of Goldstar Cable Ltd. Co.," *Proceedings of Fair Trade Commission Decisions, No. 94-242.*

According to the source, Goldstar Cable, an affiliate of Lucky-Goldstar group, favored its affiliates over non-affiliate firms in trading various commodities in 1993. It *sold* its products to affiliate buyers at much lower prices than to non-affiliate buyers (see Table B.1). It also preferentially treated its affiliates by *buying* their products at significantly higher prices than from other firms (see Table B.2). Table B.1 shows that Goldstar Cable sold electrical wires to Goldstar, its affiliate, at below-market price by 9.6–29.6 percent; it sold high voltage cables to Kukje Cable, its affiliate, at lower prices than to non-affiliate buyers by 1.1–9.1 percent; it sold electrical chillers to Lucky Engineering, its affiliate, at lower prices than to non-affiliates by 16.7–35.9 percent; it sold electrical connectors to Goldstar, its affiliate, at significantly lower prices than to the other non-affiliate buyer by 21.9–24.8 percent; and it sold coated wires to Kukje Cable, its affiliate, at lower prices than to non-affiliate buyers by 4.5–15.9 percent. Table B.2 shows that Goldstar Cable bought assembled cables from Sam-Woo Metal, its affiliate, at higher prices than from non-affiliate producers by 4.4–19.5 percent, and it bought insulated wires from

---

[1] The company changed its name from Goldstar Cable to LG Cable in 1995 in accordance with the group's name change from Lucky-Goldstar to LG.

391

Table B.1. *Sales by Goldstar Cable, within and outside Lucky-Goldstar Group*

Product	Buyer	Group Firm?	Sales*	Unit-Price*	% Price Difference
Electric Wire	Goldstar Ltd.	Yes	247,840	0.1759	
(UL3239 20KV	Dong-Yang Elec. Ltd.	No	4.041	0.250	9.6–29.6
18AWG 19/0.2	Dae-Hee Electronics	No	30,084	0.2163	
54T)	Ltd.				
	Dae-Ah Industry Ltd.	No	32,002	0.1976	
	Jang-Woo Electronics	No	18,382	0.1976	
	Damoa Electronics	No	161,157	0.1946	
High Voltage Cable	Kukje Cable Ltd.	Yes	6,093	1,489–1,960	
(SCR-A 8mm)	Man-Do Machinery	No	194	1,509–2,009	1.1–9.1
	Ltd.				
	Dong-Suh Elec. Ltd.	No	426	1,772–2,124	
	Han-Il Cable Ltd.	No	185	1,894	
	Dae-Ryuk Cable Ltd.	No	533	1,677–1,767	
	Seoul Alloy Ltd.	No	33	1,640	
	Doo-Sung Precision	No	129	1,772	
	Ltd.				
Chiller	Lucky Engineering.	Yes	25,000	2,500	
(164-SE05)	Nam-Yang Refrig. Ltd.	No	33,000	3,000	16.7–35.9
	Keumsung Refrig Ltd.	No	39,000	3,000	
	Hanlim Fishery Coop.	No	39,000	3,900	
Electrical	Goldstar Ltd.	Yes	4,969.20	0.0820	
Connector					
(GR200-11S-TS)	Inkel Ltd.	No	669.90	0.1080	24.1
(GR200-12S-TS)	Goldstar Ltd.	Yes	158.22	0.0879	
	Inkel Ltd.	No	4,270.50	0.1170	24.8
(GR200-13S-TS)	Goldstar Ltd.	Yes	7,805.28	0.0966	
	Inkel Ltd.	No	4,416.00	0.1280	24.5
(GR200-14S-TS)	Goldstar Ltd.	Yes	340.28	0.1047	
	Inkel Ltd.	No	1,112.20	0.1340	21.9
Coated Wire	Kukje Cable Ltd.	Yes	5,891	3,523	
(ICX200SQ)	Myung-Jeon Co.	No	10.708	3,966	11.2
(ICX250SQ)	Kukje Cable Ltd.	Yes	58,357	4,420	
	Dae-Sung Machine	No	61,821	4,630	4.5
	Elec.				
(ICX150SQ)	Kukje Cable Ltd.	Yes	23,373	11,335	
	Ul-Ji Electricity Ltd.	No	16,172	13,476	15.9

Notes
* For electric wire, sales are US$, and unit-price is US$ /meter.
For high voltage cable, sales are million won and unit-price is won/kg.
For chiller, sales are thousand won, and unit-price is thousand won/unit.
For electric connector, sales are US$, and unit-price is US$ /unit.
For coated wire, sales are thousand won, and unit-price is won/meter.
Source: The Korea Fair Trade Commission (1994), "A Case on the Illegal Internal Transactions of Goldstar Cable Ltd. Co.," *Proceedings of Fair Trade Commission Decisions, No. 94-242.*

Table B.2. *Purchases by Goldstar Cable, within and outside Lucky-Goldstar Group*

Product	Seller	Group Firm?	Purchases*	Unit-Price*	% Price Difference
Assembled Cable	Sam-Woo Metal Ltd.	Yes	18,169	469.8	
(A 16/0.2)	Dae-Il Sinsun	No	1,129	450	4.4
(A 20/0.18)	Sam-Woo Metal Ltd.	Yes	9,880	501.8	
	Se-Jung Industry	No	17,442	420	19.5
	Sung-Kwang Elec. Ltd.	No	21,340	420	
(A 30/0.18)	Sam-Woo Metal Ltd.	Yes	38,967	361.8	
	Sung-Kwang Elec. Ltd.	No	17,782	330	9.6
(A 34/0.18)	Sam-Woo Metal Ltd.	Yes	5,889	369.8	
	Sung-Kwang Elec. Ltd.	No	2,389	330	12.1
Insulated Wire:	Kukje Cable Ltd.	Yes	8,449	2,435	
(600V CV,1X100SQ)	Dae-Won Cable Ltd.	No	6,693	2,209	10.2
(600V CV,1X250SQ)	Kukje Cable Ltd.	Yes	281	6,245	
	Dae-Han Wire Sales	No	2,982	5,964	4.7–18.0
	Dae-Han Cable Sales Ctr.	No	16,550	5,291	
(600V CV, 2X3.5SQ)	Kukje Cable Ltd.	Yes	33,610	469	
	Han-Kuk Cable Ind. Ltd.	No	21,700	434	7.6
(600V CV,3X3.5SQ)	Kukje Cable Ltd.	Yes	41,349	617	
	Han-Kuk Cable Ind. Ltd.	No	30,968	553	11.6–22.4
	Dae-Han Elec. Sales Ltd.	No	3,024	504	
(600V CV,3X5.5SQ)	Kukje Cable Ltd.	Yes	2,968	742	
	Dae-Han Cable Ltd.	No	4,554	634	17.0
(600V CV,4X38SQ)	Kukje Cable Ltd.	Yes	123,158	6,011	
	Dae-Han Cable Ltd.	No	440,320	5,254	14.4–14.8
	Han-Kuk Cable Ind. Ltd.	No	313,501	5,238	

Notes
* For assembled cable, sales are thousand won, and unit-price is won/kg.
For insulated wire, sales are thousand won, and unit-price is won/meter.
Source: The Korea Fair Trade Commission (1994), "A Case on the Illegal Internal Transactions of Goldstar Cable Ltd. Co.," *Proceedings of Fair Trade Commission Decisions, No. 94-242.*

Kukje Cable, its affiliate, at higher prices than from non-affiliate firms by 4.7–22.4 percent.

The sales from Goldstar Cable to affiliate firms at below-market prices creates an efficiency gain within the group, although it would presumably need to be offset by some transfer of funds back to Goldstar Cable, to cover fixed costs. The *purchases* by Goldstar Cable at above-market prices are more difficult to explain on efficiency grounds, and instead, may very

Table B.3. *Purchases by Asia Automobile, within and outside Kia Group*

Product	Seller	Group Firm?	Purchases*	Unit-Price*	% Price Difference
Spider Assembly	Kia Precision Machinery Ltd.	Yes	28,958	31,285	7.0
(CC81265210)	Dae-Kwang Precision Ltd.	No	177,389	29,225	
(CC81335130)	Kia Precision Machinery Ltd.	Yes	17,422	31,000	4.8
	Dae-Kwang Precision Ltd.	No	170,523	29,576	

Note
* For spider assembly, sales are thousand won, and unit-price is won.

well serve as a device to transfer profits to the selling firms within the group.

Case 2: Asia Automobile Ltd.

Source: The Korea Fair Trade Commission (1994), "A Case on the Illegal Internal Transactions of Goldstar Cable Ltd. Co.," *Proceedings of Fair Trade Commission Decisions, No. 94-206.*

According to the source, Asia Automobile, an affiliate of Kia group, bought auto parts (spider assembly) from Kia Precision Machinery at higher prices than from other non-affiliate auto parts producers by 4.8–7.0 percent, as shown in Table B.3.

Case 3: Hyundai Electronics Ltd.

Source: The Korea Fair Trade Commission (1993), "A Case on the Illegal Internal Transactions of Hyundai Electronics Ltd. Co.," *Proceedings of Fair Trade Commission Decisions, No. 93-174.*

According to the source, in 1992 the company sold twenty-one models of electronic game machines to two of its affiliates including Hyundai General Trading at lower prices than to non-affiliate firms by 4.2–40.6 percent. It also provided sixteen models of home automation tools to three of its affiliate firms including Hyundai Construction at lower prices than to non-affiliates, Jeong-Ju Development and the like, by 8.3–52.6 percent. In selling five models of cameras, it favored five of its affiliates, Han-Moo Shopping and the like, by providing them at lower prices than to non-affiliate buyers, Dong-Yang MTS Industry and the like, by 5.2–42.9 percent. It also sold seventeen models of phones to four of its affiliates, Keum-Kang Development and the like, at lower prices than to non-affiliates, New Core and the like, by 1.0–28.1 percent. On top of these, the company preferentially treated its affiliate buyers over non-affiliates when selling personal computers, notebook computers, printers, copier parts, and car audio systems, for example, with the price differences of 4.0–56.4 percent.

Appendix C

Hypothesis Tests of the Model

Difference in Means

In Chapter 4, we perform hypothesis tests on the difference in means between our country samples for business groups and the simulated data. In the first version of the hypothesis test, we construct 95% confidence intervals around the mean of the country data and check whether the mean of the simulated data lies within this confidence interval. In this first test, the mean of the simulated data is treated as a fixed, non-stochastic value. In the second version of the hypothesis test, described here, we compare the mean of the country and the simulated samples while treating the true means of both samples as unknown. In this second version, we incorporate the standard errors of the mean of the country sample along with the standard error of the mean of the simulated data. This second test can also be used to compare the means of different types of business groups within each country, as also described subsequently.

Let $x_1, \ldots, x_M$ denote the values from the first sample, and $y_1, \ldots, y_N$ the values from the second sample, with sample means $\bar{x} = \frac{1}{M} \sum_{i=1}^{M} x_i$ and $\bar{y} = \frac{1}{N} \sum_{j=1}^{N} y_j$. We assume that these samples are independent and normally distributed, with the same variance. The standard deviation of the samples are $S_x = \sqrt{\frac{1}{(M-1)} \sum_{i=1}^{M} (x_i - \bar{x})^2}$ and $S_y = \sqrt{\frac{1}{(N-1)} \sum_{j=1}^{N} (y_j - \bar{y})^2}$, and the standard deviations of the sample means are $S_x/\sqrt{M}$ and $S_y/\sqrt{N}$. These standard deviations of the means of the country samples are reported in part (a) of Tables 4.3 and 4.4, as well as Tables C.1 and C.2.

Denote the true means of the samples by μ_x and μ_y. To test the null hypothesis that $\mu_x = \mu_y$, form the statistic (Hogg and Craig, 1970, p. 200):

$$T = \frac{(\bar{x} - \bar{y})}{\sqrt{\frac{(M-1)S_x^2 + (N-1)S_y^2}{(M+N-2)} \left(\frac{1}{M} + \frac{1}{N} \right)}}.$$

Table C.1. *Comparison of Korean Groups*

Included Groups	Statistic	Sales ($ mill.)	Internal Sales Ratio (percent)[1]	Internal Sales Ratio (no retail)[2]	Herfindahl Index (all sales)[3]	Herfindahl Index (internal inputs)[4]
(a) Korean Groups, 1989						
All 44	Mean	3,441	11.3	6.7	0.52	0.26
	St.Dev./$\sqrt{N}$	917	1.6	1.0	0.03	0.04
V-groups[5]	Mean	15,132	22.7	13.3	0.76	0.61
	St.Dev./$\sqrt{N}$	4,197	4.0	2.0	0.03	0.07
U-groups[6]	Mean	1,608	9.3	5.7	0.49	0.22
	St.Dev./$\sqrt{N}$	311	1.6	1.1	0.03	0.04
D-groups[7]	Mean	1,510	10.2	5.2	0.47	0.11
	St.Dev./$\sqrt{N}$	787	4.3	1.3	0.10	0.05
(b) Hypothesis Tests for Difference in Actual Means						
V-group mean same as U-group mean	No	No	No	No	No
V-group mean same as D-group mean	No	No	No	No	No
U-group mean same as D-group mean	Yes	Yes	Yes	Yes	Yes

Notes:
[1] Computed as the ratio of sales between firms in each group to total sales of the group.
[2] "No retail" means that the internal sales ratio is calculated without including the purchases of any trading companies or other wholesale or retail firms from within the group.
[3] The Herfindahl index equals $1 - \sum_i s_i^2$, where s_i is the share of total sales in each sector i.
[4] The Herfindahl index is computed over just internal sales of manufacturing inputs.
[5] There are six V-groups as listed in Table 4.1.
[6] There are thirty-three U-groups as listed in Table 4.1.
[7] There are five D-groups as listed in Table 4.1.

Under the null hypothesis, this is distributed as a t-statistic with $(M + N - 2)$ degrees of freedom. Roughly speaking, for $|T| > 2$ we reject the null hypotheses that the means are equal.

We can rewrite this test statistic using the standard deviation of the sample means, $S_x^\mu = S_x/\sqrt{M}$ and $S_y^\mu = S_y/\sqrt{N}$, so that: $S_x = \sqrt{M}S_x^\mu$ and $S_y = \sqrt{N}S_y^\mu$. Substituting these into the above formula we obtain:

$$T = \frac{(\bar{x} - \bar{y})}{\sqrt{\frac{(M-1)MS_x^{\mu 2} + (N-1)NS_y^{\mu 2}}{(M+N-2)}\left(\frac{1}{M} + \frac{1}{N}\right)}}.$$

To compare the means of different types of business groups within each country, for example, we could let μ_x be the true mean sales of V-groups in Korea and μ_y be the true mean sales of U-groups. The estimates of these means are $\bar{x}$ and $\bar{y}$, while the standard deviations of the sample means

Table C.2. *Comparison of Taiwan Groups*

Included Groups	Statistic	Sales ($ mill.)	Internal Sales Ratio (percent)[1]	Internal Sales Ratio (no retail)[2]	Herfindahl Index (all sales)[3]	Herfindahl Index (internal inputs)[4]
(a) Taiwan Groups, 1994						
All 80	Mean	954	7.0	4.7	0.35	0.10
	St.Dev./$\sqrt{N}$	154	0.8	0.5	0.03	0.02
D-groups[5]	Mean	1,108	7.9	3.7	0.33	0.06
	St.Dev./$\sqrt{N}$	279	1.7	0.7	0.06	0.03
U-groups[6]	Mean	908	6.1	4.6	0.36	0.12
	St.Dev./$\sqrt{N}$	195	0.8	0.6	0.03	0.02
V-groups[7]	Mean	525	14.7	14.6	0.25	0.00
	St.Dev./$\sqrt{N}$	296	3.2	3.1	0.01	0.00
(b) Hypothesis Tests for Difference in Actual Means						
D-group mean same as U-group mean		Yes	Yes	Yes	Yes	Yes
D-group mean same as V-group mean		Yes	Yes	No	Yes	Yes
U-group mean same as V-group mean		Yes	No	No	Yes	Yes

Notes:
[1] Computed as the ratio of sales between firms in each group to total sales of the group.
[2] "No retail" means that the internal sales ratio is calculated without including the purchases of any trading companies or other wholesale or retail firms from within the group.
[3] The Herfindahl index equals $1 - \sum_i s_i^2$, where s_i is the share of total sales in each sector i.
[4] The Herfindahl index is computed over just internal sales of manufacturing inputs.
[5] There are twenty-four D-groups as listed in Table 4.2.
[6] There are fifty-three U-groups as listed in Table 4.2.
[7] There are three V-groups as listed in Table 4.2.

are $S_x^\mu = S_x/\sqrt{M}$ and $S_y^\mu = S_y/\sqrt{N}$, all of which are shown in part (a) of Table C.1. Then we apply the above formula to compute the T value for the null hypothesis that $\mu_x = \mu_y$, obtaining:

$$T = \frac{(15{,}132 - 1{,}608)}{\sqrt{\frac{5 \cdot 6 \cdot 4{,}197^2 + 32 \cdot 33 \cdot 311^2}{37} \left(\frac{1}{6} + \frac{1}{33}\right)}} = 7.4,$$

because there are six V-groups in Korea and thirty-three U-groups. Because this value exceeds 2, the null hypothesis that the means sales of V-groups in Korea equal the mean sales of U-groups is soundly rejected. This is reported as a "no" in the first row of part (c) of Table C.1. Likewise, the other hypothesis tests shown for the Korean groups in Table C.1 and the Taiwanese groups in Table C.2 are performed using the above formulas.

In Chapter 4, when we compare the means of country data with the means of simulated data, then we take the standard deviation of the simulated equilibria, shown in part (b) of Tables 4.3 and 4.4, as a measure of $S_y^\mu = S_y/\sqrt{N}$. In other words, the standard deviation of the simulated sample is treated like a standard deviation of a mean. The reason for this is that the equilibrium at each of the elasticities E of the simulated economics, as shown in Figures 3.9 and 3.10, represents an economy with business groups of equal size, which equals their *mean* size. So the plots in Figures 3.9 and 3.10 should be thought of as a series of economies, which show how the *mean* size and internal sales of the groups vary across each. The dispersion in these points can, therefore, be interpreted as a *standard deviation of the mean sales (or internal sales, or other characteristics)* across economies. Using those standard deviations in part (b) of Tables 4.3 and 4.4. as a measure of $S_y^\mu = S_y/\sqrt{N}$, while the standard deviations of the country means in part (a) measure $S_x^\mu = S_x/\sqrt{M}$, then the previous formula for the T value is used to test the hypotheses in part (c). As explained in Chapter 4, this second version of the hypothesis test is generally easier to accept that the first (which is the simple confidence interval), although in practice, they usually give the same results. In the few instances where the second test allows us to conclude that the actual and simulated means are the same, but not the first test, the outcome is indicated in parentheses as "(yes)" in part (c) of Tables 4.3 and 4.4.

Notice that the test for difference in means can also be formulated as a likelihood ratio test, in which case the likelihood ratio becomes (Hogg and Craig, 1970, p. 303):

$$L = \frac{M+N-2}{M+N-2+T^2},$$

using the T value defined previously. Then the value $-2\ln L$ is asymptotically distributed as $\chi^2(1)$. Using this alternative test statistic does not rely on having a normal distribution for each sample, but does still assume that the variance of the samples are equal. Using this alternative test statistic does not affect any of the results for hypothesis tests in Tables 4.3 and 4.4, nor does it affect the results in Table C.1 or C.2.

Difference in Product Variety

In Chapter 8, we perform hypotheses tests on the difference in product variety exported from South Korea and Taiwan. In this appendix we first derive the formulas used for product variety, and then describe the structure of the hypothesis test.

For each industry, treat the U.S. imports from each country $j = 1, \ldots, J$ as differentiated across $i = 1, \ldots, N$ varieties, where each country may supply only a subset $I_j \subseteq \{1, \ldots, N\}$ of these varieties. Consistent with our notation in Appendix A, let $y_j = (y_{1j}, y_{2j}, \ldots, y_{Nj})$ denote the vector of import quantities from country j, and suppose that the total services obtained from imports of country j for the industry in question are given by the CES function $g(y_j, I_j)$:

$$g(y_j, I_j) = \left(\sum_{i \in I_j} a_i y_{ij}^{(\eta-1)/\eta} \right)^{\eta/(\eta-1)}, a_i > 0, \tag{1}$$

where the elasticity of substitution is $\eta > 1$. If the product in question is a consumer good, then $g(\cdot)$ represents the utility function for the varieties from country j, and otherwise it is a production function for importing firms. We assume that total utility or output obtained from imports from all source countries is given by the function:

$$U = F[g(y_I, I_I), \ldots, g(y_J, I_J)], \tag{2}$$

which aggregates the services obtained from each country. Equation (2) assumes that the import varieties from each country are weakly separable from each other within the function $F(\cdot)$, which is convenient in developing our indexes.

Let $Y_j = \sum_{i \in I_j} y_{ij}$ denote the total quantity of country j's imports, measured in physical units. Then the *services obtained per unit of import* is obtained by dividing total services by the physical quantity Y_j:

$$A_j \equiv g(y_j, I_j)/Y_j. \tag{3}$$

Then (2) can be rewritten as:

$$U = F[(A_I Y_I), \ldots, (A_J Y_J)]. \tag{2'}$$

The services per unit of import A_j cannot be measured directly, since it depends on the unknown level of service $g(y_j, I_j)$, but an empirical measure can be obtained by considering the ratio of relative services A_j/A_k. To develop this measure, denote the unit-cost function $c(q_j, I_j)$ dual to (1) by:

$$c(q_j, I_j) = \left(\sum_{i \in I_j} b_i q_{ij}^{1-\eta} \right)^{1/(1-\eta)}, b_i = a_i^{\eta} \tag{4}$$

where $q_j > 0$ is the price vector from country j. By definition of unit-costs, total expenditure will equal unit-costs multiplied by output, so that $E_j = c(q_j, I_j) g(y_j, I_j)$. It follows that services in (3) can be re-written as:

$$A_j = [E_j/c(q_i, I_j)]/Y_j \tag{3'}$$

Then taking the ratio of (3′) for countries j and k, we readily obtain,

$$\frac{A_j}{A_k} = \left[\frac{E_j/Y_j}{E_k/Y_k}\right] \Big/ \left[\frac{c_j(q_j, I_j)}{c_k(q_k, I_k)}\right]. \tag{5}$$

The right-hand side of expression (5) is the ratio of *unit-values* of imports from country j and k, divided by the ratio of *unit-costs* from the two countries. While the unit-values are directly obtained from import data, the unit-costs are not observed. However, their ratio can be measured by an exact price index. In particular, suppose that y_j and y_k are the cost-minimizing quantities with prices q_j and q_k, respectively, and that the set of *common* goods $I \equiv (I_j \cap I_k)$ imported from both countries is not empty. Then from Feenstra (1994), the ratio of unit-costs can be measured as:

$$c(q_j, I_j)/c(q_k, I_k) = P(q_j, q_k, y_j, y_k, I)(\lambda_j/\lambda_k)^{1/(\eta-1)}, \tag{6}$$

where the components of this expression are as follows:

1. $P(q_j, q_k, y_j, y_k, I) \equiv \sum_{i \in I} (q_{ij}/q_{ik})^{w_i(I)}$ is the price index of Sato (1976) and Vartia (1976), constructed over the common goods I. The weights $w_i(I)$ are computed as logarithmic means of the expenditure shares of the two countries over the common set of goods I, which are $s_{ij}(I) = q_{ij}y_{ij}/\sum_{i \in I} q_{ij}y_{ij}$ and $s_{ik}(I) = q_{ik}y_{ik}/\sum_{i \in I} q_{ik}y_{ik}$. Using these, the formula for the weights is $w_i(I) = [\frac{s_{ij}(I)-s_{ik}(I)}{\ln s_{ij}(I)-\ln s_{ik}(I)}]/\sum_{i \in I}[\frac{s_{ij}(I)-s_{ik}(I)}{\ln s_{ij}(I)-\ln s_{ik}(I)}]$. The numerator in this expression is a logarithmic mean of s_{ij} and s_{ik}, and lies between these cost shares. Then the weights $w_i(I)$ are a normalized version of the logarithmic means, and sum to unity.
2. $\lambda_j(I) = \sum_{i \in I} q_{ij}y_{ij}/\sum_{i \in I_j} q_{ij}y_{ij}$, with the analogous formula applying for λ_k.

The result in (6) states that the ratio of unit-costs equals the price index of the common or "overlapping" goods (in the set I) times the additional term$(\lambda_j/\lambda_k)^{1/(\eta-1)}$. To interpret this term, note that λ_j equals the proportion of the expenditure on the common goods $i \in I$ relative to the entire set of goods $i \in I_j$. Alternatively, λ_j measures one *minus* the expenditure share of the goods outside the set I. If country j has a larger share of revenue from selling products *outside* the set of common goods, so $\lambda_j < \lambda_k$, that tends to lower the unit-cost ratio by an amount depending on the power $1/(\eta-1)$. Thus, the greater the value of unique products supplied by country j, the lower will be the relative cost of obtaining import services from that country.

We can rewrite the service ratio in (5) using (6):

$$\frac{A_j}{A_k} = \frac{(E_j/Y_j)/(E_k/Y_k)}{P(q_j, q_k, y_j, y_k, I)} \left(\frac{\lambda_k}{\lambda_j}\right)^{1/(\eta-1)}$$

$$= (\text{Product Mix}) \times (\text{Product Variety})^{1/(\eta-1)}. \qquad (5')$$

Thus, the relative services per unit import of the two countries is decomposed into two sources. The first term on the right of (5') is the ratio of the unit-values to the price index, or the "product mix." A higher value for this term indicates that country j sells relatively more of the higher-priced varieties than does country k. The second term represents the relative effect of product variety. Note that the expenditure share ratio λ_k/λ_j in (5') has inverse subscripts to the quality ratio A_j/A_k. Therefore, the greater is the expenditure share on varieties from country j (or the smaller from country k) that are outside the set of common goods I, the higher will be the variety index. We will interpret the product mix index as a measure of product quality (like Aw and Roberts, 1986, 1988). Equation (5') shows that *both* the product mix and variety are components of A_j/A_k, the services per unit of country j imports relative to those of country k, so both indexes are well-motivated in terms of the preferences of importing consumers or firms.

The data used are disaggregate U.S. import statistics for 1978–94. We take each 7-digit Tariff Schedule of the United States (TSUSA) number as a variety for 1978–88, and each 10-digit Harmonized System (HS) number as a variety for 1989–94, and then construct the product mix and variety indexes within each 4- or 5-digit Standard Industrial Classification (SIC).[1] In other words, the 5-digit SIC level is taken as the "industry" for which product variety and mix are measured.[2] The period 1978–88 was broken into the two sub-periods 1978–82 and 1983–88, to check for changes in product variety and mix that may have occurred. The 5-digit industries used are those with more than three varieties exported by both countries in the full first or second period. For each of these industries, the product variety and mix indexes are calculated in each year. To determine which country dominates in product variety or mix, we compute the *mean* of

[1] The value and quantity of each 7-digit TSUSA commodity are reported in the U.S. Bureau of the Census (1978–88), which was obtained on magnetic tape. The price of each variety is a unit-value, computed by dividing total import value by total quantity at the 7-digit TSUSA level. A concordance file matching TSUSA categories with import-based SIC code numbers was used to construct the product groups. These data are described in Feenstra (1996) and Feenstra, Romalis, and Schott (2002), and available from www.internationaldata.org.

[2] An example of a 5-digit SIC category is "men's and boy's suits, coats and overcoats." We also calculated all indexes using the 8-digit SIC as the "industry" level, an example of which is "men's and boy's suits." The 5-digit and 8-digit SIC levels gave very similar results for product mix and variety; see Tzu-Han Yang (1993).

each index (measured in logs) over the years within each period, and test whether the log index is greater or less than zero at the 10% level, using a one-sided t-test.

More formally, letting z_{nt} denote the log of the product variety or mix index for some industry n in year t, and μ_n denote its mean value, we assume that:

$$z_{nt} = \mu_n + \varepsilon_{nt}, \text{ where } \varepsilon_{nt} \text{ is distributed } N(0, \sigma_n^2), \tag{7}$$

and t lies in the ranges 1978–82, 1983–88, or 1989–94. Then we test the hypotheses:

$$\begin{aligned} &H_0 : \mu_n \leq 0 \text{ versus } H_1 : \mu_n > 0, \text{ and also,} \\ &H'_0 : \mu_n \geq 0 \text{ versus } H'_1 : \mu_n < 0 \end{aligned} \tag{8}$$

The hypotheses H_0 or H'_0 are rejected if $\bar{z}_n/S > t_{0.9}(\tau - 1)$ or $\bar{z}_n/S < -t_{0.9}$ $(\tau - 1)$, respectively, where $\bar{z}_n$ is the sample mean, S is its standard deviation and τ is the number of years in each period. We have described this familiar test in detail because we shall generalize it subsequently.

In Table 8.3, measuring the index as Taiwan (T) relative to Korea (K), if the null hypothesis that $\mu_n = \ln(\lambda_{nK}/\lambda_{nT}) \leq 0$ is rejected, indicating that Taiwan has greater expenditure on varieties not in the set of common goods, then we conclude that Taiwan has greater product variety (denoted $T > K$); if on the contrary, the null hypothesis that $\mu_n = \ln(\lambda_{nK}/\lambda_{nT}) \geq 0$ is rejected, then we conclude that Korea has greater product variety (denoted $K > T$); and if neither of these hypotheses are rejected, then the conclusion is uncertain (denoted U). The same is done for the product mix index. In Table 8.3, we have summarized the results of these hypothesis tests by 2-digit categories, each of which contain multiple 5-digit industries. Entries in the columns market $T > K(K > T)$ show the *number* of 5-digit industries for which the hypothesis $\mu_n \leq 0 (\mu_n \geq 0)$ was rejected, while entries in the columns marked U are the number of 5-digit industries for which neither hypothesis was rejected.

In addition, we shall test the joint hypothesis that all *5-digit industries within a 2-digit category* have a log index that is positive, or negative. Letting n index the 5-digit industries, and $n \in N$ denote the 2-digit category, these joint hypotheses are:

$$H_0 : \mu_n \leq 0 \text{ for all } n \in N, \text{ versus } H_1 : \mu_n > 0 \text{ for some } n \in N,$$

and also,

$$H'_0 : \mu_n \geq 0 \text{ for all } n \in N, \text{ versus } H'_1 : \mu_n < 0 \text{ for some } n \in N. \tag{9}$$

For example, if there are three 5-digit industries within the 2-digit category, then these are hypotheses on the vector $\mu = (\mu_1, \mu_2, \mu_3)$. The null hypotheses H_0 specifies that μ must lie in the negative quadrant of R^3, while the alternative H_1 allows μ to lie anywhere else in R^3.

The test statistics for either hypothesis in (9) is constructed as a likelihood ratio using the model in (7). In particular, the likelihood ratio for H_0 is constructed as:

$$L = \prod_{n \in N} \left[\frac{\sum_t (z_{nt} - \bar{z}_n)^2}{\min_{\mu_n \leq 0} \sum_t (z_{nt} - \mu_n)^2} \right]^{\tau/2}, \tag{10}$$

where τ denotes the number of years in each sample, and $\bar{z}_n$ is the sample mean of z_n. The expression in the numerator of (10) is simply the sum of squared residuals (SSR) from (7), with $\bar{z}_n$ as the optimal choice for μ_n, while the expression in the denominator is the SSR when the choice of μ_n is constrained to be non-positive.

The likelihood ratio L is less than unity, and will be smaller if $\bar{z}_n$ is positive and large for some n, so that forcing $\mu_n \leq 0$ in the denominator substantially increases the SSR. For large τ, the value $-2lnL$ is asymptotically distributed as $\chi^2(q)$, where q is the number of industries within the 2-digit class N. Then a low value for L will make it more likely that H_0 is rejected, as should occur when $\bar{z}_n$ is large for some n. Like the hypotheses in (8), it is possible that neither of (9) are rejected; but in contrast to (8), it is also possible that *both* the hypotheses in (9) are rejected.

In Table 8.4, we report the results of the testing hypotheses (9) when the indexes are measured as Taiwan relative to Korea. If $H_0(H_0')$ is rejected at the 10% level and H_0' (H_0) is not rejected at the 25% level, then we conclude that Taiwan (Korea) has higher product variety or mix, which is denoted by T (K). Borderline cases occur when the first hypothesis is not rejected at the 10% level, but is rejected at the 25% level or when the second hypothesis is not rejected at the 25% level, but is rejected at the 10% level. These are denoted by U (for uncertain) followed by the letter of the country that has the higher index at the weaker significance level. Cases where the hypotheses in (9) are both rejected or both accepted are denoted by U, indicating that the conclusion is entirely uncertain.

Appendix D

The Role of Debt in the Korean Financial Crisis, 1997

Using our theoretical model of Chapter 3, we demonstrated in Chapter 4 that a drop in demand can move the economy from one equilibria (that is, structure of the business groups) to another, leading to a string of bankruptcies in the process. We argued that such a string of bankruptcies precipitated the financial crisis in Korea in 1997. In this appendix, we supplement that theoretical demonstration with two empirical arguments related to the financing of the business groups in Korea. While these arguments fall outside the narrow confines of our Walrasian model, they nevertheless offer insight into the sources of the crisis there.

First, we argue that the bankruptcies before November 17, 1997, are predicted well by the excessively high debt/equity ratios of the groups. In contrast, the bankruptcies after November 17 cannot be explained by the overall debt/equity ratios, but rather, by the excessively high levels of short-term debt of these groups. In other words, the bankruptcies before November 17 show every indication that the capital market was working as it should, whereas the bankruptcies after November 17 show the characteristics of a financial panic, in which banks are not willing to roll over short-term loans regardless of the performance of their debtors.

Second, we explain how the interaction between the bankruptcies of *chaebol* and the precarious structure of the financial system combined to create the financial crisis during the last quarter of 1997. This explanation relies on the details of financial sector reform in Korea, which expanded the role of the merchant banks in financing the *chaebol*. This financing took the form of purchasing and distributing commercial paper for the business groups, and also borrowing abroad and re-lending to them. Both these activities expose the merchant banks to considerable risk due to a mismatch between short-term and foreign-currency liabilities (borrowings) and long-term domestic currency assets (loans to the *chaebol*). This risk exposure, combined with the bankruptcies of the *chaebol*, proved to

405

be more than the financial system could withstand and led to a banking panic that culminated in the exchange rate crisis.

The Role of Debt

To support our argument that the capital market was working reasonably well during the first three quarters of 1997, we shall look empirically at the relation between the debt–equity ratios of the groups and their bankruptcies. It is well known that Korean firms in general, and the *chaebol* in particular, have exceptionally high levels of indebtedness. The debt–equity ratio for the manufacturing sectors of Korea in 1997 was 396%, while for Taiwan it was only 95%, with Japan (193%) and the United States. (154%) lying in-between these two extremes.[1] Debt-equity ratios in the range of 400% are nothing new in Korea, and the top thirty *chaebol* have been at that level for the entire decade of the 1990s, while rising from 387% at the end of 1996 to 519% at the end of 1997, after the crisis had hit.[2] Moreover, the debt-equity ratios of the largest groups that would go bankrupt – Hanbo, Sammi, Jinro and Kia – were considerably higher than the top thirty *chaebol* on average.

The high debt of these groups can be explained in part by the pattern of "affiliate payment guarantees" (APG), whereby major firms (*churyok kiop*) in a business group guarantee the bank loans made by their subsidiaries (*chahoesa*) in the group.[3] Because only large-sized firms enjoy accessibility to bank loans, the major firms in a business group play the role of financial provider for all other affiliates through APG (Yoo, 1995, pp. 180–6). By providing the banks with APG for the loans their subsidiaries make, major firms serve as the financial conduits from banks to their subsidiaries. Major firms are held accountable for bank loans of their subsidiaries made this way, so that affiliate firms' liability constitute *de facto* major firms' debt. While APG allows *chaebols* to enjoy easy access to bank loans and flexibility in financial allocation among their affiliates, it tends to increase financial vulnerability of business groups because of the liability linkage among firms.

[1] *Current Economic Situation*, Executive Yuan, Council for Economic Planning and Development, Taipei, Taiwan, July 1998; Japan value refers to 1996, and all others to 1997.
[2] These debt–equity ratios exclude the financial firms within the groups, and are obtained from the Korean Fair Trade Commission, quoted in *Business Time (Singapore)*, Online, April 16, 1998.
[3] Major firms stand out among affiliates in terms of assets and sales, represent main lines of business, and are financially most capable in a business group. For example, Samsung group owns its major firms in life insurance, electronics, semiconductor, and heavy industry, and Hyundai group has its counterparts in automobile, construction, and heavy industry.

Hanbo, Sammi, Jinro, and Kia all had higher levels of affiliate payment guarantees relative to equity than other top thirty groups in 1997. Although most of the *major* firms in these groups performed quite well and made positive net profits, bankruptcy could not be avoided due to the losses and large amounts of debts that their subsidiaries incurred (Chang and Wang, 1998, p. 130). This illustrates how the web of financial arrangement within the *chaebol* make it difficult to separate the profitable from unprofitable firms, and deal only with the latter: "affiliates are closely interlinked by cross payment guarantees, making freer withdrawals almost impossible."[4] Correcting this by insisting on consolidated financial reports by the *chaebol*, and a reduction in affiliate payment guarantees, are two of the reforms being pursued in Korea. It is noteworthy, however, that the level of affiliate payment guarantees within the *chaebol* were already decreasing prior to the crisis (Yoo, 1999, p. 197).

In Table D.1, we report the debt-equity ratios for the business groups that were among the top thirty in 1996 or 1997. Groups that went bankrupt before November 17, 1997, are shown in bold, and groups that went bankrupt after that date are shown in bold and italics (Kukdong is in the latter group, but is omitted from Table D.1 due to missing data). In total, there are fifteen groups among the top thirty that went bankrupt before or after the exchange rate crisis. Only one of these (Daewoo) is among the top five; another fourteen (including Kukdong) are in the second-tier of *chaebol* ranked between 6th and 30th; whereas ten groups (shown in Table D.1) are in the third-tier ranked between 31st and 60th in terms of assets. Thus, *one-fifth* of the largest five *chaebol* has gone bankrupt, while over *one-half* of the second-tier of groups and *one-third* of the third-tier have experienced the same. Based on these preliminary comparisons, it is apparent that the second-tier of *chaebol* experienced the greatest difficulty during the financial crisis. This is consistent with the observations of Kwon and Nam (1999) that it was exactly this group that had the highest level of nonperforming loans throughout the 1990s.

To examine the link between debt–equity ratios and bankruptcy more systematically, we performed logit regressions of bankruptcy – distinguishing those which occurred before and after November 17, 1997 – on the debt–equity ratios. The sample for these regressions is the top thirty groups shown in Table D.1, along with a few other smaller *chaebol* for which we had complete information, with results shown in Table D.2. In the first regression, we include those groups that went bankrupt *prior* to the exchange rate crisis, as well as those groups that did not fail. We find that the debt–equity ratio in 1996 is a highly significant variable ($p = 0.03$)

---

[4] Quotation from a spokesman from the Ministry of Finance and Economy, in the *Korean Herald*, July 19, 1997, "Kia Crisis to Change Government Chaebol Policies."

Table D.1. *Data for Top 30 Korean Chaebol, 1996–97*

Business Group	Sales 1996 ($million)	Debt/Equity 1996 (percent)	Debt/Equity 1997 (percent)	Short/Long debt, 1996	Short/Long debt, 1997	Prob. Of Bankruptcy
Hyundai	84,633	437	579	1.26	1.52	0.07
Samsung	70,194	270	367	0.96	0.92	0.00
LG	58,284	351	527	1.10	1.17	0.01
Daewoo	*49,636*	*382*	*474*	*1.35*	*1.70*	*0.03*
SK	28,195	350	461	2.01	2.01	0.01
Ssangyong	*22,081*	*297*	*403*	*1.66*	*3.25*	*0.00*
Kia	15,150	514	n.a.	n.a.	n.a.	0.19
Hanwha	*11,405*	*665*	*1,066*	*1.58*	*3.09*	*0.61*
Hanjin	10,810	558	920	0.43	0.26	0.30
Lotte	8,770	190	219	2.12	9.62	0.00
Hyosung	6,778	377	467	1.48	2.35	0.02
Daelim	5,976	418	508	1.42	2.16	0.05
Keumho	5,823	473	968	1.65	2.94	0.11
Kolong	4,989	341	421	1.63	0.03	0.01
Dong Ah	*4,821*	*350*	*353*	*1.80*	*3.26*	*0.01*
Halla	*3,974*	*451*	*976*	*1.99*	*3.49*	*0.08*
Doosan	3,919	743	623	1.80	4.98	0.78
Dongkuk Steel	3,817	219	323	1.10	1.21	0.00
Hanbo	**3,549**	**675**	**1,501**	n.a.	n.a.	**0.63**
Haitai	**3,227**	**521**	**814**	**1.70**	**3.09**	**0.21**
Dongbu	3,227	250	350	1.74	3.67	0.00
Kohap	*3,130*	*592*	*474*	*1.66*	*2.35*	*0.40*
Hansol	2,979	340	459	1.35	0.87	0.01
Anam	2,427	526	1820	1.73	2.88	0.22
New Core	**2,273**	**1224**	**1,784**	n.a.	n.a.	**0.99**
Dongyang	2,257	294	389	1.01	1.02	0.00
Sammi	**1,856**	**– 3,329**	n.a.	n.a.	n.a.	**1.00**
Hanil	*1,618*	*563*	*n.a.*	*n.a.*	*n.a.*	*0.31*
Jinro	**1,515**	**2,948**	**−813**	**1.45**	**2.44**	**1.00**
Daesang	1,394	471	637	2.20	3.88	0.11
Shinho	1,224	391	798	1.28	1.64	0.03
Keopyung	*1,053*	*269*	*357*	*1.57*	*2.60*	*0.00*

Notes: 1. Groups shown in bold declared bankruptcy prior to November 17, 1997; groups in bold and italics declared bankruptcy after that date.

2. Group sales have been converted to US$ using the 1996 exchange rat of 804 won/$.

3. Debt/equity ratios and short term/long term loan ratios are at end of the calendar year, and exclude financial firms in each group.

Sources: New Industry Management Academy (1999), supplemented with information from the Korean Fair Trade Commission.

Table D.2. *Regression results for Bankruptcy of Chaebol, 1996–98*

Regression 1: Those *chaebol* going bankrupt **before** November 17, 1997.

$$\text{Probability of Bankruptcy} = -47 + 7.3 \ \ln\left|\frac{\text{Dept 96}}{\text{Equity 96}}\right|, \qquad N = 35, R^2 = 0.60$$

$$(\text{s.e.} = 3.4, \ p = 0.03)$$

No. of observations **without** bankruptcy = 27 ; Successfully predicted (probability < 0.5) = 26.
No. of observations **with** bankruptcy = 8; Successfully predicted (probability > 0.5) = 6.

Regressions 2: Those *chaebol* going bankrupt **after** November 17, 1997.

(a) $\Pr(\text{Bankrupt}) = -11 + 1.73 \ \ln\left|\dfrac{\text{Dept 96}}{\text{Equity 96}}\right|, \qquad N = 36, R^2 = 0.05$

$$(\text{s.e.} = 1.3, \ p = 0.19)$$

No. of observations **without** bankruptcy = 27; Successfully predicted (probability < 0.5) = 27.
No. of observations **with** bankruptcy = 9; Successfully predicted (probability > 0.5) = 0.

(b) $\Pr(\text{Bankrupt}) = -1.8 + 0.12 \ \ln\left|\dfrac{\text{Dept 97}}{\text{Equity 97}}\right|, \qquad N = 27, R^2 = 0.00$

$$(\text{s.e.} = 0.97, \ p = 0.70)$$

No. of observations **without** bankruptcy = 20; Successfully predicted (probability < 0.5) = 20.
No. of observations **with** bankruptcy = 7; Successfully predicted (probability > 0.5) = 0.

(c) **Excluding Doosan and Lotte groups from the estimation:**

$$\Pr(\text{Bankrupt}) = -1.2 - 0.67 \ \ln\left|\frac{\text{Debt 97}}{\text{Equity 97}}\right| + 2.7 \ \ln\left(\frac{\text{Short term loans 97}}{\text{Long term loans 97}}\right),$$

$$(\text{s.e.} = 1.1, \ p = 0.55) \qquad (\text{s.e.} = 1.5, \ p = 0.06)$$
$$N = 25, R^2 = 0.22$$

No. of observations **without** bankruptcy = 18; Successfully predicted (probability < 0.4) = 15.
No. of observations **with** bankruptcy = 7; Successfully predicted (probability > 0.4) = 4.

---

in explaining the pattern of bankruptcies. The probability of bankruptcy based on regression 1 is shown in the final column of Table D.1. Of the twenty-seven groups that did not go bankrupt during this period, all but one – Doosan – are correctly predicted to survive, and of the eight groups that did go bankrupt, all but two – Kia and Haitai – are correctly predicted to fail. The cases not well explained by the regression are themselves of interest: Doosan did not fail despite its high debt, but this only because of a very aggressive restructuring effort undertaken by its head Park Yong

Maan;[5] and while Haitai had relatively low debt in 1996, it was much higher in 1997 (see Table D.1), so that using this value it would indeed be predicted to fail using regression 1. Kia's bankruptcy is another case that is not accurately predicted by the regression equation, and while it clearly had excess capacity in autos and steel, we will make some further observations on why it went bankrupt later in the text.

We see that a relatively simple consideration of debt–equity ratios goes a long way toward explaining the pattern of bankruptcies during the first three quarter of 1997. This indicates to us that the capital market was functioning as it should: penalizing those groups that had debt in excess of their ability to repay. This is not to say that the capital market could not have functioned better. Most of the groups that went bankrupt had some profitable and some unprofitable firms, and it may have been preferable to penalize the latter firms only rather than the entire group. The interlinked financial structure of the *chaebol* makes it difficult to achieve this, however. Our conclusion at this stage is that prior to the exchange rate crisis, the capital market was acting in a rational manner with the most heavily indebted groups going bankrupt.

It is worth emphasizing that allowing the groups to go bankrupt – as opposed to bailing them out – was unprecedented in Korea. This reflected a new political situation in the country. President Kim Young Sam had been elected in 1992 as the first civilian president, on the promise to "clean up" the highest-level corruption. He made good on this promise by taking a "hands off" approach towards the *chaebol* bankruptcies. Shortly after the Hanbo failure, it became apparent that the several close aides to Kim, as well as his own son, had used their influence to arrange for loans to Hanbo that had financed its prior expansion.[6] While this effectively turned the public against Kim, the fact remains that he was the first president who had allowed a large *chaebol* to fail,[7] and was at least attempting to de-link the capital market from political influence. This is quite the opposite of what we would expect from "crony capitalism."

What about after the exchange rate crisis? In the second set of regressions in Table D.2, we include those top thirty groups that went bankrupt after November 17, 1997, together with those that never failed. In regression 2(a), we again use the debt–equity ratio in 1996 as the explanatory

[5] See Charles S. Lee and Dan Biers, "Remaking Korea Inc.," *Far Eastern Economic Review*, April 30, 1998, pp. 10–13.

[6] See Shim Jae Hoon, "Hero to Zero," *Far Eastern Economic Review*, March 13, 1997, pp. 16–17.

[7] The only earlier bankruptcy of a top 30 *chaebol* was Kukje, which was completely broken up in 1985 (Nam and Kim, 1994, p. 463). It was alleged, how that this breakup was politically motivated, and occurred because the chairman of the Kukje group did not make sufficient contributions to two government organizations (see Mark Clifford, "Filing for Divorce," *Far Eastern Economic Review*, April 21, 1988, pp. 58–9).

variable, and find that it performs very poorly: the estimated equation does not predict bankruptcy for *any* of the groups, despite the fact that eight groups in the sample went bankrupt during this period. The same in true in regression 2(b), where we instead use the debt–equity ratio in 1997 as the explanatory variable, and find the equation has no predictive power at all. Given that the total amount of debt does not explain bankruptcies after November 17, we considered instead the *term structure* of debt.

Our data source (New Industry Management Academy, 1999) listed the amount of short-term and long-term loans by each group, and we used the ratio of these as another explanatory variable. When this variable is added for all available groups, it is insignificant in the regression. This is because there are two groups that did not go bankrupt despite having unusually high values of short-term debt: Doosan has short-term debt that is *five times* its long-term, while Lotte has short-term debt that is nearly *ten times* higher, as reported in Table D.2. If we exclude these two groups, as in regression 2(c), then the ratio of short-term to long-term debt is highly significant ($p = 0.06$). While the estimated equation still has difficulty in predicted bankruptcies with a probability > 0.5, if we consider instead the weaker criterion of probability > 0.4, then we successfully predict four out of the seven bankruptcies: Ssangyong, Dong Ah, Halla, and Keopyung. Most of these groups have short-term loans that are more than three times the level of long-term loans.

Although the regression including the ratio of short-term to long-term debt is clearly sensitive to its specification, the fact that this variable becomes a predictor of bankruptcy makes sense in the context of the financial crisis, but *should not* be considered an indication of a well-functioning capital market. On the contrary, among these four groups, only Halla has a level of debt relative to equity in 1997 that would justify bankruptcy according to using first regression we have estimated. Thus, the bankruptcies occurring *after* the exchange rate crisis are not predicted on the basis of "fundamentals" (that is, the debt–equity ratio), and are, therefore, attributed to some other cause. Our argument here is similar to that made by Woo, Carleton, and Rosario (2000) who used logit regressions to investigate the *countries* that experienced currency crises in 1997 and earlier. They find that the 1997 experience *does not* fit the equation estimated from earlier crises, suggesting that the events of 1997 were a financial panic. Our own estimates from the *chaebol* bankruptcies likewise suggest that there was a panic in the financial markets after November 17, such that groups were penalized based on their short-term rather than total debt. To understand the source of this financial panic, we consider next the linkages between the business groups, merchant banks, and commercial banks.

The Role of the Financial Sector

The linkages between the *chaebol* and financial institutions were greatly affected by Korea's liberalization of its financial sector during the 1990s. This included the liberalization of interest rates (November 1991),[8] overseas issuance of foreign currency denominated bonds (1991),[9] opening the Korean stock market to foreign investors (January 1992),[10] foreign currency borrowing by domestic firms (beginning 1995),[11] and also the conversion of twenty-six investment and finance companies into "merchant banks" in 1994 and 1996 (under the Act Concerning the Merger and Conversion of Financial Institutions), bringing the total number of merchant banks to thirty.[12] These actions were undertaken to improve the functioning of the capital market, and can be seen more generally as part of the globalization policy (*segyehwa*) undertaken by President Kim Young Sam (Kim, 2000b), which included Korea's entry into the Organization of Economic Cooperation and Development (OECD). Although these reforms did not cause the crisis, we believe that they were a contributing factor, especially due to their differential impact on the top five versus the second-tier of *chaebol*.

Before indicating how these reforms affected the debt structure of the *chaebol*, we first summarize the structure of the Korean financial markets and the role of the commercial banks. As is well known, the Korean government supported the business groups during the 1960s and 1970s through low-interest loans, provided by the Korean Development Bank and the commercial banks. Because of the below-market rates, the banks were forced into the position of *rationing* loans, that is, demand from the *chaebol* exceeded supply at these interest rates. As described by Nam and Kim (1994), this policy was implemented by having each of the top fifty *chaebol* assigned to specific commercial bank called the "principal transactions bank," which monitored the loans received by the group; the top thirty *chaebol* each had an upper limit on loans. These regulations were loosened in 1991, so that up to three "major corporations" within the top thirty *chaebol* were no longer subject to credit controls. Loans extended by overseas branches of Korean banks were also exempted from controls. In addition, the non-bank financial institutions (especially the merchant banks) were entirely *outside* this system of regulation, so their loans to the *chaebol* were not monitored.

---

[8] See Byrne (1993, Table 2, p. 53).
[9] Dooley and Kim (undated).
[10] Dooley and Kim (undated).
[11] "Foreign Exchange Reform Moves Forward," *Korean Business Review*, 171, April 1995, pp. 25–6.
[12] Ra and Yan (2000, p. 331, note 5).

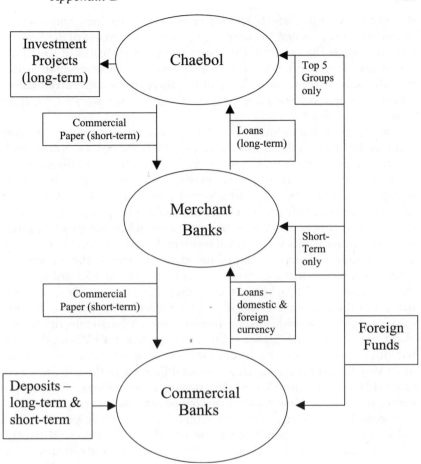

Figure D.1. Financial Structure in Korea.

The structure of the financial system between the commercial banks and business groups is illustrated in Figure D.1. At the top of that figure we show the *chaebol*, who are borrowing money to invest in long-term projects. At the bottom of the figure are the commercial banks, who are obtaining funds from domestic deposits and also foreign borrowing. As part of liberalization measures, banks were allowed to open and expand operations of overseas branches, and the foreign currency liabilities of domestic and foreign branches both roughly doubled from 1994 to 1996; the increase in external debt of the financial sector over this period exceeded that of the corporate sector.[13] In between these two are

---

[13] Dooley and Shin (undated, Tables 1 and 2). They report an increase in bank's foreign currency liabilities of $22.6 billion to $50.7 billion for domestic branches, and $31.7 billion

the merchant banks, which act as a financial intermediary and a source of funds for the *chaebol*. In contrast to Japan, where many of the *keiretsu* have a bank at the center of the group, commercial banks in Korea are legally prohibited from being a part of the *chaebol*.[14] The merchant banks play this role instead, and in fact, all but three of the top thirty *chaebol* owned one or more such non-bank financial institutions in 1996 (Lee, et al., 2000, Table 9).

The merchant banks were not subject to the regulations on the larger commercial banks, and became the scapegoat for the crisis in Korea, leading to the closure of many of them in 1998. Two activities of the merchant banks were particularly risky. First, they actively borrowed short-term on foreign markets and funneled these loans to the *chaebol*. These loans were in foreign currency (dollars or yen), but were not hedged for devaluation risk, because this had not entered anyone's mind at the time. Actually, the commercial banks were also actively borrowing in foreign currency, and in amounts *exceeding* that of the merchant banks: the foreign currency borrowings of the commercial banks peaked at 15.2 trillion won ($19 billion) in 1996, whereas the *combined* foreign plus domestic borrowing of the merchant banks were 11.6 trillion won ($14.5 billion) in the same year.[15] Nevertheless, the foreign currency borrowing of the merchant banks was much higher relative to their size: only 7% of the total liabilities of commercial banks consisted of foreign currency borrowings in 1996, whereas for the merchant banks fully 45% of the liabilities were to foreigners, and only 18% of the assets were held abroad.[16] Thus, the exposure of the merchant banks to exchange rate risk was extremely high.

A second risky activity of the merchant banks, that illustrates their close links to the *chaebol*, was issuing and dealing in "commercial paper." A commercial paper is a short-term (typically ninety days) unsecured promissory note issued by a company, which is a promise to pay back the money within three months, with nothing standing behind this promise except the good name of the company. This type of financing is used by only the most credit-worthy firms in industrial countries and only to raise a small amount of total debt: 0.1% in Germany, 1.2% in the

---

to $52.9 billion for foreign branches, over 1994–96 (Table A2). Over the same period, total external debt of the financial sector increased from $33.3 billion to $66.7 billion, with more than half of this short-term, while external debt of the corporate sector increased from $20 billion to $35.6 billion, with more than half of this short-term (Table A1).

[14] Chan Guk Huh and Sun Bae Kim, "Japan's Keiretsu and Korea's Chaebol," *Federal Reserve Bank of San Francisco Weekly Letter*, number 93–25, July 16, 1993. Nam and Kim (1994, Table A13.3, pp. 464–5) show that six of the top thirty *chaebol* in 1991 have a small equity interest in their principal transactions bank, not exceeding 5 percent.

[15] The Bank of Korea, *Monthly Statistical Bulletin*, November 1999, "Accounts of Commercial Banks," p. 31 and "Accounts of Merchant Banking Corporations," p. 45.

[16] Ra and Yan (2000), p. 336.

United States, and 0.9% in Japan.[17] In contrast, Korean manufacturing firms raised 17.5% of their funds from the commercial paper market in 1996, an amount that expanded more than seven times between 1991 and 1997.[18] For both the buyer and the seller, commercial paper is inherently risky: there is a risk for the buyer because the issuing company might not be able to repay (default risk), but in that case the seller would immediately lose the ability to refinance the debt (rollover risk). The merchant banks actively distributed the commercial paper of the *chaebol*, as well as issuing their own. And who bought this risky product? None other than the commercial banks! To understand how this unlikely situation arose, we return to the financial reform of the 1990s.

As described by Ra and Yan (2000), in 1991 the interest rates for long-term deposits (trust accounts) at the commercial banks was liberalized, leading to an inflow of long-term funds. At the same time, the interest rates on loans from the commercial banks were *not* raised, so the banks had to seek uses for their deposits that promised higher returns, and commercial paper was the answer. The commercial banks became the biggest buyers of such paper, holding about 60% of total issues, compared to 20% for pension funds and insurance companies.[19] Notice that this created a mismatch in the maturity structure of the banks, with their liabilities (that is, deposits) increasingly long-term, and their assets (including commercial paper) increasing short-term. Provided that the return on short-term commercial paper remained above the interest rates on long-term deposits, as was the case, this was profitable for the commercial banks.

But for the merchant banks, the situation was reversed. They were selling commercial paper, and also actively borrowing in the foreign market, both of which were short-term liabilities. On the asset side, they were making long-term loans to the *chaebol* to finance investment projects.[20] This is the worst situation for any financial institution to be in: with long-term assets and short-term liabilities, any increase in the short-term interest rates will quickly lead to insolvency. In terms of Figure D.1, the reader might visualize the right-hand side of the figure being pushed up by the increased inflow of foreign funds, and loans from the commercial banks, while the left-hand side of the figure is being pulled down by the outstanding issues of commercial paper; as this visual analogy is meant to suggest, the situation was precarious indeed!

Putting a strain on the whole system were the bankruptcies of *chaebol* during the first three quarters of 1997. As we have already argued, these

---

[17] Ra and Yan (2000), p. 339.
[18] Ra and Yan (2000), pp. 331 and 339.
[19] Ra and Yan (2000), pp. 333–4.
[20] In 1996, about 60% of loans from the merchant banks were made in the form of relatively illiquid assets: lease, foreign securities, and factoring (Ra and Yan, 2000, p. 336).

bankruptcies were fully justified and showed that the capital markets were doing their job. But in *combination with* the precarious financing between the *chaebol* and banks, the system barely able to withstand these shocks. Ra and Yan (2000) describe the unraveling that occurred for one group, Kia:

> ... the excessive reliance on highly risky commercial paper led the whole financial system and corporate sector to be extremely vulnerable to adverse external shocks. For example, after hearing the financial rumors about the Kia Group, Korean merchant banks recalled commercial paper worth 4.2 trillion won [$5.25 billion] in a single day in mid-July 1997 from Kia, which had used it as one of its main corporate financing sources. The recollection of loans pushed it into insolvency immediately. This punitive action further squeezed the credit pool of merchant banks that concentrated about 80 percent of their business on commercial paper. (p. 329)

> With Kia Group defaulting, Korean commercial banks, the largest buyer of commercial paper, refused to purchase and discount the paper dealt and issued by them. (p. 328)

This shows how the combination of default risk and rollover risk can quickly lead to a panic by creditor banks, and bankruptcy of a group, even if its long-term debt and financial prospects might not warrant this. Furthermore, these risks were greatest for the smaller, or second-tier *chaebol*. The reason is that the top five *chaebol* had *direct access* to foreign loans, due to their size and high credit rating, but this was not the case for the smaller *chaebol*. This is demonstrated by Lee et al (2000), who use firm-level financial data for a large sample of Korean firms over 1981–97 to investigate how the debt-structure has changed over time. They show that the top thirty *chaebol* firms have consistently had higher debt-equity ratios than non-*chaebol* firms. Within the top thirty, however, there are important distinctions between the top five and the second-tier, ranked 6–30th. The top five firms have had relative stable debt-equity ratios since 1991, but within total debt, there has been an *increasing* proportion of long-term and or foreign debt. In contrast, for the second-tier *chaebol* firms, the proportion of long-term debt has *fallen* since 1989, and the proportion of foreign debt has also *fallen* since 1992, since they have not had access to this market.

The story consistent with these empirical trends is that the top five *chaebol* gained increasing access to international markets for debt, so that the second-tier *chaebol* (ranked 6–30th) were then diverted to the domestic market for commercial paper. This increased the risks for these smaller *chaebol* because, in the event of financial difficulty, they could abruptly find themselves without access to continuing credit. Furthermore, it increased the vulnerability of the merchant banks affiliated with the *chaebol*, because in the event of bankruptcy, the banks could find themselves with bad loans in excess of their own net worth: the loans on which Kia defaulted are purported to account for 184% of the aggregate capitalization of the eight merchant banks in Seoul, and 75% of sixteen regional banks.[21]

According to Ra and Yan (2000), the event that toppled the whole system was Moody's downgrading of its credit rating for the Korea Development Bank on July 30, 1997, so that Korean banks and corporations found it increasingly difficult to borrow abroad:

> As a result, commercial banks, merchant banks, and corporations returned to the domestic financial and foreign exchange markets to raise funds. The commercial banks recalled foreign currency loans from the merchant banks. This forced the merchant banks to bid by "all-out" efforts for any available foreign currency...It accelerated the depreciation of the won and the won-dollar exchange fell to an unprecedented low...The turmoil among merchant banks was one of the key reasons behind the sharp fall of the won against the dollar. (pp. 327–8).

Notice that this account of events challenges the idea that the floating of the won was brought about by the actions of international speculators; instead, it may well have been domestic agents scrambling for foreign currency that drained the reserves of the central bank, and precipitated the exchange rate crisis.[22] Regardless, we would classify the recall of loans by the commercial banks and subsequent actions as elements of a banking crisis and financial panic, and in our view, this was the proximate cause of the bankruptcies that occurred *after* November 17, 1997. Rather than looking at long-term profitability and debt structure of groups, the financial markets focused solely on short-term accounts, leading to bankruptcy for those second-tier groups that found themselves with excessive short-term debts. Unlike the bankruptcies that occurred before November, these were not based on fundamentals, but rather, due to the financial panic brought

---

[21] Ra and Yan, (2000), pp. 327–8.
[22] Support for this idea comes from U.S. Treasury Secretary Robert Rubin, who observed in a 1998 speech about the Asian crisis: "When these crises began, foreign investors started to withdraw capital, local companies sought to hedge hard currency exposures, exporters stopped bringing their export earning home, and citizens moved their saving abroad. I think it has now become accepted that most of the pressure on these currencies comes from local sources and not foreign investors." (Address on the Asian Financial Situation to George Washington University, Washington, D.C., January 21, 1998; cited by Kim, 1998, p. 34).

about by the interconnections between the business groups, merchant banks, and commercial banks.

In summary, we view the financial crisis in Korea as the failure of a *system* of production and finance, or of economic organization, that has roots that date from well before the specific policy choices of the 1990s. This is what Nicole Woolsey Biggart (1998) calls "deep finance": the search for systemic features that explain the differential impact of the crisis in South Korea as compared to Taiwan. The fact that the government supported the *chaebol* for decades through low-interest loans, via the commercial banks, does not explain the emergence of the groups, but did indeed lead to a co-dependency between government, banks, and business groups that was extremely difficult to break. Instead of the metaphor of an "Asian flu" sweeping through the region that South Korea happened to catch (because its foreign exchange reserves were too low), we prefer to think instead of a county that was trying to "break a habit" of government-directed credit that had both contributed to, and been reinforced by, the structure of the business groups. The "deep" explanation, then, lies in the economic organization of Korea; not as an example of "crony capitalism," but as a fully rational system of production that is inherently susceptible to shocks which economies organized differently would be able to withstand.

References

Abernathy, Frederick H., John T. Dunlop, Janice H. Hammond, and David Weil. 1999. *A Stitch in Time: Lean Retailing and the Transformation of Manufacturing – Lessons from the Apparel and Textile Industries*. New York: Oxford University Press.

Abolafia, Mitchell. 1996. *Making Markets*. Cambridge, Mass.: Harvard University Press.

Aghion, Phillipe and Jean Tirole. 1997. "Formal and Real Authority in Organizations." *Journal of Political Economy* 105, 1: 1–29.

Aiyer, Sri-Ram. 1999. "The Search for a New Development Paradigm," in *Korea and the Asian Economic Crisis: One Year Later*, Joint U.S.-Korea Academic Studies 9: 21–44.

Akerlof, George A. 1984. "Gift Exchange and Efficiency-Wage Theory: Four Views." *American Economic Review* (Papers and Proceedings) 74: 79–83.

Alchian, Armen A. 1984. "Specificity, Specialization and Coalitions." *Journal of Economic Theory and Institutions* 140: 34–49.

Alchian, Armen A. and Harold Demsetz. 1972. "Production, Information Costs, and Economic Organization." *American Economic Review* 62: 777–95.

Alterman, William, W. Erwin Diewert, and Robert C. Feenstra. 1999. *International Trade Price Indexes and Seasonal Commodities*. U.S. Dept. of Labor, Bureau of Labor Statistics, Washington, D.C.

Amsden, Alice H. 1985. "The State and Taiwan's Economic Development." In *Bringing the State Back In*, edited by Peter B. Evans, Dietrich Rueschemeyer, and Theda Skocpol. Cambridge: Cambridge University Press, 78–106.

Amsden, Alice H. 1989. *Asia's Next Giant: South Korea and Late Industrialization*. New York: Oxford University Press.

Amsden, Alice H. 1991. "Big Business and Urban Congestion in Taiwan: The Origins of Small Enterprise and Regionally Decentralized Industry." *World Development* 19, 9: 1121–35.

Amsden, Alice H. 2001. *The Rise of "the Rest": Challenges to the West from Late-Industrializing Economies*. New York: Oxford University Press.

419

Amsden, Alice H. and Takashi Hikino. 1994. "Project Execution Capability, Organization Know-how and Conglomerate Corporate Growth in Late Industrialization." *Industrial and Corporate Change* 3, 1: 111–47.

Anderson, Philip W., Kenneth J. Arrow, and David Pines (eds.). 1987. *The Economy as an Evolving Complex System*. Redwood City, Calif.: Addison-Wesley Pub. Co.

Anderson, Philip W., Kenneth J. Arrow, and David Pines, editors. 1988. *The Economy as an Evolving Complex System*. Reading, Massachusetts: Addison-Wesley Publishing.

Antràs, Pol. 2003. "Firms, Contracts and Trade Structure," *Quarterly Journal of Economics* 118, 4 (November): 1374–418.

Antràs, Pol. 2005. "Incomplete Contracts and the Product Cycle," *American Economic Review* 95, 4 (September): 1054–73.

Aoki, Masahiko, ed. 1984. *The Economic Analysis of the Japanese Firm*. Amsterdam: North-Holland.

Aoki, Masahiko. 1988. *Information, Incentive, and Bargaining in the Japanese Economy*. Cambridge: Cambridge University Press.

Aoki, Masahiko. 1990. "Towards an Economic Model of the Japanese Firm." *Journal of Economic Literature* 28, 1 (March): 1–27.

Aoki, Masahiko. 1992. "Decentralization-Centralization in Japanese Organization: A Duality Principle." In *The Political Economy of Japan, Vol. 3, Cultural and Social Dynamics*, edited by Shumpei Kumon and Henry Rosovsky. Stanford: Stanford University Press, 142–69.

Aoki, Masahiko. 1998. "Organizational Conventions and the Gains from Diversity: An Evolutionary Game Approach." *Corporate and Industrial Change* 7: 399–432.

Aoki, Masahiko. 2000. *Information, Corporate Governance, and Institutional Diversity: Competitiveness in Japan, the USA, and the Transitional Economies*. Oxford, New York: Oxford University Press.

Aoki, Masahiko. 2001. *Toward A Comparative Institutional Analysis*. Cambridge, Mass.: MIT Press.

Aoki, Masahiko and Hugh Patrick. 1994. *The Japanese Main Bank System*. Oxford/New York: Oxford University Press.

Appelbaum, Richard P. and David Smith. 2001. "Governance and Flexibility: The East Asian Garment Industry." In *Economic Governance and the Challenge of Flexibility in East Asia*, edited by Frederic C. Deyo, Richard F. Doner, and Eric Hershberg. Lanham, Md.: Rowman & Littlefield, 79–106.

Arrighi, Giovanni, Takeshi Hamashita, and Mark Selden. 2003. *The Resurgence of East Asia: 500, 150, and 50-Year Perspectives*. London: Routledge.

Arrow, Kenneth J. 1968. "Economic Equilibrium." In *The International Encyclopedia of the Social Sciences*. New York: Macmillan, 376–89.

Arrow, Kenneth. 1969. "The Organization of Economic Activity: Issues Pertinent to the Choice of Market versus Nonmarket Allocation," in *The Analysis and Evaluation of Public Expenditure: The PPB System*, vol. I, U.S. Joint Economic Committee, 91st Congress, 1st Session, Washington, D.C., GPO, 59–73.

Arrow, Kenneth. 1971. "Political and Economic Evaluations, Social Effects, and Externalities." In *Frontiers of Quantitative Economics*, edited by M. D. Intriligator. Amsterdam: North Holland Press, 3–25.

Arrow, Kenneth. 1974. *The Limits of Organization*. New York: W. W. Norton.

Arrow, Kenneth J. 1990. "Kenneth J. Arrow." In *Economics and Sociology*, edited by Richard Swedberg. Princeton: Princeton University Press, 133–51.

Arrow, Kenneth and Gerard Debreu. 1954. "Existence of an Equilibrium for a Competitive Economy." *Econometrica* 22, 3 (July): 265–90.

Arthur, W. Brian. 1989. "Competing Technologies, Increasing Returns, and Lock-in by Historically Small Events." *Economic Journal* 99: 116–31.

Arthur, W. Brian. 1994. *Increasing Returns and Path Dependence in the Economy*. Ann Arbor: University of Michigan Press.

Arthur, W. Brian, Steven N. Durlauf, and David A. Lane. 1997. *The Economy as an Evolving Complex System II*. Reading, Massachusetts: Addison-Wesley.

Aw, Bee Yan and Mark J. Roberts. 1986. "Estimating Quality Change in Quota-constrained Import Markets: The Case of U.S. Footwear." *Journal of International Economics* 21: 45–60.

Aw, Bee Yan and Mark J. Roberts. 1988. Price and Quality Comparisons for U.S. Footwear Imports: An Application of Multilateral Index Numbers." In *Empirical Methods for International Trade*, edited by Robert C. Feenstra. Cambridge, Mass.: MIT Press, 257–75.

Axelrod, Robert. 1984. *The Evolution of Cooperation*. New York: Basic Books.

Baker, Hugh. 1979. *Chinese Family and Kinship*. New York: Columbia University Press.

Bates, Robert H. 1995. "Social Dilemmas and Rational Individuals: An Assessment of the New Institutionalism." In *The New Institutional Economics and Third World Development*, edited by John Harriss, Janet Hunter, and Colin M. Lewis. London: Routledge, 27–48.

Baum, Gregory. 1996. *Karl Polanyi on Ethics and Economics*. Montreal: McGill-Queen's University Press.

Beck, Peter B. 2000. "Korea's Embattled Chaebol: Are They Serious About Restructuring?" In *The Two Koreas in 2000: Sustaining Recovery and Seeking Reconciliation*. Washington, D.C.: Korea Economic Institute of America, 16–28.

Becker, Gary. 1981. *A Treatise on the Family*. Cambridge, Mass.: Harvard University Press.

Becker, Gary. 1988. "Family Economics and Macro Behavior." *American Economic Review* 78: 1–13.

Becker, Howard S. 1986. *Doing Things Together: Selected Papers*. Evanston, Illinois: Northwestern University Press.

Becker, Howard S. 1995. "The Power of Inertia." *Qualitative Sociology* 18, 3: 301–9.

Bell, Daniel. 1976. *The Cultural Contradictions of Capitalism*. New York: Basic Books.

Bellah, Robert. 1970. "Father and Son in Christianity and Confucianism." In *Beyond Belief*. New York: Harper and Row, 76–99.

Ben-Porath, Yoram. 1980. "The F-Connection: Families, Friends and Firms in the Organization of Exchange." *Population and Development Review* 6, 1: 1–30.

Berger, Suzanne and Ronald Dore (eds.). 1996. *National Diversity and Global Capitalism*. Ithaca: Cornell University Press.

Bernheim, B. Douglas and Michael Whinston.1990. "Multimarket Contact and Collusive Behavior." *Rand Journal of Economics* 21, 1 (Spring): 1–26.

Bhagwati, Jagdish N. 1992. "The Fraudulent Case against Japan." *The Wall Street Journal*, January 6.

Bhagwati, Jagdish N. 1998. "The Capital Myth." *Foreign Affairs* 77, 3: 7–12.

Biggart, Nicole Woolsey. 1990. "Institutionalized Patrimonialism in Korean Business." *Comparative Social Research* 12: 113–33.

Biggart, Nicole Woolsey. 1998. "Deep Finance: The Organizational Bases of South Korea's Financial Collapse." *Journal of Management Inquiry* 7, 4: 311–20.

Biggart, Nicole Woolsey and Mitchell Abolafia. 1991. "Competition and Markets: An Institutional Perspective." In *Perspectives on Socio-Economics*, edited by Amitai Etzioni and Paul Lawrence. Armonk, NY: M. E. Sharpe, 211–31.

Biggart, Nicole Woolsey and Mauro F. Guillén. 1999. "Developing Difference: Social Organization and the Rise of the Auto Industries of South Korea, Taiwan, Spain and Argentina." *American Sociological Review* 64: 722–47.

Biggs, Tyler S. 1988a. "Financing the Emergence of Small and Medium Enterprise in Taiwan: Heterogeneous Firm Size and Efficient Intermediation." Employment and Enterprise Policy Analysis Project. EEPA Discussion Paper No. 16.

Biggs, Tyler S. 1988b. "Financing the Emergence of Small and Medium Enterprise in Taiwan: Financial Mobilization and the Flow of Domestic Credit to the Private Sector." Employment and Enterprise Policy Analysis Project. EEPA Discussion Paper No. 15.

Blackwell, Roger D. 1997. *From Mind to Market: Reinventing the Retail Supply Chain*. New York: HarperCollins.

Blaug, Mark. 1985. *Economic Theory in Retrospect*. Cambridge: Cambridge University Press.

Block, Fred. 1987. *Revising State Theory*. Philadelphia: Temple University Press.

Block, Fred. 1990. *Postindustrial Possibilities: A Critique of Economic Discourse*. Berkeley: University of California Press.

Block, Fred and Margaret R. Somers. 1984. "Beyond the Economistic Fallacy: The Holistic Social Science of Karl Polanyi." In *Vision and Method in Historical Sociology*, edited by Theda Skocpol. Cambridge: Cambridge University Press, 47–84.

Bluestone, Barry, Patricia Hanna, Sarah Kuhn, and Laura Moore. 1981. *The Retail Revolution: Market Transformation, Investment, and Labor in the Modern Department Store*. Boston: Auburn House Publishing Company.

Bluestone, Barry and Bennett Harrison. 1982. *The Deindustrialization of America*. New York: Basic Books.

Blumer, Herbert. 1990. *Industrialization As an Agent of Social Change: A Critical Analysis*. New York: Aldine De Gruyter.

Blyth, Mark. 2002. *Great Transformations: Economic Ideas and Institutional Change in the Twentieth Century*. Cambridge: Cambridge University Press.

Bonacich, Edna and David V. Waller. 1994. "The Role of U.S. Apparel Manufacturers in the Globalization of the Industry in the Pacific Rim." In *Global Production: The Apparel Industry in the Pacific Rim*, edited by Edna Bonacich, Lucie Cheng, Norma Chinchilla, Nora Hamilton, and Paul Ong. Philadelphia: Temple University Press, 80–104.

Bonacich, Edna, Lucie Cheng, Norma Chinchilla, Nora Hamilton, and Paul Ong. 1994. *Global Production: The Apparel Industry in the Pacific Rim*. Philadelphia: Temple University Press.

Bourdieu, Pierre. 1984. *Distinction: A Social Critique of the Judgment of Taste*. Cambridge, Mass.: Harvard University Press.

Bowles, Samuel. 1986. "The Production Process in a Competitive Economy: Walrasian, neo-Hobbesian, and Marxian Models." In *The Economic Nature of the Firm, A Reader*, edited by Louis Putterman. Cambridge: Cambridge University Press, 329–55.

Bradford, C. I. 1994. "From Trade-Driven Growth to Growth-Driven Trade: Reappraising the East Asian Development Experience." Washington, DC: Organization for Economic Co-operation and Development.

Brandt, Loren and Barbara Sands. 1990. "Beyond Malthus and Ricardo: Economic Growth, Land Concentration, and Income Distribution in Early Twentieth-century Rural China." *The Journal of Economic History L*, 4 (December): 807–27.

Brinton, Mary C. and Victor Nee (eds.). 2001. *The New Institutionalism in Sociology*. Stanford: Stanford University Press.

Brown, Stephen A. 1997. *Revolution at the Checkout Counter*. Cambridge, Mass.: Harvard University Press.

Bucklin, Louis P. 1972. *Competition and Evolution in the Distributive Trades*. Englewood Cliffs, NJ: Prentice Hall Inc.

Bugra, Ayse and Behlül Üsdiken (eds.). 1997. *State, Market, and Organizational Form*. Berlin and New York: W. de Gruyter.

Burawoy, Michael. 1985. *The Politics of Production: Factory Regimes under Capitalism and Socialism*. London: Verso.

Burmeister, Larry L. 1994. "Restructuring Economic Space: Agricultural Land Policy Reforms in South Korea." Paper presented at the Annual Meeting of the Association for Asian Studies 1994.

Burnstein, Meyer. 1960. "A Theory of Full-Line Forcing." *Northwestern University Law Review 55*, February: 62–95.

Burt, Ronald S. 1992. *Structural Holes, The Social Structure of Competition*. Cambridge, Mass.: Harvard University Press.

Byrne, Tomas J. 1993. "Implications of Korea's Financial Liberalization for the National Treatment of Foreign Financial Institutions." *Korean-U.S. Financial Issues* Table 4: 53.

Cardoso, R. H. and E. Faletto. 1979. *Dependency and Development in Latin America*. Trans. Marjory Mattingly Urquidi. Berkeley: University of California Press.

Casella, Alessandra and James E. Rauch. 2002. "Anonymous Market and Group Ties in International Trade." *Journal of International Economics 58*, 1: 19–48.

Caves, Richard E. 1974. "The Economics of Reciprocity: Theory and Evidence on Bilateral Trading Arrangements." In *International Trade and Finance: Essays in Honor of Jan Tinbergen*, edited by Willy Sellekaerts. New York: International Arts and Sciences Press, 17–54.

Caves, Richard E. 1989. "International Differences in Market Structure." In *Handbook of Industrial Organization*, vol. II, edited by Richard Schmalensee and Robert D. Willig. Amsterdam: North-Holland, 1225–50.

Caves, Richard E. 1995. "Growth and Decline in Multinational Enterprises: From Equilbrium Models to Turnover Processes." In *Corporate Links and Foreign Direct Investment in Asia and the Pacific*, edited by Edward K. Y. Chen and Peter Drysdale. Pymble, Australia: HarperEducational Publishers, 9–28.

Caves, Richard E. and Masu Uekasa. 1976. *Industrial Organization in Japan*. Washington, D.C.: The Brooking Institution.

Chamberlin, Edward H. 1962 [1933]. *The Theory of Monopolistic Competition: A Reorientation of the Theory of Value*. 8th edition. Cambridge, Mass.: Harvard University Press.

Chandler, Alfred D., Jr. 1977. *The Visible Hand: The Managerial Revolution in American Business*. Cambridge, Mass: Harvard University.

Chandler, Alfred D. 1982. "The M-Form: Industrial Groups, American Style." *European Economic Review* 19: 3–23.

Chandler, Alfred D., Jr. 1990. *Scale and Scope: The Dynamics of Industrial Capitalism*. Cambridge, Mass: Harvard University.

Chang, Dukjin. 1999. *Privately Owned Social Structures: Institutionalization-Network Contingency in the Korean Chaebol*. Unpublished Ph.D. dissertation, Department of Sociology, University of Chicago.

Chang, Hyung-Soo and Yoon-Jong Wang. 1998. *IMF Cheje Hanguk Gyungje, 1997.12–1998.6: Chonghap Simchung Bogo* (Korean Economy Under the IMF Regime, December 1997–June 1998: A Comprehensive Report). Seoul: Korea Institute for International Economic Policy (in Korean).

Chang, Sea Jin and Ungwah Choi. 1988. "Strategy, Structure and Performance of Korean Business Groups: A Transactions Cost Approach." *Journal of Industrial Economics* 38, 2 (December): 141–58.

Chen, Chieh-hsuan. 1994. *Xieli wangluo yu shenhuo jiegou: Taiwan zhongxiao qiye de shehui jiji fenxi Chinese name* (Mutual aid networks and the structure of daily life: A social economic analysis of Taiwan's small- and medium-sized enterprises). Taipei: Lianjing.

Chen, Chieh-hsuan. 1995. *Huobi wangluo yu shenhuo jiegou: Difang jinrong, zhongxiao qiye Taiwan shisu shehui zhi zhuanhua* (Monetary networks and the structure of daily life: Local finances, small and medium-sized enterprises, and the transformation of folk society in Taiwan). Taipei: Lianjing.

Chen, Chieh-hsuan. 1998. *Taiwan chanye de shehuixueyanjiu.* (Sociological research on Taiwan's industries). Taipei: Lianjing.

Chen, Chieh-ying. 1997. *Gongyehua chongde chuantonghua – Hemei fangzhiye zhi yanzhou* (The traditionalism of industrialization – Research on the cotton industy in Hemei). Difang shehui (Local society) 1, 1: 211–54.

Chen, Yongmin. 1999. "Oligopoly Price Discrimination and Resale Price Maintenance." *Rand Journal of Economics* 30, 3 (Autumn): 441–55.

Chen, Yongmin. 2001. "On Vertical Mergers and their Competitive Effects." *Rand Journal of Economics* 32, 4: 667–85.

Cheng, Lu-lin and Yukihito Sato. 1998. "The Bicycle Industries in Taiwan and Japan: A Preliminary Study Toward Comparison between Taiwanese and Japanese Industrial Development." *Joint Research Program Series* No. 124. Tokyo: Institute of Developing Economies.

China Credit Information Service, various years. *Business Groups in Taiwan 1983–84* (China Credit Information Service, Ltd., Taipei).

Chiu, Stephen Wing-Kai, K. C. Ho, and Tailok Lui. 1996. *City-States in the Global Economy; Industrial Restructuring in Hong Kong and Singapore*. Boulder, Colorado: Westview Press.

Cho, Lee-Jay and Won Bae Kim. 1991. "The Population Redistribution Plan (1977) and Urbanization Problems." In *Economic Development in the Republic of Korea: A Policy Perspective*, edited by Lee-Jay Cho and Yoon Hyung Kim. Honolulu, Hawaii: East-West Center, 349–67.

Chou, Tein-Chen. 1985. *Industrial Organization in the Process of Economic Development: The Case of Taiwan, 1950–1980*. Louvain-la-Neuve: Universite Catholique de Louvain, Faculte des Science Economiques, Sociales et Politiques.

Chow, Kai-wing. 1994. *The Rise of Confucian Ritualism in Late Imperial China: Ethics, Classics, and Lineage Discourse*. Stanford: Stanford University Press.

Chow, Peter C. Y. and Mitchell H. Kellman. 1993. *Trade – The Engine of Growth in East Asia*. Oxford: Oxford University Press.

Chu, Yun-han. 1995. "The East Asian NICs: A State-led Path to the Developed World." In *Global Change, Regional Response: The New International Context of Development*, edited by Barbara Stallings. Cambridge: Cambridge University Press, 199–237.

Chung, Chi-nien. 2000. "Markets, Culture and Institutions: The Formation and Transformation of Business Groups in Taiwan, 1960s–1990s. Doctoral Dissertation, Department of Sociology, Stanford University.

Chung, Chi-nien. 2001. "Markets, Culture and Institutions: The Emergence of Large Business Groups in Taiwan, 1950s–1970s." *Journal of Management Studies* 38, 5: 719–45.

Chung, Chi-nien. 2003. "Managerial Structure of Business Groups in Taiwan: The Inner Circle System and Its Social Organization." *Developing Economies* 41, 1: 37–64.

Chung, Wai-keung and Gary G. Hamilton. 2001. "Social Logic as Business Logic: *Guanxi*, Trustworthiness, and the Embeddedness of Chinese Business Practices." In *Rules and Networks: The Legal Culture of Global Business Transactions*, edited by Richard P. Appelbaum, William L. F. Felstiner, and Volkmar Gessner. Oxford: Hart Publishing, 325–46.

Claessens, Stijn, Swati Ghosh, and David Scott. 1999. "Korea's Financial Sector Reforms," in *Korea and the Asian Economic Crisis: One Year Later*, Joint U.S.-Korea Academic Studies 9, 83–110.

Clerides, Sofronis K., Saul Lach, and James R. Tybout. 1998. "Is Learning by Exporting Important? Micro-Dynamic Evidence from Colombia, Mexico and Morocco." *Quarterly Journal of Economics* 108, 3 (August): 903–48.

Clifford, Mark L. 1994. *Troubled Tiger: Businessmen, Bureaucrats, and Generals in South Korea*. Armonk, New York: M. E. Sharpe.

Coase, Ronald. 1937. "The Nature of the Firm." *Economica* 4 (November): 386–405.

Cohen, Michael D., James G. March, and Johan P. Olsen. 1972. "A Garbage Can Model of Organizational Choice." *Administrative Science Quarterly* 17, 1 (March): 1–25.

Cohen, Nancy E. 2002. *America's Marketplace: The History of Shopping Centers*. Lyme, CT.: Greenwich Pub. Group.

Cole, David C. and Princeton N. Lyman. 1971. *Korean Development, The Interplay of Politics and Economics*. Cambridge, Mass.: Harvard University Press.

Coleman, James. 1990. *Foundations of Social Theory*. Cambridge, Mass.: Harvard University Press.

Collier, David, ed. 1979. *The New Authoritarianism in Latin American*. Princeton: Princeton University Press.

Cook, Karen S. and Margaret Levi. 1990. *The Limits of Rationality*. Chicago: University of Chicago Press.

Cox, David and Richard Harris. 1985. "Trade Liberalization and Industrial Organization: Some Estimates for Canada." *Journal of Political Economy* 93, 1 (February): 115–45.

Cox, David and Richard Harris. 1986. "A Quantitative Assessment of the Economic Impact on Canada of Sectoral Free Trade with the United States." *Canadian Journal of Economics* 19, 3 (August): 377–94.

Crouch, Colin and Wolfgang Streeck, eds. 1997. *Political Economy of Modern Capitalism*. London: Sage Publications.

Cumings, Bruce. 1984a. "The Origins and Development of the Northeast Asian Political Economy: Industrial Sectors, Product Cycles, and Political Consequences." *International Organizations* 38: 1–40.

Cumings, Bruce. 1984b. "The Legacy of Japanese Colonialism in Korea." In *The Japanese Colonial Empire, 1895–1945*, edited by Ramon Myers and Mark R. Peattie. Princeton, N.J.: Princeton University Press, 478–96.

Dalton, George. 1969. "Theoretical Issues in Economic Anthropology." *Current Anthropology* 10, 1 (February): 63–80.

Debreu, Gerard. 1959. *Theory of Value: An Axiomatic Analysis of Economic Equilibrium*. New Haven, Conn.: Yale University Press.

Demsetz, Harold. 1993. "The Theory of the Firm Revisited." In *The Nature of the Firm: Origins, Evolution, and Development*, edited by Oliver E. Williamson and Sidney G. Winter. New York: Oxford University Press, 159–78.

Deuchler, Martina. 1992. *The Confucian Transformation of Korea*. Cambridge, Mass.: Council on East Asian Studies, Harvard University.

Deyo, Frederic C. (ed.). 1987. *The Political Economy of the New Asian Industrialism*. Ithaca: Cornell University Press.

Diamond, Peter A. 1982. "Aggregate Demand Management in Search Equilibrium." *Journal of Political Economy* 90, 5 (October): 881–94.

Dicken, Peter. 1998. *Global Shift: Tranforming the World Economy*, 3rd Edition. New York: The Guilford Press.

Dinopoulos, Elias and Paul Segerstrom. 1999. "A Schumpeterian Model of Protection and Real Wages." *American Economic Review* 89, 3 (June): 450–72.

Dixit, Avinash. 1983. "Vertical Integration in a Monopolistically Competitive Industry." *International Journal of Industrial Organization* 1: 63–78.

Dixit, Avinash and Joseph Stiglitz. 1977. "Monopolistic Competition and Optimum Product Diversity." *American Economic Review* 67: 297–308.

Dobbins, Frank. 1994. *Forging Industrial Policy: The United States, Britain, and France in the Railway Age.* Cambridge: Cambridge University Press.

Dollar, David and Kenneth L. Sokoloff. 1994. "Industrial Policy, Productivity Growth, and Structural Change in the Manufacturing Industries: A Comparison of Taiwan and South Korea." In *The Role of the State in Taiwan's Development,* edited by Joel D. Aberbach, David Dollar, and Kenneth L. Sokoloff. Armonk, NY: M. E. Sharpe, 5–25.

Doner, Richard F. 1991. *Driving a Bargain: Automobile Industrialization and Japanese Firms in Southeast Asia.* Berkeley: University of California Press.

Doner, Richard F. 1992. "Limits of State Strength: Toward an Institutionalist View of Economic Development." *World Politics* 44 (April): 398–431.

Dooley, Michael P. and Inseok Shin. Undated. "Private Inflows When Crises Are Anticipated: A Case Study of Korea." University of California, Santa Cruz and Korean Development Institute, mimeo.

Dosi, Giovanni. 1982. "Technological Paradigms and Technological Trajectories." *Research Policy* 11: 147–62.

Duby, Georges. 1981. *Medieval Marriage.* Baltimore: Johns Hopkins University Press.

Dunlop, John T. and Jan W. Rivkin. 1997. "Introduction." In *Revolution at the Checkout Counter,* by Stephen A. Brown. Cambridge, Mass.: Harvard University Press, 1–38.

Duus, Peter. 1984. "Economic Dimensions of Meiji Imperialism: The Case of Korea, 1895–1910." In *The Japanese Colonial Empire, 1895–1945,* edited by Ramon Myers and Mark R. Peattie. Princeton, N.J.: Princeton University Press, 128–71.

Dyer, J. H. 1998. "Vertical keiretsu alliances and asset specialization: A new perspective on Japanese economic success." In *Networks and Markets: Pacific Rim Investigations,* edited by W. N. Fruim. New York: Oxford University Press, 233–54.

Eastman, Lloyd E. 1988. *Family, Field, and Ancestors: Constancy and Change in China's Social and Economic History, 1550–1949.* Oxford: Oxford University Press.

Eccles, R. G. 1985. *The Transfer Pricing Problem: A Theory for Practice.* Lexington, MA: Lexington Books.

Eckert, Carter. 1991. *Offspring of Empire: The Koch'ang Kims and the Colonial Origins of Korean Capitalism, 1876–1945.* Seattle: University of Washington Press.

Economic Research Center of Korea. 1962. *Industrial Structure of Korea, Vol. 1, Manufacturing Industries.* Seoul: Pyonghwa-dang Printing Co.

Egan, Mary Lou and Ashoka Mody. 1992. "Buyer–Seller Links in Export Development." *World Development* 20, 3: 321–34.

Eisenstadt, S. N. 1973. *Traditional Patrimonialism and Modern Neopatrimonialism.* Beverly Hills, California: Sage Publications.

Elster, Jon. 1986. *Rational Choice*. Oxford: Basil Blackwell.

Encaoua, David and Alexis Jacquemin. 1982. "Organizational Efficiency and Monopoly Power, The Case of French Industrial Groups." *European Economic Review* 19: 25–51.

Etzioni, Amitai. 1988. *The Moral Dimension: Toward a New Economics*. New York: Free Press.

Evans, Peter B. 1995. *Embedded Autonomy: States and Industrial Transformation*. Princeton, NJ: Princeton University Press.

Evans, Peter. 1997. "State Structures, Government–Business Relations, and Economic Transformation." In *Business and the State in Developing Countries*, edited by Sylvia Maxfield and Ben Ross Schneider. Ithaca: Cornell University Press, 63–87.

Evans, Peter B., Dietrich Rueschemeyer, and Theda Skocpol. 1985. *Bringing the State Back In*. Cambridge: Cambridge University Press.

Evans, Peter and James E. Rauch. 1999. "Bureaucracy and Growth: A Cross-Naional Analysis of the Effects of 'Weberian' State Structures on Economic Growth." *American Sociological Review* 64 (October): 748–65.

Faure, David. 1989. "The Lineage as Business Company: Patronage versus Law in the Development of Chinese Business." In *Proceedings of the Second Conference on Chinese Economic History* (January 5–7, 1989). Taipei, Taiwan: Institute of Economics, Academia Sinica, 347–76.

Feenstra, Robert C. 1994. "New Product Varieties and the Measurement of International Prices." *American Economic Review* 84, 1 (March): 157–77.

Feenstra, Robert C. 1996a. "Trade and Uneven Growth." *Journal of Development Economics* 49: 229–56.

Feenstra, Robert C. 1996b. "U.S. Imports, 1972–1994: Data and Concordances." NBER Working Paper no. 5515, March, with accompanying CD-ROM.

Feenstra, Robert C. 1997. "Business Groups in South Korea and Taiwan: A Database and Comparison." Manuscript, Pacific Rim Business and Development Program, Institute of Governmental Affairs, University of California, Davis.

Feenstra, Robert C., James Markusen, and William Zeile. 1992. "Accounting for Growth with New Inputs: Theory and Evidence." *American Economic Review, Papers and Proceedings* 82, 2 (May): 415–21.

Feenstra, Robert C., Dorsati Madani, Tzu-Han Yang, and Chi-Yuan Liang. 1999a. "Testing Endogenous Growth in South Korea and Taiwan." *Journal of Development Economics* 60: 317–41.

Feenstra, Robert C., Tzu-Han Yang, and Gary Hamilton. 1999b. "Business Groups and Product Variety in Trade: Evidence from South Korea, Taiwan and Japan." *Journal of International Economics* 48 (June): 71–100.

Feenstra, Robert C., Gary G. Hamilton and Deng-Shing Huang. 2001. "The Organization of the Taiwanese and South Korean Economies: A Comparative Equilibrium Analysis, Forthcoming." In *Networks and Markets*, edited by Alessandra Casella and James Rauch. New York: Russell Sage, 86–142.

Feenstra, Robert C., John Romalis and Peter K. Schott. 2002. "U.S. Imports, Exports and Tariff Data, 1989–2001," NBER Working Paper no. 9387, December.

Feenstra, Robert C., Deng-Shing Huang, and Gary G. Hamilton. 2003. "A Market-Power Based Model of Business Groups." *Journal of Economic Behavior and Organization* 51: 459–85.

Fei Xiaotong. 1992 [1947]. *From the Soil: The Foundations of Chinese Society.* Trans., Introduction, and Epilogue by Gary G. Hamilton and Wang Zheng. Berkeley: University of California Press.

Fields, Karl J. 1995. *Enterprise and the State in Korea and Taiwan.* Ithaca: Cornell University Press.

Fishlow, Albert, Catherine Gwin, Stephan Haggard, Dani Rodrik, and Robert Wade. 1994. *Miracle or Design? Lessons from the East Asian Experience.* Washington, DC: Overseas Development Council.

Fligstein, Neil. 1990. *The Transformation of Corporate Control.* Cambridge, Mass.: Harvard University Press.

Fligstein, Neil. 2001. *The Architecture of Markets: An Economic Sociology of Twenty-First-Century Capitalist Societies.* Princeton: Princeton University Press.

Fligstein, Neil. 2002. "Agreements, Disagreements and Opportunities in the New Sociology of Markets." In *The New Economic Sociology: Developments in an Emerging Field*, edited by Mauro F. Guillén, Randall Collins, Paula England, and Marshall Meyer. New York: Russell Sage Foundation, 61–78.

Fligstein, Neil and Iona Mara-Drita. 1996. "How to Make a Market: Reflections on the Attempt to Create a Single Market in the European Union." *American Journal of Sociology* 102, 1 (July): 1–33.

Frank, André Gunder. 1998. *Reorient: Global Economy in the Asian Age.* Berkeley, CA: University of California Press.

Frank, Robert H. and Philip J. Cook. 1995. *The Winner-Take-All Society: Why the Few at the Top Get So Much More Than the Rest of Us.* New York: Penguin Books.

Frankel, Jeffrey A. and David Romer. 1999. "Does Trade Cause Growth?" *American Economic Review* 89: 379–99.

Frenzen, Jonathan, Paul M. Hirsch, and Philip C. Zerrillo. 1994. "Consumption, Preferences, and Changing Lifestyles." In *The Handbook of Economic Sociology*, edited by Neil Smelser and Richard Swedberg. Princeton: Princeton University Press, 403–25.

Friedland, Roger and A. F. Robertson. 1990. *Beyond the Marketplace, Rethinking Economy and Society.* New York: Aldine de Gruyter.

Fu, Tsu-tan and Shun-yi Shei. 1999. "Agriculture as the Foundation for Development: The Taiwanese Story." In *Taiwan's Development Experience: Lessons on Roles of Government and Market*, edited by Erik Thorbecke and Henry Wan. Boston: Kluwer Academic Publishers, 207–30.

Fujita, Masahisa, Paul Krugman, and Anthony J. Venables. 1999. *The Spatial Economy: Cities, Regions, and International Trade.* Cambridge, Mass.: The MIT Press.

Fujita, Masahisa and Jacques-François Thisse. 2002. *Economics of Agglomeration: Cities, Industrial Location, and Regional Growth.* Cambridge: Cambridge University Press.

Fukuda, Shin-ichi and Hideki Toya. 1995. "Conditional Convergence in East Asian Countries: The Role of Exports in Economic Growth." In *Growth Theories in Light of East Asian Experience*, edited by Takatoshi Ito and Anne O. Krueger. Chicago: NBER and Univ. of Chicago, 247–62.

Fukuyama, Francis. 1995. *Trust: The Social Virtues and the Creation of Prosperity*. New York: Free Press.

Fung, K. C. 1991. "Characteristics of Japanese Industrial Groups and Their Potential Impact on U.S.–Japanese trade." In *Empirical Studies of Commercial Policy*, edited by Robert E. Baldwin. Chicago: NBER and Univ. of Chicago, 137–64.

Fung, K. C. 2002. "International Trade and Bank Groups: Welfare-Enhancing or Welfare-Reducing." *Journal of the Japanese and International Economics* 16: 212–26.

Fung, K. C. and Daniel Friedman. 1996. "International Trade and the Internal Organization of Firms: An Evolutionary Approach." *Journal of International Economics* 41(1/2) (August): 113–37.

Futatsugi, Yusaku. 1986. *Japanese Enterprise Groups*. Kobe: Kobe University, School of Business.

Galbraith, John Kenneth. 1990. *A Short History of Financial Euphoria*. Knoxville, Tenn: Whittle Direct Books.

Galenson, Walter. 1981. "How to Develop Successfully: The Taiwan Model." In *Conference on Experiences and Lessons of Economic Development in Taiwan*. Taipei: The Institute of Economies, Academia Sinica, 69–90.

Gao, Bai. 2001. *Japan's Economic Dilemma: The Institutional Origins of Prosperity and Stagnation*. Cambridge: Cambridge University Press.

Geertz, Clifford. 1963. *Peddlers and Princes: Social Development and Economic Change in Two Indonesian Towns*. Chicago: University of Chicago Press.

Gereffi, Gary. 1994. "The International Economy and Economic Development." In *The Handbook of Economic Sociology*, edited by Neil Smelser and Richard Swedberg. Princeton: Princeton University Press, 206–33.

Gereffi, Gary. 1999. "International Trade and Industrial Upgrading in the Apparel Commodity Chain." *Journal of International Economics* 48, 1 (June): 37–70.

Gereffi, Gary and Donald Wyman (eds.). 1990. *Manufacturing Miracles: Paths of Industrialization in Latin America and East Asia*. Princeton, NJ: Princeton University Press.

Gereffi, Gary and Gary G. Hamilton. 1992. "The Social Economy of Global Capitalism." Paper presented at the annual meetings of the American Sociological Association, Pittsburgh, PA.

Gereffi, Gary and Miguel Korzeniewicz (eds.). 1994. *Commodity Chains and Global Capitalism*. Westport, Conn.: Praeger.

Gereffi, Gary and Pan Mei-lin. 1994. "The Globalization of Taiwan's Garment Industry." In *Global Production: The Apparel Industry in the Pacific Rim*, edited by Edna Bonacich, Lucie Cheng, Norma Chinchilla, Nora Hamilton, and Paul Ong. Philadelphia: Temple University Press, 126–46.

Gereffi, Gary, David Spener, and Jennifer Bair. 2002. *Free Trade and Uneven Development: The North American Apparel Industry after NAFTA*. Philadelphia: Temple University Press.

Gereffi, Gary, John Humphrey, and Timothy Strugeon. 2005. "The Governance of Global Value Chains. *Review of International Political Economy*, 12, No. 1, February: 78–104.

Gerlach, Michael. 1992. *Alliance Capitalism: The Strategic Organization of Japanese Business*. Berkeley: University of California Press.

Ghatak, M. and Raja Kali. 2001. "Financially Interlinked Business Groups." *Journal of Economics and Management Strategy* 10, 4:(Winter): 591–619.

Ghemawat, P. and Tarun Khanna. 1998. "The Nature of Diversified Business Groups: A Research Design and Two Case Studies." *Journal of Industrial Economics* 46, 1 (March): 35–61.

Gilson, Ronald J. and Reiner Kraakman. 1993. "Investment Companies as Guardian Shareholders: The Place of the MSIC in the Corporate Governance Debate." *Stanford Law Review* 45: 985–1010.

Gladwell, Malcolm. 2004. "The Terrazzo Jungle." *The New Yorker*, March 15, 120–7.

Gold, Thomas B. 1986. *State and Society in the Taiwan Miracle*. Armonk, New York: M. E. Sharpe.

Goto, Akira. 1982. "Business Groups in a Market Economy." *European Economic Review* 19: 53–70.

Gould, David M. 1994. "Immigrant Links to the Home Country: Empirical Implications for U.S. Bilateral Trade Flows." *Review of Economics and Statistics* 76: 302–16.

Granovetter, Mark. 1985. "Economic Action and Social Structure." *American Journal of Sociology* 91: 481–510.

Granovetter, Mark. 1990. "The Myth of Social Network Analysis as a Separate Method in the Social Sciences." *Connections* 13, 1–2 (Spring-Summer): 13–16.

Granovetter, Mark. 1994. "Business Groups." In *Handbook of Economic Sociology*, edited by Neil Smelser and Richard Swedberg. Princeton: Princeton University Press, 453–75.

Granovetter, Mark. 1995a [1974]. *Getting a Job: A Study of Contacts and Careers*. Cambridge, Mass.: Harvard University Press.

Granovetter, Mark. 1995b. "Coase Revisited: Business Groups in the Modern Economy. *Industrial and Corporate Change* 4, 1: 93–130.

Granovetter, Mark. 2002. "A Theoretical Agenda for Economic Sociology." In *The New Economic Sociology: Developments in an Emerging Field*, edited by Mauro F. Guillén, Randall Collins, Paula England, and Marshall Meyer. New York: Russell Sage Foundation, 35–60.

Granovetter, Mark. Forthcoming. *Society and Economy: The Social Construction of Economic Institutions*. Cambridge, Mass.: Harvard University Press.

Granovetter, Mark and Roland Soong. 1986. "Threshold Models of Interpersonal Effects in Consumer Demand." *Journal of Economic Behavior and Organization* 7: 83–99.

Granovetter, Mark and Patrick McGuire. 1998. "The Making of an Industry: Electricity in the United States." In *The Laws of the Markets*, edited by Michel Callon. Oxford: Blackwell, 147–73.

Greenhalgh, Susan. 1988. "Families and Networks in Taiwan's Economic Development." In *Contending Approaches to the Political Economy of Taiwan*, edited by Edwin Winckler and Susan Greenhalgh. Armonk, NY: M. E. Sharpe, 224–45.

Greenhalgh, Susan. 1994. "De-Orientalizing the Chinese Family Firm." *American Ethnologist* 21, 4: 746–75.

Greene, Marjorie. 1974. *The Knower and the Known*. Berkeley: University of California Press.

Greenspan, Alan. 1998. "Testimony before the Committee on Foreign Relations," United States Senate, February 12.

Greif, Avner. 1994. "Cultural Beliefs and the Organization of Society: A Historical and Theoretical Reflection on Collectivist and Individualist Societies." *Journal of Political Economy* 102, 5 (October): 912–50.

Greif, Avner. 2003. "Review Essay." *Contemporary Sociology: A Journal of Reviews* 32, 2: 148–52.

Greif, Avner. Forthcoming. *Institutions and Trade during the Late Medieval Commercial Revolution: A Game Theoretical Approach*. Cambridge: Cambridge University Press.

Greif, Avner, Paul Milgrom, and Barry Weingast. 1994. "Coordination, Commitment, and Enforcement: The Case of the Merchant Guild." *Journal of Political Economy* 102, 4: 732–45.

Grossman, Gene M., ed. 1992. *Imperfect Competition and International Trade*. Cambridge, MA: MIT Press.

Grossman, Gene M. and Elhanan Helpman. 1991. *Innovation and Growth in the Global Economy*. Cambridge, Mass.: MIT Press.

Grossman, Gene M. and Elhanan Helpman. 2002. "Integration versus Outsourcing in Industry Equilibrium." *Quarterly Journal of Economics* 117, 1 (May): 85–120.

Grossman, Gene M. and Elhanan Helpman. 2004. "Global Sourcing." *Journal of Political Economy* 112: 552–80.

Grossman, Gene M. and Elhanan Helpman. 2005a. "Managerial Incentives and the International Organization of Production." *Journal of International Economics* 63: 237–62.

Grossman, Gene M. and Elhanan Helpman. 2005b. "Outsourcing in a Global Economy." *Review of Economic Studies* 72: 135–59.

Grossman, Sanford J. and Oliver D. Hart. 1986. "Costs and Benefits of Ownership: A Theory of Vertical and Lateral Integration." *Journal of Political Economy* 94, 4 (August): 691–719.

Guillén, Mauro F. 2001. *The Limits of Convergence: Globalization and Organizaitonal Change in Argentian, South Korea, and Spain*. Princeton: Princeton University Press.

Haggard, Stephan. 1990. *Pathways from the Periphery*. Ithaca: Cornell University Press.

Haggard, Stephan. 2004. "Institutions and Growth in East Asia." *Studies in Comparative International Development* 28, 4 (Winter): 53–81.

Haggard, Stephan, Byung-kuk Kim, and Chung-in Moon. 1991. "Transition to Export-Led Growth in South Korea, 1954–1966." *Journal of Asian Studies* 50, 4 (November): 850–73.

Haggard, Stephan and Chung-in Moon. 1993. "The State, Politics, and Economic Development in Postwar South Korea." In *State and Society in Contemporary Korea*, edited by Hagen Koo. Ithaca: Cornell University Press, 51–93.

Haggard, Stephan and Chien-Kuo Pang. 1994. "The Transition to Export-Led Growth in Taiwan." In *The Role of the State in Taiwan's Development*, edited by Joel D. Aberback, David Dollar, and Kenneth L. Sokoloff. Armonk, New York: M. E. Shape, 47–89.

Haggard, Stephan, David Kang, and Chung-in Moon. 1997a. "Japanese Colonialism and Korean Development: A Critique." *World Development* 25, 6: 867–81.

Haggard, Stephan, Sylvia Maxfield, and Ben Ross Schneider. 1997b. "Theories of Business and Business–State Relations." In *Business and the State in Developing Countries*, edited by Sylvia Maxfield and Ben Ross Schneider. Ithaca: Cornell University Press, 36–60.

Hamilton, Gary G. 1977. "Chinese Consumption of Foreign Commodities: A Comparative Perspective." *American Sociological Review* 42 (December): 877–91.

Hamilton, Gary G. 1984a. "Patriarchalism in Imperial China and Western Europe: A Revision of Weber's Sociology of Domination." *Theory and Society* 13, 3: 393–426.

Hamilton, Gary G. 1984b. "Configuration in History: The Historical Sociology of S. N. Eisenstadt." In *Vision and Method in Historical Sociology*, edited by Theda Skocpol. Cambridge: Cambridge University Press, 85–128.

Hamilton, Gary G. 1985. "Why No Capitalism in China." *Journal of Developing Societies* 2: 187–211.

Hamilton, Gary G. 1990. "Partriarchy, Patrimonialism, and Filial Piety: A Comparison of China and Western Europe." *British Journal of Sociology* 41: 77–104.

Hamilton, Gary G., ed. 1991. *Business Networks and Economics Development in East and Southeast Asia*. Hong Kong: University of Hong, Center for Asian Studies.

Hamilton, Gary G. 1996. "The Quest for a Unified Economics." *Industrial and Corporate Change* 5, 3: 907–16.

Hamilton, Gary G. 1997. "Organization and Market Processes in Taiwan's Capitalist Economy." In *The Economic Organization of East Asian Capitalism*, edited by Marco Orrù, Nicole Woolsey Biggart, and Gary G. Hamilton. Thousand Hills: Sage Publications, 237–96.

Hamilton, Gary G., ed. 1999. *Cosmopolitan Capitalists: Hong Kong and the Chinese Diaspora at the End of the Twentieth Century*. Seattle: University of Washington Press.

Hamilton, Gary G. and Nicole Woolsey Biggart. 1988. "Market, Culture, and Authority: A Comparative Analysis of Management and Organization in the

Far East." *American Journal of Sociology, Special Issue on Economic Sociology* 94 (July): S52–S94.

Hamilton, Gary G., William Zeile, and Wan-Jin Kim. 1989. "The Network Structures of East Asian Economies." In *Capitalism in Contrasting Cultures*, edited by Stewart Clegg and Gordon Redding. Berlin: Walter de Gruyter, 105–29.

Hamilton, Gary G. and Kao Cheng-shu. 1990. "The Institutional Foundations of Chinese Business: The Family Firm in Taiwan." *Comparative Social Research* 12: 95–112.

Hamilton, Gary G. and Robert Feenstra. 1995. "Varieties of Hierarchies and Markets." *Industrial and Corporate Change* 4, 1: 93–130.

Hamilton, Gary G., Wongi Choe, Chung Ku Kim, and Eun Mie Lim. 1999. "Riding the Tiger's Back: A Re-assessment of the Asian Development State." Paper presented at the Annual Meeting of the American Sociological Association, Chicago.

Hamilton, Gary G. and Robert C. Feenstra. 2001. "The Organization of Economies." In *The New Institutionalism in Sociology*, edited by Mary C. Briton and Victor Nee. Stanford: Stanford University Press, 153–80.

Hanchett, Thomas W. 1996. "U.S. Tax Policy and the Shopping-Center Boom of the 1950s and 1960s." *American Historical Review* 101 (October): 1082–110.

Harrison, Bennett and Barry Bluestone. 1988. *The Great U-turn: Corporate Restructuring and the Polarizing of America*. New York: Basic Books.

Hart, Oliver D. 1985. "Monopolistic Competition in the Spirit of Chamberlin: A General Model." *Review of Economic Studies* 52, 4: 529–46.

Hart, Oliver and John Moore. 1990. "Property Rights and the Nature of the Firm." *Journal of Political Economy* 98: 1119–58.

Hart, Oliver and John Moore. 1999. "Foundations of Incomplete Contracts." *Review of Economics Studies* 66: 115–38.

Hay, George A. 1973. "An Economic Analysis of Vertical Integration." *I. O. Review* 1: 188–98.

Hayek, Friedrich. 1967. *Studies in Philosophy, Politics, and Economics*. London: Routledge and Kegan Paul.

Head, Keith and John Ries. 1998. "Immigration and Trade Creation." *Journal of International Economics* 31: 47–62.

Hechter, Michael. 1987. *Principles of Group Solidarity*. Berkeley: University of California Press.

Helpman, Elhanan and Paul R. Krugman. 1985. *Market Structure and Foreign Trade*. Cambridge: MIT Press.

Henderson, Jeffrey. 1999. "Uneven Crises: Institutional Foundations of East Asian Economic Turmoil." *Economy and Society* 28, 3 (August): 327–68.

Hirsch, Paul M. 1972. "Processing Fads and Fashions: An Organization-Set Analysis of Cultural Industry Systems." *American Journal of Sociology* 77: 639–59.

Hirsch, Paul M., Stuart Michaels, and Ray Friedman. 1990. "Clean Models Vs Dirty Hands: Why Economics Is Different from Sociology." In *Structures of*

Capital: The Social Organization of the Economy, edited by Sharon Zukin and Paul DiMaggio. Cambridge: Cambridge University Press, 39–56.

Ho, Samuel P. S. 1978. *Economic Development of Taiwan, 1860–1970*. New Haven: Yale University Press.

Ho, Samuel P. S. 1982. "Economic Development and Rural Industry In South Korea and Taiwan." *World Development* 10, 11: 973–90.

Ho, Samuel P. S. 1984. "Colonialism and Development: Korea, Taiwan and Kwantung." In *The Japanese Colonial Empire, 1895–1945*, edited by Ramon Myers and Mark R. Peattie. Princeton, N.J.: Princeton University Press, 347–98.

Hogg, Robert V. and Allen T. Craig. 1970. *Introduction to Mathematical Statistics. 3rd edition*. New York: Macmillan Publishing.

Hollingsworth, J. R. and Robert Boyer, eds. 1997. *Contemporary Capitalism. The Embeddedness of Institutions*. Cambridge: Cambridge University Press.

Holmström, Bengt and John Roberts. 1998. "The Boundaries of the Firm Revisited." *Journal of Economic Perspectives* 12, 4: 73–94.

Hoshi, Takeo, Anil Kashyap, and David Scharfstein. 1990a. "The Role of Banks in Reducing the Costs of Financial Distress in Japan." *Journal of Financial Economics* 27: 67–88.

Hoshi, Takeo, Anil Kashyap, and David Scharfstein. 1990b. "Bank Monitoring and Investment: Evidence from the Changing Structure of Japanese Corporate Banking Relationships." In *Asymmetric Information, Corporate Finance and Investment*, edited by Glenn R. Hubbard. Chicago: University of Chicago and National Bureau of Economic Research, 105–26.

Hoshi, Takeo, Anil Kashyap, and David Scharfstein. 1991. "Corporate Structure, Liquidity, and Investment: Evidence from Japanese Industrial Groups." *Quarterly Journal of Economics* 106, 1 (February): 33–60.

Hsing, You-Tien. 1997. "Building *Guanxi* across the Straits: Taiwanese Capital and Local Chinese Bureaucrats." In *Ungrounded Empires. The Cultural Politics of Modern Chinese Transnationalism*, edited by Aihwa Ong and Donald Nonini. New York: Routledge, 143–66.

Hsing, You-tien. 1998. *Making Capitalism in China: The Taiwan Connection*. New York: Oxford University Press.

Hsu, Cho-yun. 1980. "The Chinese Settlement of the Ilan Plain." In *China's Island Frontier: Studies in Historical Geography of Taiwan*, edited by Ronald G. Knapp. Honolulu: The University Press of Hawaii, 69–86.

Hsu, Yi-rong Ann, Clifton W. Pannell, and James O. Wheeler. 1980. "The Development and Structure of Transportation Networks in Taiwan: 1600–1972." In *China's Island Frontier: Studies in Historical Geography of Taiwan*, edited by Ronald G. Knapp. Honolulu: The University Press of Hawaii, 167–202.

Hu, Tai-li. 1984. *My Mother-in-Law's Village: Rural Industrializaiton and Change in Taiwan*. Taipei: Institute of Ethnology, Academia Sinica.

Huang, Philip C. C. 1990. *The Peasant Family and Rural Development in the Yangzi Delta, 1350–1988*. Stanford: Stanford University Press.

Hwang, Kwang-kuo. 1987. "Face and Favor: The Chinese Power Game." *American Journal of Sociology* 92: 944–74.

Imai, Ken-ichi. 1992. "Japan's Corporate Networks." In *The Political Economy of Japan. Volume Three: Cultural and Social Dynamics*, edited by Shumpei

Kumon and Henry Rosovsky. Stanford: Stanford University Press, 198–230.

Industrial and Commercial Census Taiwan-Fukien Area, The Republic of China. Various Years, Taipei: Directorate-General of Budget, Accounting and Statistics, Ececutive Yuan.

Industrial and Commercial Census. 1983. *The Report on 1981 Industrial and Commercial Taiwan-Fukien Area, The Republich of China, Vol III, Manufacturing.* Taipei: Directorate-Feneral of Budget, Accounting and Statistics, Executive Yuan.

Institute of Developing Economies. 1975. *Development of Manufacturing in Korea in the 1960's: A Statistical Analysis.* I.D.E. Statistical Data Series, No. 17. Tokyo: Asian Economic Press.

Isett, Christopher M. 1995. "Sugar Manufacture and the Agrarian Economy of Nineteenth-Century Taiwan." *Modern China* 21, 2 (April): 233–59.

Ito, Takatoshi. 2001. "Growth, Crisis, and the Future of Economic Recovery in East Asia." In *Rethinking the East Asian Miracle*, edited by Joseph E. Stiglitz and Shahid Yusuf. New York: Oxford University Press, 55–94.

Itoh, Takatoshi. 1994. *The Japanese Economy.* Cambridge, Mass.: MIT Press.

Itoh, Takatoshi and Anne O. Krueger, eds. 1995. *Growth Theories in Light of the East Asian Experience.* Chicago: NBER and Univ. of Chicago.

Jacobs, J. Bruce. 1979. "A Preliminary Model of Particularistic Ties in Chinese Political Alliance: Kan-ch'ing and Kuan-hsi in a Rural Taiwanese Township." *China Quarterly* 78: 237–73.

Jacobs, Norman. 1985. *The Korean Road to Modernization and Development.* Urbana, IL: University of Illinois Press.

Jeanne, Olivier and Paul Masson. 2000. "Currency Crises, Sunspots and Markov-Switching Regimes." *Journal of International Economics* 50, 2: 327–50.

Jensen, Michael C. and William H. Meckling. 1976. "Theory of the Firm: Managerial Behavior, Agency Costs, and Ownership Structure." *Journal of Financial Economics* 3: 305–60.

Johnson, Chalmers. 1987. "Political Institutions and Economic Performance: The Government-Business Relationship in Japan, South Korea, and Taiwan." In *The Political Economy of the New Asian Industrialism*, edited by Frederic C. Deyo. Ithaca: Cornell University Press, 136–64.

Jones, L. P. and I. SaKong. 1980. *Government, Business, and Entrepreneurship in Economic Development: The Korean Case.* Cambridge, Mass.: Harvard University Press.

Jorgensen, Jan. J., Taieb Hafsi, and Moses N. Kiggundu. 1986. "Towards a Market Imperfections Theory of Organizational Structure in Developing Countries." *Journal of Management Studies* 24, 4: 419–42.

Jorgenson, Dale W. and Chi-Yuan Liang. 1995. "The Industry-Level Output Growth and Total Factor Productivity Changes in Taiwan, 1961–1993." Department of Economics, Harvard University and Institute of Economics, Academia Sinica, May, mimeo.

Jung, Ku-Hyun. 1984. "Trade Channel Evolution between Korea and the United States." In *From Patron to Partner: The Development of U.S.–Korean Business and Trade Relations*, edited by Karl Moskowitz. Lexington, Mass.: Lexington Books, 97–122.

Kali, Raja. 1998. "Endogenous Business Networks," mimeo, Department of Business Administration, Instituto Tecnologico Autonomo de Mexico, Rio Hondo No. 1, San Angel 01000, Mexico.

Kao, Cheng-shu. 1991. "Personal Trust in the Large Businesses in Taiwan: A Traditional Foundation for Contemporary Economic Activities." In *Business Networks And Economic Development in East And Southeast Asia*, edited by Gary G. Hamilton. Hong Kong: Center of Asian Studies, University of Hong Kong, 66–76.

Kao, Cheng-shu. 1999. *Toujia Niang* (The boss's wife). Taipei: Lien Chin Publishing Co.

Kao, Cheng-shu and Gary G. Hamilton. 2000. "Reflexive Manufacturing: Taiwan's Integration in the Global Economy." *International Studies Review* 3, 1 (June): 1–19.

Katz, Michael. 1989. "Vertical Contractual Relations." In *Handbook of Industrial Organization, Volume 1*, edited by Richard Schmalansee and Robert Willig. North-Holland: Amsterdam, 655–721.

Kenney, Martin and Richard Florida. 1993. *Beyond Mass Production: The Japanese System and Its Transfer to the U.S.* New York: Oxford University Press.

Khanna, Tarun. 2000. "Business Groups and Social Welfare in Emerging Markets: Existing Evidence and Unanswered Questions." *European Economic Review* 44, 4–6: 748–61.

Khanna, Tarun and Krishna Palepu. 1999. "Policy Shocks, Market Intermediaries, and Corporate Strategy: The Evolution of Business Groups in Chile and India." *Journal of Economics and Management Strategy* 8, 2 (Summer): 271–310.

Khanna, Tarun and Krishna Palepu. 2000a. "Is Group Affiliation Profitable in Emerging Markets: An Analysis of Indian Diversified Business Groups." *Journal of Finance* 55, 2: 867–91.

Khanna, Tarun and Krishna Palepu. 2000b. "Emerging Market Business Groups, Foreign Investors and Corporate Governance." In *Concentrated Corporate Ownership*, edited by Randall Morck. Chicago: NBER and Univ. of Chicago Press, 265–94.

Khanna, Tarun and Krishna Palepu. 2000c. "The Future of Business Groups in Emerging Markets: Long Run Evidence from Chile." *Academy of Management Journal* 43: 268–85.

Khanna, Tarun and Jan W. Rivkin. 2001. "Estimating the Performance Effects of Business Groups in Emerging Markets." *Strategic Management Journal* 22: 45–74.

Kim, E. Han. 1998. "Globalization of Capital Markets and the Asian Financial Crisis." *Journal of Applied Corporate Finance* 11, 3: 30–9.

Kim, Eun Mee. 1991. "The Industrial Organization and Growth of the Korean Chaebol: Integrating Development and Organizational Theories." In *Business Networks and Economic Development in East and Southeast Asia*, edited by Gary G. Hamilton. Hong Kong: Center of Asian Studies, University of Hong Kong, 272–99.

Kim, Eun Mee. 1993. "Contradictions and Limits of a Developmental State: With Illustrations from the South Korean Case." *Social Problems*, 40, 2 May: 228–49.

Kim, Eun Mee. 1997. *Big Business, Strong State: Collusion and Conflict in Korean Development, 1960–1990*. Albany: State University of New York Press.

Kim, Eun Mee. 2000a. "The Development of Producer-Driven Commodity Chains in the Automobile Industry in Korea: Relation to Japan and the United States." *International Studies Revie*, 3, 1 (June): 59–84.

Kim, Eun Mee. 2000b. "Globalization of the South Korean *Chaebol*." In *Korea's Globalization*, edited by Samuel S. Kim. Cambridge: Cambridge University Press, 102–25.

Kim, Hyuk-Rae. 1993. "Divergent Organizational Paths of Industrialization in East Asia." *Asian Perspective* 17: 105–35.

Kim, Hyuk-Rae. 1994. "The State and Economic Organization in a Comparative Perspective: The Organizing Model of the East Asian Political Economy." *Korean Social Science Journal* 20: 91–120.

Kim, Inchul. 1999. "Korea's Growth Potential and Crisis Management in a Changing International Environment." In *Korea and the Asian Economic Crisis: One Year Later*, Joint U.S.–Korea Academic Studies, 9: 63–81.

Kim, Kon Sik. 1995. *Corporate Governance in Korea*. Unpublished Dissertation, Department of Law, University of Washington.

Kim, Se-Jik. 2004. "Bailout and Conglomeration." *Journal of Financial Economics* 71, 2: 315–47.

King, Ambrose Yeo-chi. 1985. "The Individual and Group in Confucianism: A Relational Perspective." In *Individual and Holism*, edited by Donald Munroe. Ann Arbor: Center for Asian Studies, University of Michigan, 56–70.

King, Ambrose Yeo-chi. 1991. "Kuan-hsi and Network Building: A Sociological Interpretation." *Daedalus* 120, 2: 63–84.

Kipnis, Andrew B. 1997. *Producing Guanxi: Sentiment, Self, and Subculture in a North China Village*. Durham: Duke University Press.

Kiser, Edgar and Michael Hechter. 1991. "The Role of General Theory in Comparative-Historical Sociology." *American Sociological Review* 97: 1–30.

Kiser, Edgar and Michael Hechter. 1998. "The Debate on Historical Sociology: Rational Choice Theory and Its Critics." *American Sociological Review* 104, 3 (November): 785–816.

Knapp, Ronald G. 1980. "Settlement and Frontier Land Tenure." In *China's Island Frontier: Studies in Historical Geography of Taiwan*, edited by Ronald G. Knapp. Honolulu: The University Press of Hawaii, 55–68.

Kohli, Atul. 1994. "Where Do High Growth Political Economies Come from? The Japanese Lineage of Korea's 'Developmental State.'" *World Development* 22, 9: 1269–93.

Kohli, Atul. 1997. "Japanese Colonialism and Korean Development: A Reply." *World Development* 25, 6: 883–8.

Kohli, Atul. 1999. "Where Do High-Growth Political Economies Come From? The Japanese Lineage of Korea's 'Developmental State.'" In *The Developmental State*, edited by Meredith Woo-Cumings. Ithaca: Cornell University Press, 93–136.

Kojima, Kiyoshi and Terutomo Ozawa. 1984. *Japan's General Trading Companies: Merchants of Economic Development*. Paris: Organisation for Economic Co-operation and Development.

Köllner, Patrick. 2000. "Coping with the Legacy of Unbalanced Development." In *The Two Koreas in 2000: Sustaining Recovery and Seeking Reconciliation*, Washington, D.C.: Korea Economic Institute of America, 1–15.

Kong, Che-uk, Chong-dae Choe, and Yu-suk O. 1998. *1950-Yondae Soul Ui Chabonga* (Capitalists in Seoul in the 1950s). Soul Siriptae Sourhak Yonguso.

Kong, Jae Wook. 1993. *Analysis of the Korean Capitalists in 1950s* (in Korean). Seoul: Ilchogak.

Koo, Hagen, ed. 1993. *State and Society in Contemporary Korea*. Ithaca: Cornell University Press.

Koppl, Roger G. "'Invisible Hand' Explanations." In *The Elgar Companion to Austrian Economics*, edited by Peter J. Boettke. Aldershoot, England: Peter Elgar, 192–6.

Korea Development Bank. 1970. *Industry in Korea, 1970*. Seoul: The Korea Development Bank.

Korea Fair Trade Commission (various years). *Proceedings of Commission Decisions* (in Korean).

Kranton, Rachel E. 1996. "Reciprocal Exchange: A Self-Sustaining System." *American Economic Review*, 86, 4 (September): 830–51.

Krippner, Greta R. 2001. "The Elusive Market: Embeddedness and the Paradigm of Economic Sociology." *Theory and Society* 30: 775–810.

Krugman, Paul R. 1979. "Increasing Returns, Monopolistic Competition and International Trade." *Journal of International Economics* 9: 469–79.

Krugman, Paul R. 1980. "Scale Economies, Product Differentiation, and the Pattern of Trade." *American Economic Review* 70 (December): 950–9.

Krugman, Paul R. 1981. "Intra-Industry Specialization and the Gains from Trade." *Journal of Political Economy* 89: 959–73.

Krugman, Paul R. 1991. *Geography and Trade*. MIT Press: Cambridge, MA.

Krugman, Paul R. 1994a. *Rethinking International Trade*. Cambridge, Massachusetts: MIT Press.

Krugman, Paul. 1994b. "The Myth of Asia's Miracle." *Foreign Affairs* November/December: 62–78.

Krugman, Paul R. 1996. *The Self-Organizing Economy*. Oxford: Blackwell.

Krugman, Paul R. 1998. "What Happened to Asia?," mimeo, MIT.

Kuo, Cheng-Tian. 1995. *Global Competitiveness and Industrial Growth in Taiwan and the Philippines*. Pittsburgh: Pittsburgh University Press.

Kuo, Shirley W. Y., Gustav Ranis, and John C. H. Fei. 1981. *The Taiwan Success Story, Rapid Growth with Improved Distribution in the Republic of China, 1952–1979*. Boulder, Colorado: Westview Press.

Kuznets, Simon. 1979. "Growth and Structural Shifts." In *Economic Growth and Structural Change in Taiwan*, edited by Walter Galenson. Ithaca, NY: Cornell University Press, 15–131.

Kwon, Jae-Jung and Joo-Ha Nam 1999. "Distressed Corporate Debts in Korea." Korea Institute for International Economic Policy, Working Paper 99–11.

Lal, Deepak. 1985. *The Poverty of "Development Economics."* Cambridge, Mass.: Harvard University Press.

Lancaster, Kelvin. 1979. *Variety, Equity and Efficiency.* New York: Columbia University Press.

Landa, Janet Tai. 1994. *Trust, Ethnicity, and Identity: Beyond the New Institutional Economics of Ethnic Trading Networks, Contract Law, and Gift-Exchange.* Ann Arbor: The University of Michigan Press.

Lau, Lawrence J., ed. 1986. *Models of Development: A Comparative Study of Economic Growth in South Korea and Taiwan.* San Francisco, CA: Institute for Contemporary Studies.

Lawrence, Robert Z. 1991. Efficient or Exclusionist? The Import Behavior of Japanese Corporate Groups, *Brooking Papers on Economic Activity*, No. 2, 311–41.

Lazonick, William. 1991. *Business Organization and the Myth of the Market Economy.* Cambridge: Cambridge University Press.

Lee, Jong-Wha, Young Soo Lee, and Byung-Sun Lee. 2000. "The Determinations of Corporate Debt in Korea." *Asian Economic Journal* 14, 4: 333–56.

Lee, Keun. 1999. "Corporate Governance and Growth in the Korean Chaebols: A Microeconomic Foundation for the 1997 Crisis." Seoul National Univ., mimeo.

Lee, Seung Hoon and Ho Keun Song. 1994. "The Korean Garment Industry: From Authoritarian Patriarchism to Industrial Paternalism." In *Global Production: The Apparel Industry in the Pacific Rim*, edited by Edna Bonacich, Lucie Cheng, Norma Chinchilla, Nora Hamilton, and Paul Ong. Philadelphia: Temple University Press, 147–61.

Lee, Sheng-Yi. 1990. *Money and Finance in the Economic Development of Taiwan.* London: Macmillan.

Leff, Nathaniel. 1977. "Capital Markets in the Less Developed Countries: The Group Principle." In *Money and Finance in Economic Growth and Development: Essays in Honor of Edward S. Shaw*, edited by Ronald I. McKinnon. New York: Dekker, 97–122.

Leff, Nathaniel. 1978. "Industrial Organization and Entrepreneurship in the Developing Countries: The Economic Groups." *Economic Development and Cultural Change* 26, 4: 661–75.

Levy, Brian. 1988. "Korean and Taiwanese Firms as International Competitors: The Challenges Ahead." *Columbia Journal of World Business* (Spring): 43–51.

Levy, Brian. 1991. "Transactions Costs, the Size of Firms, and Industrial Policy: Lessons from a Comparative Case Study of the Footwear Industry in Korea and Taiwan." *Journal of Development Economics* 34: 151–78.

Lew, Seok-Choon and Byung-Young Park. 2000. "Commodity Chains in East Asia and the Development of the Electronics Industry in South Korea." *International Studies Review* 3, 1 (June): 43–58.

Li, K. T. 1988. *The Evolution of Policy Behind Taiwan's Development Success.* New Haven: Yale University Press.

Liang, Chi-Yuan. 1989. "The Sources of Growth and Productivity Change in Taiwan's Industries, 1961–1981." Discussion Paper, The Institute of Economics, Academia Sinica, Taipei, Taiwan, Republic of China.

Liao, Cheng-hung and Chun-chieh Huang. 1994. "Attitudinal Changes of Farmers in Taiwan." In *The Role of the State in Taiwan's Development*, edited by Joel D. Aberbach, David Dollar, and Kenneth L. Sokoloff. Armonk, NY: M. E. Sharpe, 354–69.

Lie, John. 1997. "Sociology of Markets." *Annual Review of Sociology* 23: 341–60.

Lie, John. 1998. *Han Unbound: The Political Economy of South Korea*. Stanford: Stanford University Press.

Lim, Eun Mie. 2002. *Big Horses Don't Die: The Chaebol Dominance in the Course of Korean Industrializaiton*. Unpublished Dissertation, Department of Sociology, University of Washington.

Lim, Haeran. 1998. *Korea's Growth and Industrial Transformation*. New York: St. Martin's Press.

Lin, Pao-an. 1991. "The Social Sources of Capital Investment in Taiwan's Industrialization." In *Business Networks and Economic Development in East and Southeast Asia*, edited by Gary G. Hamilton. Hong Kong: Centre of Asian Studies, University of Hong Kong, 94–113.

Lincoln, James R., Michael L. Gerlach, and Christina L. Ahmadjian. 1996. "Keiretsu Networks and Corporate Performance in Japan." *American Sociological Review* 61 (February): 67–88.

Lincoln, James and Michael Gerlach. 2004. *Japan's Network Economy: Structure, Persistence, and Change*. New York: Cambridge University Press.

Little, Ian M. D. 1979. "An Economic Reconnaissance." In *Economic Growth and Structural Change in Taiwan*, edited by Walter Galenson. Ithaca, NY: Cornell University Press, 448–507.

Lorch, Klaus and Tyler Biggs. 1989. "Growing in the Interstices: The Limits of Government Promotion of Small Industires." Paper presented at the annual meeting of the Association for Asian Studies, Washington, D.C.

Luhmann, Niklas. 1995. *Social Systems*. Translated by John Bednarz, Jr., with Dirk Baecker. Stanford, Calif.: Stanford University Press.

Lui, Tai-lok. 2001. "A Brief Note on Guanxi." In *Rules and Networks: The Legal Culture of Global Business Transactions*, edited by Richard P. Appelbaum, William L. F. Felstiner, and Volkmar Gessner. Oxford: Hart Publishing, 385–99.

Luo, Yadong. 1997. "Guanxi and Performance of Foreign-invested Enterprises in China: An Empirical Inquiry." *Management International Review* 37: 51–70.

Machlup, Fritz and Martha Taber. 1960. "Bilateral Monopoly, Successive Monopoly, and Vertical Integration." *Econometrica*, 28, 110 (May), 101–19.

Mankiw, Gregory N., David Romer, and David N. Weil. 1992. "A Contribution to the Empirics of Economic Growth." *Quarterly Journal of Economics* 107, 2 (May): 407–37.

Mann, Catherine L. 2000. "Korea and the Brave New World of Finance." In *The Korean Economy in an Era of Global Competition*, Joint Korea–U.S. Academic Studies 10: 55–68.

Marin, Dalia and Thierry Verdier. 2002. "Power Inside the Firm and the Market: A General Equilibrium Approach," CEPR Discussion Paper No. 3526, London.

Marin, Dalia and Thierry Verdier. 2003. "Globalization and the Empowerment of Talent." University of Munich and DELTA, Paris, manuscript.

Marion, Nancy P. 1999. "Some Parallels Between Currency and Banking Crisis." In *International Finance and Financial Crises*, edited by Peter Isard, Assaf Razin, and Andrew K. Rose. Boston: Kluwer Academic Publishers, 1–18.

Marsh, Felicity. 1983. *Japanese Overseas Investment: The New Challenge*. Special Report, No. 142. London: The Economist Intelligence Unit.

Martins, Joaquim Oliveira. 1992. "Export Behaviour with Differentiated Products: Exports of Korea, Taiwan and Japan to the U.S. Domestic Market." In M. G. Dagenais and D. A. Muet, eds., *International Trade Modeling* (Chapman and Hall).

Mathewson, G. F. and R. A. Winter. 1983. "Vertical Integration by Contractual Restraints in Spatial Markets." *Journal of Business* 56 (October): 497–517.

McKenzie, Lionel. 1951. "Ideal Output and the Interdependence of Firms." *Economic Journal* 61 (December): 785–803.

McLaren, John. 2000. "'Globalization' and Vertical Structure." *American Economic Review* 90, 5 (December): 1239–54.

McNamara, Dennis. 1990. *The Colonial Origins of Korean Enterprise, 1910–1945*. Cambridge: Cambridge University Press.

McNamara, Dennis. 1996. *Trade and Transformation in Korea, 1876–1945*. Boulder, Colorado: Westview Press.

Menkhoff, T. 1993. *Trade Routes, Trust and Trading Networks – Chinese Small Enterprises in Singapore*. Saarbracken; Fort Lauderdale: Verlag Breitenbach Publishers.

Meyer, David R. and Kyonghee Min. 1988. "Concentration and Specialization of Manufacturing in Core and Peripheral Cities during Rapid Industrialization Korea: 1960–1970." *Comparative Urban and Community Research* 1: 38–61.

Mitchell, Timothy. 1991. "The Limits of the State: Beyond Statist Approaches and Their Critics." *American Political Science Review* 85, 1 (March): 77–96.

Mody, Ashoka. 1990. "Institutions and Dynamic Comparative Advantage: The Electronics Industry in South Korea and Taiwan." *Cambridge Journal of Economics*, 14: (September): 291–314.

Moon, Chung-In and Rashemi Prasad. 1994. "Beyond the Developmental State: Networks, Politics, and Institutions." *Governance: An International Journal of Policy and Administration* 7, 4 (October): 360–86.

Morgenstern, Oskar. 1963. *On the Accuracy of Economic Observations*. Princeton: Princeton University Press.

Mortensen, Dale T. 1988. "Matching: Finding a Partner for Life or Otherwise." *American Journal of Sociology* 94 (Supplement): S215–S240.

Myers, Ramon. 1984. "The Economic Transformation of the Republic of China on Taiwan." *China Quarterly* 99: 500–28.

Myers, Ramon and Yamada Saburo. 1984. "Agricultural Development in the Empire." In *The Japanese Colonial Empire, 1895–1945*, edited by Ramon Myers and Mark R. Peattie. Princeton, NJ: Princeton University Press, 420–54.

Nam, Sang-Woo and Dong-Won Kim. 1994. "The Principal Transactions Bank System in Korea." In *The Japanese Main Bank System*, edited by Masahiko Aoki and Hugh Patrick. Oxford: Oxford University Press, 450–93.

Nelson, Richard and Sidney Winter. 1982. *An Evolutionary Theory of Economic Change*. Cambridge, MA: Harvard University Press.

New Industry Management Academy. 1999. *The Financial Analysis of the Korea's Top 30 Chaebol* (Hankuk 30dae chaebol jaemoo bunsuk) (in Korean). New York: Free Press.

Niehans, Jürg. 1990. *A History of Economic Theory: Classic Contributions, 1720–1980*. Baltimore, Maryland: Johns Hopkins University Press.

Nishiguchi, Toshihiro. 1994. *Strategic Industrial Sourcing: The Japanese Advantage*. New York: Oxford University Press.

North, Douglass C. 1990. *Institutions, Institutional Change, and Economic Performance*. Cambridge: Cambridge University Press.

North, Douglass C. and Robert P. Thomas. 1973. *The Rise of the Western World: A New Economic History*. Cambridge: Cambridge University Press.

Numazaki, Ichiro. 1986. "Networks of Taiwanese Big Business: A Preliminary Analysis." *Modern China* 12: 487–534.

Numazaki, Ichiro. 1991. "The Role of Personal Networks in the Making of Taiwan's *Guanxiqiye* (Related Enterprises)." In *Business Networks and Economic Development in East and Southeast Asia*, edited by Gary G. Hamilton. Hong Kong: Center of Asian Studies, University of Hong Kong, 77–93.

Okumura, Hiroshi. 1991. "Intercorporate Relations in Japan." In *Business Networks and Economic Development in East and Southeast Asia*, edited by Gary G. Hamilton. Hong Kong: Centre of Asian Studies, University of Hong Kong, 219–29.

Olson, Lawrence. 1970. *Japan in Postwar Asia*. New York: Praeger Publishers.

Olson, Mancur. 1982. *The Rise and Decline of Nations: Economic Growth, Stagflation, and Social Rigidities*. New Haven: Yale University Press.

Ordover, Janusz A., Garth Saloner, and Steven C. Salop. 1990. "Equilibrium Vertical Foreclosure." *American Economic Review* 80, 1 (March): 127–42.

Ordover, Janusz A., Garth Saloner, and Steven C. Salop. 1992. "Equilibrium Vertical Foreclosure: Reply." *American Economic Review* 82, 3 (June): 698–703.

Orrù, Marco, Gary G. Hamilton, and Mariko Suzuki. 1990. "Patterns of Inter-Firm Control in Japanese Business." *Organizational Studies* 10, 4: 549–74.

Orrù, Marco, Nicole Woolsey Biggart, and Gary G. Hamilton. 1991. "Organizational Isomorphism in East Asia: Broadening the New Institutionalism." In *The New Institutionalism in Organizational Analysis*, edited by Walter W. Powell and Paul J. DiMaggio. Chicago: Univ. of Chicago Press, 361–89.

Orrù, Marco, Nicole Woolsey Biggart, and Gary G. Hamilton. 1997. *The Economic Organization of East Asian Capitalism*. Thousand Hills: Sage Publications.

Pack, Howard. 2001. "Technological Change and Growth in East Asia: Marco versus Micro Perspectives." In *Rethinking the East Asian Miracle*, edited by

Joseph E. Stiglitz and Shahid Yusuf. New York: Oxford University Press, 95–142.

Padgett, John F. and Christopher K. Ansell. 1993. "Robust Action and the Rise of the Medici 1400–1434." *American Journal of Sociology* 98: 1259–319.

Page, John. 1994. "The East Asian Miracle: Four Lessons for Development Policy." In *NBER Macroeconomics Annual 1994*. Cambridge, MA: MIT Press, 219–68.

Palais, James B. 1996. *Confucian Statecraft and Korean Institutions: Yu Hyong-won and the Late Choson Dynasty*. Seattle: University of Washington Press.

Palmer, Michael J. E. 1987. "The Surface-Subsoil Form of Divided Ownership in Late Imperial China: Some Examples from the New Territories of Hong Kong." *Modern Asian Studies* 21, 1: 1–119.

Pang, Chien-Kuo. 1992. *The State and Economic Transformation: The Taiwan Case*. New York: Garland.

Patrick, Hugh and Henry Rosovsky. 1976. *Asia's New Giant: How the Japanese Economy Works*. Washington, DC: The Brookings Institution.

Pempel, T. J. 1999a. *The Politics of the Asian Economic Crisis*. Ithaca, NY: Cornell University Press.

Pempel, T. J. 1999b. "The Developmental Regime in a Changing World Economy." In *The Developmental State*, edited by Meredith Woo-Cumings. Ithaca: Cornell University Press, 137–81.

Pepall, Lynne and George Norman. 2001. "Product Differentiation and Upstream–Downstream Relations." *Journal of Economics and Management Strategy* 10, 2: 201–34.

Perotti, Enrico C. and Stanislav Gelfer. 2001. "Red Barons or Robber Barons: Governance and Financing in Russian Financial-Industrial Groups." *European Economic Review* 45, 9: 1601–17.

Perrow, Charles. 2002. *Organizing America: Wealth, Power, and the Origins of Corporate Capitalism*. Princeton: Princeton University Press.

Perry, Martin K. 1989. "Vertical Integration: Determinants and Effects." In *Handbook of Industrial Organization, volume 1*, edited by Richard Schmalansee and Robert Willig. North-Holland: Amsterdam, 185–255.

Perry, Martin K. and Robert H. Groff. 1985. "Resale Price Maintenance and Forward Integration into a Monopolistically Competitive Industry." *Quarterly Journal of Economics* 100, 1293–311.

Piore, Michael J. and Charles F. Sabel. 1984. *The Second Industrial Divide: Possibilities for Prosperity*. New York: Basic Books.

Podolny, Joel M. 1993. "A Status-based Model of Market Competition." *American Journal of Sociology* 98, 4 (January): 829–72.

Podolny, Joel M. 2001. "Networks as the Pipes and Prisms of the Market." *American Journal of Sociology* 107, 1 (July): 33–60.

Podolny, Joel M., Toby Stuart, and Michael Hannan. 1996. "Networks, Knowledge and Niches: Competition in the Worldwide Semiconductor Industry." *American Journal of Sociology* 102, 3 (November): 659–89.

Polanyi, Karl, C. Arensberg, and H. Pearson. 1957. *Trade and Market in the Early Empires*. New York: Free Press.

Porter, Michael E. 1990. *The Competitive Advantage of Nations*. New York: Free Press.

Powell, Walter W. 1990. "Neither Market Nor Hierarchy: Network Forms of Organization." *Research in Organizational Behavior* 12: 295–336.

Powell, Walter W. and Paul J. DiMaggio, eds. 1991. *The New Institutionalism in Organizational Analysis*. Chicago: University of Chicago Press.

Powell, Walter W. and Peter Prantley. 1992. "Competitive Cooperation in Biotechnology: Learning Through Networks?" In *Organizations and Networks*, edited by Nitin Nohria and Robert Eccles. Cambridge, Mass.: Harvard Business School Press, 366–94.

Puga, Diego and Daniel Trefler 2002. "Knowledge Creation and Control in Organizations." University of Toronto, manuscript.

Putterman, Louis, ed. 1986. *The Economic Nature of the Firm: A Reader*. Cambridge: Cambridge University Press.

Quack, Sigrid, Glen Morgan, and Richard Whitley, eds. 2000. *National Capitalisms, Global Competition, and Economic Performance*. Amsterdam: John Benjamins Publishing Company.

Ra, Sungsup and Gong Yan. 2000. "Bad Credit Equilibria with the Abnormally Utilized Commercial Paper: A Catalyst of the Korean Currency Crisis." *The Journal of the Korean Economy* 1, 2 (Fall): 325–53.

Rauch, James E. 1993a. "Productivity Gains from Geographic Concentration of Human Capital: Evidence from the Cities." *Journal of Urban Economics* 34, 3 (November): 380–400.

Rauch, James E. 1993b. "Does History Matter Only When It Matters Little? The Case of City-Industry Location." *Quarterly Journal of Economics* 108, 3 (August): 843–67.

Rauch, James E. 1999. "Networks versus Markets in International Trade." *Journal of International Economic* 48, 1 (June): 7–36.

Rauch, James E. 2001a. "Business and Social Networks in International Trade," *Journal of Economic Literature*, 39, December: 1177–203.

Rauch, James E. 2001b. "Black Ties Only? Ethnic Business Networks, Intermediaries, and African American Retail Entrepreneurship." In *Networks and Markets*, Alessandra Casella and James E. Rauch, eds. New York: Russell Sage, 270–309.

Rauch, James E. and Alessandra Casella. 2001. *Networks and Markets*. New York: Russell Sage.

Rauch, James E. and Vitor Trindade. 2002. "Ethnic Chinese Networks in International Trade." *Review of Economics and Statistics* 84, 1 (February): 116–30.

Rauch, James E. and Vitor Trindade. 2003. "Information, International Substitutability, and Globalization." *American Economics Review* 93, (June): 775–91.

Rauch, James E. and Alessandra Casella. 2003. "Overcoming Informational Barriers to International Resource Allocation: Prices and Group Ties." *Economic Journal*, forthcoming.

Rauch, James E. and Joel Watson. 2004. "Entrepreneurship and International Trade."

Rawski, Evelyn Sakakida. 1972. *Agricultural Change and the Peasant Economy of South China*. Cambridge, Mass.: Harvard University Press.

Reardon, Thomas, C. Peter Timmer, Christopher B. Barrett, and Julio Berdegue. 2003. "The Rise of Supermarkets in Africa, Asia, and Latin America." *American Journal of Agricultural Economics* 85, 5: 1140–7.

Redding, Gordon. 1991. "Weak Organizations and Strong Linkages: Managerial Ideology and Chinese Family Business Networks." In *Business Networks and Economic Development in East and Southeast Asia*, edited by Gary G. Hamilton. Hong Kong: Centre of Asian Studies, University of Hong Kong, 30–47.

Redding, S. Gordon. 1990. *The Spirit of Chinese Capitalism*. Berlin: Walter de Gruyter.

Regan, Kevin. 1999. "The Retail Industry – Trends in the Next Century." Pp. 389–407 in *Workouts and Turnarounds II: Global Restructuring Strategies for the Next Century*, edited by Dominic DiNapoli. New York: Wiley.

Rhee, Yung Whee, Bruce Ross-Larson, and Garry Pursell. 1984. *Korea's Competitive Edge: Managing the Entry into World Markets*. Baltimore: Johns Hopkins University Press.

Rigobon, Roberto and Dani Rodrik. 2004. "Rule of Law, Democracy, Openness, and Income: Estimating the Interrelationships." NBER Working Paper no. 10750.

Ringer, Fritz. 1997. *Max Weber's Methodology: The Unification of the Cultural and Social Sciences*. Cambridge, Mass.: Harvard University Press.

Robinson, Joan. 1969 [1933]. *The Economics of Imperfect Competition*. 2nd edition. London: Macmillan.

Rodriguez, Francisco and Dani Rodrik. 2000. "Trade Policy and Economic Growth: A Skeptic's Guide to the Cross-National Evidence." In *NBER Macroeconomics Annual 2000*, edited by Ben S. Bernanke and Kenneth Rogoff. Cambridge, Mass.: MIT Press, 261–325.

Rodrik, Dani. 1993. "Industrial Organization and Product Quality: Evidence from South Korean and Taiwanese Exports." In *Empirical Studies of Strategic Trade Policy*, edited by Paul Krugman and Alasdair Smith. NBER and Univ. of Chicago, 195–210.

Rodrik, Dani. 1994. "King Kong Meets Godzilla: The World Bank and the *East Asian Miracle*." In *Miracle or Design? Lessons from the East Asian Experience*, Albert Fishlow and Catherine Gwin. Washington, DC: Overseas Development Council, 13–54.

Rodrik, Dani. 1995. "Getting Interventions Right: How South Korea and Taiwan Grew Rich." *Economic Policy* 10, 21: 53–107.

Rodrik, Dani. 1996. "Coordination Failures and Government Policy: A Model with Applications to East Asia and Eastern Europe." *Journal of International Economics* 40, 1–2 (February): 1–22.

Rodrik, Dani. 1997. "Trade Strategy, Exports, and Investment: Another Look at East Asia." *Pacific Economic Review* 2, 1: 1–29.

Rodrik, Dani. 1999. *The New Global Economy and Developing Countries: Making Openness Work*. Baltimore: Overseas Development Council and Johns Hopkins Univ. Press.

Romer, Paul. 1990. "Endogenous Technological Change." *Journal of Political Economy* 98, 5 (October): S71–S102.

Romer, Paul. 1994. "New Goods, Old Theory, and the Welfare Costs of Trade Restrictions." *Journal of Development Economics* 43: 5–38.

Rosser, J. Barkley Jr. 1999. "On the Complexities of Complex Economic Dynamics." *Journal of Economic Perspectives* 13, 4 (Fall): 169–92.

Rowe, William T. 1985. "Approaches to Modern Chinese Social History." Pp. 236–96 in *Reliving the Past: The Worlds of Social History*, edited by Olivier Zunz. Chapel Hill: University of North Carolina Press.

Roy, William G. 1997. *Socializing Capital: The Rise of the Large Industrial Corporation in America*. Princeton: Princeton University Press.

Ruskola, Teemu. 2000. "Conceptualizing Corporations and Kinship: Comparative Law and Development Theory in a Chinese Perspective." *Stanford Law Review* 52 (July): 1599–729.

Ruskola, Teemu. 2002. "Law Without Law, or Is 'Chinese Law' an Oxymoron?" *William & Mary Bill of Rights Journal* 11 (2002): 65–670.

Sali-i-Martin, Xavier X. 1997. "I Just Ran Two Million Regressions." *American Economic Review, Papers and Proceedings* May: 178–83.

Sato, Kazuo. 1976. "The Ideal Log-Change Index Number." *Review of Economics and Statistics* 58, 2 (May): 223–8.

Saxenian, AnnaLee. 1994. *Regional Advantage: Culture and Competition in Silicon Valley and Route 128*. Cambridge, Massachusetts: Harvard University Press.

Saxenian, AnnaLee. 1998. "Silicon Valley's New Immigrant Entrepreneurs and Their Asian Networks." Paper presented at the International Conference on Business Transformation and Social Change in East Asia, May 22–23, Tunghai University, Taiwan.

Saxenian, AnnaLee. 1999a. "Comment on Martin Kenney and Urs Van Burg 'Technology, Entrepreneurship, and Path Dependence: Industrial Clustering in Silicon Valley and Route 128.'" *Industrial and Corporate Change* 8, 1: 105–10.

Saxenian, AnnaLee. 1999b. *Silicon Valley's New Immigrant Entrepreneurs*. San Francisco, CA: Public Policy Institute of California, June 1999.

Saxenian, AnnaLee. 2000a. "Networks of Immigrant Entrepreneurs." *The Silicon Valley Edge: A Habitat for Innovation and Entrepreneurship*, edited by Chong-Moon Lee, William F. Miller, Marguerite Gong Hancock, and Henry S. Rowen. Stanford: Stanford University Press, 248–75.

Saxenian, AnnaLee. 2000b. "Transnational Entrepreneurs and Regional Industrialization: The Silicon Valley–Hsinchu Connection." In *Embeddedness and Corporate Change in a Global Economy*, edited by Rueyling Tzeng and Brian Uzzi. New York: Peter Lang, 283–302.

Saxenian, AnnaLee and Jinn-Yuh Hsu. 2000. "The Limits of Guanxi Capitalism: Transnational Collaboration Between Taiwan and the U.S." *Environment and Planning A* 32, 11 (November): 1991–2005.

Saxenian, AnnaLee and Jinn-Yuh Hsu. 2001. "The Silicon Valley–Hsinchu Connection: Technical Communities and Industrial Upgrading." *Industrial and Corporate Change* 10, 4: 893–920.

Saxonhouse, Gary. 1993. "What Does Japanese Trade Structure Tell Us about Japanese Trade Policy?" *Journal of Economic Perspectives* 7, 3: 21–43.

Schelling, Thomas C. 1978. *Micromotives and Macrobehavior*. New York: W. W. Norton and Company.

Scherer F. M. and David Ross. 1990. *Industrial Market Structure and Economic Performance*. Boston: Houghton Mifflin.

Schott, Peter K. 2004. "Across-Product versus Within-Product Specialization in International Trade." *Quarterly Journal of Economics* 119, 2(May): 647–78.

Scitovsky, Tibor. 1986. "Economic Development in Taiwan and South Korea: 1965–81." In *Models of Development: A Comparative Study of Economic Growth in South Korea and Taiwan*, Lawrence J. Lau. San Francisco, CA: Institute for Contemporary Studies.

Segerstrom, Paul, T. C. A. Anant, and Elias Dinopoulos. 1990. "A Schumpeterian Model of the Product Life Cycle." *American Economic Review* 80: 1077–99.

Semkow, Brian W. 1994. *Taiwan's Capital-Market Reform: The Financial and Legal Issues*. New York: Oxford University Press.

Shafer, Michael. 1997. "The Political Economy of Sectors and Sectoral Change: Korea Then and Now." In *Business and the State in Developing Countries*, edited by Sylvia Maxfield and Ben Ross Schneider. Ithaca: Cornell University Press, 88–121.

Shieh, G. S. 1992. *"Boss" Island: The Subcontracting Network and Micro-Entrepreneurship in Taiwan's Development*. New York: Peter Lang.

Shiga, Shuzo. 1978. "Family Property and the Law of Inheritance in Traditional China." In *Chinese Family Law and Social Change in Historical and Comparative Perspective*, edited by David C. Buxbaum. Seattle: University of Washington Press, 109–50.

Shin, Gi-Wook. 1994. "The Historical Making of Collective Action: The Korean Peasant Uprisings of 1946." *American Journal of Sociology* 99, 6 (May): 1596–624.

Shin, Gi-Wook. 1996. *Peasant Protest and Social Change in Colonial Korea*. Seattle: University of Washington Press.

Shin, Gi-Wook. 1998. "Agrarian Conflict and the Origins of Korean Capitalism." *American Journal of Sociology* 103, 5 (March): 1309–51.

Shin, Yong-ha. 1978. "Landlordism in the Late Yi Dynasty." *Korea Journal*, June and July, pp. 25–32.

Smelser, Neil J. and Richard Swedberg. 1994. *The Handbook of Economic Sociology*. Princeton, NJ: Princeton University Press and Russell Sage Foundation.

Smitka, Michael J. 1991. *Competitive Ties: Subcontracting in the Japanese Automotive Industry*. New York: Columbia University Press.

Sohn, Chan-Hyun and Junsok Yang, eds. 1998. *Korea's Economic Reform Measures Under the IMF Program: Government Measures in the Critical First Six Months of the Korean Economic Crisis.* Seoul: Korea Institute for International Economic Policy.

Solow, Robert. 1956. "A Contribution to the Theory of Economic Growth." *Quarterly Journal of Economics* 60, 1: 65–94.

Solow, Robert. 1995. "Review of Francis Fukuyama, Trust: The Social Virtues and the Creation of Prosperity." *The New Republic.* September 11, 1995: 37–9.

Somers, Margaret R. 2003. "'We're No Angels': Realism, Rational Choice, and Relationality in Social Science." *American Journal of Sociology* 104, 3 (November): 722–84.

Speare, Alden Jr. 1992. "Taiwan's Rural Populace: Brought in or Left out of the Economic Miracle?" In *Taiwan: Beyond the Economic Miracle,* edited by Denis Fred Simon and Michael Y. M. Kau. Armonk, NY: M. E. Sharpe, 211–36.

Spence, Michael E. 1976. "Product Selection, Fixed Costs and Monopolistic Competition." *Review of Economic Studies* 43: 217–36.

Spulber, Daniel F. 1996. "Market Microstructure and Intermediation." *Journal of Economic Perspectives* 10, 3 (Summer): 135–52.

Spulber, Daniel F. 1998. *Market Microstructure: Intermediaries and the Theory of the Firm.* Cambridge: Cambridge University Press.

Steers, Richard M., Yoo, Keun Shiv, and Gerardo Ungson. 1989. *The Chaebol: Korea's New Industrial Might.* New York: Harper & Row.

Stigler, George J. 1951. "The Division of Labor Is Limited by the Extent of the Market." *Journal of Political Economy* 54, 3 (June): 185–93.

Stigler, George J. 1966. *The Theory of Price.* New York: Macmillan.

Stigler, George J. 1968. *The Organization of Industry.* Homewood, IL: Irwin.

Stiglitz, Joseph E. 1994. "Economic Growth Revisited." *Industrial and Corporate Change* 3, 1: 65–110.

Stiglitz, Joseph E. 2000. "The Insider: What I Learned at the World Economic Crisis." *The New Republic,* April 17 & 24, issues 4,448 & 4,449, 56–60.

Stiglitz, Joseph E. and Shahid Yusuf, eds. 2001. *Rethinking the East Asian Miracle.* New York: Oxford University Press.

Swedberg, Richard. 1991. *Schumpeter, A Biography.* Princeton: Princeton University Press.

Swedberg, Richard, ed. 1993. *Explorations in Economic Sociology.* New York: Russell Sage Foundation.

Swedberg, Richard. 1998. *Max Weber's Economic Sociology.* Princeton, NJ: Princeton University Press.

Swedberg, Richard. 2003. *Principles of Economic Sociology.* Princeton: Princeton University Press.

Swidler, Ann. 1986. "Culture in Action: Symbols and Strategies." *American Sociological Review* 51 (April): 273–86.

Taiwan Statistical Data Book, Various years. Taipei: Council for Economic Planning and Development.

Taniura, Takao. 1989. "Management in Taiwan: The Case of the Formosa Plastics Group." *East Asian Cultural Studies* 28, 1–4 (March): 63–90.

The Oriental Economist. 1984. *Japanese Overseas Investment: A Complete Listing by Firms and Countries, 1984–85*. Tokyo: The Oriental Economist.

Thorbecke, Erik. 1979. "Agricultural Development." In *Economic Growth and Structural Change in Taiwan: The Postwar Experience of the Republic of China*, edited by Walter Galenson. Ithaca: Cornell University Press, 132–205.

Tirole, Jean. 1989. *The Theory of Industrial Organization*. Cambridge, MA: MIT Press.

Tong, Chee Kiong and Yong Pit Kee. 1998. "*Guanxi* Bases, *Xinyong* and Chinese Business Networks." *British Journal of Sociology* 49, 1: 75–96.

Trefler, Daniel. 2001. "The Long and the Short of the Canada–U.S. Free Trade Agreement." Institute for Policy Analysis, National Bureau of Economic Research working paper no. 8293, May.

Tsai, Henry Shih-shan. 1996. *The Eunuchs in the Ming Dynasty*. Albany: State University of New York Press.

Tsang, Steve, ed. 1993. *In the Shadow of China: Political Developments in Taiwan since 1949*. Hong Kong: Hong Kong University Press.

Tsurumi, Yoshi. 1984. *Sogoshosha: Engines of Export-Based Growth*. Montreal: The Institute for Research on Public Policy.

Tuan, Chyau. 1976. *Determinants of Financial Savings in Taiwan Farmers' Associations, 1960 to 1970*, Monograph Series No. 1. Taipei: Institute of the Three Principles of the People, Academia Sinica.

Turner, Matthew. 1996. "Hong Kong Design and the Roots of Sino-American Trade Disputes." *The Annals of the American Academy* 547 (September): 37–53.

Twitchett, Denis. 1959. "The Fan Clan's Charitable Estate, 1050–1760." In *Confucianism in Action*, edited by David S. Nivison and Arthur F. Wright. Stanford: Stanford University Press, 97–133.

U.S. Bureau of the Census, 1978–88. U.S. general imports for consumption, schedule a, commodity by country, FT135. U.S. Department of Commerce, Government Printing Office, Washington, D.C.

Uzzi, Brian. 1996. "The Sources and Consequences of Embeddedness for the Economic Performance of Organizations: The Network Effect." *American Sociological Review* 61, 4 (August): 674–98.

Vallas, Steven P. 1999. "Rethinking Post-Fordism: The Meaning of Workplace Flexibility." *Sociological Theory* 17, 1 (March): 68–101.

Vancil, R. F. 1978. *Decentralization: Managerial Ambiguity by Design*. Homewood, IL: Dow Jones-Irwin.

Vartia, Yrjo O. 1976. "Ideal Log-Change Index Numbers." *Scandinavian Journal of Statistics* 3, 3: 121–6.

Veblen, Thorstein. 1953 [1899]. *The Theory of the Leisure Class*. New York: Mentor.

Vernon, John M., and Daniel A. Graham. 1971. "Profitability of Monopolization by Vertical Integration." *Journal of Political Economy* 79, 4 (July/August): 924–5.

Wade, Robert. 1990. *Governing the Market: Economic Theory and the Role of Government in East Asian Industrialization.* Princeton: Princeton University Press.

Wade, Robert and Frank Veneroso. 1998. "The Asian Crisis: The High Debt Model vs. the Wall Street-Treasury-IMF Complex." *New Left Review*, March–April, pp. 3–23.

Wallerstein, Immanuel. 1974. *The Modern World-System: Capitalist Agriculture and the Origins of the European World-Economy in the Sixteenth Century.* New York: Academic Press.

Wallerstein, Immanuel. 1984. *The Politics of the World-Economy.* Cambridge: Cambridge University Press.

Walras, Léon. 1977. *Elements of Pure Economics or the Theory of Social Wealth.* Fairfield, NJ: Augustus M. Kelley Publishers.

Walton, Gary M. and Hugh Rockoff. 1994. *History of the American Economy*, 7th ed. Fort Worth: The Dryden Press.

Wang, I-shou. 1980. "Cultural Contact and the Migration of Taiwan's Aborigines: A Historical Perspective." In *China's Island Frontier: Studies in Historical Geography of Taiwan*, edited by Ronald G. Knapp. Honolulu: The University Press of Hawaii, 31–54.

Wank, David L. 1999. *Commodifying Communism: Business, Trust, and Politics in a Chinese City.* Cambridge: Cambridge University Press.

Warren-Boulton, Frederik R. 1974. "Vertical Control with Variable Proportions." *Journal of Political Economy* 82 (August/September): 783–802.

Weber, Max [1921–22]. 1978. *Economy and Society.* Trans. and ed. G. Roth and C. Wittich. 3 vols. Berkeley: University of California Press.

Weinstein, David E. and Yishay Yafeh. 1995. "Japan's Corporate Groups: Collusive or Competitive? An Empirical Investigation of Keiretsu Behaviour." *Journal of Industrial Economics* 43: 359–76.

Weinstein, David E. and Yishay Yafeh. 1998. "On the Costs of a Bank-Centered Financial System: Evidence from the Changing Main Bank Relations in Japan." *Journal of Finance* 53, 2 (April): 635–72.

Westfield, Fred M. 1981. "Vertical Integration: Does Product Price Rise or Fall?" *American Economic Review* 71, 3 (June): 334–46.

White, Harrison C. 1981. "Where Do Markets Come From?" *American Journal of Sociology* 87: 517–47.

White, Harrison C. 1992. *Identity and Control: A Structural Theory of Social Action.* Princeton, New Jersey: Princeton University Press.

White, Harrison C. 1993. "Markets in Production Networks." In *Explorations in Economic Sociology*, edited by Richard Swedberg. New York: Russell Sage Foundation, 161–75.

White, Harrison C. 2002. *Markets from Networks: Socioeconomic Models of Production.* Princeton: Princeton University Press.

Whitehead, Alfred North. 1929. *Process and Reality.* New York: Harper.

Whitley, Richard D. 1990. "Eastern Asian Enterprise Structures and the Comparative Analysis of Forms of Business Organization." *Organization Studies* 11, 1: 47–74.

Whitley, Richard D. 1992. *Business Systems in East Asia*. London: Sage.

Whitley, Richard D. 1999. *Divergent Capitalisms: The Social Structuring and Change of Business Systems*. New York: Oxford University Press.

Williams, Jack F. 1980. "Sugar: The Sweetener in Taiwan's Development." In *China's Island Frontier: Studies in Historical Geography of Taiwan*, edited by Ronald G. Knapp. Honolulu: The University Press of Hawaii, 219–52.

Williamson, Oliver E. 1971. "The Vertical Integration of Production: Market Failure Considerations." *American Economic Review* 51, 2 (May): 112–23.

Williamson, Oliver E. 1975. *Markets and Hierarchies: Analysis and Antitrust Implications*. New York: Free Press.

Williamson, Oliver E. 1981. "The Economics of Organization." *American Journal of Sociology* 87: 548–77.

Williamson, Oliver E. 1985. *The Economic Institutions of Capitalism*. New York: The Free Press.

Williamson, Oliver E. 1991. "Comparative Economic Organization: The Analysis of Discrete Structural Alternatives." *Administrative Science Quarterly* 36 (June): 269–96.

Williamson, Oliver E. 1994. "Transaction Cost Economics and Organization Theory." In *The Handbook of Economic Sociology*, edited by Neil Smelser and Richard Swedberg. Princeton: Princeton University Press, 77–107.

Williamson, Oliver E. and Sidney G. Winter. 1993. *The Nature of the Firm: Origins, Evolution, and Development*. New York: Oxford University Press.

Winckler, Edwin A. and Susan Greenhalgh, eds. 1988. *Contending Approaches to the Political Economy of Taiwan*. Armonk, NY: M. E. Sharpe.

Winn, Jane Kaufman. 1991. "Banking and Finance in Taiwan: The Prospectis for Internationalization in the 1990s." *The International Lawyer* 25, 4 (Winter): 907–52.

Winn, Jane Kaufman. 1994. "Relational Practices and the Marginalizaiton of Law: Informal Financial Practices of Small Businesses in Taiwan." *Law and Society Review* 28, 2: 193–232.

Wong, Siu-Lun. 1985. "The Chinese Family Firm: A Model." *British Journal of Sociology* 36: 58–72.

Woo, Jung-en (see also Woo-Cumings). 1991. *Race to the Swift: State and Finance in Korean Industrialization*. New York: Columbia University Press.

Woo, Wing Thye. 1990. "The Art of Economic Development: Markets, Politics, and Externalities." *International Organization* 44, 3 (Summer): 403–29.

Woo, Wing Thye, Jeffrey D. Sachs, and Klaus Schwab, eds. 2000. *The Asian Financial Crisis: Lessons for a Resilient Asia*. Cambridge, Mass.: MIT Press.

Woo, Wing Thye, Patrick D. Carleton, and Brian P. Rosario. 2000. "The Unorthodox Origins of the Asian Currency Crisis: Evidence from Logit Estimation." *ASEAN Economic Bulletin*. August.

Woo-Cumings, Meredith (see also Woo, Jung-en). 1999a. "The State, Democracy, and the Reform of the Industrial Sector in Korea." In *The Politics of the Asian Economic Crisis*, T. J. Pempel. Ithaca: Cornell University Press, 116–142.

Woo-Cumings, Meredith. 1999b. *The Developmental State*. Ithaca: Cornell University Press.

Woo-Cumings, Meredith. 2001. "Miracle as Prologue: The State and the Reform of the Corporate Sector in Korea." In *Rethinking the East Asian Miracle*, edited by Joseph E. Stiglitz and Shahid Yusuf. New York: Oxford University Press, 343–78.

World Bank. 1993. *The East Asian Miracle: Economic Growth and Public Policy*, Washington, D.C. Yang, Mayfair Mei-hui. 1994. *Gifts, Favors, and Banquets: The Art of Social Relationships in China*. Ithaca: Cornell University Press.

Wu, Silas H. L. 1970. *Communication and Imperial Control in China*. Cambridge, Mass.: Harvard University Press.

Yan, Yunxiang. 1996. *The Flow of Gifts: Reciprocity and Social Networks in a Chinese Village*. Stanford: Stanford University Press.

Yang, Jun-sok. 2000. "Korea's Trade Relations: Conflict and Opportunity." In *The Korean Economy in an Era of Global Competition*, Joint Korea-U.S. Academic Studies, 10, 105–38.

Yang, Mayfair Mei-hui. 1994. *Gifts, Favors, and Banquets: The Art of Social Relationships in China*. Ithaca: Cornell University Press.

Yang, Tzu-Han. 1993. *Industrial Structure and Trade patterns: Evidence from South Korea and Taiwan*. Ph.D. Dissertation, University of California, Davis.

Yao, Souchou. 1987. "The Fetish of Relationships: Chinese Business Transactions in Singapore." *Sojourn* 2: 89–111.

Yarbrough, Beth V. and Robert M. Yarbrough. 1987. "Institutions for the Governance of Opportunism in International Trade." *Journal of Law, Economics, and Organization* 3, 1 (Spring): 129–42.

Yeung, Henry Wai-chung and Kris Olds, eds. 2000. *Globalization of Chinese Business Firms*. New York: St. Martin's Press.

Yoo, In-Hak. 1995. *Gyungje Gaehyuk Gwa Chaebol* (Economic reform and Chaebol) Seoul: Chayuchiseongsa (in Korean).

Yoo, Seong Min. 1999. "Corporate Restructuring in Korea." In *Korea and the Asian Economic Crisis: One Year Later*, Joint U.S.-Korea Academic Studies 9: 131–200.

Yoshino, M. Y. and Thomas B. Lifson. 1986. *The Invisible Link: Japan's Sogo Shosha and the Organization of Trade*. Cambridge, Mass.: The MIT Press.

Young, Alwyn. 1992. "A Tale of Two Cities: Factor Accumulation and Technical Change in Hong Kong and Singapore." In Olivier Blanchard and Stanley Fischer, eds. *NBER Macroeconomics Annual, 1992*. MIT Press: Cambridge, MA, 13–53.

Young, Alwyn. 1993. "Lessons from the East Asian NICs: A Contrarian View." *European Economic Review* 38: 964–73.

Young, Alwyn. 1995. "The Tyranny of Numbers: Confronting the Statistical Realities of the East Asian Growth Experience." *Quarterly Journal of Economics* 60, 3 (August): 641–80.

Yun, Minkyung. 2000. "Foreign Direct Investment: A Catalyst for Change?" In *The Korean Economy in an Era of Global Competition*, Joint U.S.-Korea Academic Studies 10: 139–63.

Zeile, William. 1991. "Industrial Policy and Organizational Efficiency: The Korean Chaebol Examined." In *Business Networks and Economics Development in East and Southeast Asia*, edited by Gary G. Hamilton. Hong Kong: Center of Asian Studies.

Index

Other Books in the Series (*continued from page iii*):